PUBLIC ADMINISTRATION

PUBLIC ADMINISTRATION

CONCEPTS & CASES

FOURTH EDITION

Richard J. Stillman II
George Mason University

HOUGHTON MIFFLIN COMPANY   BOSTON
Dallas   Geneva, Illinois   Palo Alto   Princeton, New Jersey

For my wife, Kathleen
my daughter, Shannon Marie
my son, Richard J. III

Printed in the U.S.A.

Library of Congress Catalog Card Number: 87–80690

ISBN: 0–395–35969–4

DEFGHIJ-H-99876543210

Contents

CHAPTER 7
Key Decision Makers in Public Administration:
The Concept of the Professional State   *179*

PART II   THE MULTIPLE FUNCTIONS OF PUBLIC
ADMINISTRATORS: THEIR MAJOR ACTIVITIES,
RESPONSIBILITIES, AND ROLES   *218*

CHAPTER 8
Decision Making: The Concept of Incremental Public
Choice   *221*

CHAPTER 9
Administrative Communications: The Concept of Information
Networks   *250*

PART III   ENDURING AND UNRESOLVED RELATIONSHIPS: CENTRAL VALUE QUESTIONS, ISSUES, AND DILEMMAS OF CONTEMPORARY PUBLIC ADMINISTRATION 402

Preface

Bureaucracy; administrative power; informal groups; third-party government; issue networks; implementation; incremental decisions; personnel motivation; moral ambiguities of public choice: this textbook introduces students to these and other fundamental concepts that serve as the framework for public administration.

Format and Approach

The same methodological format and design of the first three editions remain intact in the fourth edition. This approach seeks to interrelate many of the authoritative conceptual works in public administration with contemporary case studies.

By pairing a reading with a case study in each chapter, the text serves four important purposes:

1. The concept-case study method permits students to read firsthand the work of many leading administrative theorists who have shaped the modern study of public administration. This method aims at developing in students a critical appreciation of the classic administrative ideas that serve as the basis of modern public administration.
2. The text encourages a careful examination of practical administrative problems through the presentation of contemporary cases—often involving major national events—that demonstrate the complexity, the centrality, and the challenge of the current administrative processes of public organizations.
3. The book seeks to promote a deeper understanding of the relationship between the theory and the practice of public administration by allowing readers to test for themselves the validity of major ideas about public administration in the context of actual situations.
4. Finally, the concept-case method develops a keener appreciation of the eclectic breadth and interdisciplinary dimensions of public administration by presenting articles—both conceptual and case writings—from a wide variety of sources, using many materials not available in the average library.

The immense quantity of literature in the field has made it particularly difficult to select the writings. I sought, therefore, to answer four basic questions affirmatively in making choices of material:

1. Do the writings focus on the central issues confronting public administrators?
2. Do the writings, individually and collectively, give a realistic view of the contemporary practice of public administration?

3. Do the individual conceptual readings and case studies relate logically to each other?
4. Are the writings interesting and long enough to convey the true sense and spirit intended by the authors?

The arrangement of the selections follows an order of topics used by many instructors in the field, moving from a definition of public administration to increasingly specific issues and problems. Many subjects (such as productivity and personnel recruitment), though not treated separately, are discussed as part of other chapters.

A diagram may help readers to understand the design of the book more clearly.

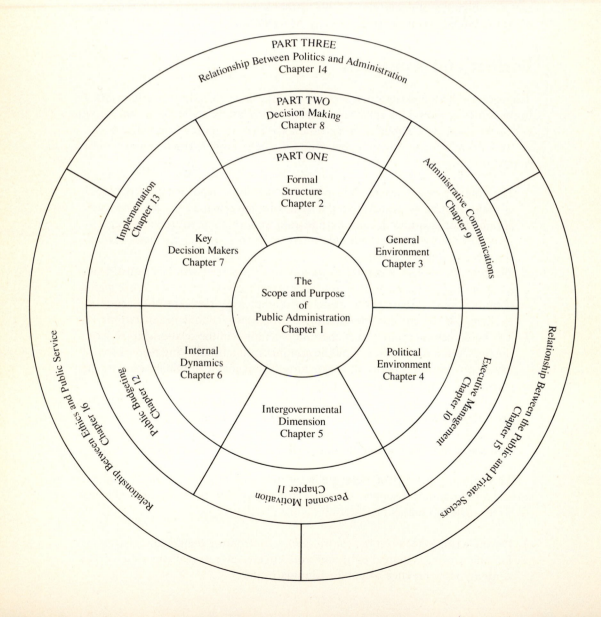

At the center of this schematic figure is Chapter 1, which discusses "The Scope and Purpose of Public Administration," perhaps the most difficult, central intellectual problem in public administration today. The first ring outward is Part One, "The Environment of Public Administration." These six chapters present concepts and cases pertaining to the broad environment surrounding public administration and the work of public administrators. The second ring is Part Two, "The Multiple Functions of Public Administrators." These six chapters focus on the major activities, roles, and responsibilities of practicing administrators in the public sector. The exterior ring is Part Three; these three chapters discuss "Enduring and Unresolved Relationships" in public administration.

New Material in the Fourth Edition

To ensure that the text stays current and continues to reflect the ideas and events shaping public administration today, two new topics—implementation (Chapter 13) and the relationship between public and private sectors (Chapter 15)—have been added to this edition. Readings and cases have also been carefully selected with an eye to readability and contemporary appeal.

Six (roughly one-third) new readings appear in this edition:

Reading 1: "What Is Public Administration?" (Dwight Waldo)

Reading 2: "Bureaucracy" (Max Weber)

Reading 5: "Intergovernmental Relations in the 1980s: A New Phase of IGR" (Deil S. Wright)

Reading 6: "Informal Organizations and Their Relation to Formal Organizations" (Chester I. Barnard)

Reading 13: "The Conditions of Effective Implementation: A Guide to Accomplishing Policy Objectives" (Paul Sabatier and Daniel Mazmanian)

Reading 15: "Rethinking Public Management: Third-Party Government and the Changing Forms of Government Action" (Lester M. Salamon)

Nine (roughly one-half) case studies are also new to this edition:

Case Study 2: "The Rescission of the Passive Restraints Standard" (David M. Kennedy)

Case Study 4: "The Changing FBI—The Road to Abscam" (James Q. Wilson)

Case Study 5: "The Love Canal Relocation" (Martin Linsky)

Case Study 6: "The Two Faces of Organization" (Fred I. Greenstein)

Case Study 10: "The Space Shuttle *Challenger* Accident" (Presidential Commission on the Space Shuttle *Challenger* Accident)

Case Study 12: "The Employment and Training Administration: Budget Cuts by the President and Congress" (Irene S. Rubin)

Case Study 13: "The Florida Freeze" (Frank R. Durr)

Case Study 14: "Target Qaddafi" (Seymour M. Hersh)

Case Study 15: "Cornwall County School District" (David Kennedy and Robert Leone)

Revised introductions, alerting students to the main ideas that follow, open each selection. Also updated are the review questions, key terms, and suggestions for further reading that conclude each chapter, as well as the subject and topic indexes.

Instructor's Guide

The *Instructor's Guide* contributes to the usefulness of the text. Revised carefully from the previous edition, the manual offers numerous insights, practical guides, and resources for teaching introductory and graduate students. The guide is organized as a set of memoranda from myself to the instructor. Each memo addresses a separate important topic, for instance, "How to use case studies in the classroom." The guide also includes sample quizzes, exams, and course evaluation forms. Appendices include the Federalist Papers, nos. 10 and 51, and Woodrow Wilson's essay, "The Study of Public Administration."

Acknowledgments

Various people have contributed to this book either by helping to shape its focus in the early stages or by reviewing the finished manuscript. Special thanks are due to Virginia Bott, California State University at Fullerton; John Burke, University of Vermont; Brian Donnelly, Southern Illinois University at Edwardsville; Susan S. Lederman, Kean College of New Jersey; Nancy S. Lind, Illinois State University; Thomas Roback, Virginia Polytechnic Institute; Lana Stein, University of Missouri at St. Louis; L. Nolan Walker, University of West Florida; and J. D. Williams, University of Utah.

Several faculty colleagues at George Mason University offered invaluable suggestions and ideas for preparing this fourth edition. Thanks must also go to Ross Brown, a GMU undergraduate who provided helpful research assistance for this project; my editors at Houghton Mifflin for their generous support and enthusiastic encouragement throughout this difficult writing and editing assignment; and the entire Fenwick Library staff at George Mason University, who gave me a quiet place to work during the summer and put up with my ceaseless requests to track down yet another obscure document on public administration. To these and many others, I owe a great debt of gratitude for their assistance.

R.J.S. II

The Search for the Scope and Purpose of Public Administration

"The central idea of public administration is rational action, defined as action correctly calculated to realize desired goals. Public administration both as a study *and as an* activity *is intended to maximize the realization of goals; and often the two blend into each other, since in the last analysis study is also a form of action."*

Dwight Waldo

READING 1

Introduction

A definition of the parameters of a field of study, that is, the boundaries, landmarks, and terrain that distinguish it from other scientific and humanistic disciplines, is normally considered a good place to begin any academic subject. Unfortunately, as yet, no one has produced a simple definition of the study of public administration—at least one on which most practitioners and scholars agree. Attempting to define the core values and focus of twentieth-century public administration provides lively debates and even deep divisions among students of the field.

A major difficulty in arriving at a precise and universally acceptable definition arises in part from the rapid growth in the twentieth century of public administration, which today seems to be all-encompassing. Public administrators are engaged in technical, although not necessarily mundane details: they prepare budgets for a city government or classify jobs in a post office or evaluate the performance of drug treatment centers in a central city. At the same time, they are also vitally concerned with the major goals of society and the development of resources for achieving those goals within the context of a rapidly changing political environment. For instance, if an engineering staff of a state agency proposes to build a highway, this decision appears at first glance to be a purely administrative activity. However, it can and indeed does involve a wide range of social values related to pressing concerns like community land use patterns, energy consumption, the control of pollution, and mass transit planning. The broad problems of race relations, the general economic well-being of a community, and the allocation of scarce physical and human resources affect even simple administrative decisions about highway construction.

Public administration does not operate in a vacuum but is deeply intertwined with the critical dilemmas confronting the entire society. The issue then becomes: how can a theorist reasonably and concisely define a field so interrelated with all of society?

The rapidly increasing number and scope of activities involving public administration have led major theorists to attempt a variety of definitions. Consider some offered recently by leading textbook writers:

Public Administration is the production of goods and services designed to serve the needs of citizens-consumers.

Marshall Dimock, Gladys Dimock, and Douglas Fox,
Public Administration (Fifth Edition, 1983)

Public administration:
  1. is a cooperative group effort in a public setting.
  2. covers all three branches—executive, legislative, and judicial—and their interrelationships.
  3. has an important role in the formulation of public policy, and is thus part of the political process.
  4. is different in significant ways from private administration.
  5. is closely associated with numerous private groups and individuals in providing services to the community.

Felix A. Nigro and Lloyd G. Nigro,
Modern Public Administration (Sixth Edition, 1984)

We suggest a new conceptual framework that emphasizes the perception of public administration as *design,* with attendant emphasis on participative decision making and learning, purpose and action, innovation, imagination and creativity, and social interaction and "coproduction."

Jong S. Jun,
Public Administration (1986)

In ordinary usage, public administration is a generic expression for the entire bundle of activities that are involved in the establishment and implementation of public policies.

Cole Blease Graham, Jr., and
Steven W. Hays,
Managing the Public Organization (1986)

Traditionally, public administration is thought of as the accomplishing side of government. It is supposed to comprise all those activities involved in carrying out the policies of elected officials and some activities associated with the development of those policies. Public administration is . . . all that comes after the last campaign promise and election-night cheer.

Grover Starling,
Managing the Public Sector (Third Edition, 1986)

Public administration is the use of managerial, political, and legal theories and processes to fulfill legislative, executive, and judicial governmental mandates for the provision of regulatory and service functions for the society as a whole or for some segments of it.

David H. Rosenbloom,
Public Administration (1986)

Generally, these attempts at defining public administration seem to identify public administration with the following: (1) the executive branch of government (yet it is related in important ways to the legislative and judicial branches); (2) the formulation and implementation of public policies; (3) the involvement in a considerable range of problems concerning human behavior and cooperative human effort; (4) a field that can be differentiated in several ways from private administration; and (5) the production of public goods and services. However, trying to pin down public administration in much more specific detail becomes, according to some specialists like Harold Stein, a fruitless endeavor. The many variables and complexities of public administration make almost every administrative situation a unique event, eluding any highly systematic categorization. As Stein writes: "public administration is a field in which every man is his own codifier and categorizer and the categories adopted must be looked on as relatively evanescent."[1]

For some writers like Frederick C. Mosher, the elusiveness of a disciplinary core for public administration gives the subject its strength and fascination, for students must draw upon many fields and disciplines, as well as their own resources, in order to solve a particular administrative problem. As Mosher writes: "Perhaps it is best that it [public administration] not be defined. It is more an area of interest than a discipline, more a focus than a separate science. . . . It is necessarily cross-disciplinary. The overlapping and vague boundaries should be viewed as a resource, even though they are irritating to some with orderly minds."[2]

But for others like Robert Parker, the frustrations of dealing with such a disorderly discipline mitigate against its being a mature, rewarding academic field of study. "There is really no such subject as 'public administration'," writes Parker. "No science or art can be identified by this title, least of all any single skill or coherent intellectual discipline. The term has no relation to the world of systematic thought. . . . it does not, in itself, offer any promising opportunity to widen or make more precise any single aspect of scientific knowledge."[3]

Despite Parker's pessimistic assessment of the present and future status of public administration, the search for a commonly accepted definition of the field, both in its academic and professional applications, continues by many scholars.

[1]Harold Stein, *Public Administration and Policy Development: A Case Book* (New York: Harcourt Brace Jovanovich, 1952), p. xxv.

[2]Frederick C. Mosher, "Research in Public Administration," *Public Administration Review,* 16 (Summer 1956), p. 177.

[3]Robert S. Parker, "The End of Public Administration," *Public Administration,* 34 (June 1965), p. 99.

Indeed, defining public administration—its boundaries, scope, and purpose—has been a central, perhaps *the* central preoccupation and difficulty confronting administrative theorists in recent years. Within the last two decades the field's "identity crisis," as Dwight Waldo once labeled the dilemma,[4] has become especially acute because a plethora of models, approaches, and theories now purport to define what public administration is all about. In the following selection from *The Study of Public Administration,* Dwight Waldo, one of the foremost contemporary scholars of the field, wrestles with the problem of defining public administration. Waldo begins this selection by pointing out how complicated the task is to define this subject in any clear or concise manner. What is public administration all about, he asks, and responds: "in truth there is no good definition of public administration. Or, perhaps there are good short definitions, but no good short explanations. The immediate effect of all one-sentence or one-paragraph definitions of public administration is mental paralysis rather than enlightenment and stimulation."

But with that said, Waldo then proceeds to construct his own definition of public administration. Note carefully his approach. One by one he addresses key issues in the field: Is administration an art or a science? Is it action or study? What is the meaning of *administration?* Of the term *public?* How do *management* and *organization* differ from *public administration?* Only by this painstaking, deliberate process of dissecting each issue and distinguishing the key terms from each other does Waldo arrive at his own "model" of the field in "A Summary Explanation."

In the area of public administration scholarship, Dwight Waldo (1913–   ) is perhaps the most respected and thoughtful theorist. Waldo devoted much of his 40-year academic career to thinking and writing about administrative ideas, institutions, and practices. After serving during World War II in the Bureau of the Budget and Office of Price Administration, Waldo taught at the University of California, Berkeley, and the Maxwell School, Syracuse University. He is particularly well-known for such influential books as *The Administrative State* (1948), *Perspectives on Administration* (1956), and *The Enterprise of Public Administration* (1980). Throughout his career he exercised important leadership roles as editor-in-chief of the *Public Administration Review* for a dozen years (1966–1977); president of the National Association of Schools of Public Affairs and Administration (1977–1978); and the Albert Schweitzer Chair in the humanities at the Maxwell School (1967–1979), where he gave his critical support for developing the Minnowbrook Conference of younger scholars in 1968 to consider the future of the field.

As you read this selection from Waldo's *The Study of Public Administration,* keep in mind the following questions:

Why is it so complicated, according to Waldo, to assign a precise meaning to the term *public administration?* Why do one-sentence definitions usually fail to capture the essence of the field?

---

[4]Dwight Waldo, "Public Administration, 1948–68," *Journal of Politics,* 30 (May 1968).

Why does Waldo emphasize the importance of distinguishing between public administration as a "field of study" and public administration as "an activity or process"? Can you give an example of the common usage of each meaning and why the two meanings of this same term might lead to confusion? Do you think he makes a valid point here?

How does Waldo define the concept of rational action? Why is it so critical for an adequate understanding of the field?

According to Waldo, how do concepts of "culture" and "structural-functional analysis" assist us with defining public administration? Do these ideas, in your view, help or hinder our comprehension of the meaning of public administration?

DWIGHT WALDO

What Is Public Administration?

Because we have lived from birth in a society with an advanced technology of cooperation and have learned so much of this technology without awareness, we accept the miracles of human cooperation all about us as though they were natural or indeed inevitable. But they are not. Far from it. This technology was achieved through incalculable human industry, much systematic thought, and the flashes of inspiration of occasional geniuses. The technology of human cooperation must be learned afresh with each generation. Still fuller achievement of human purposes depends upon its extension by study and invention.

This essay is intended as an introduction to the study of one phase or aspect of human cooperation, namely, public administration. Public administration is much less than the whole process or concept of human cooperation. Those who study law, or anthropology, or economics, for example, are also studying human cooperation. There are specialized technologies within the technology of human cooperation; and there

are also varying conceptual apparatuses by which study *in* or the study *of* these technologies may be approached. Public administration in our society is one of the technologies within the technology, and has its own special conceptual apparatuses in its practice and in its study.

The Problem of Definition

Logic and convention both require that we now deal more carefully with the problem of definition, What is public administration? But in truth there is no good definition of public administration. Or perhaps there are good short definitions, but no good short explanation. The immediate effect of all one-sentence or one-paragraph definitions of public administration is mental paralysis rather than enlightenment and stimulation. This is because a serious definition of the term— as against an epigrammatical definition, however witty—inevitably contains several abstract words or phrases. In short compass these abstract words and phrases can be explained only by other abstract words and phrases, and in the process the reality and importance of "it" become fogged and lost. With this warning let us consider two typical definitions:

(1) Public administration is the organization and management of men and materials to achieve the purposes of government.

(2) Public administration is the art and science of management as applied to affairs of state.

These are the ways public administration is usually defined. There is nothing wrong with such definitions—except that in themselves they do not help much in advancing understanding. Perhaps these definitions do evoke sharp concepts and vivid images in the reader's mind. But if they do not, it is better to proceed, rather than puzzle over each word, in the hope that the following explanations, descriptions, and comments will bring understanding in their train.

Administration: Art or Science?

Let us give a moment's attention to a traditional dispute in the definition of public administration, and a related source of frequent confusion in the use of the term. The conflict has concerned whether public administration is an art or science. Some students and administrators, impressed with the achievements of the natural and physical sciences, have been insistent that public administration can and should become a science in the same sense. Other students and administrators, impressed with a fluid, creative quality in actual administration, with such intangibles as judgment and leadership, have been equally insistent that public administration cannot become a science, that it is an art.

Much nonsense has resulted from the debates of the science-art controversy, but also considerable clarification of concepts and agreement on usage. It is fashionable nowadays to refer to the "art *and* science" of public administration, in the manner of the second definition above. This usage reflects a general conclusion that public administration has important aspects of *both* science and art. It reflects also, however, a desire to bypass the definitional problems, to compromise the issues by yielding to both sides,

to get on with the study and practice of public administration, whatever it is. This disposition to get on is no doubt healthy, and diminishes a picayune and wasteful squabbling over words alone. But it must not be forgotten that definitions are important to fruitful study and effective action. The problem of how people are to be educated or trained for participating in public administration, for example, is one that can be solved only after a decision as to what, after all, is meant by public administration.[1]

Dual Usage of the Words *Public Administration*

A fertile source of confusion and error, closely related to the science-art controversy, is the fact that the words "public administration" have two usages. They are used to designate and delineate both (1) an area of intellectual inquiry, a discipline or study, and (2) a process or activity—that of administering public affairs. While the two meanings are of course closely related, they are nevertheless different; it is a difference similar to that between biology as the study of organisms and the organisms themselves.

Now if this distinction seems so obvious as not to warrant the making, the excuse must be that it is nevertheless a distinction often missed. It is obvious, in retrospect, that a great deal (but not all) of the controversy over whether public administration is a science or an art stemmed from failure to agree on which public administration was being discussed, the discipline or the activity. It is quickly apparent that it is easier to make the case for science on the *systematic study,* and the case for art on the *practice,* of public administration.

A student of public administration must cultivate a sharp eye for the two usages of the term.

---

[1]Another distinction, related and similar to the distinction between science and art, is that between pure and applied, or theoretical and practical, science. This distinction . . . has important uses. . . . For a statement of it see Herbert A. Simon: *Administrative Behavior: A Study of Decision-Making Processes in Administrative Organization* (New York, The Macmillan Co., 1947), Appendix.

Sometimes the meaning will be clear from definition or context, but often there is simply ambiguity and confusion. Sometimes this is true because a writer begins with a definition of public administration as a process or activity, and then proceeds, abruptly or gradually, to use the term also to refer to the systematic study of public administration. Sometimes too the attempt is made to embrace both meanings within the same definition, which opens great opportunity for confusion. (Turn back now and scrutinize the two definitions given on an earlier page. In terms of the distinction made, is their intent clear?)

Let us confess that in attempting to clarify a distinction which is important we have made it sharper than it is in fact. To explain, recall the analogy drawn above between biology as the study of organisms and the organisms themselves. In this case the distinction is sharp, because while biology includes the study of man as an organism, this is but a small part of the whole; and on the other hand, no organism except man makes much of a study of other organisms. In the case of public administration, however, the central concern of the study is man himself, in certain aspects and sets of relationships; and on the other hand, much studying of public administration is carried on by men while engaged in the activities and process of public administration. The file clerk meditating on a better filing system for his needs, the supervisor deciding upon a new distribution of work among his staff, the group of publicly employed social scientists making an elaborate study of how employee morale can be maintained, are all studying public administration in some sense or aspect.

The Concept of Rational Action

The point will be made clearer by the introduction of the concept of *rational action,* defined here as action correctly[2] calculated to realize given desired goals with minimum loss to the realization of other desired goals. We will use the concept somewhat crudely, and not pause here to consider such interesting and important questions as whether man does wish or should wish that all his actions be rational. We will be content for the moment with the general observation or belief that man can and does maximize his goal achievement by taking thought, by correctly relating means to ends.

Now public administration in *both* senses is rational action as just defined. It is action designed to maximize the realization of goals that are public by definition. In public administration *as an activity* there is continuous calculation of the means to maximize public goals, although there is great variation in the goal awareness, knowledge, and level of abstraction of those engaged in the activity. A top leader may be highly trained and spend his time and energy in a conscious and careful calculation of means to realize given public goals. A machine-operator, on the other hand, may not know or care about the "public" goals of the agency for which he works. Still, the work of the machine-operator will be rational, in the sense that it is a joining of means to ends—say, the operation of a calculating machine for the solving of arithmetical problems. Rationality may be built into a mechanical operation or even a profession. The task of a leader or administrator is then to relate such built-in rationality to goals which *he* seeks in such a way that these goals are maximized.

In public administration *as a study* there is also continuous calculation of the means by which public goals may be maximized. In fact this is not only a central concern of the discipline but, many would say, its sole legitimate concern. In this case too, however, there is great

---

[2]This is an important—and difficult—word. One source of difficulty lies in the fact that given actions may produce desired results for the wrong reasons. Thus actions enjoined by superstition are found sometimes to be correct (i.e. goal-maximizing) by science, but the explanations in the two systems of interpretation are quite different. Another source of difficulty or ambiguity is discussed under The Nature of Management.

variation—in types of approach, in level of abstraction, in size of problem, in the generality or particularity of goals to be maximized, and so forth. Time-and-motion studies of mechanical operations, leadership decision-making, community value-structures affecting administration, auditing procedures, trade-union characteristics in public administration—these are random examples suggesting the range and variation of studies.

To visualize how study and action can blend together in the concept of rational action, let us imagine a case. Suppose that a firm of management consultants is hired on contract by a state department of public works, with the specific task of determining whether use of mechanical equipment might be made more rational. The persons assigned to the study would observe and gather data and enlist the interest and support of those employees in the department who are concerned with mechanical equipment. Eventually they would present recommendations, and these recommendations might be accepted and put into effect immediately, by the consultants working together with those in the department. In such a case, study and action are so blended that the distinction does not make much sense; and of course study is also a form of action, in the final analysis. Still, at the extreme instead of at the mean, the distinction is a very useful one. A helpful analogy is the familiar range of the spectrum: between the extreme bands are many variations and gradations.

The Meaning of Administration: Cooperative Rational Action

Up to this point we have invariably dealt with the expression *public administration* and at no time with the noun *administration* alone. An appropriate next step is to examine into the meaning of the noun alone, and then into that of the adjective.

We may proceed by analogy: Public administration is a species belonging to the genus administration, which genus in turn belongs to a family which we may call *cooperative human action.* The word *cooperative* is here defined in terms of results: human activity is cooperative if it has effects that would be absent if the cooperation did not take place. Thus—to take a frequently used illustration—when two men roll a stone which neither could roll alone, they have cooperated. The result, the rolled stone, is the test. But what if one of the two men has lent his effort unwillingly, perhaps under threat of bodily harm from the other: Is this cooperation? It is, in the meaning here assigned. Cooperation as ordinarily used suggests willingness, even perhaps enthusiasm; so we are straining the customary meaning. But the English language seems to have no word better adapted to the meaning here desired. The expression *antagonistic cooperation,* incidentally, is sometimes used in the social sciences to distinguish unwilling from willing cooperation.

We are now in a position to describe administration. Administration is a type of cooperative human effort that has a high degree of rationality. This description in turn needs some qualification.

First, administration is not necessarily the only type of human cooperation that is rational. For example, the American economic system utilizes competition between companies—antagonistic cooperation—as well as administration within them to achieve rational action in the production and distribution of economic goods.[3]

Second, there is an important question implicit in the phrase "high degree of rationality."

[3]See *Politics, Economics and Welfare* (New York, Harper & Brothers, 1953) by Robert A. Dahl and Charles E. Lindblom for a discussion of different forms of rational cooperation.

It is well to note this question, though it cannot be discussed fully here. Whose goals or ends shall be used in assessing rationality? A little reflection will suggest that the *personal* goals of many if not all of the people in a particular administrative system are different from the formally stated goals of that system; sometimes, indeed, a product (for example, a military item) may be secret, its use unknown to many of those engaged in its manufacture. The idea of purpose or goal is essential to the definition of administration. But like quicksilver it is hard to grasp; it eludes and scatters. What shall we say is the purpose or goal of the Chevrolet Division of General Motors? In one sense certainly to make automobiles; and in another sense certainly to make profits for the stockholders. But the personal goals of all officers and employees are certainly in some senses neither of these, or at least not wholly these.[4]

Administration was described as a type of cooperative human endeavor with a high degree of rationality. What distinguishes it as a *type?* The answer depends in part upon the perspective. In one perspective the sociologist views the distinguishing characteristics as those he subsumes under the concept of *bureaucracy.* In the conventional perspective of the student of administration these characteristics are best subsumed under the two terms *organization* and *management.*

The Nature of Organization

The terms *organization* and *management* require explanation in turn. We may begin with another analogy: organization is the anatomy, management the physiology, of administration. Organization is structure; management is functioning. But each is dependent upon and inconceivable without the other in any existing administrative system, just as anatomy and physiology are intertwined and mutually dependent in any living organism.[5] We are close to the truth, in fact, when we assert that organization and management are merely convenient categories of analysis, two different ways of viewing the same phenomena. One is static and seeks for pattern; the other is dynamic and follows movement.

More precisely, organization may be defined as *the structure of authoritative and habitual personal interrelations in an administrative system.* In any administrative system some persons give orders to others, for certain activities if not for all, and these orders or instructions are habitually followed by other persons; that is to say, some have more power than others, as evidenced by habitual command-obedience or instruction-response relationships. Usually there is an official theory or statement of what the authoritative interrelationships should be in a given administrative system. In an army unit, for example, authority is officially exercised according to the ranks (lieutenant, major, etc.) in the chain of command.

There may be considerable discrepancy, however, between the official theory or statement of authoritative interrelations and the actual, habitual exercise of authority, as evidenced by the actual giving and following of orders or directions. In truth, in any actual administrative system there is usually some discrepancy between the official theory or statement and the facts of authority as evidenced by customary

---

[4]Sometimes a distinction is made between *purpose* and *function* in an attempt to deal with this problem. Dahl and Lindblom (p. 38) apply the idea of *net* goal achievement to the problem of multiple goals. "What do we mean by 'rationality'? And how can one test whether one action is more rational than another? The first question is easier to answer than the second. An action is rational to the extent that it is 'correctly' designed to maximize goal achievement, given the goal in question and the real world as it exists. Given more than one goal (the usual human situation), an action is rational to the extent that it is correctly designed to maximize *net* goal achievement."

[5]This analogy is for introductory and explanatory purposes, and is to be viewed in this light. The definitions of organization and management admittedly comprehend less than the whole of societal anatomy and physiology respectively. And we are not here concerned with the familiar sociological distinction between patterns and consequences, or with distinguishing between static and dynamic models.

action; and in some cases the official theory or statement may even be no more than a polite fiction, so far do the facts depart from it. Moreover, all or nearly all so-called subordinates, those we think of as docilely taking orders, have means or techniques for changing the behavior of their superiors—for example, the workers' slowdown, or the secretary's smile or frown. A pure one-way power relationship in human affairs is very rare, if indeed it exists. In short, the word *authoritative* in the above definition is ambiguous, since the test of authority may be either the official theory or habitual response. The definition was framed in the knowledge of this ambiguity, which is important but cannot be explored further here. In any case—this is our present point—there are more or less firm structures of personal interrelationships in an administrative system, and these we designate *organization*.

The Nature of Management

Turning to *management,* we may define it as *action intended to achieve rational cooperation in an administrative system.* An administrative system is what we are seeking to explain, and rational cooperation has already been defined. Our attention focuses, then, upon the phrase *action intended to achieve.*

Action is to be construed very broadly: *any change intended to achieve rational cooperation.* It includes self-change or activity, all effects of man upon man, and all effects of man upon nonhuman things. In the postal system, for example, action includes the deliberations of the Postmaster General on such a matter as the desirability of a system of regional postal centers, the instructions of a city postmaster in supervising his staff, and the activities of a deliverer in sorting his daily batch of mail. There is an authoritative quality involved in many of these actions: some men habitually give more instructions (which are followed) than others. Hence some writers define management in terms of direction or control. But this definition

is likely to lead to an undesirable narrowing of attention.

The word *intended* in the definition has this significance: there may be a distinction between actions intended to achieve rational cooperation and actions which in fact do so. The reason for this is that in terms of given goals, actions intended to be rational may fail because not all the relevant facts and conditions are known or properly included in judgments and decisions—something which occurs in private life as well as in group activity. On the other hand, actions which are not part of any conscious rational calculation may nevertheless contribute to rational cooperation. Such actions may be sheerly accidental, or they may be actions we associate with emotions, personality, and so forth—areas beyond full scientific statement and calculation, for the present at least. *Management* is customarily used of actions *intended* to achieve rationality (and carries the presumption that the intention is usually realized), but of course an astute practitioner or student will be aware of the difference between intention and actuality and will never forget the large area still unmanageable. Incidentally, a great deal of political theory, especially in modern centuries, has concerned itself with the question of the general scope and the particular areas of human manageability. Students of administration can profit from the literature of this debate. And their findings and experience are in turn an important contribution to it.

The Meaning of Public

After this attempt at a formal definition of administration we return to the question, What is *public* administration? What qualities are signified by the adjective? How is public administration distinguished from administration in general, the species differentiated from the genus?

This is a difficult question. We might begin by defining *public* in terms of such words as government and *state,* as is often done. An attempt to understand these words in turn leads to an inquiry into such legal and philosophical concepts as sovereignty, legitimacy, and general welfare. These are important matters, and a student or practitioner of public administration ought to have made serious inquiry into general political theory. Such inquiry helps in understanding various phenomena, such as the coercions sometimes exercised in public administration.

Or we might take a quite different, empirical tack and attempt to define *public* simply by the test of opinion: In a particular society what functions or activities are believed to be public? This proposal has a certain crude truth or usefulness. In the United States, for example, there is certainly a general opinion that, say, the administration of military affairs is public, whereas the administration of automobile sales is private. But complications arise quickly in following this approach. People's opinions differ and are extremely hard to determine and assess (and to suggest another type of complication, the administration of automobile sales is subject to much public control, even in peacetime).

Or we might take the common-sense approach and ask simply, Does the government carry on the function or activity? For many common-sense purposes this approach is quite adequate. It will satisfy most of the purposes of the citizen, and many of those of the student and practitioner of administration. But for many purposes of study, analysis, and informed action it is quite inadequate. Even at the level of common sense it is not completely adequate. For example, there are unstable political situations in which it is difficult to identify "the government" and what is "legal." And there are borderline activities of which one is hard put to it to say whether the government carries them on or not, such are the subtleties of law and circumstances. For example, the development of atomic energy is public in the sense that the government of the United States is in charge. Indeed, there is much secrecy, and tight con-

trols; the situation is sometimes referred to as a monopoly. Yet this program involves an intricate network of contractual relationships, not only with state and local authorities, but with private corporations and individuals. Shall we call developmental programs carried on under contract by Union Carbide and Carbon Corporation public administration?

The most fruitful approach to the meaning and significance of *public* for the student of administration is through use of certain concepts which have been developed most fully in such disciplines as sociology and anthropology. The ones suggested as being particularly useful are associated with the expressions *structural-functional analysis* and *culture.* The concepts involved in these terms are by no means completely clear and precise. About them highly technical and intense professional debates are carried on. Nevertheless they are very useful to the student of administration even if used crudely. They provide needed insight, if not firm scientific generalizations.

Clarification through Structural-Functional Analysis

Structural-functional analysis seeks the basic or enduring patterns of human needs, wants, dispositions, and expressions in *any* society. Recognizing the great diversity in human societies, it yet seeks for common denominators, for the universal grammar and syntax of collective living.

Such studies provide the basis for a meaning of *public* which one could designate universal or inherent. What is indicated—if not precisely concluded—is that institutions and activities that are associated with the identity of a group, with group life as a whole, have special coercive, symbolic, and ceremonial aspects. There is inevitably a sacred aura surrounding some aspects of government. In some societies, of course, Church and State are one, or closely joined. But even where they are officially separated, and even indeed when religion, as such, is officially proscribed by the government, the government—if it is "legitimate"—has this sacred quality. (Nationalism is, of course, often described as a secular religion.)

This approach helps us to understand the special public quality of certain functions of government, for example, the apprehension and trial at law of persons accused of crimes, and the punishment or incarceration of the convicted; the manufacture and control of money; the conduct of foreign relations; or the recruitment, training, and control of armed forces. There is about such activities a monopoly aspect, and they are heavily vested with special coercions, symbolisms, and ceremonies. It is especially in such areas of activity that when a private citizen becomes a public official we expect him to play a new role, one which gives him special powers and prestige, but also requires of him observance of certain proprieties and ceremonies.

Incidentally, though the concept of rational action seems the most useful one in defining administration, we could also use the ideas and findings of structural-functional analysis for this purpose. We could, that is to say, construct a model of what an administrative system is like as a general type, using the concepts and idiom of structural-functional analysis.

Clarification through the Concept of Culture

The concept of culture is used in the social sciences—especially anthropology and sociology—to denote the entire complex of beliefs and ways of doing things of a society. We may analyze it as follows for our purposes: By *beliefs* is meant the systems of ideas held with respect to such matters as religion, government, economics, philosophy, art, and personal interrelations. By *ways of doing things* is meant patterns of activity with respect to food, clothing, shelter, courtship and marriage, child-rearing, entertainment, aesthetic expression, and so forth. The concept implies or asserts that there is a close connection between beliefs and ways of

doing things—for example, between ideas concerning art, and modes of aesthetic expression. It further implies or asserts that the various beliefs and ways of doing things in a particular culture are a system in the sense that they are dependent one upon the other, in such a way that a change in one sets off a complicated (and given the present state of our knowledge, at least, often unanticipated and uncontrollable) train of results in others. For example, the introduction of firearms or of the horse into the culture of a primitive people is likely ultimately to affect such matters as artistic expression and marriage customs.

Now the concept of culture tends somewhat to turn attention in the opposite direction from structural-functional analysis. It emphasizes the variety of human experience in society rather than the recurrent patterns. Indeed, the concept has been used in arguing the almost complete plasticity of human beings and of society—and this is the source of one of the professional controversies referred to above. The professional controversies as to the *limits* of the truth or usefulness of concepts should not mislead us, however. The two concepts or sets of concepts we are dealing with here are not necessarily antithetical, but rather are customarily supplementary over a large area of social analysis.

As structural-functional analysis provides tools for dealing with recurrent phenomena, the concept of culture provides tools for dealing with *variety*. The feeling or intuition that administration is administration wherever it is comes very quickly to the student of administration; and this theme is heavily emphasized in the American literature dealing with administration. Yet the student will also become aware, as he advances, that there are important *differences* between administrative systems, depending upon the location, the tasks, the environment, and the inhabitants of the system. And he needs handles by which he can grasp and deal with the differences.

Our present concern is with the differences between private and public administration. The thesis here is that unless we take the broad view provided by intercultural comparison, we are likely to fall into error, designating a distinction as universal when it is a true or important distinction only in our own country or cultural tradition. There come to mind here the common generalizations of writers in the United States which are true of a significant part or aspect of public administration in liberal democratic societies, but are by no means true of public administration by definition, as is implied or suggested. Precisely, consider the generalization that public administration is distinguished by special care for equality of treatment, legal authorization of and responsibility for action, public justification or justifiability of decisions, financial probity and meticulousness, and so forth. It does not take much knowledge of comparative administration to appreciate the very limited applicability of these characteristics to some "public" administration.

The concept of culture—plus knowledge about the actual culture—enables us to see administration in any particular society in relation to all factors which surround and condition it: political theories, educational system, class and caste distinctions, economic technology, and so forth. And enabling us to see administration in terms of its environment, it enables us to understand differences in administration between different societies which would be inexplicable if we were limited to viewing administration analytically in terms of the universals of administration itself. *For as the constituent parts of culture vary within a society, or between societies, so does administration vary as a system of rational cooperative action in that society, or between societies.* Administration is a part of the cultural complex; and it not only is acted upon, it acts. Indeed, by definition a system of rational cooperative action, it inaugurates and controls much change. Administration may be thought of as the major invention and device by which civilized men in complex societies try to control their culture, by which they seek simultaneously to achieve— within the limitations of their wit and knowledge—the goals of stability and the goals of change.

What Is Public Administration? A Summary Explanation

Let us return again to the question: What is *public* administration? The ideas associated with structural-functional analysis and culture will not enable us to *define* public with precision, but they help us in understanding the significance and implications of the term. They help us to understand why public administration has some general or generic aspects but also why the line between public and private is drawn in different places and with differing results—why "public" doesn't have precisely the same meaning in any two different cultural contexts. They help make some sense of the undoubted facts of similarity in diversity and diversity in similarity that characterize the Universe of Administration.

Whether public administration is an art or a science depends upon the meaning and emphasis one assigns these terms. The answer is affected too by the kind of public administration referred to—the study or discipline on the one hand, the activity or process on the other.

The central idea of public administration is rational action, defined as action correctly calculated to realize given desired goals. Public administration both as a *study* and as an *activity* is intended to maximize the realization of goals; and often the two blend into each other, since in the last analysis study is also a form of action.

Administration is cooperative human action with a high degree of rationality. Human action is *cooperative* if it has effects that would be absent if the cooperation did not take place. The significance of *high degree* of rationality lies in the fact that human cooperation varies in effectiveness of goal attainment, whether we think in terms of formal goals, the goals of leaders, or the goals of all who cooperate.

The distinguishing characteristics of an administrative system, seen in the customary perspective of administrative students, are best subsumed under two concepts, organization and management, thought of as analogous to anatomy and physiology in a biological system. *Organization* is the structure of authoritative *and* habitual personal interrelations in an administrative system. *Management* is action intended to achieve rational cooperation in an administrative system.

The significance of *public* can be sought in varying ways, each having some utility. For some purposes, for example, a simple determination of the legal status of an administrative system will suffice. For some important purposes, however, it is desirable to go beyond the boundaries of public administration as it has conventionally been studied and to adopt some of the concepts and tools of sociology and anthropology. *Structural-functional analysis* helps to identify the generic meaning or enduring significance of *public* in all societies. The concept of culture, on the other hand, helps in identifying and dealing with the varying aspects of *public* between societies, as well as with various relations of administration within a society.

The Importance of Nonrational Action

In this attempt to define and explain public administration in brief compass we have constructed a simple model. Of necessity many concepts of importance in the study of public administration have been omitted, and some of the concepts included have been dealt with rather summarily. . . . This is the appropriate place, however, to deal with what is perhaps a bias or distortion in our model, since the basis or source of the distortion largely lies outside of the later discussions.

The point is this: perhaps the model, by stressing rational action, creates a false impression of the amount of rationality (as defined) existing or possible in human affairs.

Now we may properly hold that the concept of rational action is placed at the center of administrative study and action. This is what it is about, so to speak. But the emphasis needs to be qualified—mellowed—by knowledge and appreciation of the nonrational. It is now generally agreed that earlier students of administration had a rationalist bias that led them to overestimate the potentialities of man (at least in the foreseeable future) for rational action.

Most of the streams of modern psychology emphasize—indeed perhaps overemphasize—the irrational component in human psychology: the role of the conditioned response, the emotive, the subconscious. Much of anthropology and sociology stresses complementary themes: the large amount of adaptive social behavior that is below the level of individual—and even group—conscious choice of goals and means to realize the goals. (The fact that goals are not chosen consciously does not mean that there are no goals in this behavior, nor that the goals are necessarily unimportant, nor even that they are any less true or meaningful than those consciously chosen. A baby responding to food stimuli, for example, is not choosing the goal of survival—but survival is usually thought a highly important goal. Actually, though such words as *conscious* and *unconscious* or *deliberate* and *adaptive* suggest two different realms of behavior, there is probably no sharp break, but rather varying levels of awareness of ends and means.)

The general picture that the nonrationalist conclusion of the psychologists, anthropologists, and sociologists (and others—the sources and manifestations of this mode of thought are many) present for the student of administration is this: An administrative organization has an internal environment and an external environment that are largely nonrational, at least so far as the formal goals of the administrative organization are concerned. People do not come into administrative organizations as pieces of putty, as units of abstract energy, nor as mere tools sharpened to some technical or professional purpose. They bring with them their whole cultural conditioning and their personal idiosyncrasies. Each is genetically unique, and all are members of institutions—families, churches, clubs, unions, and so forth—outside the administrative organization; and within the administrative organization they form into natural or adaptive groups of various kinds—friendships, cliques, car pools, and so forth—that flow across the lines of formal administrative organization, sometimes darkening, sometimes lightening, and sometimes erasing these lines.

Students of administration have become increasingly aware of the nonrational factors that surround and condition administration. They have broadened the base of their study to include much information that was formerly either unavailable or ignored. The goal of rationality has not been abandoned. Rather, it has been put in a new perspective: to achieve rationality demands a respect for the large area of the nonrational and much knowledge of it. Partly this new perspective is but a more serious heeding of Bacon's maxim: "Nature to be commanded must be obeyed." (These nonrational factors are not to be understood as, by definition, working against formal organization goals, but rather, paradoxically, as phenomena which, properly understood, can often be directed toward the realization of organization goals. They are resources as well as liabilities. Thus personal rivalries can be channeled—as by an official contest—to help rather than hinder goal achievement.) Partly the new perspective is a philosophical or psychological reorientation, as implied in the word *respect*. Students of administration now know that they are not going to take heaven by storm, that is to say, quickly reduce human affairs to rule and chart. Some of them, even, without ceasing to desire and strive for more rationality than we have now achieved, are heard to say that complete rationality in human affairs is not the proper goal; that a world in which *all* is orderly and predictable, with no room for spontaneity, surprise, and emotional play, is an undesirable world.

CASE STUDY 1

Introduction

The foregoing essay by Dwight Waldo underscored the difficulty in defining contemporary public administration. You may agree with its author's thesis regarding what is the substance of public administration, or you may have formulated your own conception of the scope of the field. In either case, the following story may shed some further insight into the role of public administration in modern society. The story, "The Blast in Centralia No. 5: A Mine Disaster No One Stopped," is an excellent account of a mine disaster that occurred a generation ago in Centralia, Illinois, taking the lives of 111 miners. This article is an unusual case study in public administration, for not only does the author, John Bartlow Martin, carefully recount the facts of the catastrophe, but he also attempts to understand the reasons behind the disaster. In his search for clues, the writer reveals much about the inner complexities of the administrative framework of our modern society—a coal company sensitive only to profit incentives; state regulatory agencies inadequately enforcing mine safety legislation; federal officials and mine unions complacent about a growing problem; and the miners incapable of protecting themselves against the impending disaster.

Here is an example of administrative reality that, for some, will only confirm their suspicions about the inherent corruption of modern administrative enterprises. The victims died, they might argue, because the mine owners were only interested in profits, not in human lives. But is this the correct interpretation? Martin does not blame any one individual or even a group of individuals but stresses the ineffectiveness of the administrative structure on which all the disaster victims were dependent for survival.

After reading this story you will probably be struck by how much modern society depends on the proper functioning of unseen administrative arrangements—for safeguarding our environment; for protecting the purity of our food; for transporting us safely by road, rail, or air; for sending us our mail; or for negotiating an arms limitations agreement at some distant diplomatic conference. All of us, like the miners in Centralia No. 5, rely throughout our lives on the immovable juggernaut of impersonal administrative systems. A functioning, ordered public administration, as this story illustrates, is an inescapable necessity for maintaining the requisites of a civilized modern society.

As you read this selection, keep the following questions in mind:

What is this case study's relevance to the problems of defining the essential qualities of public administration as outlined in the foregoing essay by Dwight Waldo?

How would you frame a suitable definition of the field based on your understanding of this case study's central theme? Does it "square" with Waldo's?

What does the case say about the special *public* obligations of public administrators compared to those engaged in private administration?

Finally, if you had actually been one of the leading administrative officials in the case—Driscoll O. Scanlan, Dwight Green, or Robert Medill—what would have been your view of public administration, and how might such a perspective on administration have helped to shape the outcome of the story?

JOHN BARTLOW MARTIN

The Blast in Centralia No. 5: A Mine Disaster No One Stopped

Already the crowd had gathered. Cars clogged the short, black rock road from the highway to the mine, cars bearing curious spectators and relatives and friends of the men entombed. State troopers and deputy sheriffs and the prosecuting attorney came, and officials from the company, the Federal Bureau of Mines, the Illinois Department of Mines and Minerals. Ambulances arrived, and doctors and nurses and Red Cross workers and soldiers with stretchers from Scott Field. Mine rescue teams came, and a federal rescue unit, experts burdened with masks and oxygen tanks and other awkward paraphernalia of disaster. . . .

One hundred and eleven men were killed in that explosion. Killed needlessly, for almost everybody concerned had known for months, even years, that the mine was dangerous. Yet nobody had done anything effective about it. Why not? Let us examine the background of the explosion. Let us study the mine and the miners, Joe Bryant and Bill Rowekamp and some others, and also the numerous people who might have saved the miners' lives but did not. The miners had appealed in various directions for help but got none, not from their state government nor their federal government nor their employer nor their own union. (In threading the maze of officialdom we must bear in mind four agencies in authority: The State of Illinois, the United States Government, the Centralia Coal Company, and the United Mine Workers of America, that is, the UMWA of John L. Lewis.) Let us seek to fix responsibility for the disaster. . . .

The Centralia Mine No. 5 was opened two miles south of Centralia in 1907. Because of its age, its maze of underground workings is extensive, covering perhaps six square miles, but it is regarded as a medium-small mine since it employs but 250 men and produces but 2,000 tons of coal daily. It was owned by the Centralia Coal Company, an appendage of the Bell & Zoller empire, one of the Big Six among Illinois coal operators. . . . The Bell & Zoller home office was in Chicago (most of the big coal operators' home offices are in Chicago or St. Louis); no Bell & Zoller officers or directors lived at Centralia.

There are in coal mines two main explosion hazards—coal dust and gas. Coal dust is unhealthy to breathe and highly explosive. Some of the dust raised by machines in cutting and loading coal stays in suspension in the air. Some subsides to the floor and walls of the tunnels, and a local explosion will kick it back into the air where it will explode and, in turn, throw more dust into the air, which will explode; and as this chain reaction continues the explosion will propagate throughout the mine or until it reaches something that will stop it.

The best method of stopping it, a method in use for some twenty-five years, is rock dusting. Rock dusting is simply applying pulverized stone to the walls and roof of the passageways; when a local explosion occurs it will throw a cloud of rock dust into the air along with the coal dust, and since rock dust is incombustible the explosion will die. Rock dusting will not prevent an explosion but it will localize one. Illinois law requires rock dusting in a dangerously dusty mine. Authorities disagreed as to whether the Centralia mine was gassy but everyone agreed it was exceedingly dry and dusty. The men who worked in it had been complaining about the dust for a long time—one recalls "the dust was over your shoetops," another that "I used to cough up chunks of coal dust like walnuts after work"—and indeed by 1944, more than two years before the disaster, so widespread had dissatisfaction become that William Rowekamp, as recording secretary of Local Union 52, prepared an official complaint. But even earlier, both state and federal inspectors had recognized the danger.

Let us trace the history of these warnings of disaster to come. For in the end it was this dust which did explode and kill one hundred and eleven men, and seldom has a major catastrophe of any kind been blueprinted so accurately so far in advance.

Driscoll O. Scanlan (who led the rescue work after the disaster) went to work in a mine near Centralia when he was 16, studied engineering at night school, and worked 13 years as a mine examiner for a coal company until, in 1941, he was appointed one of 16 Illinois state mine inspectors by Governor Green upon recommendation of the state representative from Scanlan's district. Speaking broadly, the job of a state inspector is to police the mine operators—to see that they comply with the state mining law, including its numerous safety provisions. But an inspector's job is a political patronage job. Coal has always been deeply enmeshed in Illinois politics.

Dwight H. Green, running for Governor the preceding fall, had promised the miners that he would enforce the mining laws "to the letter of the law," and however far below this lofty aim his administration fell (as we shall see), Scanlan apparently took the promise literally. Scanlan is a stubborn, righteous, zealous man of fierce integrity. Other inspectors, arriving to inspect a mine, would go into the office and chat with the company officials. Not Scanlan; he waited outside, and down in the mine he talked with the miners, not the bosses. Other inspectors, emerging, would write their reports in the company office at the company typewriter. Not Scanlan; he wrote on a portable in his car. Widespread rumor had it that some inspectors spent most of their inspection visits drinking amiably with company officials in the hotel in town. Not Scanlan. Other inspectors wrote the briefest reports possible, making few recommendations and enumerating only major violations of the mining law. Scanlan's reports were longer than any others (owing in part to a prolix prose style), he listed every violation however minor, and he made numerous recommendations for improvements even though they were not explicitly required by law.

Scanlan came to consider the Centralia No. 5 mine the worst in his district. In his first report on it he made numerous recommendations, including these: "That haulage roads be cleaned and sprinkled. . . . That tamping of shots with coal dust be discontinued and that clay be used. . . ." Remember those criticisms, for they were made February 7, 1942, more than five years before the mine blew up as a result (at least in part) of those very malpractices.

Every three months throughout 1942, 1943, and 1944 Scanlan inspected the mine and repeated his recommendations, adding new ones: "That the mine be sufficiently rock dusted." And what became of his reports? He mailed them to the Department of Mines and Minerals at Springfield, the agency which supervises coal mines and miners. Springfield is dominated by the Statehouse, an ancient structure of spires and towers and balconies, of colonnades and domes; on its broad front steps Lincoln stands in stone. Inside all is gloom and shabby gilt. The Department of Mines and Minerals occupies three high-ceilinged rooms in a back corner of the second floor. The Director of the Department uses the small, comfortable, innermost office, its windows brushed by the leaves of trees on the Statehouse lawn, and here too the Mining Board

meets. In theory, the Mining Board makes policy to implement the mining law, the Director executes its dictates; in practice, the Director possesses considerable discretionary power of his own.

In 1941 Governor Green appointed as Director Robert M. Medill, a genial, paunchy, red-faced man of about sixty-five. Medill had gone to work in a mine at sixteen; he rose rapidly in management. He had a talent for making money and he enjoyed spending it. He entered Republican politics in 1920, served a few years as director of the Department of Mines and Minerals, then returned to business (mostly managing mines); and then, after working for Green's election in 1940, was rewarded once more with the directorship. Green reappointed him in 1944 with, says Medill, the approval of "a multitude of bankers and business men all over the state. And miners. I had the endorsement of all four factions." By this he means the United Mine Workers and its smaller rival, the Progressive Mine Workers, and the two associations of big and little operators; to obtain the endorsement of all four of these jealous, power-seeking groups is no small feat. As Director, Medill received $6,000 a year (since raised to $8,000) plus expenses of $300 or $400 a month. He lived in a sizable country house at Lake Springfield, with spacious grounds and a tree-lined driveway.

To Medill's department, then, came Driscoll Scanlan's inspection reports on Centralia Mine No. 5. Medill, however, did not see the first thirteen reports (1942–44); they were handled as "routine" by Robert Weir, an unimaginative, harassed little man who had come up through the ranks of the miners' union and on recommendation of the union had been appointed Assistant Director of the Department by Green (at $4,000 a year, now $5,200). When the mail brought an inspector's report, it went first to Medill's secretary who shared the office next to Medill's with Weir. She stamped the report [with date of receipt] . . . and put it on Weir's desk. Sometimes, but by no means always, Weir read the report. He gave it to one of a half-dozen girl typists in the large outer office. She edited the inspector's recommendations for errors in grammar and spelling, and incorporated them into a form letter to the owner of the mine, closing:

"The Department endorses the recommendations made by Inspector Scanlan and requests that you comply with same.

"Will you please advise the Department upon the completion of the recommendations set forth above?

"Thanking you . . ."

When the typist placed this letter upon his desk, Weir signed it and it was mailed to the mine operator.

But the Centralia company did not comply with the major recommendations Scanlan made. In fact, it did not even bother to answer Weir's thirteen letters based on Scanlan's reports. And Weir did nothing about this. Once, early in the game, Weir considered the dusty condition of the mine so serious that he requested the company to correct it within ten days; but there is no evidence that the company even replied.

This continued for nearly three years. And during the same period the federal government entered the picture. In 1941 Congress authorized the U.S. Bureau of Mines to make periodic inspections of coal mines. But the federal government had no enforcement power whatever; the inspections served only research. The first federal inspection of Centralia Mine No. 5 was made in September of 1942. In general, the federal recommendations duplicated Scanlan's—rock dusting, improving ventilation, wetting the coal to reduce dust—and the federal inspectors noted that "coal dust . . . at this mine is highly explosive, and would readily propagate an explosion." In all, they made 106 recommendations, including 33 "major" ones (a government official has defined a "major" hazard as one that "could . . . result in a disaster"). Four months passed before a copy of this report filtered through the administrative machinery at Washington and reached the Illinois Department at Springfield, but this mattered little: the Department did nothing anyway. Subsequent federal reports in 1943 and 1944 showed that the "major" recommendations had not been complied with. The federal bureau lacked the power to force compliance; the Illinois Department possessed the power but failed to act.

What of the men working in the mine during these three years? On November 4, 1944, on instructions from Local 52 at Centralia, William Rowekamp, the recording secretary, composed a letter to Medill: "At the present the condition of those roadways are very dirty and dusty . . . they are getting dangerous. . . . But the Coal Co. has ignored [Scanlan's recommendations]. And we beg your prompt action on this matter."

The Department received this letter November 6, and four days later Weir sent Inspector Scanlan to investigate. Scanlan reported immediately:

"The haulage roads in this mine are awful dusty, and much dust is kept in suspension all day. . . . The miners have complained to me . . . and I have wrote it up pretty strong on my inspection reports. . . . But to date they have not done any adequate sprinkling. . . . Today . . . [Superintendent Norman] Prudent said he would fix the water tank and sprinkle the roads within a week, said that he would have had this work done sooner, but that they have 20 to 30 men absent each day." (This last is a claim by the company that its cleanup efforts were handicapped by a wartime manpower shortage. This is controversial. Men of fifty-nine—the average wartime age at the mine—do not feel like spending weekends removing coal dust or rock dusting, a disagreeable task; winter colds caused absenteeism and miners are always laying off anyway. On the other hand, the company was interested in production and profits: as Mine Manager Brown has said, "In the winter you can sell all the coal you can get out. So you want top production, you don't want to stop to rock dust.")

At any rate, Rowekamp's complaint got results. On December 2, 1944, he wrote Scanlan: "Well I am proud to tell you that they have sprinkled the 18th North Entry & 21st So. Entry and the main haulage road. . . . Myself and the Members of Local Union #52 appreciate it very much what you have done for us." It is apparent from this first direct move by Local 52 that Scanlan was working pretty closely with the Local to get something done.

But by the end of that month, December 1944, the mine once more had become so dirty that Scanlan ended his regular inspection report, ". . . if necessary the mine should discontinue hoisting coal for a few days until the [cleanup] work can be done." But all Weir said to the company was the routine "The Department endorses. . . ."

Early in 1945 it appeared that something might be accomplished. Scanlan, emerging from his regular inspection, took the unusual step of telephoning Medill at Springfield. Medill told him to write him a letter so Scanlan did:

"The haulage roads in this mine are in a terrible condition. If a person did not see it he would not believe. . . . Two months ago . . . the local officers [of Local Union 52] told me that . . . if [the mine manager] did not clean the mine up they were going to prefer charges against him before the mining board and have his certificate canceled. I talked them out of it and told them I thought we could get them to clean up the mine. But on this inspection I find that practically nothing has been done. . . . The mine should discontinue hoisting coal . . . until the mine is placed in a safe condition. . . . The coal dust in this mine is highly explosive. . . ."

This stiff letter was duly stamped "Received" at Springfield on February 23, 1945. A few days earlier a bad report had come in from Federal Inspector Perz. And now at last Medill himself entered the picture. What did he do? The Superintendent at Centralia had told Scanlan that, in order to clean up the mine, he would have to stop producing coal, a step he was not empowered to take. So Medill bypassed him, forwarding Scanlan's letter and report to William P. Young, Bell & Zoller's operating vice-president at Chicago: "Dear Bill. . . . Please let me have any comments you wish to make. . . . Very kindest personal regards." From his quiet, well-furnished office near the top of the Bell Building overlooking Michigan Avenue, Young replied immediately to "Dear Bob" [Medill]: "As you know we have been working under a very severe handicap for the past months. The war demand for coal . . . we are short of men. . . . I am hopeful that the urgent demand of coal will ease up in another month so that we may have available both the time and labor to give proper attention to the recommendations of Inspector Scanlan. With kindest personal regards. . . ."

A week later, on March 7, 1945, Medill forwarded copies of this correspondence to Scanlan, adding: "I also talked with Mr. Young on the phone, and I feel quite sure that he is ready and

willing. . . . I would suggest that you ask the mine committee [of Local 52] to be patient a little longer, inasmuch as the coal is badly needed at this time."

The miners told Scanlan they'd wait till the first of April but no longer. On March 14 Medill was to attend a safety meeting in Belleville. Scanlan went there to discuss Centralia No. 5 with him. According to Scanlan, "When I went up to his room he was surrounded with coal operators . . . all having whiskey, drinking, having a good time, and I couldn't talk to him then, and we attended the safety meeting [then] went . . . down to Otis Miller's saloon, and I stayed in the background drinking a few cokes and waited until the crowd thinned out, and went back up to his hotel room with him. . . . I told him that the mine was in such condition that if the dust became ignited that it would sweep from one end of the mine to the other and probably kill every man in the mine, and his reply to me was, 'We will just have to take that chance.' " (Medill has denied these words but not the meeting.)

On the first of April the president of Local Union 52 asked Scanlan to attend the Local's meeting on April 4. The miners complained that the company had not cleaned up the mine and, further, that one of the face bosses, or foreman, had fired explosive charges while the entire shift of men was in the mine. There can be little doubt that to fire explosives on-shift in a mine so dusty was to invite trouble—in fact, this turned out to be what later caused the disaster—and now in April 1945 the union filed charges against Mine Manager Brown, asking the State Mining Board to revoke his certificate of competency (this would cost him his job and prevent his getting another in Illinois as a mine manager). Rowekamp wrote up the charges: ". . . And being the Mine is so dry and dusty it could of caused an explosion. . . ."

Weir went to Centralia on April 17, 1945, but only to investigate the charges against Brown, not to inquire into the condition of the mine. He told the miners they should have taken their charges to the state's attorney. Nearly a month passed before, on May 11, Weir wrote a memorandum to the Mining Board saying that the company's superintendent had admitted the shots had been fired on-shift but that this was done "in an emergency" and it wouldn't happen again; and the Board refused to revoke Manager Brown's certificate.

Meanwhile, on April 12 and 13, Scanlan had made his regular inspection and found conditions worse than in February. He told the Superintendent: "Now, Norman, you claim Chicago won't give you the time to shut your mine down and clean it up. Now, I am going to get you some time," and he gave him the choice of shutting the mine down completely or spending three days a week cleaning up. The Superintendent, he said, replied that he didn't know, he'd have to "contact Chicago," but Scanlan replied: "I can't possibly wait for you to contact Chicago. It is about time that you fellows who operate the mines get big enough to operate your mines without contacting Chicago." So on Scanlan's recommendation the mine produced coal only four days a week and spent the remaining days cleaning up. For a time Scanlan was well satisfied with the results, but by June 25 he was again reporting excessive dust and Federal Inspector Perz was concurring: "No means are used to allay the dust." Following his October inspection Scanlan once more was moved to write a letter to Medill; but the only result was another routine letter from Weir to the company, unanswered.

Now, one must understand that, to be effective, both rock dusting and cleanup work must be maintained continuously. They were not at Centralia No. 5. By December of 1945 matters again came to a head. Scanlan wrote to Medill, saying that Local 52 wanted a sprinkling system installed to wet the coal, that Mine Manager Brown had said he could not order so "unusual" an expenditure, and that Brown's superior, Superintendent Prudent, "would not talk to me about it, walked away and left me standing." And Local 52 again attempted to take matters into its own hands. At a special meeting on December 12 the membership voted to prefer charges against both Mine Manager Brown and Superintendent Prudent. Rowekamp's official charge, typed on stationery of the Local, was followed next day by a letter, written in longhand on two sheets of dime-store notepaper, and signed by 28 miners.... At Springfield this communication too was duly stamped "Received." And another Scanlan report arrived.

Confronted with so many documents, Medill called a meeting of the Mining Board on December 21. Moreover, he called Scanlan to Springfield and told him to go early to the Leland Hotel, the gathering place of Republican politicians, and see Ben H. Schull, a coal operator and one of the operators' two men on the Mining Board. In his hotel room, Schull (according to Scanlan) said he wanted to discuss privately Scanlan's report on Centralia No. 5, tried to persuade him to withdraw his recommendation of a sprinkling system, and, when Scanlan refused, told him, "you can come before the board." But when the Mining Board met in Medill's inner office, Scanlan was not called before it though he waited all day, and after the meeting he was told that the Board was appointing a special commission to go to Centralia and investigate.

On this commission were Weir, two state inspectors, and two members of the Mining Board itself, Schull and Murrell Reak. Reak, a miner himself, represented the United Mine Workers of America on the Mining Board. And Weir, too, owed his job to the UMWA but, oddly, he had worked for Bell & Zoller for twenty years before joining the Department, the last three as a boss, so his position was rather ambiguous. In fact, so unanimous were the rulings of the Mining Board that one cannot discern any management-labor cleavage at all but only what would be called in party politics bipartisan deals.

The commission had before it a letter from Superintendent Prudent and Manager Brown setting forth in detail the company's "absentee experience" and concluding with a veiled suggestion that the mine might be forced to close for good (once before, according to an inspector, the same company had abandoned a mine rather than go to the expense entailed in an inspector's safety recommendation). Weir wrote to Prudent, notifying him that the commission would visit Centralia on December 28 to investigate the charges against him and Brown; Medill wrote to the company's vice-president, Young, at Chicago ("You are being notified of this date so that you will have an opportunity to be present or designate some member of your staff to be present"); but Medill only told Rowekamp, "The committee has been appointed and after the investigation you will be advised of their findings and the action of the board"—he did not tell the Local when the commission would visit Centralia nor offer it opportunity to prove its charges.

Rowekamp, a motorman, recalls how he first learned of the special commission's visit. He was working in the mine and "Prudent told me to set out an empty and I did and they rode out." Prudent—remember, the commission was investigating charges against Prudent—led the commission through the mine. Rowekamp says, "They didn't see nothing. They didn't get back in the buggy runs where the dust was the worst; they stayed on the mainline." Even there they rode, they did not walk through the dust. Riding in a mine car, one must keep one's head down. In the washhouse that afternoon the men were angry. They waited a week or two, then wrote to Medill asking what had been done. On January 22, 1946, Medill replied: the Mining Board, adopting the views of the special commission, had found "insufficient evidence" to revoke the certificates of Prudent and Brown.

He did not elaborate. Next day, however, he sent to Scanlan a copy of the commission's report. It listed several important violations of the mining law: inadequate rock dusting, illegal practice in opening rooms, insufficient or improperly placed telephones, more than a hundred men working on a single split, or current, of air. In fact, the commission generally concurred with Scanlan, except that it did not emphasize dust nor recommend a sprinkling system. Thus in effect it overruled Scanlan on his sprinkling recommendation, a point to remember. It did find that the law was being violated yet it refused to revoke the certificates of the Superintendent and the Mine Manager, another point to remember. Weir has explained that the board felt that improvements requiring construction, such as splitting the airstream, would be made and that anyway "conditions there were no different than at most mines in the state." And this is a refrain that the company and the Department repeated in extenuation after the disaster. But actually could anything be more damning? The mine was no worse than most others; the mine blew up; therefore any might blow up!

The miners at Centralia were not satisfied. "It come up at the meeting," Rowekamp recalls.

Local 52 met two Wednesday nights a month in its bare upstairs hall. The officers sat at a big heavy table up front; the members faced them, sitting on folding chairs which the Local had bought second-hand from an undertaker. Attendance was heavier now than usual, the men were aroused, some were even telling their wives that the mine was dangerous. They wanted to do something. But what? The state had rebuffed them. Well, why did they not go now to the higher officials of their own union, the UMWA? Why not to John L. Lewis himself?

One of them has said, "You have to go through the real procedure to get to the right man, you got to start at the bottom and start climbing up, you see? If we write to Lewis, he'll refer us right back to Spud White." Spud White is Hugh White, the thick-necked president of the UMWA in Illinois (District 12), appointed by Lewis. Now, Lewis had suspended District 12's right to elect its own officers during the bloody strife of the early 1930's, when the members, disgusted with what they called his "dictator" methods and complaining of secret payrolls, expulsions, missing funds, stolen ballots, and leaders who turned up on operators' payrolls, had rebelled; in the end the Progressive Mine Workers was formed and Lewis retained tight control of the UMWA. A decade later the Illinois officers of UMWA demanded that he restore their self-government, but Lewis managed to replace them with his own men, including Spud White. By 1946 President White, a coal miner from the South, was consulting at high levels with Lewis, he was receiving $10,000 a year plus expenses (which usually equal salary), and he was maintaining a spacious house on a winding lane in the finest residential suburb of Springfield, a white house reached by a circular drive through weeping willows and evergreens.

Evidently the perplexed miners at Centralia already had appealed to District 12 for help, that is to White. Certainly Murrell Reak, the UMWA's man on the Mining Board and a close associate of White's, had asked Weir to furnish him with a copy of the findings of the special commission: "I want them so I may show the district UMWA. So they in turn may write Local Union down there, and show them that their charges are unfounded or rather not of a nature as to warrant the revocation of mine mgr. Certificate. . . ." Jack Ripon, the bulky vice-president of District 12 and White's right-hand man, said recently, "We heard there'd been complaints but we couldn't do a thing about it; it was up to the Mining Department to take care of it."

And yet in the past the UMWA has stepped in when the state failed to act. One unionist has said, "White could have closed that mine in twenty-four hours. All he'd have had to do was call up Medill and tell him he was going to pull every miner in the state if they didn't clean it up. It's the union's basic responsibility—if you don't protect your own wife and daughter, your neighbor down the street's not going to do it."

Perhaps the miners of Local 52 knew they must go it alone. They continued to address their official complaints to the State of Illinois. On February 26 Rowekamp wrote once more to Medill: "Dear Sir: At our regular meeting of Local Union 52. Motion made and second which carried for rec. secy. write you that the members of local union 52 are dissatisfied with the report of the special investigation commission. . . ." No answer. And so the members of Local 52 instructed Rowekamp to write to higher authority, to their Governor, Dwight H. Green.

It took him a long time. Elmer Moss kept asking if he'd finished it and Rowekamp recalls, "I'd tell him, Elmer, I can't do that fast, that's a serious letter, that'll take me a while." He wrote it out first in pencil and showed it to a couple of the boys and they thought it sounded fine. Then, sitting big and awkward at his cluttered little oak desk in the living room of his home outside town, he typed it, slowly and carefully—"anything important as that I take my time so I don't make mistakes, it looks too sloppified." He used the official stationery of the Local, bearing in one corner the device of the union—crossed shovels and picks—and in the other "Our Motto—Justice for One and All." He impressed upon it the official seal—"I can write a letter on my own hook but I dassen't use the seal without it's official"—and in the washhouse the Local officers signed it. Rowekamp made a special trip to the post office to mail it. It was a two-page letter saying, in part:

Dear Governor Green:

We, the officers of Local Union No. 52, U. M. W. of A., have been instructed by the members . . . to write a letter to you in protest against the negligence and unfair practices of your department of mines and minerals . . . we want you to know that this is not a protest against Mr. Driscoll Scanlan . . . the best inspector that ever came to our mine. . . . But your mining board will not let him enforce the law or take the necessary action to protect our lives and health. This protest is against the men above Mr. Scanlan in your department of mines and minerals. In fact, Governor Green this is a plea to you, to please save our lives, to please make the department of mines and minerals enforce the laws at the No. 5 mine of the Centralia Coal Co. . . . before we have a dust explosion at this mine like just happened in Kentucky and West Virginia. For the last couple of years the policy of the department of mines and minerals toward us has been one of ignoring us. [The letter then recited the story of the useless special commission.] We are writing you, Governor Green, because we believe you want to give the people an honest administration and that you do not know how unfair your mining department is toward the men in this mine. Several years ago after a disaster at Gillespie we seen your pictures in the papers going down in the mine to make a personal investigation of the accident. We are giving you a chance to correct the conditions at this time that may cause a much worse disaster. . . . We will appreciate an early personal reply from you, stating your position in regard to the above and the enforcement of the state mining laws.

The letter closed "Very respectfully yours" and was signed by Jake Schmidt, president; Rowekamp, recording secretary; and Thomas Bush and Elmer Moss, mine committee. Today, of these, only Rowekamp is alive; all the others were killed in the disaster they foretold.

And now let us trace the remarkable course of this letter at Springfield. It was stamped in red ink "Received March 9, 1946, Governor's Office." In his ornate thick-carpeted offices, Governor Green has three male secretaries (each of whom in turn has a secretary) and it was one of these, John William Chapman, that the "save our lives" letter, as it came to be called, was routed. Two days later Chapman dictated a memorandum to Medill: ". . . it is my opinion that the Governor may be subjected to very severe criticism in the event that the facts complained of are true and that as a result of this condition some serious accident occurs at the mine. Will you kindly have this complaint carefully investigated so I can call the report of the investigation to the Governor's attention at the same time I show him this letter?" Chapman fastened this small yellow memo to the miners' letter and sent both to Medill. Although Medill's office is only about sixty yards from the Governor's, the message consumed two days in traversing the distance.

The messenger arrived at the Department of Mines and Minerals at 9:00 A.M. on March 13 and handed the "save our lives" letter and Chapman's memorandum to Medill's secretary. She duly stamped both "Received" and handed them to Medill. He and Weir discussed the matter, then Medill sent the original letter back to the Governor's office and dictated his reply to Chapman, blaming the war, recounting the activities of the special commission, saying: "The complaint sounds a good deal worse than it really is. The present condition at the mine is not any different than it has been during the past ten or fifteen years. . . . I would suggest the Governor advise Local Union No. 52, U. M. W. of A., that he is calling the matter to the attention of the State Mining Board with instructions that it be given full and complete consideration at their next meeting."

This apparently satisfied Chapman for, in the Governor's name, he dictated a letter to Rowekamp and Schmidt: "I [*i.e.,* Governor Green] am calling your letter to the attention of the Director of the Department of Mines and Minerals with the request that he see that your complaint is taken up at the next meeting of the State Mining Board. . . ." This was signed with Governor Green's name but it is probable that Green himself never saw the "save our lives" letter until after the disaster more than a year later. Nor is there any evidence that the Mining Board ever considered the letter. In fact, nothing further came of it.

One of the most remarkable aspects of the whole affair was this: An aggrieved party (the miners) accused a second party (Medill's department) of acting wrongfully, and the higher authority to which it addressed its grievance simply, in effect, asked the accused if he were guilty and, when he replied he was not, dropped the matter. A logic, the logic of the administrative mind, attaches to Chapman's sending the complaint to the Department—the administrative mind has a pigeonhole for everything, matters which relate to law go to the Attorney General, matters which relate to mines go to the Department of Mines and Minerals, and that is that— but it is scarcely a useful logic when one of the agencies is itself accused of malfunction. Apparently it did not occur to Chapman to consult Inspector Scanlan or to make any other independent investigation.

And Jack Ripon, Spud White's second-in-command at the District UMWA, said recently, "If I get a letter here I turn it over to the department that's supposed to take care of it, and the same with Governor Green—he got some damn bad publicity he shouldn't have had, he can't know everything that's going on." Ripon's sympathy with Green is understandable—he must have known how Green felt, for he and Spud White received a copy of the same letter. Ripon says, "Oh, we got a copy of it. But it wasn't none of ours, it didn't tell us to do anything. So our hands was tied. What'd we do with it? I think we gave it to Reak." Perhaps Murrell Reak, the UMWA's man on the Mining Board, felt he already had dealt with this matter (it was Reak who, to Scanlan's astonishment, had joined the other members of the special commission in upholding the Superintendent and Mine Manager in their violations of the law and then had been so anxious to help White convince the members of Local 52 "that their charges are unfounded"). At any rate, Reak apparently did not call the Board's attention to the "save our lives" letter, even though it was a local of his own union which felt itself aggrieved. And White took no action either.

As for Medill, on the day he received the letter he called Scanlan to Springfield and, says

Scanlan, "severely reprimanded" him. According to Scanlan, Medill "ordered me to cut down the size of my inspection report," because Medill thought that such long reports might alarm the miners, "those damn hunks" who couldn't read English (Medill denied the phrase); but Scanlan took this order to mean that Medill wanted him to "go easy" on the operators—"it is the same thing as ordering you to pass up certain things." And one day during this long controversy, Medill buttonholed Scanlan's political sponsor in a corridor of the Statehouse and said he intended to fire Scanlan; Scanlan's sponsor refused to sanction it and but for this, Scanlan was convinced, he would surely have lost his job.

But now hundreds of miles away larger events were occurring which were to affect the fate of the miners at Centralia. In Washington, D.C., John L. Lewis and the nation's bituminous coal operators failed to reach an agreement and the miners struck, and on May 21, 1946, President Truman ordered the mines seized for government operation. Eight days later Lewis and Julius A. Krug, Secretary of the Interior, signed the famous Krug-Lewis Agreement. Despite strenuous protests by the operators, this agreement included a federal safety code. It was drawn up by the Bureau of Mines (a part of the U.S. Department of the Interior). And now for the first time in history the federal government could exercise police power over coal mine safety.

Thus far the efforts of the miners of Local 52 to thread the administrative maze in their own state had produced nothing but a snowfall of memoranda, reports, letters, and special findings. Let us now observe this new federal machinery in action. We shall learn nothing about how to prevent a disaster but we may learn a good deal about the administrative process.

"Government operation of the mines" meant simply that the operators bossed their own mines for their own profit as usual but the UMWA had a work contract with the government, not the operators. To keep the 2,500 mines running, Secretary Krug created a new agency, the Coal Mines Administration. CMA was staffed with only 245 persons, nearly all naval personnel ignorant of coal mining. Theirs was paper work. For technical advice they relied upon the Bureau of Mines plus a handful of outside experts. More than two months passed before the code was put into effect, on July 29, 1946, and not until November 4 did Federal Inspector Perz reach Centralia to make his first enforceable inspection of Centralia No. 5. Observe, now, the results.

After three days at the mine, Perz went home and wrote out a "preliminary report" on a mimeographed form, listing 13 "major violations" of the safety code. He mailed this to the regional office of the Bureau of Mines at Vincennes, Indiana. There it was corrected for grammar, spelling, etc., and typed; copies then were mailed out to the Superintendent of the mine (to be posted on the bulletin board), the CMA in Washington, the CMA's regional office at Chicago, the District 12 office of the UMWA at Springfield, the UMWA international headquarters at Washington, the Bureau of Mines in Washington, and the Illinois Department at Springfield. While all this was going on, Perz was at home, preparing his final report, a lengthy document listing 57 violations of the safety code, 21 of them major and 36 minor. This handwritten final report likewise went to the Bureau at Vincennes where it was corrected, typed, and forwarded to the Bureau's office in College Park, Maryland. Here the report was "reviewed," then sent to the Director of the Bureau at Washington. He made any changes he deemed necessary, approved it, and ordered it processed. Copies were then distributed to the same seven places that had received the preliminary report, except that the UMWA at Springfield received two copies so that it could forward one to Local 52. (All this was so complicated that the Bureau devised a "flow sheet" to keep track of the report's passage from hand to hand.)

We must not lose sight of the fact that in the end everybody involved was apprised of Perz's findings: that the Centralia Company was violating the safety code and that hazards resulted. The company, the state, and the union had known this all along and done nothing, but what action now did the new enforcing agency take, the CMA?

Naval Captain N. H. Collison, the Coal Mines Administrator, said that the copy of the inspector's preliminary report was received at his office in Washington "by the head of the Production and Operations Department of my headquarters staff . . . Lieutenant Commander Stull. . . . Lieutenant Commander Stull would review such a report, discuss the matter with the Bureau of Mines as to the importance of the findings, and then . . . await the final report"—unless the preliminary report showed that "imminent danger" existed, in which case he would go immediately to Captain Collison and, presumably, take "immediate action." And during all this activity in Washington, out in Chicago at the CMA's area office a Captain Yates also "would receive a copy of the report. His duty would be to acquaint himself with the findings there. If there was a red check mark indicating it fell within one of the three categories which I shall discuss later, he would detail a man immediately to the mine. If it indicated imminent danger . . . he would move immediately." The three categories deemed sufficiently important to be marked with "a red check mark" were all major hazards but the one which killed 111 men at Centralia No. 5 was not among them.

These, of course, were only CMA's first moves as it bestirred itself. But to encompass all its procedures is almost beyond the mind of man. Let us skip a few and see what actually resulted. The CMA in Washington received Perz's preliminary report November 14. Eleven days later it wrote to the company ordering it to correct one of the 13 major violations Perz found (why it said nothing about the others is not clear). On November 26 the CMA received Perz's final report and on November 29 it again wrote to the company, ordering it to correct promptly *all* violations and sending copies of the directive to the Bureau of Mines and the UMWA. Almost simultaneously it received from Superintendent Niermann a reply to its first order (Niermann had replaced Prudent, who had left the company's employ): "Dear Sir: In answer to your CMA8-gz of November 25, 1946, work has been started to correct the violation of article 5, section 3c, of the Federal Mine Safety Code, but has been discontinued, due to . . . a strike. . . ." This of course did not answer the CMA's second letter ordering correction of all 57 violations, nor was any answer forthcoming, but not until two months later, on January 29, 1947, did the CMA

repeat its order and tell the company to report its progress by February 14.

This brought a reply from the company official who had been designated "operating manager" during the period of government operation, H. F. McDonald. McDonald, whose office was in Chicago, had risen to the presidency of the Centralia Coal Company and of the Bell & Zoller Coal Company through the sales department; after the Centralia disaster he told a reporter, "Hell, I don't know anything about a coal mine." Now he reported to CMA that "a substantial number of reported violations have been corrected and others are receiving our attention and should be corrected as materials and manpower become available." For obvious reasons, CMA considered this reply inadequate and on February 21 told McDonald to supply detailed information. Three days later McDonald replied ("Re file CMA81-swr"): He submitted a detailed report—he got it from Vice-President Young, who got it from the new General Superintendent, Walter J. Johnson—but McDonald told the CMA that this report was a couple of weeks old and he promised to furnish further details as soon as he could get them. The CMA on March 7 acknowledged this promise but before any other correspondence arrived to enrich file CMA81-swr, the mine blew up.

Now, the Krug-Lewis Agreement set up two methods of circumventing this cumbersome administrative machinery. If Inspector Perz had found what the legalese of the Agreement called "imminent danger," he could have ordered the men removed from the mine immediately (this power was weakened since it was also vested in the Coal Mines Administrator, the same division of authority that hobbled the state enforcers). But Perz did not report "imminent danger." And indeed how could he? The same hazardous conditions had obtained for perhaps twenty years and the mine hadn't blown up. The phrase is stultifying.

In addition, the Krug-Lewis Agreement provided for a safety committee of miners, selected by each local union and empowered to inspect the mine, to make safety recommendations to the management, and, again in case of "an immediate danger," to order the men out of the mine (subject to CMA review). But at Centralia

No. 5 several months elapsed before Local 52 so much as appointed a safety committee, and even after the disaster the only surviving member of the committee didn't know what his powers were. The UMWA District officers at Springfield had failed to instruct their Locals in the rights which had been won for them. And confusion was compounded because two separate sets of safety rules were in use—the federal and the state—and in some instances one was the more stringent, in other instances, the other.

Meanwhile another faraway event laid another burden upon the men in the mine. John L. Lewis' combat with Secretary Krug. It ended, as everyone knows, in a federal injunction sought at President Truman's order and upheld by the U.S. Supreme Court, which forbade Lewis to order his miners to strike while the government was operating the mines. (Subsequently Lewis and the UMWA were fined heavily.) The members of Local 52 thought, correctly or not, that the injunction deprived them of their last weapon in their fight to get the mine cleaned up—a wildcat strike. A leader of Local 52 has said, "Sure we could've wildcatted it—and we'd have had the Supreme Court and the government and the whole public down on our necks."

The miners tried the state once more: Medill received a letter December 10, 1946, from an individual miner who charged that the company's mine examiner (a safety man) was not doing what the law required. Earlier Medill had ignored Scanlan's complaint about this but now he sent a department investigator, who reported that the charges were true and that Mine Manager Brown knew it, that Superintendent Niermann promised to consult Vice-President Young in Chicago, that other hazards existed, including dust. Weir wrote a routine letter and this time Niermann replied: The examiner would do his job properly. He said nothing about dust. This letter and one other about the same time, plus Young's earlier equivocal response to Medill's direct appeal, are the only company compliance letters on record.

There was yet time for the miners to make one more try. On February 24, 1947, the safety committee, composed of three miners, wrote a short letter to the Chicago area office of the Coal Mines Administration: "The biggest grievance is dust. . . ." It was written in longhand by Paul Compers (or so it is believed: Compers and one of the two other committee members were killed in the disaster a month later) and Compers handed it to Mine Manager Brown on February 27. But Brown did not forward it to the CMA; in fact he did nothing at all about it.

And now almost at the last moment, only six days before the mine blew up, some wholly new facts transpired. Throughout this whole history one thing has seemed inexplicable: the weakness of the pressure put on the company by Medill's Department of Mines and Minerals. On March 19, 1947, the St. Louis *Post-Dispatch* broke a story that seemed to throw some light upon it. An Illinois coal operator had been told by the state inspector who inspected his mine that Medill had instructed him to solicit money for the Republican Chicago mayoralty campaign. And soon more facts became known about this political shakedown.

Governor Dwight H. Green, a handsome, likeable politician, had first made his reputation as the young man who prosecuted Al Capone. By 1940 he looked like the white hope of Illinois Republicans. Campaigning for the governorship, Green promised to rid the state of the Democratic machine ("there will never be a Green machine"). He polled more votes in Illinois than Roosevelt; national Republican leaders began to watch him. Forthwith he set about building one of the most formidable machines in the nation. This task, together with the concomitant plans of Colonel Robert R. McCormick of the Chicago *Tribune* and others to make him President or Vice-President, has kept him occupied ever since. He has governed but little, permitting subordinates to run things. Reelected in 1944, he reached the peak of his power in 1946 when his machine succeeded in reducing the control of the Democratic machine over Chicago. Jubilant, Governor Green handpicked a ward leader to run for mayor in April of 1947 and backed him hard.

And it was only natural that Green's henchmen helped. Among these was Medill. "Somebody," says Medill, told him he was expected to raise "$15,000 or $20,000." On January 31, 1947, he called all his mine inspectors to the state mine rescue station in Springfield (at state expense), and told them—according to Inspector Scanlan who was present—that the money must be raised among the coal operators "and that he had called up four operators the previous day and two of them had already come through with a thousand dollars . . . and that he was going to contact the major companies, and we was to contact the independent companies and the small companies." Medill's version varied slightly: he said he told the inspectors that, as a Republican, he was interested in defeating the Democrats in Washington and Chicago, that if they found anybody of like mind it would be all right to tell them where to send their money, that all contributions must be voluntary.

After the meeting Scanlan felt like resigning but he thought perhaps Governor Green did not know about the plan and he recalled that once he had received a letter from Green (as did all state employees) asking his aid in giving the people an honest administration: Scanlan had replied to the Governor "that I had always been opposed to corrupt, grafting politicians and that I wasn't going to be one myself; and I received a nice acknowledgement . . . the Governor . . . told me that it was such letters as mine that gave him courage to carry on. . . ." Scanlan solicited no contributions from the coal operators.

But other inspectors did, and so did a party leader in Chicago. So did Medill: he says that his old friend David H. Devonald, operating vice-president of the huge Peabody Coal Company, gave him $1,000 and John E. Jones, a leading safety engineer, contributed $50 (Jones works for another of the Big Six operators and of him more later). No accounting ever has been made of the total collected. The shakedown did not last long. According to Medill, another of Governor Green's "close advisers" told Medill that the coal operators were complaining that he and his inspectors were putting pressure on them for donations and if so he'd better stop it. He did, at another conference of the inspectors on March 7.

Since no Illinois law forbids a company or an individual to contribute secretly to a political campaign we are dealing with a question of political morality, not legality. The Department of Mines and Minerals long has been a political agency. An inspector is a political appointee and during campaigns he is expected to contribute

personally, tack up candidates' posters, and haul voters to the polls. Should he refuse, his local political boss would have him fired. (Soliciting money from the coal operators, however, apparently was something new for inspectors.) Today sympathetic Springfield politicians say: "Medill was just doing what every other department was doing and always has done, but he got a tough break." But one must point out that Medill's inspectors were charged with safeguarding lives, a more serious duty than that of most state employees, and that in order to perform this duty they had to police the coal operators, and that it was from these very operators that Medill suggested they might obtain money. A United States Senator who investigated the affair termed it "reprehensible."

What bearing, now, did this have on the Centralia disaster? Nobody, probably, collected from the Centralia Coal Company. But the shakedown is one more proof—stronger than most—that Governor Green's department had reason to stay on friendly terms with the coal operators when, as their policemen, it should have been aloof. As a miner at Centralia said recently: "If a coal company gives you a thousand dollars, they're gonna expect something in return."

Here lies Green's responsibility—not that, through a secretary's fumble, he failed to act on the miners' appeal to "save our lives" but rather that, while the kingmakers were shunting him around the nation making speeches, back home his loyal followers were busier building a rich political machine for him than in administering the state for him. Moreover, enriching the Green machine dovetailed nicely with the personal ambitions of Medill and others, and Green did not restrain them. By getting along with his old friends, the wealthy operators, Medill enhanced his personal standing. Evidence exists that Bell & Zoller had had a hand in getting him appointed Director, and remember, Weir had worked as a Bell & Zoller boss. By nature Medill was no zealous enforcer of laws. As for the inspectors, few of them went out of their way to look for trouble; some inspectors after leaving the Department have obtained good jobs as coal company executives. Anyway, as one inspector has said, "If you tried to ride 'em, they'd laugh at you and say, 'Go ahead, I'll just call up Springfield.' " As one man has said, "It was a cozy combination that worked for everybody's benefit, everybody except the miners." And the miners' man on the Board, Murrell Reak of the UMWA, did not oppose the combination. Nor did Green question it.

As the Chicago campaign ground to a close, down at Centralia on March 18 Federal Inspector Perz was making another routine inspection. General Superintendent Johnson told him the company had ordered pipe for a sprinkler system months earlier but it hadn't arrived, "that there would be a large expenditure involved there . . . they had no definite arrangements just yet . . . but he would take it up with the higher officials of the company" in Chicago. Scanlan and Superintendent Niermann were there too; they stayed in the bare little mine office, with its rickety furniture and torn window shades, till 7:30 that night. No rock dusting had been done for nearly a year but now the company had a carload of rock dust underground and Scanlan got the impression it would be applied over the next weekend. (It wasn't.) Perz, too, thought Johnson "very conscientious . . . very competent." Scanlan typed out his report—he had resorted wearily to listing a few major recommendations and adding that previous recommendations "should be complied with"—and mailed it to Springfield. Perz went home and wrote out his own report, acknowledging that 17 hazards had been corrected but making 52 recommendations most of which he had made in November (the company and the CMA were still corresponding over that November report). Perz finished writing on Saturday morning and mailed the report to the Vincennes office, which presumably began processing it Monday.

The wheels had been turning at Springfield, too, and on Tuesday, March 25, Weir signed a form letter to Brown setting forth Scanlan's latest recommendations: "The Department endorses. . . ." But that day, at 3:26 P.M., before the outgoing-mail box in the Department was emptied, Centralia Mine No. 5 blew up. . . .

The last of the bodies was recovered at 5:30 A.M. on the fifth day after the explosion. On "Black Monday" the flag on the new city hall flew at half staff and all the businesses in town closed. Already the funerals had begun, 111 of them. John L. Lewis cried that the 111 were "murdered by the criminal negligence" of Secretary Krug and declared a national six-day "mourning period" during this Holy Week, and though some said he was only achieving by subterfuge what the courts had forbidden him—a strike and defiance of Krug—nonetheless he made the point that in the entire nation only two soft coal mines had been complying with the safety code; and so Krug closed the mines.

Six separate investigations began, two to determine what had happened, and four to find out why. Federal and state experts agreed, in general, that the ignition probably had occurred at the extreme end, or face, of the First West Entry, that it was strictly a coal-dust explosion, that the dust probably was ignited by an explosive charge which had been tamped and fired in a dangerous manner—fired by an open-flame fuse, tamped with coal dust—and that the resulting local explosion was propagated by coal dust throughout four working sections of the mine, subsiding when it reached rock-dusted areas. . . .

And what resulted from all the investigations into the Centralia disaster? The Washington County Grand Jury returned no-bills—that is, refused to indict Inspector Scanlan and five company officials ranging upward in authority through Brown, Niermann, Johnson, Young, and McDonald. The Grand Jury did indict the Centralia Coal Company, as a corporation, on two counts of "willful neglect" to comply with the mining law—failing to rock dust and working more than 100 men on a single split of air—and it also indicted Medill and Weir for "palpable omission of duty." The company pleaded *nolo contendere*—it did not wish to dispute the charge—and was fined the maximum: $300 on each count, a total of $1,000 (or less than $10 per miner's life lost). The law also provides a jail sentence of up to six months but of course you can't put a corporation in jail.

At this writing the indictments against Medill and Weir are still pending, and amid interesting circumstances. Bail for Medill was provided by Charles E. Jones, John W. Spence, G. C. Curtis, and H. B. Thompson; and all of these men, oddly enough, are connected with the oil and gas division of the Department from which Medill was fired. And one of them is also one of Medill's defense attorneys. But this is not all. Medill and Weir filed a petition for a change of venue, supported by numerous affidavits of Washington County residents that prejudice existed. These affidavits were collected by three inspectors for the oil and gas division. They succeeded in getting the trial transferred to Wayne County, which is dominated by a segment of Governor Green's political organization led locally by one of these men, Spence. Not in recent memory in Illinois has the conviction of a Department head on a similar charge been sustained, and there is little reason to suppose that Medill or Weir will be convicted. Medill performed an act of great political loyalty when he shouldered most of the blame at Centralia, in effect stopping the investigation before it reached others above him, and this may be his reward.

Why did nobody close the Centralia mine before it exploded? A difficult question. Medill's position (and some investigators') was that Inspector Scanlan could have closed it. And, legally, this is true: The mining law expressly provided that an inspector could close a mine which persisted in violating the law. But inspectors have done so very rarely, only in exceptional circumstances, and almost always in consultation with the Department. Scanlan felt that had he closed the Centralia mine Medill simply would have fired him and appointed a more tractable inspector. Moreover, the power to close was not his exclusively: it also belonged to the Mining Board. (And is not this divided authority one of the chief factors that produced the disaster?) Robert Weir has said, "We honestly didn't think the mine was dangerous enough to close." This seems fantastic, yet one must credit it. For if Scanlan really had thought so, surely he would have closed it, even though a more pliable inspector reopened it. So would the federal authorities, Medill, or the company itself. And surely the miners would not have gone to work in it.

Governor Green's own fact-finding committee laid blame for the disaster upon the Department, Scanlan, and the company. The Democrats in the Illinois joint legislative committee submitted a minority report blaming the com-

pany, Medill, Weir, and Green's administration for "the industrial and political crime . . ."; the Republican majority confessed itself unable to fix blame. After a tremendous pulling and hauling by every special interest, some new state legislation was passed as a result of the accident, but nothing to put teeth into the laws: violations still are misdemeanors (except campaign solicitation by inspectors, a felony); it is scarcely a serious blow to a million-dollar corporation to be fined $1,000. Nor does the law yet charge specific officers of the companies—rather than the abstract corporations—with legal responsibility, so it is still easy for a company official to hide behind a nebulous chain of command reaching up to the stratosphere of corporate finance in Chicago or St. Louis. It is hard to believe that compliance with any law can be enforced unless violators can be jailed.

As for the Congress of the United States, it did next to nothing. The Senate subcommittee recommended that Congress raise safety standards and give the federal government power to enforce that standard—"Immediate and affirmative action is imperative." But Congress only ordered the Bureau of Mines to report next session on whether mine operators were complying voluntarily with federal inspectors' recommendations. . . .

After the Centralia disaster each man responsible had his private hell, and to escape it each found his private scapegoat—the wartime manpower shortage, the material shortage, another official, the miners, or, in the most pitiable cases, "human frailty." Surely a strange destiny took Dwight Green from a federal courtroom where, a young crusader, he overthrew Capone to a hotel in Centralia where, fifteen years older, he came face to face with William Rowekamp, who wanted to know why Green had done nothing about the miners' plea to "save our lives." But actually responsibility here transcends individuals. The miners at Centralia, seeking somebody who would heed their conviction that their lives were in danger, found themselves confronted with officialdom, a huge organism scarcely mortal. The State Inspector, the Federal Inspector, the State Board, the Federal CMA, the company officials—all these forever invoked "higher authority," they forever passed from hand to hand a stream of memoranda and letters, decisions and laws and rulings, and they lost their own identities. As one strives to fix responsibility for the disaster, again and again one is confronted, as were the miners, not with any individual but with a host of individuals fused into a vast, unapproachable, insensate organism. Perhaps this immovable juggernaut is the true villain in the piece. Certainly all those in authority were too remote from the persons whose lives they controlled. And this is only to confess once more that in making our society complex we have made it unmanageable.

Chapter 1 Review Questions

1. How did Dwight Waldo define the scope, substance, and purpose of public administration? How does "public administration" differ from "management" or "bureaucracy," according to Waldo?
2. Why does Waldo at the end of his essay stress "the importance of nonrational action" in public administration? What does he mean by that? For example?
3. Did the case, "The Blast in Centralia No. 5," help you to formulate your own view of what the scope and purpose of the field are or should be today? Does the case contradict or support the conclusions about the theory of the field made in the Waldo essay?
4. Based on your reading of the case, what do you see as the central causes of the tragedy in "The Blast in Centralia No. 5"? Why did these causes develop?
5. What reforms would you recommend to prevent the tragedy from reoccurring elsewhere? How could such reforms be implemented?
6. Based on your analysis of "The Blast in Centralia No. 5," can you generalize about the importance of public administration for society? Can you list some of the pros *and* cons of having a strong and effective administrative system in order to perform essential services in society?

Key Terms

rational action	culture
cooperative human action	structural-functional analysis
bureaucracy	art and science of administration
organization	nonrational action
management	public

Suggestions for Further Reading

The seminal book on the origins and growth of public administration in America remains Dwight Waldo, *The Administrative State: A Study of the Political Theory of American Public Administration* (New York: Ronald Press, 1948), which has been reissued in 1984, with a new preface, by Holmes and Meier Publishers. For other writings by Waldo, see "The Administrative State Revisited," *Public*

Administration Review, 25 (March 1965), pp. 5–37, and *The Enterprise of Public Administration: A Summary View* (Navato, Calif.: Chandler and Sharp Publishers, 1980). For a helpful commentary on Waldo's ideas and career, see Brack Brown and Richard J. Stillman II, *A Search for Public Administration* (College Station: Texas A&M University Press, 1986).

Much can be learned from the writings of important contributors to the field, like Woodrow Wilson, Frederick Taylor, Luther Gulick, Louis Brownlow, Herbert Simon, and Charles Lindblom. For an excellent collection of many of those classic writings with insightful commentary, see Frederick C. Mosher, ed., *Basic Literature of American Public Administration 1787–1950* (New York: Holmes and Meier, 1981), and for a recent selection of key theorists, read Frederick S. Lane, ed., *Current Issues in Public Administration,* Third Edition (New York: St. Martin's Press, 1986). Equally valuable is the four-volume history of public administration prior to 1900 by Leonard D. White: *The Federalists* (1948); *The Jeffersonians* (1951); *The Jacksonians* (1954); and *The Republican Era* (1958), all published by Macmillan. Some of the important books that document the rise of public administration in the twentieth century are Jane Dahlberg, *The New York Bureau of Municipal Research* (New York: New York University Press, 1966); Robert H. Wiebe, *The Search for Order, 1877–1920* (New York: Hill & Wang, 1967); Don K. Price, *America's Unwritten Constitution* (Baton Rouge, La.: Louisiana State University Press, 1983); John A. Rohr, *To Run a Constitution: The Legitimacy of the Administrative State* (Lawrence: University of Kansas Press, 1986); Barry Karl, *Executive Reform in the New Deal* (Cambridge, Mass.: Harvard University Press, 1963); and Stephen Skowronek, *Building a New American State: The Expansion of National Administrative Capacities, 1877–1910* (New York: Cambridge University Press, 1982).

Numerous shorter interpretative essays on the development of the field include Herbert Kaufman, "Emerging Conflicts in the Doctrines of Public Administration," *American Political Science Review* (December 1956), pp. 1057–1073; David H. Rosenbloom, "Public Administration Theory and the Separation of Powers," *Public Administration Review,* 43 (May/June 1983), pp. 213–227; Laurence J. O'Toole, Jr., "Harry F. Byrd, Sr. and the New York Bureau of Municipal Research: Lessons from an Ironic Alliance," *Public Administration Review,* 46 (March/April 1986), pp. 113–123; Lynton K. Caldwell, "Novus Ordo Seclorum: The Heritage of American Public Administration," and Barry Karl, "Public Administration and American History: A Century of Professionalism"—both appeared in *Public Administration Review,* 36 (September/October 1976), pp. 476–505. Several excellent essays are also found in Frederick C. Mosher, ed., *American Public Administration: Past, Present, Future* (University, Ala.: University of Alabama Press, 1975); Ralph Clark Chandler, ed., *A Centennial History of the American Administrative State* (New York: Free Press, 1987); as well as the bicentennial issue of the *Public Administration Review* (January/February 1987), entitled, "The American Constitution and Administrative State," edited by Richard J. Stillman II.

The past decade has witnessed an outpouring of new, rich, and diverse perspectives on what public administration is and ought to be. Among the recent, more challenging points of view include: E. S. Savas, *Privatizing the Public Sector* (Chatham, N.J.: Chatham, 1982); William G. Scott and David K. Hart, *Organizational America* (Boston: Houghton Mifflin, 1979); Frederick C. Thayer, *An End to Hierarchy and Competition: Administration in the Post-Affluent World* (New York: New Viewpoints, 1981); Robert B. Denhardt, *In the Shadow of Organization* (Lawrence, Kan.: The Regents Press of Kansas, 1981); Donald F. Kettl, *Government by Proxy* (Washington, D.C: CQ Press, 1988); H. George Frederickson, *New Public Administration* (University, Ala.: University of Alabama Press, 1980); Michael M. Harmon, *Action Theory for Public Administration* (White Plains, N.Y.: Longman, 1981); Jonathan B. Bendor, *Parallel Systems: Redundancy in Government* (Berkeley, Calif.: University of California Press, 1985); and Herbert Kaufman, *Time, Chance, and Organizations* (Chatham, N.J.: Chatham House, 1985). Where we are in the 1980s with regard to contemporary trends in public administration theory is probably best summarized in Robert B. Denhardt's *Theories of Public Organization* (Monterey, Calif.: Brooks/Cole, 1984); Michael M. Harmon and Richard T. Mayer, *Organization Theory for Public Administration* (Boston: Little, Brown, 1986); or Jay D. White, "On the Growth of Knowledge in Public Administration," *Public Administration Review,* 46 (January/February 1986), pp. 15–24. For a useful comprehensive guide to public administration literature, see Howard E. McCurdy, *Public Administration: A Bibliographic Guide to the Literature* (New York: Marcel Dekker, 1986).

PART ONE

THE ENVIRONMENT OF PUBLIC ADMINISTRATION: THE PATTERN OF PUBLIC ADMINISTRATION IN AMERICA

Public administrators are surrounded by multiple environments that serve to shape decisively what they do and how well (or how poorly) they do it. Part One discusses the major conceptual ideas about the key environmental factors that profoundly influence the nature, scope, and direction of contemporary public administration. Each reading in Part One outlines one of these important environmental concepts, and each case study illustrates that concept. The significant environmental concepts featured in Part One include:

CHAPTER 2 *The Formal Structure: The Concept of Bureaucracy* What are the formal elements of the bureaucratic structure that serve as core building blocks in the administrative processes?

CHAPTER 3 *The General Environment: The Concept of Ecology* How does the general administrative environment significantly influence the formulation, implementation, and outcomes of public programs?

CHAPTER 4 *The Political Environment: The Concept of Administrative Power* What is the nature of the political landscape in which public agencies operate, and why is administrative power key to their survival, growth, or demise?

CHAPTER 5 *The Intergovernmental Dimension to Public Administration: The Concept of Calculative IGR* Why do intergovernmental relationships create complex problems for modern American public administrators?

CHAPTER 6 *Internal Dynamics: The Concept of the Informal Group* How does the internal environment of organizations affect the "outcomes" of the administrative processes?

CHAPTER 7 *Key Decision Makers in Public Administration: The Concept of the Professional State* Who are the key decision makers in public agencies today?

The Formal Structure: The Concept of Bureaucracy

"Under normal conditions, the power position of a fully developed bureaucracy is always overtowering. The 'political master' finds himself in the position of the 'dilettante' who stands opposite the 'expert.' . . ."

Max Weber

READING 2

Introduction

To most Americans, "bureaucracy" is a fighting word. Few things are more disliked than bureaucracy, few occupations held in lower esteem than the bureaucrat. Both are subjected to repeated criticism in the press and damned regularly by political soap box orators and ordinary citizens alike. "Inefficiency," "red tape," "stupidity," "secrecy," "smugness," "aggressiveness," and "self-interest" are only a few of the emotionally charged words used to castigate bureaucrats.

There may very well be considerable truth to our dim view of bureaucrats. We may also be justified in venting our spleens occasionally at the irritating aspects of bureaucracy that arise almost daily—we may even experience a healthy catharsis in the process. But this understandably testy outlook should not prevent us from grasping the central importance and meaning of this phenomenon of bureaucracy.

From the standpoint of public administration and social science literature in general, "bureaucracy" means much more than the various bothersome characteristics of modern organizations. The term in serious administrative literature denotes the general, formal structural elements of a type of human organization, particularly a governmental organization. In this sense bureaucracy has both good *and* bad qualities; it is a neutral term rather than one referring to only the negative traits of organizations. It is a lens through which we may dispassionately view what Carl Friedrich has appropriately tagged "the core of modern government."

The German social scientist, Max Weber (1864–1920) is generally acknowledged to have developed the most comprehensive classic formulation of the characteristics of bureaucracy. Weber not only pioneered ideas about bureaucracy, but ranged across a whole spectrum of historical, political, economic, and social thought. As Reinhard Bendix observed, Weber was "like a man of the Renaissance who took in all humanity for his province." In his study of Hindu religion, Old Testament theology, ancient Roman land surveying, Junker politics, medieval trading companies, and the Chinese civil service, he sought to analyze objectively the nature of human institutions and to show how ideas are linked with the evolution of political, economic, and social systems. One of his best works, *The Protestant Ethic and the Spirit of Capitalism*, established the critical intellectual ties between the rise of Protestantism and capitalism in the sixteenth and seventeenth centuries. He constantly pressed for answers to enormously complex problems. What is the interplay between ideas and institutions? What distinguishes the Western culture and its ideas? Why has a particular society evolved the way it has?

We cannot summarize here the numerous ideas formulated by Max Weber's fertile mind, but we can examine a few aspects of his thought that bear directly on his conception of bureaucracy. Weber believed that civilization evolved from the primitive and mystical to the rational and complex. He thought that human nature progressed slowly from primitive religions and mythologies to an increasing theoretical and technical sophistication. World evolution was one-way in Weber's nineteenth-century view: he visualized a progressive "demystification" of humanity and humanity's ideas about the surrounding environment.

In keeping with his demystification view of progress, Weber describes three "ideal-types" of authority that explain why individuals throughout history have obeyed their rulers. One of the earliest, the "traditional" authority of primitive societies, rested upon the established belief in the sanctity of tradition. Because a family of rulers has always ruled, people judge them to be just and right and obey them. Time, precedent, and tradition gave rulers their legitimacy in the eyes of the ruled.

A second ideal-type of authority, according to Weber, is "charismatic" authority, which is based on the personal qualities and the attractiveness of leaders. Charismatic figures are self-appointed leaders who inspire belief because of their extraordinary, almost superhuman, qualifications. Military leaders, warrior chiefs, popular party leaders, and founders of religions are examples of individuals whose heroic feats or miracles attract followers.

Weber postulated a third ideal-type of authority that is the foundation of modern civilizations, namely, "legal-rational" authority. It is based on "a belief in the legitimacy of the pattern of normative rules and the rights of those elevated to authority under such rules to issue commands." Obedience is owed to a legally established, impersonal set of rules, rather than to a personal ruler. Legal-rational authority vests power in the office rather than in the person who occupies the office; thus anyone can rule as long as he or she comes to office "according to the rules."

This third type of authority forms the basis for Weber's concept of bureaucracy. According to Weber, bureaucracy is the normal way that "legal-rational" authority appears in institutional form; it holds a central role in ordering and controlling modern societies. "It is," says Weber, "superior to any other form in precision, in stability, in stringency of its discipline, and in its reliability. It thus makes possible a particularly high degree of calculability of results for the heads of organizations and for those acting in relation to it." It is finally superior in its operational efficiency and "is formally capable of application to all kinds of administrative tasks." For Weber, bureaucracy is indispensable to maintaining civilization in modern society. In his view, "however much people may complain about the evils of bureaucracy it would be sheer illusion to think for a moment that continuous administrative work can be carried out in any field except by means of officials working in offices."

A great deal of Weber's analysis of bureaucracy dealt with its historical development. According to Weber, modern bureaucracy in the Western world arose during the Middle Ages when royal domains grew and required bodies of officials to oversee them. Out of necessity, princes devised rational administrative techniques to extend their authority, frequently borrowing ideas from the church, whose territories at that time encompassed most of Europe. "The proper soil for bureaucratization of administration," writes Weber, "has always been the development of administrative tasks." Bureaucracy grew because society needed to do things—to build roads, to educate students, to collect taxes, to fight battles, and to dispense justice. Work was divided and specialized to achieve the goals of a society.

Weber also identified a monied economy as an important ingredient for the development of bureaucracy. "Bureaucracy as a permanent structure is knit to the presupposition of a constant income for maintenancy. . . . A stable system of taxation is the precondition for the permanent existence of bureaucratic administration." Other cultural factors contributing to the rise of highly structured bureaucracies were the growth of education, the development of higher religions, and the burgeoning of science and rationality.

Weber listed in a detailed fashion the major elements of the formal structure of bureaucracy. Three of the most important attributes in his concept of bureaucracy were the division of labor, hierarchical order, and impersonal rules—keystones to any functioning bureaucracy. The first, specialization of labor, meant that all work in bureaucracy is rationally divided into units that can be undertaken by an individual or group of individuals competent to perform those tasks. Unlike traditional rulers, workers do not *own* their offices in bureaucracy but enjoy tenure based upon their abilities to perform the work assigned. Second, the hierarchical order of bureaucracy separates superiors from subordinates; on the basis of this hierarchy, remuneration for work is dispensed, authority recognized, privileges allotted, and promotions awarded. Finally, impersonal rules form the life-blood of the bureaucratic world. Bureaucrats, according to Weber, are not free to act in any way they please because their choices are confined to prescribed patterns of conduct imposed by legal rules. In contrast to "traditional" or "charismatic" authority, bureaucratic rules provide for the systematic control of subordinates by superiors, thus limiting the opportunities for arbitrariness and personal favoritism.

Weber theorized that the only way for a modern society to operate effectively was by organizing expertly trained, functional specialists in bureaucracies. Although Max Weber saw bureaucracy as permanent and indispensable in the modern world, he was horrified by what he believed was an irreversible trend toward loss of human freedom and dignity:

> It is horrible to think that the world could one day be filled with nothing but those little cogs, little men clinging to little jobs and striving towards bigger ones—a state of affairs which is to be seen once more, as in the Egyptian records, playing an ever-increasing part in the spirit of our present administrative system and especially of its offspring, the students. This passion for bureaucracy . . . is enough to drive one to despair.[1]

And although he despaired over the increasing trend toward bureaucratization in the modern world, Weber also observed the leveling or democratizing effect of bureaucracy upon society. As Reinhard Bendix wrote of Weber's idea: "The development of bureaucracy does away with . . . plutocratic privileges, replacing unpaid, avocational administration by notables with paid, full-time administration by professionals, regardless of their social and economic position. . . . Authority is exercised in accordance with rules, and everyone subject to that authority is legally equal."[2]

Over the last fifty years, certain elements in Max Weber's conception of bureaucracy have given rise to repeated academic debate and scholarly criticism.[3] Nevertheless, the main outline of his classic formulation is generally accepted as true and significant. For students of public administration, his concept forms one of the essential intellectual building blocks in our understanding of the formal institutional structure of public administration.

As you read this selection, keep the following questions in mind:

Where can you see evidence of Weber's concept of bureaucracy within familiar organizations?

In what respects does Weber's characterization of bureaucracy as a theoretical "ideal-type" miss the mark in describing the practical reality? In what respects is it on target?

How is Weber's bureaucratic model relevant to the previous case, "The Blast in Centralia No. 5"? On the basis of that case as well as your own observations, can you describe some positive and negative features of modern bureaucracy?

[1]As quoted in Reinhard Bendix, *Max Weber: An Intellectual Portrait* (New York: Doubleday and Co., 1960), p. 464.

[2]Ibid., p. 429.

[3]For an excellent discussion of general academic criticism and revision of Weber's ideas, read either Alfred Diamant, "The Bureaucratic Model: Max Weber Rejected, Rediscovered, Reformed," in Ferrel Heady and Sybil L. Stokes, *Papers in Comparative Public Administration* (Ann Arbor, Mich.: Institute of Public Administration, 1962) or Peter M. Blau and Marshall W. Meyer, *Bureaucracy in Modern Society* (New York: Random House, 1971).

Bureaucracy[1]

Characteristics of Bureaucracy

Modern officialdom functions in the following specific manner:

I. There is the principle of fixed and official jurisdictional areas, which are generally ordered by rules, that is, by laws or administrative regulations.

1. The regular activities required for the purposes of the bureaucratically governed structure are distributed in a fixed way as official duties.

2. The authority to give the commands required for the discharge of these duties is distributed in a stable way and is strictly delimited by rules concerning the coercive means, physical, sacerdotal, or otherwise, which may be placed at the disposal of officials.

3. Methodical provision is made for the regular and continuous fulfilment of these duties and for the execution of the corresponding rights; only persons who have the generally regulated qualifications to serve are employed.

In public and lawful government these three elements constitute 'bureaucratic authority.' In private economic domination, they constitute bureaucratic 'management.' Bureaucracy, thus understood, is fully developed in political and ecclesiastical communities only in the modern state, and, in the private economy, only in the most advanced institutions of capitalism. Permanent and public office authority, with fixed jurisdiction, is not the historical rule but rather the exception. This is so even in large political structures such as those of the ancient Orient, the Germanic and Mongolian empires of conquest, or of many feudal structures of state. In all these cases, the ruler executes the most important measures through personal trustees, table-companions, or court-servants. Their commissions and authority are not precisely delimited and are temporarily called into being for each case.

II. The principles of office hierarchy and of levels of graded authority mean a firmly ordered system of super- and subordination in which there is a supervision of the lower offices by the higher ones. Such a system offers the governed the possibility of appealing the decision of a lower office to its higher authority, in a definitely regulated manner. With the full development of the bureaucratic type, the office hierarchy is monocratically organized. The principle of hierarchical office authority is found in all bureaucratic structures: in state and ecclesiastical structures as well as in large party organizations and private enterprises. It does not matter for the character of bureaucracy whether its authority is called 'private' or 'public.'

When the principle of jurisdictional 'competency' is fully carried through, hierarchical subordination—at least in public office—does not mean that the 'higher' authority is simply authorized to take over the business of the 'lower.' Indeed, the opposite is the rule. Once established and having fulfilled its task, an office tends to continue in existence and be held by another incumbent.

From *Max Weber: Essays in Sociology,* translated and edited by H. H. Gerth and C. Wright Mills. Copyright © 1946 by Oxford University Press, Inc. Renewed copyright 1973 by Hans H. Gerth. Reprinted by permission of the publisher.

[1] *Wirtschaft und Gesellschaft,* part III, chap. 6, pp. 650–78.

III. The management of the modern office is based upon written documents ('the files'), which are preserved in their original or draught form. There is, therefore, a staff of subaltern officials and scribes of all sorts. The body of officials actively engaged in a 'public' office, along with the respective apparatus of material implements and the files, make up a 'bureau.' In private enterprise, 'the bureau' is often called 'the office.'

In principle, the modern organization of the civil service separates the bureau from the private domicile of the official, and, in general, bureaucracy segregates official activity as something distinct from the sphere of private life. Public monies and equipment are divorced from the private property of the official. This condition is everywhere the product of a long development. Nowadays, it is found in public as well as in private enterprises; in the latter, the principle extends even to the leading entrepreneur. In principle, the executive office is separated from the household, business from private correspondence, and business assets from private fortunes. The more consistently the modern type of business management has been carried through the more are these separations the case. The beginnings of this process are to be found as early as the Middle Ages.

It is the peculiarity of the modern entrepreneur that he conducts himself as the 'first official' of his enterprise, in the very same way in which the ruler of a specifically modern bureaucratic state spoke of himself as 'the first servant' of the state. The idea that the bureau activities of the state are intrinsically different in character from the management of private economic offices is a continental European notion and, by way of contrast, is totally foreign to the American way.

IV. Office management, at least all specialized office management—and such management is distinctly modern—usually presupposes thorough and expert training. This increasingly holds for the modern executive and employee of private enterprises, in the same manner as it holds for the state official.

V. When the office is fully developed, official activity demands the full working capacity of the official, irrespective of the fact that his obligatory time in the bureau may be firmly delimited. In the normal case, this is only the product of a long development, in the public as well as in the private office. Formerly, in all cases, the normal state of affairs was reversed: official business was discharged as a secondary activity.

VI. The management of the office follows general rules, which are more or less stable, more or less exhaustive, and which can be learned. Knowledge of these rules represents a special technical learning which the officials possess. It involves jurisprudence, or administrative or business management.

The reduction of modern office management to rules is deeply embedded in its very nature. The theory of modern public administration, for instance, assumes that the authority to order certain matters by decree—which has been legally granted to public authorities—does not entitle the bureau to regulate the matter by commands given for each case, but only to regulate the matter abstractly. This stands in extreme contrast to the regulation of all relationships through individual privileges and bestowals of favor, which is absolutely dominant in patrimonialism, at least in so far as such relationships are not fixed by sacred tradition.

The Position of the Official

All this results in the following for the internal and external position of the official:

I. Office holding is a 'vocation.' This is shown, first, in the requirement of a firmly prescribed course of training, which demands the entire capacity for work for a long period of time, and in the generally prescribed and special examinations which are prerequisites of employment. Furthermore, the position of the official is in the nature of a duty. This determines the internal structure of his relations, in the following manner: Legally and actually, office holding is not considered a source to be exploited for rents or emoluments, as was normally the case during the Middle Ages and frequently up to the threshold of recent times. Nor is office holding considered a usual exchange of services for equivalents, as is the case with free labor contracts. Entrance into an office, including one in the private economy, is considered an acceptance of a specific obligation of faithful management in return for a secure existence. It is decisive for the specific nature of modern loyalty to an office that, in the pure type, it does not establish a relationship to a *person,* like the vassal's or disciple's faith in feudal or in patrimonial relations of authority. Modern loyalty is devoted to impersonal and functional purposes. Behind the functional purposes, of course, 'ideas of culture-values' usually stand. These are *ersatz* for the earthly or supra-mundane personal master: ideas such as 'state,' 'church,' 'community,' 'party,' or 'enterprise' are thought of as being realized in a community; they provide an ideological halo for the master.

The political official—at least in the fully developed modern state—is not considered the personal servant of a ruler. Today, the bishop, the priest, and the preacher are in fact no longer, as in early Christian times, holders of purely personal charisma. The supra-mundane and sacred values which they offer are given to everybody who seems to be worthy of them and who asks for them. In former times, such leaders acted upon the personal command of their master; in principle, they were responsible only to him. Nowadays, in spite of the partial survival of the old theory, such religious leaders are officials in the service of a functional purpose, which in the present-day 'church' has become routinized and, in turn, ideologically hallowed.

II. The personal position of the official is patterned in the following way:

1. Whether he is in a private office or a public bureau, the modern official always strives and usually enjoys a distinct *social esteem* as compared with the governed. His social position is guaranteed by the prescriptive rules of rank order and, for the political official, by special definitions of the criminal code against 'insults of officials' and 'contempt' of state and church authorities.

The actual social position of the official is normally highest where, as in old civilized countries, the following conditions prevail: a strong demand for administration by trained experts; a strong and stable social differentiation, where the official predominantly derives from socially and economically privileged strata because of the social distribution of power; or where the costliness of the required training and status conventions are binding upon him. The possession of educational certificates—to be discussed elsewhere—are usually linked with qualification for office. Naturally, such certificates or patents enhance the 'status element' in the social position of the official. For the rest this status factor in individual cases is explicitly and impassively acknowledged; for example, in the prescription that the acceptance or rejection of an aspirant to an official career depends upon the consent ('election') of the members of the official body. This is the case in the German army with the officer corps. Similar phenomena, which promote this guild-like closure of officialdom, are typically found in patrimonial and, particularly, in prebendal officialdoms of the past. The desire to resurrect such phenomena in changed forms is by no means infrequent among modern bureaucrats. For instance, they have played a role among the demands of the quite proletarian and expert officials (the *tretyj* element) during the Russian revolution.

Usually the social esteem of the officials as such is especially low where the demand for expert administration and the dominance of status conventions are weak. This is especially the case in the United States; it is often the case in new settlements by virtue of their wide fields for profitmaking and the great instability of their social stratification.

2. The pure type of bureaucratic official is *appointed* by a superior authority. An official elected by the governed is not a purely bureaucratic figure. Of course, the formal existence of an election does not by itself mean that no appointment hides behind the election—in the state, especially, appointment by party chiefs. Whether or not this is the case does not depend upon legal statutes but upon the way in which the party mechanism functions. Once firmly organized, the parties can turn a formally free election into the mere acclamation of a candidate designated by the party chief. As a rule, however, a formally free election is turned into a fight, conducted according to definite rules, for votes in favor of one of two designated candidates. . . .

3. Normally, the position of the official is held for life, at least in public bureaucracies; and this is increasingly the case for all similar structures. As a factual rule, *tenure for life* is presupposed, even where the giving of notice or periodic reappointment occurs. In contrast to the worker in a private enterprise, the official normally holds tenure. Legal or actual life-tenure, however, is not recognized as the official's right to the possession of office, as was the case with many structures of authority in the past. Where legal guarantees against arbitrary dismissal or transfer are developed, they merely serve to guarantee a strictly objective discharge of specific office duties free from all personal considerations. In Germany, this is the case for all juridical and, increasingly, for all administrative officials.

Within the bureaucracy, therefore, the measure of 'independence,' legally guaranteed by tenure, is not always a source of increased status for the official whose position is thus secured. Indeed, often the reverse holds, especially in old cultures and communities that are highly differentiated. In such communities, the stricter the subordination under the arbitrary rule of the master, the more it guarantees the maintenance of the conventional seigneurial style of living for the official. Because of the very absence of these legal guarantees of tenure, the conventional esteem for the official may rise in the same way as, during the Middle Ages, the esteem of the nobility of office rose at the expense of esteem for the freemen, and as the king's judge surpassed that of the people's judge. In Germany, the military officer or the administrative official can be removed from office at any time, or at least far more readily than the 'independent judge,' who never pays with loss of his office for even the grossest offense against the 'code of honor' or against social conventions of the salon. For this very reason, if other things are equal, in the eyes of the master stratum the judge is considered less qualified for social intercourse than are officers and administrative officials, whose greater dependence on the master is a greater guarantee of their conformity with status conventions. Of course, the average official strives for a civil-service law, which would materially secure his old age and provide increased guarantees against his arbitrary removal from office. This striving, however, has its limits. A very strong development of the 'right to the office' naturally makes it more difficult to staff them with regard to technical efficiency, for such a development decreases the career-opportunities of ambitious candidates for office. This makes for the fact that officials, on the whole, do not feel their dependency upon those at the top. This lack of a feeling of dependency, however, rests primarily upon the inclination to depend upon one's equals rather than upon the socially inferior and governed strata. The present conservative movement among the Badenia clergy, occasioned by the anxiety of a presumably threatening separation of church and state, has been expressly determined by the desire not to be turned 'from a master into a servant of the parish.'

4. The official receives the regular *pecuniary* compensation of a normally fixed *salary* and the

old age security provided by a pension. The salary is not measured like a wage in terms of work done, but according to 'status,' that is, according to the kind of function (the 'rank') and, in addition, possibly, according to the length of service. The relatively great security of the official's income, as well as the rewards of social esteem, make the office a sought-after position, especially in countries which no longer provide opportunities for colonial profits. In such countries, this situation permits relatively low salaries for officials.

5. The official is set for a *'career'* within the hierarchical order of the public service. He moves from the lower, less important, and lower paid to the higher positions. The average official naturally desires a mechanical fixing of the conditions of promotion: if not of the offices, at least of the salary levels. He wants these conditions fixed in terms of 'seniority,' or possibly according to grades achieved in a developed system of expert examinations. Here and there, such examinations actually form a character *indelebilis* of the official and have lifelong effects on his career. To this is joined the desire to qualify the right to office and the increasing tendency toward status group closure and economic security. All of this makes for a tendency to consider the offices as 'prebends' of those who are qualified by educational certificates. The necessity of taking general personal and intellectual qualifications into consideration, irrespective of the often subaltern character of the educational certificate, has led to a condition in which the highest political offices, especially the positions of 'ministers,' are principally filled without reference to such certificates. . . .

Technical Advantages of Bureaucratic Organization

The decisive reason for the advance of bureaucratic organization has always been its purely technical superiority over any other form of organization. The fully developed bureaucratic mechanism compares with other organizations exactly as does the machine with the nonmechanical modes of production.

Precision, speed, unambiguity, knowledge of the files, continuity, discretion, unity, strict subordination, reduction of friction and of material and personal costs—these are raised to the optimum point in the strictly bureaucratic administration, and especially in its monocratic form. As compared with all collegiate, honorific, and avocational forms of administration, trained bureaucracy is superior on all these points. And as far as complicated tasks are concerned, paid bureaucratic work is not only more precise but, in the last analysis, it is often cheaper than even formally unremunerated honorific service.

Honorific arrangements make administrative work an avocation and, for this reason alone, honorific service normally functions more slowly; being less bound to schemata and being more formless. Hence it is less precise and less unified than bureaucratic work because it is less dependent upon superiors and because the establishment and exploitation of the apparatus of subordinate officials and filing services are almost unavoidably less economical. Honorific service is less continuous than bureaucratic and frequently quite expensive. This is especially the case if one thinks not only of the money costs to the public treasury—costs which bureaucratic administration, in comparison with administration by notables, usually substantially increases—but also of the frequent economic losses of the governed caused by delays and lack of precision. The possibility of administration by notables normally and permanently exists only where official management can be satisfactorily discharged as an avocation. With the qualitative increase of tasks the administration has to face, administration by notables reaches its limits—today, even in England. Work organized by collegiate bodies causes friction and delay and requires compromises between colliding interests and views. The administration, therefore, runs less precisely and is more independent of superiors; hence, it is less unified and slower. All advances of the Prussian administrative organization have been and will in the future be advances of the bureaucratic, and especially of the monocratic, principle.

Today, it is primarily the capitalist market economy which demands that the official business of the administration be discharged precisely, unambiguously, continuously, and with as much speed as possible. Normally, the very large, modern capitalist enterprises are themselves unequalled models of strict bureaucratic organization. Business management throughout rests on increasing precision, steadiness, and, above all, the speed of operations. This, in turn, is determined by the peculiar nature of the modern means of communication, including, among other things, the news service of the press. The extraordinary increase in the speed by which public announcements, as well as economic and political facts, are transmitted exerts a steady and sharp pressure in the direction of speeding up the tempo of administrative reaction towards various situations. The optimum of such reaction time is normally attained only by a strictly bureaucratic organization.*

Bureaucratization offers above all the optimum possibility for carrying through the principle of specializing administrative functions according to purely objective considerations. Individual performances are allocated to functionaries who have specialized training and who by constant practice learn more and more. The 'objective' discharge of business primarily means a discharge of business according to *calculable rules* and 'without regard for persons.'

'Without regard for persons' is also the watchword of the 'market' and, in general, of all pursuits of naked economic interests. A consistent execution of bureaucratic domination means

the leveling of status 'honor.' Hence, if the principle of the free-market is not at the same time restricted, it means the universal domination of the 'class situation.' That this consequence of bureaucratic domination has not set in everywhere, parallel to the extent of bureaucratization, is due to the differences among possible principles by which polities may meet their demands.

The second element mentioned, 'calculable rules,' also is of paramount importance for modern bureaucracy. The peculiarity of modern culture, and specifically of its technical and economic basis, demands this very 'calculability' of results. When fully developed, bureaucracy also stands, in a specific sense, under the principle of *sine ira ac studio.* Its specific nature, which is welcomed by capitalism, develops the more perfectly the more the bureaucracy is 'dehumanized,' the more completely it succeeds in eliminating from official business love, hatred, and all purely personal, irrational, and emotional elements which escape calculation. This is the specific nature of bureaucracy and it is appraised as its special virtue.

The more complicated and specialized modern culture becomes, the more its external supporting apparatus demands the personally detached and strictly 'objective' *expert,* in lieu of the master of older social structures, who was moved by personal sympathy and favor, by grace and gratitude. Bureaucracy offers the attitudes demanded by the external apparatus of modern culture in the most favorable combination. As a rule, only bureaucracy has established the foundation for the administration of a rational law conceptually systematized on the basis of such enactments as the latter Roman imperial period first created with a high degree of technical perfection. During the Middle Ages, this law was received along with the bureaucratization of legal administration, that is to say, with the displacement of the old trial procedure which was bound to tradition or to irrational presuppositions, by the rationally trained and specialized expert. . . .

---

*Here we cannot discuss in detail how the bureaucratic apparatus may, and actually does, produce definite obstacles to the discharge of business in a manner suitable for the single case.

The Permanent Character of the Bureaucratic Machine

Once it is fully established, bureaucracy is among those social structures which are the hardest to destroy. Bureaucracy is *the* means of carrying 'community action' over into rationally ordered 'societal action.' Therefore, as an instrument for 'societalizing' relations of power, bureaucracy has been and is a power instrument of the first order—for the one who controls the bureaucratic apparatus.

Under otherwise equal conditions, a 'societal action,' which is methodically ordered and led, is superior to every resistance of 'mass' or even of 'communal action.' And where the bureaucratization of administration has been completely carried through, a form of power relation is established that is practically unshatterable.

The individual bureaucrat cannot squirm out of the apparatus in which he is harnessed. In contrast to the honorific or avocational 'notable,' the professional bureaucrat is chained to his activity by his entire material and ideal existence. In the great majority of cases, he is only a single cog in an ever-moving mechanism which prescribes to him an essentially fixed route of march. The official is entrusted with specialized tasks and normally the mechanism cannot be put into motion or arrested by him, but only from the very top. The individual bureaucrat is thus forged to the community of all the functionaries who are integrated into the mechanism. They have a common interest in seeing that the mechanism continues its functions and that the societally exercised authority carries on.

The ruled, for their part, cannot dispense with or replace the bureaucratic apparatus of authority once it exists. For this bureaucracy rests upon expert training, a functional specialization of work, and an attitude set for habitual and virtuoso-like mastery of single yet methodically integrated functions. If the official stops working, or if his work is forcefully interrupted, chaos results, and it is difficult to improvise replacements from among the governed who are fit to master such chaos. This holds for public administration as well as for private economic management. More and more the material fate of the masses depends upon the steady and correct functioning of the increasingly bureaucratic organizations of private capitalism. The idea of eliminating these organizations becomes more and more utopian.

The discipline of officialdom refers to the attitude-set of the official for precise obedience within his *habitual* activity, in public as well as in private organizations. This discipline increasingly becomes the basis of all order, however great the practical importance of administration on the basis of the filed documents may be. The naive idea of Bakuninism of destroying the basis of 'acquired rights' and 'domination' by destroying public documents overlooks the settled orientation of *man* for keeping to the habitual rules and regulations that continue to exist independently of the documents. Every reorganization of beaten or dissolved troops, as well as the restoration of administrative orders destroyed by revolt, panic, or other catastrophes, is realized by appealing to the trained orientation of obedient compliance to such orders. Such compliance has been conditioned into the officials, on the one hand, and, on the other hand, into the governed. If such an appeal is successful it brings, as it were, the disturbed mechanism into gear again.

The objective indispensability of the once-existing apparatus, with its peculiar, 'impersonal' character, means that the mechanism—in contrast to feudal orders based upon personal piety—is easily made to work for anybody who knows how to gain control over it. A rationally ordered system of officials continues to function smoothly after the enemy has occupied the area; he merely needs to change the top officials. This body of officials continues to operate because it is to the vital interest of everyone concerned, including above all the enemy.

During the course of his long years in power, Bismarck brought his ministerial colleagues into unconditional bureaucratic dependence by eliminating all independent statesmen. Upon his retirement, he saw to his surprise that they continued to manage their offices unconcerned and undismayed, as if he had not been the master mind and creator of these creatures, but rather as if some single figure had been exchanged for some other figure in the bureaucratic machine. With all the changes of masters in France since the time of the First Empire, the power machine has remained essentially the same. Such a machine makes 'revolution,' in the sense of the forceful creation of entirely new formations of authority, technically more and more impossible, especially when the apparatus controls the modern means of communication (telegraph, et cetera) and also by virtue of its internal rationalized structure. In classic fashion, France has demonstrated how this process has substituted *coups d'état* for 'revolutions': all successful transformations in France have amounted to *coups d'état*.

Economic and Social Consequences of Bureaucracy

It is clear that the bureaucratic organization of a social structure, and especially of a political one, can and regularly does have far-reaching economic consequences. But what sort of consequences? Of course in any individual case it depends upon the distribution of economic and social power, and especially upon the sphere that is occupied by the emerging bureaucratic mechanism. The consequences of bureaucracy depend therefore upon the direction which the powers using the apparatus give to it. And very frequently a crypto-plutocratic distribution of power has been the result.

In England, but especially in the United States, party donors regularly stand behind the bureaucratic party organizations. They have financed these parties and have been able to influence them to a large extent. The breweries in England, the so-called 'heavy industry,' and in Germany the Hansa League with their voting funds are well enough known as political donors to parties. In modern times bureaucratization and social leveling within political, and particularly within state organizations in connection with the destruction of feudal and local privileges, have very frequently benefited the interests of capitalism. Often bureaucratization has been carried out in direct alliance with capitalist interests, for example, the great historical alliance of the power of the absolute prince with capitalist interests. In general, a legal leveling and destruction of firmly established local structures ruled by notables has usually made for a wider range of capitalist activity. Yet one may expect as an effect of bureaucratization, a policy that meets the petty bourgeois interest in a secured traditional 'subsistence,' or even a state socialist policy that strangles opportunities for private profit. This has occurred in several cases of historical and far-reaching importance, specifically during antiquity; it is undoubtedly to be expected as a future development. Perhaps it will occur in Germany.

The very different effects of political organizations which were, at least in principle, quite similar—in Egypt under the Pharaohs and in Hellenic and Roman times—show the very different economic significances of bureaucratization which are possible according to the direction of other factors. The mere fact of bureaucratic organization does not unambiguously tell us about the concrete direction of its economic effects, which are always in some manner present. At least it does not tell us as much as can be told about its relatively leveling effect socially. In this respect, one has to remember that bureaucracy as such is a precision instrument which can put itself at the disposal of quite varied—purely political as well as purely economic, or any other sort—of interests in domination. Therefore, the measure of its parallelism with democratization must not be exaggerated, however typical it may be. Under certain conditions, strata of feudal lords have also put bureaucracy into their service. There is also the possibility—and often it has become a fact, for instance, in the Roman principate and in some forms of absolutist state structures—that a bureaucratization of administration is deliberately connected with the formation of *estates,* or is entangled with them by the force of the existing groupings of social power. The express reservation of offices for certain status groups is very frequent, and actual reservations are even more frequent. The democratization of society in its totality, and in the *modern* sense of the term, whether actual or perhaps merely formal, is an especially favorable basis of bureaucratization, but by no means the only possible one. After all, bureaucracy strives merely to level those powers that stand in its way and in those areas that, in the individual case, it seeks to occupy. We must remember this fact—which we have encountered several times and which we shall have to discuss repeatedly: that 'democracy' as such is opposed to the 'rule' of bureaucracy, in spite and perhaps because of its unavoidable yet unintended promotion of bureaucratization. Under certain conditions, democracy creates obvious ruptures and blockages to bureaucratic organization. Hence, in every individual historical case, one must observe in what special direction bureaucratization has developed.

The Power Position of Bureaucracy

Everywhere the modern state is undergoing bureaucratization. But whether the *power* of bureaucracy within the polity is universally increasing must here remain an open question.

The fact that bureaucratic organization is technically the most highly developed means of power in the hands of the man who controls it

does not determine the weight that bureaucracy as such is capable of having in a particular social structure. The ever-increasing 'indispensability' of the officialdom, swollen to millions, is no more decisive for this question than is the view of some representatives of the proletarian movement that the economic indispensability of the proletarians is decisive for the measure of their social and political power position. If 'indispensability' were decisive, then where slave labor prevailed and where freemen usually abhor work as a dishonor, the 'indispensable' slaves ought to have held the positions of power, for they were at least as indispensable as officials and proletarians are today. Whether the power of bureaucracy as such increases cannot be decided *a priori* from such reasons. The drawing in of economic interest groups or other non-official experts, or the drawing in of non-expert lay representatives, the establishment of local, inter-local, or central parliamentary or other representative bodies, or of occupational associations—these *seem* to run directly against the bureaucratic tendency. How far this appearance is the truth must be discussed in another chapter rather than in this purely formal and typological discussion. In general, only the following can be said here:

Under normal conditions, the power position of a fully developed bureaucracy is always overtowering. The 'political master' finds himself in the position of the 'dilettante' who stands opposite the 'expert,' facing the trained official who stands within the management of administration. This holds whether the 'master' whom the bureaucracy serves is a 'people,' equipped with the weapons of 'legislative initiative,' the 'referendum,' and the right to remove officials, or a parliament, elected on a more aristocratic or more 'democratic' basis and equipped with the right to vote a lack of confidence, or with the actual authority to vote it. It holds whether the master is an aristocratic, collegiate body, legally or actually based on self-recruitment, or whether he is a popularly elected president, a hereditary and 'absolute' or a 'constitutional' monarch....

CASE STUDY 2

Introduction

How does Max Weber's conceptualization of the formal elements of bureaucracy apply to the United States? What is America's bureaucracy? What are bureaucracy's patterns in this country? Does Weber's bureaucratic model fit or fail to fit the American experience?

In light of Weber's ideas about bureaucracy, consider the following case, "The Recission of the Passive Restraints Standard," by David M. Kennedy. Raymond A. Peck, head of the National Highway Traffic Safety Administration (NHTS), on October 23, 1981, announced that the agency would rescind sections of the Federal Motor Vehicle Safety Standards (FMVSS) 208 that required passive restraints—i.e., either air bags or passive safety belts (not manually operated)—in all cars sold after September 1, 1983, in America.

The mandatory passive restraint regulation had been a hotly contested issue since the late 1960s. Proponents such as consumer groups and the insurance industry argued that it would save lives as well as significantly prevent or reduce injuries in auto accidents. Opponents such as car manufacturers and dealers said it would add expense without clearly demonstrated benefits.

The case study traces the long, complex history of FMVSS 208 from its conceptual origins in the 1960s, through various attempts to develop it by the Nixon and Ford administrations and its implementation by the Carter administration, until its recission by the Reagan administration. Far from being a neutral, rational bureaucratic rule-making process, as suggested by the Weber reading, FMVSS 208 rode "a regulatory seesaw" with various interest groups, career bureaucrats, politicians, and the courts fiercely contesting its value during almost two decades. The story culminates in an interesting examination of Raymond Peck's decision to rescind sections of FMVSS 208.

As you read this case study, try to think about it in light of Max Weber's foregoing analysis of bureaucracy and its characteristics:

What were the origins of FMVSS 208 in the first place? Do they "square" with Weber's notions of how and why bureaucratic rules develop?

Why was this bureaucratic rule so hard to develop and then settle? Why did it not acquire any easy final permanence?

What powerful interests in this case kept things stirred up and undecided? What were their motivations? Does Weber, in your view, adequately consider the influence of special interests on (or inside) bureaucracy as well as shaping its choices? Is bureaucracy as depicted here, in reality, so "overtowering" (as Weber stresses)?

Did Peck, in your opinion, make the correct choice at the end? How did his personality, position in the bureaucracy of NHTS, and way of thinking influence his choice about rescinding the passive restraints? Do you think Weber's conception of bureaucrats accounts for such factors as those that shaped Peck's decision?

How might you modify Weber's position to take better account of such factors?

DAVID M. KENNEDY

The Rescission of the Passive Restraints Standard

No decision within the foreseeable future will have the impact of this one on traffic safety. It is a question of thousands of lives or deaths per year and tens of thousands of serious injuries. . . . In 1974 and again in 1975, we saw significant fatality and injury reductions compared to previous years because millions of people changed their driving habits. The next reduction of that magnitude within predictable time can come only through increased use of occupant restraints.

NHTSA head Dr. James Gregory to
Transportation Secretary William Coleman, 1976

On October 23, 1981, National Highway Traffic Safety Administration (NHTSA) head Raymond A. Peck, Jr., announced the rescission of those sections of Federal Motor Vehicle Safety Standard (FMVSS) 208 which would have required passive restraints in all passenger cars sold in the United States after September 1, 1983. Passive restraints—which safeguard auto occupants against crash injuries without their having to do anything beyond what is required to operate the car—have ridden a regulatory seesaw since the concept first graced the pages of the *Federal Register* in the late sixties. Peck's rescission proved just another downswing: the decision was overturned by the District of Columbia Court of Appeals and by the U.S. Supreme Court. This case traces the issues and events involved in Peck's decision and reviews in brief the ensuing litigation.

Background

NHTSA, created by the National Traffic and Motor Vehicle Safety Act of 1966 and given its

This case was prepared by David M. Kennedy under the supervision of Stephanie Gould, for use in the U.S. Government Subcabinet Seminars in Professional Public Management. Funds were provided for the case through contract MB3C02. This material may be reproduced by or for the U.S. Government pursuant to the copyright license under DAR clause 7-104.9(a). (0284). Copies of Kennedy School cases are available from the Kennedy School Case Program Distribution office. For information, call (617) 495-9523. Copyright © 1985 by the President and Fellows of Harvard College.

current name in 1970, was charged by its enabling legislation with establishing motor vehicle safety standards that are "reasonable, practicable, and appropriate. . . . meet the need for motor vehicle safety, and . . . [are] stated in objective terms." The latter phrase, along with the legislative history of the act, made it clear that NHTSA was empowered to set performance standards for safety equipment, but not to mandate the specific design of that equipment—the intent being both to encourage private sector development of new and more effective technologies and to keep the federal government out of the engineering business.

FMVSS 208 was among the first standards set by NHTSA. In its earliest form, it sets out safety standards which were met by the manually fastened lap and shoulder seat belts. In 1968, a new and attractive occupant restraint, the airbag, came to the attention of NHTSA officials. Equipped with a sensor, which activates the bag in the event of a frontal crash, the airbag in its current form is a fabric sack which inflates with pyrotechnically generated nitrogen gas within one twenty-fifth of a second following the onset of deceleration to keep occupants from hitting the windshield, dashboard or steering wheel. Although airbag technology had not yet been perfected, NHTSA deemed the concept promising enough to warrant the publication in 1969 of an Advance Notice of Proposed Rulemaking (ANPRM) titled, "Inflatable Occupant Restraint Systems." Congress had given NHTSA authority (later confirmed in the 1972 *Chrysler vs. DOT* decision) to require "reasonable" development of technology if in the interests of safety. Apparently, inexperience with both the concept of passive restraints (inflatable restraints were the only passive restraints under much consideration in 1969) and the standard-setting process led NHTSA to issue such a specific ANPRM. In keeping with NHTSA's congressional mandate to issue performance rather than design standards, a subsequent NPRM published in 1970 retrenched somewhat from the "inflatable system" idea to the more general concept of passive restraints, requiring that all passenger cars be equipped with some kind of passive restraint (in addition to airbags, various net and automatic barrier systems were being investigated in the early seventies) by January 1, 1973.

Besides their intrinsic value as crash protection devices, airbags and other passive restraints attracted NHTSA officials because of the failure of manual seat belts to catch on with the driving public. According to NHTSA surveys, less than 20% of all drivers used seat belts in the late sixties, and in the main the percentage continued to slide over the course of the seventies. Belief in the appropriateness of airbags, however, was not shared by the auto manufacturers—particularly the three largest domestic companies, General Motors (GM), Ford and Chrysler—who early on registered their opposition. Arguing that the airbag was an expensive and unwieldy device of unproven efficacy, the automakers managed to obtain the first of a series of delays in the implementation of the passive restraint standard. NHTSA initially delayed implementation in passenger cars until July 1, 1973, in response to manufacturers' requests for more time for testing and tooling up for production. Meanwhile various devices were considered that would boost seat belt usage, and, as an interim measure, NHTSA required the installation of a continuous warning buzzer indicating unfastened seat belts on all 1972 and 1973 cars. Consumers, however, quickly learned to deactivate the device.

Following publication of a final rule in 1971 requiring passive restraints by July 15, 1973, NHTSA again received numerous petitions requesting a delay in the effective date, but the agency granted petitioners only a month's respite, moving the effective date to August 15, 1973. A group of automakers (excluding GM) took the agency to court, claiming among other things that the standard had been improperly promulgated, and that, in light of the current level of technology, the agency's action had been arbitrary and capricious. While that suit, titled *Chrysler vs. DOT,* was in litigation, Henry Ford and President Lynn Townsend of Chrysler met first with President Richard Nixon and subsequently with his top aides John Ehrlichman and Peter Flanigan to register a general protest against the extent of government regulation of the auto industry. According to a House subcommittee investigative report, soon after that meeting:

> The White House took a direct interest in NHTSA's passive restraint rulemaking. A series of high level briefings and exchanges of views took place between NHTSA, DOT, and White House officials. Then Secretary of Transportation, John Volpe, a firm advocate of the passive restraint proposal, was reported to have returned despondently from sessions with White House officials who rejected his efforts to defend the proposal. Eventually, in a White House confidential memorandum to DOT, Presidential aides John Ehrlichman and Peter Flanigan ordered both a delay in passive restraints and a requirement for the ignition interlock. NHTSA duly complied.

In compliance with these instructions, the ignition interlock, which kept a vehicle from starting until occupants' seatbelts were fastened, was added to FMVSS 208 as an acceptable alternative to passive restraints in 1972.

On December 5, 1972, the U.S. District Court of Appeals for the Sixth Circuit decided the automakers' suit in favor of NHTSA (apparently somewhat to the dismay of the Administration), on all grounds except for the automakers' charge that test dummy specifications were too vague. The court remanded the standard to NHTSA with instructions to revise those specifications. In response, NHTSA set a new implementation date of September 1, 1973; but in the interim, the availability of the interlock option appeared to auto manufacturers to offer a much cheaper and simpler avenue of compliance than airbags. Thus it happened that in late 1973 cars equipped with ignition interlocks hit the market, to the outrage of consumers. In the ensuing public melee, Congress specifically forbade the agency from ever again mandating the ignition interlock, as well as any buzzer lasting longer than eight seconds, and trimmed the NHTSA regulators' sails. Henceforth NHTSA would be required to submit to Congress any regulatory action regarding automobile restraints which could be met otherwise than with normal, active seat belts. Such a standard, which would almost inevitably include an airbag mandate or some measures to coerce passengers to wear seat belts, would stand only if both houses did not pass a concurrent resolution of disapproval within sixty days.

The public case against airbags was bolstered by various publications in widely read journals: in 1969 the *New York Times,* in 1971 *Parade* magazine, and in 1972 the American Automobile Association printed critical reviews of the technology, characterizing it as inconclusively researched and reporting alleged dangers from both routine and accidental activation. Also, the public's experience with the interlock and continuous buzzers had earned little sympathy for NHTSA's regulatory zeal in general, or for airbags in particular.

In the wake of the Congressional veto of the interlock and in a new spirit of circumspection, NHTSA issued a new standard offering three options, one of which had to be implemented in passenger cars by August 15, 1975: full passive protection in frontal, angular and lateral crashes and rollovers; passive protection for all but the rollover combined with lapbelts at all seating positions and a "fasten seatbelt" warning system; or a combination of lap and shoulder belts combined with a warning system. These three options were subsequently extended through August 15, 1976. Public hearings held by NHTSA in 1975 and 1976 elicited allegations from consumer groups of excessive influence of the industry on NHTSA and its parent DOT; from the auto industry, complaints that they needed more time, that the efficacy of airbags

remained unproven, and that consumer resistance to airbags was likely; and from the economically interested insurance industry, enthusiastic endorsements of passive restraints. General Motors announced plans to produce 100,000 airbag-equipped cars in 1974 and 1975, and proceeded—with, apparently, something less than a whole heart—to produce 10,000 such cars before discontinuing the airbag option in 1976. (The *Wall Street Journal* reported heavy pressure on GM dealers from the company to discourage customers from buying airbags.)

The Coleman Decision

Finally, in 1976, came an attempt to review and resolve the passive restraint issue. In June of that year President Ford's Secretary of Transportation, William T. Coleman, Jr., issued a Notice of Proposed Rulemaking (NPRM) in order to begin a new, exhaustive look at the merits of passive restraints. Exquisitely conscious of the skepticism with which Congress and the public were regarding NHTSA following the interlock debacle, Coleman wrote in his NPRM:

> To achieve further reduction in deaths and injuries will require increased use of occupant restraints. It is a question involving thousands of lives or deaths and tens of thousands of injuries per year. Furthermore, the annual cost to our society in terms of lost resources represented by those who are killed or maimed in traffic accidents is perhaps incalculable. . . . The success of governmental regulatory policy in any area, however, will ultimately depend upon the support it receives within the body politic. Recent Congressional action to ban ignition interlock systems . . . reflect the belief of many that there are limits to the federal government's role in forcing the individual to protect herself or himself. Thus this case presents a problem of balancing the need for motor vehicle safety with a concern for the limitations on the federal government's role in regulating aspects of our national life.

This decision also involves the difficult task

of assessing and comparing the safety benefits and costs of alternative occupant restraint systems. While the legislative history of the Safety Act indicates that safety is the overriding consideration, the cost of a standard must also be examined. Marginal increments in safety benefits which can be achieved only at great cost are not in the public interest.

Coleman proposed five alternative versions of FMVSS 208. The first was an extension of the standard then in force, which permitted manufacturers a choice of complying via completely passive protection for all accident modes (frontal impacts, side impacts, and rollover accidents), via passive protection (practically speaking, airbags) for frontal crashes and a manual lapbelt for other modes, or via manual lap and shoulder belts for the driver and front outboard passenger and lapbelts in the rear and front-center seats. All manufacturers had chosen the latter option. Coleman's second alternative would have required that the states "adopt and enforce safety belt usage laws or otherwise to achieve a usage level much higher than being experienced today." Congress would have had to legislate such a standard. Similar proposals had frequently been made by the automobile industry as it worked to oppose airbags.

As his third option Coleman proposed that passive restraints be subjected to an extensive federally-sponsored field test. The testing, to be accomplished by insinuating passive restraints into consumers' or government fleet cars by one of several methods, was projected to cost $50 million to $150 million and could not have been undertaken without Congressional approval of a supplementary appropriation for NHTSA. Supporters of such an idea, Coleman wrote,

. . . generally believe that while passive restraints may be mandated eventually, there is insufficient data regarding effectiveness and practicability to justify such a requirement at this time. In view of the substantial cost of mandatory passive restraints and the relatively small cost of a field test, they would argue, the federal government must ensure

that these questions are settled before embarking on such a program.

Coleman's fourth alternative would have amended FMVSS 208 so as to require manufacturers to put passive restraints in all cars manufactured after August 31, 1979 (although that date was subject to amendment if it conflicted with the lead time manufacturers required to work passive restraints into their designs). Finally, Secretary Coleman considered amending 208 to

. . . require that automobile manufacturers provide consumers with the option of passive restraints in some or all of their models. . . . Those in favor of this option would argue that this alternative would realize the advantages of passive restraint systems for those who choose them while preserving the consumer's freedom of choice. . . . Those opposing this option would argue that the safety benefits of passive restraints would not be realized because consumers would choose the less expensive, less protective, active systems. And the optional nature of passive systems would raise their unit cost even higher, thus further discouraging the purchase of passive systems.

On December 6, 1976, Secretary Coleman announced his verdict: none of the above. While he had been convinced by the rulemaking proceedings that passive restraints were technologically feasible and would be effective, Coleman was afraid the public might react badly to an airbag mandate:

. . . the overall goal of motor vehicle safety would not be served by a mandate of passive restraints which is ultimately rejected by the public. The consequences of such rejection once consumers were required to purchase passive-restraint-equipped cars would be extremely destructive. Reversal would result in a vast waste of the national resources spent in developing and producing the discarded systems and, equally important, in a poisoning of popular sentiment toward other promising safety equipment. Both the public record and our past experience with occupant restraint systems indicate that there would be a large measure of hostility to a new government requirement that people riding in cars protect themselves with relatively costly, unfamiliar devices. While such a conclusion is clearly a matter of judgment, I believe that if the public does not have an opportunity to become familiar with the benefits of such systems before they are installed in all cars, such a rejection is a real possibility.

Accordingly, Coleman proposed that automakers agree to manufacture and market half a million airbag-equipped cars beginning with the 1979 model year in order to demonstrate to the public the salutary nature of passive restraints. The Secretary hoped that the concretely demonstrated effectiveness of airbags would ultimately result in a strong market demand for the devices, making a federal mandate unnecessary.

Negotiations between the DOT and Ford and GM—reportedly conducted under threat of a full-fleet mandate if the firms didn't come through—resulted in a January 18, 1977 announcement that 60,000 such vehicles would be produced. In a separately negotiated agreement, Volkswagen committed itself to producing at least 125,000 more cars equipped with a new kind of passive restraint the firm had introduced in its 1975 Rabbit: the passive, or automatic, belt. Designed to relieve automobile occupants of the responsibility for fastening their seatbelts, the Volkswagen passive belt resembled a conventional shoulder strap anchored to the upper trailing edge of the door rather than to the car's floor or seat. Merely entering the car and closing the door was enough to wrap the belt around the occupant. The Volkswagen design replaced the conventional lap belt with a padded knee bar; other manufacturers later incorporated the conventional lap belt into the passive system. Cheaper and simpler than airbags, passive belts found little favor with manufacturers of large cars because they were impossible to install except at the front outboard seats—thus destroying the capability of large cars to seat three in front—and because of fears that purchasers of expensive luxury cars would find them declasse compared to the unobtrusive airbag.

Provisions in the agreements allowed the manufacturers to back out if NHTSA should later issue any kind of mandatory passive restraint rule. On January 27 Coleman issued the final rule and closed the docket. The passive restraint issue had, at last, been settled.

The Adams Decision

In that final rule, though, was a phrase which must surely have made Detroit wince. "I want to make it clear, however," wrote the lame-duck Secretary Coleman,

> . . . that by . . . amending Standard 208 to extend indefinitely, the current occupant crash protection requirements for passenger cars, I have not in any way foreclosed on future Secretary or Administrator of NHTSA from instituting at any time a rulemaking to amend Standard 208 either to place a termination date on Standard 208 or to mandate passive restraints on some or all passenger cars.

Indeed, only two months later—on March 24, 1977—President Carter's Secretary of Transportation, Brock Adams, issued another NPRM on FMVSS 208. In that notice Secretary Adams said,

> I am concerned that this recent decision by the Department may not be entirely consistent with the statutory mandate of the National Traffic and Motor Vehicle Safety Act . . . to issue standards to reduce highway deaths and injuries. Section 103(a) of the Act directs that,
>
> (a) the Secretary shall establish by order appropriate federal motor vehicle safety standards. Each such federal motor vehicle safety standard shall be practicable, shall meet the need for motor vehicle safety, and shall be stated in objective terms.
>
> I believe a decision based upon anticipated consumer resistance needs reconsideration because I cannot agree that consumers would respond to passive restraints in the same fashion as the ignition-interlock. The igni-

tion-interlock was a "forced action" system that required the vehicle occupant to operate the seatbelts each time the car was started. This represented a constant interference with the occupant's behavior and understandably became a source of irritation. In direct contrast, the passive restraint system requires no action to be effective. In the case of inflation-cushion-type restraints, it is not even visible to the occupant.

I am also concerned that the negotiated contracts represent a 5- to 8-year delay in any decision to install passive restraints in all passenger cars. At this time, the Department is promulgating fuel efficiency standards ... that are expected to result in the reduction of the size and weight of many passenger cars. ... It is accepted that, between vehicles with comparable structures, the lighter vehicle is less safe for the occupant, because less vehicle mass and crush distance are available to absorb crash forces. Improved vehicle structures are expected to compensate for reduction in weight and size to some degree, but it appears that the safety need for occupant protection may increase in the near future.

Following yet another public hearing—this one in April 1977—Secretary Adams issued his final rulemaking on July 5. FMVSS 208 was amended to mandate passive restraints in large cars as of September 1, 1981 (September 1 is the traditional opening of Detroit's new-model year), mid-size cars as of September 1, 1982, and small cars as of September 1, 1983. The effective dates were staggered in order to ease the burden on airbag manufacturers, allow the automobile companies to redesign vehicle interiors at a pace roughly commensurate with their normal design practices, to permit some lingering technical problems with small-car airbags to be overcome, and to avoid placing a huge number of the still somewhat experimental airbags on the road simultaneously. Adams expected the rule to save 9,000 lives a year once the full fleet was equipped with airbags. As for the Coleman Proposal, Adams wrote:

The issue of occupant crash protection has been outstanding too long, and a decision would have been further delayed while the demonstration programs was [sic] conducted. A rigorous review of the findings made by the Department in December 1976 demonstrates that they are in all substantial aspects correct as to the technological feasibility, practicability, reasonable cost, and life-saving potential of passive restraints. The decision set forth in this notice is the logical result of those findings.

Ford and GM—but not Volkswagen—promptly backed out of their commitments to the Coleman Proposal, and the Department of Transportation was almost immediately sued by two parties in simultaneous opposition to both the Secretary's decision and to each other: Ralph Nader, who considered the lead time granted the manufacturers to be unconscionably long, and the Pacific Legal Foundation, a conservative public-interest law organization which argued that Adams had wrongly ignored anti-airbag public sentiment. The cases were combined into one and decided in Adams' favor by the Sixth Circuit of the U.S. District Court of Appeals which ruled that—contra Adams' opinion in his final rule—the Department *was* obliged to consider public reaction but—contra the Pacific Legal Foundation—Adams had so acted when differentiating in his rulemaking between the public's probable response to passive restraints and that engendered by the ignition interlock. The rule stood, and manufacturers began implementing plans to comply.

The Politics Change

The Reagan Administration swept into Washington in January 1981 promising a program of rapid and comprehensive deregulation. NHTSA and the passive restraint rule had not escaped the conservatives' notice. Candidate Reagan had made political capital of the issue on the stump in Detroit:

... the requirement for elaborate new passenger restraints—such as automatic seat belts and air bags—discriminates against [domestic] automakers because the phase-in of the rule, beginning in 1982, starts with large cars, and won't affect small cars—and hence, foreign imports—until 1984. In addition, the expensive airbags will be required only on cars which seat more than two people in the front seat, again generally exempting foreign imports.

The conservative and influential Heritage Foundation had excoriated the agency:

NHTSA's actions in the fields of both safety and fuel economy regulation have been blamed as causing, in large part, the financial problems which domestic manufacturers such as Chrysler and Ford have recently encountered.

The controversies stirred by NHTSA result largely not from any congressional directives to the agency, but from specific policy decisions made by NHTSA in exercising its administrative discretion. It is these policy decisions, rather than any structural reorganization, which must be addressed in considering the agency.

Two of NHTSA's most controversial standards—ignition interlocks and passive restraints—were established not to increase the safety potential of automobiles, but to overcome the refusal of many car occupants to use an existing safety device—seatbelts. . . . The result of all this will be cars which in all likelihood will be no safer, but (in the case of airbag equipped vehicles) much more expensive, than current models containing conventional seatbelts utilized by the occupants.

President Carter's NHTSA administrator, Joan Claybrook, who had made implementation of the passive restraint rule her primary concern during her tenure, was particularly worried about the new administration's intentions toward 208.

That's why I worked on legislation in the summer and fall of 1980, because I knew that the manufacturers would never meet a standard unless it were legislated into law, or the Democrats were in office, and there was enough question about it that I felt that the important thing to do was to legislate it into

law. And we lost by three votes on the House floor. And when that happened, I think that everyone inside the agency and everyone who cared about this issue knew that the Republicans were going to tackle it as A-number one.

Detroit and the business world, however, weren't so sure. In December 1980 the *Wall Street Journal* commented editorially on Claybrook's legislative efforts, saying

The fact that this silly struggle has gone on for so long tells us how deeply Congress has tangled itself in matters it is ill-equipped to deal with—the engineering of automobiles, for example. And the fact that a Republican Senator, one John W. Warner of Virginia, was one of the co-conspirators in the effort to sneak an airbag mandate into federal law warns us not to expect miracles from the new Republican Senate.

And in Detroit the Reagan Administration's intentions towards 208 were considered far from a sure thing. Christopher Kennedy, Manager of Government and Safety Relations for Chrysler, says that, "All we expected here in my office—all I expected—was to get a review of it with new people. And we really had no idea what they would do. Honest—none. Except that we thought they'd look at it." Dick Kimball, then Ford Motor Company's Executive Engineer on Rules and Regulations, had similar, if more world-weary, feelings:

I didn't know what to expect. I've watched several administrations since 1966—Republican and Democrat—and somehow I never was able to second-guess any of them accurately. I gave up having great expectations in any direction—all I had was a hope. If you look at the history of it you'll see that it didn't matter much whether it was a Democrat or Republican administration in the past. Things just kept rolling onward and upward. So all we could hope was that with the Reagan Administration saying that there was too much regulation burdening private enterprise in this country we'd say, "Yeah, man, we believe you. Now let's see if you can perform." But I long since gave up having any great expectations.

President Reagan wasted no time demonstrating his intent to act, against both regulations in general and against automobile regulations in particular. On January 22 he announced that Vice President Bush would chair a Presidential Task Force on Regulatory Relief. A press release noted that ". . . at least five federal agencies directly regulate the auto industry, and these five agencies are now considering more than fifty significant new auto rules." On January 29 Reagan asked the heads of twelve departments and agencies, including Transportation, to refrain from allowing any pending regulations to become effective before March 29 and to avoid beginning rulemaking on any new regulations during those sixty days. Reagan fired the last shot of his first deregulatory skirmish on February 17, when he issued Executive Order 12291, "Federal Regulation," ordering (among other things) every department to delay, if legally possible, any major rule that had not yet become effective to give the issuing agency time to review the regulation, checking its cost effectiveness and that it takes "into account the condition of the particular industries affected by regulations, the condition of the national economy, and other regulatory actions contemplated for the future." EO 12291 also required that OMB have 30 days to review all major rules before their promulgation.

Secretary of Transportation Drew Lewis didn't wait for EO 12291, however, and the Acting Administrator of NHTSA, Diane Steed, didn't wait for Lewis. As soon as she was appointed to the agency in January, Steed directed a standard-by-standard review of NHTSA's regulations.* Steed's Special Assistant, Erica Jones, recalls that

One of the important ways that the agenda for review and reform was set by the new

administration was Diane's standard by standard review. In each case the staff, the technical staff, was asked to describe what was in the regulations and to discuss the reason why it was added to the rules, and to discuss whether it continued to be needed, continued to be effective, and continued to warrant its original purpose or examination. . . . From these meetings a list was made by this agency of the regulations that were in the vice president's announcement of what regulations and standards would be reviewed. That's not our regular process.

That list was sent to the Secretary of Transportation's office, and of its 17 items 3 concerned FMVSS 208: two on the merits of the passive restraint issue and one addressing the September 1, 1981, effective date for the passive restraint rule. On February 9 Secretary Lewis took action to postpone that effective date, issuing a NPRM

. . . to delay for one year the effective date of the first phase of the automatic restraint requirements of the standard . . . in light of the dramatic decrease in production plans for large cars and a similar increase in small ones, and in light of the fact that economic circumstances have changed since the standard was adopted in 1977.

At issue in the delay was the auto industry's devastated financial position and the effect the rule might have on its competitive status. Only large cars were to be required to have passive restraints in 1982, and the Department echoed Reagan's campaign comments:

. . . implementation now may shift some demand from large cars to mid-size cars at a time when large car sales are already slumping . . . the practical effect of the implementation schedule is to require domestic manufacturers to begin compliance in model year 1982 while almost all foreign manufacturers need not begin compliance until model year 1984. This disparate effect results from the concentration of foreign manufacturers almost exclusively in the smaller size classes.

---

*Although Steed—who as Acting Administrator did not require Senate confirmation—was then in charge of the agency and the review of its standards, soon-to-be Administrator Raymond Peck—although without official status—was at this time at the agency and was involved in the review proceedings.

The NPRM also suggested that it might be advisable to reverse the 1977 rule's priorities for implementation, mandating instead that small cars receive passive restraints effective September 1, 1982, mid-size cars September 1, 1983, and large cars September 1, 1984. This would serve safety in two ways: by placing passive restraints in a larger number of cars in the first year of the standard, and by placing them first in those cars whose occupants are at greatest risk.

If the proposed delay of 208 was in accord with a popular conception of an Administration dedicated to gutting regulations, Lewis' suggestion that it might be best to resolve the issue by mandating passive restraints in a larger number of small cars sooner was not. Neither was that suggestion, or indeed the proposed delay itself, commensurate with pressures on Lewis from within the Reagan Administration. Mark Aron, then Acting General Counsel for the Department of Transportation, recalls that

> There were a series of OMB staff people who wanted it [208] turned around immediately. ... We couldn't do it—I told them they'd better send over the facts [to justify immediate revocation] because otherwise I was going to have to be in court the next day. They had a theory that the President could at least suspend rules that had not gone into effect, based on inherent executive powers. In fact they used some of that, throughout the government. We, frankly, thought that was very questionable. ... Lewis was not about to be ordered around. He was quite willing to take them on. I didn't find [Lewis] totally antagonistic [to 208]. He didn't *know* anything about it when he came in—he wasn't a safety advocate, just a businessman. I don't know if it's in the record, but he did sit in a car and have an airbag explode in his face, and he said it was pretty impressive. There were a lot of prototypes floating around, and I seem to recall him saying, "These look pretty impressive."

On April 6, however, as part of the Program for the U.S. Auto Industry announced that day by the White House, the DOT chose to delay the rule. Pride of place in the Program went to Reagan's Economic Recovery Program, but the plan gave great importance to regulatory relief, which was to save the stricken auto industry $1.3 billion and consumers $8 billion over five years:

> The Presidential Task Force and the Executive branch regulatory agencies will give high priority to relief for the auto industry.... The Acting Administrators of the Environmental Protection Agency (EPA) and the National Highway Traffic Safety Administration (NHTSA) have today submitted to the *Federal Register* notices of intent to rescind, revise, or repropose a total of 34 specific regulations.

The 208 delay was the first NHTSA measure; the agency cited excessive economic costs to manufacturers, reduced safety benefits, and consumer dissatisfaction as justification.

The second NHTSA offering was a new NPRM on FMVSS 208. The agency solicited comment on three proposed treatments of the rule: reversal, under which passive restraints would be mandated for small cars in 1983, mid-size cars in 1984, and large cars in 1985; simultaneous implementation, affecting all cars March 1, 1983; and—for the first time since the passive restraint rule was first proposed—rescission.

Reagan had shown he could perform, and Detroit was delighted. *Automotive News* reported GM as considering delay and the proposed changes "a sensible step toward making regulation more cost-effective." Ford found the notice "... very encouraging.... We at Ford believe the changes can be implemented without in any way checking progress toward . . . safer vehicles." Chrysler remarked that "the Task Force report is a big step in the right direction," and Volkswagen of America enthused that "the Administration has taken a giant step toward restoring the economic health of the American automotive industry."

Congressman Timothy Wirth, Chairman of the House Committee on Telecommunications, Consumer Protection, and Finance (NHTSA's House authorization committee), was not nearly so pleased. A strong supporter of passive restraints, Wirth wrote Lewis regarding the proposed amendment of 208:

> There is no question, of course, that the economic health of the industry has deteriorated

seriously since June 1977, the date NHTSA completed its last thorough review of the entire automatic crash protection standard. In addition, the dramatic rise in gasoline and other energy prices since that date have induced an unanticipated shift in consumer demand toward small cars.

To the extent the economic condition of the industry has changed, it is my considered opinion that such a fact is relevant not to the agency's deliberations, which must be guided solely by safety related concerns under its statutory mandate, but only to *Congress.* In passing the National Traffic and Motor Vehicle Safety Act, Congress did not intend that safety requirements should move up and down with the fortunes of the general economy or with the economic conditions of the automobile industry, in particular. Such factors can be considered by Congress in any future legislative deliberations, but are not to enter into the agency's decisions on auto safety regulations.

Wirth closed his letter to Lewis with a host of questions about the procedural integrity of NHTSA's rulemaking, among which were:

. . . Why did OMB regulatory Chief James Miller . . . state that the deadline for the automatic belt and airbag requirements had "already" been delayed when the period for public comment on the one-year delay proposal was still open?

. . . Why did Secretary of Treasury Donald Regan state on March 24 that "airbags would be delayed" at a time when DOT was still in rulemaking to consider whether or not it would delay the implementation of Standard 208?

. . . Why did Secretary of Transportation Lewis declare on April 27 that encouraging the use of manual seatbelts could probably save more lives than requiring automatic crash protection at a time when the Department was engaged in a rulemaking proceeding whose purpose supposedly was to compile a record which would furnish a basis for answering just that?

. . . In light of the comments by Mr. Miller, Secretary Regan, and Secretary Lewis, is the ongoing rulemaking no more than a charade designed to reach a pre-ordained result?

Fortunately, perhaps, for Secretary Lewis, the issue was no longer in his hands. On April 14 NHTSA finally got an administrator.

The Administrator

Former environmental counsel to the Department of Commerce, director of energy regulatory policy in the Treasury Department, and then a natural resources lawyer in private practice in Washington, Raymond Peck believes that he was very carefully chosen for the job of NHTSA administrator:

I think that from the standpoint of the qualifications of the incoming administrator I have every reason to believe that they were very carefully defined, and then sought. They recognized, I believe, that they could not choose anyone from the auto industry or anyone from the opposing [Nader's] side without very serious confirmation problems. This was just too high profile and too highly charged politically to take someone out of the existing field. Because it was highly charged politically and highly sensitive from a public relations standpoint they wanted someone who was extremely skilled by way of background and past experience in the regulatory process. . . . [They wanted] someone who had had experience in the government, who had a regulatory background, and who was not afraid of controversial issues.

Reluctant to accept the post, Peck nonetheless met with Lewis and White House officials to discuss the agency shortly after Lewis was named Secretary in December 1980.* As he recounts it,

---

*That Peck was willing to take unpopular positions did not mean that he was eager to do so. He recently explained his reservations about taking over the head job at NHTSA:

Who needs this kind of a headache? I mean, this is a job that in the job description should have—willing to be

both his and their knowledge of NHTSA in general and the passive restraint issue in particular was minimal. Lewis, however, was reassuring:

> Drew said, "I want you to know we are not abolishing NHTSA and we are not downgrading the agency and we have no intention of having a heavy hand on the rulemaking exercise." By then I had gone through the organizational chart of NHTSA and had some idea of the statutes but nothing else. And I gave a very general five minute discussion. It seemed to me that this agency had in the process of becoming politicized—polarized on the issues—surrendered an awful lot of opportunities to make meaningful contributions to highway safety. . . . We did not discuss a single substantive issue, because they didn't know anything about the substantive issues. . . . All I really knew was what a major reader of newspapers would know about the agency, and Joan [Claybrook's] tenure [as administrator] and what have you. It seemed to me in looking at the statute that there were a lot of dumb things happening and a lot of opportunities that weren't being seized. One of which was, and one of my first questions in the agency was, why aren't you trying to get people to wear seatbelts? And that was formulated—this issue was formulated in my own mind—as early as that. It had nothing to do—I would not have *known* what the passive restraint issue was. I did not know what the passive restraint standard was.

Peck took over the job of NHTSA administrator on April 14, 1981. Personal reassurances by

President-elect Ronald Reagan immediately before the inauguration were instrumental in his decision to accept the post.

> . . . [Reagan] gave me the only five minutes that could possibly have caused me to take the job. He didn't give me five minutes on deregulation, five minutes on regulatory reform, five minutes on *anything* substantive. He gave me five minutes on the importance of not throwing out the baby with the bathwater. He gave me five minutes on how important it was and how sophisticated a set of judgments it was going to be to look at an agency as controversial as NHTSA and not lose sight of the safety mission. That's what he wanted to stress. And I appear to have taken the job during that interview . . . if he had said one word about deregulation I would have walked away from it. I had really decided not to take it.

Once he had accepted the position, however, Peck claims to have had no doubts whatsoever that he was in charge. DOT Secretaries Coleman and Adams had both removed the decision making on FMVSS 208 from NHTSA; Secretary Lewis, says Peck, would have none of it:

> About two weeks after the August hearing on the ruling I was up meeting with Drew on something else and he said, "Listen, I know you have had your hearing on the 208 decision, and I know you have it on your desk. I probably don't have to say this, and I hope I don't have to say it. . . . But I want to emphasize that when we put you in that job we made you our expert. You know more about it than I do. You know more about it than the President does. . . . There is a common public view, as a result of when the issue came up in the campaign, that this administration has a view on that standard. I want you to be absolutely clear that you are the expert. And if your decision is, after you have reviewed all of this, that that view usually attributed to us is wrong, I want you to know I can and will sell that wherever I have to." So I was entirely unconstrained. As a matter of fact, there were many days when I wished I was constrained. I kept trying to give Drew responsibility to

lied about. In public. Willing to be the point man in an issue that has become over time one of the most sensitive of all, from the standpoint of citizen activists. I mean, if Ralph Nader is going to take on Joan Claybrook as administrator no one has any right to assume that whoever is sitting in this chair is not going to be under an unrelieved, unrelenting barrage of fire. What do I need that for?

[In an episode notorious in the history of the auto safety movement, Nader publicly demanded that Claybrook, long his close associate, resign as NHTSA administrator when then-Secretary Adams gave manufacturers four years to prepare for compliance with his 1977 passive restraint mandate.]

make this [decision], kept volunteering that this was an important decision which should be made by the Secretary. He kept pointing out that he had just sat through the air traffic controllers [controversy] and had no intention of taking on another.*

The Rulemaking

NHTSA staff had begun a substantive review with the publication of the April NPRM. The review followed standard NHTSA procedure, although it proceeded quickly, with each of the NHTSA offices involved proceeding with its task simultaneously rather than sequentially, as was more commonly the case. The Office of Rulemaking, under Associate Administrator Michael Finkelstein, prepared for delivery to Peck a Rulemaking Support Paper (RSP) which analyzed the April NPRM without—as would usually be the case—making any recommendations as to which of the notice's three options ought to be pursued. Finkelstein recalls why:

> I was very nervous about it. I think everybody else was very nervous about it because we had a new administration in office. They were not known as to how they would react. The level of paranoia at

NHTSA here was reasonably high. We were the agency with the highest ideological content, certainly, within the DOT. The rest of the department builds stuff. They will occasionally get into a controversial situation, like the controllers' strike, but they're not part of the ideological rhetoric that was being kicked around by the new Administration, as we were. Plus we had an administrator [Joan Claybrook] who was the most political animal in the department prior to that. So I was very conscious to do a Rulemaking Support Paper that was as neutral as possible. Now had I done a Rulemaking Support Paper in the past when Claybrook was here it would have taken a very strong position. The Rulemaking Support Paper that we prepared for Peck discussed the regulation and the Administrator's choices in detail, but it did not have a recommendation section. My recommendations were made to the new Administrator in person.

The Office of Plans and Programs headed by Associate Administrator Barry Felrice produced a Regulatory Impact Analysis (RIA) which, although released to the public only after the decision was made in October, was circulated throughout NHTSA and was available to the Administrator as a distillation of the staff's expertise on all sides of the issue. It weighted the costs and benefits of all three options proposed in the April NPRM. Normally the Office of Plans and Programs, serving as NHTSA's office of internal review, prepared the RIA subsequent to taking delivery of the RSP. In the case of 208, preparation of the two documents proceeded concurrently in order to expedite the rulemaking. Both documents went to NHTSA's Chief Counsel's Office—Felrice recalls sending over a draft RIA in August—and were then recirculated and rewritten. Peck commissioned no new studies to support the rulemaking, but the research—and rationale—that had informed Secretary Adam's decision making in 1977 was soon seen to be largely inapplicable to the situation as it existed in 1981. There were two crucial differences. Felrice explains that:

*The issue of Administrator Peck's independence from Lewis and the rest of the Reagan Administration has been a favorite topic for speculation among NHTSA-watchers both inside and outside the DOT. Given the political sensitivity of FMVSS 208, many have found it highly unlikely that Peck should have been given the unqualified freedom under which he claims to have acted. One highly placed DOT official, however, found it plausible, if perhaps not wholly altruistic on Lewis' part:

> I wouldn't be surprised if that occurred. Lewis is a very smart political animal. . . . Just guessing, I would think that Lewis and John Fowler, who became his general counsel, would feel that [having to decide the passive restraint issue] was a no-win situation, that they might be in between the White House and the press, and get out of it and let Peck do it. It obviously was not the kind of thing Lewis is that interested in. . . . [He is primarily interested in] the finance type of thing, or a management type of thing, and I just don't think he saw it as a big-ticket item.

. . . [E]arlier, in 1977, the standard was really viewed as an airbag standard, by the public, in the industry, and I think within the agency. And I think the agency and the industry really felt that most cars would comply with airbags. And the new data was that it was a big shift: one, in the mix of vehicles being sold, and two, even more of a shift in the means of compliance by the manufacturers.

The two changes were closely related. The 1977 rulemaking had been predicated upon predictions of fleet mix for the years 1982–1985 of roughly 22% large cars, 41% mid-size cars, and 37% small cars. 75% of these vehicles were expected to comply with FMVSS 208 via airbags, with the remaining 25%—mostly small cars—using passive belts.

It can be argued that the Ayatollah Khomenei killed the airbag. After the 1979 oil crisis a radical restructuring of the automobile market toward fuel-efficient vehicles occurred. Now, NHTSA anticipates that in 1983 small cars will comprise 65% of the market, mid-size 22% and large cars but 13%. Manufacturers claim that there remain lingering technical barriers to installing airbags in small cars; they had always planned to comply with 208 by putting the simpler, cheaper passive belts in their smaller offerings. As the market segments of large and mid-size cars shrank, the volume of airbags which would be manufactured for those cars shrank correspondingly. The price of airbags is very closely—and inversely—linked to production volume; during the 1981 rulemaking manufacturers submitted to NHTSA estimates that the cost of an airbag had jumped as high as $1000 from the $2–$300 cost estimated for Adams' decision. As a result, by the time Peck began his rulemaking manufacturers were planning to incorporate airbags into less than 1% of new cars, relying instead on passive belts for mid-size and large, as well as small, cars. NHTSA wrote in the preamble to the decision that the industry's plans were fully understandable from a competitive point of view:

Manufacturers have stated that they chose belt systems for compliance because of the competitive disadvantage of offering the rela-

tively expensive, inadequately understood airbag when other manufacturers would have been providing automatic belts. These explanations seem credible.

Former administrator Claybrook scoffs at this rationale:

It was all verbal. It was all coming out of the mouths of Detroit. It was like press releases being issued. There was nothing solid. They didn't show us any documented orders to the seatbelt manufacturers. They didn't make any. They kept all their options open. They had [airbag] suppliers on contingencies, and they had belt manufacturers on contingencies. They had the whole thing all just ready to go, whichever way they decided to go.

Finkelstein, however, had no doubts of the industry's veracity: "I am absolutely convinced that they were going to put in what they were telling us. We had engineering plans, we had [engineering] tear downs, we knew what their orders were."

The 1977 decision had been made using analyses centered around the effectiveness of the airbag. Finkelstein recalls that,

. . . when the regulation was issued in 1977—again—all the debate that had preceded it was presuming that it was going to be largely an airbag regulation and all of the numbers derived on [the usage and effectiveness] of [automatic] seatbelts were made up. Not made up. They were very rough estimates that nobody examined carefully because they weren't relevant.

Rough estimates were no longer adequate, however. The question of automatic belt usage had become the central issue in the 208 rulemaking. The only data available for addressing the issue were NHTSA contractors' observations of usage levels in the field for some 350,000 1975–1980 model Volkswagen Rabbits and telephone polls of owners of 21,000 1978–1980 model Chevrolet Chevettes equipped with automatic belts. The results were extremely encouraging. NHTSA's RIA shows automatic belt use of close to 90% in

Rabbits and 72% in Chevettes—at least three times the 23% usage rate set by NHTSA as its minimum cost-benefit break-even point.* The agency, however, stated in the RIA that *"it is impossible to predict with precision the level of automatic belt usage if all cars were to be so equipped"* (emphasis in original), arguing that the research did not apply to the systems which would actually be used to comply with 208. It was to become an enormously controversial point.

The agency's doubts about the Rabbit/Chevette data stemmed mainly from the presence in these cars' passive belts of coercive features that would not be built into cars equipped with passive belts as the result of a full-fleet passive restraint mandate. The Rabbit belt and one of the Chevette designs had conventional buckles so that the belts could be separated in emergencies, but they also incorporated an ignition interlock (which Congress had specifically forbidden NHTSA to require after the 1973 debacle) in order to prevent occupants from simply unlocking their belts and leaving them that way. The other Chevette design was a "spool-release" design which could not be detached but allowed a length of webbing to unreel for emergency exits. GM had successfully petitioned NHTSA in 1978 for permission to use the spool-release design. The manufacturer was apparently motivated by fears that, in the absence of an interlock, usage rates for detachable belts would be so low as to compel NHTSA to prohibit passive belts as a means of compliance with FMVSS 208. On several occasions, however, the agency had declined to either prohibit detachable belts or to mandate spool-release designs. Fearing that a tangle of webbing would trap occupants in submerged or burning vehicles, NHTSA continued to hold that position in its 1981 rulemaking, asserting that it "would be unable to find the cause of safety served by imposing any requirement which would further complicate the extrication of any occupant from his car."**

Automobile manufacturers, convinced that consumers would regard passive belts with the same dark fury they had visited upon the ignition interlock, generally planned to include neither interlocks nor continuous designs in their offerings. Purchasers of cars produced under a FMVSS 208 passive restraint mandate would be free to simply unbuckle the devices. Once detached the belts would have to be manually rebuckled to be effective, just like a common active belt. Presto: no passive restraint.

Since Congress prohibited NHTSA from requiring ignition interlocks and NHTSA declined to mandate spool-release (also called "continuous") belts, the agency found itself somewhat unexpectedly in the dark about the usage rates it could anticipate with the detachable automatic belts industry would use to comply with 208. Administrator Peck recounts how

> Everyone had just gone on blithely assuming—without having looked at the facts—that the success of the VW Rabbit and the Chevy Chevette in terms of usage was going to be translated over to the success of the belt usage rate under the passive restraint standard. It was only when you actually had to make that finding that all of the nasty questions like, "What about the ignition interlock present in the Rabbit? What about the ignition interlock and a continuous belt/shoulder system in the Chevy Chevette? How do you account for the presence of those technologies bearing in mind that they're not going to appear in the new belts?" It was really only—exactly as it should—in the process of developing the docket and developing the record that these issues got focused on for the first time.

NHTSA had other doubts about the applicability of the Rabbit/Chevette data. Felrice says that

> There were several reasons the agency felt it could not rely on that data to determine automatic seat belt usage. First is we only have

---

*NHTSA has always performed cost-benefit analyses, but is very cautious about relying on them for decisionmaking. See discussion in text below.

**Despite, as critics later pointed out, GM's testimony at NHTSA hearings on FMVSS 208 that, ". . . under the

emergency conditions of an accident, we think . . . [the spool release] would be a highly satisfactory solution."

data on a single car size, subcompact cars. People who drive subcompact cars behave differently than people who drive bigger cars. When we look at manual seatbelt usage by car size we find between a doubling and tripling of seatbelt usage in subcompacts as compared to full size cars. About 7% in full size cars, and it's up about 17% in subcompacts. So, one, you have that phenomenon of the inverse relationship between usage and car size. That would tend to give you a higher value for usage than you would expect in the whole fleet. . . . The second thing is the people who buy VW Rabbits, which was the only car that we had what we like to call real world data on [field observation data], have a much higher income level than the average car buyer. Many of the studies that we've done on seatbelt usage . . . [show] that the higher the income level, the greater the propensity to wear a seatbelt. So we had *that* bias. We had the bias that these people had voluntarily purchased the belt [the Rabbit belt was available only as part of an extra-cost option package] . . . When someone voluntarily spends money on something you would expect that they would tend to use it more than people who don't spend money on it. And then from the Chevette data we have the problem . . . that people tend to give socially responsible answers to [telephone] interviewers. And all those biases would yield higher numbers in usage than we would expect [to see if the standard went into effect].

Detroit didn't have any doubts about the question. GM's comments to NHTSA on the April NPRM are typical of submissions for both the domestic industry and foreign manufacturers:

We believe this is no longer a technical issue, but that it hinges squarely on what the American public is willing to accept in terms of economic or behavioral burden [sic]. Inflatable restraints are too costly to be acceptable to most and the cost will remain high in relation to belts because of their complexity. Automatic belts that are coercive will be rejected by

the public. Non-coercive (separable) automative [sic] belts will not significantly increase belt use over that achievable with manual belts, and thus will not be cost effective.

Chrysler's Kennedy has much the same feeling; and, given the independence of auto dealers from the manufacturers of the cars they sell, an additional worry:

If you simply give consumers a car with a passive belt without any further motivation, they are perfectly free to push the button and take it off. In the absence of some additional motivation we feel sure that the response by car occupants will be exactly as it is today. In fact, many of these cars, we feel sure, will be delivered [to the consumer] with the passive belts in the stowed position and people will never even know they have them.

Despite the uncertainty of usage rates, NHTSA's senior analytic staff strongly advocated retaining some form of the standard: not on cost-benefit grounds, but rather on grounds of the irrelevance of cost-benefit concerns relative to other issues. Michael Finkelstein said:

I think where I came out was that there was enough uncertainty with belt use information that a reasonable man honestly looking at the issue could possibly come out and say you ought to get rid of it. I wouldn't though. . . . I think that what happens is that people who get into the [automobile safety] field and stay in it any length of time discover that the currency you're dealing with is not dollars-and-cents currency; when you do the cost-benefit analyses they can be useful tools to select among choices. But the real question is—I argue with Ray [Peck] that it's not a philosophical issue. You go to a trauma center and you see people being brought in with their bodies mangled because they've smashed into an instrument panel . . . and you know philosophically that they could have taken care of themselves with the available seatbelts. But you're asking people to pay an enormous price for failure to use seatbelts when there are other solutions available. And so from my perspective . . . when you're dealing with uncertainty, such as automatic belt use levels, if the cost of the regulation is not enormous you go through with it. That's where I would have come out. I believe that the initial costs were higher than the long-run figures would have been with respect to the cost of the regulation, and I thought it really would have saved lives. Whether it would have saved 2,000 or 3,000, or 1,000, I can't predict with certainty, but I thought it was in the range of one or two thousand lives (annually). And to me, that's a lot of people.

Barry Felrice had a very similar sense of the agency's priorities:

. . . we all, myself included, advised him to retain it in some form. Not because we expected the 9,000 or 10,000 estimates of lives saved [annually] going around, because none of us believes in that anymore, but because we felt it had the potential to yield significant benefits. Probably more so than any rulemaking activity that this agency could initiate in the next four years or more than any we did in the last four years. Probably more than we did in the last four years of promulgating 208 combined. Because you only need—well, for each percent increase in usage you get nearly 200 lives saved as a benefit once all cars are equipped with passive restraints. That's big numbers.

I think the feeling of the staff was that there would be a large negative public reaction and that there would be very little if any increase in usage. What we could not advise the administrator on—we could not translate that increase into numbers for him. I probably did most of the analysis in my office, and I could not tell Ray that usage would increase by two percentage points, or ten, or twenty. The Agency's been accused of [making the decision] on benefit-cost grounds: that usage would have had to go up from 11% to 23% to justify the societal costs involved. We never did that kind of analysis. In fact we publicly stated that we don't do that kind of analysis and we don't like to translate lives and arms and legs and faces into dollars. It's abhorrent, repellant, to us, and we only address that issue at all because the Insurance Institute [for Highway Safety] raised it. No one in this agency is forcing us to, or even suggesting that we do dollar-based cost benefit analysis. What I did tell Ray was that I did not think usage would go anywhere near that 23% and I think that's what the other advisors told Ray also. And it was his judgment as to how much it would increase, if any, and whether that small increase was worth the cost of compliance.

Chapter 2 Review Questions

1. What are the formal elements of Weber's model of bureaucracy? Based on your reading of the case or your own experiences with public bureaucracies, did Weber fail to mention any attributes of bureaucracy in his description?

2. After reading the foregoing case study, where would you modify Weber's model to account more accurately for the pattern of growth and the characteristics of America's bureaucracy?

3. Does the case in your view support or contradict Weber's arguments about the monolithic power position of bureaucracy in society? About the nature of bureaucratic rationality? Its hierarchy? Specialization? Narrow latitude of bureaucratic rule enforcement? High degree of efficiency?

4. What are the chief causes, based on your reading of Weber and the case study, for bureaucratic growth?

5. According to Weber and the case study, is bureaucracy hard to change? What are the main causes of "bureaucratic inertia"? What, according to the case, are the sources prompting change?
6. Think about the case, "The Rescission of the Passive Restraint Standard," and what it says about the value of bureaucratic rules in modern society. Why are they important? And yet so hard to determine? To decide upon and then put into practice?

Key Terms

ideal-types	objective experts
traditional authority	bureaucratic rules
charismatic authority	monied economy
legal-rational authority	bureaucratic power
bureaucratic hierarchy	bureaucratic secrecy
tenure in office	

Suggestions for Further Reading

For a thoughtful understanding of Weber's background, his intellectual development, and continuing influence read the introduction of H. H. Gerth and C. Wright Mills, eds., *From Max Weber: Essays in Sociology* (New York: Oxford University Press, 1946); Reinhard Bendix, *Max Weber: An Intellectual Portrait* (New York: Doubleday, 1960); and Marianne Weber, *Max Weber: A Biography* (New York: John Wiley, 1975). For a short but insightful piece, see Alfred Diamant, "The Bureaucratic Model: Max Weber Rejected, Rediscovered, and Reformed," in *Papers in Comparative Administration,* edited by Ferrel Heady and Sybil L. Stokes (Ann Arbor, Mich.: The University of Michigan Press, 1962).

The current literature on bureaucracy is vast but uneven and should be read selectively. Some of the better introductions include Graham Allison, *Essence of Decision: Explaining the Cuban Missile Crisis* (Boston: Little, Brown, 1971); Peter M. Blau and Marshall W. Meyer, *Bureaucracy in Modern Society,* Second Edition (New York: Random House, 1971); Francis E. Rourke, *Bureaucracy, Politics and Public Policy,* Third Edition (Boston: Little, Brown, 1984); Peter Woll, *American Bureaucracy,* Second Edition (New York: W. W. Norton, 1977); Kenneth J. Meier, *Politics and the Bureaucracy: Policy Making in the Fourth Branch of Government,* Second Edition (North Scituate, Mass.: Duxbury Press, 1987); Douglas Yates, *Bureaucratic Democracy: The Search for Democracy and Efficiency in American Government* (Cambridge, Mass.: Harvard University Press, 1982); Harold Seidman and Robert Gilmour, *Politics, Position, and Power,* Fourth Edition (New York: Oxford University Press, 1986); Gary C. Bryner, *Bureaucratic Discretion* (New York: Pergamon Press, 1987); and Richard J. Stillman II, *The American Bureaucracy* (Chicago: Nelson-Hall, 1987). Francis E. Rourke's *Bureaucratic Power in National Politics,* Fourth Edition (Boston: Little,

Brown, 1986), is a balanced, up-to-date collection of various excerpts from seminal writings on this subject.

For three excellent historic treatments of the rise of bureaucratic institutions, see the two volumes of E. N. Gladden, *A History of Public Administration* (London: Frank Cass, 1972); Ernest Barker, *The Development of Public Services in Western Europe, 1660–1930* (New York: Oxford University Press, 1944); and Frederick C. Mosher, *Democracy and the Public Service,* Second Edition (New York: Oxford University Press, 1982). Leonard D. White's four-volume history of American public administration up to 1900 (cited in the previous chapter's "Suggestions for Further Reading") is certainly valuable reading on this topic. Martin Albrow, *Bureaucracy* (New York: Praeger, 1970); Stephen Skowronek, *Building a New American State: The Expansion of National Administrative Capacities, 1877–1920* (New York: Cambridge University Press, 1982); Don K. Price, *America's Unwritten Constitution* (Baton Rouge, La.: Louisiana University Press, 1983); Martin J. Schiesl, *The Politics of Efficiency* (Berkeley, Calif.: University of California Press, 1977); Guy Benueniste, *The Politics of Expertise,* Second Edition (San Francisco: Boyd & Fraser, 1977); Thomas K. McCraw, *Prophets of Regulation* (Cambridge, Mass.: Harvard University Press, 1984); Frederick C. Mosher, *A Tale of Two Agencies* (Baton Rouge, La.: Louisiana University Press, 1984); and Mathew Crenson, *The Federal Machine* (Baltimore: Johns Hopkins University Press, 1975) offer unique and highly original conceptual and historical perspectives, as well as James Q. Wilson's essay, "The Rise of the Bureaucratic State," in *The Public Interest* (Fall 1975).

Serious students of bureaucracy should examine primary materials—executive orders, legislative acts, and official reports. Many key materials are contained in Frederick C. Mosher, ed., *Basic Documents of American Public Administration, 1776–1950* (New York: Holmes and Meier, 1976), and Richard J. Stillman II, ed., *Basic Documents of American Public Administration Since 1950* (New York: Holmes and Meier, 1982). For the best recent defense of bureaucracy, see Charles T. Goodsell, *The Case for Bureaucracy* (Chatham, N.J.: Chatham House, 1983).

The General Environment:
The Concept of Ecology

"An ecological approach to public administration builds, then, quite literally from the ground up. . . ."

John M. Gaus

Introduction

Ecology entered the lexicon of social science and public administration literature long before it became popular in the media and on college campuses in the 1970s as a word synonymous with protecting the natural beauty of the landscape. Originally, the term was derived from the ancient Greek word *oikos,* meaning "living place," and was used extensively by nineteenth-century Darwinian botanists and zoologists to describe how organisms live and adapt to their environments. Sociologists during the 1920s borrowed the ideas of plant and animal ecology and applied the concept to human life; they emphasized the *interdependence* of human life within an increasingly complex organic system and the tendency of living systems to move toward an *equilibrium,* or stabilization of life forms in relation to the surrounding environment.

Ecology was introduced into the public administration vocabulary primarily through the writings of the late Harvard Professor John M. Gaus (1894–1969), one of the early pioneers of public administration; he elaborated on ecology in a series of famous lectures at the University of Alabama in 1945, later published as *Reflections on Public Administration.*

In this work, as well as in his other writings, Gaus was particularly adept at weaving the patterns and ideas of public administration into the total fabric of the issues and events of modern American society. Better than most observers, he showed how public administration, its development, and its activities were influenced by its setting, or its ecology. In his words, ecology "deals with all interrelationships of living organisms and their environment." Thus, "an ecological approach to public administration builds . . . quite literally from the ground up; from the elements of a place—soils, climate, location, for example—to the people who live there—their numbers and ages and knowledge, and the ways of physical and social technology by which from the place and in relationships with one another, they get their living." For Gaus, administrative systems were inextricably intertwined with the fabric of society. In particular, he delineated several important elements that he found useful "for explaining the ebb and flow of the functions of government: people, place, physical technology, social technology, wishes and ideas, catastrophe, and personality." He addressed himself to the importance of these ecological factors in the following selection abridged from his *Reflections on Public Administration.*

Gaus began teaching political science shortly after World War I (prior to Harvard, he taught at the University of Wisconsin) with an early interest in public administration. He interspersed teaching with numerous state and national administrative assignments, and he brought these practical experiences to his classes. Throughout his career, Gaus was fascinated by the interplay of forces between public administration and the larger society.

Gaus shared much in common with Frederick Jackson Turner, an early twentieth-century American historian who poured over maps, soil samples, statistical data of regions, and voting records in his empirical study of the growth of the American nation. Similarly, Gaus asked students of public administration to observe the environment of administration so as to understand how the characteristics of its ecology influence the development of administrative institutions. For Gaus, the term *ecology* was relevant not only to cloistered scholars of administration at work on universal theories of the administrative process, but also to on-the-line practitioners of administration. A conscious awareness of ecological factors permits administrators to respond more wisely to the demands and challenges of the external environment of their organizations. Thus, in the hands of the practitioner, ecology can become a diagnostic tool; it can help in visualizing the major elements in the administrative processes and provide a yardstick for measuring their impact on an organization. However, Gaus was aware that prediction would not be simple: "The task of predicting the consequences of contemporary action, of providing the requisite adjustment, is immensely difficult with the individual or in family life. The difficulty increases with the size and complexity of the unit and expansion and range of variables."

Gaus's concern with ecology of administration was prompted by a special concern with "change." He was a member of the generation rocked by the hardships of a catastrophic economic depression in the 1930s, and he saw the American landscape rapidly being transformed in myriad ways. As he observed, "Change which we have found to be so characteristic of American life, change that has disrupted neighborhoods, that has destroyed cultural stabilities, that has reflected the sweep across the continent, the restless migration to city and back to farm, from one job to another, has brought widely hailed merits. Its merits have been so spectacular, indeed, that we speak of it as progress. . . . Its costs are also becoming clearer, registered in the great dramatic collapses of the depression, more subtly in the defeat, disintegration and frustration of individuals. . . ." Gaus looked to public administration "to find some new source of content, of opportunity for the individual to assert some influence on the situation in which he finds himself." In one essay, "American Society and Public Administration," he stated: "My thesis is that through public instruments some new institutional bases which will enable the individual to find development and satisfaction can be created and some sense of purpose may flower again."[1]

Gaus was both pessimistic and optimistic about the condition of human society. His pessimism welled up when he saw change destroying the patterns of existence familiar to his generation, breaking down the stabilizing institutional arrangements, and confronting individuals with serious economic and personal hardships. Yet Gaus perceived a bright hope in applied social science: through an ecological approach to public administration he believed that new and renewed institutional patterns could be devised for individuals living in an age of change. Ecology in public administration became for Gaus a vital instrument for comprehending, directing, and modulating the forceful shocks of change in contemporary life. In the more than 40 years that have passed since Gaus's studies of ecology were published, younger scholars in the field, like Fred Riggs, have been active in the wider application of the ecological approach, especially in the newer areas of developmental and comparative public administration.

As you read this selection, keep the following questions in mind:

Why does Gaus argue that knowledge of the general environment is so critical for administrators?

If you were to revise this essay for today's readers, what other environmental factors that affect modern public administration might you add to Gaus's list? (You might include, for example, the generation gap or ethnic or sexual factors.)

In what ways can administrators recognize changes in the general environment?

What might be the price paid for the failure of organizations to respond swiftly and correctly to external environmental change?

As you read Gaus's essay, reflect on its relevance to Case Study 1, "The Blast in Centralia No. 5." How did ecological factors influence the outcome of this case?

---

[1]John Gaus, "American Society and Public Administration," in John M. Gaus, Leonard D. White, and Marshall E. Dimock, *The Frontiers of Public Administration* (Chicago: University of Chicago Press, 1936).

JOHN GAUS

The Ecology of Public Administration

The study of public administration must include its ecology. "Ecology," states the Webster Dictionary, "is the mutual relations, collectively, between organisms and their environment." J. W. Bews points out that "the word itself is derived from the Greek *oikos,* a house or home, the same root word as occurs in economy and economics. Economics is a subject with which ecology has much in common, but ecology is much wider. It deals with all the interrelationships of living organisms and their environment."[1] Some social scientists have been returning to the use of the term, chiefly employed by the biologist and botanist, especially under the stimulus of studies of anthropologists, sociologists, and pioneers who defy easy classification, such as the late Sir Patrick Geddes in Britain. In the lecture of Frankfurter's already quoted, the linkage between physical area, population, transport and government is concretely indicated. More recently, Charles A. Beard formulated some axioms of government in which environmental change is linked with resulting public administration. "I present," he stated, "for what it is worth, and may prove to be worth, the following bill of axioms or aphorisms on public administration, as fitting this important occasion.

1. The continuous and fairly efficient discharge of certain functions by government, central and local, is a necessary condition for the existence of any great society.

Abridged from *Reflections on Public Administration* by John Gaus, pp. 6–19. Copyright 1947 by The University of Alabama Press. Reprinted by permission of the Estate of Janette Gaus.
[1]J. W. Bews, *Human Ecology* (London: Oxford University Press, 1935), p. 1.

2. As a society becomes more complicated, as its division of labor ramifies more widely, as its commerce extends, as technology takes the place of handicrafts and local self-sufficiency, the functions of government increase in number and in their vital relationships to the fortunes of society and individuals.

3. Any government in such a complicated society, consequently any such society itself, is strong in proportion to its capacity to administer the functions that are brought into being.

4. Legislation respecting these functions, difficult as it is, is relatively easy as compared with the enforcement of legislation, that is, the effective discharge of these functions in their most minute ramifications and for the public welfare.

5. When a form of government, such as ours, provides for legal changes, by the process of discussion and open decision, to fit social changes, the effective and wise administration becomes the central prerequisite for the perdurance of government and society—to use a metaphor, becomes a foundation of government as a going concern.

6. Unless the members of an administrative system are drawn from various classes and regions, unless careers are open in it to talents, unless the way is prepared by an appropriate scheme of general education, unless public officials are subjected to internal and external criticism of a constructive nature, then the public personnel will become a bureaucracy dangerous to society and to popular government.

7. Unless, as David Lilienthal has recently pointed out in an address on the Tennessee Valley Authority, an administrative system is so constructed and operated as to keep

alive local and individual responsibilities, it is likely to destroy the basic well-springs of activity, hope, and enthusiasm necessary to popular government and to the following of a democratic civilization."[2]

An ecological approach to public administration builds, then, quite literally from the ground up; from the elements of a place—soils, climate, location, for example—to the people who live there—their numbers and ages and knowledge, and the ways of physical and social technology by which from the place and in relationships with one another, they get their living. It is within this setting that their instruments and practices of public housekeeping should be studied so that they may better understand what they are doing, and appraise reasonably how they are doing it. Such an approach is of particular interest to us as students seeking to cooperate in our studies; for it invites—indeed is dependent upon—careful observation by many people in different environments of the roots of government functions, civic attitudes, and operating problems.

With no claim to originality, therefore, and indeed with every emphasis on the collaborative nature of the task, I put before you a list of the factors which I have found useful as explaining the ebb and flow of the functions of government. They are: people, place, physical technology, social technology, wishes and ideas, catastrophe, and personality. I have over many years built up a kind of flexible textbook in a collection of clippings, articles and books illustrative of each, as any one can do for himself. Such illustrations of the "raw material of politics" and hence administration are in themselves the raw material of a science of administration, of that part of the science which describes and

interprets why particular activities are undertaken through government and the problems of policy, organization and management generally that result from such origins.[3]

By illustrating concretely the relation of these environmental factors, a cooperative testing of the theory will be facilitated. The changes in the distribution of the people of a governmental unit by time, age and place throw light on the origins of public policy and administration. At our first census we were a people 80 per cent of whom lived on farms; at our last census, one hundred and fifty years later, 80 per cent of us did not live on farms. Over a third are now living in a relatively few metropolitan areas; but the growth of these areas is not in the core or mother city; it is in the surrounding suburbs, separate political entities, frequently also separate economic-status and cultural entities, yet sharing with the mother city, which is often absolutely declining in population, the public housekeeping problems of a metropolitan organism for which no—or no adequate—political organization exists. Our population is increasingly one with a larger proportion distributed among the older age classes. These raw facts—too little known and appreciated by citizens, which should be at once placed before them in discussing many of our public questions—in themselves explain much about our functions of government. Coupled with factors of place and technology, they clarify many an issue that is usually expressed in sterile conflicts. For example, the old people in the more frequent large family on a farm of a century ago, where more goods and services were provided on the farm, had a function still to perform and a more meaningful place in the lives of younger genera-

---

[2]From "Administration, A Foundation of Government," by Charles A. Beard, in *American Political Science Review,* XXXIV, No. 2 (April, 1940), p. 232. Reprinted by permission of the American Political Science Association.

[3]The methods as well as the substantive interpretations of Frederick Jackson Turner should be familiar to students of public administration so far as the printed page permits. It was a rich experience to be present as he worked over maps and statistical data of a county, state or region, putting geology, soils, land values, origins of residents, and voting records together for light on the resulting social action.

tions of the family. In a more pecuniary economy, separated from the family-subsistence economy, ignored in the allocation of the work and rewards of an industrial society, the demand for pensions became irresistible.

The movement of people (by characteristic age and income groups) from the mother city to suburbs (as guided by factors of time-space and cost in the journey to work, the dispersal of shopping centers, the search of industry for land space for straight-line production facilitated by paved roads, trucks and distribution of power by wires, and other technological changes, and changes in what we wish for in residential environment) produces its repercussion in the values of land and buildings, in the tax basis for public services already existent in older areas and demanded in the new, in the differential requirements and capacities-to-pay of people for housing (including the site and neighborhood equipment) and in the adjustment of transport and utility requirements for the ever-changing metropolitan organism.

Thus the factors of people and place are inextricably interwoven. And not merely in crowded urban centers. I have watched the same process of change in sparsely settled areas of farm and forest, and its potent effect on government.

Where there are extensive cut-over areas in the Lake States, where the older farm lands of New England or New York are no longer profitable to agriculture and reforestation is too recent to yield timber crops, in the Great Plains where lands best suited to grazing and with limited rainfall have been subjected to the plough, in the cut-over and eroded lands of the Southern Piedmont, or in the anthracite region of Pennsylvania, physical conditions—the exhaustion of the resource which originally brought settlement—have produced a chain of institutional consequences. Land values and tax payments decline, tax delinquent land reverts to county or state, public schools, roads and other services can no longer be locally financed. Immediate relief through state financial aids or state administered services in turn are inadequate when

widespread catastrophic economic depression undermines state revenues. Efforts aimed at restoring a source of production, such as encouragement of cropping timber through favoring taxation or the building up of public forests adequate for permanent wood-using industries, or the restoration of soil, will require a long period of time for efficacy, and equally require an atmosphere in which political leadership, the careful integration of national, state, local, and individual and corporate policies, and skilled technical personnel can be established and supported steadily. Such an atmosphere, however, is not likely to be present among the frustrate population of such areas, or the better-provided populations of other areas called upon to tax themselves for local units of government in areas which they have never seen or whose problems they do not understand. Thus changes in place, or the use of the resources and products of a place, are coercive in their effect upon public administration.[4]

My own generation has had a great lesson in the importance of change in physical technology in witnessing the adoption of the automobile and the role it has come to play. It may be noted that its widespread use was made possible by the development of paved highways provided necessarily as a public service. Highway expansion and design have been affected by the coercion of political forces created by the physical invention. Groups of automobile users, manufacturers, hotel proprietors, road builders, road machinery and materials suppliers, persons seeking jobs in highway construction and administration and many others, have contended with those using horses, carriage and harness makers and persons opposed to the increased taxation that paved roads would require. The original causes—a combination of physical in-

---

[4] A reverse picture is the sudden demand on the use of ores in the Adirondack region during the world war because of changes in the conditions of ocean shipment. In one remote village a public housing project, to take care of the expanded work force, was a consequence, again, of the catastrophe of war.

ventions such as the internal combustion engine and the vulcanization of rubber—get obscured in the ultimate disputes over taxation, jurisdiction, requirement of liability insurance and examination for drivers' licenses, or over the merits or defects of systems of traffic control or the financing of overhead crossings or express highways. The citizen blames "bureaucrats" and "politicians" because the basic ecological causes have not been clarified for him. This process of public function adoption may also be reversed by other changes—as we see, for example, in the abandonment of many publicly financed and constructed canals, when new technologies of transport rendered them obsolete.

Changes in physical technology, however slowly their institutional influences may spread, are more obvious even to the point of being dramatic, to the citizen. But he sometimes forgets the importance of the invention of social institutions or devices, and their continuing influences which coerce us. Thus the pooling and application of the savings of many through the invention of the corporation has set new forces to ripple through the social order, disarranging human relationships and creating new possibilities of large scale enterprise financially capable of utilizing extensive equipment and personnel and creating new relationships between buyer and seller, employer and employee—from which coercions for a new balance of forces, through consumer, labor and investor standards, have resulted.

You will have noted how interrelated all of these factors are in their operation. Perhaps the subtlest one is that for which I have difficulty in finding a satisfactory term. I have used the words "wishes and ideas." What you don't know, it is said, won't hurt you. I wonder whether this is true. If you do know that some new drug, or method of treatment of disease, will prevent the illness or perhaps death of those dear to you, you will have a new imperative for action, even if that action requires a public program. If you know or think you know that a combination of legislative and administrative

measures will safeguard your bank deposit or insurance from destruction, that idea will have a coercive effect upon your political action. If you think that public officials are corrupt, that a tariff act or a regulation of a trade is a "racket," that too will influence the political decisions of your time. If you value material well-being, and if that desire takes so definite a form as a house and yard and garden, there are inevitable consequences in standards of public services that will facilitate the realization of your desire. Down that long road one will find the public insurance of mortgages to achieve lower interest rates and longer-term financing and zoning ordinances.

The originators of ideas and of social as well as physical invention are persons. We students of public administration will do well to study the elements in the influences which Bentham, the Webbs, the city planner Burnham, the health officer Biggs, the pioneers in the New York Bureau of Municipal Research and its Training School for Public Service have wielded. Relevant preparation, longevity, personal or institutional resources for research, sympathetic disciples, frequently some catastrophic situation in which prevailing attitudes were sufficiently blasted to permit the new ideas to be applied, channels of publication and of communication generally, as well as inner qualities of industry and integrity all, or nearly all in some combination, will be found. We each will have touched some one of this kind, perhaps, in our own community; if not a pioneer in original invention, an enlightened civic interpreter, agitator, or organizer. Thus the late Governor Alfred E. Smith had a genius for relating his sense of people's needs, his experience in party and legislative processes and his position as Governor to a political and administrative program in which the special knowledge of many persons was most effectively used in the service of the State of New York.

Catastrophe, especially when leadership and knowledge are prepared with long-time programs into which the immediate hurried relief action can be fitted, has its place in the ecology of administration. It not only is destructive, so that relief and repair are required on a scale so large that collective action is necessary, but it also disrupts, jostles or challenges views and attitudes, and affords to the inner self as well as to others a respectable and face-saving reason for changing one's views as to policy. The atomic bomb gave to many, perhaps, a determining reason for a change of attitude toward international organization. But I incline to the view that the effects of catastrophe on our thinking are relatively short-lived, and confined to relatively smaller institutional changes, and that older forces flood back with great strength to cancel most of the first reaction. A frightened and frustrated society is not one in which really significant changes will take root, unless careful preparation and wise administration of the relief period are available. The night club fire in Boston in recent years in which so many service men from various parts of the country were killed is a tragic example of one role of catastrophe. In the lurid glare of that fire, weaknesses in building codes and the administration of them were revealed. So many vested interests of materials, construction and crafts center in building codes that they are difficult to keep in tune with invention and changing social needs. The fact that many in the fire were from remote places, and were men in the armed services, gave unusually wide reporting of the tragedy for some days, especially as many victims lingered on in hospitals. One result of the shock of the catastrophe was therefore action in cities throughout the world to inspect their places of public amusement and survey their fire-prevention legislation and administration. On a vaster scale, the catastrophe of economic world depression led to a varied array of responses through collective action in which there was much similarity despite regional and ideological differences among the various states of the world, since there were also like ecological factors, common to modern power industry and the price system. World wars illustrate the extent to which a large area of collective action is necessarily adopted under modern conditions of total war—and equally illustrate the tremendous pull of older customary views at the close, when the pressure to remove the controls rises, and individuals in office are held responsible for the frustrations once borne as a patriotic offering. Wise and fortunate indeed is that community that has so analyzed its problems and needs, and has so prepared to make use of catastrophe should it come by plans for carrying out programs of improvements, that the aftermath of tragedy finds its victims as well cared for as humanly possible and in addition some tangible new advance in the equipment and life of the community. I have seen some communities which, because they had equipped themselves with personnel capable of fresh thinking, had obtained from depression work-relief programs recreation facilities that were their first amenities.

Such an approach as this to our study of public administration is difficult, in that it makes demands upon our powers to observe, upon a sensitive awareness of changes and maladjustment and upon our willingness to face the political—that is, the public-housekeeping —basis of administration. These factors—you may improve upon my selection—in various combinations lie behind a public agency. In their combination will be found the reasons for its existence, and the reasons for attack upon it as well. Only in so far as we can find some essentially public core in the combination can we hope to have an agency free from spoils or abuse of power. The process of growth and formulation of a public policy out of these environmental materials links environment and administration. We may be too responsive to change, or we may fail to achieve our best selves by ignoring what we might do to advantage ourselves by collective action, if we perform this task of politics badly.

"When I pay taxes," wrote Justice Holmes to his friend Sir Frederick Pollock, "I buy civilization." It is no easy task of the citizen in this complicated world to get fair value in what he buys. That task is one of discovery of the causes of problems, of the communication of possible remedies, of the organizing of citizens, of the formulation of law. It is the task, in short, of politics. The task will be more fruitfully performed if the citizen, and his agents in public offices, understand the ecology of government.

CASE STUDY 3

Introduction

The concept *ecology of administration* can be well illustrated by most case studies on public administration, for it would be a rare public administrator who was *not* influenced by at least a few of the major ecological factors that John Gaus outlined in the preceding essay. The theme of ecology runs throughout administrative activities, serving to shape and reshape the course and direction of public policy. The following case study, "Dumping $2.6 Million on Bakersfield," is a good example of how ecological factors can affect public administration and what can happen to administrators who fail to take these external factors into account before initiating a public program.

Michael Aron, a California-based journalist, writes an interesting account of the planning and implementation of a federal program sponsored by the U.S. Department of Health, Education, and Welfare to build health clinics for migratory farm workers near the small central California town of Bakersfield. Formulated with good intentions, the program sounded ideal in the initial planning stage, but it nearly failed because inadequate attention was paid to the surrounding social ecology of administration. Aron ably details the ensuing intense struggle between various local forces for control of the health program—the black community, Mexican-American groups, local politicians, and established medical groups. HEW's Washington office and its regional San Francisco office soon became caught in the middle of a conflict that they neither wanted nor had anticipated.

When reading this selection, keep the following questions in mind:

If you had been the administrator at HEW responsible for the planning of this migratory health program, how would you have assessed the local administrative ecology and better adapted your program to suit its characteristics?

Who were the interest groups, and what were their individual points of view?

In what ways did HEW's own actions in implementing the program intensify the conflict among the major interest groups? In particular, what environmental factors did they fail to recognize in designing and implementing this program?

What were the various viewpoints of the Bakersfield situation *within* HEW? How did these conflicting forces, in turn, influence the course of development of HEW's program?

Do Gaus's ideas on the ecology of administration need adjusting to conform more closely to the current demands and problems confronting modern public administrators, such as those outlined in the case study? If so, specifically in what ways?

MICHAEL ARON

Dumping $2.6 Million on Bakersfield (Or How *Not* to Build a Migratory Farm Workers' Clinic)

Like the coming of the railroad, the arrival of big federal money in a small, out-of-the-way California town causes a certain amount of uproar, especially when it is dumped in a bundle by an agency that has to get rid of it quick. In this case, the money comes from the Department of Health, Education, and Welfare, for one of its 131 migrant health programs, and the town that has to fight over the grant is Bakersfield.

But it could just as well have been one of the other 130 migrant health programs, or any federal effort where the bureaucrat is mandated both to spend money fast and also to insure that local people control their own destinies. Controlling your own destiny, in these days of decentralization and revenue sharing, really means that the locals can help decide how to divvy up federal money among themselves. Bakersfield is a consequence of the whole idea of community participation in federal projects, but in this instance, the town only began participating after the money was pumped in—for very obvious reasons and with some very disruptive results.

Our story begins in Washington, D.C., in March, 1970, with the passage by Congress of the Migrant Health Act. Senator Walter Mondale's Migratory Labor subcommittee drafted the legislation, authorizing an $11-million appropriation for migrant programs in fiscal 1970, and it was Mondale, personally, who pressed for insertion of an amendment providing that "persons broadly representative of all elements of the population to be served [be] given an opportunity to participate in the implementation of such programs."

Since this was the time the Nixon Administration was striving to decentralize the "vast" federal bureaucracy, it fell to the regional offices of HEW to implement the legislation. Region IX, headquartered in San Francisco, and responsible for seven Western states (it has since lost Oregon and Washington), proposed four areas with heavy migrant "homebase" populations as possible locations for health projects. Three were in rural California counties, the fourth in the state of Washington. One was Bakersfield, Kern County, California.

HEW's plan was to find a chicano community group in each area to become its delegate agency for day-to-day administration of a project, in the same way that local anti-poverty groups became delegate agencies of the Office of Economic Opportunity. But there was a time problem: the legislation had been passed relatively late in the fiscal year, giving HEW only a few months in which to spend the money or else forfeit it back to Treasury. Compounding the problem was the fact that Bakersfield seemed to have no chicano community groups—20,000 chicanos, but no groups.

With the end of the fiscal year only six weeks away, anxious rural health officials turned their attention to a black group, the Kern County Liberation Movement (KCLM). Born six months earlier in the waning hours of a poor people's workshop and designated a consumers' auxiliary of the local anti-poverty agency, KCLM was little more than a collection of low-income citizens. As its first official act, KCLM had applied to HEW for a $70,000 planning grant to assay the health needs of Bakersfield's black ghetto; that application was still in the pipeline when regional HEW asked KCLM if it would accept $2.6 million to immediately establish a health center.

KCLM responded enthusiastically: certainly they would accept a grant—who wouldn't? In late May, 1970, an official from the Rural Health Office of the Community Health Service of the Health Services and Mental Health Administration (HSMHA) of the Public Health Service of the regional office of HEW flew to Bakersfield to help KCLM prepare a formal application. All this was done very quietly, without fanfare. Final contracts were signed in June, three weeks before the end of the fiscal year.

It wasn't until July that Kern County's health establishment got wind of the news—and when they did, all hell broke loose. The entire roster of local health agencies—the county medical society, the dental society, Kern General Hospital, the county health department, the board of supervisors, the state health department, the California Medical Association; and the congressionally mandated regional planning bodies, Comprehensive Health Planning and Regional Medical Programs—vented their spleen because none had been consulted prior to the awarding of the grant. The medical society had a special reason for bitterness: it had been operating its own federally-funded migrant clinic for years in two old trailers outside of town, and HEW was cutting the budget on that program at the same time it was handing $2.6 million to a bunch of poor people with no experience whatsoever in the administration or delivery of health care.

Creative Fumbling

For five days the flap over the award commanded headlines in the *Bakersfield Californian* (in sky-blue ink, no less); the paper also editorialized against the grant ("More Fumbling and Bumbling") and even ran a two-part feature on the medical society's "wonderful clinic." Bakersfield's two Republican state assemblymen called press conferences to denounce the award. Congressman Robert Mathias sent an angry telegram to HEW Secretary Elliot Richardson questioning how the department could possibly sanction such behavior on the part of its regional office. "Is this what the Administration means by 'creative federalism'?" Mathias asked. For the next three weeks the Bakersfield health establishment would virtually convulse in an effort to get the grant canceled.

On July 14, Dr. James Cavanaugh, deputy assistant secretary for health, announced a "full review" of the conditions surrounding the awarding of the grant, intimating that the con-

tract would be canceled "if irregularities are detected."

On July 15, Cavanaugh flew from Washington to the regional office in San Francisco. In what is reported to have been a rather stormy session, Cavanaugh and regional officials rewrote the guidelines on community health grants so as to insure consultation with all appropriate state and local agencies. In Washington, meanwhile, Mathias' staff had done some checking and discovered that the Kern County Liberation Movement was not registered with OEO as an official delegate arm of the local antipoverty agency. Mathias called Cavanaugh to ask if this were sufficiently "irregular" to warrant cancellation of the contract. When Cavanaugh said he didn't think so, Mathias asked if the contract could possibly be renegotiated under the new guidelines just promulgated. Cavanaugh said he doubted it. A Mathias press release the next day called HEW's action "inexcusable" and fixed the blame on "middle-level bureaucrats [who] ignored the letter of the law" (a reference to their failure to consult the congressionally mandated regional planning bodies).

While Mathias was busy reverse pork-barreling in Washington, physicians and politicians in Bakersfield were writing letters to anyone they could think of who might be able to reverse the decision. Let me quote from some of these letters:

Kern General Hospital Administrator Dr. Owen Hatley, to Dr. Vernon Wilson, an HEW official in Rockville, Maryland:

When an independent, unbiased consulting firm, experienced in developing health delivery systems, presents a program for Kern County, then and only then will I support any sponsoring agency in any of these endeavors. Reputable, experienced consulting firms are available, in contrast to falsefront organizations [KCLM] created to obtain desired answers to fuzzy-minded hypotheses conjured up by some social planners.

Congressman Barry Goldwater, Jr. (representing a neighboring district) to Secretary Richardson:

This group [KCLM] has absolutely no experience that would even remotely qualify them for a grant of this magnitude. . . . I request that you immediately investigate this matter and withdraw the grant.

State Assemblyman William Ketchum to HEW Undersecretary John Veneman, his former colleague in the California legislature:

I object to the "cart before the horse" manner in which this has been handled and request that you immediately stop funding . . . [HEW's] "better to spend now than undertake planning" philosophy is a classic symptom of the whole OEO syndrome.

On July 27, KCLM held a press conference to refute the "numerous unfounded charges leveled against us in recent days." Considering the group's relative inexperience, it was an artful performance. One moment they were militant: "The low income community of Kern County wants to see a migrant health center that will meet their needs and they want to see it not after a two- or three-year planning study. Frankly we are *tired* of being studied. We want direct medical services now." The next moment, conciliatory: "Naturally we welcome the cooperation and support of any agencies interested in meeting the common goal of comprehensive health care for the entire community."

In San Francisco, meanwhile, regional HEW was kept busy trying to explain its actions to HEW officials in Washington. An assistant regional director recalls: "Washington was not terribly happy with us, and that's the understatement of the year. Of course, we knew what we were doing all along. We were going to get funding into that area no matter who it upset, and not by the traditional route of currying favor with conservative county medical societies. To get things done, you go do them and fight the political battles after—especially in this Administration. We like to think of ourselves as 'bureaucratic guerrillas' fighting for what we believe in."

By July 29, it was compromise time. Cavanaugh and Mathias flew to Bakersfield together to announce that HEW was suspending project funds for 90 days pending a "restructuring" of the KCLM board of directors. The suspension, Cavanaugh told a press conference, would be lifted only when the board, then made up entirely of "consumers," added professional health-care "providers" to its membership. Cavanaugh's, too, was an artful performance (which may help explain why he is now on the White House staff). He seemed genuinely pained by "this unfortunate misunderstanding." He urged the Bakersfield health establishment to play an "activist" role on the consumer-provider board, and assured his good friends that "this sort of thing will not happen again." Privately, he told Mathias that HEW would consider canceling the grant if KCLM should fail in any way to execute its provisions. And when the man from HEW left town that night, KCLM was still the beneficiary of the potential $2.6 million.

Although project funds were technically suspended, regional HEW began sending "emergency" funds to KCLM to keep it on its feet. The grant had called for expenditures of $391,000 in the first year—$248,000 for staff salaries and the rest for clinic facilities and supplies. (And when they tell you they're putting X million dollars into programs for poor people, remember: professionals, clericals, and private businesses get the money; the poor get services.) Before any of this money could be spent, however, it would be necessary to hire a project director, preferably one who could court the favor of the health establishment and orchestrate a restructuring of the board.

Regional HEW proposed that a young dental school graduate from San Francisco become interim project director until a permanent director could be found. KCLM agreed, and Robert Isman, D.D.S., assumed his duties in August.

Through the fall months Isman worked hard to win the cooperation of local health agencies, but two things were working against him: his longish hair and what they call in Bakersfield "ultraliberal leanings." City officials, whose own budgets only added up to something like $12 million, simply could not understand why HEW would select such a character to supervise a $2.6-million project. He had no experience, either dental or administrative. He showed up for meetings with bankers and lawyers wearing cut-off jeans and thongs. To this day, people talk about Isman as if his eight months in Bakersfield had been profitably spent dealing hashish on the side.

It took much persuasion and several trips to Bakersfield by regional HEW officials, but in November the KCLM board was restructured to include 10 professional health providers representing various agencies in the county, including the medical society, which put its migrant clinic director on the board but instructed him not to vote. (The argument is sometimes advanced that the medical society joined only to sabotage the project, because free health care for the poor takes money out of the pockets of local physicians and the county hospital; but there's too much conspiracy theory there, or at least not enough money involved to make it credible.)

That the consumers still outnumbered the providers 25 to 10 irked some people, however. Mathias' local aide called the restructuring "a token effort to appease the community." Assemblyman Stacey branded it "a sham and a fraud" and joined the ranks of the countless politicians who at one time or another have accused HEW of "strong-arm tactics."

With the board restructured, everyone expected funding to resume, but HEW suddenly attached new conditions to the lifting of the suspension. KCLM either had to demonstrate broad-based community support, or hire a permanent project director.

In the meantime, forces were still at work trying to get the grant canceled. In December, the medical society applied to HEW for $325,645, ostensibly to expand its existing clinic program, in effect proposing itself as an alternative to KCLM. In Washington, Mathias continued to warn HEW that the project was "doomed to failure" unless local agencies were brought into the fold and given more say in board policy. Quietly, Mathias also asked the Government Accounting Office for a full investigation of the activities of the local anti-poverty umbrella agency, the Kern County Economic Opportunities Corporation.

Three months went by with no progress made toward filling the project director's job and mounting hostility towards Isman from the establishment. Then in April, 1971, HEW decided to step in and temporarily take over the project itself. Vincent Garza, a Mexican-American public health officer stationed at headquarters, was dispatched to replace Isman as interim project director for 90 days. To complement this action, regional HEW abruptly canceled the dental component of the project, thus insuring Isman's complete removal from the scene. Both sides in Bakersfield welcomed the two moves—the health establishment because Garza was a professional like themselves; KCLM because it meant immediate resumption of funding.

From this point on, the struggle ceases to be one pitting organized medicine and its friends against poor people. As you will see, it evolves into a struggle pitting poor people of one race against poor people of another. There are no Machiavellian plots here, no designs by the establishment to divide and conquer. That's just the way it happens.

Dude Ranch Junket

Most of the farm workers of Kern County are Mexican-Americans; maybe 20 per cent are Mexican nationals who came north to follow the soft-fruit season (legally or illegally) and managed to linger longer.

For years, these people have lived in shacks and camps or slept unsheltered on the banks of irrigation canals. Their general health is not good. They get skin diseases from working in fields sprayed with pesticides; they suffer high incidences of venereal disease, eye defects, heart trouble, and nervous disorders; obesity, hypertension, and diabetes are so prevalent that local health authorities believe these conditions to be hereditary in Mexicans; 90 per cent of the children have serious dental problems. "They're learning that an unhealthy body produces nothing," one official said, adding as an afterthought, "They've certainly learned it the hard way." It used to be that when someone got sick, he worked it off or waited it out—unless he got real sick, in which case his family piled him into a car and drove the 20 miles to Kern General Hospital where they would wait for hours in the emergency room hoping that the next intake nurse spoke Spanish. Of course, there was also the medical society's migrant clinic in trailers in La-mont, but it operated only during "the season" (May to September; the actual season is eight to 10 months), and then only three nights a week from 6 p.m. to 10 p.m. At regional HEW the clinic is still referred to as a "band-aid station."

The first thing on Garza's agenda when he arrived in Bakersfield was to find a suitable loca-tion for a health center. For several days he, an architect, and Mathias' local aide drove around the Lamont-Arvin-Weedpatch area looking for a site—and immediately a conflict arose. KCLM thought they ought to be looking in the Lake-view district, where blacks live. Garza explained that these were *migrant* funds and that it had been HEW's intention all along to put a health center someplace where the campesinos would have easy access to it. But this had not been KCLM's understanding at all; they had been led to believe, they said, that the center would be located in a black neighborhood and that cam-pesinos from all over the county would be en-couraged to use it and think of it as their own.

KCLM felt suddenly betrayed. After fighting off the encroachments of the health establish-ment for almost a year, they now learned that HEW wanted to put the health center in a part of the county where less than one per cent of the population is black. A bitter pill; several KCLM board members chose to resign rather than swal-low it.

To sweeten it, perhaps, Garza organized a weekend outing for KCLM board members at a ranch-retreat 80 miles north of Bakersfield and invited the HEW regional director to come along and to bring some of his staff. A good time was presumably had by all, and the regional director soothed ruffled feathers by promising that no matter what happened in the future, KCLM's efforts would not go unrewarded; but folks in Bakersfield took a different view of the outing. Garza returned to Bakersfield on a Monday morning to find himself being blasted on the front page of the *Californian* for his $2,500 dude ranch junket financed by "the taxpayers." (The story was written by the son of the county health superintendent, which says something about small cities.) Three weeks later, Garza left Ba-kersfield and the Public Health Service and went to Yale on a fellowship.

Garza was replaced in July, 1971, by Charles Pineda, a Mexican-American native of Kern County, the son of a fruit picker and holder of a master's degree in social work. Pineda continued the search for a clinic site and also began to think about recruiting a medical staff.

Hmm . . . Federal Funding

In September, 15 months after the awarding of the grant, a makeshift clinic was finally opened in Lamont. Pineda had found a young doctor from Los Angeles to become clinic physician ($25,000), had lured an aging South American from a hospital in the Bronx to become medical director ($27,500), and the three of them had talked the medical society into renting its trailers to KCLM until a permanent location could be found ($1,600, which has never been paid). As soon as the medical society clinic shut down for the "winter," KCLM occupied the trailers and began treating its first farmworker patients. Pineda, meanwhile, found an old grocery store in Weedpatch, leased it, and gradually moved the project into it over the next three months.

The clinic in Weedpatch is a shock when you first see it. Somehow the term "migrant health center" leads you to expect a depressing store-front, partitioned in half, and dimly lit, with maybe a purple curtain separating the waiting room from the examining room, and a wizened old doctor inside waiting to grab you in his pal-sied, age-blotched hands. You walk into the clinic in Weedpatch, however, and your first thought is "hmmm . . . federal funding." The clinic is partitioned all right, but partitioned into a large reception room, two intake offices, five examining rooms, a treatment room, a labora-tory, a records library, staff offices, and a lounge. The staff numbers about 25. The equipment is brand new, ultra-modern, and *clean.* When you open your mouth to say "aaahh . . ." in this clinic, you're opening it to an electronic implement coming out of a wall console.

To the campesinos and their families, the clinic is a godsend. It heals them, soothes them, educates them, trains them, employs a few of them—all free of charge, for the time being. HEW wants the clinic to become self-sufficient, so patient billings will begin in the near future;

but treatment will still be "free" (sort of) for the 90 per cent who belong to the union's "Robert F. Kennedy Farm Workers' Medical Plan" (for which a small premium is deducted from their paychecks). At last count, the clinic had given treatment to 6,000 patients from 1,200 families, and thanks to the imperatives of bureaucracy, each one now has a detailed record of his medical history, probably for the first time in his life. Ask the campesinos whom they thank for all this, and you get a surprising—no, not surprising—answer. Senator Kennedy, of course. The young one.

Chicanos in the Wings

But don't get the idea that just because the clinic opened, the infighting ceased. On the contrary, now there was something tangible to fight over.

An interesting bit of correspondence circulated around Bakersfield at this time, copies of an exchange between HEW Secretary Richardson and Senators Walter Mondale and Adlai Stevenson III, past and present chairmen of the Migratory Labor subcommittee. Richardson's letter to the subcommittee requested "clarification of congressional intent" regarding the consumer-participation amendment to the Migrant Health Act. Mondale wrote back: "I was shocked to learn that there is still substantial doubt as to your Department's implementation of an amendment which became effective in March of 1970." Stevenson wrote: "I am extremely concerned that Migratory Health Program relations and guidelines provide the basis for 'meaningful' farm-worker participation, rather than a degree of 'tokenism.' This, of course, requires a policy-making function for the farm-worker participants rather than merely an advisory role."

It was regional HEW that flooded Bakersfield with copies of the exchange. And for a reason. KCLM was still the delegate agency administering the project, but it no longer could be said to represent the true "consumers." Now that the clinic had opened in Weedpatch, the consumers were campesinos. It was *they* who should be doing the community-participating.

This was fine with project director Pineda, a chicano whose father was still out in the fields;

it was fine, as well, with the clinic staff, half of whom were Mexican, and others who had to have been sympathetic to the plight of farm workers in the first place in order to have accepted a job in a town as Godforsaken as Weedpatch. KCLM, on the other hand, was naturally upset: first, they had "lost" the clinic itself; now they were faced with possible loss of control over it and forfeiture of their status as a bona fide government delegate agency.

Acting on their own authority, but with behind-the-scenes encouragement from regional HEW, Pineda and several clinic staff members appointed five reasonably intelligent, but non-English-speaking, campesinos to a "campesino board," a kind of shadow cabinet that would wait in the wings ready to take over at the earliest signal from HEW. That they were non-English-speaking meant that they had to rely on people like Pineda to tell them what was going on. This was in October.

On December 14, KCLM voted to fire Pineda. The official reasons are not worth going into—basically they questioned Pineda's competence. The actual reason was that Pineda had been attempting to serve two masters at once, KCLM and the campesinos, and his allegiance to the former seemed to be flagging. Informed of the dismissal, regional HEW immediately ordered him reinstated, saying that KCLM no longer had legal authority to make such a decision (because it no longer represented "consumers").

At its next regular meeting, on December 22, KCLM voted to change its name to the Kern County Health Committee (KCHC). This is not insignificant. It represents a conscious grab at respectability and tacitly acknowledges its new position in the battle configuration. How can you call yourself a liberation movement when you're fighting to preserve a vested interest?

Culturally Unfit

Two things of consequence happened in January. First, elections for a new campesino board were held in Lamont-Arvin-Weedpatch; four of the five men who had been appointed by Pineda in October won election to the board. (The fifth would have won, too, had he chosen to run.) The board then incorporated itself as Clinica De Los Campesinos, Inc. (CDLC). Second, the clinic's South American medical director failed his state medical board examination, meaning he was without a license to practice in California.

In February, the roof caves in.

On February 14, 24 hours before KCHC was supposed to transfer authority to CDLC, the KCHC board notifies Pineda of his dismissal in a memo listing eight specific grievances, one claiming he hired the South American medical director without consulting the board and another charging him with "loading" the clinic staff with Mexican-Americans.

On February 15: KCHC, citing election "irregularities," rejects the legitimacy of the CDLC board and refuses to transfer control of the project.

On February 16: 200 chicano demonstrators mass in front of the clinic, Pineda and two clinic staff members among them, carrying picket signs and threatening to "shut it down" (in Spanish). The black chairman of KCHC wades into the angry mob and fires the two staff members on the spot. Half of the demonstrators move down the highway to the KCHC administrative office in Lamont. The demonstrations last until midnight without serious incident.

February 17: The clinic has been splattered with paint during the night. There are bullet holes in the plate glass window. KCHC's black chairman appoints himself "acting project director." Regional HEW officials fly down from San Francisco in the hope of restoring order; they put the KCHC chairman on notice that his assumption of the project directorship constitutes a flagrant conflict of interest. Two-thirds of the clinic staff send individual letters to HEW declaring their allegiance to CDLC.

February 18: A provider member of the KCHC board calls the executive secretary of the medical society at midnight and, on behalf of KCHC, pleads for help. The executive secretary calls his 30-year-old assistant, Riley McWilliams, at 2:30 a.m. and orders him to report to KCHC the next day to become interim project director.

February 23: Telegram to KCHC from regional HEW states: actions of KCHC in direct contradiction to agreements; therefore, project funds would be suspended indefinitely and funding to KCHC would terminate on April 15, 1972.

February 24: Local aide sends confidential memo to Mathias in Washington warning of black-brown racial conflict that could engulf the county; says black community promises reprisals if any harm comes to KCHC chairman; surmises that United Farm Workers are involved in demonstrations.

February 26: CDLC writes to Secretary Richardson—letter begins, "Honorable Sire"; informs that Riley McWilliams made project director without HEW approval; ends with veiled threat to close clinic down as "last resort."

February 28: Medical society applies to HEW for $155,891 grant to expand its own clinic; application states, "basic to this proposal is removal of the existing clinic."

February 29: KCHC chairman reports alleged threats to his person.

March 10: CDLC submits application to HEW to take over administration of project; application actually written by four clinic staff members.

March 17: Twelve clinic staff draft joint letter to HEW threatening to resign if CDLC not made delegate agency; claim Riley McWilliams culturally unfit to be project director.

Bent in the Fields

April 15, the date HEW said it would terminate the project funding to KCHC, came and went, with no word from San Francisco. Three weeks later, the regional director sent letters to KCHC and CDLC proposing a joint luncheon meeting on May 10 at the posh (for Bakersfield) Casa Royale motel. He also sent a letter to the medical society announcing an award of $67,000 to continue their clinic-on-wheels, providing they move it to Buttonwillow, in the southwest part of the county. (Buttonwillow's one physician raised a stink, but that is another story.)

The regional director, the black project officer, and the chicano Public Health Service officer from Los Angeles arrived in Bakersfield the morning of the 10th. At noon they joined the KCHC board for lunch. The CDLC board had been invited to come at 1 p.m., but the hour passed 2 p.m. and the five campesinos had yet to show. Someone suggested that they might have gotten lost, since surely they had never been to the Casa Royale before. Someone else was delegated to go look for them. He found them in their customary positions for that hour, bent over in the fields in 95-degree heat. They said they had not been notified of the meeting. There was reason to think that one of their advisors on the clinic staff had intercepted the letter for reasons she believed to be in their best interests. The meeting proceeded without them. A radical Lutheran minister acted as their unofficial spokesman.

When it was over, an elaborate compromise had been drawn up: 1) the CDLC board would be absorbed into the KCHC board; 2) four providers mutually agreed upon by KCHC and CDLC would join the five campesinos, together to constitute a separate board-within-a-board; 3) the mini-board would serve in a "policy-recommending" capacity and receive the benefit of "whatever training and experience is available"; 4) on or before January 1, 1973, KCHC would transfer administrative control of the project to CDLC, retaining for itself only the role of fiscal intermediary. A fifth provision went unstated, but was well understood nonetheless: in return for its great efforts and considerable sacrifice, KCHC would become HEW's "umbrella agency" for all future projects in the county.

HEW and KCHC signed the compromise that afternoon. In the evening the five campesinos met with their supporters in the basement of the Lutheran Church in Lamont. Heated debate lasted past midnight, but the campesinos finally decided to sign the compromise. "It was not a victory, it was not a defeat," said CDLC chairman, Natividad Arreolo, weary perhaps in the knowledge that he was due out in the fields again at 4 A.M.

If Weedpatch Had Movies

That should be the end of the story. You know it's not. In the months since, there have been controversial hirings and firings, protest resignations, accusations of petty theft, and at least one false rumor of a sexual nature deliberately planted to discredit a potential project director. Dr. Garcia, the South American medical director, took his state boards again in June, and the delay in reporting his grade leads to speculation that it is being deliberately held up in channels for political reasons. As of September 1, the young medical society executive was still project director, a fact from which few but the medical society derive any comfort, and yet he is there.

The question remains as to whether KCHC will cede its little fiefdom to the campesinos by January 1, as agreed. HEW says it is committed to seeing the campesinos take over on schedule, and it is hard to imagine what KCHC could possibly gain by holding out. One also can't help but wonder whether the campesinos really are capable of running the project.

The real problem with this project, and, one suspects, with others as well, has been the ease with which political considerations were able to obscure the stated objective, namely, comprehensive health care for farm workers—combined with the fact that HEW would seem to have subordinated the stated objective to an unstated, or at least secondary one, namely, Mexican-American community organization. Thus, it took 15 months of sparring and jockeying before a single patient was seen. And once opened, the clinic had to shorten its hours anytime HEW felt it necessary to suspend funds in order to reprimand this faction or that. The community of 20,000 is still without a dentist because of an essentially political decision.

The medical society seems to think that because doctors can save lives on a surgical table, their expertise necessarily embraces all facets of medicine, including how it should be delivered to people whom the doctors barely understand, can't talk to, and don't especially like—and the medical society fights to preserve the integrity of that idea. The poor people, black and brown, want better medical care than they are accustomed to receiving, but they also want power and respectability and anything else that might foster the illusion that they are swimming into the mainstream, and if a government health project is the only game in town, they'll jump at the chance to play it, and they'll play it as fiercely and seriously as they imagine it to be played elsewhere, and so what if the brothers and sisters have to wait a little longer for something they have never had anyway. And the whites on the clinic staff and the others lurking in the background all the time probably wouldn't be so eager to stir up the waters if only Weedpatch had a movie theater.

The government, through all this, has been like a ship captain steering the project towards shores the crew can't see yet. For the crowd in San Francisco, the project has been, and continues to be, "an interesting social experiment" (an assistant regional director's words), originally conceived to meet a singular need, but taking on added dimensions as it unfolds. Can blacks and browns work together? Are illiterate campesinos capable of self-administration? What adjustments can we make to keep the community from blowing apart? "I would say we've basically been more interested in using the clinic as an instrument of long-range social change than in meeting the short-run health needs of the target community," one HEW official admitted, fully aware that this is the kind of statement bureaucrats get roasted for every day.

To date $400,000 has been spent on the project, a mere fraction of the $13 billion HEW spends every year on health programs. One shudders at the thought of KCLMs and medical societies and campesino-equivalents plotting and maneuvering against each other and intramurally in every community where federal grants have been won; and yet, that is probably what happens, and is happening, all over the country at this moment.

"Kern County?" a project officer asked rhetorically. "Oh, it's not so bad there. These things are usually much worse in urban areas."

Chapter 3 Review Questions

1. What were the chief elements in the administrative ecology that HEW planners failed to take into account prior to developing the migratory farm workers' health clinic in Bakersfield? If you had been in charge of the project at HEW Regional Headquarters in San Francisco, what would you have done to ensure that the project began properly?

2. What was the role of the local press, politicians, and special interest groups in affecting the outcome of this federally supported program? Can you generalize about the impact of such special interest groups on national programs?

3. Can you distinguish between the institutional factors (such as the budgetary process) and the personnel leadership factors (such as the various persons assigned by HEW to administer the program at the local level) that prevented effective long-term comprehensive planning for this local public program? What reforms would you recommend to enhance better program planning in the future?

4. Compare Case Study 1, "The Blast in Centralia No. 5," with this case. How did the geographical distances in both cases influence the administrative decisions that were made? Can you generalize about the difficulties of effective administrative actions as the *distances* between the administrator and the "administered" expand?

5. Why were there various points of view about the purposes of this program *within* HEW? What were these competing viewpoints? Can you generalize about the difficulties of effective administrative actions as the *levels of bureaucracy* between the administrator and the "administered" expand?

6. After reviewing this case study, how would you modify Gaus's ideas about the

nature of modern administrative ecology? In your view, for instance, does he adequately cover the problems of ethnic differences? Class differences? Media influence? Leadership factors? Fragmented government oversight?

Key Terms

administrative ecology

physical technology

social technology

general environment

wishes and ideas

catastrophe

Suggestions for Further Reading

Gaus spent much of his life thinking about the ecology of public administration; therefore you would do well to begin by reading the entire book from which the reading in this chapter was reprinted, *Reflections on Public Administration* (University, Ala.: University of Alabama Press, 1947). In recent years comparative administrative scholars are perhaps the ablest group carrying on Gaus's investigations in this area; see Fred Riggs, *The Ecology of Administration* (New York: Asia Publishing House, 1967), as well as Ferrel Heady, *Public Administration: A Comparative Perspective,* Third Edition (New York: Marcel Dekker, 1985).

Biographies and autobiographies offer some of the finest observations on the interplay between social forces and public administration, and the five most outstanding ones are Louis Brownlow, *A Passion for Anonymity* (Chicago: University of Chicago Press, 1958); Robert Caro, *The Power Broker: Robert Moses and the Fall of New York City* (New York: Random House, 1974); Leroy F. Harlow, *Without Fear or Favor: Odyssey of a City Manager* (Provo, Utah: Brigham Young University Press, 1977); Thomas K. McCraw, *Prophets of Regulation* (Cambridge, Mass.: Harvard University Press, 1984); and David Stockman, *The Triumph of Politics: The Inside Story of the Reagan Revolution* (New York: Harper & Row, 1986). There are several classic social science studies of this subject, including Philip Selznick, *TVA and the Grass Roots: A Study of the Sociology of Formal Organization* (Berkeley: University of California Press, 1949); Herbert Kaufman, *The Forest Ranger—A Study in Administrative Behavior* (Baltimore: Johns Hopkins University Press, 1960); Arthur Maass, *The Army Engineers and The Nation's Rivers* (Cambridge, Mass.: Harvard University Press, 1951); Milton D. Morris, *Immigration: The Beleaguered Bureaucracy* (Washington, D.C.: Brookings Institute, 1985); and Paul Light, *Artful Work: The Politics of Social Security Reform* (New York: Random House, 1985).

You should not overlook the rich case studies available through the Inter-University Case Program (P.O. Box 229, Syracuse, N.Y. 13210) as well as the John F. Kennedy School of Government Case Program (Kennedy School of Government, Case Program, Harvard University, 79 JFK Street, Cambridge, Mass. 02138), most of which explore and highlight various dimensions of administrative ecology. The first ICP case book, Harold Stein, ed., *Public Adminis-*

tration and Policy Development: A Casebook (New York: Harcourt Brace Jovano-vich, 1952), contains an especially good introduction by Stein focusing on this topic.

Two short but useful pieces that should be read as well are Herbert G. Wilcox, "The Culture Trait of Hierarchy in Middle Class Children," *Public Administration Review* (March/April 1968), pp. 222–232, and F. E. Emery and E. L. Trist, "The Causal Texture of Organizational Environments," *Human Relations,* 18 (February 1965), pp. 21–32.

Certainly *must* reading for comprehending the whole cultural-social milieu within which American public administration operates remains the two volumes of Alexis de Tocqueville, *Democracy in America* (New York: Vintage, 1945), or for that matter, several of the better historical treatments of the American experi-ence: James Bryce, *The American Commonwealth,* 2 volumes (New York: Mac-millan, 1888); Richard Hofstadter, *The American Political Tradition* (New York: Vintage Book, 1948); Michael Kammen, *People of Paradox* (New York: Vintage Books, 1972); Henry Steele Commanger, *The Empire of Reason* (New York: Doubleday, 1977); and Samuel P. Huntington, *American Politics; The Promise of Disharmony* (Cambridge, Mass.: Harvard University Press, 1981). For contem-porary trends in the American social, economic, political, and fiscal landscape, read either John Naisbitt, *Megatrends* (New York: Warner Books, 1984) or David R. Young, *America in Perspective* (Boston: Houghton Mifflin, 1986).

The Political Environment: The Concept of Administrative Power

"The lifeblood of administration is power."

Norton E. Long

Introduction

While John Gaus stressed the broad, evolutionary perspective of administrative ecology, Norton E. Long (1910–   ) of the University of Missouri at St. Louis, a contemporary American political scientist and former New Deal civil servant, zeroes in on the immediate environment of public administration, namely, that of administrative power. In his classic essay, "Power and Administration," Long argues that administrative institutions—public agencies, departments, bureaus and field offices—are engaged in a continual battle for political survival. In this fierce administrative contest bureaucrats contend for limited power resources from clientele and constituent groups, the legislative and executive branches, and the general public in order to sustain their organizations. As he writes, "The lifeblood of administration is power. Its attainment, maintenance, increase, and losses are subjects the practitioner and student can ill afford to neglect." And yet, "it is the most overlooked in theory and the most dangerous to overlook in practice."

For Long, the concept of power cannot be bottled in a jar and kept safely tucked away for future use; nor can its nature be revealed by simply examining the U.S. Constitution, the legislative mandates, or the formal hierarchy of an organizational chart. It is, rather, an ephemeral substance that is part of the disorderly, fragmented, decentralized landscape of American public administration—a landscape reminiscent more of tenth-century warring medieval fiefs than of twentieth-century modern government. Power in this chaotic terrain is everywhere, flowing "in from the sides of an organization, as it were; it also flows up the organization to the center from the constituent parts."

This fluid situation arises partly, in Long's view, from the failure of the American party system to protect administrators from political pressures and to provide adequate direction and support for government bureaus and agencies.

The American party system "fails to develop a consensus on a leadership and a program that makes possible administration on the basis of acceptable decisional premises." Left to their own devices and discretion, public agencies are forced to enter the "business of building, maintaining and increasing their political support."

Administrators seek to build strong public relations and mobilize political support by developing a "wide range of activities designed to secure enough 'customer' acceptance to survive and, if fortunate, develop a consensus adequate to program formulation and execution." If public servants are to succeed, they must understand the political environment in which they operate and the political resources at their disposal. On this point, Long has direct relevance to some of the central political problems faced by administrators in Case Study 1, "The Blast in Centralia No. 5," and in Case Study 3, "Dumping $2.6 Million on Bakersfield."

How can Long's disorderly array of narrow interests weld itself together to develop an overall scheme of the national purpose? Rational schemes of coordination always run counter to "the self-centered demands of primary groups for funds and personnel." Again Long visualizes the power factor as significant in any reorganization plan for government. Improved coordination through any governmental reorganization plan will "require a political power at least as great as that which tamed the earlier feudalism." "Attempts to solve administrative reorganization in isolation from the structure of power and purpose in the polity are bound to prove illusory" and have "the academic air of South American Constitution-making."

In his perceptive essay, Long raises another important issue, namely, that because the decentralized nature of the American political system puts administrators in the midst of numerous competing interest groups, they are plagued with the continual problem, "To whom is one loyal—unit, section, branch, division, bureau, department, administration, government, country, people, world history, or what?" A precise consensus on what should be done and who should be obeyed rarely exists and will not so long as the American system fails to establish organized, disciplined political parties or so long as presidents are unable to find firm and continuing majorities in Congress for their legislative programs. Unlike the Parliamentary system, according to Long, each agency in the American executive branch must fend for itself in the political arena, grasping for its own share of political resources to sustain its programs. Therefore Long advises American administrators to read Machiavelli, La Rochefoucauld, Duc de Saint Simon, or Madison on the reality of power rather than the classic texts on public administration that often only stress the formal components of public organizations.

The following excerpt from Long's essay, "Power and Administration," is based on his perceptive understanding, his training in classical political philosophy, as well as his practical administrative experiences while working at the local, state, and national levels during the Depression, World War II, and the postwar period, particularly his experience at the National Housing Administration in New York City and the Office of Price Administration in Washington. Long's perspectives on power were also significantly shaped by the "new realism" of such insightful students of governmental administration during the 1930s and 1940s as E. Pendleton Herring, Paul Appleby, and Herbert Simon who, like Long, were sober realists about the nature and substance of administrative power. For some traditionalists, Long may seem uncomfortably iconoclastic and politically cynical in his thinking, offering few simple answers to the questions he poses. Nevertheless, his essay raises several perplexing problems that are still critical in public administration today.

As you read this selection, keep the following questions in mind:

How does Long define administrative power? Why is it important? Are there any differences between political power and administrative power? How is administrative power attained and maintained?

What are the appropriate "ends" or "purposes" of the contest for power in administration?

Will the administrative struggle necessarily, if left unchecked, produce a coordinated, effective, and responsible public policy?

How can better planning and rationality be incorporated into the administrative system?

How does Long's approach differ from Weber's or Gaus's approach?

NORTON LONG

Power and Administration

There is no more forlorn spectacle in the administrative world than an agency and a program possessed of statutory life, armed with executive orders, sustained in the courts, yet stricken with paralysis and deprived of power. An object of contempt to its enemies and of despair to its friends.

The lifeblood of administration is power. Its attainment, maintenance, increase, dissipation, and loss are subjects the practitioner and student can ill afford to neglect. Loss of realism and failure are almost certain consequences. This is not to deny that important parts of public administration are so deeply entrenched in the

habits of the community, so firmly supported by the public, or so clearly necessary as to be able to take their power base for granted and concentrate on the purely professional side of their problems. But even these islands of the blessed are not immune from the plague of politics. . . . To stay healthy one needs to recognize that health is a fruit, not a birthright. Power is only one of the considerations that must be weighed in administration, but of all it is the most overlooked in theory and the most dangerous to overlook in practice.

The power resources of an administrator or an agency are not disclosed by a legal search of titles and court decisions or by examining appropriations or budgetary allotments. Legal authority and a treasury balance are necessary but politically insufficient bases of administration.

Reprinted with permission from *Public Administration Review,* © 1949 by The American Society for Public Administration, 1120 G Street, N.W., Suite 500, Washington, D.C. All rights reserved.

Administrative rationality requires a critical evaluation of the whole range of complex and shifting forces on whose support, acquiescence, or temporary impotence the power to act depends.

Analysis of the sources from which power is derived and the limitations they impose is as much a dictate of prudent administration as sound budgetary procedure. The bankruptcy that comes from an unbalanced power budget has consequences far more disastrous than the necessity of seeking a deficiency appropriation. The budgeting of power is a basic subject matter of a realistic science of administration.

It may be urged that for all but the top hierarchy of the administrative structure the question of power is irrelevant. Legislative authority and administrative orders suffice. Power adequate to the function to be performed flows down the chain of command. Neither statute nor executive order, however, confers more than legal authority to act. Whether Congress or President can impart the substance of power as well as the form depends upon the line-up of forces in the particular case. A price control law wrung from a reluctant Congress by an amorphous and unstable combination of consumer and labor groups is formally the same as a law enacting a support price program for agriculture backed by the disciplined organizations of farmers and their Congressmen. The differences for the scope and effectiveness of administration are obvious. The presidency, like Congress, responds to and translates the pressures that play upon it. The real mandate contained in an executive order varies with the political strength of the group demand embodied in it, and in the context of other group demands.

Both Congress and President do focus the general political energies of the community and so are considerably more than mere means for transmitting organized pressures. Yet power is not concentrated by the structure of government or politics into the hands of a leadership with a capacity to budget it among a diverse set of administrative activities. A picture of the presidency as a reservoir of authority from which the lower echelons of administration draw life and vigor is an idealized distortion of reality.

A similar criticism applies to any like claim for an agency head in his agency. Only in varying degrees can the powers of subordinate officials be explained as resulting from the chain of command. Rarely is such an explanation a satisfactory account of the sources of power.

To deny that power is derived exclusively from superiors in the hierarchy is to assert that subordinates stand in a feudal relation in which to a degree they fend for themselves and acquire support peculiarly their own. A structure of interests friendly or hostile, vague and general or compact and well-defined, encloses each significant center of administrative discretion. This structure is an important determinant of the scope of possible action. As a source of power and authority it is a competitor of the formal hierarchy.

Not only does political power flow in from the sides of an organization, as it were; it also flows up the organization to the center from the constituent parts. When the staff of the Office of War Mobilization and Reconversion advised a hard-pressed agency to go out and get itself some popular support so that the President could afford to support it, their action reflected the realities of power rather than political cynicism.

It is clear that the American system of politics does not generate enough power at any focal point of leadership to provide the conditions for an even partially successful divorce of politics from administration. Subordinates cannot depend on the formal chain of command to deliver enough political power to permit them to do their jobs. Accordingly they must supplement the resources available through the hierarchy with those they can muster on their own, or accept the consequences in frustration— a course itself not without danger. Administrative rationality demands that objectives be determined and sights set in conformity with a realistic appraisal of power position and potential. . . .

The theory of administration has neglected the problem of the sources and adequacy of power, in all probability because of a distaste for the disorderliness of American political life and a belief that this disorderliness is transitory. An idealized picture of the British parliamentary system as a Platonic form to be realized or approximated has exerted a baneful fascination in the field. The majority party with a mandate at the polls and a firmly seated leadership in the cabinets seems to solve adequately the problem of the supply of power necessary to permit administration to concentrate on the fulfillment of accepted objectives. It is a commonplace that the American party system provides neither a mandate for a platform nor a mandate for a leadership.

Accordingly, the election over, its political meaning must be explored by the diverse leaders in the executive and legislative branches. Since the parties have failed to discuss issues, mobilize majorities in their terms, and create a working political consensus on measures to be carried out, the task is left for others—most prominently the agencies concerned. Legislation passed and powers granted are frequently politically premature. Thus the Council of Economic Advisors was given legislative birth before political acceptance of its functions existed. The agencies to which tasks are assigned must devote themselves to the creation of an adequate consensus to permit administration. The mandate that the parties do not supply must be attained through public relations and the mobilization of group support. Pendleton Herring and others have shown just how vital this support is for agency action.

The theory that agencies should confine themselves to communicating policy suggestions to executive and legislature, and refrain from appealing to their clientele and the public, neglects the failure of the parties to provide either a clear-cut decision as to what they should do or an adequately mobilized political support for a course of action. The bureaucracy under the American political system has a large share of responsibility for the public promotion of policy and even more in organizing the political basis for its survival and growth. It is generally recognized that the agencies have a special competence in the technical aspects of their fields which of necessity gives them a rightful policy initiative. In addition, they have or develop a shrewd understanding of the politically feasible in the group structure within which they work. Above all, in the eyes of their supporters and their enemies they represent the institutionalized embodiment of policy, an enduring organization actually or potentially capable of mobilizing power behind policy. The survival interests and creative drives of administrative organizations combine with clientele pressures to compel such mobilization. The party system provides no enduring institutional representation for group interest at all comparable to that of the bureaus of the Department of Agriculture. Even the subject matter committees of Congress function in the shadow of agency permanency.

The bureaucracy is recognized by all interested groups as a major channel of representation to such an extent that Congress rightly feels the competition of a rival. The weakness in party structure both permits and makes necessary the present dimensions of the political activities of the administrative branch—permits because it fails to protect administration from pressures and fails to provide adequate direction and support, makes necessary because it fails to develop a consensus on a leadership and a program that makes possible administration on the basis of accepted decisional premises.

Agencies and bureaus more or less perforce are in the business of building, maintaining, and increasing their political support. They lead and in large part are led by the diverse groups whose influence sustains them. Frequently they lead and are themselves led in conflicting directions. This is not due to a dull-witted incapacity to see the contradictions in their behavior but is an almost inevitable result of the contradictory nature of their support.

Herbert Simon has shown that administrative rationality depends on the establishment of uniform value premises in the decisional centers of organization. Unfortunately, the value premises of those forming vital elements of political support are often far from uniform. These elements are in Barnard's and Simon's sense "customers" of the organization and therefore parts of the organization whose wishes are clothed with a very real authority. A major and most time-consuming aspect of administration consists of the wide range of activities designed to secure enough "customer" acceptance to survive and, if fortunate, develop a consensus adequate to program formulation and execution.

To varying degrees, dependent on the breadth of acceptance of their programs, officials at every level of significant discretion must make their estimates of the situation, take stock of their resources, and plan accordingly. A keen appreciation of the real components of their organization is the beginning of wisdom. These components will be found to stretch far beyond the government payroll. Within the government they will encompass Congress, Congressmen, committees, courts, other agencies, presidential advisors, and the President. The Aristotelian analysis of constitutions is equally applicable and equally necessary to an understanding of administrative organization.

The broad alliance of conflicting groups that makes up presidential majorities scarcely coheres about any definite pattern of objectives, nor has it by the alchemy of the party system had its collective power concentrated in an accepted leadership with a personal mandate. The conciliation and maintenance of this support is a necessary condition of the attainment and retention of office involving, as Madison so well saw, "the spirit of party and faction in the necessary and ordinary operations of government." The President must in large part be, if not all things to all men, at least many things to many men. As a consequence, the contradictions in

his power base invade administration. The often criticized apparent cross-purposes of the Roosevelt regime cannot be put down to inept administration until the political facts are weighed. Were these apparently self-defeating measures reasonably related to the general maintenance of the composite majority of the administration? The first objective—ultimate patriotism apart—of the administrator is the attainment and retention of the power on which his tenure of office depends. This is the necessary pre-condition for the accomplishment of all other objectives.

The same ambiguities that arouse the scorn of the naive in the electoral campaigns of the parties are equally inevitable in administration and for the same reasons. Victory at the polls does not yield either a clear-cut grant of power or a unified majority support for a coherent program. The task of the presidency lies in feeling out the alternatives of policy which are consistent with the retention and increase of the group support on which the administration rests. The lack of a budgetary theory (so frequently deplored) is not due to any incapacity to apply rational analysis to the comparative contribution of the various activities of government to a determinate hierarchy of purposes. It more probably stems from a fastidious distaste for the frank recognition of the budget as a politically expedient allocation of resources. Appraisal in terms of their political contribution to the administration provides almost a sole common denominator between the Forest Service and the Bureau of Engraving.

Integration of the administrative structure through an overall purpose in terms of which tasks and priorities can be established is an emergency phenomenon. Its realization, only partial at best, has been limited to war and the extremity of depression. Even in wartime the Farm Bureau Federation, the American Federation of Labor, the Congress of Industrial Organizations, the National Association of Manufacturers, the Chamber of Commerce, and a host of lesser interests resisted coordination of themselves and the agencies concerned with their interests. A presidency temporarily empowered by intense mass popular support acting in behalf of a generally accepted and simplified purpose can, with great difficulty, bribe, cajole, and coerce a real measure of joint action. . . . Only in crises are the powers of the executive nearly adequate to impose a common plan of action on the executive branch, let alone the economy.

In ordinary times the manifold pressures of our pluralistic society work themselves out in accordance with the balance of forces prevailing in Congress and the agencies. Only to a limited degree is the process subject to responsible direction or review by President or party leadership. . . .

The difficulty of coordinating government agencies lies not only in the fact that bureaucratic organizations are institutions having survival interests which may conflict with their rational adaptation to overall purpose, but even more in their having roots in society. Coordination of the varied activities of a modern government almost of necessity involves a substantial degree of coordination of the economy. Coordination of government agencies involves far more than changing the behavior and offices of officials in Washington and the field. It involves the publics that are implicated in their normal functioning. To coordinate fiscal policy, agricultural policy, labor policy, foreign policy, and military policy, to name a few major areas, moves beyond the range of government charts and the habitat of the bureaucrats to the marketplace and to where the people live and work. This suggests that the reason why government reorganization is so difficult is that far more than government in the formal sense is involved in reorganization. One could overlook this in the limited government of the nineteenth century but the multi-billion dollar government of the mid-twentieth permits no facile dichotomy between government and economy. Economy and efficiency are the two objectives a laissez faire society can prescribe in peacetime as overall government objectives. Their inadequacy either as motivation or standards has long been obvious. A planned economy clearly requires a planned government. But, if one can afford an unplanned economy, apart from gross extravagance, there seems no compelling and therefore, perhaps, no sufficiently powerful reason for a planned government.

Basic to the problem of administrative rationality is that of organizational identification and point of view. To whom is one loyal—unit, section, branch, division, bureau, department, administration, government, country, people, world history, or what? Administrative analysis frequently assumes that organizational identification should occur in such a way as to merge primary organization loyalty in a larger synthesis. The good of the part is to give way to the reasoned good of the whole. This is most frequently illustrated in the rationalizations used to counter self-centered demands of primary groups for funds and personnel. Actually the competition between governmental power centers, rather than the rationalizations, is the effective instrument of coordination.

Where there is a clear common product on whose successful production the subgroups depend for the attainment of their own satisfaction, it is possible to demonstrate to almost all participants the desirability of cooperation. The shoe factory produces shoes, or else, for all concerned. But the government as a whole and many of its component parts have no such identifiable common product on which all depend. Like the proverbial Heinz, there are fifty-seven or more varieties unified, if at all, by a common political profit and loss account.

Administration is faced by somewhat the same dilemma as economics. There are propositions about the behavior pattern conducive to full employment—welfare economics. On the other hand, there are propositions about the economics of the individual firm—the counsel of the business schools. It is possible to show with considerable persuasiveness that sound considerations for the individual firm may lead to a depression if generally adopted, a result desired by none of the participants. However, no single firm can afford by itself to adopt the course of collective wisdom; in the absence of a common power capable of enforcing decisions premised on the supremacy of the collective interest, *sauve qui peut* is common sense.

The position of administrative organizations is not unlike the position of particular firms. Just as the decisions of the firms could be coordinated by the imposition of a planned economy so could those of the component parts of the government. But just as it is possible to operate a formally unplanned economy by the loose coordination of the market, in the same fashion it is possible to operate a government by the loose coordination of the play of political forces through its institutions.

The unseen hand of Adam Smith may be little in evidence in either case. One need not believe in a doctrine of social or administrative harmony to believe that formal centralized planning—while perhaps desirable and in some cases necessary—is not a must. The complicated logistics of supplying the city of New York runs smoothly down the grooves of millions of well adapted habits projected from a distant past. It seems naive on the one hand to believe in the possibility of a vast, intricate, and delicate economy operating with a minimum of formal overall direction, and on the other to doubt that a relatively simple mechanism such as the government can be controlled largely by the same play of forces. . . .

It is highly appropriate to consider how administrators should behave to meet the test of efficiency in a planned polity; but in the absence of such a polity and while, if we like, struggling to get it, a realistic science of administration will teach administrative behavior appropriate to the existing political system.

A close examination of the presidential system may well bring one to conclude that administrative rationality in it is a different matter from that applicable to the British ideal. The

American presidency is an office that has significant monarchical characteristics despite its limited term and elective nature. The literature on court and palace has many an insight applicable to the White House. Access to the President, reigning favorites, even the court jester, are topics that show the continuity of institutions. The maxims of La Rochefoucauld and the memoirs of the Duc de Saint Simon have a refreshing realism for the operator on the Potomac.

The problem of rival factions in the President's family is as old as the famous struggle between Jefferson and Hamilton. . . . Experience seems to show that this personal and factional struggle for the President's favor is a vital part of the process of representation. The vanity, personal ambition, or patriotism of the contestants soon clothes itself in the generalities of principle and the clique aligns itself with groups beyond the capital. Subordinate rivalry is tolerated if not encouraged by so many able executives that it can scarcely be attributed to administrative ineptitude. The wrangling tests opinion, uncovers information that would otherwise never rise to the top, and provides effective opportunity for decision rather than mere ratification of prearranged plans. Like most judges, the executive needs to hear argument for his own instruction. The alternatives presented by subordinates in large part determine the freedom and the creative opportunity of their superiors. The danger of becoming a Merovingian is a powerful incentive to the maintenance of fluidity in the structure of power.

The fixed character of presidential tenure makes it necessary that subordinates be politically expendable. The President's men must be willing to accept the blame for failures not their own. Machiavelli's teaching on how princes must keep the faith bears rereading. Collective responsibility is incompatible with a fixed term of office. As it tests the currents of public opinion, the situation on the Hill, and the varying strength of the organized pressures, the White House alters and adapts the complexion of the administration. Loyalties to programs or to groups and personal pride and interest frequently conflict with whole-souled devotion to the presidency. In fact, since such devotion is not made mandatory by custom, institutions, or the facts of power, the problem is perpetually perplexing to those who must choose.

The balance of power between executive and legislature is constantly subject to the shifts of public and group support. The latent tendency of the American Congress is to follow the age-old parliamentary precedents and to try to reduce the President to the role of constitutional monarch. Against this threat and to secure his own initiative, the President's resources are primarily demagogic, with the weaknesses and strengths that dependence on mass popular appeal implies. The unanswered question of American government—"who is boss?"—constantly plagues administration.

CASE STUDY 4

Introduction

In the foregoing essay, Long discusses how critically important it is for public administrators at all levels of government to understand the dynamics and realities of administrative power—its sources, influences, and impacts on their programs and on themselves, as well as the methods for maintaining and effectively using the power. Long's realism about the nature of administrative power, however, was primarily a theoretical study of the subject. But how do Long's ideas apply to actual administrative situations?

Perhaps one of the most insightful recent studies of administrative power—its redirection and application—is found in the following account by James Q. Wilson, "The Changing FBI—The Road to Abscam." Here Wilson recounts the background of the highly publicized FBI undercover "sting operations" that took place in the early 1980s and were code-named "Abscam." Operation Abscam originated from a tip by an informant who had been useful for several years in locating stolen art works. The Bureau was told by the informant that he could put agents in touch with congressmen who were "for sale." Since the death of J. Edgar Hoover in the early 1970s, the FBI had been prodded by Congress to place greater priority on investigating political corruption and "white-collar crimes" and to move away from its more traditional emphasis on auto thefts and bank robbery cases. Abscam was a case that seemed to fit the new mandates for the Bureau as established by Congress—namely, cracking down on high-level political corruption.

The FBI thus accepted the informant's offer and set up an elaborate Abscam operation by having an FBI agent pose as a wealthy Arab businessman who said he would buy political favors from congressmen in order to help his businesses. Several members of Congress were then brought individually to a house leased by the Bureau in Washington, D.C., and the negotiations between the congressmen and the mythical Arab businessman were recorded on film by a hidden camera. Abscam ultimately resulted in the arrest and imprisonment of several of these individuals. Although sting operations were and still are fairly commonplace law enforcement activities, as Wilson writes, "What is different is that in this case

Congressmen were apparently involved and the operation was leaked to the press before indictments were issued." Wilson not only looks carefully at the development of Abscam but also probes thoughtfully the reasons for this fundamental shift in Bureau priorities as well as the possible ramifications of the new application for administrative power by the Bureau.

When reading this case, keep in mind the following questions:

Traditionally, why had the FBI stayed away from investigating white-collar crime and high-level political corruption?

What caused the Bureau to shift its investigative resources toward these new directions?

In particular, what role did Congress, key subcommittee members, the director of the FBI, and others have in initiating such changes?

How did the FBI agents, individually and collectively, respond to such shifts in the Bureau's priorities? Do you think their responsiveness is characteristic of bureaucrats in other public organizations or is the Bureau's political responsiveness unique in several ways?

In general, what does this case say about the nature and use of administrative power? Does the case support Long's ideas on this subject?

JAMES Q. WILSON

The Changing FBI—The Road to Abscam

It is inconceivable that J. Edgar Hoover would ever have investigated members of Congress to gather evidence for possible prosecution. Hoover's FBI learned a great deal about congressmen, and may have gone out of its way to collect more information than it needed, but all this would have been locked discreetly away, or possibly leaked, most privately, to a President or attorney general whose taste for gossip Hoover wished to gratify or whose personal loyalty he wished to assure. The Bureau's shrewd cultivation of congressional and White House opinion, effective for decades, was in time denounced as evidence that the FBI was "out of control," immune from effective oversight.

From *The Public Interest* (Spring 1980), pp. 3–14. Copyright © 1980 by James Q. Wilson. Reprinted by permission of the author.

Today, of course, the Bureau is again being criticized, albeit circumspectly, by various congressmen who complain of the manner (and possibly also the fact) of its investigation of possible legislative bribery. Congressmen wonder whether the FBI is launched on a "vendetta" against its erstwhile allies turned critics. Once again there are angry mutterings that the Bureau is "out of control," this time because it is using its most powerful technique—undercover operations—to discover whether congressmen are corrupt.

It would be tempting to ascribe the changes in the Bureau's relations with Congress to nothing more than personal pique amplified into organizational vengeance. After years of congressional adulation of Hoover and the FBI, the mood suddenly turned nasty with revelations of how far the Bureau was prepared to go in using its investigative powers to maintain political support. The list of Bureau excesses is long, familiar, and dismaying; the wrath visited upon it by several congressional committees combined a proper outrage at abuse of power with a hint of romance gone sour. For the FBI now to turn on those who had turned on it would be precisely the sort of thing one might suppose a Hoover-style agency might relish.

This is not what has happened. No doubt there are some FBI agents who are enjoying the sight of congressmen scurrying for cover, but that was not the motive for "Operation Abscam." The Bureau has in fact changed, and changed precisely in accordance with the oft-expressed preferences of Congress itself. Congressional and other critics complained that the Bureau in the 1960's was not only violating the rights of citizens, it was wasting its resources and energies on trivial cases and meaningless statistical accomplishments. Beginning with Director Clarence Kelley, the Bureau pledged that it would end the abuses and redirect its energies to more important matters. This is exactly what has happened.

This rather straightforward explanation is hard for official Washington to accept, and understandably so. Bureaucracies are not supposed to change, they are only supposed to claim to have changed. It tests the credulity of a trained congressional cynic to be told that a large, complex, rule bound organization such as the FBI would or could execute an about-face.

But the FBI is not just any bureaucracy, and never has been. Next to the Marine Corps, it is probably the most centrally controlled organization in the federal government. Its agents do not have civil service or union protection, its disciplinary procedures can be swift and draconian, and despite recent efforts to decentralize some decision making, the director himself, or one of his immediate subordinates, personally approves an astonishingly large proportion of all the administrative decisions made in the Bureau. Not long ago, a decision to install sanitary-napkin dispensers in women's lavoratories in Bureau headquarters could not be made until Director William Webster endorsed the recommendation. FBI agents have complained for

decades about the heavy-handed supervision they received from headquarters; though that has begun to change, the visit of an inspection team to an FBI field office continues to instill apprehension bordering on terror in the hearts of the local staff. The inspectors sometimes concentrate on the minutiae at the expense of the important, but whatever its defects, nit-picking insures that field offices will conform to explicit headquarters directives pertaining to observable behavior.

But even for the Bureau, the change in investigative strategy that culminated in Operation Abscam was no easy matter. For one thing, much of what the Bureau does is not easily observable and thus not easily controlled by inspection teams and headquarters directives. Law enforcement occurs on the street in low-visibility situations that test the judgment and skill of agents but do not lend themselves to formal review. Many laws the FBI enforces—particularly those pertaining to consensual crimes such as bribery—place heavy reliance on the skill and energy of agents and field supervisors who must find ways of discovering that a crime may have been committed before they can even begin the process of gathering evidence that might lead to a prosecution. Relations between an agent and an informant often lie at the heart of the investigative effort, but these are subtle, complex, and largely unobservable. Finally, what the Bureau chooses to emphasize is not for it alone to decide. The policies of the local United States Attorney, who though nominally an employee of the Justice Department is in reality often quite autonomous, determine what federal cases will be accepted for prosecution and thus what kinds of offenses the local FBI office will emphasize.

Changing the Bureau

Given these difficulties, the effort to change the investigative priorities of the Bureau was a protracted, controversial, and difficult struggle. Several things had to happen: New policies had to be stated, unconventional investigative techniques had to be authorized, organizational changes had to be made, and new incentives had to be found.

As is always the case, stating the new policies was the easiest thing to do. Attorney General Edward Levi and Director Kelley pledged that the Bureau would reduce its interest in domestic security cases, especially of the sort that led to such abuses as COINTELPRO, and in the investigation of certain routine crimes (such as auto theft or small thefts from interstate shipments) that had for years generated the impressive statistics that Hoover was fond of reciting. The domestic security cases were constitutionally and politically vulnerable; the criminal cases that produced evidence of big workloads but few significant convictions were unpopular among the street agents. The man Kelley brought in to close down virtually all the domestic security investigations was, ironically, Neil Welch, then in charge of the Bureau's Philadelphia office and later to be in charge of the New York office and of Operation Abscam. In a matter of months, thousands of security cases were simply terminated; hundreds of security informants were let go; domestic security squads in various field offices were disbanded and their agents assigned to other tasks. New attorney-general guidelines clarified and narrowed the circumstances under which such cases could be opened in the future. The number of FBI informants in organizations thought to constitute a security risk became so small that it was kept secret in order, presumably, to avoid encouraging potential subversives with the knowledge that they were, in effect, free to organize without fear of Bureau surveillance.

Kelley also announced a "quality case program" authorizing each office to close out pending investigative matters that had little prosecutive potential and to develop priorities that would direct its resources toward important cases. Almost overnight, official Bureau caseloads dropped precipitously, as field offices stopped pretending that they were investigating (and in some cases, actually stopped investigating) hundreds of cases—of auto thefts, bank robberies, and thefts from interstate commerce and from government buildings—where the office had no leads, the amounts stolen

were small, or it was believed (rightly or wrongly) that local police departments could handle the matter.*

Headquarters made clear what it regarded as the "priority" cases that the field should emphasize: white-collar crime, organized crime, and foreign counterintelligence. But saying that these were the priorities, and getting them to *be* the priorities, were two different things. Permitting field offices to stop reporting on high-volume, low-value cases did not automatically insure that the resources thereby saved would be devoted to, say, white-collar crime. For that to occur, some important organizational changes had to be made.

The most important of these was to reorganize the field-office squads. Traditionally, a field office grouped its agent personnel into squads based on the volume of reported criminal offenses—there would be a bank robbery squad, an interstate theft squad, an auto theft squad, and so on. These squads reacted to the incoming flow of reported crimes by assigning an agent to each case. What we now call white-collar crime was typically the province of a single unit—the "accounting squad"—composed, often, of agents with training as accountants, who would handle bank complaints of fraud and embezzlement. Occasionally, more complex cases involving fraud would be developed; many offices had individual agents skilled at detecting and investigating elaborate political, labor, or business conspiracies. But attention to such matters was not routinized because the internal structure of a typical field office was organized around the need to respond to the reports of crimes submitted by victims. Elaborate conspiracies often produced no victims aware of their victimization or enriched the participants in ways that gave no one an incentive to call the FBI. Taxpayers generally suffer when bribes are offered and taken, and innocent investors may be victimized by land frauds, but either the citizen is unaware he is a victim or the "victim" was in fact part of the conspiracy, drawn in by greed and larcenous intent.

---

*A fuller account of these changes can be found in James Q. Wilson, *The Investigators: Managing FBI and Narcotics Agents* (Basic Books, 1978).

Again Neil Welch enters the scene. The Philadelphia office was one of the first to redesign its structure so that most of its squads had the task, not of responding to victim complaints, but of identifying ("targeting") individuals, groups, and organizations for intensive scrutiny on the grounds that they were suspected of being involved in organized crime, major conspiracies, labor racketeering, or political corruption. Though almost every FBI field office would from time to time make cases against corrupt politicians or businessmen, the cases made in Philadelphia were spectacular for their number and scope. Judges, state legislators, labor leaders, businessmen, police officers, and government officials were indicted and convicted. The more indictments that were handed down, the more nervous accomplices, frightened associates, or knowledgeable reporters would come forward to volunteer more information that spurred further investigations.

During the period when Welch and the Philadelphia office were making headlines (roughly, 1975 to 1977), the rest of the Bureau was watching and waiting. Experienced FBI officials knew that under the Hoover regime, the only safe rule was "never do anything for the first time." Taking the initiative could result in rapid promotions but it could also lead to immediate disgrace; innovation was risky. What if the allies of the powerful people being indicted (one was Speaker of the Pennsylvania House of Representatives) complained? Hoover had usually rebuffed such complaints, but you could never be certain. More important, how would Bureau headquarters react to the fact that the *number* of cases being handled in Philadelphia had dropped owing to the reassignment of agents from the regular high-volume squads to the new "target" squads? In the past, resources—money, manpower—were given to field offices that had high and rising caseloads, not to ones with declining statistics.

Kelley's response was clear—he increased the number of agents assigned to Philadelphia and gave Welch even more important responsibilities (it was at this time that Welch was brought to headquarters to oversee the winding down of the domestic security program). There were still many issues to resolve and many apprehensive supervisors to reassure, but the momentum was growing: More and more field offices began to reorganize to give structural effect to the priority-case program, and thus to an aggressive stance regarding white-collar crime.

Emphasizing Priority Offenses

The incentives to comply with the emphasis on priority offenses came from within and without the Bureau. Inside, the management information system was revised so that investigations and convictions were now classified by quality as well as number. The criminal offenses for which the FBI had investigative responsibility were grouped into high- and low-priority categories, and individual offenses within these categories were further classified by the degree of seriousness of the behavior under investigation (for example, thefts were classified by the amount stolen). It is far from clear that the statistics generated were used in any systematic way by Bureau headquarters—in the FBI as in many government agencies, such data are often perceived as a "numbers game" to be played and then forgotten—but at the very least these statistics reinforced the message repeated over and over again in the statements of the director, first Kelley and then William H. Webster: Go after white-collar and organized crime.

Outside the Bureau, key congressmen were pressing hard in the same direction. Nowhere was this pressure greater than in the chambers of the Subcommittee on Civil and Constitutional Rights of the House Judiciary Committee, chaired by Congressman Don Edwards of California—who had once been, briefly, a member of the FBI. This Subcommittee had become one of the centers of congressional attacks on the Bureau. Kelley and Webster spent hours answering questions put by its members, who included in addition to Chairman Edwards, Elizabeth Holtzman of New York and Robert Drinan of Massachusetts. The attack on the FBI's performance began with criticism of the domestic security programs, but came to include criticisms of the Bureau's weaknesses in the area of white-collar crime. This latter concern reflected, in part, the Subcommittee members' genuine conviction that white-collar offenses were serious matters.

But it also reflected the Subcommittee members' suspicion that the FBI was "soft" on "establishment" crimes while being excessively preoccupied with subversion, and thus inclined merely to go through the motions when investigating the former and to put its heart and resources into inquiries regarding the latter. Thus, getting the Bureau to emphasize white-collar crimes was not only good in itself, it was a way, the Subcommittee seemed to think, of keeping it out of domestic security work.

In 1977, staff members of the Subcommittee toured various FBI field offices and spoke as well to several U.S. Attorneys. Their report sharply criticized the FBI for continuing to devote manpower to street crimes such as bank robberies and hijacking—all of which, in the opinion of the staff, could better be handled by the local police. In some cases, the staff claimed, the FBI's idea of white-collar crime was welfare cheating and other examples of individual, and presumably small-scale, frauds against the government. The staff lamented the "reluctance on the part of FBI personnel, particularly at the supervisory level, to get involved in more complex investigations that may require significant allocation of manpower for long periods of time." And the report criticized the field offices for not mounting more undercover operations.

Whatever shortcomings the FBI may have, indifference to congressional opinion has never been one of them. The pressure inside the Bureau to develop major white-collar-crime cases mounted. The Bureau had always thoroughly investigated reported violations of federal law whatever the color of the collar worn by the suspects. Businessmen, politicians, and labor leaders had been sent to prison as a result of FBI inquiries. But most of these cases arose out of a complaint to the Bureau by a victim, followed by FBI interviews of suspects and an analysis of documents. Sometimes wiretaps were employed. The number, scope, and success of such investigations depended crucially on the skill and patience of the agents working a case. One legendary FBI agent in Boston was personally responsible for making several major corruption cases as a result of his tenacity, his ability to win the confidence of reluctant witnesses and accomplices, and his knowledge of complex financial

transactions. But finding or producing large numbers of such agents is difficult at best. Far easier would be the development of investigative techniques that could generate reliable evidence in large amounts without having to depend solely on an agent's ability to "flip" a suspect, who then would have to testify in court against his former collaborators.

Undercover Operations

One such method was the undercover operation. Narcotics agents in the Drug Enforcement Administration and in local police departments had always relied extensively on undercover agents buying illegal drugs in order to produce evidence. Traditionally, however, the FBI had shied away from these methods. Hoover had resisted any techniques that risked compromising an agent by placing him in situations where he could be exposed to adverse publicity or tempted to accept bribes. Hoover knew that public confidence in FBI agents was the Bureau's principal investigative resource and that confidence should not be jeopardized by having agents appear as anything other than well-groomed, "young executive" individuals with an impeccable reputation for integrity. From time to time, an agent would pose as a purchaser of stolen goods, but these were usually short-lived operations with limited objectives. For most purposes, the FBI relied on informants—persons with knowledge of or connections in the underworld—to provide leads that could then, by conventional investigative techniques, be converted into evidence admissible in court in ways that did not compromise the informant.

The FBI's reliance on informants rather than undercover agents had, of course, its own costs. An informant was not easily controlled, his motives often made him want to use the FBI for personal gain or revenge against rivals, and either he would not testify in court at all or his testimony would be vulnerable to attacks from defense attorneys. Moreover, it is one thing to find informants among bank robbers, jewel thieves, and gamblers with organized crime connections; it is something else again to find informants among high-level politicians, business executives, and labor leaders. An undercover operation came to be seen as a valuable supplement to the informant system: Though created with the aid of an informant, it could be staffed by FBI agents posing as thieves, fences, or businessmen, carefully monitored by recording equipment, used to develop hard physical evidence (such as photographs of cash payoffs), and operated so as to draw in high-level suspects whose world was not easily penetrated by conventional informants.

In 1974 the Law Enforcement Assistance Administration (LEAA) began supplying money to make possible the now-famous "Sting" operations in which stolen property would be purchased from thieves who thought they were selling to criminal fences. LEAA insisted initially that a Sting be a joint federal-local operation, and so the FBI became partners in these early ventures, thereby acquiring substantial experience in how to mount and execute an undercover effort in ways that avoided claims of entrapment. In 1977, the FBI participated in 34 Sting operations. Soon, however, the requirement of federal participation was relaxed and the Sting became almost entirely a state and local venture (albeit often with LEAA money). After all, most of the persons caught in a Sting were thieves who had violated state, but not federal, law.

The experience gained and the success enjoyed by the FBI in the Stings were now put in service of undercover operations directed at the priority crimes—especially white-collar crimes and racketeering. During fiscal year 1978, the Bureau conducted 132 undercover operations, 36 of which were aimed at white-collar crime. They produced impressive (and noncontroversial) results, and led to the indictment of persons operating illegal financial schemes, trying to defraud the government, engaging in union extortion, and participating in political corruption.

Each of these operations was authorized and supervised by FBI headquarters and by the local United States Attorney or by Justice Department attorneys (or both). Among the issues that were reviewed was the need to avoid entrapment. In general, the courts have allowed undercover operations—such as an agent offering to buy illegal narcotics—as a permissible investigative technique. In *Hampton v. United States,* the Supreme Court held in 1976 that the sale to government agents of heroin supplied to the defendant by a government informant did not constitute entrapment. In an earlier case, Justice Potter Stewart tried to formulate a general rule distinguishing a proper from an improper undercover operation: "Government agents may engage in conduct that is likely, when objectively considered, to afford a person ready and willing to commit the crime an opportunity to do so." It is noteworthy that this formulation appeared in a dissenting opinion in which Stewart argued that the case in question *had* involved entrapment; thus, it probably represents the opinion of many justices who take a reasonably strict view of what constitutes entrapment. As such, it affords ample opportunity for undercover operations, especially those, such as Abscam, in which lawyers can monitor agent activity on almost a continuous basis.

Congress was fully aware that the FBI was expanding its use of undercover operations. The House Appropriations Committee, as well as others, were told about these developments—without, of course, particular cases then in progress being identified. Moreover, Congress by law had to give permission for the Bureau to do certain things necessary for an undercover operation. These prerequisites to FBI undercover operations involve the right to lease buildings or to enter into contracts in ways that do not divulge the fact that the contracting party or the lessee are government agents, and that permit advance payment of funds. Indeed, one statute prohibits a government agency from leasing a building in Washington, D.C., without a specific appropriation for that purpose having first been made by Congress. If that law had been in force, the FBI would not have been able to lease the Washington house in which Operation Abscam was conducted. At the request of the FBI, however, Congress exempted the Bureau from compliance with statutes that might have impeded such operations. The proposed FBI Charter, now before Congress, would specifically authorize undercover operations and would grant a continuing exemption, whenever necessary, from the statutes governing contracts and leases.

Though the FBI learned a great deal about undercover operations by its early participation in Stings, Operation Abscam is not, strictly speaking, a Sting at all. In a Sting, a store is opened and the agents declare their willingness to buy merchandise from one and all. Much of what they buy involves perfectly legitimate sales; some of what they buy is stolen, and when that is established, the ground is laid for an arrest. Operation Abscam followed a quite different route. It resulted from the normal exploitation of an informant who had been useful in locating stolen art works. The informant apparently indicated that he could put agents in touch with politicians who were for sale; the agents accepted, and set up Abscam by having an agent pose as a wealthy Arab interested in buying political favors to assist his (mythical) business enterprises. Several important congressmen, or their representatives, were brought to the house used for Abscam and their negotiations with the agents recorded. The operation is no different in design from those used in many other cases that earned praise for the Bureau. What is different is that in this case congressmen were apparently involved and the operation was leaked to the press before indictments were issued.

Congress, Law Enforcement, and the Constitution

For congressmen to be in trouble with the law is nothing new. During the 95th Congress alone, 13 members or former members of the House of Representatives were indicted or convicted on criminal charges. Most if not all of these cases resulted from the use of conventional investigative methods—typically, a tip to a law enforcement officer or reporter by a person involved in the offense (bribery, payroll padding, taking kickbacks) who then testified against the official. Law enforcement in such cases is ordinarily reactive and thus crucially dependent on the existence and volubility of a disaffected employee, businessman, or accomplice. Operation Abscam was "proactive"—it created an opportunity for persons to commit a crime who were (presumably) ready and willing to do so.

Congress has never complained when such methods were used against others; quite the contrary, it has explicitly or implicitly urged—and

authorized—their use against others. There is no small element of hypocrisy in the complaints of some congressmen that they did not mean a vigorous investigation of white-collar crime to include *them*.

But it is not all hypocrisy. It is worth discussing how such investigations should be conducted and under what pattern of accountability. An unscrupulous President with a complaisant FBI director could use undercover operations to discredit political enemies, including congressmen from a rival party. Hoover was a highly political FBI director, but he saw, rightly, that his power would be greater if he avoided investigations of Congress than if he undertook them. Clarence Kelley and William H. Webster have been sternly nonpartisan directors who would never consider allowing the Bureau's powers to be put in service of some rancid political purpose. But new times bring new men, and in the future we may again see partisan efforts to use the Bureau. What safeguards can be installed to prevent schemes to embarrass political enemies by leaked stories is worth some discussion.

But there is a dilemma here: the more extensive the pattern of accountability and control, the greater the probability of a leak. The only sure way to minimize leaks is to minimize the number of persons who know something worth leaking. In the case of Operation Abscam, scores of persons knew what was going on—in part because such extensive efforts were made to insure that it was a lawful and effective investigation. In addition to the dozens of FBI agents and their supervisors, there were lawyers in the Justice Department and U.S. Attorneys in New York, Newark, Philadelphia, and Washington, D.C., together with their staffs, all of whom were well informed. Any one of them could have leaked. Indeed, given their partisan sponsorship and what is often their background in political activism, U.S. Attorneys are especially likely to be sources of leaks—more so, I should surmise, than FBI agents. If, in order to prevent abuses of the Bureau's investigative powers, we increase the number of supervisors—to include, for example, members of the House or Senate ethics committees—we also increase the chances of leaks (to say nothing of other ways by which such investigations could be compromised).

In the meantime, the debate will not be helped by complaints that the Bureau has launched a "vendetta" against Congress or that it is "out of control." It is nothing of the kind. It is an organization that is following out the logic of changes and procedures adopted to meet the explicit demands of Congress.

Chapter 4 Review Questions

1. On the basis of your reading of the Long essay and the case study, how would you define the term *administrative power?* Can it be measured? If so, how?

2. Based on the case study, "The Changing FBI—The Road to Abscam," by James Q. Wilson, how did Hoover effectively use the Bureau's administrative power? How did he influence its direction and enhancement of power? Why did he avoid investigating political corruption and white-collar crime?

3. After Hoover's death, what prompted the redirection of Bureau priorities? How did FBI agents respond to these new priorities?

4. In your view, was Abscam a responsible or irresponsible use of FBI administrative power? How can one determine "responsible" or "irresponsible" use of administrative power?

5. Can you list the pros and cons of having the Bureau involved in "sting operations" like Abscam?

6. On the basis of Long's essay and your analysis of the case study, can you list the specific factors that can strengthen or detract from an organization's administrative power? Are there specific ways that administrators protect or enhance their power positions? If so, how?

Key Terms

interest groups

organizational fragmentation

administrative rationality

balance of power

coordination of government

sources of conflict

sources of cohesion

maintaining political support

Suggestions for Further Reading

The classic works on interest groups and their influence on the governmental process are Arthur F. Bentley, *The Process of Government* (Cambridge, Mass.: Harvard University Press, 1908); E. Pendleton Herring, *Public Administration and the Public Interest* (New York: Russell and Russell, 1936); and David Truman, *The Governmental Process* (New York: Alfred A. Knopf, 1951). The influence of politics on public administration and the general power politics within administrative processes were especially emphasized and popularized by the "new postwar realism" of authors such as Paul H. Appleby, *Big Democracy* (New York: Alfred A. Knopf, 1945) and *Policy and Administration* (University, Ala.: University of Alabama Press, 1949); Robert A. Dahl and Charles E. Lindblom, *Politics, Economics, and Welfare* (New York: Harper and Brothers, 1953); and Herbert Simon et al., *Public Administration* (New York: Alfred A. Knopf, 1950). Of course, Long's numerous essays did much to explore as well as contribute to this topic and they are available in a single volume, *The Polity* (Chicago: Rand McNally and Co., 1962).

The last two decades have witnessed an enormous outpouring of books and articles on this subject. Some of the best that illuminate our understanding of the complex interplay between administration and politics have been more narrowly focused book-length cases of policy dilemmas such as A. Lee Fritchler, *Smoking and Politics*, Second Edition (Englewood Cliffs, N.J.: Prentice-Hall, 1975); Daniel P. Moynihan, *The Politics of a Guaranteed Income* (New York: Random House, 1973); Jeffrey L. Pressman and Aaron Wildavsky, *Implementation,* Second Edition (Berkeley: University of California Press, 1979); and Stephen K. Bailey and Edith K. Mosher, *ESEA: The Office of Education Administers a Law* (Syracuse: Syracuse University Press, 1968). There are many, many more such cases, particularly those available through the Inter-University Case Program (P.O. Box 229, Syracuse, N.Y. 13210), and the John F. Kennedy School of Government Case Program, Kennedy School of Government, Case Program, Harvard University, 79 JFK Street, Cambridge, Mass. 02138. For recent books about administrative power based on some careful case studies, read: Gary C. Bryner, *Bureaucratic Discretion* (New York: Pergamon Press, 1987); Irene S. Rubin, *Shrinking the Federal Government* (New York: Longman, 1985); and James P. Pfiffner, *The Strategic Presidency* (Chicago: The Dorsey Press, 1988).

Perhaps some of the very best contemporary analyses of the aspects of power influencing administrative actions are found in Harold Seidman and Robert Gilmour *Politics, Position, and Power,* Fourth Edition (New York: Oxford University Press, 1986); Francis E. Rourke, *Bureaucracy, Politics and Public Policy,* Third Edition (Boston: Little, Brown, 1984); as well as Rourke's excellent edited collection entitled *Bureaucratic Power in National Policy Making,* Fourth Edition (Boston: Little, Brown, 1986). The late Stephen K. Bailey's "Improving Federal Governance," *Public Administration Review,* 30 (November/December 1980), pp. 548–553, is also excellent; as well as Frederick C. Mosher, "The Changing Responsibilities and Tactics of the Federal Government," in the same issue, pp. 541–548; and James D. Carroll, A. Lee Fritchler, and Bruce L. R. Smith, "Supply-Side Management in the Reagan Administration," *Public Administration Review,* 45 (November/December 1985), pp. 805–814.

You should not overlook biographies and autobiographies as offering worthwhile insights, particularly Joseph A. Califano, Jr., *Governing America* (New York: Simon and Schuster, 1981); William Manchester, *American Caesar: Douglas MacArthur, 1880–1964* (Boston: Little, Brown, 1978); Norman Polmar and Thomas B. Allen, *Rickover: A Biography* (New York: Simon and Schuster, 1982);

or Robert Caro, *The Power Broker,* cited in Chapter 3; and David Stockman, *The Triumph of Politics,* cited in Chapter 3. During the 1980s the Urban Institute in Washington, D.C. published several interesting books assessing, in part, the Reagan presidency's influence on political-administrative relationships, see especially: Lester M. Salamon and Michael S. Lund, eds., *The Reagan Presidency and the Governing of America* (1985); and John L. Palmer, ed., *Perspectives on the Reagan Years* (1986).

The Intergovernmental Dimension to Public Administration: The Concept of Calculative IGR

"[The calculative phase of IGR] is a phase that still contains many of the surface trappings of federalism. Local and state governments have the appearance of making significant policy choices. A few such choices may still remain, but they seem to be few and elusive. The chief choice that most nonnational participants have is deciding whether to participate in federal assistance programs. Once that choice is made, a large array of more limited choices appears open to those who have entered the federal assistance arena. A great deal of bargaining and negotiation takes place within that arena. But these are constrained chiefly, if not exclusively, by nationally specified rules of the game."

Deil S. Wright

READING 5

Introduction

In most countries, the concept of intergovernmental relations is not a topic that is discussed much. Unitary forms of government, found in communist societies, third world or developing nations, and many developed Western countries, allow for little or no semiautonomous local units of government. In these governments, power flows from the top downward, and no competition with national sovereignty from governmental subunits is tolerated. Local autonomy is simply unknown.

By contrast, the government of the United States has always been based on the idea of federalism. The federal structure under the U.S. Constitution distributes authority among the various levels of federal, state, and local government. Thus, in the United States, public administrators work within an unusual, complex framework in which authority over agency and program activities is frequently shared by various levels, jurisdictions, and units of government. Because of this "scattering" of authority, administrative problems arise, leading, in turn, to the important study of intergovernmental relations (IGR).

Understandably, the study of IGR has become increasingly important to public administrators since their programs (and indeed often their own survival) may involve actions, activities, and funding that are supported by other levels of government. In recent years, academic and practitioner concern over IGR has increased because of reliance on federal block grants and categorical programs to support local government's activities.[1] Rarely, today, is a successful administrator's work not in some manner affected by IGR. Therefore, it is likely that the importance of IGR will continue to grow in the years ahead.

In the seminal text on the subject, *Understanding Intergovernmental Relations,* by Deil Wright, the concept of IGR is defined as more than federal aid to states or localities. It "includes as objects of proper study all the permutations and combinations of relations among the units of government in the American system."[2] Wright also would include the formal as well as the informal relationships between elected and nonelected officials in a definition of IGR. He writes, "Strictly speaking . . . there are no relationships among *governments;* there are only relations among *officials* who govern different units. The individual actions and attitudes of public officials are at the core of IGR."[3]

Most of this reading reviews the development of IGR, showing how the concept evolved through six distinct phases that the author outlines carefully and how, according to Wright, the growth of IGR was largely because of the federal government's massive effort to combat the economic and social havoc of the Great Depression. Wright goes on, however, to point out that "during the 1960s and 1970s formal use of the concept of IGR expanded and was employed on national, state, and local levels," largely given impetus through the Intergovernmental Cooperation Act of 1968 (PL 90-577) and the Intergovernmental Personnel Act of 1970 (PL 91-648). The major features of IGR are explained in the reading, with particular attention given to the characteristics of IGR that became evident during the 1970s and 1980s, or what Wright labels the phase of *calculative IGR.*

Those involved in IGR must think ahead about their actions. Therefore, according to Wright, being *calculative* involves (1) "deliberating and weighing one or more avenues of action"; (2) having the ability "to forecast or predict the consequences of anticipated actions"; and (3) being able "to count, to figure, or to compute—in a numerical sense" the best strategic option available for a unit of government. Within the IGR setting, such calculative behavior translates into specific actions that are exhibited by the "tendency to estimate the 'costs' as well as the 'benefits' of getting a federal grant," or secondly, by playing the "formula game," where formula grants are created

---

[1]The important distinctions between these major forms of federal assistance to states and localities are presented in detail in the following essay.

[2]Deil S. Wright, *Understanding Intergovernmental Relations,* Second Edition (Monterey, Calif.: Brooks/Cole Publishing Co., 1982).

[3]Ibid.

or revised to favor one's particular locale. Wright cites the following statement by a close observer of IGR who captures the essence of the present calculative era of IGR: "Public interest groups come into Washington with computer printouts with the [formula] weighting and what will happen if a certain weighting is approved."

In this perceptive analysis of contemporary IGR, Wright argues further that the calculative behavior by the IGR "actors" has turned much of federalism into a facade. For Wright, *facade federalism* has two meanings: the "false front put forth by some (or several?) participants in intergovernmental exchanges [that] may be contrived or artificial to bluff other participants" (as in a game of poker); and "the absence or falseness of federalism," reflecting the idea that "in some contemporary circumstances power has gravitated so heavily toward national officials that federalism, in its historic and legal sense, is nonexistent." Wright's arguments about the present calculative IGR reveal both a clear-eyed realism as well as an irritating pessimism about the nature and practice of contemporary IGR. Certainly these ideas cannot be ignored for their implications about the future of government and public administration in the United States are serious ones.

A word here about Deil Wright (1930–   ). Currently professor of Political Science at the University of North Carolina at Chapel Hill, he served as director of the Master of Public Administration Program from 1973–1980. For two decades he has taught and published extensively in the intergovernmental field, especially on the topics of fiscal behavior of state and local governmental units, and actions and attitudes of administrative officials. Indeed, today he is an eminent scholar in this field. In 1981, he was awarded the Donald C. Stone Prize for his distinguished contributions to this academic area.

As you read this selection, keep the following questions in mind:

According to Wright, how did IGR evolve in the United States? What are its six basic phases and their key features?

Which major events, official studies, scholarly ideas, and congressional acts contributed to the rise of IGR in this century?

Specifically, what are the differences between the concepts of IGR and federalism?

Why does Wright characterize the present era as "calculative IGR" and as "facade federalism"? Do you agree with his analysis?

Why does Wright pay special attention to the human dimensions of IGR? Why does he believe that careful attention to human behavior ultimately will enable us to understand better the policy outcomes in IGR?

In the case study in Chapter 3, what calculative human behaviors were exhibited in IGR processes and what "impacts" did this behavior have on the policy outcomes as well as the administration of public programs in Bakersfield?

DEIL S. WRIGHT

Intergovernmental Relations in the 1980s

A New Phase of IGR

It is an accepted fact that since 1900 the U.S. political system has experienced significant changes that border on major but evolutionary upheavals. One approach to systematizing and understanding the events and shifts of nearly a century-long period of national-state-local relationships is to think of phases of IGR (intergovernmental Relations). This approach has been elaborated elsewhere [1]. The aim here is to identify and explore only the most recent and current phase of IGR—the calculative phase. A short sketch of the five previous phases will provide a basis for exploring the current calculative phase.

The six phases of IGR and their approximate periods of prominence are:

Conflict:	pre-1930s
Cooperative:	1930s to 1950s
Concentrated:	1940s to 1960s
Creative:	1950s to 1960s
Competitive:	1960s to 1970s
Calculative:	1970s to 1980s

A condensed chart of the distinctive features of each phase is provided in Table 5.1.

For each phase of IGR three substantive components are identified. (See the second through fourth columns of Table 5.1.) First, what policy issues dominated the public agenda during each phase? Second, what dominant perceptions did the chief participants seem to have?

Deil S. Wright, "A New Phase of IGR," in *Intergovernmental Relations in the 1980s,* edited by Richard H. Leach, Marcel Dekker, Inc., N.Y., 1983, pp. 15–32. Reprinted with permission from the publisher.

What orientations or mind-sets guided their behavior in each phase? Third, what mechanisms and techniques were used to implement intergovernmental actions and objectives during each period? The fifth column of the table lists a metaphorical characterization of each phase. The metaphors most commonly used are forms of federalism.

The dates for each period are approximate at best. Indeed, the phases actually overlap. Therefore, the idea of climax period is important—not only because it conveys a time of peak prominence but because it does not preclude the continuation of a phase beyond the dates given. For example, although the conflict phase climaxed before and during the 1930s, conflict patterns did not end then. They regularly recur today as subsidiary events during the current dominant calculative phase.

Thus, like successive, somewhat porous strata that have been superimposed on each other (by the interactions and perspectives of public officials), no phase ends at an exact point—nor does it in fact disappear. Each phase is continuously present in greater or lesser measure, bearing the weight, so to speak, of the overlying strata (subsequent phases) and producing carry-over effects much wider than the climax periods indicated in Table 5.1. Indeed, the present state of IGR results from multiple overlays of each of the six phases. The task of an IGR analyst is like that of a geologist: to drill or probe the several strata and from the samples make inferences about the substructure of the terrain.

Short sketches of the first five phases serve as backdrops for the more extended analysis of the sixth phase. The conflict, cooperative, concentrated, creative, and competitive phases are reviewed below.

Table 5.1   Phases of Intergovernmental Relations (IGR)

Phase descriptor	Main problems	Participants' perceptions	IGR mechanisms	Federalism metaphor	Approximate climax period
Conflict	Defining boundaries Proper spheres	Antagonistic Adversary Exclusivity	Statutes Courts Regulations	Layer-cake federalism	19th Century–1930s
Cooperative	Economic distress International threat	Collaboration Complimen-tarity Mutuality Supportive	National planning Formula grants Tax credits	Marble-cake federalism	1930s–1950s
Concentrated	Service needs Physical development	Professionalism Objectivity Neutrality Functionalism	Categorical grants Service standards	Water taps (focused or channeled)	1940s–1960s
Creative	Urban-metropoli-tan Disadvantaged clients	National goals Great Society Grantsmanship	Program planning Project grants Participation	Flowering (proliferated and fused)	1950s–1960s
Competitive	Coordination Program effectiveness Delivery systems Citizen access	Disagreement Tension Rivalry	Grant consolidation Revenue sharing Reorganization	Picket fence (fragmented)	1960s–1970s
Calculative	Accountability Bankruptcy Constraints Dependency Federal role Public confidence	Gamesmanship Fungibility Overload	General aid-entitlements Bypassing Loans Crosscutting regulations	Facade (confronta-tional)	1970s–1980s

Source: From *Understanding Intergovernmental Relations* by Deil S. Wright. Copyright © 1982 by Brooks/Cole Publishing Company. Reprinted by permission of the publisher.

Conflict Phase

Until the 1930s the relationships between the national, state, and local governments were known largely for the conflicts they generated. Courts, legislative bodies, and elected executives seemed to be propelled by concerns over who had the "right" to act (or not act) on a problem, such as regulating child labor, promoting public health, or assuring a minimum standard of welfare. Various governmental bodies made an effort to define clearly the boundaries and "proper" spheres of action of local, state, and national governments. Scholars have correctly noted that submerged below the prominent conflicts were elements of cooperation [2, 3]. Nevertheless, it was common to use a culinary metaphor in describing IGR prior to and into the 1930s—layer-cake federalism.

Cooperative Phase

The economic distress of the 1930s and the international demands and tensions of the 1940s brought public officials together in a spirit of cooperation. Collaboration between the national government and the states in the welfare field was a noteworthy result of the Depression. All governments and officials, of course, supported the war effort of 1941 to 1945. One perceptive observer [4] noted that:

> cooperative government by federal-state-local authorities has become a byword in the prodigious effort to administer civilian defense, rationing, and other war-time programs. Intergovernmental administration, while it is a part of all levels of government, is turning into something quite distinct from them all.

The degree of cooperation between national, state, and local officials in administrative affairs did not stop at the end of World War II. The continuing intertwining of IGR contacts gave rise to a new metaphor—marble-cake federalism.

Concentrated Phase

IGR became increasingly concentrated around a rising number of specific federal grant-in-aid programs. Over 20 major functional, highly focused grant programs were established in a 15-year postwar period, including programs for airports, defense education, libraries, sewage treatment, and urban renewal. The number, focus, fiscal size, and specificity of these grant programs produced an incremental but distinct policy shift in national-state and national-local relations.

The contacts now involved or were even dominated by exchanges between specialists and professionals in particular fields, such as airport engineering, library science, and health. Administrators, who were also program professionals, entered the scene as important participants. This rising professionalism was reflected in the entire public service and is the reason this phase is labeled *"concentrated."* Mosher has referred to the 1950s as the "triumph of the professional state" [5].

In addition, between 1953 and 1955 a temporary presidential commission devoted considerable attention to policy and administrative questions involving IGR. Continuing attention to IGR has been assured since 1959, when the Congress created the permanent Advisory Commission on Intergovernmental Relations (ACIR). The ACIR is a representative body that conducts studies and makes recommendations to improve the functioning of the federal system. It is composed of 26 members: 3 private citizens, 9 national officials (3 each from the executive branch, House, and Senate), and 14 representatives of state and local governments.

Creative Phase

The cooperative and concentrated phases constituted the pilings if not the full foundation on which the creative phase of IGR was erected. The word for this phase comes from President Johnson's Great Society era, when he called for numerous program and policy initiatives under the banner of "Creative Federalism." The impact of the Johnson initiatives on IGR was stupendous. Over a hundred major new categorical grant programs were enacted (nearly 300 specific legislative authorizations). More significant from an administrative point of view was that the bulk of the new grant authorizations were *project* grants. Historically, most grants had formula provisions that apportioned the grant monies among the states (or occasionally among cities). But project grant funds for programs such as Model Cities and Urban Mass Transit were available for open competition, so to speak. Large numbers of cities could (and did) apply with specific and detailed project proposals, which were required to fit guidelines and regulations. Not only did federal program administrators write the regulations, but they also made most (if not all) of the decisions on which cities' projects were approved and funded. State and local administrators were similarly thrust into the policy-making limelight, in part because of the additional resources available to them and the clientele-building tasks needed to sustain new programs.

The revolution in IGR during the 1960s can be noted in financial terms. Federal aid to state and local governments more than tripled from $7 billion in 1960 to about $24 billion in 1970. A similar increase also characterized state aid to local units—from almost $10 billion in 1960 to almost $29 billion in 1970. Detailed breakdowns on the intergovernmental flows of funds are important but are too numerous for specific comment. Overall, the amounts show the magnitude of the links in 1970 between national, state, and local governments. The creative phase of IGR produced a highly interdependent, tightly bonded set of relationships. The IGR links were sometimes referred to as *"fused federalism,"* and it was said that "when national policy makers sneeze, the state and local ones catch pneumonia."

Competitive Phase

The apparent tight links of the creative phase of IGR overstated reality. Even before the creative phase peaked (in dollar terms) at the end of the 1960s, there were signs of tension, disagreement, and dissatisfaction among many IGR participants, especially those at the state and local levels. Senator Edmund Muskie perceptively pinpointed the nature of the tension. He had been a governor, and as a senator he chaired the Subcommittee on Intergovernmental Relations. As early as 1966 the senator observed, "The picture, then, is one of too much tension and conflict rather than coordination and cooperation all along the line of administration—from top federal policymakers and administrators to the state and local professional administrators and elected officials" [1; p. 62]. One example might be the case of a state health department head supporting provi-

sions in national health legislation that differ from the policy position taken by his/her state's governor.

The tension and conflict to which Muskie referred between the "line of administration" and "professional administrators" laid bare a new type of fracture in IGR. This was the split between policy-making generalists, whether elected or appointed, and the professional program specialists. Figure 5.1 displays what ex-governor Terry Sanford (of North Carolina) called picket-fence federalism [6]. The metaphor illuminates the friction between the vertical functional allegiances of administrators to their specialized programs and the horizontal coordination intentions of the policy generalists—represented by the position-based associations of the "big seven" groups in Figure 5.1.

The "picket-fence" metaphor is an oversimplification in several respects [1, 7]. Nevertheless, it conveys some sense of the concerns and tensions present in IGR during the 1960s and early 1970s. Selective empirical research has shown the strong presence of specialized, functional attitudes among program administration officials [8].

The tolerance and support of the officials in the seven public interest groups had worn thin on behalf of categorical grant programs of both formula and project varieties. References were made to the "vertical functional autocracies," "balkanized bureaucracies," and the "management morass" that seemed associated with categorical forms of federal aid. The public interest groups shifted toward new policy stances, including support of general revenue sharing (enacted in 1972), broad-based block grants (several were passed), grant consolidations, and other similar proposals. A concise statement about the autonomous and fragmenting impacts of federal aid in the competitive IGR phase of the late 1960s and the 1970s came from a local official (in 1969) who observed that "our city is a battleground among warring Federal cabinet agencies" [9]. He was referring to the fact that various federal departments were funding, operating, and controlling "their" semiautonomous programs within the city.

Calculative Phase

Previous discussion has pointed out that the time periods tied to each phase are imprecise and approximate. That point holds for the climax span of the current IGR phase—the calculative period. If forced to identify a precise date and event that signaled the rise of this phase, however, I would select 1975 and the event would be the near-bankruptcy of New York City. Telescoped into that episode, and into the continuing fiscal/social/economic plight of that city, were several issues that re-

flected some of the core problems of our society and our political system. Those problems range from accountability, bankruptcy, and constraints, to dependency, the federal role, and the loss of public confidence (see Table 5.1).

Main Problems

For years it had been difficult for New York City's citizens to identify and hold accountable those officials who were making major and costly public decisions [10–12]. For example, bond monies, ostensibly for capital construction, were used for equipment and even operating expenses. It finally took the private banking community, which was not without its share of blame for the malaise, to call a halt and push the city to the brink of bankruptcy. Constraints and severe cutback management were clamped on

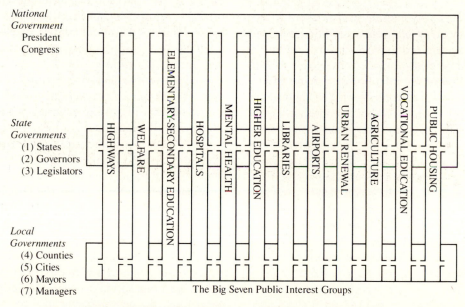

Figure 5.1 Picket-fence federalism: A schematic representation. (Deil S. Wright, "A New Phase of IGR," in *Intergovernmental Relations in the 1980's,* edited by Richard H. Leach, Figure 1. Marcel Dekker, Inc., N.Y., 1983.)

the city largely by national requirements connected with a temporary federal loan. The city also found itself attempting to cope with other externally mandated and less yielding constraints—the three E's of economy (especially stagflation), energy, and environment.

New York City's route into, and thus far its provisional route through, the crisis is illustrative of another common current problem in IGR—dependency. And dependency is intimately attached to a larger problem: What is the appropriate role of the federal government? (As we shall see shortly, this issue has reasserted itself in a manner and with a force that is reminiscent of the conflict phase.) What are the boundaries and appropriate spheres within which the national government should (or should not) act? Finally, the problems of citizen confidence or public trust in government(s) can likewise be discerned in the New York City crisis.

New York City is a microcosm, albeit a large one, of an array of problems confronting our political system and its IGR dimensions. Fortunately, most other jurisdictions have not suffered, and hopefully will not experience, the convergence of such a problem-set. The significance and the dispersion of the six problems mentioned above . . . across the nation are sufficient, however, to demand attention and precautionary or preventive actions. Perhaps the worst outlook or approach to adopt is to conclude that New York City's plight is completely irrelevant to the difficulties, issues, and operations of other governments—national, state, and local. Other entities and officials should avoid the complacent attitude expressed in the famous (or infamous) phrase: "It can't happen here!"

Participants' Perceptions and Behavior

What happened in IGR during the 1970s? What can be projected to extend well into the 1980s? What are the current prominent per-

ceptions of the main participants in IGR processes? Three chief perceptions are suggested as dominating the calculative phase. (There may well be others.) The three are fungibility, gamesmanship, and overload. All three are tied directly to the characterization of this phase as calculative.

The word *calculative* is used in at least three senses. First, it means to think in advance of taking action, deliberating and weighing one or more avenues of action. A second meaning is to forecast or predict the consequences of anticipated actions; it implies the adoption of a rather sophisticated, quasi-scientific mode of thinking, perhaps best expressed in the form of the hypothetical statement: "If . . ., then . . ." Third, calculative means to count, to figure, or to compute—in a numerical sense. In other words, quantitative forecasting, usually measured in dollar units, is a prominent (but not universal) part of the term's meaning. There are several types of behavior identifiable in contemporary IGR that are calculative in character, and these behavior patterns are expected to prevail in the near future.

One current calculative feature is the increased tendency to estimate the "costs" as well as the benefits of getting a federal grant. Two illustrations will suffice.

In 1976 the coordinator of state-federal relations for New York State reported that New York refused to pursue over $2 million in funds available to New York under the Developmental Disabilities Act. He notes that: "It would have cost us more than the two million we would receive to do the things that were required as a condition for receipt of the funds; my recommendation was not to take it and that was a hard one to make" [13]. Similarly at the local level, the city manager of a town with a population of 30,000 indicated (to the author) that unless a federal grant exceeded $40,000 he declined to inquire about or pursue it. Only a grant in excess of that "break-even" amount was sufficient to make it worth seeking. The calculation-based comment was made in 1973;

subsequent inflation and increased federal regulations may have doubled that earlier threshold-seeking amount. It is clear from these illustrations that state and local administrators had become more cautious and calculative about their IGR fiscal efforts.

A second type of calculation involves the *formula game*. The formula game is the strategic process of attempting to change, in a favorable direction, one or more formulas by which federal funds are allocated among state and local governments. Increased attention to grant formulas has occurred since 1975 for two reasons. One is the widely heralded conflict between the snow belt and sun belt regions of the country. A second is that despite enactment of a large number of project grant programs, new as well as older formula grant programs account for nearly 80% of the $96 billion in estimated federal aid distributed in 1981.

An example of calculational strategy on a formula grant occurred with the extension of the Community Development Block Grant (CDBG) Program in 1977. The factors used in allocating $3.4 billion in 1978 CDBG funds were changed chiefly by substituting for "housing overcrowding" the "age of housing" (built prior to 1940) in a city. This formula revision heavily favored older industrial cities in the northeast and north central states at the expense of newer, younger, and smaller cities in southern and western states [14].

The stakes involved in calculative IGR can be huge. In any given year several formula grant programs totaling billions of dollars expire and must be reauthorized. It is easy to understand why experts, statistics, and computers have become commonplace in the present phase of IGR. A close observer of contemporary IGR captured the calculative propensities of this phase when he noted: "Public interest groups come into Washington with computer printouts with the [formula] weighting and what will happen if a certain weighting is approved" [15, 16].

Calculative behavior in three other areas of activity can be described in general terms. One involves coping with constraints and developing skills in cutback management. The International City Management Association, for example, has developed a program seminar with the title: "Managing with Declining Resources." The purpose of the sessions is to perfect operational techniques, quantitative and analytical, wherever possible, for making deliberate decisions on program reductions. Extensive attention has been devoted in the past few years to cutback management and coping with fiscal stress [17, 18].

A second example of calculation involves profits of $300 to $400 million that will accrue to several states from making federally subsidized loans to students attending colleges and technical schools. These profits, accumulating between 1980 to 1985, will be realized by the 18 states issuing student loan bonds plus the 10 other states that may do so for the first time in 1980 [19].

This situation occurs as a result of high interest rates, recent national tax and education legislation, and the active entry of several states, and even some local governments, into the student loan field. The profits will accrue to state (or local) governments in a manner that is best explained by two paragraphs from a Congressional Budget Office report. The report formally identified and calculated the estimated costs to the national government—and profit for the states.

Student loan bonds are issued to provide students better access to loans. For a number of years, the federal government has induced commercial lenders to make student loans voluntarily, by offering them interest subsidies (a "special allowance") and insurance against student default. Even with these inducements, however, commercial lenders have been unwilling to lend to all student applicants because of the high cost of servicing student loans. As a result, some students have had trouble finding banks willing to lend to them, and an increasing number of states responded by issuing student loan bonds and then relending the proceeds to students.

States and localities raise money by issuing bonds at low, tax-exempt interest rates and use the proceeds to buy or make federally guaranteed student loans at significantly higher interest rates, paid in large part by the federal government. Although the interest costs of nearly all student loan bond authorities were under 7 percent in 1979, for example, the yield they received on student loans fluctuated between 11 and 16 percent. The profits accruing to the bond issuers is the difference between the yield on student loans and the level of associated expenses—interest on the bonds and administrative costs. Lenders receive 7 percent interest paid by the federal government until students leave school and by students thereafter. In addition, lenders receive special allowance payments from the federal government. The special allowance rate is recalculated each quarter and averaged 6.5 percent in 1979. [19; p. ix]

A final illustration of calculative behavior might best be summarized as the *risk* of noncompliance. This feature derives directly from the rising regulatory dimensions of IGR. A recent Office of Management and Budget (OMB) study identified 59 crosscutting or general national policy requirements [20]. These requirements are called *crosscutting* because they apply to the national assistance programs of more than one agency or department. In some cases they apply to *all* assistance programs in *every* department or agency, for example, nondiscrimination because of race, color, national origin, or handicapped status.

The significance and relevance of these requirements to the calculative phase of IGR are straightforward and twofold. One is the cost of compliance with the regulations by the recipi-

ents of federal assistance. Estimated costs of compliance with the equal access provisions for handicapped persons [21] in the public transportation field alone are estimated at $3 to $4 *billion.*

Recently a systematic study of local government compliance costs was conducted by Muller and Fix of the Urban Institute [22]. The researchers examined the incremental costs of complying with six major regulations in seven communities. The local units were Alexandria (Va.), Burlington (Vt.), Cincinnati, Dallas, Fairfax Co. (Va.), Newark, and Seattle. Among the regulations were bilingual education and transit accessibility for the handicapped. The study encompassed both capital and operating costs. The locally funded incremental costs varied from $6 per capita in Burlington to $52 per capita in Newark. The average across the seven units was $25 per capita. The authors set these compliance costs within the larger federal aid framework with the following observation: "One statistic can put the figures . . . into sharp perspective: the aid that the seven jurisdictions received under federal revenue sharing averaged about $25 per capita a year—essentially the same as what it cost them, on average, to comply with these regulatory programs" [22; p. 31].

Another type of "cost" associated with these crosscutting requirements is one of noncompliance or, more accurately, incomplete compliance. It is hard to imagine any recipient of federal assistance that can fully comply with all the applicable policy requirements. The calculations laid on assistance recipients are ones that require tradeoffs or choices between these mandates, *provided* that the recipient is even aware of the applicability of a particular requirement. The OMB study described the forced choices and costs of the policy mandates and also allowed for the possibility that recipients might not know of some requirements because no one in the national government has been charged with knowing what they are.

Individually, each crosscutting requirement may be sound. But cumulatively the conditions may be extraordinarily burdensome on federal agencies and recipients. They can distort the allocation of resources, as the conditions are frequently imposed with minimal judgement as to relative costs and benefits in any given transaction. Frequently, the recipients must absorb substantial portions of the costs. While the recipients may feel the full impact of these multiple requirements, there has been no one place in the federal government charged even with the task of knowing what all the crosscutting requirements are. [20; p. 20]

The 1970s as the starting period for the calculative phase of IGR is supported in part by temporal data on the 59 crosscutting requirements. About two-thirds of the socioeconomic policy requirements are a product of the 1970s. Over half of the administrative/fiscal requirements were placed in effect during the 1970s. Continuation of the calculative phase through the 1980s seems assured based on the likely permanence of this regulatory dimension of national assistance programs.

The remaining aspects of the calculative phase of IGR (see Table 5.1) deserve mention and brief exposition. The perceptions of participants are summarized with three terms—gamesmanship, fungibility, and overload. The first refers to the way in which participants in IGR processes engage in strategic behavior. They play various "games." Grantsmanship, for example, is one well-established game which, while identified with the creative phase, has been perfected through the competitive phase to the point that it is possible to specify some of the rules by which the grantsmanship game is played [23].

Fungible means interchangeable or substitutive. In intergovernmental terms fungibility means the ability to shift or exchange resources received for one purpose and accomplish another purpose. Several state governments will receive federal monies to subsidize student education loans. Those funds, once received by the states, are fungible after entering a state government's treasury and may be used for any purpose. General revenue sharing and block grant funds are noteworthy for their fungible or displacement effects. The receipt of such funds may permit the recipient unit to reduce the amount of its own resources devoted to the federally assisted program. The funds that are released from this substitution process can be allocated to other purposes or the process can result in a tax decrease.

An illustration of fungibility in connection with CETA funds in North Carolina is contained in Figure 5.2, "Fungible Funds from Federal Grants." CETA funds were used in 1975 to hire several hundred temporary employes by the Division of Highways. It was difficult to determine, however, how many of the federally funded positions were new jobs and how many were persons who were simply replacements in jobs that were previously state-funded. The average of state-paid jobs in 1974 was 1821 but dropped to 1532 in 1975. Peak state-paid employment in 1974 was about 2400; in 1975 it was below 2000.

Overload is a third dimension of participants' perspectives. The term gained considerable currency in the late 1970s, and it fits well the tone and temper of the calculative phase. A broader phrase, *political overload,* was used by James Douglas in 1976 to mean that "modern democratic governments [are] overwhelmed by the load of responsibilities they are called upon—or believe they are called upon—to shoulder" [24; p. 5]. Applied to the United States as a term criticizing governmental performance, the phrase has been interpreted to stand for excessive cost, ineffectiveness, and overregulation [24, 25]. These themes, when combined with the prior discussion of the crosscutting requirements, should adequately amplify the concept of overload.

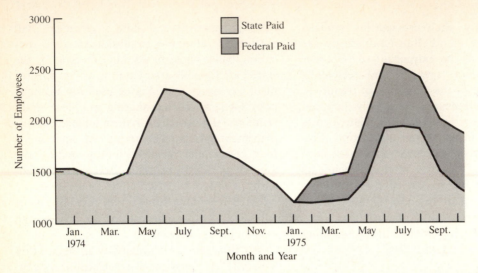

Figure 5.2 Fungible funds from federal grants. (From *The News and Observer*, Raleigh, N.C., Sunday, Dec. 7, 1975. Copyright © 1975 by The News and Observer Publishing Company. Reprinted by permission of the publisher.)

A "weighty" example of overload recently surfaced at a New Jersey meeting attended by a staff member of the U.S. Regulatory Council (an interagency group that attempts to coordinate the 90 federal agencies issuing 2000 or more rules annually). Among the attendees was a mayor who had collected and weighed (literally) all the regulations and directives his city had received over the prior 18 months from different national and state agencies. The physical mass exceeded 2000 pounds [26]!

IGR Mechanisms and Metaphors

Several mechanisms are used to implement IGR activities in the calculative phase. One, as implied previously, is discretionary aid— general aid and block grants. These funds are dispensed on a formula basis. The legal term used in connection with the disbursements is indicative of a shift in participants' mindset about aid funds. The funds obtained by recipients are called *entitlements*. Jurisdictions are legally entitled to receive funding.

This not only specifies the self-interest stake of the recipients; it escalates the possessive and proprietary *rights* of recipients. One consequence of these altered perspectives has been the rise of a new body of case law. One part of the large OMB study for *Managing Federal Assistance in the 1980s* identified nearly 500 court cases dealing with grants, and this was a "quick-and-dirty" effort to inventory the area [27]. A special conference held by the ACIR in late 1979 focused exclusively on the current status of grant law [28]. Explaining the sudden rise in grant-related cases (over three-fourths of the cases have originated since 1975), one conference participant observed that "the financial strains on state and local governments and the resultant paring down of available funds have brought about numerous lawsuits challenging the denial of grants or regulations which limit eligibility for grants" [29]. Shortly thereafter, the District of Columbia Bar sponsored a conference on "Federal Grant Litigation," with the candid subtitle: "Suing the Hand That Feeds You" [30].

Associated with the mechanism of general aid is the technique of bypassing. Bypassing is the process of allocating federal monies directly to local governments without the funds passing through state government coffers. In 1960 only 8% of $7.2 billion, or $570 million, bypassed the states. This was an increase from $100 million in 1950. By 1970 about 16% of federal aid, or $3.5 *billion,* bypassed state governments. In 1980 about one-third of all federal aid went directly to local governments—approximately $30 billion.

Loans constitute a third implementing mechanism for IGR in the calculative phase. Many examples of loans in the IGR processes could be provided, two of which have been mentioned— to New York City and to students. The latter involved combined state and national financing participation with several states reaping handsome profits. Profit, however, was far from the mind of New York City officials during and after the bleak days of 1975.

The temporary federal loan in 1975 attached conditions which put the U.S. Secretary of the Treasury in the unique position of overseer of the city's financial operations and fiscal obligations. In statements and admonitions to city officials then Secretary William Simon called for reductions in expenditures, program cuts, management improvements, and so forth. But the Secretary also had several Simon-says mandates, for example, phasing out rent control and promptly implementing accounting and financial control systems. New York City's fiscal status remained in a near-crisis state for the remainder of the 1970s. It remained solvent only through the subsequent infusion of federal loans and grants. Yet the anomaly of a national cabinet official sitting in continuous oversight of the governance of New York City, or any other city, is no longer novel. It seems to be accepted as a normal state of affairs.

Regulation is the fourth and final implementing mechanism identified with the calculative phase. References to the *Federal Register,* cross-cutting requirements, and grant law convey the prominence and significance of this subject. Perhaps the connecting point should be made with the participants' perceptions column. Without the *Federal Register* and the *Catalog of Federal Domestic Assistance,* it is difficult to become involved in IGR gamesmanship and grantsmanship. Furthermore, it is hazardous to engage in fungibility without an intimate knowledge of the assistance-related regulations associated with these and other documents. It is, however, difficult to cope with these mountainous materials without political and administrative overload. Therein lies the crux and the paradox of the calculative phase of IGR.

It is a phase that still contains many of the surface trappings of federalism. Local and state governments have the appearance of making significant policy choices. A few such choices may still remain, but they seem to be few and elusive. The chief choice that most nonnational participants have is deciding whether to participate in federal assistance programs. Once that choice is made, a large array of more limited choices appears open to those who have entered the federal assistance arena. A great deal of bargaining and negotiation takes place within that arena. But these are constrained chiefly, if not exclusively, by nationally specified rules of the game. That is why *facade federalism* is selected as the metaphor characterizing the calculative phase of IGR.

The term "facade" is used in both of its two usual meanings. First, it means the front or forward part of anything (usually a building). In this sense, the leading or frontal parts of governmental units' laws, structures, and officials are involved in the IGR exchanges. In other words, executives, legislative bodies, and courts are active and prominent participants. Associated with such involvement is the tendency toward confrontations, that is, face-to-face exchanges (such as court proceedings) that may or may not be amicably resolved.

Facade also means an artificial or false front. Dual aspects of this meaning are pertinent to the calculative phase of IGR. First, the false front put forth by some participants in intergovernmental exchanges may be contrived or artificial to bluff the other participants. Some IGR "games" played in the calculative phase may be like poker, a good bluff may win a "pot."

The other possible meaning of facade federalism is the absence or falseness of federalism. In other words, it could be argued that in some contemporary circumstances power has gravitated so heavily toward national officials that federalism, in its historical and legal sense, is nonexistent.

Whatever meaning is attached to facade federalism, it is clear that the 1980s will be a time in which the character and content of national-state-local relationships will continue to be debated and contested, refined and perhaps redefined. The nature and significance of the contests of refinements can be probed and understood, by student and practitioner alike, in minute events such as the making of student loans or in the passage of multibillion dollar aid programs, for example, the renewal of General Revenue Sharing.

Conclusion

One approach to understanding the contemporary character of intergovernmental relations is to see the present scene as the accretion of past patterns and relationships which fit a series of phases. These phases are analogous to layers of sedimentary rock in which the most evident is the current or surface layer. This present phase is called calculative, in part because of the emphasis on strategic or game-type behavior. This behavior has been encouraged, if not induced, by a startling array of events, problems, and difficulties that have confronted IGR participants and organizations.

Several elements of the calculative phase seem likely to persist through the 1980s. Indeed, the attitudes, actions, accomplishments, and proposals pursuant to the New Federalism of the Reagan administration seem destined to intensify calculative behavior among IGR participants. President Reagan's New Federalism is the fourth instance or variety of twentieth century policy initiatives designed to produce *new* departures in the arena of federalism and intergovernmental relations [31]. It may not be the last. But its four prominent thrusts of deconcentration, devolution, decrementalism, and deregulation appear likely to accentuate over the short run several of the patterns and perceptions of the calculative phase. To the extent that the current New Federalism is implemented, however, over the longer run it may produce a significant shift in intergovernmental patterns and result in yet another phase of IGR.

References

1. Wright, Deil S. (1982). *Understanding Intergovernmental Relations.* Brooks/Cole, Monterey, California.
2. Elazar, Daniel J. (1962). *The American Partnership: Intergovernmental Cooperation in the Nineteenth Century,* University of Chicago Press, Chicago.
3. Grodzins, Morton (1966). *The American System: A New View of Governments in the United States,* (Daniel J. Elazar ed.)., Rand McNally, Chicago.
4. Bromage, Arthur W. (1943). Federal-state-local relations. *American Political Science Review 37:*35.
5. Mosher, Frederick (1968). *Democracy and the Public Service,* Oxford University Press, New York. See especially Ch. 4, "The Professional State."

6. Sanford, Terry (1967). *Storm Over the States,* McGraw Hill, New York.

7. Hale, George E., and Marian Lief Palley (1979). Federal grants to the states: who governs? *Administration and Society 11* (May):3–26.

8. Light, Alfred R. (1976). *Intergovernmental Relations and Program Innovation: The Institutionalized Perspectives of State Administrators,* Ph.D. Dissertation, University of North Carolina at Chapel Hill.

9. Sundquist, James, with David W. Davis (1969). *Making Federalism Work: A Study of Program Coordination at the Community Level,* Brookings Institution, Washington, D.C.

10. Sayre, Wallace, and Herbert Kaufman (1965). *Governing New York City,* Russell Sage Foundation, New York.

11. Caro, Robert A. (1974). *The Power Broker: Robert Moses and the Fall of New York,* Alfred A. Knopf, New York.

12. Auletta, Ken (1979). *The Streets Were Paved with Gold,* Random House, New York.

13. Greenblatt, Robert (1976). A comment on federal-state relations. In *Intergovernmental Administration: 1976– Eleven Academic and Practitioner Perspectives,* James D. Carroll and Richard W. Campbell, (eds.). Maxwell School of Citizenship and Public Affairs, Syracuse University, Syracuse, New York, pp. 143–171.

14. Adams, Jerome R., Thad L. Beyle, and Patricia J. Dusenbury (1979). The new "dual formula" for community development funds. *Popular Government 44:* 33–37.

15. Walker, David B. (1979). Is there federalism in our future? *Public Management 61:* 11.

16. Stanfield, Rochelle L. (1978). Playing computer politics with local aid formulas. *National Journal* (December 9):1977–1981.

17. Levine, Charles H. (1978). Organizational decline and cutback management. *Public Administration Review 38:* 315–325.

18. Levine, Charles H. (1980). *Managing Fiscal Stress: The Crisis in the Public Sector,* Chatham House Publishers, Inc., Chatham, New Jersey.

19. Congressional Budget Office (1980). *State Profits on Tax-Exempt Student Loan Bonds: Analysis of Options,* CBO Background Paper, Washington, D.C.

20. Office of Management and Budget (1980). *Managing Federal Assistance in the 1980's.* Government Printing Office, Washington, D.C.

21. Sec. 504, Rehabilitation Act of 1973, P.L.93–112.

22. Muller, Thomas, and Michael Fix (1980). Federal solicitude and local costs: the impact of federal regulation on municipal finances. *Regulation 4:* 29–36.

23. Wright, Deil S. (1980). Intergovernmental games: an approach to understanding intergovernmental relations. *Southern Review of Public Administration 3:* 383–403.

24. Beer, Samuel H. (1977). Political overload and federalism. *Polity 10:* 5–7.

25. Heclo, Hugh (1977). A question of priorities. *The Humanist 37:* 21–24.

26. Petkas, Peter J. (1981). The U.S. regulatory system: partnership or maze? *National Civic Review 70:* 297–301.

27. Office of Management and Budget (1979). *Managing Federal Assistance in the 1980's: Working Papers—(A-7),* Survey of Case Law Relating to Federal Grant Programs, Executive Office of the President, Washington, D.C.

28. Advisory Commission on Intergovernmental Relations (ACIR) (1980). *Awakening the Slumbering Giant: Intergovernmental Relations and Federal Grant Law,* Government Printing Office, Washington, D.C.

29. *Public Administration Times* (1980). Aid Program Growth Spurs Rise of Grant Law, *3:* 1.

30. Peters, Charles (1980). A way to control spending: FDR and Kennedy, and the games bureaucrats play. *The Washington Post,* April 25:F5.

31. Wright, Deil S. (1983). New federalism: recent varieties of an older species. *American Review of Public Administration* (forthcoming).

CASE STUDY 5

Introduction

"Love Canal." These words evoke memories of an ecological nightmare that became a highly charged, emotional, front-page issue in the 1980s. On an old toxic waste dump site in upstate New York, near Niagara Falls, where 21,000 tons of chemicals had been buried by Hooker Chemical Company in the 1940s, moderate income housing had been built in the 1950s. By the 1970s the Love Canal residents began complaining of the noxious fumes, burns, ill health, and other dangerous side effects caused by toxic wastes leaking out of the ground.

On one hand, the Love Canal story is about hazardous waste, its effects on human beings and their environment, as well as the physical complexities of its clean-up. But on another level, the Love Canal story is very much about how government attempts to respond to such a serious problem, particularly the difficulties associated with taking administrative action involving so many levels of government and different agencies within each level. As one sees in the following case, "The Love Canal Relocation," by Martin Linsky, the major problem in dealing with the Love Canal situation stemmed, to a large extent, from intergovernmental rivalries. An increasingly adversarial relationship, fueled by intensive media coverage, developed among local, state, and federal authorities, who argued whether Love Canal was a problem in the first place, which level had jurisdiction over it, what needed to be done, how relocation should be handled, who should assume the financial burdens, and who ought to get the credit *and* blame for the results. Intergovernmental calculations, in the words of Deil Wright's foregoing essay, played no small role in determining the outcomes of this issue.

As you review this case, you might want to think about the following questions:

How did the "intergovernmental dimension" create problems for solving the Love Canal situation?

Who were the major IGR actors in this case? Why were they motivated—or not motivated—to get involved? How did they "calculate" their moves? Who was, in your view, the most successful in handling these calculations? Why?

Does the case support—or fail to support—Deil Wright's conceptualization of contemporary IGR as "calculative"? If so, why? Or, if not, in your view, why not?

Can you generalize, based on your reading of "The Love Canal Relocation" case study, why understanding IGR and being able to cope with its many aspects are so significant to modern public administrators' on-the-job performance and their capacity to deal with problems that they confront? How can administrators learn to handle IGR responsibilities effectively?

MARTIN LINSKY

The Love Canal Relocation

The History at Love Canal

The history of the tension, the environment, industry, and people around the site of the Love Canal began over two hundred years ago. The basic geography is not hard to absorb. The Niagara River flows north, from Lake Erie to Lake Ontario. Its most dominant feature, of course, is its 186-foot plunge halfway along the course known to honeymooners around the world as Niagara Falls. Settlers in the area realized that a river moving that fast had great potential as a power-generating source—as early as 1757 a small canal was built for a sawmill—and by the late 19th century, power from the river was being used to light the parks adjoining the falls.

Then in the 1890s the possibilities for future development attracted a resourceful entrepreneur by the name of William T. Love. Love had a plan: build a canal, a navigable waterway, that would divert the river away from the falls for about seven miles, falling some 280 feet before it reconnected to the old river route. That way, he reasoned, he could harness the river's power and provide free energy to industry, and to the

This case study was written by Martin Linsky as part of a research project of the Center for Press, Politics and Public Policy at the Institute of Politics, John F. Kennedy School of Government, Harvard University. This study was made possible by the support of the Charles H. Revson Foundation. Copies of Kennedy School cases are available from the Kennedy School Case Program Distribution office. For information, call (617) 495-9523. Copyright © 1985 by the President and Fellows of Harvard College.

community he planned to construct along the route of the canal, near the northernmost point. It was to be called Model City, and Love's vision was sufficiently compelling that he was accorded the privilege of addressing a joint session of the New York State Senate and Assembly, which promptly passed a law permitting him to carry on, and, not so incidentally, divert as much of the Niagara as he deemed necessary to see his project through. He began to dig, a factory and a few homes were built, and then, in the late 1890s, his fantasy withered away. The depression of those years caused his investors to pull back, and the U.S. Congress passed a law barring him from removing water from the Niagara in order to preserve the falls. Love abandoned the project, but left a gaping hole, nearly a mile long, ten feet deep and sixty feet wide among the fields of a quiet town known as LaSalle, situated just east of Niagara Falls.

Love's Model City never came to pass, but his vision of cheap energy was not lost. Plentiful inexpensive power is essential in the chemical business, and it was no surprise when industry began to look to the Niagara Falls area. Elon Hooker started Hooker Electrochemical Company there in 1905 in a three-room farmhouse, and by 1906 the first plant, producing caustic soda from salt brine, was already in operation. There were about seventy-five employees at that point, not a huge number but important in that small community. The company prospered, in part because it had invested in a device which was later to be central to the production of chlorine. By 1915, the company was growing rapidly and providing essential materials for the war effort. Sales reached $20 million by 1940, its stock was publicly traded, and its manufacturing facilities went national and eventually worldwide. Sales continued to rocket, climbing from $75 million in 1955 to $1.7 billion in 1978 and in the 1960s Hooker was bought by Occidental Petroleum. The Niagara Falls operation continued to be its largest, employing as many as 3,000 people. Hooker's corporate headquarters remained in Niagara Falls and the company was always special in the area, even though many other corporate chemical-producing giants followed it into the region.

Hooker's growth produced, inevitably, a need to find a way to get rid of the huge amounts of chemical waste produced by its operations. The town of LaSalle had been annexed by Niagara Falls in 1927, and the canal and its surrounding fields were used by the residents of the city for swimming in the warm weather, ice skating in the winter, and all-purpose year-round fishing/outdoor recreation. The canal had been sold at public auction in 1920 and later began to be used for some municipal dumping. In 1942, the Niagara Power and Development Company gave Hooker permission to dump its wastes in the canal. The stuff was brought to the site in 55-gallon barrels which were dropped into the canal. In 1947, Niagara Power sold the canal and two adjoining seventy-foot wide strips of land to Hooker, and the dumping continued. By 1952, the old canal was nearly full. Hooker had deposited some 21,000 tons of chemical wastes on the site.

According to standards of that era, the old Love Canal was an ideal site for dumping. No one worried about such esoteric matters as toxic chemical leaking into the water supplies. The issue was only whether the site was deep enough and well protected enough so that it would not attract an undue supply of flies and vermin. The canal's deep trough and thick clay walls seemed fine for those purposes. In retrospect, however, those who lived in the homes closest to the canal apparently knew that once Hooker started using the site, something different was going on.

A letter to the editor of the *Niagara Gazette* recounted that as early as 1943 the smell was unbearable and the white cloud that came from

the site "killed the grass and trees and burnt the paint off the backs of the houses and made the other houses all black." There were stories of workers who were dumping the wastes running to the nearest homes to use garden hoses to wash themselves off when some of the substances spilled on them. Children played on the site and enjoyed picking up phosphorous rocks, throwing them against the cement and watching them explode. In the hot weather, there were spontaneous fires on the site and industrial-type odors wafting through open windows of the nearby homes.

In 1953, with the site almost full and covered over with earth and clay, Love Canal came to another turning point in its tortuous history. The exact nature of the politics of the transaction is difficult to recover, but on April 28, 1953, for consideration of $1, Hooker transferred the land to the Niagara Falls Board of Education. Hooker maintains that the board was threatening to condemn the land and take the property for a new school site. Board members and staff have suggested that Hooker was dumping the site now that they had finished dumping the wastes. Hooker tried to transfer the property with a limitation in the deed that it could only be used as parkland, but the Board had already developed plans for a school on the site. The deed that was finally accepted included a clause shifting to the Board all "risk and liability" for use of the site from the chemical wastes buried there. The clause identified the wastes in a general way; Board representatives had the year before toured the site with Hooker officials and taken test borings which showed chemicals in two locations only four feet below the surface. The Board proceeded with its plans, even after construction workers found what the architect described as a "pit filled with chemicals" on the site. Despite the architect's warning that it was "poor policy" to continue with the project, the Board simply resited the building some eighty-five feet north of the original location. The school was completed and opened in February, 1955. The next year, with the approval of school officials, the architect ordered the contractor to relocate a kindergarten play area because it was located directly over the chemical dump.

In 1957, the next public incident over Love

Canal occurred. The Board's Buildings and Grounds Committee agreed to a trade of land with some homebuilders. The builders wanted part of the Love Canal site for houses, and were willing to part with parcels they owned that were desired by the Board, plus pay the Board $11,000. At a meeting of the Board on November 7, 1957, representatives of Hooker appeared and strongly opposed the sale to the subdividers, saying that they had made it clear at the time of the original transfer that the site was unsuitable for any construction which required basements and sewer lines. In November, a divided Board voted against the trade with the subdividers. During the same period, however, the city was busily constructing sewers right through the canal walls as part of the finishing and paving of a street that went over the Hooker property. Several other incursions into the canal's walls were made in the next few years. In addition, in the two years after the Board accepted the deed in 1953, the Board had voted to remove 17,000 cubic feet of fill for use at other sites. In 1960, the Board gave the northern portion of the site to the city; and in 1961 it sold the southern portion at auction. During the 1960s and early 1970s homes were built in the area and sewer lines were laid. An expressway was constructed at the southern end of the site, necessitating the relocation of a main street and uncovering chemical wastes which Hooker agreed to cart away. On the surface, the neighborhood was a quiet, modest family area. No one connected some apparently random but disturbing incidents to the chemicals underground.

In 1958, for example, Hooker investigated when the company was told that three or four children had been burned by debris at the property. Members of the crew building streets in the area complained of itchy skin and blisters. Black sludge was reported seeping into basement walls as early as 1959. Sump pumps had to be regularly replaced. City Hall records showed complaints from residents and reports from inspectors about hazardous conditions. The chemical odors began to be noticeable after every heavy rain. Backyards became unusable, holes opened up on the baseball diamond, trees and shrubbery that backed onto the canal site were dying. Yet it was almost by accident that in 1976

the first official public investigation began to link these events with the earlier dumping.

Earlier that year, the International Joint Commission, which monitors the water quality in the Great Lakes, had found traces of an insecticide called Mirex in fish in Lake Ontario. Mirex is an extremely toxic substance which, according to Michael Brown in his book, *Laying Waste,* had been used in the South to control ants and as a "flame retardant and placticizer" (*Laying Waste,* p. 65) before being restricted by the FDA. While there were no studies on the effect of Mirex on humans, its devastating effects on laboratory animals were uncontroverted. In addition, it exhibited properties known to be characteristic of cancer-causing agents, and the damage caused to humans exposed to a closely related chemical, Kepone, was known and included a high incidence of sterility and liver ailments. Mirex was made in part from C-56, a highly toxic substance "capable of causing damage to every organ in the body" (*Laying Waste,* p. 16). The New York State Department of Environmental Conservation (DEC) began trying to establish the source of the insecticide; on October 1, a story in the *Niagara Gazette* reported that a team of DEC investigators were to pay a visit to Hooker's Niagara Falls plant and to nearby chemical disposal sites, including Love Canal. At about the same time, the *Gazette* ran a letter complaining about the health problems of families near Love Canal and charging that they were connected to unaccounted-for discharges seeping into their cellars and the like.

Reporter David Pollack was assigned the story and his report, which appeared on page one on October 3, was a significant milestone on the Love Canal story. It provided what the residents needed in order to be taken seriously: public disinterested outside support for their fears that there was a connection between the illnesses in their families and the chemicals in the canal. Pollack recounted the history of Love Canal as a repository for chemical wastes, and detailed the unanswered complaints from residents during the past four years. Pollack followed up on his story by returning to the home of a Love Canal family he had spotlighted in the first piece, scooping up some of the sludge in their basement to see if it could be identified and traced. His paper was able to persuade a company called Chem-Trol Pollution Services to analyze the sample. Chem-Trol agreed to cooperate but only on the condition that its anonymity be protected; Hooker was one of the company's biggest clients. Chem-Trol's report confirmed both that the sludge contained toxic chemicals and that Hooker was their source. That information was reported in the *Gazette* on November 2. The story stimulated the first coverage in the larger Buffalo daily newspapers and seems to have spurred the DEC investigation as well. By this time the DEC regional director had already asked Hooker for a full accounting of what had been deposited in the canal and the State Department of Health for an analysis of some samples taken from the area. The newspapers pursued the story in early November, but there were no new developments for several months while DEC tried to cajole local officials and Hooker representatives into agreeing to tackle the clean-up problem. Hooker's people continued to deny responsibility, and the local officials seemed uninterested. A *Gazette* story on November 4 quoted a county health official as suggesting that individual homeowners ought to take steps to stop the discharges by, for example, cementing over the drainage holes in their basements.

DEC did not have the resources to force corrective action, but in the spring of 1977 the agency was able to direct the city to develop a clean-up plan. The city hired a consultant to devise a program, and by early May the consultant reported that conditions were serious, that more toxic chemicals were found, and that some of the drums which were filled with chemicals and buried in the canal were at or close to the surface. Local officials were still dismissing the problem, and again, Love Canal dropped out of the news for a brief period of time. But the problem would not go away and two events occurred, one in August and the other in September, which were to change the character of the Love Canal issue forever.

First, Michael Brown, a young suburban reporter for the *Gazette,* while covering a committee meeting on a related matter, heard a Love Canal resident make an eloquent plea for action. Brown returned to the office, researched the old stories, called local officials, and learned that the

consulting firm had proposed a $425,000 clean-up plan. He wrote a front page story reporting all this on August 10, and the newspaper followed up ten days later with a strong editorial urging the city to move forward. The city turned down the recommendation as too expensive, but it could not turn off Michael Brown, who became the primary journalist involved with the story for over two years. His work, not only in the *Gazette,* but through articles in the *New York Times Sunday Magazine* and in the *Atlantic* in 1979 and a book in 1980, helped make Love Canal into a national story. But equally important in this regard was the first visit to the site, in early September, of the U.S. Congressman who represented the area, John LaFalce. LaFalce was upset by what he saw and heard and also urged the city to act. For his efforts he was criticized by a local city councillor for "grandstanding" and stonewalled by local officials who not only rejected his suggestions, but discouraged others from cooperating. Now there was present an aggressive journalist, backed by a committed newspaper, and a responsive United States Congressman, both deeply involved in rectifying what they perceived to be an injustice. Yet Hooker and local public officials continued to look the other way in the vain hope that when they turned around, the *Gazette,* LaFalce, and the residents' complaints would simply disappear. But with those forces engaged, Love Canal was no longer a local matter, able to be resolved in a quiet friendly way between the area's political establishment and the executives of Hooker. They wanted to believe that until someone proved a direct connection between Hooker, the chemicals in the canal, and the health problems of the residents, there was no need to act. Brown and LaFalce, however, were doing what good reporters and good representatives are supposed to do: to listen to legitimate complaints, find people who might be responsible for the problem or in a position to solve it, and keep the heat on them until they respond.

LaFalce would not let go of Love Canal. He arranged for another tour of the site, this time accompanied by EPA officials. In October 1977, soon after the visit, the regional EPA administrator wrote, in an internal memorandum, that based on what he had seen at Love Canal, "serious thought should be given to the purchase of some or all of the houses affected. . . ." During that same month, DEC requested that EPA test the air in the basements of Love Canal homes. For the next several weeks, EPA and DEC continued to do tests of the air, water, and soil, while local officials continued to assume that the fuss would go away. In February 1978, Brown, then covering City Hall, returned to the story, pointing out that there was a "full-fledged environmental crisis" going on whether or not the local officials acknowledged it. As the results of the tests began coming in during the spring, federal and state officials became increasingly alarmed. The local authorities still declined to act, but gradually the test results, all confirming that a serious health hazard existed, became known through leaks to Michael Brown and his subsequent articles in the *Gazette.* People read that their basements were dangerous places. Brown's stories understandably increased the anxiety among Love Canal residents and spurred them to organize to seek help. The Buffalo papers were now paying more attention to the Love Canal issue.

State health and environmental authorities visited the site again, and, at the end of April, the state ordered the Niagara County Health Commission to take a series of steps to do something about the problem. The Commissioner responded slowly. He tried to take care of the most visible signs of trouble by covering the exposed drums and the standing water with dirt. But he failed to take other basic remedial steps, such as putting a fence around the site and posting "No Trespassing" signs, until several more weeks had elapsed.

Slowly, but surely, New York State officials began to become more concerned—and more involved—with Love Canal. Meetings with residents were held in May, including one in which state and local officials argued on stage about the seriousness of the problem. State officials continued to express concern and Brown continued to report what they told him. He quoted a state biophysicist who said that, knowing what he knows, if he lived at Love Canal and could afford to move, he would do so.

In June, the state took blood samples from residents and asked those who lived right on the

canal to fill out health questionnaires. In response to inquiries from other residents, the state agreed to test and provide questionnaires for all those who lived in the area. The public meetings between state officials and the residents increasingly assumed an air of confrontation. In the last week of June, the state began to systematically test air samples in the homes, and in early July the residents received forms from the state indicating levels of chemicals found in their houses, but providing very little information or guidance about what it all meant.

Relations between the state officials and the residents were not smooth, but at least the state appeared to be doing something. Local officials continued to run for cover. On the advice of its bond counsel, the City of Niagara Falls even withdrew from a multi-party study group trying to devise an engineering plan for the area. There were persistent rumors that the U.S. Army had contributed to the problem by disposing of materials in the canal decades before, but after conducting a brief investigation, the Army declared that it had not done any dumping. Then, in mid-July, residents learned that there would be an important announcement on August 2 at a meeting held by the New York Commissioner of Health, Robert Whalen. The Whalen announcement was to take place in Albany, 300 miles from Love Canal, thus assuring (although it was not arranged there for that purpose) that few of the residents would be able to hear the long-awaited declaration of policy in person.

For weeks, Whalen had been studying the test results and consulting with experts from all over the country. His statement was short and to the point. Ten carcinogenic compounds had been found in vapors in homes around Love Canal. A disproportionate number of spontaneous abortions was another indication of potential toxicity. Whalen declared a public health emergency and concluded by saying that there existed "a great and imminent peril" to the health of the people living in and around Love Canal. He made several recommendations; among the most startling were that residents should not eat food from their gardens or use their basements. If that wasn't alarming enough, he urged that pregnant women and children under two years old living at the southern end of the area be relocated. It was a dramatic acknowledgement that Love Canal was a risky place to live.

Among those in attendance at the meeting was Lois Gibbs, who was to become a major force in the organization of Love Canal homeowners and a national spokesperson for their interests. Gibbs returned to Niagara Falls and almost immediately began to assume responsibilities as the leader of the residents' group. Meetings were held on the day of the announcement, and the following day, with the families increasingly concerned about the implications of Whalen's recommendations, and the unwillingness of the state to commit financial help for those who were relocating. The State of New York was then the first governmental entity to acknowledge the Love Canal problem, and the first to propose strong steps to deal with it. But being willing to step out in front also meant becoming the focus of all the residents' fears and frustrations. Whalen's response was forthright enough, but it did not adequately address the inevitable consequences of what he had to say. Telling people not to go into their basements, or eat from their gardens, or send their children to the local school were powerful and frightening messages. If children under two should be relocated, what about those who were 2½ or 3? If pregnant women should move, what about those who wanted to conceive?

Governor Carey was not yet publicly involved, but there was tremendous pressure for him to be. He was in the middle of a reelection campaign and Love Canal had suddenly been acknowledged as a state problem. On August 4, two days after the Whalen announcement, the Love Canal Homeowners Association was officially established at a meeting at which Congressman LaFalce reported that President Carter was supporting legislation to provide some federal financial help. The Governor's opponent in the Democratic primary, his own Lieutenant Governor, Mary Ann Krupsak, was calling for state action and wholesale relocation from the area.

On Monday, August 7, after a visit to Love Canal by Federal Disaster Assistance Administration officials, President Carter declared Love Canal an emergency. That evening, Governor Carey toured the area for the first time and an-

nounced to the crowd that the state would buy the homes bordering the canal. There was also some confusion about where the Governor was drawing the line, but it was quickly sorted out and 239 families living in the so-called inner ring of homes on the Canal site were to be moved.

Between August 1978 and December 1979, Love Canal residents and the state struggled toward solutions. A $9.2 million dollar state-financed construction program to secure the site by diverting the leaching and placing an eight-foot-thick clay cap on the canal was bogged down for a long time over the question of an adequate safety program; residents were understandably anxious about living in the area while engineers and construction crews were disturbing the ground in and around the canal. There were studies and more studies, and fierce disagreements among federal, state, and the residents' scientists about what the studies meant and how much danger continued to exist for those who remained in their homes. There was continuing action, particularly by LaFalce at the federal level, to push for a more comprehensive federally-funded relocation. The state was already committed to spending about $11.6 million on the relocation in addition to the construction. Carey continued to feel the pressure from the residents. And Love Canal stayed in the news, whether it was a temporary relocation for a few families because they had become ill from the fumes during the construction project, or a much ballyhooed visit from Jane Fonda, who added her voice to those calling for relocation.

By the end of 1979, the construction was nearly complete, but the residents who remained were dissatisfied with their lot and there was no scientific consensus on the continuing health risk for them. The Love Canal story was far from complete.

Setting the Stage for Public Policymaking

Late in 1979, senior officials at the Environmental Protection Agency decided to do something about the public perception that the government was not acting decisively about the problems of hazardous waste. From the agency's point of view, there was little legal authority to deal with incidents involving hazardous waste and too little support for the Superfund legislation, then pending in the Congress and which would, if enacted, give the government the legal tools and money to clean up the worst dumps. A Hazardous Waste Enforcement Task Force, organized and headed by Jeffrey Miller, then the Acting Head of the Enforcement Division at the EPA, was formed to try, as Miller recalls, "to piece together whatever authorities the government had to deal with the situations." The task force's strategy, according to Miller, was to develop lawsuits against Love Canal and other hazardous waste sites with two purposes in mind: "to affect legislation, and to try to turn the press around from criticism of the agency's handling of the hazardous waste problem, to acceptance that the agency was doing what it could but lacked all the tools it needed." One of the first products of the work of the task force was a lawsuit filed on December 20, 1979 by the Department of Justice against Hooker Chemical, the City of Niagara Falls, the Niagara County Health Department, and the Board of Education of the City of Niagara Falls. The suit asked for $124.5 million and for an end to the discharge of toxic chemicals in the area surrounding Love Canal, clean-up of the site, and relocation of the residents if necessary. It was a landmark suit, the first time that the federal government had gone after a private company which had dumped wastes into a site many years ago and no longer controlled the area. If successful, the suit would have established nationwide industry liability for the effects of abandoned toxic wastes that endangered people or the environment. It also represented a collaboration between the Justice Department's beefed-up Land and Natural Resources Division and its newly-created Hazardous Waste Section and the EPA's Enforcement Division. The suit had been developed over several months by the two agencies working together and was filed by Justice on behalf of EPA.

Proving that the actions of Hooker had harmed Love Canal residents was essential to establishing the company's liability. All the ear-

lier tests had showed that the area was a toxic, and therefore dangerous, place to live. But no study had proven that health damage suffered by some of the residents could be directly traced to Hooker's wastes. Sometime in January, the lawyers handling the case at Justice decided that they needed to know more about the possible evidence of damage. Justice and EPA agreed that EPA would conduct a quick "pilot study" to see whether there was enough potential to go ahead with a full-blown rigorous scientific examination of the possible effects. The theory behind the pilot study was to look for chromosomal damage among Love Canal residents since such damage is evidence that people have been exposed to toxic chemicals. As subjects for the pilot study, they targeted people who would be most likely to show chromosomal damage because they had already exhibited some manifestations, such as cancer or children with birth defects. The study was a lawyer's "fishing expedition," according to Dr. Stephen Gage, the EPA Assistant Administrator for Research and Development, who said at the time that if it showed "promise" the agency would commission a full-scale project, which, if supportive, could be used in the court case.

Two other elements of the study are important to mention. First, EPA selected Dr. Dante Picciano and the firm of which he was scientific director, Biogenics of Houston, to do the study. Picciano was a somewhat controversial person in the chromosomal testing business as a result of a well-publicized fight he had with a former employer, Dow Chemical. Picciano, who had been testing Dow employees for chromosomal breakage, charged that Dow had refused to publicize his results when he found undue breakage among employees who had been exposed to certain chemicals. Second, the study lacked a control group. Picciano said at the time the EPA wanted the study done so quickly that there was no time for a control group to be tested, but Beverly Paigen, who helped him select the subjects for the study, says that the EPA used money, not time, as the excuse for not using controls.

At the time the study was commissioned, none of the senior administrators at EPA, surprisingly enough, were aware of it; the political, legislative, and public relations arms of the agency were uninvolved. Miller recalls the study being mentioned to him a couple of times during briefings on the case, but "no particular significance was attached to it" and he himself did not consider the potential impact of finding chromosomal damage among Love Canal residents.

While this potentially explosive study was unobtrusively moving forward during the spring of 1980, the attention of the Carter Administration was understandably elsewhere. It was already well into an election year. The President seemed to be surviving a serious, time-consuming, and expensive intraparty challenge from Senator Edward M. Kennedy (D-Mass.) and was relying primarily on surrogates to campaign in his behalf around the country. But the economy was not in good shape; Ronald Reagan appeared to be the likely Republican nominee and his photogenic appeal and ideological clarity were certain to cause problems. There were still American hostages in Iran and, although the President had managed to keep them off the front pages, their fate remained unresolved.

In addition, in early April there were the first inklings of the possibility of large numbers of Cubans being allowed to leave the island and seek refuge in other countries. Carter agreed on April 14 to accept 3500 of them. Then, on April 24, the President's secret hostage rescue mission stalled, literally and figuratively, on an Iranian desert causing embarrassment, tragedy, the resignation of his Secretary of State, and a lot of unexpected questions which had to be answered. On the same day, John Anderson, the moderate Republican Congressman from Illinois, further complicated Carter's reelection hopes by announcing that he was no longer a candidate for the Republican nomination for President, but would run in November as an Independent. Within a week, the trickle of Cuban refugees became a flood and by May 15, just before the Love Canal study became public, over 46,000 Cubans had arrived in the United States, needing housing, food, relocation assistance, and jobs. By the end of Love Canal week, that figure would rise to 67,000.

As the Love Canal decision came into focus over the weekend of May 16–18, the President could hardly be faulted for not making it his number one priority. On Saturday night, Miami exploded with race riots that resulted in 14 dead, 300 injured, and over $100 million in property damage. And the next day there was another eruption: Mt. St. Helens. Carter declared the region a disaster area, as rescue workers began the task of cleaning up the bodies.

Finally, if there were to be an environmental crisis to solve, it was double trouble for Carter that it had to occur in New York State. Relations between the state and the federal government had been strained over Love Canal for at least two years. Governor Carey had been forced to assume the financial and administrative responsibilities for the first relocation. During that time, Carey had been trying to get the federal government to reimburse the state for its expenses, to share them, or to take over the problem. On the political front, the Governor had been no friend at all. Carey was personally close to Kennedy, although he never endorsed Kennedy's candidacy. New York was critical to any Democratic Presidential candidate and was one state where the presence on the ballot of John Anderson was likely to be particularly volatile. There was even talk of a Carey draft at the Democratic convention, if California's Governor Jerry Brown were to manage to win enough delegates to keep the nomination from either Kennedy or Carter. On May 9, the week before Love Canal was to become a major issue between them again, Carey announced that he was urging both Carter and Kennedy to release their delegates so that there could be an "open" Democratic convention. It was hardly an idea designed to win over the hearts and minds of Carter and his friends. Eugene Eidenberg, then deputy assistant to President Carter for intergovernmental affairs, called Carey "as serious a political problem as we had" at the time. And in the first major White House focus on the newest Love Canal problem, Jane Hansen, an aide to Jack Watson, who was Secretary of the Cabinet and Assistant to the President for Intergovernmental Affairs (and in the process of becoming Chief of Staff in the White House), wrote in a memo marked "Administratively Confidential" that "we're up against the politics of Governor Carey and the poor working relationship we have with him."

Sometime in April, Hansen began to become involved in the Love Canal matter. No one is clear now exactly how that happened, but there had been continuing pressure from Governor Carey for federal funds and from Congressman LaFalce for federal action. In addition, Mayor Michael O'Laughlin of Niagara Falls had requested use for Love Canal residents of apartments in the area no longer needed by the Air Force for its personnel. Hansen began to put together a compendium of all the health studies of Love Canal residents, presumably to determine whether or not to recommend making those housing units available. In the course of pulling together the existing material, Hansen learned of the existence of the Justice/EPA pilot study.

Around the first of May, Dante Picciano spoke on the phone with Frode Ulvedal, head of the EPA's Health Effects Division, and gave him the preliminary results of the study. He reported that he had found chromosome aberrations in 12 of the 36 individuals tested. Shortly thereafter, he sent a letter, dated May 5, confirming the content of the telephone conversation. In part, the letter said:

> . . . these results are believed to be significant deviations from normal, but in the absence of a control population, prudence must be exerted in the interpretation of such results.

Picciano recommended a larger study be undertaken. Miller recalls that there was a lot of activity at the EPA after the phone call from Picciano, before the report or even the letter had actually arrived. He remembers that it was assumed from the outset that the federal government would make a public release of the results:

> . . . the thought process that we went through was that if we have a piece of scientific information which indicates dangers to people living in that area, it is the responsibility of the agency to make that information known to those people. Otherwise, you may well be adding to the medical difficulties in the area, which would be irresponsible. Well, at that point, you have to ask two questions. One, is this scientifically okay or not? And second, what kind of response should the govern-

ment itself make, or should it make a response?

On Thursday, May 8, Hansen met with LaFalce, who briefed her on all the activity around Love Canal since 1977. He discussed Carey's role in the matter and focused her attention on the issue of permanent relocation and the possibility of the government purchasing the homes of the residents. On Friday, Hansen was fully briefed on the Picciano study, although the report itself had not yet been received, only the May 5 letter and the phone call. Doug McMillan, who had succeeded Miller as the head of the EPA Hazardous Waste Task Force, did the briefing. Notes from that meeting reflect agreement with Miller's assumption that the government would have to announce the results of the study. There was discussion about the timing of the announcement, and Jim Moorman, who was responsible for the lawsuit at Justice, was quoted as saying that the EPA was "leaky" and the study would not stay out of the press. There was a general consensus that the announcement of the study would affect the course of the Superfund bill through the Congress and that it should be done in coordination with LaFalce and not before the government had organized its response to the findings.

It was noted that Beverly Paigen, who had been the on-site coordinator for the study, already knew the results and so did Lois Gibbs, President of the Love Canal Homeowners Association, although in her own recounting of the events, Gibbs says that she did not know the results of the study until several days later.

That was the situation at the end of the week. Senior administrators at both Justice and the EPA were aware of the results of the Picciano study through telephone calls and a brief letter outlining them. The full report had not yet arrived. The White House was already involved, although neither Jack Watson nor the President even knew of the existence of the Picciano study, never mind the results. All involved assumed that the government would have to make public the results, both because eventually they would leak to the press and also out of a sense of responsibility to the residents of Love Canal. At that point, pressure was mounting but those

officials who were talking about the problem believed that time was not yet of the essence and
that the government would be able to make a
reasoned and thoughtful judgment about what
to do. Although some of those involved now
recall thinking about the need for establishing
the scientific credibility of the study, there are no
clear references to that issue in notes taken at the
time. There was no sense in Washington at that
point that the federal government would sup-
plant the state and local governments as the lead
actor in dealing with Love Canal, although it
was clear that the government would have to
have some response.

On Monday evening, May 12, Hansen, along
with Robert Harris and Robert Nicholas of the
Council on Environmental Quality, went to
Watson to brief him on the study. They told him
that they were exploring the statutes to see
whether the federal government had the legal
authority to pay for the relocation of residents.
Watson's reply was a clear directive to Hansen to
pull together the pieces for the federal response:
to "expedite the use of the 90 Air Force housing
units, have GSA [the General Services Adminis-
tration] do a survey of available housing, have
HUD [the Department of Housing and Urban
Development] assume responsibility for the
250-unit public housing project, and research
the legal authority for the feds to do anything."

During the next couple of days, the pace of
activity began to increase. The government was
trying to figure out what it could do, what it
could pay for, and who or what agency would
pick up the bill. Jeffrey Miller remembers that
"for a week, I did nothing else but run around on
this, talking to Barbara [Blum, EPA's Deputy
Administrator], talking to Steve [Gage], talking
to my people, going over to the White House,
talking to people at Justice. It all runs together.
Later in the week, perhaps on Thursday, May 15,
it was apparent that the press knew something
about the study, if not anything more than its
existence." Miller recalls hearing about inquiries
from the *New York Times* to the EPA press office
on Thursday. And the situation there was compounded by the fact that Marlin Fitzwater, the
EPA's Public Information officer, was on vacation. Watson and Hansen do not remember
fielding any similar inquiries at the White House

during that period, but by Thursday, Hansen
realized that the time for decisionmaking was
beginning to shrink. She wrote a long memo to
Watson stressing the need for urgent action:

I am concerned that momentarily the press/
media will have the results of health studies
which reveal chromosomal abnormalities,
peripheral nerve damage, and unsuccessful
pregnancies among residents of Love Canal.

After commenting on the complications stem-
ming from Carey's involvement and her own
efforts to put together federal funds for relocation from several different sources, Hansen continued with her action plan:

I think we should take the offensive *quickly*
[her emphasis] in announcing the results of
the studies ourselves. At that time, I recommend we also announce the following:

- The state health department and EPA
  are verifying the data and will determine within a week whether or not it
  constitutes a health hazard. (Dr. Rall of
  HHS is prepared to have a team of
  scientists start as early as this weekend.)
- The federal government is making 90
  units of excess military housing available immediately as alternative housing
  for those who want it. We will negotiate
  with state and local governments on
  rehabilitation, payments, and maintenance costs.
- If the area is deemed uninhabitable at
  the end of the week, the federal government will work with the state to temporarily relocate the residents of the area
  while the federal and state governments pursue their lawsuits with the
  Hooker Chemical Company.

This announcement will provide us with
some flexibility and give us at least a week to
answer some important questions and determine our own course of action. . . . Carey will
probably blast us for whatever we decide to do
since he's still arguing that we should pay him

the $10 million he used to buy up homes in Ring One. We might as well get on the offensive, express our concern by releasing the results of the study and announce some positive steps. Then we should call in the state by early next week and begin negotiating. . . .

The Hansen memo had the desired effect. Watson asked for a meeting for Friday, the purpose of which, he recalled, was "to get to the bottom of the situation. There were a lot of stories, internal stories, being circulated about what was going on and how serious it was, and what the life-threatening 'quotient' was. And I wanted to understand that. I therefore had to gather in some of the technical people from the EPA and other places, who could speak directly to that, so that I could understand the degree of the risk and the nature of the risk. We were also very concerned . . . with the public's perception, not so much the public at large, but the public that was directly affected. . . . I was very concerned about wrong, rumor-filled, distorted information getting to them through the press, through other means, which would cause them to be in a state of great panic. . . ."

The meeting was scheduled for 11:00 A.M. on Friday, May 16, in Room 248 of the Old Executive Office Building. There were at least fifteen people invited, senior administrators from Justice, EPA, the Federal Emergency Management Agency (FEMA), the Council on Environmental Quality (CEQ), and the Department of Health and Human Services (HHS).

According to Watson, in conversations before the meeting Dr. Rall of HHS indicated that he could verify the results of the study with a panel of experts in about a week. There had been some interagency tension between HHS and EPA over who had the lead for the government in the environmental health area and Rall seemed eager to take responsibility for examining the EPA study's scientific validity. During the meeting, Rall noted that whatever the results of the study, it would be impossible to say with scientific certainty that there was a connection between the release of chemicals and the health problems of the residents because of the difficulty of knowing for sure what caused the chromosomal damage. This line of reasoning was frustrating to

Watson, who remembers saying that "that sort of academic view of this matter was unacceptable. We had a number of people's lives potentially grievously affected or literally at stake, and we did not have the time, nor did I have the inclination, to sit around while scientists debated rather maliciously with each other about whose process was right."

Notes taken at the meeting make it clear that there was agreement that time was precious, that people in Niagara Falls knew the study had been completed, and that there was a good chance that if they did not act soon, the report would be in the press before the people who had been tested were notified of the results. The decision was made to inform the subjects immediately and to hold a press conference the next day, Saturday, to release the study and announce the response of the federal government. There was some pressure from the representatives of the Justice Department to make the public announcement on Friday, but the need first to inform the study participants was deemed to be an overriding consideration: they deserved to be informed officially what their own tests showed. Language discussed at the meeting was to find its way into the public statements: steps were being taken with an "abundance of caution," the data was "preliminary" and the government was acting "prudently" in the matter. Those present at the meeting recall no debate over the general plan that was developed, no argument in favor of not releasing the results immediately. It was agreed that Wednesday would be the day for making the next decision.

After the meeting, Miller went back to his office to draft a memo for Watson with a schedule of the activities for the next 24 hours, including a draft of the press release and a form letter to be provided to the Love Canal residents from whom blood samples were taken. During that afternoon, it became evident that the officials' fears were realized: the study had leaked, and the *New York Times* was going to have a story about it in the Saturday paper. According to Watson and Hansen, the White House was not called by either the *Times* or the upstate papers that published the story on Saturday. The calls did come to the EPA and for the moment at least it was an EPA story, not a White House one.

Watson called EPA Deputy Administrator Barbara Blum, who was in Atlanta at the time, and told her to return to Washington because she was going to hold a press conference the next day announcing the results of the study. According to the plan, each of those who had been subjects of the study would be informed individually of their results; late Friday afternoon the EPA called Lois Gibbs and asked her to notify the thirty-six families involved and arrange appointments for them between 8:00 A.M. and noon. According to Gibbs, the EPA official told her that it had to be done immediately because someone had already leaked the results of the study to the press. Gibbs and a colleague reached thirty-four of the families by 8:00 P.M.; the other two were away for the weekend. Hansen called LaFalce and reached him in his Niagara Falls office late Friday afternoon. LaFalce describes himself as being "stunned" by the news relayed by Hansen: "I had never heard about this [study] and [it] was going to be devastating when released."

LaFalce convinced them to have the press conference in his Niagara Falls office "where we could limit the number of people, where it wouldn't be wide open in an auditorium with questions from the audience. With TV cameras there it could lead to absolute chaos."

The plans for Saturday were set. While reporters for the *Times,* the *Buffalo Courier Express,* and the *Niagara Gazette* were preparing page one stories, federal officials were organizing a complex series of events that included a Washington press conference, a briefing for each of the study subjects at Lois Gibbs' Homeowners offices, a briefing for local officials followed by a press conference for local press in Congressman LaFalce's Niagara Falls office, and late morning phone calls to inform Carey and the two United States Senators from New York, Daniel Patrick Moynihan and Jacob Javits.

Keeping Up with the Story

There was nothing quiet about Saturday, May 17, for those involved with Love Canal. On the front page of the *New York Times* was a story by Irvin Molotsky, attributing to "federal officials" who "asked not to be identified" the results from the Biogenics study. The story suggests strongly that the information did not come from EPA, but originated from someone who had been involved in the Friday meeting at the White House and therefore knew of the impending press conferences. Hooker spokespersons criticized the release of the study, pointed to the preliminary nature of the findings, and expressed concern that the publicity would cause panic among Love Canal residents. The article mistakenly reported that the study had only reached Washington on Thursday and that the decision to go public had been made on the day after it was received, lending further credence to the idea that this was done in haste because of the seriousness of the results. Similar front page stories appeared in both the Niagara Falls and Buffalo morning newspapers.

For Lois Gibbs, the day started before dawn. She had only a few hours' sleep, after having finally reached the last of the Biogenics subjects to schedule their meetings. As she recalls that day in her book on Love Canal:

> . . . The tension in the office increased as people went in and out of the doctors' rooms. Most of the families were as confused when they came out as when they went in. Tempers grew shorter; people were visibly upset. Even those families with negative findings were upset, wondering whether they had been told the truth or whether their children might yet be affected. . . . I tried to keep things running as smoothly as best I could, but it was difficult to keep from being deeply moved by my friends' tears and their shock. I kept wondering how much more those people could take! One of these days, they will go crazy, I thought.

It was not much quieter for Congressman LaFalce. He had done little more than provide the site for the briefing and press conference scheduled at noon in Niagara Falls. The theory was that local officials would be briefed by EPA scientists and then be available for the press. LaFalce recalls that Gibbs had done most of the work informing people that the event was to take place, but about 30 minutes before the conference began he realized that the Niagara Falls Mayor had not been notified and hurriedly called him. LaFalce says he did not know until well after the press conference that the study was preliminary and without a control group. He remembers that when the conference was over the EPA officials were preparing to go back to Washington and he took them into his office:

> I cornered them and I said, "no way can you come in and toss a bombshell at my constituents and tell them that they have this chromosomal damage possibilities and just walk away. You better stay here all weekend until you decide what you are going to do." . . . They were totally unprepared for this. We got the message across and they in fact did stay.

LaFalce says he talked with Carey that afternoon; Regional EPA Administrator Charles Warren had failed to reach state officials until minutes before the press conference, undoubtedly adding to Carey's frustration with Washington. LaFalce says that he and Carey discussed pushing for another declaration of emergency from the White House and for permanent relocation.

An important feature of the press conference was that despite LaFalce's warnings, the space used was big enough to accommodate some of the residents as well as the representatives of the media. Gibbs remembers that there were a hundred residents there; the *New York Times* says twenty. Which report is right is less relevant than the fact that the residents made themselves heard at the press conference, and seen on the nightly news that evening. LaFalce recalls, with begrudging respect, watching Lois Gibbs moving around the room, encouraging residents to yell questions to the officials, and doing some of that herself.

Back in Washington, Barbara Blum and Stephen Gage, the Assistant Administrator for Research and Development at the EPA, were simultaneously holding their press conference for the national press. The language of Blum's press statement was cautious, as it was supposed to be, although the press release issued by EPA was headlined, by the agency itself, "EPA finds chromosomal damage at Love Canal," thereby undermining the effort to put the study in the context of a preliminary effort which needed fur-

ther review and suggesting that the EPA was interested in keeping the pressure on for the Superfund bill and in emphasizing its aggressive actions against Hooker. Whatever the intent of the government had been, the Washington press conference resulted in reports which framed the key issues which were to occupy the energies of officials at all levels of government and residents of the affected area for the next few days. On the question of relocation, Blum said that the decision would be made "probably by Wednesday" on the basis of a review of the Biogenics study. On the question of who would pay for relocation she said, "We certainly can't let money stand in the way . . . if that should prove to be necessary." She characterized the Biogenics findings as "alarming." Caution was expressed by lawyers for Hooker (who attended both press conferences) and by Gage, who noted that "The science of studying cells is not advanced enough to say definitively that there is a causal relationship between an abnormality and a disease." But the main thrust of the day's activities was clearly that something of enormous import had taken place. As LaFalce notes:

> EPA was making a big deal out of this. EPA was not saying "there is a study and we hold this study suspect." EPA was saying "we have a serious study that has created serious problems." . . . EPA handled it with such immediacy and such alarm and such a sense of urgency, that it created an aura that was impossible to cope with rationally.

LaFalce's assessment of the Saturday morning press conferences seems correct. The leak and the Saturday morning stories may have added some momentum and created a sense of urgency surrounding the issue, but the White House EPA strategy of deliberately publicizing the study results stood on its own as an expression of major concern on the part of the government. Perhaps the most significant consequence of the press conferences was that the coverage following them—unlike the Saturday morning coverage—focused more on the issue of relocation than on the Biogenics study itself. Had the study been the story, perhaps Blum's carefully worded warnings about its lack of definitiveness would not have gotten lost. In any event, there is nothing in the records of the meetings leading up to Saturday's events or in conversations with several of the participants which suggests that the federal officials involved had anticipated that they would ignite a tinderbox, both among the media and the residents of Love Canal. No one in the government seems to have suggested that publicizing the study as seriously as they did would create an irreversible demand for relocation from potentially-affected Love Canal families, whose anxieties, in turn, would be fed by a national sense of outrage and compassion stoked with enormous press coverage.

The press conference in Washington made the CBS and NBC nightly news, with both networks including a Niagara Falls segment showing families in distress. The Sunday *New York Times* was a Love Canal cornucopia. There were two stories on page 1, one by Molotsky on the press conference in Washington which led with the relocation question, and one by Josh Barbanel from Niagara Falls, which led with a family receiving the bad news from the EPA doctors and detailed the press conference hosted by LaFalce, with emphasis on the residents' demands for relocation. Barbanel quoted one resident as saying "Governor Carey doesn't want to do anything and the President is killing us." There was a sidebar on chromosomes and the connection between chromosomal damage and problems such as birth defects and cancer. Even the Book Section chipped in with a laudatory review of Michael Brown's book, *Laying Waste,* which, coincidentally, had just been published and included sixty pages on the history of the problems at Love Canal, laying most of the blame at the feet of Hooker Chemical.

Blum describes her role that day as being called on to "mitigate" the damage from the leak by showing that the federal government was in control and taking responsive and responsible steps. She says that the White House reaction was to "panic" and that the situation from Saturday forward was "like two people standing down in the field and being pelted with five hundred balls." What was an effort to control the flow of events did not succeed because "the situation just rolled on faster than the management of it."

That may be a view enhanced by the benefit of hindsight; while most of those who were directly involved were aware that time was of the essence, they recall feeling that they were still going to be able to make a deliberative and rational decision about relocation, that they could wait until the results of the Rall review were available midweek, and that if they decided to relocate they would be able first to put together a package of legal authority, necessary funding, and cooperation with New York State that would help ensure an orderly process.

Sometime early Saturday, Jack Watson composed a memorandum for the President. It was carefully written, with measured language seemingly designed to neither overstate nor understate the situation but to clearly reflect Watson's instinct that relocation was probably just around the corner. Presumably, it was the first the President had heard of the activity around the new Love Canal crisis which had consumed so much of the time and energy of senior federal officials for the past few days. Watson began:

> I wish to apprise you of a situation which has arisen during the last few days and will no doubt gain national attention. . . .

> This week the Justice Department informed me that they had received rather alarming results of a study conducted in the course of their lawsuit against Hooker Chemical Company. While the results must be validated, health experts who have reviewed the data within the last couple of days claim that if the study is accurate, residents' health is in danger and they should leave the area as soon as possible. Justice lawyers are attempting to get Hooker to pay for temporary relocation of residents by threatening to ask the Court for a temporary injunction if they refuse to assume responsibility voluntarily. In the meantime, however, it appears that the residents face an immediate health hazard that demands speedier response than litigation.

Watson went on to discuss the Friday meeting which he chaired and then continued:

. . . Justice and I did not feel that we could conceal the information until then [Wednesday, when the study could be validated]. . . .

If we are faced with such an emergency, people will have to be moved when validation is in.

The state has been characteristically uncooperative and I anticipate problems with Governor Carey in defining state and federal responsibilities. . . .

I . . . will attempt to avoid a lengthy public battle resulting in no action and growing hysteria among Love Canal residents.

Watson seemed to be suggesting that the handwriting was already on the wall; he was not going to allow the Carter administration to be in the position of opposing assistance to Love Canal residents who were understandably upset about the continuing danger to their health. In retrospect, it appears that he was already paving the way for a federally-financed relocation decision.

For Dr. David Rall, Saturday was the beginning of the effort to confirm the study. Wednesday was his deadline and his plan was to assemble a team at the Biogenics offices in Houston on Saturday to begin looking at the data. This was not Rall's first experience with Love Canal; as chief of the National Institute of Environmental Health Science (NIEHS), he had been head of an interagency task force which had reviewed the existing Love Canal health studies in 1979. On Friday, after the White House meeting, the EPA had called Dr. Picciano to tell him that the panel was coming to look at his work. Picciano says that he agreed to the review, but that he objected to one member of the Rall panel because there were rumors that the individual was planning to start a consulting firm. Picciano said that Rall could replace him with anyone else and also add one person from a list of five suggested by Biogenics. Chris Carter, scientific director at NIEHS, chaired the panel and apparently spent time over the weekend with Rall determining the appropriate response to Picciano's conditions. Concurrent with the NIEHS review, Doug MacMil-

lan at the EPA continued putting together a compendium of all the health studies of Love Canal residents.

At the White House, Hansen was continuing to work on the effort to pull together the federal funds and authority that she and Watson felt were necessary should a decision to relocate be forthcoming. She had received a call from Larry Hammond at the Office of the Legal Counsel at the Justice Department on Friday saying that he needed more time to do the research on what statutes and what funds would cover relocation.

Gene Eidenberg was the White House official handling the wave of Cuban refugees flooding Florida. As of that weekend, there had been 46,000 arrivals in three weeks. Eidenberg spent much of his time flying back and forth between Washington and Miami. Hansen had sent him a copy of her May 15th memo to Watson and Eidenberg was present at the Friday meeting chaired by Watson. On Saturday he was off again to Miami for the day and remembers riding out to Andrews Air Force Base with Jane Hansen briefing him on further Love Canal developments. Eidenberg had to be involved because as the chief of intergovernmental relations it would fall to him to take on the sticky negotiations with Carey. According to Eidenberg, Hansen said that the situation was "becoming unglued," and they both realized that there would be little time to work out a deal with Carey with respect to costs and responsibility before the decision had to be made.

Carey, for his part, was already frustrated by the way the federal government had handled him and the study. Sunday was the day for him to organize his response to the new Love Canal crisis. He met with his Love Canal task force at the Governor's mansion in Albany to plan his strategy. The focus of attention was not on the Love Canal residents, but on the residents of the White House, as Carey believed at that point that relocation had become inevitable and the central issue was who—or which government—was going to pay the bill. Later in the day Carey and his state health commissioner, Dr. David Axelrod, spoke to the press and, in effect, opened up negotiations with the White House. He was taking a very hard line, and sending a very strong message to the Carter Administration.

Carey and Axelrod criticized the study because of the lack of a control group, criticized the release of the study, and said that making the information public was "devastating psychologically" whether or not the results were later validated. Finally Carey estimated the costs of relocation as between $30 and $60 million, a far cry from the $3 to $5 million estimate Barbara Blum had given to the press the day before. Carey's figures included money he had already spent and probably estimated the costs of permanent, rather than temporary relocation. Whatever his calculations, Carey's message was received. An anonymous "high ranking Carter Administration official" characterized Carey as trying to embarrass the Administration and avoid responsibility for Love Canal. Before the face-to-face negotiations even began, the *New York Times* was carrying declarations of war back and forth between the parties.

The issue of how the report became public was another sore spot. Senior Carter officials say, and their notes confirm, that they made a decision to go public hours before they knew that the results had been leaked. In fact, there was some suggestion by them that it was someone at the Friday meeting who began the chain of events resulting in the Saturday morning stories. Yet as part of their defense of their handling of the situation, they responded to Carey and others as if the Saturday press conference was scheduled because the information had already leaked and that they were trying to control the damage. The EPA's Stephen Gage was quoted in the *Times* as saying that "We would not have had a public release of information if it had not already leaked. . . . We felt it was a responsible thing to do to lay things out." From the perspective of the Carter Administration, the relocation decision and what it would entail if it was made were still open questions, so they did not want it to seem at all as if they had been responsible for creating the crisis. For instance, over the weekend Donald L. Baieder, President and Chief Operating Officer of Hooker, wrote to Moorman declining to share in the relocation costs, agreeing to assist in a further study, and attaching a copy of his company's press release issued "after the *New York Times* carried a story which I can only conclude was inadvertently leaked to them." When Hansen prepared Eidenberg on

Sunday for the beginning of the negotiations with Carey over money, she noted, "if he wants to know why we released the study before validated, tell him it was out of control because of leaks." Sunday was also the day for arranging another White House meeting, with essentially the same participants as before, to try to anticipate options when the results of the Rall review were in hand later in the week.

Eidenberg talked with Carey and Carey's chief aide, Robert Morgado, late at night. "It was a very hard conversation," Eidenberg recalls, "because Carey had criticized us for having made the information public, and [he] was basically saying, 'look, you guys are the inept ones, you don't know how to handle it, you put this thing in the public domain . . . you pay for it.'" Eidenberg remembers negotiating the conditions under which Carey would request a declaration of emergency and the White House would agree. Eventually, during conversations held in the following twenty-four hours, the deal was cut: Carey would request the declaration and they agreed that the state and the federal government would essentially share whatever costs were involved. Even as they spoke, however, the White House and EPA were still waiting for the results of the Rall review and trying to put together the money to pay the bills. Eidenberg says that it was already clear that there was a psychological emergency which had to be solved whether or not there proved to be a health one as well.

The Rall review was moving slowly. Picciano remembers receiving a call on Monday from Charles Carter, "acting for Rall." Picciano says that Carter first told him that no one would be removed from the committee but that they would add one of his nominees. He then recalls another call, later in the day, informing him that none of his nominees had been selected. This call came from Carter's secretary and also carried the message that Carter and his review team were on their way to Houston to visit Biogenics. Picciano told the secretary to have Carter call when he arrived. Carter called about midnight. Picciano tried to re-open the membership issue. Carter declined to do so. There was a round of calls again on Tuesday, this time between Picciano and Blum. Finally, the review committee rejected the last nominee from Picciano and decided to make whatever review was possible without visiting the laboratory. Carter and his associates went home.

In Washington on Monday there was another White House strategy meeting, chaired by Eidenberg. At this session there was discussion of what should happen if the results of the Picciano study could not be validated and consideration was given to recommending relocation even in that case. No decision was made. The remainder of the meeting was spent on the continuing search for federal funds and authority, some updating on the results of the search for other health tests of Love Canal residents, and some awareness that EPA and HHS were not completely in accord on the question of which agency ought to have the lead role in doing health tests in this area.

But despite the continuing rational discussion of the problem at the meeting, matters were clearly getting out of White House control. White House officials, including Stuart Eizenstat, Eidenberg, and Hansen, met with LaFalce and Senator Moynihan in Moynihan's office. The two legislators expressed their anger at the way the situation was being handled, particularly at the leak of the study before the residents had been informed, and pushed the White House people on whether the study was sound and whether money was available for relocation.

Meanwhile, up at Love Canal, residents and the press spent the day at the Love Canal Residents Association offices, anxiously awaiting further word from Washington on what was going to happen. Gibbs recalls that in the early afternoon someone showed her a newspaper headline from the Buffalo *Evening News* which blared across the front page: "White House blocked Canal pullout." The headline fired up the residents there, and as the word spread the crowd grew from 50 to 100. People stopped passing cars and ignited gasoline on a lawn across the street forming the letters EPA. The police arrived. Lois Gibbs tried to locate the two EPA officials left in Niagara Falls to ask them to come to the site, hoping that "the residents would focus their anger on them." The two had stayed in the area to answer residents' questions. One was a public information officer, the other a doctor. She finally reached one of them, Frank Napal, the public information officer, and he agreed to come to the office. Napal arrived at

about 4:00 P.M. Gibbs urged him to call the doctor so that there would be someone there to talk about the health issues. Napal called the physician, James Lucas, and shortly he, too, appeared at the Association headquarters. Once the two officials were inside the building, Gibbs informed them that they were being held hostage. Here is her account of what happened next:

I told them no harm would come to them, but that if they left the office, I could not be responsible for what the crowd, now numbering nearly 500 people, would do. We had no guns, no other weapons; but for their own protection, I advised them to stay in our office. We had plenty of food, all homemade, and they could use the phone as they wished. My office was so packed with reporters and residents, no one could walk through it. I had no idea of what one did holding hostages. I thought to myself: Why didn't I watch TV more carefully!

It wasn't hard to figure out that we should tell someone, never thinking the press was already telling the whole world. I decided to call the White House. I knew I would never be able to talk to the President, and I didn't want to talk to a lackey. So I put in a call to Jack Watson. . . .

When the crowd quieted down, I said I had notified the White House that the officials were being held hostage by the Love Canal residents. The crowd cheered. Then I said, "I don't know what Washington is going to do, but I expect a call back soon." I stressed that they should stay calm and orderly. "We have not been destructive or violent in the past. Let's not do it now. As soon as I hear something, I'll tell you." I restricted the building to no more than five people at a time and only one person from media at a time. That would ensure the safety of the hostages. The crowd was hostile: "They ain't ensuring our safety. Why should we ensure theirs?" and: "To hell with them! Let them suffer just like we have the past two years!" I had forgotten for a moment how touchy the crowd was; but they reminded me quickly enough.

I went back into the office and asked everyone to leave. I let Marie Pozniak decide who would stay.... [Later] we heard a man's voice shouting. I couldn't make out what he was saying. I hoped Marie had posted large people at the door! At first, I couldn't tell who it was, but then my heart sank and I recognized the voice. The person hated me and the association. He repeatedly accused us of holding secret meetings with officials. He could not be described as cool and collected; in fact he was just the opposite.

Marie told us he was outside and her "guards wouldn't let him in." He was accusing us of holding a secret meeting with EPA. She said he had gone off again and was furious. She no sooner closed the door than there was a crash. The window next to me splattered in a thousand pieces. I was as frightened as everyone else in the room. I looked around to see if anyone was hurt. Jim Quimby came charging through the door to see what happened. Our hostages, sensing the crowd's mood, were becoming edgy themselves. . . .

The phone rang. It was Chuck Warren, from the EPA regional office in New York City. He wanted to know what was going on. I explained about the five hundred angry people out front, the broken window, and the EPA officials whom we were calling hostages to keep the crowd happy. I said that, in all truth, we were protecting them—in hopes they wouldn't arrest us. He asked me to let them go. I reminded him of the crowd and the broken window. I told him it was impossible; they would never make it off the porch before the crowd attacked them. I said that I felt a responsibility to protect people from possible harm, which was more than the government felt toward us.

Warren asked to talk to Napal, who reassured him that the hostage-taking was somewhat benign. Napal said that he didn't feel "physically threatened." It was just that he couldn't leave.

The next caller was LaFalce. He was furious at Gibbs, and told her that the incident was "going to work against her." He warned her that, however innocent it began, holding people against their will with an angry crowd outside had the potential for disaster. Gibbs told LaFalce that she wanted to talk with the President. LaFalce told her that he was going to have dinner with the President that evening and would talk to him about the problems at Love Canal.

LaFalce was telling the truth, but not quite all of it. Just by coincidence he was scheduled to have dinner with Mr. Carter at the White House, but along with 50 or 75 other members of the House of Representatives. At any rate, that dinner date seemed to give both Gibbs and LaFalce a little breathing space. LaFalce urged her to release the hostages, and the conversation ended. Gibbs went outside, told the crowd that LaFalce was meeting with the President to discuss the residents' concerns, and that LaFalce wanted them to release the EPA officials. The crowd cheered the news of the LaFalce–Carter meeting, but clearly was opposed to the idea of letting Napal and Lucas go free. According to Miller, the FBI brought its kidnap team to the EPA and established telephone contact with Gibbs and the hostages. During the early evening, Gibbs repeatedly went outside to speak to the crowd and her colleagues brought the hostages some supper.

In Washington, Blum issued a statement in response to the news of the hostage-taking to the effect that the EPA was moving as rapidly as possible to evaluate the study and that the "well-being of the Love Canal residents is our highest priority." Meanwhile LaFalce was having his "dinner meeting" with Carter. When he went to the White House, LaFalce did not know whether he would get a chance to speak with the President so he typed a letter for Carter, urging relocation as soon as possible, calling the White House actions to that point "unresponsive," and expressing anger at what he called a "lack of federal leadership."

By a stroke of good fortune, LaFalce was seated for dinner at the same table as the President. As he recalls, "It was a round table, and there were perhaps three other members of Congress at the same table as well as some members of the Administration. Assistant Secretary of the

Treasury Fred Bergsten was on my right, and the President was two or three people to my left. He was terribly preoccupied, and it was difficult to engage him in conversation . . . I did try to address Love Canal, . . . but he wanted to discuss social events. He was having a great conversation about jogging with Congressman Butler Derek of South Carolina, and when I tried to bring up Love Canal . . . it was really not appropriate. When I told him that at this very moment people of Love Canal were holding officials of the EPA hostage, he sort of laughed and said, 'I don't know what the problem is, nobody is keeping them at Love Canal. They can leave any time they want.' "

LaFalce never reported that part of the conversation to the Love Canal residents, but he did call them after dinner to let them know that he had talked with the President and that the President was going to take all their requests "under serious consideration." That gave Gibbs another excuse to go out and talk to the crowd and, more important, to the assembled television cameras and reporters, who were instrumental in keeping the story alive and keeping the heat on federal and state officials. "It was all media hoopla," LaFalce commented recently. "But the media was the victim there. They were the ones being manipulated."

At 9:00, the FBI called Gibbs and told her that she had seven minutes to release the EPA officials. She went outside to face the crowd, hoping to win their approval or at least acquiescence for what appeared to be the desirable option of letting them go, rather than having the FBI storm the place. She made a fiery speech, suggesting, among other things, that the hostage-taking would be like a "Sesame Street picnic" compared with what would happen next if no action was taken. Finally, three FBI agents, four U.S. marshals, and six members of the Niagara Falls Police Department entered the building and escorted Napal and Lucas away. The crowd hooted and spat as the contingent made its way to the awaiting cars. There were no arrests, and Washington officials now downplay the impact of the event, but in retrospect it seems to have played some role in making relocation even more inevitable than it was before.

The Decision and Its Aftermath

The decision to relocate the families at Love Canal seems to have been made by Tuesday morning, even if only implicitly. Hansen and Watson remember stopping to talk between the White House and the Old Executive Office Building on Monday evening or perhaps Tuesday morning. She recalls Watson saying "something like, 'I think these people have been jerked around enough . . . we'll just have to go ahead and do it and suffer whatever the political consequences are.' "

If there was an actual decision meeting, it was the one held at 9:00 Tuesday morning, chaired by Eidenberg. The White House had already made a special point of alerting both OMB and the Congressional liaison office that they were going to have to come up with some money to pay for relocation, although the estimate was still in the $5–$10 million range. And EPA had completed its review of all the federal, state, and private studies which had ever been done on Love Canal residents. It was an impressive list: thirteen separate studies, all suggesting, but none irrevocably concluding that there was some connection between the leakage from Love Canal and the health of the residents. No one was any longer arguing for waiting until the review of the Picciano study was finished.

At the Tuesday morning meeting, the conflict between the scientists and the politicians was evident. The experts from HHS were quoted as saying that they "feel in their gut there's a problem, but that they wouldn't recommend relocation based on the science." And the surgeon general was represented as "probably" favoring relocation although he "wouldn't say there was a health emergency." This attitude did not sit well in the White House. Remember that Watson had been similarly frustrated at the first big Love Canal meeting the previous Friday, and referred to this syndrome as the "writing-a-scientific-treatise-on-the-head-of-a-pin." Eidenberg recalls the gap between the "scientific doubt within the expert scientific community . . . and the absolute certainty among the public at large and the residents of the Love Canal area." The representative from FEMA, William Wilcox, said that there was no choice but to relocate. The representative from Justice, Larry Hammond, urged that the decision not be dependent on precedent. Realizing that the scientists were in doubt, the precedent and legal authority were not clear, and the money was not yet in hand, Eidenberg stated the position that was to become the key justification for relocation. "In light of the suggestive data," he said, "prudence requires action to minimize further exposure."

He then moved the meeting on to a discussion of the "exact steps" to be taken to get ready for an announcement on the following day, Wednesday. First, of course, was the negotiation with Carey. Eidenberg was to call Morgado to discuss the request from the Governor for a declaration of emergency, but "no request would be entertained without a commitment of $5 million" from the state, representing 50% of the high side of the federal estimate of the costs. Eidenberg and Hansen would ask Watson to talk with James McIntyre at OMB before going to the President. FEMA was to be responsible for the actual relocation negotiations and logistics. Jeffrey Miller of the EPA was to work on a draft statement for the announcement. Justice was to provide a memo on why relocation would not set a precedent for future similar situations involving environmental risk. And FEMA was to do the same on the possibilities for temporary housing.

The temporariness—or permanence—of the relocation was apparently never addressed head on. The federal officials seemed to assume that it would be temporary, but LaFalce and others close to the residents realized that the notion of temporary relocation did not make much sense in either practical or financial terms. The costs of long term "temporary" relocation were potentially much higher than the costs of buying the homes of the residents at their market value before the trouble started, and letting them make their futures elsewhere.

After the negotiations with Morgado and Carey were completed, Watson sent a memorandum to the President. "Since Barbara Blum made the announcement this weekend," it began, "two federal employees were taken hostage by a frustrated populace who are demanding reloca-

tion by the state and/or federal government." Watson then recommended that the President declare an emergency, noting that New York State "is willing to split the costs of whatever we do by 50%." Arguing that the "human element of this cannot be overlooked," Watson went on to lay out the action plan:

The understandable concern and anxiety which has been precipitated by the release of this most recent study requires our immediate response. If you approve my recommendation to declare an emergency, a team of people whom I've appointed immediately will begin working with the state in drafting a request from the Governor to you. We would announce jointly with the state tomorrow that we both are amending our lawsuits against Hooker whom we hold ultimately accountable; that we are undertaking further, more conclusive studies; but that in the meantime we are responding prudently and immediately to the human need which is evident at Love Canal.

Tuesday's *New York Times* was full of Love Canal again. In addition to the fifth front page story in the past four days—this one on the hostage-taking—there was an editorial urging compensation for the "psychological effect" of the "premature" release of information about the study. A piece under the headline "Caution Urged on Data from Love Canal," in the science section, suggested that the link between damage to health of humans and hazardous waste was tough to make and, in any event, would not necessarily mean future danger even if the connection to existing health problems was proven. The *CBS Evening News* ran a long segment on the whole situation, including the hostage-taking and the dispute over the make-up for the panel reviewing the Picciano study.

While the CBS story was airing, Eidenberg and Carey were deep in negotiations over the details of the request for an emergency declaration and the sharing of the costs. The federal leverage was that the state desperately wanted help; the state leverage was that Carey knew how much pressure Carter was under to act. The two crucial issues, how much each would pay and whether the federal commitment was for permanent or temporary relocation, were not resolved. The two sides finally agreed on language for Carey's telegram requesting help. Looking back on it, it seems clear that the intergovernmental tussle was going to get a lot worse before it got better. During the negotiations, Carey talked with Vice President Mondale and members of the New York congressional delegation in an effort to force a bigger federal commitment. At least twice, Carey and Eidenberg talked on the phone, with Carey insisting that the federal government agree to buy the homes and Eidenberg arguing that federal law would not permit it. As Eidenberg later said to reporters, "The Governor's problem is that he can't understand that . . . we have no legal authority to get into the real estate business." Carey did not get all he wanted in the agreement on the language of the telegram: buying the homes was not mentioned and New York State was asking for federal sharing of costs, not a full financial bailout. Yet it did contain a dig at the Administration's handling of the problem; Carey was requesting the help, it said, because of the publicized EPA report.

Word of on-going, intense negotiations was leaking out and those involved at the White House were frantically trying to work out the agreement with Carey, respond to the press inquiries, and prepare for the press conference, all at the same time. It was decided that Blum would again be the spokesperson, supported by John Macy, Jr., Administrator of FEMA. Hansen, Eidenberg, and Watson all participated in the briefing session for them, cautioning them to "get the rhetoric and hyperbole down," and to "make points about other studies, not just EPA's." There was specific discussion about the likelihood of a question on permanent relocation and the advice there was to suggest that they were conducting further studies and that there was no authorization for buying homes, "but if the situation warrants it" the federal government would respond.

Wednesday, the day of the press conference, began predictably enough. On Tuesday night Carey's office told the *New York Times'* Robin Herman the details of the negotiated agreement between the state and the federal governments so that the *Times* was able to go with another front page Love Canal story preempting an announcement from the Carter Administration. Headlined "Accord is Reported on Evacuation of Last 710 Love Canal Families," Herman's story did everything the Governor could have wanted. In addition to stealing the thunder from the press conference, it focused attention on the two issues which were still unresolved: whether the relocation would be permanent or temporary, and how much the feds would pay. In addition, the Herman article cast more doubt on EPA's management revealing that Dr. Robert S. Gordon, a member of the team reviewing the Picciano study, had written an "internal memorandum" critical of the study, saying its findings could be no more than "suggestive." If the Herman story were not enough of a backdrop for the press conference, the *Times* also ran two other Love Canal stories, one from Niagara Falls reporting that the Love Canal residents were holding a peaceful vigil as they awaited word from Washington, and the other reporting the results of a new study of the residents which found nerve damage in the majority of those tested.

At noon, Blum and Macy held the press conference, announcing that the President had agreed to declare a federal emergency and that the federal government would pay for temporary relocation. During the press conference, Blum put the federal share at $3–$5 million. While she tried to stress, as she later recalled, that the decision was made "not on the study, but on the panic caused in Love Canal," the coverage of the announcement stressed the studies. Carey, for his part, immediately criticized the federal response and reiterated his call for permanent relocation, purchase of homes, and a federal financial commitment to "match" the $35 million he said the state had already spent at Love Canal.

At Love Canal itself, Lois Gibbs had been trying all morning to find out what the federal government was going to say. She remembers being told by the woman handling the press for the EPA that she would have to wait until noon, just like everyone else. She finally found someone at EPA who read the press release to her just as the press conference was getting underway, and she repeated it word for word so that the Love Canal residents who had come to the Homeowners Association office during the morning could hear. When the relocation commitment was announced, pandemonium followed. Gibbs recalled in her biography that "everyone was hugging me. TV and newspaper people were congratulating us. . . . Someone brought a case of champagne. Corks were popping. . . . People were laughing, crying, hugging each other, dancing around and saying: 'We won! We won! We're out.'" Families began packing and moving immediately to area motels, not even awaiting detailed instructions from the government.

The relief in Niagara Falls and the continued determination in Albany were matched by frustration in Washington about the process of decisionmaking, and the realization that things are often not as they appear to be. For Eidenberg there was the difficulty of having the White House in an election year appearing to be responsible for what he believed was essentially a problem for the state government. For Blum, there was the difficulty of being the spokesperson for what she recently termed "the worst public policy decision made during my four years with the government." And for Hansen, it was returning to her office *after* the relocation decision and finally receiving the HHS assessment of the Picciano study, whose findings had prompted the relocation. The Picciano study, according to the report, provided "inadequate basis for any scientific or medical inferences from the data (even of a tentative or preliminary nature) concerning exposure to mutogenic substances because of residence in the Love Canal area."

The Aftermath of the Relocation Announcement

Given the significance of the decision to relocate and vagueness about the federal-state commitments to relocation, it was not surprising that the Love Canal issue did not move quickly off the desks of the policymakers or out of sight of the press corps.

Coverage of the EPA press conference was straightforward, perhaps even understated because the story had leaked the day before. All

three networks covered the story Wednesday night, with reports on each of them from both Washington and Niagara Falls. All three noted a connection between the relocation and the Picciano study, although Dan Rather at CBS added that the HHS panel had warned that the chromosomal damage found in the study was not necessarily related to chemicals from the canal. The front page of Thursday's *New York Times* reported the relocation decision, with emphasis on the studies and on Carey's concerns. There were inside stories on Carey's position and on the reaction of Love Canal families to the decision, and an editorial headlined "More Cruelty at Love Canal," which was critical both of the EPA and of Biogenics, and called Carter's action "the only humane decision" in light of the justifiable panic of the residents.

Carey kept the public pressure on. On Thursday, May 22, he let it be known that the state had tried to get the federal government to do a comprehensive and well-designed study of the health effect on Love Canal residents in 1979. His Administration estimated that it would cost more to temporarily relocate the families for a year than to buy the homes and thus offer permanent relocation. Congress held hearings at which government scientists reiterated their lack of confidence in the studies, prompting one Congressman, Long Island Republican Norman Lent, to suggest that if it wasn't science that dictated the relocation it must have been politics. On Friday, Carey released his "plan," a detailed permanent relocation proposal which would have the federal government assuming $20 million of the $25 million cost. Adding to the confusion, the researchers who had done the study which had found the nerve damage began to back off their earlier statements that the findings were significant. All the while, FEMA was trying to manage the relocation while the White House was trying to continue the dialogue with Carey and stave off an increasing financial or logistical commitment.

Love Canal had touched a broad-based fear about the dangers of toxic wastes. In ten days there had been an enormous amount of national coverage; 31 separate articles in the *New York Times,* including eight front page stories and three editorials; and thirty-one and a half minutes on the nightly network news programs. There was only one thing left: a *60 Minutes* story. That came on Sunday, May 25. It focused more on inaction by the State of New York than on the federal role, although Harry Reasoner ended the piece by asking "Who's going to pay for all this?" That, of course, was Carey's question, too, and he managed to keep it alive as the relocation began.

The White House and EPA continued to state publicly that they had no authority to buy the homes and that they were not committed to spending more than the original $3–$5 million that was estimated, but residents of Love Canal were getting a distinctly different impression. They were led to believe by federal and state officials that the decision on permanent relocation—which really meant purchase of their homes—would depend in some way on the results of further studies or more complete review of the existing studies.

By May 26, only five days after the relocation decision, FEMA's Macy was writing to the EPA's Blum asking for assurances that no permanent federal role in the area was being contemplated and suggesting that the quicker that the EPA could make a decision on permanent relocation the better he would like it. The next day, Dr. Stephen Gage of EPA telephoned a meeting of Love Canal area leaders, regional EPA and FEMA officials, and members of the governor's task force to say that the federal government could not undertake permanent relocation whatever the outcome of further tests. The reaction was swift. The Love Canal Homeowners Association began remobilizing, Macy wrote Jack Watson suggesting that Gage's comments "essentially refuted the federal position and residents' understanding," and LaFalce, Moynihan, and Javits began to grease the congressional wheels to break the state-federal deadlock. Blum wrote Watson, complaining that "The Administration is not talking in one voice," suggesting that there must be an effort "to involve the residents enough to make them part of the process without having them serve an omnipresent, antagonistic role that keeps the federal agency representatives from working openly and efficiently with each other." At the end of May, there was another Love Canal

meeting in the Old Executive Office Building. Watson reiterated the Administration position that permanent relocation was not an option, that the temporary relocation did not hinge on the chromosome study but on the "preponderance of the evidence," and that Blum should be the single voice for federal policy on the question.

With the New York congressional delegation in gear, the Democratic convention approaching, Senator Kennedy announcing hearings on Love Canal, and Carey keeping the heat on, the permanent relocation of the residents of Love Canal had become the proverbial political football. As Hansen wrote to Watson on May 31st,

> Many of the political types around the White House are beginning to involve themselves in the Love Canal situation, especially now that Sen. Kennedy has called the hearings. . . . In my opinion, the discussion reflects an overreaction to, and limited focus on, the New York press. People have got to understand that, short of declaring that the federal government will purchase people's homes, we cannot win with Carey, the state, Love Canal residents, or the New York press. The best we can do is cut our losses, both in New York and with Kennedy.
>
> On the other hand, there is substantial national press, which basically conveys that President Jimmy Carter is the one who has finally, after 2½ years of requests for help from all levels of government, responded to the tragic plight of these people. . . .

She predicted that until the Administration caved in and agreed, Carey would ensure that the residents continued to press their case and that the New York media would continue to "dramatize their plight." She wrote that memo the day after the *New York Times* had waded in again, this time with an editorial strongly urging permanent federally financed relocation.

Contrary to Hansen's expectation, Love Canal did not remain simply a local New York state story during the summer months. In early June Carey and FEMA signed a relocation agreement and Congress began to move on both the environmental Superfund legislation and special legislation to authorize and fund the purchase of the Love Canal homes. A week later Carey announced that he was asking the federal government for a loan of $20 million to purchase the homes, and at the end of July the Carter Administration finally agreed to loan New York State $15 million to buy up to 550 of the residences. Lois Gibbs made appearances on *Good Morning America* and the *Phil Donahue Show,* and Tom Hayden and Jane Fonda sponsored a California speaking tour for her. She also led and organized a demonstration at the Democratic National Convention in New York City, keeping the pressure for permanent relocation squarely on the President. Gibbs believes her appearance on *Good Morning America,* during which she continued her criticism of Carter, catalyzed the Administration into working out the final agreement on permanent relocation. Less than two weeks after her appearance, and after Congress had approved the necessary appropriations and authorizations, Carter signed the agreement with New York State at a well-publicized and well-attended meeting in Niagara Falls.

The original Picciano study and the nerve damage study continued to be reviewed by panels of scientists throughout the summer. In October, a panel authorized by the state legislature and headed by Dr. Lewis Thomas made a report on all the health studies that was widely interpreted as dismissing their findings. The Thomas report moved some of the continuing controversy into the scientific community, since at that point the immediate political stalemate had been broken. The scientific controversy was covered in *Science* magazine and lent enough credence to the criticism of the Picciano study that he sued the magazine. In December, the Congress enacted the Superfund bill and Carter, then a lame-duck President, signed it into law. By February 1981, over 400 families had been permanently relocated from Love Canal, with others still making arrangements.

With the relocation, coverage of the plight of Love Canal residents has faded but the controversy over what the evidence means still endures. In 1982, the federal government released an EPA report which concluded, after monitoring the chemicals at Love Canal for two years, that the area was habitable. The conclusion was buttressed by another federal report, this one by the Department of Health and Human Services, on the health effects. The following year, the federal government released another two-year study of the health effects and concluded that "no specific relationship existed between exposure to chemical agents in the Love Canal area and increased frequency of chromosomal damage."

On the other side, the Congressional Office of Technology Assessment released its own report, in June of 1983, which criticized the two 1982 federal reports and said that the conclusion that it was okay for people to resettle at the Love Canal had no scientific basis. In the early fall, another study, this one of animals around the Love Canal area (done under the direction of a professor at SUNY/Binghampton), indicated there were continuing problems on the site.

Finally, in September 1983, the EPA discovered chemical leaks and backed off the declaration of habitability made a year before. The EPA's answer to when it would reach a final determination was March . . . of 1985. Or maybe, they added, it would not be until 1988. Hooker's parent company, Occidental Petroleum, settled some of the Love Canal lawsuits in October, and in December the EPA sued Hooker to try to recover the $45 million that had been spent to that date cleaning up the site.

Four years after President Carter declared the emergency and agreed to the temporary relocation, most of the families had moved. Local officials had tried to begin revitalizing the area. The future was not clear. But one thing was certain: no one can say for sure what the scientific evidence concludes about the damage to residents as a result of the chemicals buried at Love Canal, but anyone can add up the lives that have been altered and the dollars that have been spent since the day the results of the Justice Department's pilot study were leaked to the press.

Chapter 5 Review Questions

1. Why are intergovernmental relations so critical to effective program performance in the public sector today? What were the major historic phases in IGR's development?

2. What is the difference between calculative IGR and facade federalism? Do you think "calculative" is an apt description of contemporary IGR? Why or why not?

3. In what ways did the Love Canal case study illustrate some of the characteristics and dilemmas of modern federalism?

4. Who were the key IGR actors in this case and how did they "calculate" to secure their own interests? Who was in your view the most successful handling these calculations?

5. What does the Love Canal case study say about the role and importance of experts involved in IGR? Who were the experts in this case and how did they derive their professional standards? Is there a problem that their specialized expertise may not always be applied in the public interest? What safeguards are available to ensure that these experts will be guided by the broad public interest?

6. What does the Love Canal case study say about the significance of political bargaining and coalition-building in IGR and the role of the press in influencing outcomes? Can these political dimensions of IGR be pointed out in Case Study 3, "Dumping $2.6 Million on Bakersfield"?

Key Terms

intergovernmental relations
categorical grants
block grants
Advisory Commission on
    Intergovernmental Relations (ACIR)
formula game
crosscutting requirements
facade federalism
political overload
"layer-cake" federalism

"picket-fence" federalism
cooperative federalism
creative federalism
competitive federalism
calculative federalism
IGR policy purposes and
    policy expectations
grant formulas
participant perspectives
IGR gamesmanship

Suggestions for Further Reading

Some of the best up-to-date sources of information on the changing world of intergovernmental relations can be found in the frequent authoritative studies published by the Advisory Commission on Intergovernmental Relations, as well as in the ACIR journal, *Intergovernmental Perspective,* which can be obtained free of charge by writing to the ACIR, Washington, D.C. Particularly, see Carl W. Stenberg, "Federalism in Transition," *Intergovernmental Perspective,* 6 (Winter 1980), pp. 13+; and such ACIR reports as *The Intergovernmental Grant System as Seen by Local, State and Federal Officials* (1977), and *Citizen Participation in the Federal System* (1980). Also refer to some of the recent ACIR reports: *Significant Features of Fiscal Federalism, 1987* (1987); *Devolving Federal Program Responsibilities and Revenue Sources to State and Local Governments* (1986); *Reflections on Garcia and its Implications for Federalism* (1986); *The Question of State Government Capacity* (1985); *Intergovernmental Service Arrangements for Delivering Local Services* (1985); *Regulatory Federalism* (1984); *Strengthening the Federal Revenue System* (1984); *Emerging Issues in American Federalism* (1985); *The Condition of American Federalism* (1986); and *The Future of Federalism in the 1980s* (1981). The *National Journal* also contains excellent IGR coverage.

There are a number of excellent textbooks available on IGR, including Parris N. Glendening and Marvis M. Reeves, *Pragmatic Federalism: An Intergovernmental View of the American Government* (Pacific Palisades, Calif.: Palisades Publishing, 1977); Deil S. Wright, *Understanding Intergovernmental Relations,* Second Edition (Monterey, Calif.: Brooks/Cole Publishing, 1982); Michael D. Reagan and John D. Sanzone, *The New Federalism,* Second Edition (New York: Oxford University Press, 1981); Richard H. Leach, ed., *Intergovernmental Relations in the 1980s* (New York: Marcel Dekker, 1983); and David B. Walker, *Toward a Functioning Federalism* (Cambridge, Mass.: Winthrop, 1981).

The several more scholarly and focused studies of IGR that should be examined as well include James D. Carroll and Richard W. Campbell, eds., *Intergovernmental Administration* (Syracuse, N.Y.: Maxwell School, 1976); Martha Derthick, *The Influence of Federal Grants: Public Assistance in Massachusetts* (Cambridge, Mass.: Harvard University Press, 1970); and Jeffrey L. Pressman, *Federal Programs and City Politics: The Dynamics of the Aid Process in Oakland* (Berkeley: University of California Press, 1975). Serious students of IGR also should read the Kestnbaum Commission Report (June 1955), which contains information still helpful for understanding modern IGR, as well as other basic documents on IGR contained in Richard J. Stillman, *Basic Documents of American Public Administration Since 1950* (New York: Holmes and Meier, 1982). Laurence J. O'Toole, Jr., ed., *American Intergovernmental Relations* (Washington, D.C.: Congressional Quarterly, 1985); Lewis G. Bender and James A. Stever, *Administering the New Federalism* (Boulder, Colo.: Westview Press, 1986); as well as Deil S. Wright and Harvey L. White, eds., *Federalism and Intergovernmental Relations* (Washington, D.C.: American Society for Public Administration, 1984) offer outstanding collections of current and classic IGR essays.

Internal Dynamics: The Concept of the Infomal Group

" 'Learning the organizational ropes' in most organizations is chiefly learning who's who, what's what, why's why, of its informal society. One could not determine very closely how the government of the United States works from reading its Constitution, its court decisions, its statutes, or its administrative regulations. Although ordinarily used in a derogatory sense, the phrase 'invisible government' expresses a recognition of informal organization."

Chester I. Barnard

READING 6

Introduction

Public administration was never the primary concern of Elton Mayo and Fritz Roethlisberger. Most of their research efforts centered around the study of business enterprises at the Harvard Business School, yet their impact on general administrative thought has been significant principally because from their investigations developed the *human relations* or *industrial sociological school* in organization theory. This school of thought emphasizes understanding and improving the dynamics of the internal human group within complex organizations; it was both a product of and a reaction to the scientific-management movement of the early part of this century. Frederick W. Taylor, an early founder of scientific management, had stressed that from the rational study of industrial organizations, "principles" of efficient, economical management could be derived.

Similarly, Elton Mayo, Fritz Roethlisberger, and a team of researchers from the Harvard Business School set out in 1927 at Western Electric's Hawthorne Electric Plant in Cicero, Illinois, near Chicago, to measure scientifically the effect of changes in the external environment on workers' output; they studied such matters as more or less lighting, shorter or longer lunch breaks, and increased or decreased hours in the work week. Their goal at first, like the goal of scientific management, was to discover the most efficient way to motivate workers. The Hawthorne Plant manufactured phones and telecommunications equipment for American Telephone and Telegraph (AT&T), employing at the time more than 40,000 workers. The company encouraged the Mayo-Roethlisberger experiments as part of its generally considered progressive management practices (progressive at least for that era).

While following the same methods as Taylor's scientific-management research, the Mayo-Roethlisberger team paradoxically arrived at different conclusions and insights from those of Taylor and his followers. The results of five years of intense study at the Hawthorne Plant revealed that the *primary work group* (that is, the relationships between workers and their supervisors and among workers themselves), had as much if not more impact on productivity as the formal physical surroundings and economic benefits derived from the job. For many, the Hawthorne experiment came "as the great illumination," or as Roethlisberger more modestly described it, "the systematic exploitation of the simple and obvious." It underscored a fundamental truth, obscured for some time by scientific-management theories, namely, that the employees of an organization constituted its basis, and that industrial effectiveness and productivity depended ultimately on their attitudes, behavior, and morale within their primary groups. As Roethlisberger wrote:

> It is my simple thesis that a human problem requires a human solution. First, we have to learn to recognize a human problem when we see one; and second, upon recognizing it, we have to learn to deal with it as such and not as if it were something else.[1]

The Hawthorne investigators shifted the focus of management studies from simply the external elements of organizations to its internal and non-rational aspects. By interviewing techniques and by close observations of the dynamics of primary groups, i.e., interrelations between workers, the investigators sought to understand the social codes and norms of behavior of informal work groups that were rarely displayed on the formal organization chart. "They studied the important social functions these groups perform for their members, the histories of these informal work groups, how they spontaneously appear, how they tend to perpetuate themselves, multiply, and disappear, how they are in constant jeopardy from technical change, and hence how they tend to resist innovation." In essence, like Freud and Jung in clinical psychology, they attempted to rationalize the irrational nature of human beings in the organizational context and find cures for the psychotic disorders of industrial institutions.

The Hawthorne experimenters also challenged the prevailing scientific management view of the individual employee, i.e., that the greatest motivating factor for the worker was his or her pay check. Rather, Roethlisberger argued, "Most of us want the satisfaction that comes from being accepted and recognized as people of worth by our friends and work associates. Money is only a small part of this social recognition. . . . We want the feeling of security that comes not so much from the amount of money we have in the bank as from being an accepted member of a group. A man whose job is without social function is like a man

---

[1]Fritz J. Roethlisberger, *Management and Morale* (Cambridge, Mass.: Harvard University Press, 1941), p. 7.

without a country; the activity to which he has to give the major portion of his life is robbed of all human meaning and significance."

After the termination of the Hawthorne Plant experiments Mayo's writings led to broad speculations about administration and the problems of human society. In these later works, *The Human Problems of an Industrial Civilization* (1933), *The Social Problems of an Industrial Civilization* (1945), and *The Political Problems of an Industrial Civilization* (1947), his central thesis emphasized that social skills have lagged behind technical skills. While the techniques of specialists like engineers, chemists, and doctors were important, it was by the leadership of administrators, in particular business people, that human cooperation could be advanced and the problems of organization in society solved. In the deepest sense, Mayo became a social reformer who believed that improving the quality of administrative talent could help to build a better world. In his view, the administrator "becomes the guardian or preserver of the morale through the function of maintaining a condition of equilibrium which will preserve the social values existing in the cooperative system."

While Mayo, Roethlisberger, and the Hawthorne Plant researchers should rightly be credited with "the discovery" of the informal organization and its enormous influence over formal organizational life, it was Chester I. Barnard who drew on this research and perhaps most effectively synthesized its findings involving the informal group into a broader conceptual overview of how modern organizations function. In many respects, Barnard most succinctly summarized their research and developed its implications for the generic theory of organizations.

Who was Chester I. Barnard, and how did he draw on the Hawthorne Plant discoveries for his writings?

Chester I. Barnard (1887–1961) came to writing late in life, after forty years with New Jersey Bell Telephone. Unlike many administrative theorists, Barnard was in his own right a successful chief executive of both public and private enterprises, having served as president of New Jersey Bell, president of the United Service Organization, president of the Rockefeller Foundation, and chairman of the National Science Foundation.

In 1937 Barnard was invited to give a series of lectures on administration at the Lowell Institute in Boston. These lectures were eventually published as a major administrative classic, *The Functions of the Executive* (1938). This book, from which the following selection is drawn, was an ambitious undertaking; the author wrote in the preface: "To me it has long seemed probable that there are universal characteristics of organization . . . which can be perceived by careful and astute observers and students." Barnard's search for these universal characteristics of organization led to his development of a comprehensive, integrated theoretical system, or model, of the organizational world. This concept he described in the *Harvard Business Review* as "labored, abstract and abstruse";[2] it is, however, importantly original in its view of organizations and has contributed

---

[2]Chester I. Barnard, "Comments on the Job of the Executive," *Harvard Business Review,* 18 (Spring 1940), p. 307n.

significantly to the writings of many later administrative theorists, particularly Herbert Simon (see Chapter 9).

Central to Barnard's view of organizations is the idea that basically they are integrated social systems of cooperative human action between two or more people. He sees organizations as a series of transactions between people, not as static material objects. As he observed, "Each part is related to every other part and the system is held together by some common purpose, by the willingness of certain people to contribute to the operation of the organization and by the ability of them to communicate with each other." Barnard believed that the executive should seek to secure from individuals within the organization a willingness to cooperate with each other, should facilitate internal communication, and should encourage people to work towards achieving a common purpose. Barnard also thought that organizational efficiency was not measured by merely maximizing output but rather "in the capacity of an executive to offer effective inducements in sufficient quantities to maintain the equilibrium of the organizational system." Barnard focuses on the problems faced by executives who are attempting to foster cooperative efforts inside organizations by offering a variety of inducements.

What persuades individuals to want to contribute their activities to the operations of an organization? Barnard posits the view that individuals continuously face choices about where to put their energies, and that people will make their contributions in those organizations that offer the highest return. The author visualizes a *contribution-satisfaction equilibrium* in which the existence of an organization depends on an exchange between the contributions of employees to the organization and the net satisfaction or returns that employees receive from their work. If employees get back only what they put in, there is no incentive, that is, no net satisfaction, for them in cooperating. What they get back must give them an advantage in terms of satisfaction, which almost always means returns as additions over and above what they contribute.

At the root of Barnard's organizational theory is the assumption that organizations function largely because of the effective work of executives in gaining the support of informal organizations of employees and directing their efforts. Here Barnard is clearly influenced by the work of the Hawthorne researchers (whom he knew personally) who had concluded their work by the time he wrote *The Functions of the Executive* and whose ideas he gratefully acknowledges in his text.

In the following selection from *The Functions of the Executive,* Barnard focuses on the informal organization, which he argues serves as the basic building block of formal organizations: "By informal organization I mean the aggregate of the personal contacts and interactions and the associated groupings of people. . . ."

Unlike the formal organization that is based on rational purposes and concrete structures, the informal organization described by Barnard is "indefinite" and "structureless," "a shapeless mass of quite varied densities." It results, according to Barnard, from "the external factors affecting the closeness of the people geographically" or the "formal purposes which bring them specifically into contact for conscious joint efforts." The proximity of people who are engaged in specific tasks is thus the root cause of the creation of informal organizations. Such frequent contact and interactions change "the experience, knowledge, attitudes, and emotions of the individuals affected" and thereby decisively affect the direction and activities of the formal organization. Indeed, for Barnard, the informal organization is the very source of the development of the formal organization.

As you read this selection, think about the following questions:

What are the chief attributes that distinguish formal and informal organizations?

What functions do informal groups perform in organizations?

Why is it so critical that managers recognize informal organizations and learn to work with them?

Why does Barnard argue that "informal organizations create the conditions under which formal organizations may arise"? Do you agree?

Do informal organizations exist and operate the same way in *both* private and public settings?

Can you point out an informal organization in any of the previous case studies that you read in this book? How did it influence (if at all) the work of the formal organization?

CHESTER I. BARNARD

Informal Organizations and Their Relation to Formal Organizations

I. What Informal Organizations Are

It is a matter of general observation and experience that persons are frequently in contact and interact with each other when their relationships are not a part of or governed by any formal organization. The magnitude of the numbers involved varies from two persons to that of a large mob or crowd. The characteristic of

Reprinted by permission of the publishers from *The Functions of the Executive* by Chester I. Barnard, Cambridge, Mass.: Harvard University Press. Copyright 1938, 1968 by the President and Fellows of Harvard College; © 1966 by Grace F. N. Barnard.

these contacts or interactions is that they occur and continue or are repeated without any specific conscious *joint* purpose. The contact may be accidental, or incidental to organized activities, or arise from some personal desire or gregarious instinct; it may be friendly or hostile. But whatever the origins, the fact of such contacts, interactions, or groupings changes the experience, knowledge, attitudes, and emotions of the individuals affected. Sometimes we are aware of the fact that our emotions are affected, for example, by being in a crowd; more often we observe effects of such relationships in others; still more frequently we are not aware of any permanent effects either in ourselves or in others by direct observation. But we nevertheless currently show that we infer such effects by using the phrase "mob psychology," by recognizing imitation and emulation, by understanding that there are certain attitudes commonly held, and very often by our use of the phrases "consensus of opinion" and "public opinion." The persistence of such effects is embodied in "states of mind" and habits of action which indicate the capacities of memory, experience, and social conditioning. As a result of these capacities some of the effects of contacts of persons with limited numbers of persons can spread through very large numbers in a sort of endless chain of interaction over wide territories and through long periods of time.

By informal organization I mean the aggregate of the personal contacts and interactions and the associated groupings of people that I have just described. Though common or joint purposes are excluded by definition, common or joint results of important character nevertheless come from such organization.

Now it is evident from this description that informal organization is indefinite and rather structureless, and has no definite subdivision. It may be regarded as a shapeless mass of quite varied densities, the variations in density being a result of external factors affecting the closeness of people geographically or of formal purposes which bring them specially into contact for conscious joint accomplishments. These areas of special density I call informal organizations, as distinguished from societal or general organization in its informal aspects. Thus there is an informal organization of a community, of a state. For our purposes, it is important that there are informal organizations related to formal organizations everywhere.

II. Consequences of Informal Organizations

Informal organization, although comprising the processes of society which are unconscious as contrasted with those of formal organization

which are conscious, has two important classes of effects: (a) it establishes certain attitudes, understandings, customs, habits, institutions; and (b) it creates the condition under which formal organization may arise.

(a) The most general direct effects of informal organization are customs, mores, folklore, institutions, social norms and ideals—a field of importance in general sociology and especially in social psychology and in social anthropology. No discussion of these effects is necessary here, except on two points. The first is that as a result, as I think, of the inadequate attention to formal organization there is much confusion between formal institutions, resulting directly from formal organizational processes, and informal institutions resulting from informal organization; for example, a practice established by legal enactment, and a custom, the latter usually prevailing in the event of conflict. Not only locally, in restricted collectivities, but in broad areas and large collectivities, there is a divergence, and a corrective interaction, between institutions informally developed and those elaborated through formal organization practices. The first correspond to the unconscious or non-intellectual actions and habits of individuals, the second to their reasoned and calculated actions and policies. The actions of formal organizations are relatively quite logical.

(b) Informal association is rather obviously a condition which necessarily precedes formal organization. The possibility of accepting a common purpose, of communicating, and of attaining a state of mind under which there is willingness to cooperate, requires prior contact and preliminary interaction. This is especially clear in those cases where the origin of formal organization is spontaneous. The informal relationship in such cases may be exceedingly brief, and of course conditioned by previous experience and knowledge of both informal and formal organization.

The important consideration for our purposes, however, is that informal organization compels a certain amount of formal organization, and probably cannot persist or become extensive without the emergence of formal organization. This partly results from the recognition of similarity of needs and interests which continuation of contact implies. When these needs and interests are material and not social, either combination and cooperation—at least to the extent of the development of a distributive purpose—or conflict of interest, antagonism, hostility, and disorganization ensue.

Even when the needs and interests are not material but are social—that is, there is a gregarious need of interaction for its own sake—it likewise requires a considerable concentration upon definite purposes or ends of action to maintain the association. This is especially true if instead of gregarious impulses one goes back to a *need of action* as a primary propensity or instinct. It is an observable fact that men are universally active, and that they seek objects of activity. Correlative with this is the observation that enduring social contact, even when the object is exclusively social, seems generally impossible without activity. It will be generally noted that a purely passive or bovine kind of association among men is of short duration. They seem impelled to *do something*. It is frequently the case that the existence of organizations depends upon satisfactions in mere association, and that this is the uniform and only motive of all participants. In these cases, nevertheless, we can, I think, always observe a purpose, or concrete object of action, which may be of minor importance or even trivial. In these cases it may make no difference in a direct and substantial sense whether the objective is accomplished or not. For example, the discussion of some subject (or subjects) is essential to conversation which is socially desirable, yet the participants may be and frequently are rather indifferent to the subject itself. But the personal associations which give the satisfactions depends upon discussing *something*. This is easily observed in ordinary social affairs.

Thus a concrete object of action is necessary to social satisfactions. The simplest form of doing something together is, of course, conversation, but it is evident that any particular form

of activity for one reason or another is exhausted usually in a short time and that alternative methods of activity are on the whole not easy to devise either by individuals or groups. Hence, the great importance of established patterns of activity. Where circumstances develop so that a variety of outlets for activity involving associations are not readily available—as is often the case, for example, with unemployed persons—the situation is one in which the individual is placed in a sort of social vacuum, producing a feeling and also objective behavior of being "lost." I have seen this a number of times. Where the situation affects a number of persons simultaneously they are likely to do any sort of mad thing. The necessity for action where a group of persons is involved seems to be almost overwhelming. I think this necessity underlies such proverbs as "Idle hands make mischief," and I have no doubt that it may be the basis for a great deal of practice within armies.

The opposite extreme to lack of concrete objectives of action is a condition of social complexity such that action may take a great many different forms involving the possibilities of association with many different groups. In such situations the individual may be unable to decide which activity he wishes to indulge in, or what groups he wishes to be associated with. This may induce a sort of paralysis of action through inability to make choice, or it may be brought about by conflict of obligations. The resulting condition was described by the French sociologist Durkheim as "anomie." This I take to be a state of individual paralysis of social action due to the absence of effective norms of conduct.

The activities of individuals necessarily take place within local immediate groups. The relation of a man to a large organization, or to his nation, or to his church, is necessarily through those with whom he is in *immediate* contact. Social activities cannot be action at a distance. This seems not to have been sufficiently noted. It explains, or justifies, a statement made to me that comradeship is much more powerful than patriotism, etc., in the behavior of soldiers. The essential need of the individual is association, and that requires local activity or immediate interaction between individuals. Without it the man is lost. The willingness of men to endure onerous routine and dangerous tasks which they could avoid is explained by this necessity for action at all costs in order to maintain the sense of social integration, whether the latter arises from "instinct," or from social conditioning, or from physiological necessity, or all three. Whether this necessity for action in a social setting arises exclusively from biological factors, or is partly inherent in gregarious association, need not be considered.

Finally, purposive cooperation is the chief outlet for the logical or scientific faculties of men, and is the principal source of them as well. Rational action is chiefly a purposive cooperative action, and the personal capacity of rational action is largely derived from it.

For these reasons, either small enduring informal organizations or large collectivities seem always to possess a considerable number of formal organizations. These are the definite structural material of a society. They are the poles around which personal associations are given sufficient consistency to retain continuity. The alternative is disintegration into hostile groups, the hostility itself being a source of integrating purposes (defense and offense) of the groups which are differentiated by hostility. Thus as formal organization becomes extended in scope it permits and requires an expansion of societal cohesiveness. This is most obviously the case when formal organization complexes of government expand—government itself is insufficient, except where economic and religious functions are included in it. Where with the expansion of formal government complexes there is correlative expansion of religious, military, economic, and other formal organizations, the structure of a large-scale society is present. When these formal complexes fail or contract, social disintegration sets in. There appear to be no societies which in fact are not completely structured by formal organizations—beginning with families and ending in great complexes of states and religions.

This is not to deny, but to reaffirm, that the attitudes, institutions, customs, of informal society affect and are partly expressed through formal organization. They are interdependent aspects of the same phenomena—a society is structured by formal organizations, formal organizations are vitalized and conditioned by informal organization. What is asserted is that there cannot be one without the other. If one fails the other disintegrates. Nor is this to say that when disintegrated the separated or conflicting societies (except isolated societies) have no affect upon each other. Quite the contrary; but the effect is not cooperative but polemic; and even so requires formal organization within the conflicting societies. Complete absence of formal organization would then be a state of nearly complete individualism and disorder.

III. The Creation of Informal by Formal Organizations

Formal organizations arise out of and are necessary to informal organization; but when formal organizations come into operation, they create and require informal organizations.

It seems not easily to be recognized without long and close observation that an important and often indispensable part of a formal system of coöperation is informal. In fact, more often than not those with ample experience (officials and executives of all sorts of formal organizations) will deny or neglect the existence of informal organizations within their "own" formal organizations. Whether this is due to excessive concentration on the problems of formal organization, or to reluctance to acknowledge the existence of what is difficult to define or describe, or what lacks in concreteness, it is unnecessary to consider. But it is undeniable that major executives and even entire executive organizations are often completely unaware of widespread influences, attitudes, and agitations within their organizations. This is true not only of business organizations but also of political organizations, governments, armies, churches, and universities.

Yet one will hear repeatedly that "you can't understand an organization or how it works from its organization chart, its charter, rules and regulations, nor from looking at or even watching its personnel." "Learning the organization ropes" in most organizations is chiefly learning who's who, what's what, why's why, of its informal society. One could not determine very closely how the government of the United States works from reading its Constitution, its court decisions, its statutes, or its administrative regulations. Although ordinarily used in a derogatory sense, the phrase "invisible government" expresses a recognition of informal organization.

Informal organizations as associated with formal organization, though often understood intuitively by managers, politicians, and other organization authorities, have only been definitely studied, so far as I know, at the production level of industrial organizations.[1] In fact, informal organization is so much a part of our matter-of-course intimate experience of everyday association, either in connection with formal organizations or not, that we are unaware of it, seeing only a part of the specific interactions involved. Yet it is evident that association

---

[1] See especially the following: Elton Mayo, *The Human Problems of an Industrial Civilization* (New York: The Macmillan Co., 1933); T. N. Whitehead, *Leadership in a Free Society* (Cambridge: Harvard University Press, 1936) and *The Industrial Worker,* 2 vols. (Cambridge: Harvard University Press, 1938); F.J. Roethlisberger and W.J. Dickson, *Management and the Worker,* Business Research Studies No. 9 (Harvard Graduate School of Business Administration, 1938). See also works of Mary P. Follett, who had great insight into the dynamic elements of organization; see especially her paper reprinted in *Papers on the Science of Administration,* edited by Gulick & Urwick (New York: Institute of Public Administration, 1937).

of persons in connection with a formal or specific activity inevitably involves interactions that are incidental to it.

IV. The Functions of Informal in Formal Organizations

One of the indispensable functions of informal organizations in formal organizations—that of communication—has already been indicated. Another function is that of the maintenance of cohesiveness in formal organizations through regulating the willingness to serve and the stability of objective authority. A third function is the maintenance of the feeling of personal integrity, of self-respect, of independent choice. Since the interactions of informal organization are not consciously dominated by a given impersonal objective or by authority as the organization expression, the interactions are apparently characterized by choice, and furnish the opportunities often for reinforcement of personal attitudes. Though often this function is deemed destructive of formal organization, it is to be regarded as a means of maintaining the personality of the individual against certain effects of formal organizations which tend to disintegrate the personality.

The purpose of this . . . has been to show (I) that those interactions between persons which are based on personal rather than on joint or common purposes, because of their repetitive character become systematic and organized through their effect upon habits of action and thought and through their promotion of uniform states of mind; (2) that although the number of persons with whom any individual may have interactive experience is limited, nevertheless the endless-chain relationship between persons in a society results in the development, in many respects, over wide areas and among many persons, of uniform states of mind which crystallize into what we call mores, customs, institutions; (3) that informal organization gives rise to formal organizations, and that formal organizations are necessary to any large informal or societal organization; (4) that formal organizations also make explicit many of the attitudes, states of mind, and institutions which develop directly through informal organizations, with tendencies to divergence, resulting in interdependence and mutual correction of these results in a general and only approximate way; (5) that formal organizations, once established, in their turn also create informal organizations; and (6) that informal organizations are necessary to the operation of formal organizations as a means of communication, of cohesion, and of protecting the integrity of the individual.

CASE STUDY 6

Introduction

The following case study is drawn from a recent award-winning book, *The Hidden-Hand Presidency: Eisenhower as Leader* by Fred I. Greenstein, a political scientist at Princeton University. As its subtitle suggests, the book analyzes the leadership qualities of Dwight Eisenhower when he was president. Ironically, as Greenstein argues, Eisenhower, the ex-military officer, was viewed at the time of his presidency as someone who relied mainly on the formal chain-of-command for achieving his goals. But the reality, based on documentary evidence and in-depth interviews by the author with leading participants in the Eisenhower administration, was quite different. As Greenstein notes, "Eisenhower ran organizations by deliberately making simultaneous use of both formal and informal organization." Although Eisenhower was "highly attentive to finding orderly formal procedures for insuring routine or repetitive tasks were carried out reliably," he "placed at least equal emphasis on informal aspects of organizational leadership." How Eisenhower nurtured and pursued this dual strategy of using *both* the formal and informal organizations to govern and what the overall consequences of this complex leadership method were for his presidency are ably described in the following account.
As you read this selection, keep the following questions in mind:

What gave Eisenhower his unique background for understanding and using formal and informal organizations to run his administration?

How were the formal and informal organizations in this story different—yet related to each other?

What strategies did Eisenhower pursue in developing his staff and cabinet into an effective informal group of "team players"?

How did he handle differences and disputes among its members?

In the practice of setting domestic policies, why was the development and effective use of the informal group so important? Can you cite an example of how this worked during Eisenhower's presidency? Or from a current presidency?

Despite Eisenhower's apparent ability to use the informal group to get results during his presidency, why did the popular image persist that he was only good at using the formal chain-of-command? Do you think that misconception was deliberately "planted" by Eisenhower? What are the lessons here for modern administrators?

Does this case study "square" with the essential points about informal groups made by Chester Barnard? Based on your reading of this case, where might you revise or amend his views?

Finally, although this case focuses on the workings of an informal group at the very highest levels of government, namely the White House, do you think informal groups function much the same way and play just as significant a role at state and local levels in the 1980s (think back to Case Study 3, "Dumping $2.6 Million on Bakersfield")? Explain why or why not.

FRED I. GREENSTEIN

The Two Faces of Organization

There was a major parallel between Eisenhower's political strategies and the organization of his day-to-day working procedures. In each case the visible side of how he worked was complemented by an equally significant unpublicized side. His strategies involved making the chief of state aspect of the president's job evident, while veiling much of his political leadership. His organizational style drew attention to the formal face of his policy machinery and did not publicize his flexible use of informal organization.

There are both formal and informal components in any entity sufficiently institutionalized to warrant being called an organization. Formal organization consists of rules and regulations, power relationships outlined in organization charts, and officially sanctioned operating procedures. But organizations do not operate by formal means alone. Members' personalities are too complex to mesh with official job descriptions, and the subtle choices posed by each new decision cannot be anticipated by regulations, no matter how detailed. Invariably any formal organization is intertwined with an informal network of personalities, practices, and relation-

ships. The informal will sometimes impair the formal organization, but it can also provide the lubricants that make it work.[1]

Eisenhower ran organizations by deliberately making simultaneous use of both formal and informal organization. This style of organizational leadership is underrepresented in the standard analyses of statecraft. In fact, one well-recognized classification of how presidents organize their aides distinguishes between "formalistic" organization of the presidency and various informal methods, taking no account of the organizer who simultaneously turns both ingredients to effective use.[2]

---

[1]See Peter Blau, *The Dynamics of Bureaucracy* (Chicago: University of Chicago Press, 1955); Philip Selznick, *Leadership in Administration* (New York: Harper & Row, 1957); Peter Blau and W. Richard Scott, *Formal Organizations: A Comparative Approach* (San Francisco: Chandler, 1962); and Charles Perrow, *Complex Organizations* (Glenview, Ill.: Scott, Foresman, 1979), chap. 1.

[2]Richard Tanner Johnson, *Managing the White House* (New York: Harper & Row, 1974), and his "Presidential Style," in *Perspectives on the Presidency* ed. Aaron Wildavsky (Boston: Little, Brown, 1979), pp. 262–300. Johnson uses the somewhat pejorative suffix "-ic" to identify presidential organizational procedures that emphasize official channels. He contrasts "formalistic" presidential organization with two types of informally organized advising systems—the "collegial" in which advisors have equal status and interact flexibly with the president on an amiable basis

Eisenhower was, as all accounts of the organization of his presidency recognize, highly attentive to finding orderly formal procedures for insuring that routine or repetitive tasks were carried out reliably, consistently, and systematically. Yet as president, and in his prepresidential thought and practice, he placed at least equal emphasis on informal aspects of organizational leadership.

Undoubtedly Eisenhower's binocular perspective on leadership accounts for the universal recognition of his prowess as an organizer during his pre-White House years. From his West Point graduation in 1915, through World War II to NATO, his assignments either required organizational management or gave him vantage points from which to view and reflect on the problems of guiding large-scale collective endeavors. With this preparation he proved superlative as wartime supreme commander, a role that demanded supervision of the largest invasion force ever assembled; alliance management; mediation among fractious personalities; and maintainance of the morale of fellow leaders, troops, and the civilians on the home front. Ironically, for a man whose presidency gave the contemporary impression of reflecting narrow, militarily derived formalism, he was universally recognized in his military capacities (even by critics of his skill as a soldier) as outstandingly gifted in "political generalship"—that is, management of the personal (and by this token informal) component of leadership.

Given Eisenhower's many tours of duty in Washington holding positions that enabled him to observe the presidency, it is not surprising that he assumed that office with a strong sense of how he would set it up. When he arrived in Washington in the late 1920s, the White House was so unbureaucratized that the term "organi-

zation" was not applicable. Herbert Hoover had conducted business with the aid of a few clerks. In that simpler era, the president still held periodic public receptions and shook hands with any citizen willing to wait in the line that trailed from the Corcoran Gallery to the White House. The parklike White House grounds were surrounded by a low fence rather than the present electronically wired barrier. Open gates permitted Eisenhower to stroll from his office in the State, War and Navy Department building across the White House grounds when he visited his brother at the Department of Agriculture.[3]

Before Eisenhower left Washington in 1935 for his tour of duty in the Philippines, however, the presidential office had become a beehive. Franklin Roosevelt employed a host of advisors, using them informally and flexibly. Some received their paychecks as nominal employees of executive branch agencies and others served without remuneration. By the time Eisenhower returned to Washington shortly after Pearl Harbor, Roosevelt, while still exercising his informal and improvisatory approach to using aides and conducting his leadership, had initiated the process of giving the presidency a formal organization with an official staff. A much enlarged and activated Bureau of the Budget (now the Office of Management and Budget) was by then ensconced in the building in which Eisenhower previously worked, providing the president with a cadre of career civil servants. The West Wing by then housed a new entity called the White House Office, composed of politically appointed middle-management aides officially assigned to help the president advance his program.

During his two postwar years as Truman's chief of staff, Eisenhower saw the Budget Bureau and the White House Office grow in size and importance and the Council of Economic Advisors and National Security Council become part of the new Executive Office of the President (EOP). Truman paid more attention than Roose-

---

and the "competitive" in which the advisors vie for influence and attention. Johnson classifies the Eisenhower and Nixon arrangements as formalistic, those of Roosevelt as competitive, and those of the other modern presidents he discusses—Truman, Kennedy, and Johnson—as collegial. Alexander L. George suggests ways that formal and informal organization of advisors can be combined in a single president's operating procedures in *Presidential Decision-making in Foreign Policy: The Effective Use of Information and Advice* (Boulder, Colo.: Westview Press, 1980), pp. 164–69.

[3]Longtime White House Chief Clerk William J. Hopkins provides a good description in his John F. Kennedy Library oral history. See also Fred I. Greenstein, "Change and Continuity in the Presidency," in *The New American Political System* ed. Anthony King (Washington, D.C.: American Enterprise Institute, 1978), pp. 45–85.

velt to using orderly, official procedure, but even his more formalized presidency had the aura of a conclave of Missouri politicians conducting their business in a casual manner rather than that of an orderly staff of disciplined policy analysts.

Reflecting on his own experience as an administrator and what he had seen of the presidency, Eisenhower described in his memoirs the cast of mind he brought to organizing the presidency:

> For years I had been in frequent contact with the Executive Office of the White House and I had certain ideas about the system, or lack of system, under which it operated. With my training in problems involving organizations it was inconceivable to me that the work of the White House could not be better systemized than had been the case during the years I observed it.[4]

To this he added a more general observation about organizational planning: although "organization cannot make a genius out of an incompetent," nor "make the decisions which are necessary to trigger action, disorganization can scarcely fail to result in inefficiency and can easily lead to disaster."[5]

President watchers in the 1950s were fully aware of Eisenhower's preoccupation with organizing the presidency.[6] Many of them argued that he overorganized and overformalized a position which by virtue of being political required informal flexibility. In their view his years of training in the hierarchies of the military had led him to fall into the trap of seeking to run the presidency as if the chief executive's tasks could be mechanically codified, after the fashion of a field manual.

The evidence seemed plain. In the White House, rather than following Roosevelt's and Truman's practices of setting themselves astride their own advisory networks, Eisenhower introduced a staff chief. To his critics it seemed clear that this patently military practice would reduce the quantity and quality of information and advice the president received. Their impression was that Eisenhower was fed predigested information, largely through "channels." This surmise appeared to be confirmed by the press conference exchanges in which he claimed ignorance of currently publicized events and issues.

In discussing his relations with cabinet members, Eisenhower and his aides stressed that he was delegating significant authority to them. Such a practice again seemed to fit the military model—a supreme commander necessarily would be accustomed to relying on his many field commanders to use their knowledge of local conditions and make their own tactical and strategic decisions. Critics felt he was misapplying a principle of military organization to government. This impression was corroborated by Eisenhower's practice at press conferences, of directing questions concerning the specifics of a policy or event to the appropriate cabinet secretary.

Finally, Eisenhower's approach toward his cabinet as a collective entity appeared unlike those of a skilled politician. Roosevelt, for example was famous for trivializing the cabinet meeting. Those who have followed American politics have read the many accounts of how an FDR cabinet meeting was the last place a department secretary would consider raising an important issue. After each haphazard, unfocused meeting, individual members crowded in the "Amen corner" to speak to Roosevelt alone and raise the matters they considered significant. The prevailing view held that part of Roosevelt's genius was to foster competition among his aides and to reach out informally to a great diversity of people in many walks of life for advice, thus maximizing his information and his options. Truman took his cabinet meetings more seriously than Roosevelt did, but he too acted on the assumption that in the United States, cabinet secretaries battled for their departments' programs and constituencies, while resisting being encroached upon by the programs of other departments and even by the president. So he too conducted serious business outside the formal cabinet meet-

---

[4]Dwight D. Eisenhower, *The White House Years: Mandate for Change, 1953–1956* (Garden City, N.Y.: Doubleday, 1963), p. 87.

[5]Eisenhower, *Mandate for Change,* p. 114.

[6]To take one of the great many examples see Charles J. V. Murphy, "Eisenhower's White House," *Fortune,* July 1953, 75.

ings, and he also made extensive use of unofficial advisors.[7]

Eisenhower, on the other hand, met regularly with his cabinet, thus conveying the impression both that these sessions were central for conducting the business of his administration and that he had departed from his predecessors' practice of making decisions in informal contexts. His reliance on official meetings seemed, like his use of a staff chief and his extensive delegation of authority, to have military roots— in this case in the planning conferences of top military commanders.

The likely outcome of these procedures when transferred to politics, his critics argued, was "government by committee," which in turn would surely smother creativity by fostering compromises that reduce policies to the lowest denominator acceptable to the committee members. Moreover, the cabinet was not the only committee meeting Eisenhower regularly held. His week began with a session with Republican congressional leaders; Thursdays he met at length with the NSC; Friday was cabinet meeting day. These formal routines, however, were the outward face of his organizational leadership. While their significance was far from trivial, they did not begin to represent the full texture of his organizational practices. . . .

Eisenhower Organizes His Presidency: The Hotel Commodore Meeting

Shortly after noon on January 12, 1953, at his campaign and transition headquarters in New York's Hotel Commodore, Eisenhower presided over a rare if not unprecedented gathering in the history of the presidency, a preinauguration cabinet meeting. He used the meeting for three purposes: to brief the cabinet, the vice-president-elect, and key White House aides on changes he planned in formal operating procedures; to solicit advice on the immediate issues of what to cover in his inaugural address and how to deal with a potential political conflict with senior congressional Republicans; and, most importantly, to build rapport and cohesion. In so doing, he was organizing the informal even more than the formal side of his organizational changes.

Early in the session Eisenhower stressed that he planned to operate his cabinet differently from those of his predecessors. Even at this stage Eisenhower's cabinet meeting was more formalized than cabinet meetings of other presidents. There was a written agenda, minutes were kept, and digression was kept to a minimum. Noting that "I have attended in the past a number of Cabinet meetings . . . as a specialist to talk about the European problem or a military problem of some kind," Eisenhower said that the preinaugural meeting gave him

a good chance to express a very definite opinion in front of all of you. Sometimes I have had to sit while the Cabinet, so called, went through its gyrations, and there is certainly no more charitable word that you could use with respect to what I have seen. My hope will be to make this a policy body, to bring before you and for you to bring up subjects that are worthy of this body as a whole.[8]

Eisenhower described another step he was taking to systematize the organization of his presidency. He was strengthening the White House staff by adding aides who were to have the ability and stature of department secretaries. These aides, who also attended the meeting, were assigned to jobs "I have filled on the theory that those positions are equally important with any Cabinet position that we have." While some were assigned to new staff positions, others were in old positions, which required better-qualified

[7]See the account of the informal approaches to operating the presidency of Roosevelt and Truman by Richard E. Neustadt, *Presidential Power: The Politics of Leadership from FDR to Carter* (New York: Norton, 1980), chap . 7, "Men in Office," which originally appeared in the 1960 edition of this classic work.

[8]All quotations from the Hotel Commodore meeting are from the verbatim transcript of it, January 12–13, 1953, WF-C.

personnel and demanded more responsibility than had previously been the case. Noting that holding comparable "positions down in Washington now [are] men who are, at least in one or two instances that I know of, scarcely above the clerical level," Eisenhower observed that if a president's staff aides are not given substantial status and stature they "cannot bring . . . problems to the attention of Cabinet officers and get something done on them." Therefore his own aides were to be sufficiently elevated so that "people . . . can walk into the offices of any one of [them] and say, 'Bill, this thing is wrong. We have got to do something.' "

The most prominent new position was assigned to former New Hampshire Governor Sherman Adams. He was chief of staff, but bore the deliberately nonmilitary title the assistant to the president. Another Eisenhower innovation was to introduce a special assistant to the president for national security. This new position was occupied by Robert Cutler, a Boston banker with extensive experience as a wartime aide to Marshall and senior advisor to Truman's NSC. When his turn came to brief the cabinet, Cutler explained that, like the cabinet itself, the NSC was to become a significant element in the new administration's operating procedures. Cutler's job was to reorganize the NSC so that it could meet its new responsibilities and to manage its operations.*

Eisenhower's old friend, longtime War Department congressional liaison worker, Wilton ("Jerry") Persons, presided over still another increment in formal organization. He headed the newly established White House congressional relations unit. Persons, who had risen to major general as army congressional liaison specialist, left retirement first to manage Eisen-

hower's NATO congressional relations and then, enlisting several other veterans of the legislative corridors, he set up and ran Eisenhower's White House congressional lobbying operation.

Cutler, Persons, and Adams were much more experienced than most of the cabinet members, a number of whom, like former General Motors president Charles Wilson, were political neophytes. It was consistent with Eisenhower's Washington-wise mode of conducting the less visible side of official business to put political insiders in the White House Office and Executive Office of the President to back up those of the cabinet members who were politically inexperienced.

Another presidential aide with substantial political savvy was Joseph Dodge, who had worked with Eisenhower in overseeing occupied Germany and, like Cutler, was a banker with considerable experience in the foreign policy-making community. Eisenhower had made up his mind before the election that he wanted Dodge to head the most important agency in the EOP. He invited Dodge to spend election night with him, and immediately signed him up for the Budget Bureau job. Dodge was instructed to spend the preinauguration period observing the preparation of Truman's outgoing budget and to become acquainted with Budget Bureau career officials, so that Truman's budget request could quickly be reduced to proportions consistent with Eisenhower's commitment to lower expenditures. Still another political veteran sitting among the staff aides at the Hotel Commodore meeting was Press Secretary James Hagerty, who had been New York Governor Thomas Dewey's press chief and had managed media relations in Dewey's 1940 nomination bid and the 1944, 1948, and 1952 Republican election campaigns.

Eisenhower explained to his incoming cabinet that the disciplined cabinet and NSC meetings he would hold, coupled with the strengthened White House staff, would help the team coordinate its activities, because most significant policy issues overlapped departmental jurisdictions. The changes in the formal organization of the presidency were designed to help make certain that a secretary proposing an activity could

---

*This position, augmented to include many more responsibilities than Cutler was assigned, became highly visible in later presidencies where it served as a base for advocating and enunciating foreign policy, when filled by such men as McGeorge Bundy, Walt Rostow, Henry Kissinger, and Zbigniew Brzezinski. Eisenhower's principle, however, was that staff aides had the job of compiling information and coordinating and clarifying options, but that recommending, deciding, and, especially, publicly discussing decisions was the job of the cabinet secretaries, other line officials, and ultimately the president.

be sure that his "group is properly coordinated with Labor, with Agriculture, with Defense and State, and all the way around."

At this meeting he also urged the members to practice what he had long ago concluded was essential for effective organization—spontaneous mutual coordination. "I hope," he preached, "that before we have gone very long each one of you will consider the rest of you here your very best friends in the world so that you can call up and do your own coordinating. That is the perfect way." By "friendship" he did not mean that his colleagues had to be bosom companions; his aim was that they develop comfortable, compatible working relationships. To this end he had chosen some associates already well-connected with one another: Attorney General Herbert Brownell, Press Secretary Hagerty, and Appointments Secretary Thomas Stephens were longtime co-workers in the Dewey organization. General Persons, too, chose as staff aides men he had worked with in the past, such as former House Armed Services Committee staff chief Bryce Harlow.

Eisenhower had already started to put the cabinet to work as a unit in early December. Fulfilling his campaign promise to visit Korea, he took along several of his designees. Together they planned the new administration as well as inspected the military situation. On the return trip, they met many of Eisenhower's remaining associates flown to Wake Island at his request. The uninterrupted sea voyage to the United States gave the president-elect's party a chance to ponder policy and learn each other's ways.

On concluding the January 12 session, Eisenhower gave the group another nudge toward learning to practice friendly, spontaneous coordination. He asked his associates to get together for small dinner meetings to discuss mutual interests, rather than convening them for a formal banquet. In general he staged a meeting that was remarkable in tone and content. He managed both to convey that routines would be more orderly than in other presidencies and yet to induce a lively camaraderie. In spite of the formal innovations announced at the meeting, the discussion was if anything more flexible, relaxed, and constructive than it was in Truman and Roosevelt cabinet meetings.

Eisenhower began discussion of his inaugural address by reading its most recent draft. After cutting short the applause that followed, he explained that

I read it far more for your blue pencils than I did for your applause. At first in our attempt to state a philosophy of government and of intent we were not close enough down to our daily living. So we have been gradually rewriting it, but it is very difficult to abandon in our own thinking and your own writing an original conception. One reason I wanted to read it now is so that you can think it over and be ready to tear it to pieces.

He stressed he did not want to be as colloquial as a campaign address, rather, "I deliberately tried to stay on the level of talk that would make as good reading as possible at the Quai d'Orsay or at No. 10 Downing." Nevertheless, in establishing a high tone, "I particularly tried to make the words that would sound good to the fellow digging the ditch in Kansas."

The group was enthusiastic about the speech but was quick to offer suggestions. There were comments on both its phrasing and content. When Eisenhower agreed with them, he passed them on to speech writer Emmet Hughes to be incorporated into the next draft. When he disagreed, he said so and explained his objections. Thus in responding to comments on speech rhetoric, he was also able to make certain that the group understood his policy objectives and the reasoning behind them.

Defense Secretary-designate Charles Wilson, for example, was distressed at the implication that the United States might begin trade in nonstrategic goods with Iron Curtain countries. Wilson grumbled that he had never liked the idea of selling "firearms to the Indians." "Remember this," Eisenhower replied,

You are trying to set up out of Moscow what you might call a series of centrifugal forces. The last thing you can do is to begin to do things that force all these peripheral countries—the Baltic states, Poland, Czechoslovakia and the rest of them—to depend on Moscow for the rest of their lives. How are you going to keep them interested in you? If you trade with them, Charlie, you have got something pulling their interest your way. . . . You just can't preach abstraction to a man who has to turn for his daily living in some other direction.

Not convinced, Wilson announced, "I think I am going to be on the tough side of this one." Eisenhower settled the issue agreeably but decisively, remarking, "Charlie, I am talking common sense." The final speech read, "We shall strive to foster everywhere, and to practice ourselves, policies that encourage productivity and profitable trade."

The speech markup was lively, but a rolled-up-sleeves sense that this was a group of working politicians planning strategy was more evident when they tackled the potential conflict with Republican congressmen. At stake was another formal innovation, the President's Advisory Commission for Governmental Organization (PACGO), which Eisenhower set up in the Executive Office of the President. This was designed to be a continuing unit to propose ways of organizing executive branch operations more efficiently, which the president could then submit to Congress for approval. Under prevailing procedures, reorganization plans would go into effect unless Congress voted otherwise. Eisenhower demonstrated his commitment to PACGO by announcing its existence and membership at the same time that he announced his cabinet and key White House staff appointments and by including his closest advisor, Milton Eisenhower, as one of the three members of the panel. (The others were Nelson Rockefeller as chairman, and Arthur Flemming.)

But two influential Republican congressmen, Representative Clarence Brown of Ohio and Senator Homer Ferguson of Michigan, were already on record favoring an instrument for proposing reorganizations that could readily have clashed with PACGO proposals, a "second Hoover Commission," modeled on the independent study group Truman had instituted under the chairmanship of ex-president Herbert Hoover. From the standpoint of Eisenhower and his associates, a Hoover II would have the disadvantage of being independent of administration control. Moreover, by having to recruit staff and hold hearings it would delay the reorganization procedures Eisenhower wanted to put into effect as soon as possible.

The Commodore meeting participants considered two options: they could either override Brown and Ferguson or they could placate them by devising an outcome that would give the congressmen a nominal victory but would not impede the activities of PACGO. As the discussion came to a head, Eisenhower joined those who favored the second approach, and revealed that he had already taken steps that were consistent with initiating it. That morning he had met with Brown and Ferguson. Since the two had traveled from Washington to New York with Dodge, who as a Detroit civic leader knew Ferguson well and also happened to know Brown slightly, the congressmen were aware of the potential conflict and assured Eisenhower that they did not want a "dog fight."

Stating to the group his strategy for calming this political minitempest he began with his customary disclaimer: "I am no politician as you well know." Then, in effect contradicting the disclaimer, he outlined his proposal for defusing the issue, following the approach he favored to resolve conflict—yield on symbolism, win on substance—and a basic assumption for dealing with Congress—defer to its coordinate constitutional status, but seek to lead it. No matter how misguided or unnecessary Brown and Ferguson's proposal was, he did not doubt the intensity and sincerity of the views of these men whose support would be essential in the narrowly Republican Eighty-third Congress.

"Those two men have both introduced their resolutions," he observed, "and they just act like they are newborn children." Eisenhower's recommended solution was to constitute Hoover II well after the start of the legislative session, assign it intractable problems, and insure that it not report until late in the legislative session, meanwhile expeditiously dispatching PACGO-initiated resolutions to Congress. The members of the new Hoover Commission were not named until July. They included Brown and Ferguson as well as the Republican ex-president whose special merit as a diagnostician of executive branch inefficiency they so much admired. The commission reports were deeply conservative. In contrast to PACGO recommendations, most of which were accepted by Congress, few Hoover II recommendations were adopted.

Turning to the general issue of working with congressional Republicans, the president-elect went on to refute the widespread impression (one he cultivated) that he did not intend to seek legislative influence. He planned a reeducation program to encourage Capitol Hill Republicans to "reverse their philosophy that they are the opposition group" and learn that with a Republican president their job "is to hold up the hands of the Executive departments." "They have not learned that yet," Eisenhower explained.

> There is no Republican in Congress today who was ever there under a Republican President, with the result that anything the Executive proposes is almost automatically opposed by the Republican Congress. . . . [Therefore] we must come at it on the basis of nurturing and carrying along these people until they understand that we . . . are their friends, that we are the guys they have to help, not kick in the teeth.

Eisenhower then described still another innovation he was adding to the formal organization of his presidency. He would meet weekly with the Republican congressional leadership. Unlike Truman's personal conferences with the Big Four—the two top Democrats in each House—Eisenhower's legislative meetings would comprise a larger, more varied group of his party's congressional leaders and would also include the newly instituted legislative liaison aides as well as cabinet members responsible for legislative issues to be discussed at a particular meeting. The meetings would help provide an early warning system, minimizing occasions for Republicans in the two branches to collide because of sheer lack of coordination or over disagreements that could be straightened out in advance. "I think," the president explained, "we can gradually sell them some way under which we don't have to suddenly say 'Here, that is wrong.'"

Late in the first day's session of the pre-inauguration meeting Adams announced that a transcript of the discussion would be at everyone's place at the table in the morning. "Someone has got to edit the transcript very carefully," Eisenhower warned. "We talked about Senator Ferguson and some of the others," he reminded the group. "I don't want anything in the transcript here to look like it is critical of anybody or anything when we talk about our problems." Pressing the matter, Eisenhower added that he saw no need to circulate a transcript "unless you people want it." None did.

What then should Hagerty tell the press about the day's meeting, Adams asked? Eisenhower suggested blandly uninformative wording: "I would say we are having discussions about our future duties. We are getting acquainted with each other and so on." Hagerty, he added, should put this noncommittal announcement "in nice words."

The Cabinet and Domestic Policy Making

In many administrations the cabinet would meet so rarely that the term referred mainly to the collective department heads, not to a functioning collegial body. The importance Eisenhower attached to cabinet meetings is evident from their profusion—ten in eighty days—during the formative, policy- and team-shaping period immediately after he took office. (Kennedy, in contrast, held only three in his first eighty days.) Eisenhower held an average of thirty-four cabinet meetings a year over his two terms, never pulling back from the commitment he made at the Hotel Commodore meeting to use the cabinet as a "policy body."

Indeed, in seeking to live up to his promise "to bring up subjects that are worthy of this body as a whole," he evolved more systematic formal machinery than that used in any other presidency to shape cabinet agendas, to insure that the participants had advance briefings, and to record and implement the decisions he announced in the meetings. He instituted the new machinery, a cabinet secretariat, in the fall of 1954, by drawing on a study he commissioned by Carter Burgess,[9] an organization planner who had designed the staff procedures for several wartime and postwar governmental agencies, and Bradley Patterson, a civil servant in the State Department's secretariat.

Late in the previous year Eisenhower had begun systematizing cabinet deliberations and had given White House aide Maxwell Rabb, the added job of cabinet secretary. The Burgess-Patterson study specified the operating procedures Rabb and his successor, Robert Gray, were to use and provided them with a deputy in the form of Patterson, whom Rabb and Adams invited to transfer to the White House staff.

It is one thing to have a cabinet secretariat, however, and another to curb the powerful impulse of department secretaries to avoid jeopardizing valued projects by airing them in meetings. The department heads, Patterson notes, were indisposed to "hasten to suggest items for discussion." Rather, it was up to the cabinet secretary "to dig, wheedle, persuade and finesse Cabinet members to bring to the common table what were clearly common matters, but which department heads . . . would much prefer to bring privately to the Oval Office." But how could a mere White House aide force department secretaries to go public with programs that might then be rejected because of a colleague's criticisms, or be turned over to other departments? The cabinet secretary was able to overcome departments' reticence because cabinet members "knew that Eisenhower wanted it this way and no other."[10]

The secretariat saw to it that departments with business on the agenda prepared background papers explaining their proposals in advance of the meetings and circulated the papers and agenda to all members in time for them to arrive briefed at the Friday meeting. Bringing in the secretaries' executive assistants immediately following each cabinet session, it conducted virtual replicas of each meeting to initiate implementation of the proposals and to review the

cabinet discussion. The secretariat further insured implementation of administration policies by preparing a Record of Actions—a summary of the decisions Eisenhower approved at each meeting—and followed that up with a Status of Actions report every three months. Sherman Adams's task was to needle departments with "significant delinquencies, bringing them back on schedule."[11]

Note, however, that Eisenhower had said that the cabinet would serve only as a "policy body," not a policy-*making* or policy-*initiating* body, much less the *only* source of domestic policy. (The NSC was the main formal forum for foreign policy.) This leads to a number of observations about the overall domestic policy-making process and the relationship between the formal cabinet meetings (which were well publicized especially among audiences likely to approve of businesslike efficiency) and Eisenhower's unpublicized informal means of policy shaping and making. (1). The Record of Actions was of Eisenhower's actions, not the cabinet's. There was no voting in the cabinet. After listening to discussion, Eisenhower would make his decisions, including decisions to let an issue ripen while awaiting further information. He was scrupulous about explaining the rationale behind his decisions, but he did not make them on the basis of nose counts. (2). Much cabinet activity was advisory in nature; the cabinet served more as a sounding-board than as a policy-considering body— that is, it functioned much as it did in the Hotel Commodore discussions, where at least as much of the significance of the meeting was in its give-and-take discussions and their contribution to solidifying the administration team as in its influence on Eisenhower's own decisions. (3). Many of the issues that came before the cabinet had already been decided upon by Eisenhower, though he was often prepared to reopen an issue, change his mind, or modify details if discussion (in or outside of the formal cabinet meeting) seemed to him persuasive enough to do so. Thus, these meetings often functioned to brief the cabinet members on and discuss ways of implementing policies already worked out by Eisenhower.

[9]Carter Burgess, COHC; and Bradley H. Patterson, Jr., "The President's Cabinet: Issues and Answers," Special Publication, American Society for Public Administration, May 1976, pp. 106–11.

[10]Bradley Patterson, "The President's Cabinet," p. 108.

[11]Ibid., p. 110.

In his December 22, 1953, memorandum to Budget Director Dodge, for example, Eisenhower tells Dodge not to cut and if possible to increase certain welfare and public works programs in order to signal to the public the administration's progressive philosophy.... Had such a presidential domestic policy decision made its way to the cabinet and been registered in that meeting's Record of Action, the record, though seemingly of a cabinet action, would have been of a decision announced in cabinet but not made there. (4). The cabinet minutes show that not all meeting time was devoted to policy discussions. Some time was spent briefing members on matters of broad concern, such as the vice-president's findings on his trips abroad. (5). Finally, certain issues were too sensitive, or divisive, or in need of tactical day-by-day management to be suitable for cabinet discussion....

Why should Eisenhower have insisted on devoting so much time to carefully planned conferences with a group that was not the nexus of policy making? Part of the answer can be found in Bedell Smith's comment concerning Eisenhower's longstanding use of consultation as a means of exercising leadership. Eisenhower knew that advice seeking was an effective tool for winning the willing support of those he consulted, even though he might not take their advice.

By being consulted, particularly by someone displaying open eagerness, Eisenhower's associates were encouraged to think of themselves as part of a collective enterprise rather than as individual entrepreneurs. They believed the president respected them sufficiently to consider their recommendations when making final policy decisions, although as loyal team members they recognized that many factors influenced Eisenhower's final decisions. Therefore, it was incumbent on them to fall in line, even if their particular recommendation was not followed.

When Eisenhower asked advice in the cabinet meeting, he could contribute in still further ways to what plainly was the primary function of the formal component of his domestic policy machinery—administration consolidator. By knowing what their colleagues were doing, members could coordinate their activities. The attorney general, for example, on finding pro-

posals requiring legal back-up in the form of precedents and orders, could immediately set his staff to work. Members who attended the briefings and read briefing papers were in a position to defend aspects of administration policy falling outside their immediate areas. Being privy to high-level information outside their own departmental domains added to their feeling that their opinions were valued and that the consultation was not perfunctory. This reinforced Eisenhower's explicit message that in the cabinet the members were to view themselves as general statesmen, not simply defenders of departmental positions. So viewing themselves the cabinet members had still another reason (whatever their private disagreements) to unite behind Eisenhower's program. His administration suffered remarkably few cabinet-level leaks, feuds, or reports initiated by members indicating that they were at variance with Eisenhower's policies.

Above all, the meeting was his bully pulpit. It was here that he personally conveyed the general principles behind his policies, giving them added force by displaying his strength of conviction and "force of personality." Bradley Patterson, although impressed with the Eisenhower cabinet procedures, considering them superior to the option papers and employment of White House intermediaries that replaced Eisenhower's approach in later presidencies, stresses that no impersonal procedure or staff aide

can equal the impact, on a group of Cabinet officers, of hearing the President, in person, deliver private remarks about his own decisions and priorities, his disappointments of the past, his hopes for the future. Coming from an emphatic and articulate man ... often with some purple language added, Cabinet remarks by the Chief Executive carry a strength and an indelibility which the senior most White House aide cannot duplicate.[12]

Because cabinet meetings had functions other than that of debate, Eisenhower never expressed to the cabinet or the secretariat his feeling that

[12]Ibid., p. 112.

"in some instances . . . to fill out an agenda . . . items are not of the caliber that should come before the Cabinet,"[13] a view of his that Mrs. Whitman transmitted to Milton Eisenhower. An example of this might have been a meeting that Under Secretary of State Douglas Dillon remembered where "we sat around looking at plans for Dulles airport. They had a model and everything, and we would say why don't you put a door there, and they would say why they didn't."[14] Neither this nor any other item in Patterson's seven years of preparing the agenda produced a single Eisenhower complaint "that the agenda contained an item he didn't want to discuss at the table."[15]

His reason for not complaining is contained in a private diary entry in which he evaluated the cabinet after his first year in office. (By this time the one member who was ideologically and temperamentally unsuited to function with his colleagues, the former union president who served as his first labor secretary, Martin Durkin, had resigned.) He judged his cabinet members, and by extension their regular meetings, in terms of the degree to which they had come to fit together, in their informal as much as their formal capacities, as a harmonious team.

[A]s now constituted, I cannot think of a single position that I could strengthen by removal of the present incumbent and appointment of another. By no means do I mean to imply that any one of my associates . . . is perfect in his job—any more than I deem myself to be perfectly suited to my own! I merely mean to say that I have had a good many years of experience in selecting people for positions of heavy responsibility, and I think the results so far achieved by this Cabinet and by other close associates, justify my conviction that we have an extraordinarily good combination of personalities. . . . I think the individuals in the Cabinet and other offices like each other. At least, I can detect no sign

of mutual dislike among the group. I know that I like them all; I like to be with them; I like to converse with them; I like their attitude toward their duty and toward governmental service.[16]

Long before he was president, Eisenhower's thinking about how a body formally constituted as a policy council could be informally guided in a manner designed to foster its members' cohesion had taken shape. Eisenhower dispatched a lengthy memorandum to Defense Secretary James Forrestal on February 7, 1948, his final day as army Chief of Staff, containing a remarkable discussion of the practical aspects combining formal and informal organization. His particular concern in the memorandum paralleled his concern as president with mitigating departmental "parochialism." He was advising the defense secretary on how to win the support of the service chiefs for a coherent, overall defense program, discouraging the impulse of each chief to attempt to centralize maximum resources in his own branch.

"The old saying 'centralization is the refuge of fear,'" Eisenhower observed, "is partially rooted in the natural human feeling that every man wants under his own hand complete control and authority over every factor or unit that has a possible function in the discharge of his responsibilities." Eisenhower's suggestions to Forrestal on how to wean the service chiefs away from acting on this feeling were, like his means of running the cabinet, grounded on a formal secretariatlike procedure that relied on informal leadership for its dynamics.

He urged Forrestal to employ a neutral formal body—the Defense Department Research and Development Board—as the instrument for framing the agenda of discussions between the secretary and the Joint Chiefs of Staff. This body was to use the most recent Defense Department "concept of war" formulation of the nation's overall military requirements and to identify exactly which department was doing what with how much expense and overlap in function. "In this way," he explained, "the matter will be

[13]Ann Whitman to Milton Eisenhower, August 28, 1956, WF-N (Eisenhower, Milton).

[14]C. Douglas Dillon quoted by Arthur Schlesinger, Jr., *A Thousand Days* (Boston: Houghton Mifflin, 1965), p. 136.

[15]Patterson, "The President's Cabinet," p. 109.

[16]PD January 18, 1954.

taken out of the realm of generality and brought down to specific recommendation."

He then sketched the politics and persuasive techniques that could be used to encourage genuine cooperation among the chiefs. First, although the secretary was "not expected to interfere in detailed administration of the several services," nevertheless he should work to insure the appointment of the "right type" of men in terms of intellectual commitments—that is, "officials who he has determined in advance to be completely sold on the idea of achieving greater efficiency and economy through maximum interdependence among the services." Secondly, the men chosen should be psychologically suited to working in groups. This was no idle homily for Eisenhower. It was at the core of his principles of leadership: "In organizing teams, personality is equally important with ability. . . . Leadership is as vital in conference as it is in battle."

Underscoring the word he used both in his preinauguration meeting to advise his cabinet members how to regard one another and in his description of the cabinet after its first year, Eisenhower then emphasized that "the work of the Secretary will never be successful unless the principal members of his team are *friends.*"

In dealing with problems, friends develop among themselves a natural selflessness that is the outgrowth of their regard for the other. Personal antagonism enjoys the defeat of the opponent—consequently objectivity and selflessness cannot be attained when it is present.

Finally, he discussed how the man conducting a council of organization chiefs should seek to encourage them to transcend the impulse simply to advance their departments. Exercising "patience and a sense of humor," the man in charge should "habitually and assiduously" bring "into the open in informal meetings major controversial issues in the attitude of one seeking *general* professional assistance so that he may make decisions on the basis of the national welfare." (Eisenhower's emphasis) To this end, Eisenhower advised that "whenever . . . any individual showed a tendency to become a special pleader," the subject should be "skillfully

changed and a constant effort made to achieve unanimity of conclusion, first upon broad generalities and these gradually brought closer to concrete application.[17]

Although Chief of Staff Eisenhower's 1948 memorandum to the Secretary of Defense foreshadows how President Eisenhower was to make informal use of an official policy advising body to promote cohesion among its members, Eisenhower's formal meetings were only one of the vehicles he used for making team players of his associates. Consider the case of one of the most independent-minded—and in Eisenhower's view, valuable—cabinet members, Treasury Secretary George Humphrey. (As former president of Hanna Steel, he was one of the most conspicuous sources of the somewhat inaccurate aphorism that the cabinet consisted of nine millionaires and a plumber.) Humphrey was the only cabinet member who joined Eisenhower's personal circle of bluff, hearty, intelligent-but-not-intellectual golf and bridge friends. Humphrey's economic conservatism undoubtedly helped Eisenhower buttress his own somewhat inchoate similar views, but Eisenhower did not accept Humphrey's most conservative views, especially those bearing on international activity. Since it was an article of faith of both men not to publicize their disagreements, and since Eisenhower's many social visits to Humphrey's Georgia plantation were a matter of record, observers who thought of Eisenhower as a liberal in the captivity of conservatives, typically saw Humphrey as his principal "mind guard." In fact, however, membership on the Eisenhower team was profoundly liberalizing for Humphrey.

Eisenhower did not rely on Humphrey alone for economic advice. He frequently gathered and acted on dissenting views, for example, those of Council of Economic Advisors Chairman Arthur Burns.[18] And he frequently pressed Humphrey to change his views. Humphrey became a strong defender of foreign aid, for example, and he was

[17]Eisenhower to James V. Forrestal, February 7, 1948, PDDE, vol. 9, pp. 2242–56.

[18]On Burns winning out over Humphrey see the Vanderbilt University collection of oral histories of former heads of the Council of Economic Advisors, publication forthcoming. I am indebted to Professor Erwin Hargrove for making this available to me.

a firm opponent to the restraints on presidential foreign policy making power in the various versions of the Bricker Amendment. Had he remained with Hanna Steel from 1953 to 1957, he surely would have taken a businessman's stance on the opposing side of these issues. (He seems to have told Bricker as much in connection with the Ohio senator's proposed curb on presidential treaty-making powers.)[19] Moreover, when Humphrey did disagree with an administration policy, his loyalty prevailed. On one occasion, Milton Eisenhower informed the president he had just learned that Humphrey did not approve of a program for liberalizing aid and loan terms to Latin America, which Milton and Humphrey had been assigned to propose at a forthcoming meeting of the Western Hemisphere nations. The president replied:

> So long as he is the good soldier that I believe him to be, I must say that I don't see that anything is hurt by the presence in the highest councils of different kinds of thinking. It is in the combination of these various attitudes that we hammer out acceptable policies; enthusiasts for anything go too far.[20]

Shortly thereafter Milton wrote back describing a conversation with Humphrey in which the latter said that, having been told by the president that he was "a general in the cold war," he would be a "good general" and "support the State Department Program."[21]

Humphrey's behavior, however, did not invariably comport with his intentions. Through inadvertence rather than through insubordination, he provoked the most widely publicized seeming breach of cabinet unity during Eisenhower's presidency. In 1957, on the day that the administration's budget was released, the press reported that Humphrey had claimed the budget was too large and that such budgets would lead to a "depression that will curl your hair." The report was a misrepresentation of Humphrey's public statement, since in using the phrase he

was not referring to the current budget. When in a preliminary cabinet meeting Humphrey had expressed his desire to release a statement warning against *future* big budgets, several members advised against making an announcement that might be viewed "as a break within the Administration."[22] Thus, Humphrey issued to the press a carefully worded letter that in no way undermined the current year's budget request.[23] Two minutes before the close of the press conference that began with his release of the letter, however, Humphrey used the "hair curling" phrase in a reference to long-run spending.[24] The story in the *New York Times* elided it with a remark Humphrey had made early in the conference about the possibility that savings could be made in the present budget. This created an account that gave precisely the impression Humphrey had been warned to avoid. Humphrey had no sooner used the picturesque phrase than the reporters asked that the stenotype be read back for quotation.[25] A professional politician no doubt would have seized upon that signal to withdraw the remark or to qualify it even more carefully. But Eisenhower had to pay a price for taking into his cabinet several corporate leaders who, though they had the technical knowledge and administrative experience, often were not politically astute.*

[22]Cabinet Meeting, January 9, 1957, WF-C.

[23]See Nathan R. Howard, ed., *The Basic Papers of George M. Humphrey as Secretary of the Treasury* (Cleveland: Western Reserve Historical Society, 1965) for the text of Humphrey's statement and a transcript of his news conference—"Remarks concerning the President's 1958 Budget," January 15, 1957, pp. 236–52. Also see Ellis Slater, *The Ike I Knew* (Published privately by the Ellis Slater Trust, 1980), p. 50.

[24]Howard, *The Basic Papers of George M. Humphrey,* "Remarks Concerning the President's 1958 Budget," January 15, 1957, pp. 236–52.

[25]*New York Times,* January 17, 1957. The request to the stenotypist is reproduced on p. 252 of Howard, *The Basic Papers of George M. Humphrey.*

*Richard Neustadt's use of the episode as evidence of Eisenhower's nonprofessionalism in Washington politics captures a complaint that Eisenhower himself occasionally voiced about the businessmen he appointed to executive branch positions. They had special virtues gained in their private sector experience, but they often could be outmaneuvered by the professional politicians with whom they dealt.[26]

[26]Richard Neustadt, *Presidential Power,* chapter 6.

[19]John Bricker, COHC.

[20]Eisenhower to Milton Eisenhower, November 23, 1954, WF-N (Eisenhower, Milton).

[21]Milton Eisenhower to Eisenhower, "Monday" (no further date), WF-N (Eisenhower, Milton).

Although the cabinet, as a so-called policy body, was largely concerned with team building, Eisenhower clearly also valued it as one of the many forums in which he could hear and take part in debate over policy. The cabinet minutes show that there was indeed genuine debate, though it did not take the form of heated exchanges or cutting repartee, but rather the good-natured discourse one might expect in a cabinet of friends. The exchanges were consistent with Patterson's view (formed in the course of attending virtually all of the meetings after the summer of 1954) that "discussions at Eisenhower's Cabinet table were candid and lively, reflecting . . . the basic divergence in the Republican Party which was evident in the convention of 1952 itself: between conservatives and moderates."[27]

The greatest intensity reached in a cabinet debate is reflected in the January 19, 1959, discussion of aid to education, which so impressed Patterson that he transcribed rather than summarized his shorthand notes. That meeting, which clearly brought out the conservative-moderate division in the cabinet, was the occasion for a defense by Secretary of Health, Education and Welfare Arthur Flemming of his proposal that the administration request legislation authorizing poor school districts to finance the building of classrooms by issuing federally guaranteed bonds.

Eisenhower prefaced Flemming's presentation by acknowledging his own resistance in principle to federal aid to education, a basic attitude the members knew he held even though he had allowed school-aid legislative proposals to be part of the official administration legislative program under both of Flemming's predecessors in the HEW post, Oveta Culp Hobby and Marion Folsom. Nodding as it were to his conservative colleagues, Eisenhower remarked "the principle . . . still shocks me," but putting Flemming's proposal in a favorable context, he noted that it was "peanuts" compared with the sweeping aid to education package being advanced by liberals in the heavily Democratic Eighty-sixth Congress that had just convened. Then amiably saying, "having put that much of a noose around your

head . . . Arthur," he asked Flemming to make his presentation.

Flemming's defense of the program—it transcended principles of fiscal conservatism and avoidance of federal involvement in education, he argued, because facilities to accommodate the population-bulge of post-World War II children were a national necessity—met with a conservative barrage. Treasury Secretary Robert Anderson argued at length that subsidized bonds were economically unsound and would compete unfairly with Treasury borrowing, while the arch-conservatives, Commerce Secretary Lewis Strauss,* Agriculture Secretary Ezra Taft Benson, and Budget Bureau Director Maurice Stans, based their arguments largely on ideology.

Flemming held his own, stressing "national need," the argument most likely to sway Eisenhower from conservative principles. Another cabinet moderate, Labor Secretary James Mitchell, backed Flemming, using the rhetoric of "investing in human resources." Flemming's strongest supporter was Vice-President Nixon, who, as in many other controversies, examined the political side of the question. Nixon remarked that, although he knew conservative opposition to aid to education extended to the Republican party's own congressional leaders, the group the cabinet should be concerned about was not the leaders, but rather those moderate Republicans who had to run against liberal Democrats in closely divided congressional districts. They would suffer if they had no alternative to the Democratic school-aid program to offer their constituents. "Nothing hits people more directly than their kids in school," Nixon observed. Whatever the views of the congressional leaders, he thought "the ultimate majority of people will say there is a need." Anticipating what was to be Eisenhower's resolution of the debate, Nixon concluded that "We cannot win on this issue by saying 'there is no need' or that 'the need will soon be met.'"

Wrapping up the discussion, Eisenhower told Flemming to present his proposal at the next

---

[27]Patterson, "The President's Cabinet," p. 109.

*Strauss had been appointed as Commerce Secretary in November 1958 when Congress was not in session and served in that position until the Senate refused to confirm him in June 1959.

White House Legislative Leadership meeting. In effect ruling against the conservative positions taken by a majority of the cabinet members, he indicated that he was sure "we are going to put up some kind of program," granting that "I do not know of anything I *hate* as much."* Having encouraged debate between the cabinet moderates and conservatives, Eisenhower made a final remark which seemed to satisfy everyone: "We have had a good growl."[28]

. . . Eisenhower drew for advice on many White House aides, other administration members, and friends and acquaintances for what appears to have been as rich—if not as palpably contrived—a flow of face-to-face conversation, questioning, and thinking out loud as occurred under Roosevelt. By the same token the key aides freely exchanged tactical and substantive ideas with each other. . . .

Press Secretary Hagerty had particularly close access to Eisenhower, because Eisenhower valued his views and appreciated his many sources of off-the-record information. Moreover, Hagerty traveled with Eisenhower to the president's public appearances, and in the course of doing so, had numerous opportunities to chat informally with him. Hagerty's diary provides many illustrations of how the president continually sought his and other aides' ideas and mined them for information. His reports accord with the Nixon observation that Eisenhower frequently engaged in "mindstretching" ruminations, tossing out ideas he did not necessarily plan to act on:

With people he knew well and trusted, Eisenhower liked to think out loud. He would sometimes make what would seem to be completely outlandish and politically naive remarks, just to test them, perhaps even believ-

ing in some of them momentarily. He was very bold, imaginative and uninhibited in suggesting and discussing new and completely unconventional approaches to problems. Yet he probably was one of the most deliberate and careful Presidents the country had ever had where action was concerned.†[29]

Milton Eisenhower was probably the single most important influence in the informal organization of the Eisenhower White House. Since he could be completely trusted, he served as a superlative sounding board. During the 1950s as president first of Pennsylvania State University and then of Johns Hopkins University, Milton arranged with the trustees of both institutions to devote four days a week to university business, and the remaining to serving three days as aide to his brother. When in Washington, he often met with his brother at times not covered by the appointment log—at breakfast and in the evenings or by a back door to the Oval Office. He wrote numerous advisory letters to Eisenhower, typing them himself when he felt they were too sensitive to pass through a secretary. And the two brothers were connected by a secure direct telephone line, insuring that their conversations would not be monitored.‡[30]

Informal, regularly-held stag dinners con-

*Later in the year, Flemming forwarded a proposed administration bill to Congress. Like other school-aid proposals, it was not acted upon because of the stalemate on domestic policy making caused by the collision of the liberal Eighty-sixth Congress with Eisenhower conservatism, and the preoccupation in both parties with position taking rather than policy resolution as the 1960 nominations and election campaigns loomed.

[28]"Excerpt of Cabinet Discussion," "Minutes of the Cabinet Meeting," January 16, 1959, WF-C.

†The passage continues: "Because of his military experience, he was always thinking in terms of alternatives, attack and counter-attack. This was true of every problem he handled. I cannot, for instance, imagine him countenancing the plan for the 1961 rebel attack against Cuba without air power before asking: 'What is our position if the landings fail? . . . (But) he could be very enthusiastic about half-baked ideas in the discussion."

[29]Richard M. Nixon, *Six Crises* (New York: Doubleday, 1962), p. 169 (paperback).

‡Milton Eisenhower was at least as important to his brother as Robert Kennedy was to John F. Kennedy. The contrast between the tactful, low visibility modus operandi of the Eisenhower brothers and the controversial public approach and teamwork of the Kennedys epitomizes the differences between the Eisenhower mode of seeking results without apparent controversy and the Kennedy emphasis on establishing the president and his team as visibly tough, "hard ball" political operators.

[30]My sources include interviews with Milton Eisenhower, concerning his letters to his brother, WF-N (Eisenhower, Milton), and with Bernard Stanley and Thomas Stephens concerning their respective tenure as appointments secretary.

stituted another of Eisenhower's advisory resources. Guest lists of dozens of such events are available and reveal the close attention paid to the choice of guests and even to seating arrangements. Those best represented at these dinners were the well-established or rising businessmen, usually in prominent positions of responsibility. Guests also included executive branch officials, party leaders, celebrities, leading clergymen, academics (especially natural scientists), and a few labor leaders, usually craft unionists who had supported Eisenhower's candidacy.

Typically, those invited would meet the president at 7:30 P.M. for drinks followed by dinner, and would then gather for conversation in the White House residential quarters. Although the tone was easygoing, Eisenhower would consistently direct the conversation to discussion of immediate and long-run problems about which he wanted information, insight, and advice. The meetings inevitably had a rallying as well as informative function. Not surprisingly, those favored with invitations usually left these gatherings as enthusiastic Eisenhower supporters, stimulated both by the distinction of being invited to the White House and by Eisenhower's compelling presence.

The stag dinners were the most formal manifestation of what might be called Eisenhower's "White House behind the White House," a wholly informal institution, operating as much in the living as in the working quarters of 1600 Pennsylvania Avenue, and extending to Camp David, Augusta, and Eisenhower's other favorite sites outside of Washington. He had an extraordinarily broad network of acquaintances and friends with whom he corresponded and met.

Some of these friends were people with whom he could simply relax, while others, such as publisher and public-relations man William Robinson and General Clay were men whose views, breadth of acquaintance, and support he had long found valuable. In all, unofficial and official associates combined to provide Eisenhower with at least as diverse a flow of information and advice as any of the other modern presidents.

The Eisenhower Parallels

The man, his strategies, and his organizational style provide a lens for re-examining specific episodes in Eisenhower's presidential leadership; the congruence of organizational style, strategies, and man is striking. His organizational style seemed from public evidence to be highly formalistic, but its unpublicized face was directed to the informal subtleties of administrative politics. He left a public impression that he was not a political strategist, but rather a head of state who was above politics. Looked at from the inside, however, he revealed himself as a self-conscious practitioner of a leadership style that enabled him to maintain the popular support needed by a successful head of state without foregoing direct participation in the controversial politics of leadership. And at the personal level he showed a striking capacity to think in politically astute ways but presented himself as a guileless folk hero. He also worked hard at carrying off his distinctive style of leadership, but left the impression that it was all effortless.

Chapter 6 Review Questions

1. What is your definition of an informal group in organizations?
2. How are informal groups formed and how do they influence the activities of public organizations?
3. Do informal groups emerge and have an impact upon *public* organizations in the same ways as they do upon *business* organizations?
4. Why was President Eisenhower so successful, according to the case study, at using the informal group to run his presidency? Do you think the same

strategies could be used by modern presidents? If so, how? Or for state and local public managers? Why or why not?

5. Can you see any evidence of the influence of informal groups in organizations with which you are familiar? If so, how did these groups emerge and in what ways do they affect the policies and activities of those organizations?

6. Based on your personal observations of the workings of informal groups, would you modify the informal group concept as described by Barnard in any way? For example, could you add more specifics about how to identify informal groups? Measure their strength? Identify sources of influence in organizations? Reasons for weakness? Methods for achieving the support of management? Ways of communication? Means of motivation?

Key Terms

informal group	Hawthorne experiments
"great illumination"	need of action
"anomie"	purposive cooperation
immediate groups	formal organization
"learning the organizational ropes"	functions of informal organizations

Suggestions for Further Reading

The best book about the Hawthorne experiments is Fritz Roethlisberger and W.J. Dickson, *Management and the Worker* (Cambridge, Mass.: Harvard University Press, 1939). For a less complicated view, see Fritz Roethlisberger, *Management and Morale* (Cambridge, Mass.: Harvard University Press, 1941). Elton Mayo's broad philosophic interpretations are contained in his "trilogy": *The Human Problems of an Industrial Organization* (New York: Macmillan Co., 1933); *The Social Problems of an Industrial Civilization* (Boston: Graduate School of Business Administration, Harvard University, 1945); and *The Political Problems of an Industrial Civilization* (same publisher, 1947). For an excellent retrospective on Hawthorne, refer to "An Interview with Fritz Roethlisberger," *Organizational Dynamics,* 1 (Autumn 1972), pp. 31–45, and "Hawthorne Revisited: The Legend and the Legacy," *Organizational Dynamics,* 4 (Winter 1975), pp. 66–80.

Two excellent and now classic interpretations of Hawthorne are George Homans, *The Human Group* (New York: Harcourt, Brace, 1950) and Henry Landsberger, *Hawthorne Revisited* (Ithaca, N.Y.: Cornell University Press, 1958). By contrast, to taste a small sampling of the scholarly arguments over Hawthorne, read Alex Carey, "The Hawthorne Studies: A Radical Criticism," *American Sociological Review,* 32 (June 1967), pp. 403–416; and for a review of small group theory applied to public administration, see Robert T. Golembiewski, "The Small Group and Public Administration," *Public Administration Review,* 19 (Summer

1959), pp. 149–156. For some interesting new perspectives on the psychological dimensions of public management, see Richard L. Schott, "The Psychological Development of Adults: Implications for Public Administration," *Public Administration Review,* 46 (November/December 1986), pp. 657–667.

The legacy of Hawthorne can be found in numerous examples of the prolific postwar authors associated with the Human Relations School of Management, Chris Argyris, Warren Bennis, Frederick Herzberg, Daniel Katz, Robert Kahn, Rensis Likert, Douglas McGregor, Leonard Sayles, William Whyte, and many, many others who owe a tremendous debt to Hawthorne. In turn, their "spinoffs" and "impacts" on public administration have been profound and numerous but largely uncharted by scholars in the field, though for a useful compilation of many of their writings, refer to Jay Shafritz et al., eds., *Classics of Public Administration,* Second Edition, (Chicago: Dorsey Press, 1987); Thomas H. Patten, *Classics of Personnel Management* (Chicago: Moore Publishing, 1979); and Louis E. Boone and Donald D. Bowen, eds., *The Great Writings in Management and Organizational Behavior* (Tulsa, Okla.: The Petroleum Publishing Co., 1980). For a current overview of this topic, read Charles Perrow, *Complex Organizations: A Critical Essay,* Second Edition (Glenview, Ill.: Scott, Foresman, 1979). Interestingly, it is perhaps the success of Japanese business in recent years that has brought renewed attention on the informal group as the basis for effective management by Americans, as reflected in such popular texts as William Ouchi, *Theory Z: How American Business Can Meet the Japanese Challenge* (New York: Avon Books, 1982). Note the heavy influence of Hawthorne thinking in this and other such writings about the Japanese success story.

Key Decision Makers in Public Administration: The Concept of the Professional State

"For better or worse—or better and worse—much of our government is now in the hands of professionals. . . ."

Frederick C. Mosher

Introduction

Nearly five million people work for the federal government, and another ten million work in state and local governments in the United States. They may be engineers working on the Panama Canal, foresters in Alaska, city managers in Texas, highway patrol officers in California, or public school teachers in Boston—all are public servants who carry out the varied important and not-so-important tasks that society calls on government to undertake.

Frederick C. Mosher (1913–   ) is a distinguished scholar and practitioner of public administration, who recently retired after more than three decades of teaching in the field, first at the Maxwell School, Syracuse University, later at the University of California, Berkeley, and finally as the Doherty Professor of Government and Foreign Affairs at the University of Virginia. In his brilliant study *Democracy and the Public Service* (now updated in its Second Edition), which won the first Brownlow prize for the outstanding book published in the field, Professor Mosher gives us perhaps the best and most convincing analysis of the character of contemporary American public service. His central argument is that the people who work for government today in appointed positions are increasingly becoming professionalized in terms of their skills and the substance of their work. His statistics show that more than one-third of government employees are now engaged in professional or technical pursuits—"three times the comparable proportion in the private sector." The number of professionals working in the public sector has increased since the first quarter of this century, when the U.S. Classification Act of 1923 established a professional and scientific service, and has continued to rise over the years as civil service ratings have offered increasing incentives for specialized training and advanced skills. The demands for skilled workers have also grown because the tasks of government, particularly since the Depression and World War II, have become increasingly more complex in nature and broader in scope. In short, Mosher characterizes the public service at all levels of bureaucracy as "the professional state."

By *professional* Mosher means: "1) a reasonably clear-cut occupational field, 2) which ordinarily requires higher education at least through the bachelor's level, 3) which offers a lifetime career to its members." These individuals include lawyers and physicians who happen to hold government jobs as well as public professionals like diplomats or military officers whose professions are generated within government and are dependent solely on public sector employment. Individual professional specialists have come to dominate public agencies, e.g., military officers in the Defense Department, physicians in the Public Health Service, and lawyers in the Justice Department.

Mosher identifies several common traits in bureaucracy's public professionalism. One is the desire of professional groups to elevate their status and strengthen their public image as a profession, frequently by defining certain kinds of work as their exclusive domain, thereby protecting career opportunities for their members. There is also an emphasis on "work substance," particularly in terms of training in scientific skills as preparation for their jobs. Another common tendency among professional groups, Mosher contends, is "a built-in aversion between professions and politics." Professional public servants seek continually to escape the control and influence of politicians and concentrate instead on "the correct ways of solving problems and doing things." And if politics are to be avoided, so also are bureaucratic controls. Bureaucracy is viewed as a threat to professional freedoms, for traditional professions like law and medicine have a high regard for their own autonomy and their control over establishing the rules, fees, and ethics of their profession. Mosher cites various ways in which public service severely restricts the scope of professional autonomy.

Within each public profession, Mosher finds a core of individuals that constitute its professional elite: "it is at the center of the agency, controls the key line positions, and provides the main, perhaps the exclusive, source of its leadership." This elite is also usually the group most closely identified with the central purposes and basic work objectives of the organization—pilots in the Air Force, engineers in the highway department, educators in the Department of Education, geologists in the Geological Survey Office, or scientists and physicians in the National Institutes of Health. Mosher asserts that the real tensions that develop within government occur not between workers and management, but rather "arise between those in different professions (or segments)." "A professional's status is not threatened by his or her secretary, bookkeeper, or janitor. The professional can, and often does, 'go to bat' for them, and they may look upon him or her as their principal advocate. Not so professionals in other segments and professions who are free to challenge the other's competence or judgment." Peer groups, not subordinates or superiors, are chief sources of conflict within administrative agencies.

Professional elites also are the essential decision makers of government, forming the nucleus within professions for determining key personnel policies, hiring criteria, and standards for advancement. Elites sit on promotion boards and draw up job policy and personnel procedures. In general, professional elites in the more established professions exercise greater control over employment practices than those in the newer ones.

Unlike many public administration theorists, Mosher attempts to come to grips with the essential question: who rules the bureaucracy? As he concludes:

> For better or worse—or better *and* worse—much of our government is now in the hands of professionals (including scientists). The choice of these professionals, the determination of their skills, and the content of their work are now principally determined, not by general governmental agencies, but by their own professional elites, professional organizations, and the institutions and faculties of higher education. It is unlikely that the trend toward professionalism in or outside of government will soon be reversed.

As you read this selection, keep the following questions in mind:

How can the appropriate balance be struck between, on the one hand, freedom for professionals to apply expertise in their respective fields of government and, on the other hand, general public control and oversight of their activities?

What ensures that professionals will maintain the broad public view, rather than become narrow special interests seeking only their self-advancement?

What is the appropriate relationship between public professionals and publicly elected officials?

Can you point out the public professionals' influence in any of the cases of chapters three and four? Was professional authority exercised wisely and responsibly?

FREDERICK C. MOSHER

The Professional State

There is a curious aura of unreality about much that has been said and done in the last half-century with regard to public executives and public managers. A good many otherwise enlightened citizens are not aware of their existence—other than the President, who is of

course the chief executive. They know there is a chief of police and a secretary of defense and a county clerk, but these are politicians or bureaucrats, or worse, a combination of the two. They may be aware too that there is a county director of public health, a superintendent of schools, a director of the Forest Service; but these are professionals—a doctor, an educator, a forester. They are not thought of as executives or managers. And a great many of the incum-

From *Democracy and the Public Service,* Second Edition, by Frederick C. Mosher. Copyright © 1982 by Oxford University Press, Inc. Reprinted by permission.

bents of such positions do not think of themselves in those terms either. I have talked with a number of members of the Senior Executive Service who said that they had never thought of themselves as executives. They were engineers, biologists, lawyers, economists. They did not consider themselves managers or executives although they have made or participated in decisions affecting thousands of subordinates, millions of citizens, and sometimes billions of dollars. Some years ago, the president of one of the great universities in the world described himself in these words: "I am first of all a professor."

It may prove over the years that the greatest contributions of the Brownlow Committee on Administrative Management, the two Hoover Commissions, and Carter's personnel reform (as well as a great many other efforts) were to lend credence to the importance of what public executives were doing and therefore to the importance of selecting, preparing, and motivating them for their jobs. The faulty public image and self-image of career public servants are probably a product of developments over the last century or longer toward professionalism in American society. Although its seeds appeared earlier, the professional ethos really began to make its mark in the latter decades of the nineteenth century. It fostered, and was fostered by, a number of parallel social movements: the development of universities (or, in Clark Kerr's apt term, multiversities); increasing occupational specialism; meritocracy; careerism off the farm; the growth of an enormous, fluid, and amorphous middle class; and faith in progress.[1] In the 1960s, Daniel Bell wrote of an emerging new society in which old values and social power associated with property, wealth, production, and industry

are giving way to knowledge, education, and intellect.

To speak rashly: if the dominant figures of the past hundred years have been the entrepreneur, the businessman, and the industrial executive, the "new men" are the scientists, the mathematicians, the economists, and the engineers of the new computer technology. And the dominant institutions of the new society—in the sense that they will provide the most creative challenges and enlist the richest talents—will be the intellectual institutions. The leadership of the new society will rest, not with businessmen or corporations as we know them . . . but with the research corporation, the industrial laboratories, the experimental stations, and the universities.[2]

Viewed broadly, the professions are social mechanisms, whereby knowledge, particularly new knowledge, is translated into action and service. They provide the means whereby intellectual achievement becomes operational.

The extent to which the professions have become dominant in American society has been noted by a number of commentators. Several years ago, Kenneth S. Lynn maintained that "Everywhere in American life, the professions are triumphant."[3] And Everett C. Hughes wrote: "Professions are more numerous than ever before. Professional people are a larger proportion of the labor force. The professional attitude, or mood, is likewise more widespread; professional status more sought after."[4]

In statistical terms, data of the U.S. Census

---

[1] There is a growing volume of literature about the growth and effects of professionalism, mostly by sociologists. I have here relied heavily upon Burton J. Bledstein, *The Culture of Professionalism: The Middle Class and the Development of Higher Education in America* (New York, Norton, 1976).

[2] "Notes on the Post-Industrial Society," I *The Public Interest,* 6 (Winter, 1967), p. 27.

[3] Kenneth S. Lynn, "Introduction," *Daedalus,* 92 (1963), p. 649. This issue of *Daedalus* was wholly dedicated to a discussion of the development of the professions within America.

[4] Everett C. Hughes, "Professions," *Daedalus,* 92 (1963), p. 655.

and the Bureau of Labor Statistics reflect the accelerating increase of "professional, technical, and kindred" workers, who grew from 4 to 15 percent of the American labor force between 1920 and 1978. The fastest growth has been since World War II; it continues today and probably will do so well into the future.

The Professions and Government

The prominent role of American governments in the development and utilization of professions went largely unnoticed for a long time. Governments are the principal employers of professionals. According to estimates of the Bureau of Labor Statistics, about two of every five workers classified as "professional, technical, and kindred" (39.4%) were employed by governments in 1978, a proportion which has been stable since 1970.[5] This category does not include the multitude of engineers, scientists, and others on private rolls who are actually paid from government contracts, subsidies, and grants. Looked at another way, more than one third (36.7%) of all government employees were engaged in professional or technical pursuits, more than three times the comparable proportion in the private sector (10.9%). The governmental proportion is swollen by the education professions, especially elementary and secondary school teachers. But even if education is removed from both sides of the ledger,

[5]Data in this paragraph are drawn from "The 1978 Class of Worker Matrix for the United States," an unpublished table furnished by the Bureau of Labor Statistics. The definition of "professional, technical, and kindred" includes occupations that some might not construe as professional, such as applied scientists, athletic coaches, embalmers, writers, artists, and entertainers. On the other hand, it excludes others that might be considered professional, including all of those who describe themselves as "managers, officials, proprietors" (of whom governments employed some 1,170,000 in 1978), military officers, and police.

the percentage of professional and technical personnel in government (21.2%) is nearly double the comparable percentage in the private sector (11.6%).

Leaving aside the political appointees at or near the top of our public agencies and jurisdictions, the administrative leadership of government became increasingly professional in terms of educational and experiential backgrounds. This is not to say that public leadership as such is an administrative profession, rather that it consists of a very wide variety of professions and professionals in diverse fields, most of them related to the missions of the organizations in which they lead.

In government, the professions are the conveyor belts between knowledge and theory on the one hand, and public purpose on the other. The interdependencies of the professions and government are many. Governments are, or have been:

> the creators of many professions;
>
> the *de jure* legitimizers of most of those which have been legitimized;
>
> protectors of the autonomy, integrity, monopoly, and standards of those which have such protections;
>
> the principal supporters of their research and of that of the sciences upon which they depend;
>
> subsidizers of much of their education;
>
> among their principal employers and the nearly exclusive employers of some of them; which means also
>
> among the principal utilizers of their knowledge and skills.

For their part, the professions:

> contribute to government a very substantial proportion of public servants;

provide most of the leadership in a considerable number of public agencies;

through their educational programs, examinations, accreditation, and licensing, largely determine what the content of each profession is in terms of knowledge, skills, and work;

influence public policy and the definition of public purpose in those many fields within which they operate;

in varying degree and in different ways provide or control the recruitment, selection, and other personnel actions for their members;

shape the structure as well as the social organization of many public agencies.

There is nothing very new about professionalism in government. The principal spawning period for educational programs for many of the professions . . . was the first quarter of this century, and the U.S. Classification Act of 1923 established as the most distinguished segment a professional and scientific service. In all probability the number of professionally educated personnel in all American governments has been rising for the past century. Yet there appears to have been very little recognition of, or concern about, the significance of professionalism in the public service and its leadership until quite recently. For example, the Brownlow report and those of the two Hoover commissions, for all of their emphasis upon administrative management, paid scant attention to professionals in fields other than management as such.

The degree to which individual professional specialisms have come to dominate public agencies is suggested by the small table here. The right hand column indicates both the primary professional field in the agency and the normal professional source of its career leadership.

FEDERAL

All military agencies	military officers
Department of State	foreign service officers
Public Health Service	public health doctors
Forest Service	foresters
Bureau of Reclamation	civil engineers
Geological Survey	geologists
Department of Justice	lawyers
Department of Education	educators
Bureau of Standards	natural scientists

STATE AND LOCAL

Highways and other public works agencies	civil engineers
Welfare agencies	social workers
Mental hygiene agencies	psychiatrists
Public health agencies	public health doctors
Elementary and secondary education offices and schools	educators
Higher education institutions	professors
Attorneys general, district attorneys, legal counsel	lawyers

I define the word "profession" liberally as 1. a reasonably clear-cut occupational field, 2. which ordinarily requires higher education at least through the bachelor's level, and 3. which offers a lifetime career to its members.[6] The

[6]The definition is unquestionably too loose to satisfy many students of occupations, who would like to add other requi-

professions in government may conveniently be divided into two classes: first, those in fields employed in the public *and* the private sectors and for whom the government must compete in both recruitment and retention. This category, which I shall call "general professions," includes most of the callings commonly understood as professions: law, medicine, engineering, architecture, and many others. I also include among them applied scientists in general and college professors. Second are those employed predominantly and sometimes exclusively by governmental agencies, which I shall call "public service professions." Most of these were generated within government in response to the needs of public programs, and although there has been a tendency in the direction of increased private employment for many of them, governments are still the predominant employers. They consist of two groups: first, those who are employed exclusively by a single agency such as military officers, Foreign Service officers, and Coast Guard officers; and, second, those employed by a number of different governmental jurisdictions, such as school teachers, educational administrators, social workers, public health officers, foresters, agricultural scientists, and librarians.

Most of those listed above in both categories may be described as "established professions" in the sense that they are widely recognized as professions, and with only a few exceptions their status has been legitimized by formal state action through licensing, credentialing, commissioning, recognizing educational accreditation, or a combination of these.

In addition to these professions, there are many "emergent professions" which have not been so recognized and legitimized but which are valiantly and hopefully pulling themselves up by their vocational bootstraps to full professional status. In this group are included specialists in personnel, public relations, computer technology, and purchasing. Emergent in the "public service" category are governmental subdivisions of all of these and some which are more exclusively governmental: e.g., assessors, police, penologists, employment security officers, air pollution specialists.

The professions—whether general or public service, whether established or emergent—display common characteristics which are significant for democracy and the public service. One of these is the continuing drive of each of them to elevate its stature and strengthen its public image as a profession. In a very few highly esteemed fields, such as law and medicine, the word "maintain" is perhaps more appropriate than "elevate." A prominent device for furthering this goal is the establishment of the clear and (where possible) expanding boundaries of work within which members of the profession have *exclusive* prerogatives to operate. Other means include: the assurance and protection of career opportunities for professionals; the establishment and continuous elevation of standards of education and entrance into the profession; the upgrading of rewards (pay) for professionals; and the improvement of their prestige before their associates and before the public in general.

A second common denominator of the professions is their concentration upon the *work substance* of their field, both in preparatory education and in journeyman activities, and the differentiation of that field from other kinds of work (including other professions) and from work at a lower or subprofessional level in the same field. Accompanying this emphasis upon work substance has been a growing concentration, particularly in preprofessional education, upon the sciences, which are considered foundational for the profession in question, whether they be natural or biological or social (behavioral). This emphasis is an inevitable consequence of the explosive developments of science

---

sites, such as: professional organization; or eleemosynary or service orientation; or legal establishment; or individual autonomy in performance of work; or code of ethics. In terms of governmental consequences, the liberal usage is more appropriate. For example, in terms of their group behavior in government, the officers of the U.S. Navy are at least as "professionalized" as are lawyers.

in the last several decades, and unquestionably it has contributed to the betterment of professional performance in the technical sense.

Partially in consequence of the concentration upon science and work substance there has been a much less than parallel treatment of the *ecology* of the profession in the total social milieu: of the consequences and purposes of the profession and of the constraints within which it operates. There are signs in a good many fields today that attention to these topics is increasing, particularly in the public service professions. Yet much of professional education and practice is still so focused on substance and science as to obscure the larger meaning of the profession in the society. Except for those few professionals who grow beyond their field, the real world is seen as by a submariner through a periscope whose direction and focus are fixed.

One of the most obscure sectors of the real world in professional education and much of its practice is the realm of government and politics. There is a built-in animosity between the professions and politics. Its origin is historical: Most of the professions, and particularly those in the public service category, won their professional spurs over many arduous years of contending against the infiltration, the domination, and the influence of politicians (who to many professionals are amateurs at best and criminals at worst). Compare, for example, the evolution of such fields as the military, diplomacy, social welfare, and city management. The aversion to politics also has contemporary support. Professionalism rests upon specialized knowledge, science, and rationality. There are *correct* ways of solving problems and doing things. Politics is seen as being engaged in the fuzzy areas of negotiation, elections, votes, compromises—all carried on by subject-matter amateurs. Politics is to the professions as ambiguity to truth, expediency to rightness, heresy to true belief.

Government as a whole comes off not much better than politics in the eyes of most professions, particularly the "general" ones. By definition, it carries the political taint. It also violates or threatens some of the treasured attributes and myths of true professionalism: individual and professional autonomy, and freedom from "bureaucratic" control; service to, and fees from, individual clients; vocational self-government. Among those general professions with large numbers of members employed privately, preservice education usually treats government as an outside agency with or against which one must deal. This seems to be true of most education in law, engineering, accounting, and other business fields, upon which government is heavily dependent. It is also true of medicine and most of its subspecialties. Even in many public service professions—public school education provides an excellent example—there is a considerable aversion to government *in general* and to politics, which may be another word for the same thing. Government is all right in those particular areas in which the specified profession has dominant control; but beyond those perimeters, it is equated with "politics" and "bureaucracy" in their more invidious senses.

I doubt that it is appropriate to speak of "strategies" of the professions in government, because some of their consequences seem to have "just growed" rather than to have been consciously planned. Yet those consequences are fairly consistent, particularly among the established professions, whether of the public service or the general category. And the emergent professions are varying distances down the road. The pattern has these features:

1. the given profession has staked its territory within the appropriate governmental agency or agencies, usually with boundaries approximately coterminous with those of the organization itself;
2. within its organization, it has formed an elite corps with substantial control over the operations of the agency, significant influence on agency policies, and high prestige within and outside the agency;
3. to the extent possible, it has assumed control over employment policies and individual per-

sonnel actions for its own members in the agency and also over the employment of persons not in the elite profession;

4. it has provided its members the opportunities, assurances, and protections of a career system of employment.

The following two sections will deal with items 2 and 3 above. . . .

Professional Elites

Our study and hence our understanding of public administrative organizations have for some time been conditioned by two primary considerations. One is simply the past, when most organizations were not professionalized and when it seemed logical to build on the premise that organization consisted of two essential elements: management and workers. The focus was upon the problems, the skills, the content of management viewed as a single, common task, regardless of the differing activities and objectives of the organizations.[7] The second source of our lore about public organizations derives principally from studies of organizations in the realm of private business, but augmented by cases and analyses about some public or semi-public organizations usually at a fairly subordinate level of operations: military units, hospitals, mental institutions, prisons, schools, and scientific laboratories. The more recent of the organizational literature has recognized and even dwelt upon a third element of organization: the professionals, usually viewed as *staff*. They are organizationally below management but are often considered to be superior in educational and social terms.

So we begin our organizational analysis from a *trichotomy* which consists of management, workers, and professionals or staff. The professionals are categorized according to whether they are dedicated to their organizations (the "locals") or to their professions (the "cosmopolitans"). There are presumed conflicts of prospects and goals between management and workers, between professionals and workers, and between management and professionals.

One hesitates to generalize as to the validity or usefulness of either the dichotomous or the trichotomous premises in nonpublic organization today. Undoubtedly they are still applicable in many industrial and commercial organizations. They seem quite inapplicable, however, in most of the professionalized agencies of government, and these include the most important ones. In these agencies:

the managers are professionals in the specialized occupational fields of their agencies—but not as managers per se, for few have been trained for management;

most of those designated as staff are also professionals, but typically in fields of specialism different from that of management;

many of the workers—and most of those in middle-management positions—are also professionals, usually in the same professions as management.

Commonly there is a mutually supportive relationship between the professional managers and the professional workers in the same profession. The former see themselves, and are viewed by the latter, as representative of the interests of both.

Further, there may be no conflict between the organization and its objectives on the one hand and the aspirations and standards of its professional workers and executives on the other. In a good many cases, the goals and standards of public agencies, as seen by their officers and employees, are identical with the goals and standards of the professions as they are seen by their members. This is true of most public organizations in fields such as public health, wel-

---

[7]For examples see the works of Frederick Taylor, Henri Fayol, or Chester Barnard. Their main tenets were reinforced by the writings of Max Weber.

fare, geology, forestry, education, and military affairs. The public organizations, the bureaucracies, not only heavily influence but actually determine and epitomize the goals of the professions which provide the leaders and many of the workers under them. In other words, the bureaucracies, with their official powers, funds, and activities, and the elite professions which people and often dominate bureaucracies with their educational backgrounds, cultures, standards, and prestige are mutually supportive and have common objectives.[8]

A more useful model of most sizable public organizations in government—at the department level and below in state and local units and at the bureau or service level and below in the federal government—would be one which recognized the internal professional and other vocational groupings and the stratification of these within each agency in terms of both prestige and power. In most public agencies which have been in operation for some time, there is a single occupational group whose knowledge, skills, and orientations are closely identified with the mission and activities of the agency. If the work is seen as requiring intellectual capacity and background education to the level of college graduation—and as we have seen, this is the case in an increasing majority of agencies— the group comes to constitute a professional elite. It is a *corps*—a body of men and women closely associated with each other and with the enterprise—and it is sometimes so designated. It is also a *core:* it is at the center of the agency, controls the key line positions, and provides the main, perhaps the exclusive, source of its leadership. If at the time the elite developed there was no existing profession clearly identified with the

activities of the agency, it is likely to be a unique *public service profession*—military, Foreign Service, or public health, for example. If on the other hand there was a clearly related, existing, outside profession or if one subsequently developed, the elite may consist of members of a *general profession*—such as civil engineers in highway departments, psychiatrists in mental hygiene institutions, and lawyers in departments of justice. In some cases, the clearly different nature of the work of the public agencies has occasioned a split-off from an established profession and the birth of a new public service profession, which, however, has retained the educational base of the older one—as in the case of public health doctors and the emerging professions of public works engineers and educational administrators.

There are five principal types of exceptions to the professional elite structure. One is found in relatively new agencies where no existing profession can yet make a clear claim to status as the appropriate elite. A second exception occurs in agencies of the business type, such as the Postal Service and some publicly owned utilities, where the trichotomy of management, staff, and workers may be more descriptive. (In many utility operations, however, line management consists of professional engineers.) A third exception is found in those public agencies whose work does not, or does not yet, require higher education to the graduating level. Police and fire protection are examples of this, though both are moving in the direction of professionalization. Fourth are agencies which are controversial, unstable or temporary, or which, for political reasons, must avoid the appearance of permanence. Professional elitism entails a career orientation. (The Agency for International Development is a good current example in which the development of a technical assistance elite has been politically inhibited.) Finally, a few agencies were deliberately designed in such a way as to prevent dominance by a single occupation through their multipurpose missions. An historic example is the Tennessee Valley Author-

[8]Most of the relevant literature has emphasized the opposition of the professions and their values to organizations and their values, laying stress upon the demands of individual professionals for autonomy against organizational demands for group or social goals. It has ignored the frequent affinity between professions and the organizations which they govern and the organizational efforts, in many cases, to protect the professional autonomy of employees.

ity, but interdisciplinary research laboratories offer abundant illustrations.

Professional elites in larger agencies tend to specialize into subdivisions under the general professional canopy. These may be reflections of well-recognized divisions of the profession, determined outside the agency and extending back into educational specialization, as in medicine and engineering. They may be grounded in specializations of work in the agency itself, sometimes highly formalized as in various arms and services of the Army (Engineer, Quartermaster, Infantry, Ordnance). Or they may be based upon continuing kinds of work assignments not formally recognized as separate corps or segments—e.g., the distinctions among personnel officers in activities such as recruiting, examining, classification, labor relations. Among such subgroups there is normally a pecking order of prestige and influence. The most elite of them is likely to be the one which historically was most closely identified with the end purpose, the basic content of the agency—the officers of the line in the Navy, the pilots in the Air Force, the political officers in the Foreign Service, the civil engineers in a construction agency which also employs electrical and mechanical engineers.

No organization of substantial size can consist solely of members of one occupation. There must always be supportive activities, carried on by individuals who are not members of the elite profession. Indeed, the number in the professional elite may constitute only a small minority of all employees; e.g., public health doctors in a local health office, psychiatrists in mental health institutions, social workers in welfare offices. Complex government agencies employ sizable numbers of professionals, specialists, and workers in fields other than the elite one. These may be grouped in the following main categories:

Supporting Line Professions: professionals who carry on and contribute to the substantive work of the agency, but are trained and experienced in different fields. Thus in a state mental health department and in state mental institutions the psychiatrists are the elite, but by far the greater numbers are psychologists, psychiatric nurses, and social workers. A forestry operation includes agronomists, botanists, engineers, and many others.

Staff Professions: advisers and technicians for their specialized knowledge in areas related to, but not central to, the line work of the agency—as economists, sociologists, legal counsel, design engineers, computer analysts in many kinds of agencies. These are usually few in number and relatively high in grade and position, though not at the very top.

Administrative Professions: officials engaged in personnel, budget, finance, communications, purchasing, supply. Some of these can be found in almost every large agency, although in some the positions are filled by members of the elite professions, particularly at the level of leadership. Most of these are "emergent" rather than established professions.

Workers: paraprofessionals, supervisors, clerical, service, skilled, and unskilled personnel.

Figure 7.1 is a "still picture" of the composition of a hypothetical public agency, well-established and operating in a professional field. (Hypothetical examples of the schema in particular kinds of agencies are shown in Table 7.1.) The vertical dimension is organizational rank or level of pay, and may be assumed to equate very roughly with the level of day-to-day responsibility of incumbents. The horizontal dimension represents the numbers of persons at each grade. The horizontal lines at the bottom of the figures represent the normal and the sometimes exclusive entering-level of beginners when they are appointed in the various categories. The horizontal lines and points at the top of the various figures represent the highest grade an individual in each category can expect to reach.

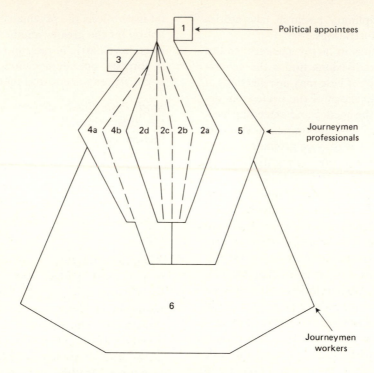

Key: 1. Political appointees from outside the agency
      2. The elite profession:
         a. The elite segment of the elite profession
         b,c,d. Other segments of the elite profession
      3. Staff professions
      4. Line professions
         a. Reserve Officers
         b. Civil Service
      5. Administrative professions
      6. Workers, including supervisors, paraprofessionals, clerical,
         manual, and others

Figure 7.1   Schematic diagram of composition of a professionalized government agency. (From *Democracy and the Public Service.* Second Edition by Frederick C. Mosher. Copyright © 1982 by Oxford University Press, Inc. Reprinted by Permission.)

For an employee to cross lines from one category to another is usually difficult and, where professional standards are high and clear-cut, may be impossible, even illegal. The diamond shapes of the elite profession (2) and of the other professional groups (4 and 5) are typical of most such groups in government where professionals are hired soon after completing their education on a junior basis and advance rapidly to journeyman-level work. The trapezoidal (as distinguished from the familiar pyramidal) shape of the organization as a whole is also representa-

tive, although in most agencies the percentage of the total who are professional personnel is much smaller than is represented on the chart. Over the course of time, the normal progress of an employee in any category is upward, but obviously only a few will make it all the way to the top.

At the top of the diagram are represented a small number of political appointees, recruited from outside, who may or may not be professional. With these are included some political appointees drawn from the elite segment of the

Table 7.1   Illustrative but Hypothetical Examples of Social Organizations of Public Agencies

	Department of State	Department of Air Force	State Department of Highways	State Department of Mental Health	Local Department of Health
1. Political appointees	Secretary, undersecretaries, and some assistant secretaries	Secretary, undersecretaries and assistant secretaries	Department head and deputies	Department head and deputies	Department head
2. Elite profession a. Elite segment b. Other segment c. Other segment d. Other segment	FSO's Political officers Economic officers Consular officers Administrative officers	Air Force officers Flying officers Logistics officers Maintenance officers Administrative officers	Engineers Civil engineers Electrical engineers Mechanical engineers Industrial engineers	M.D.s Psychiatrists Surgeons Pathologists	M.D.s Public health M.D.s Pediatricians
3. Staff professions	Legal advisers Scientific advisers Public relations officers	General counsel Scientific advisers Public information officers	Counsel Economists Public relations officers Real estate appraisers	Counsel Sociologists Statisticians	Counsel Sociologists Biostatisticians
4. Line professions	a. Reserve officers (various fields) b. Civil service (various fields)	Reserve officers (various fields) Civil service (various fields)	Scientists—civil service (various fields) Technicians—civil service (various fields)	Clinical psychologists Psychiatric social workers Psychiatric nurses	Sanitary engineers Public health nurses Social workers
5. Administrative professions	Officers in finance, budget, personnel, training, supply, communications, purchasing, etc. (Civil service and F.S. staff officers)	(Civil service and noncom. enlisted)	(Civil service)	(Civil service)	(Civil service)
6. Nonprofessional employees	Subprofessional, clerical, labor, custodial, etc. (Civil service and F.S. staff)	(Civil service and enlisted)	(Civil service)	(Civil service)	(Civil service)

elite profession. Most of the very top career jobs are also filled from this group, and almost all of such jobs are filled by the elite profession. The incumbents of these jobs constitute very roughly what Morris Janowitz has described as the "elite nucleus."[9]

The diagram suggests that those who make it to the very top, the "elite of the elite," have pursued a more or less orthodox and "proper" type of career. The implication appears to be erroneous in some cases and may indeed be widely untrue. Janowitz found a substantial proportion of the military elite nucleus to be individuals who had pursued unorthodox, innovative careers. A study of the U.S. Foreign Service some years ago indicated that among the Foreign Service Officers in executive positions in Washington and overseas, a disproportionate number had entered the service laterally (i.e., unorthodoxly).[10] Whether these findings about the top leadership in the Foreign Service and the military are typical of professionalized public agencies or arise from certain special circumstances is a significant though largely unexplored question.

Note that the arrangement of professional elites within different agencies does not necessarily reflect the status and prestige of the different professions in the society at large, nor does it reflect the amount of education beyond the bachelor's degree. The determining element is the historic and current identification of the specialty with the central content and purpose of the agency's work. Registered nurses are the elite of a visiting nurse association but not of a hospital. Engineers are the elite of a state highway department but not of a scientific laboratory. Masters of social work are elite in a welfare department but not in a mental hospital. Psychiatrists are the elite profession (or a segment if medical doctors are considered a single profession) in a mental hospital but not in a general hospital or in a local, state, or national public health office. Scientists are the elite in a scientific laboratory, but not in a U.S. embassy overseas.

Note also that within large departments there may be a number of different systems of elitism at different levels in the organization. Professionals in a given field tend to form an associational community which is often the basis for formal organizational differentiation. To a considerable extent, therefore, the suborganization of many departments conforms to professional definitions. Within each major unit there is a professional elite, which may not be the same as the elite of the larger organization. Thus architects are likely to be the elite *within* an architectural division which includes many engineers among other professionals; but if the division is a part of a department of public works, the architects yield in elite status to the civil engineers at the departmental level. Similarly, geologists are the elite in the U.S. Geological Survey but not in the Department of Interior.

Thirdly, it may be noted that the elite status of professions in many different public agencies is relatively but not completely stable. The knowledge, technique, and orientation of the older professions tend toward obsolescence in the face of growing science, new kinds of problems, and new understandings about how to deal with them. These tendencies cast the older professional elites in a stance that is defensive and conservative vis-à-vis their positions and their control over agency objectives and programs. The intra-agency structure of elitism is, in many organizations, a battleground between a professional elite, or an elite segment, and other professions, other segments, and nonprofessionals. Political leaders desirous of rapid development of new programs may, and frequently do, endeavor to tip the balance against the elite professionals by appointing or selecting for promotion individuals who represent points of view at variance with the elite.

[9]*The Professional Soldier: A Social and Political Portrait* (Glencoe, Ill., The Free Press, 1964), Chapter 8.

[10]John E. Harr, *The Anatomy of the Foreign Service: A Statistical Profile* (New York, Carnegie Endowment for International Peace, Foreign Affairs Study No. 4, 1965), Chapter VI.

The key zones of potential tension and conflict in agencies of this kind lie not between management and workers, though these are not absent; nor between management and professionals, because most of the managers are themselves professional; nor between professionals and workers as such, since many of the workers are professionals. Rather they are delineated by the vertical lines (solid and dotted) in Figure 7.1. Specifically, they include tensions between:

1. politically appointed officials and the elite profession (or its elite segment), especially if the political leaders are not members of the profession (or segment);
2. different and competing segments of the elite profession;
3. the elite profession (or elite segment) and other professions in the agency, including especially those in line and administrative professions.

My unproven observation is that the most conflictive situations in professionalized but not unionized public agencies arise between those in different professions (or segments) and in different personnel systems who are approximately equal in level of responsibility and pay, but where one is "more elite" than the other. That is, the principal tensions are horizontal and diagonal rather than vertical. Personnel who are clearly subordinate are more likely to look upon their professional superiors as defenders and representatives than as competitors or opponents; and the professional superiors regard their own role in the same somewhat paternalistic fashion. This is less true in programs staffed by unionized employees, and with the growing organization of public employees it has changed substantially in the recent past. Still, a professional's status is not threatened by his or her secretary, bookkeeper, or janitor. The professional can, and often does, "go to bat" for them, and they may look upon him or her as their principal advocate. Not so professionals in other segments and professions who are free to challenge the other's competence or judgment.

Each profession brings to an organization its own particularized view of the world and of the agency's role and mission in it. The perspective and motivation of each professional are shaped, at least to some extent, by the lens provided by professional education, prior professional experience, and professional colleagues. These distinctive views are further molded and strengthened through training and experience in the agency itself; and where the professional corps within the agency is one of long standing, where it operates through a well-entrenched career system, and where there is a vigorously defended stratification between the professional elite and others in the organization, these postentry forces can be very strong indeed.

The analysis of different public organizations in terms of their professional structure and intraprofessional and interprofessional systems of relationships is basic to a true understanding of how they work. Important decisions are likely to be the product of intraprofessional deliberation, representing the group views of the elite profession in the agency, compromised in some cases to satisfy the demands of other professions and nonprofessionals. Social relationships outside the office usually parallel professional relationships within. Members of the same profession in an agency are "colleagues," like professors in a university; and the flavor of their work is similarly collegial. Toward members of other professions, their behavior is likely to be more formal, sometimes suspicious or even hostile. Toward paraprofessionals and other workers, the relationship may more frequently be paternalistic, patronizing, or dictatorial. Members of the elite profession identify their own work and that of the agency with their profession; the others are a little "outside," they are supplementary or supporting. The "climate" of an organization as well as its view of mission and its effectiveness in carrying it out are in considerable part a product of its professional structure and professional value system.

The Public Employment of Professionals

As the professional composition of public agencies has substantially revolutionized their internal anatomy, physiology, and nervous systems, so has the emergence of professions revolutionized the precepts and practices of public employment. Both revolutions continue with the development and solidification of new fields and new subspecialties. Although there are large differences in precepts and practices among different jurisdictions of government, the basic directions in public service employment are clear. They also are probably inevitable. They apply to virtually all professional fields, whether or not under civil service laws. They are often at odds with the most central—and most cherished—principles associated with civil service reform in this country: equal opportunity to apply and compete for jobs; competitive examinations for selection and (sometimes) promotion; equal pay for equal work; neutral and objective direction and control of the personnel system.

The most important of the changes is the last one, which involves the direction of personnel activities; it underlies the others. In general, what has happened (and is happening) is a *delegation* of real personnel authority, formal and/or informal, from a central personnel office or civil service commission to the professions and the professionals themselves.[11]

A basic drive of every profession, established or emergent, is *self-government* in deciding policies, criteria, and standards for employment and advancement, and in deciding individual personnel matters. The underlying argument for such professional hegemony is that no one outside—no amateur—is equipped to judge or even to understand the true content of the profession or the ingredients of merit in its practice. This thesis is difficult to challenge, particularly in highly developed, specialized, and scientized fields with which an amateur—or a professional in personnel administration—can have only a passing acquaintance.

The means whereby the professionals assert their control over personnel policies and actions are many and diverse. Some are specified and required by law or regulation; others grow out of gentlemen's agreements within—or in spite of—civil service laws; some reflect a silent abdication by the civil service agencies or a failure to assume an effective role; and some are unintended (or mayhap intended) consequences of others. I shall discuss them under three headings: influence and control by the professional elites within governmental agencies; influence and control by "outside" professions and their organizations; and influence and control by institutions of professional education.

Professional Elites

The extreme examples of professional control within agencies are provided by the various commissioned corps in the federal government which have never been under a general civil service system. Here one finds the most consolidated mechanisms of internal control by the elite group and particularly by senior members—the *elite cadre,* as Janowitz termed it. They determine the standards and criteria for entrance; the policies and procedures of assignment; the appropriate work content of elite corps positions; the criteria for promotion. They also set up the machinery for personnel operations, usually including boards, all or a majority of whose members are drawn from the corps itself. They also superintend the policies and operations of personnel management for other employees, including other professionals, who are not in the elite, yielding as little as they must to civil service requirements, to other employee groups, to outside professional interests, and to political pressures.

Much of this personnel control is sanctioned

---

[11]The word "delegation" is not precisely accurate in a good many fields, since many developed independently of any central personnel office, and there was no real *process* of delegation. But delegation is a reasonably accurate description of the product, whatever the nature of the evolution which preceded it.

by law. It is significant that personnel matters in the various corps carry such preeminent weight and importance. Historically in the Army the handling of personnel was long entrusted to the staff division known as G-1 (A-1 in the Air Force); today the officers in charge of personnel are first deputy chiefs of staff. In the State Department the Board of Foreign Service has, since its founding, been essentially a personnel board, as the Director General of the Foreign Service has been primarily concerned with matters of personnel. It may be noted too that in these cases the professional elites have assumed control over the administration of agency personnel who are not in the corps: reserve officers, enlisted personnel (or Foreign Service staff), and civil servants.

Among the agencies not dominated by a commissioned corps, professional control over personnel matters has been less conspicuous but still effective. In many cases it is carried out under the canopy of civil service laws and regulations. The professional elites normally have the most influential voice in determining personnel policies, standards, and criteria within broad prescriptions of civil service law. The recent trend toward decentralization, both at the federal level and in other large jurisdictions, has of course facilitated this development. Personnel selection for professionals is in many places left to boards, which are usually dominated by agency professionals. As will be seen later, competitive written and performance examinations in most of the established professional fields have largely been abandoned in favor of evidences of qualification determined outside the agency and indeed outside the civil service system. What is left—normally an "unassembled" examination of the candidates' records and/or an oral examination—is conducted by boards composed principally of members of the agency's elite profession. The same situation pertains to other personnel actions: assignments, promotions, disciplinary actions. In most cases the central influence is that of the agency; and if it is controlled by a professional elite, the basic control lies with that elite. The

civil service or personnel agency provides assistance in recruitment, a certain amount of professional personnel guidance, certain procedural requisites, and participation and perhaps inspection to ensure conformance with regulations. The substance of personnel policy and decision rests, however, in the professional elite.

Our studies conducted some years ago of employment practices of federal, state, and local jurisdictions in California in general confirmed the tendency toward professional elite control of policies, standards, and actions within the agencies in which there was a professional elite. There were, of course, variations in the degree of control and in the techniques whereby it was made effective. In general, these variations seemed responsive to two factors: first, the degree to which the professional group had established itself as truly elite within a given agency; and second, the degree to which demand exceeded supply for professionals in the field in question. The better established, more recognized professions had greater control, as did those in which supply was scarcest. In our California studies, we found this to be true at all levels of government in the employment of lawyers, natural scientists, engineers, doctors, social workers, and health professionals. In the federal government, we found it true also for foresters, architects, and some others. In the state of California, it applied to psychiatrists in mental hygiene; among local governments, it applied in varying degrees to recreation workers, city planners, librarians, and some others.

The Professionals and Their Organizations

Among the established general professions, the practice of licensing practitioners is an old one. Indeed, it is a common index of whether or not a profession is truly "established," and many of the aspiring newer fields are seeking it to give them official and legal sanction. The licensing of professionals, as of craftsmen, is normally accomplished by the legal delegation of state powers to a board, itself composed exclusively or predominantly of members of the profession. It normally requires the passing of an examination, drafted and graded by the board or other professional group. In all of this, the public personnel organization usually plays no part, and the examinations themselves are directed almost exclusively to the knowledge and skills required for private practice, not to governmental policy and managerial problems, nor to those of large organizations of any kind. In well-established fields, such as law, medicine, dentistry, architecture, some kinds of engineering, and school teaching, licensing is normally requisite to practice at the journeyman level. In others, it is essential to advancement to higher levels of responsibility and supervision: accounting and nursing, for example.

Governmental agencies, other than the licensing boards themselves, play little part in the licensing process and have little influence upon or even interest in the content and standards of the examinations. Very probably, the finding of James W. Fesler in his 1942 study *The Independence of State Regulatory Agencies* is still accurate: "Professional licensing boards are virtually the creatures of the professional societies. . . ."[12] Yet it is clear that these examinations significantly affect the education and the qualifications which make for a professional man or woman. The governments by and large accept those qualifications as gospel in their own employment. In some fields (e.g., law, medicine) a license is an absolute requisite to employment at any professional level. In others, while not required, it may be sufficient evidence for hiring—without further evidence of qualification—and a basis for preferential treatment for advancement as well. Professionals who have gained their credentials in most fields are likely to escape any further tests of competence and knowledge if they aspire to enter government employ. For them the governments have abandoned to the professions the testing of merit insofar as it can be determined by examinations of knowl-

edge and skill. Further, the licensing tests are noncompetitive among the candidates. Qualifications are measured only in terms of passing a minimum standard—which may of course be a high one.

But perhaps most important is the effect of the licensing structure upon the content, the dimensions, and the boundaries of the individual professions. As Corinne Lathrop Gilb has observed: "Public administrators generally fail to acknowledge *the extent to which the structure and composition of regulatory boards affect the division of labor and authority in the work world.*"[13] And the "work world" of course includes the administration of government itself.

Professional Education

Over the long pull, the most profound impact upon the professional public services is that of the universities—their professional schools, their departments in the physical and social sciences which produce professionals, and their faculties in general. Higher education produces the bulk of future professionals. By their images, and by their impressions upon students, the schools have a great influence upon who opts for what fields and what kinds of young people—of what quality, what interests, what values—go where. It is clear too that they influence the choices by students among employers—whether government or other, and which jurisdictions and agencies of government. By their curricula, their faculties, their teaching, they define the content of each different specialism and the expectations and aspirations of the students in each. These students will of course include the principal operators in government tomorrow and the principal leaders the day after tomorrow.

In most professional fields, governments have accepted, without much question or

---

[12]Chicago, Public Administration Service, pp. 60–61.

[13]*Hidden Hierarchies: The Professions and Government* (New York, Harper & Row, 1966), p. 194. (Author's emphasis.)

knowledge, the academic definition of content and the academic criteria of qualification and merit. Most governments, like other employers, rely heavily upon credentials; possession of the sheepskin from an accredited institution is enough. Accreditation itself is normally based upon a review and approval of a given school's program by a committee of a larger organization composed of, or dominated by, professional educators in the same field. It reflects a consensus among academics as to the minimal curricular and faculty requirements necessary to produce qualified practitioners. In some fields accreditation and high academic standing (grade point average) are more important to governmental employers than professional licenses. In fields for which licensing has been provided in only a few states (or in none)—like social work, city planning, or librarianship—accreditation and grades become almost the sole criteria. Accreditation moreover is sometimes a requirement for licensing. Where government employers have any significant choice among candidates for jobs in the recognized professions, their reliance is placed upon 1. whether they come from accredited schools, 2. their grade point averages, and 3. the recommendations of professors. All three are of course academic determinants.

In the main, governments have yielded to the universities and professional educators the significant influences, the criteria, and the choices about public employment. Few of our larger governmental units give any competitive examinations on substance—that is, knowledge and skill—for candidates in professional fields. They leave it largely to the universities to determine what knowledges and skills are appropriate, and who among the graduating students are deserving of appointment. In a few fields, they also rely upon licensing examinations, themselves controlled by practitioners and educators outside of government. Among the agencies dominated by an elite professional corps, personnel decisions are largely dictated by the corps.

It is interesting that the Congress reaffirmed

in the Veterans' Preference Act of 1944 its long-standing suspicion of formal academic qualifications for civil service jobs:

No minimum educational requirement will be prescribed in any civil service examination except for such scientific, technical, or professional positions the duties of which the Civil Service Commission decides cannot be performed by a person who does not have such education.[14]

The Civil Service Commission (now the Office of Personnel Management) has since excepted virtually all of the established and general professional fields, a great many emergent professions including some that are exclusive to government, and a majority of the natural, life, and social scientists. The omissions from the civil service exceptions are more conspicuous than the exceptions themselves. Attorneys are of course omitted since they are not in the classified service anyway. Officials in administrative fields, such as budgeteers, personnel specialists, purchasing officers, tax administrators, and administrative officers are not excepted. None of the fields normally considered among the humanities at universities is excepted; and among social scientists, the political scientists, public administrators, and historians are conspicuous in not being excepted from the Congressional fiat. Anthropologists, economists, psychologists, and sociologists are all excepted.

The professional suspicion and opposition toward politics and government, suggested earlier, are probably even more vigorous among university professors. Here they are strength-

[14]The wording but not the sense of this provision was subsequently modified. See 80 Stat. 89–554, Sept. 6, 1966, p. 419. For an overview and explanation of the rationale for the exception of particular professions from the prohibition against minimum educational requirements see U.S. Office of Personnel Management, *Qualification Standards for Positions under the General Schedule:* Handbook X-118, (Washington, D.C., Government Printing Office, January 1979).

ened by the creeds of academic freedom and professional autonomy. Apparently, the further one progresses through higher education, the less he or she is enticed by governmental employment; and this must reflect to some extent the influence of university faculties.[15]

. . . We have come full circle. Near the beginning, I discussed the impact of the knowledge explosion upon our society; near the end, I discussed the impact of the universities upon public employment. The latter is a facet of the former. As knowledge has grown and as occupations have been increasingly professionalized, the public services have become more dependent upon the founts of knowledge, the universities. In their own organizations, governments have both reflected and influenced the occupational structure of the society. In so doing they have benefited tremendously through the advancement in the level of knowledge and skill in every field. They may also have

suffered in the degree to which the central governments could control and direct operations in the general interest. For in the process, they have yielded a great deal of influence over *who* will conduct and direct individual programs, and how the content of programs will be defined as well.

For better or worse—or better *and* worse— much of our government is now in the hands of professionals (including scientists). The choice of these professionals, the determination of their skills, and the content of their work are now principally determined, not by general governmental agencies, but by their own professional elites, professional organizations, and the institutions and faculties of higher education. It is unlikely that the trend toward professionalism in or outside of government will soon be reversed. But the educational process through which the professionals are produced and later refreshed (in continuing educational programs) can be restudied and conceivably changed. The need for broadening, for humanizing, and in some fields for lengthening professional education programs may in the long run prove more crucial to governmental response to societal problems than any amount of civil service reform.

[15]On this point, see especially Franklin P. Kilpatrick, Milton C. Cummings, Jr., and M. Kent Jennings, *The Image of the Federal Service* and the accompanying *Source Book* (Washington, D.C., The Brookings Institution, 1964).

CASE STUDY 7

Introduction

On March 24, 1976, President Gerald R. Ford officially announced the start of the National Influenza Immunization Program, the title for what popularly became referred to as the "swine flu program." In both timing and scope this federal program was unprecedented. Fearing a new strain of killer flu comparable with the massive 1918 flu epidemic that swept America, federal officials aimed to inoculate every man, woman, and child in the United States by December 1976—or 210 million people in 9 months!

A $135 million appropriation for the program was quickly rushed through Congress, buttressed by special legislation in the field of liability after the president's announcement. State health departments with special technical assistance from several Health, Education, and Welfare agencies were rapidly prepared to conduct the program. On October 1, 1976, the mass inoculations of Americans began. By December 16, after only 2.5 months, the swine flu program was suspended to assess the statistical evidence of a serious side effect appearing after some flu shots, known as the Guillain-Barré syndrome. Finally the swine flu program was halted entirely in March 1977 by President Jimmy Carter's new HEW secretary, Joseph A. Califano, Jr. As a full-scale operation, the swine flu program did not even last 1 year—indeed it really ran for only 2.5 months—and the killer flu never came!

In the following account, "The Swine Flu Affair," Richard E. Neustadt and Harvey V. Fineberg, two distinguished Harvard University faculty members (Neustadt in the Government Department and Fineberg in Public Health), carefully reconstruct the details of the decision-making processes that went into launching this one-of-a-kind national program. Their case study was originally commissioned by Secretary Califano, who, in his words, requested the study "in search of lessons for the future, not of fault in the past. I asked them to give me as objective and clinical a report as they could write."[1]

The two authors took painstaking care in recounting the factual events of what actually occurred. "In establishing what happened," write Neustadt and Fineberg, "we have sought not less than three and preferably five opinions when there were as many or more persons present. In the case of actions taken by one person we have sought both his account and the impressions of contemporary bystanders, along with written records if available. Throughout we have sought views from informal observers."[2]

What were their central findings? As the two writers stressed in their introduction: "One thing we are convinced the [swine flu] program was not . . . it wasn't party politics; President Ford wanted to protect the public health."[3]

Rather than politics, the authors discovered that the problems involved the decision-making processes that launched the swine flu program in the first place. Advice from the experts in the public health field—much of which was highly technical, beyond the competency of the lay public to evaluate or comprehend—was accepted to a large extent uncritically and without much debate. The public health professionals had incorrectly perceived that the swine flu problem was a national problem and then convinced the president and Congress to undertake emergency actions on a massive scale. Thus, this case study relates quite cogently to the critical issues raised in Mosher's essay involving the role and importance of public professionals in American government.

As you read this selection, keep the following questions in mind:

What should the appropriate relationship be between the politically elected or appointed representatives of government and the professional experts working in government?

How can top political officials deal effectively with highly technical subject matter from the experts and make sound judgments on complex issues when

---

[1]Joseph A. Califano, Jr., in his Introduction to Richard E. Neustadt and Harvey V. Fineberg, *The Swine Flu Affair: Decision-Making on a Slippery Disease* (Washington, D.C.: U.S. Government Printing Office, 1978), p. v.

[2]Neustadt and Fineberg, *The Swine Flu Affair*, p. 2.

[3]Ibid., p. 3.

the "facts" (as in this case) are so uncertain and understood by relatively few experts in the field?

How can the public interest be well served when public policymaking increasingly turns on knowledge about issues that largely is in the purview of a few experts?

RICHARD E. NEUSTADT AND HARVEY V. FINEBERG

The Swine Flu Affair: Decision-Making on a Slippery Disease

The New Flu

The proximate beginning of this story is abrupt. On the East Coast of the United States, January 1976 was very cold. At Fort Dix, New Jersey, training center for Army recruits, new men fresh from civilian life got their first taste of barracks and basics. A draft of several thousand came in after New Year's Day to be instructed by a cadre back from Christmas leave. The fort had been almost emptied; now in the cold it was full again. By mid-January many men began reporting respiratory ailments. A relative handful were hospitalized. One, refusing hospitalization, went on an overnight hike and died.

After a county medical meeting on another subject, the state's chief epidemiologist bet the senior Army doctor that Fort Dix was in the midst of an influenza virus epidemic. To win, the latter sent a sample set of cultures for analysis in the state laboratory. He lost. The lab turned up several cases of flu traceable to the Victoria virus which had been since 1968 the dominant cause of human influenza. But the lab also found other cases of flu caused by a virus it could not identify. With foreboding, Dr. Martin Goldfield, the civilian epidemiologist, sent those cultures to Atlanta, to the Federal government's Center for Disease Control (CDC). A similar

Reprinted from a public document entitled *The Swine Flu Affair*, published by the U.S. Department of Health, Education, and Welfare (Washington, D.C.: U.S. Government Printing Office, 1978) pp. 1–30.

virus, also unidentified, was isolated from the dead man and a culture sent to CDC. In the evening of February 12, the Center's laboratory chief, Dr. Walter Dowdle, reported the result to his superiors—in four cases including the fatality, the unknown was swine flu. At CDC this caused more concern than surprise.

Four things combined to create the concern. First, these four recruits could have been infected through human-to-human transmission. Not since the late 1920's had this form of influenza been reported in as many persons out of touch with pigs. There might have been a number of occasions unreported; no one knew. Second, for a decade after World War I a virus of this sort was believed to have been the chief cause of flu in human beings. Since then it had confined itself to pigs. Were it returning now to humans, none younger than 50 would have built up specific antibodies from previous infection. Third, the Fort Dix virus differed in both its surface proteins, termed "antigens," from the influenza virus then circulating in the human population. This difference, in expert terms an "antigenic shift," would negate any resistance carried over from exposure to the other current viruses. In 1976, it was assumed by leading experts that pandemics follow antigenic shifts as night from day.

And finally, in 1918, a pandemic of the swine flu virus, the most virulent influenza known to modern medicine, had, in a so-called "killer wave," been associated with some 20 million deaths worldwide, 500,000 here. Many were taken by bacterial pneumonia, a complication of influenza now treatable with antibiotics, but an unknown number succumbed to the flu itself. Among the hardest hit then had been able-bodied persons in their twenties and early thirties. Parents of small children died in droves. So did young men in uniform. Virulence cannot as yet be tested in the lab. Could the Fort Dix swine flu be a comparable killer? No one at CDC knew any reason to suppose it was—contrast the 1920's and the circumstances of the one death now—but still. . . .

The absence of surprise reflected expert views at that time about epidemic cycles and about the reappearance of particular types of viruses in people. It was widely thought—on rather scanty evidence—that antigenic shifts were likely about once a decade (interspersed with slighter changes, "drifts," each second or third year). There had been shifts in 1957 and in 1968, both followed by pandemics—Asian flu and Hong Kong flu respectively—and public health officials were expecting another by, say, 1978 or 1979. 1976 was close. The very day the Fort Dix cases were identified at CDC, the *New York Times* carried an Op Ed piece by Dr. Edwin D. Kilbourne, one of the country's most respected influenza specialists, extolling cycles and affirming that pandemics occur every eleven years—another one of which, he warned, was surely coming soon:

> Worldwide epidemics, or pandemics, of influenza have marked the end of every decade since the 1940's—at intervals of exactly eleven years—1946, 1957, 1968. A perhaps simplistic reading of this immediate past tells us that 11 plus 1968 is 1979, and urgently suggests that those concerned with public health had best plan without further delay for an imminent natural disaster.

Also, an influenza virus recycling theory was just then receiving attention, and this suggested swine-type as a likely next strain to appear. The idea was that the flu virus had a restricted antigenic repertoire and a limited number of possible forms, requiring repetition after a time period sufficient for a large new crop of vulnerable people to accumulate. The Asian flu of 1957 was thought to have resembled flu in the pandemic

year of 1889. The Hong Kong flu of 1968 was thought to be like that of 1898. Swine flu, absent for 50 years, fit well enough, no surprise. The theory had been originally proposed by two doctors who wrote in 1973:

> A logical sequel to the data presented and supported here would be the emergence in man of a swine-like virus about 1985–1991. . . . Regardless of one's view as to the origin of recycling of human strains of influenza, the matter of being prepared to produce swine virus vaccine rapidly should receive consideration by epidemiologists. Man has never been able to intervene effectively to prevent morbidity and mortality accompanying the emergence of a major influenza variant, but the opportunity may come soon.

Though some experts were skeptical about the regularity with which previous strains might be expected to reappear, no one doubted that a swine flu virus might well re-emerge in the human population.

On February 12, alerted by preliminary lab reports, Dr. David Sencer, CDC's Director, asked a number of officials from outside his agency to join him there for a full lab report on February 14. The Army responded as did Goldfield from New Jersey. And from two other parts of CDC's parent entity in HEW, the Public Health Service (PHS), Dr. Harry Meyer and Dr. John Seal came as a matter of course. Meyer was Director of the Bureau of Biologics (BoB) in the Food and Drug Administration; Seal was the Deputy Director of the National Institute for Allergy and Infectious Diseases (NIAID) in the National Institutes of Health. (NIAID's director left these relations to Seal.) The BoB was responsible for licensing and testing flu vaccines, the NIAID for federally sponsored flu research. The duties of Meyer and Seal overlapped, but they were accustomed collaborators. Both were accustomed also to work closely with CDC, its labs and its state services.

Among their recent objects of collaboration had been workshops held at intervals since 1971 on how to better the quite dismal record of 1957 and of 1968 in getting vaccine to Americans ahead of a pandemic. This matter was much on Seal's mind and especially on Meyer's. His bureau had been the subject of a Senate inquiry three years before and needed nothing less than the black-marketing and discrimination characteristic of vaccine distribution in 1957.

To this group, enlarged by CDC staff, Dowdle reported his laboratory findings. The question at once became whether four human cases were the first appearance of incipient pandemic or a fluke of some kind, a limited transfer to a few humans of what remained an animal disease which would not thrive in people. All agreed that on the present evidence there was no means of knowing. Surveillance was the task at hand. Since their uncertainty was real, they agreed also that there should be no publicity until there were more data: why raise public concern about what might turn out an isolated incident? Some days later CDC scrapped this agreement on the plea that uninformed press leaks were imminent, and Sencer called a press conference for February 19. He must have hated the thought that an announcement might come from some place other than CDC. However that may be, the press conference got national attention.

In the *New York Times* Harold Schmeck reported, February 20:

The possibility was raised today that the virus that caused the greatest world epidemic of influenza in modern history—the pandemic of 1918–19—may have returned.

This story (on page 1) was headed:

U.S. Calls Flu Alert On Possible Return of Epidemic Virus

The 1918 reference was included in brief notices that night, on CBS and ABC news telecasts. NBC went them one better and showed 1918 still pictures of persons wearing masks. Lacking further information, the media did not follow up the story for a month. But 1918 left a trace in certain minds, some of them TV producers and reporters. From within CDC, we have encountered a good deal of retrospective criticism at press tendencies to "harp" on 1918 prematurely, with no evidence whatsoever about prospective virulence or even spread through 1976. These NBC pictures are cited along with the *New York Times* headline. But the reference was included

in the CDC press briefing and indeed without it what was known about Fort Dix so far was scarcely news at all. What sense to a conference that did not bring it up?

Publicity had no effect upon the effort to establish what the Fort Dix outbreak meant. In Fort Dix itself, where the Army conducted its own investigation shielded from civilians, the Victoria strain proved dominant, at least for the time being. There were plenty of new influenza cases, none was caused by the swine virus. On the other hand, that virus was isolated from a fifth soldier who had been sick in early February, and blood tests confirmed eight more old cases of swine flu, none of them fatal. Moreover, a sampling of antibody levels among recruits suggested that as many as 500 had been infected by swine flu. This implied human transmission on a scale that could not reasonably be viewed lightly. Around Fort Dix, however, in the civilian population—which was Goldfield's territory for investigation—analysis of every case of flu reported, by a medical community on the alert, showed only Victoria. Elsewhere in New Jersey Goldfield's inquiries turned up no swine flu. The Army's inquiries turned up none at camps other than Fort Dix. The NIAID network of university researchers and the state epidemiologists in touch with CDC reported none untraceable to pigs. The World Health Organization, pressed by CDC, could learn of none abroad. One death, thirteen sick men and up to 500 recruits who evidently had caught and resisted the disease, all in one Army camp, were the only established instances of human-to-human swine flu found around the world as February turned into March, the last month of flu season in the Northern Hemisphere.

On March 10 the group that had met February 14 reassembled at CDC and under Sencer's chairmanship reviewed their findings with the Advisory Committee on Immunization Practices (ACIP). That committee was in form a set of outside experts appointed by the Surgeon General, independently advising CDC; in fact it was almost a part of CDC, nominated, chaired and staffed at Sencer's discretion. BoB deadlines now forced his pace. One ACIP function was to make vaccine recommendations for the next flu season available to manufacturers. The annual questions were: vaccine against what viruses, aimed at which population groups? For 1976 these questions had already been reviewed in a January ACIP meeting. The committee had recommended Victoria vaccine for the "high-risk groups" as then defined, some 40 million people over 65 in age or with certain chronic diseases. By March 10, the four active manufacturers had produced in bulk form about 20 million doses of Victoria vaccine for the civilian market. If Fort Dix meant a change or addition, now was the time to decide. Indeed for a regulatory body like the BoB, responsible for setting standards and for quality control, March was already late. Vaccine is grown in eggs; a vaccine against swine flu would require new supplies replacing those just used for Victoria vaccine. Then immunization trials would be needed if there were a new vaccine, also extensive testing. And what about the vaccine now in bulk? Whatever surveillance had turned up by now would have to suffice for some sort of decision.

Sencer Decides

Sencer was an able, wily autocrat with a devoted staff. The CDC was wholly his. He knew everything about it, everybody in it, and took care to put his own imprint on policy. Swine flu was no exception.

He spent March 9 preparing for the ACIP meeting in informal get-togethers with his laboratory people and some other senior aides. Dowdle recalled when we interviewed him:

It was clear we could not say the virus would spread. But it was clear that there had been human-to-human spread at Fort Dix. It was also clear that there was not any immunity in the population to this virus, not if you were under 50 (or maybe 62). Usual "high risk" categories did not apply. Most people were at risk, especially young adults. An epidemic spreading into a pandemic had to be anticipated *as a possibility.*

. . . Army recruits were a unique population group . . . maybe they would be the only ones affected. But the current disappearance of the virus did not prove that. Flu could do strange things. Six weeks was a short time.

We had to report our fundamental belief that a pandemic was indeed a possibility.

This was the scientist speaking. What could not be disproved must be allowed for. Dowdle also recalls his frustration with the lack of data and his sadness at the thought of "changing all those lives," disrupting CDC by action on so little information. Influenza was a slippery phenomenon. Not much was known about pandemic spread. Aside from the three years of 1918, 1957, 1968, the past was mostly conjecture. And recorded spread in those years varied quite enough to buttress contradictory arguments about what now was happening. Since February, swine flu might have sunk back into pigs. Or was it spreading in humans subclinically, "seeding itself" to erupt explosively next flu season? Nothing quite like Fort Dix and the lack of spread beyond it had been seen before. One could guess but not know. And even among specialists, guesses diverged. Dowdle reportedly was cool to claims that a swine virus readily dominated by Victoria at Fort Dix would shortly arise and sweep around the world. In the circumstances he was not much afraid of subclinical spread. But others were. Kilbourne, for one, who would be with them the next day.

In the then hierarchy of virologists, as several tell us now, Dowdle was the Coming Man but Kilbourne an Old Great, while Sencer was a well-informed bystander. Of the few generally acknowledged "Greats" in Kilbourne's class, none was a current member of the ACIP and he himself would be there out of interest, not entitlement (he had just been appointed for a term not yet begun). His presence was to count. It counted more as others recall it than as he does.

Save for some epidemiologists, whose eyes shine even yet with remembered excitement, many CDC-ers were at least as cool as Dowdle on March 9. More precisely they remember being at once apprehensive and resigned. As one of those who sat through Sencer's staff sessions explained to us:

There was nothing in this for CDC except trouble. Here we were at the end of one flu season with time to try to do something before the next flu season. The obvious thing to do was immunize everybody. But if we tried to do that, guide it, help it along, we might have to interrupt a hell of a lot of work on other diseases . . . work here, and in the states, a lot of places.

Then if a pandemic came, lots of people—maybe millions—would be angry . . . because they couldn't get shots when they wanted. . . . Or they got sick of something else that they mistook for flu and thought our shots weren't working. Most people in this country (including half the doctors) call all kinds of things flu that aren't. As for "another 1918," I didn't expect that, but who could be sure? . . . It would wreck us.

Yet, on the other hand, if there weren't a pandemic we'd be charged with wasting public money . . . crying wolf . . . causing all that inconvenience for nothing . . . and not only the people who got shots . . . the people who administered the shots . . . our friends out in the states . . . what would they think of us? It was a no-win situation . . . we saw that . . . talked about it. . . .

But institutional protection could not override the ethic of preventive medicine. Disease prevention was the professional commitment of them all, including those who cared for CDC the most. They felt themselves trapped. With a pandemic possible and time to do something about it, and lacking the time to disprove it, then *something* would have to be done. So ran the logic of what Sencer heard from his staff.

The next day, at the March 10 ACIP meeting, staff spelled out the situation (couched of course in Dowdle's terms, not those of institutional protection). It was an open meeting, though with minimal press attendance. After hours of discussion a consensus emerged:

First, the possibility of pandemic existed. None thought it negligible. Kilbourne thought it very likely. Most seem to have thought privately of likelihoods within a range from two to twenty percent; each was prepared to bet, however, with nobody but himself. These probabilities, after all, were based on personal judgment, not scientific fact. They voice them to us now, they did not argue them then.

Second, while severity could not be estimated, one death in a dozen was worrisome. Besides, somewhere in everybody's mind lurked 1918. No one thought there literally could be a repetition; antibiotics would hold down the death rate. Deaths aside, few thought the virus would be so severe. When last seen in the '20's it was mild. But nobody could bring himself to argue that such mildness was assured. It wasn't.

Third, traditional definition of high-risk groups did not apply. People under 50 had no natural protection, and young adults had suffered unusually high mortality in the 1918 pandemic. This argued for producing enough vaccine to inoculate them all before the next flu season. All meant all, or as many as possible, because one could not count on "herd" immunity to stifle epidemic spread. In influenza nothing on this scale had ever been attempted. But not since 1957 had the timing of discovery allowed for it. And then we did not have vaccines as safe or as effective as the ones developed since. Nor did we have the guns for swift injection. With a decision now the manufacturers could buy their eggs and make the vaccine fast enough so that inoculations could begin in summer, when the chance of flu was slightest and the risk of panic least. Meanwhile plans could be made for mass immunization.

Predisposition buttressed that consensus. It reflected the agendas several ACIP members drew from other aspects of their working lives. Kilbourne, for one, not only championed his theories, but was keen to make the country see the virtues of preventive medicine. Swine flu seemed to him a splendid opportunity. Others also saw the chance to demonstrate the value of public health practice. Dr. Reuel Stallones, Dean of the Public Health School at the University of Texas, recalled for us:

This was an opportunity to try to pay something back to society for the good life I've had as a public health doctor. Society has done a lot for me—this is sheer do-goodism. It was also an opportunity to strike a blow for epidemiology in the interest of humanity. The rewards have gone overwhelmingly to molecular biology which doesn't do much for humanity. Epidemiology ranks low in the hierarchy—in the pecking order, the rewards system. Yet it holds the key to reducing lots of human suffering.

Consensus thus supported might have dissolved over one issue which at this meeting was never joined: should one move automatically from ordering the vaccine and preparing for its use to using it? If so, what evidence about the spread of the disease would make one stop and stockpile it instead? If not, what evidence would make one move from stockpiling into mass immunization?

Dr. Russell Alexander of the Public Health School at the University of Washington was the principal proponent of a pause for further evidence. His concern was more medical than managerial. As he put it to us in retrospect:

My general view is that you should be conservative about putting foreign material into the human body. That's always true . . . especially when you are talking about 200 million bodies. The need should be estimated conservatively. If you don't need to give it, don't.

He also had a glimmering of one aspect of management, public understanding and acceptance. He told us:

If you have spread combined with high surveillance then the surrounding communities will really go to work and the public will really cooperate each time flu is reported in a new place. If it hit Denver you could immunize Seattle, because everybody would move fast.

Alexander did not make a speech. He put in questions or made comments when he could. An unimpassioned man, he was so mild that other members we have seen recall but vaguely something about "stockpiling." He himself makes light of it. Known as a voice of caution in past meetings, he was easy to discount on this occasion. But Schmeck, the *New York Times* man, there as an observer, stressed to us:

Alexander seemed serious about stockpiling. He wanted to know "at what point do we stop going on with our preparations to immunize everybody and turn to stockpiling instead— what point in terms both of progress of our preparations and progress of the disease." He asked this seriously. It was not answered.

If so, the term "stockpiling" trivializes, even distorts Alexander's suggestion, which embraced not alone the issue of a waiting game, but also the criteria for playing it. And failure to pursue them both, *especially* criteria, appears by hindsight sad, an opportunity lost. From this we draw a lesson for next time.

That they were not pursued in the ACIP meeting was Sencer's choice from the chair. It could not have escaped him that there was some nascent sentiment for separating manufacture from inoculation. Goldfield and a colleague, in particular, spoke for it from their vantage point, New Jersey, and were evidently bursting to elaborate, if asked. Sencer seems to have wanted none of that. The day before he had discussed stockpiling with his staff, and they had ended by dismissing it. Inoculation took two weeks to bring immunity. Infection brings on the disease within a few days. In two weeks flu could spread throughout a city. Add air travel and how prevent its spreading through the country unless everyone were immunized beforehand? Besides there was the issue of response-time by state clinics, private doctors, volunteers, and citizens at large, the objects of it all. Even a short lag could be too long. "Jet-spread" and slow response combined to make a stockpile option moot. So staff had said.

Staff aside, Seal tells us he and Meyer talked with Sencer at some point. One of them, Seal no longer remembers which, observed for Sencer's benefit (one career executive to another):

Suppose there is a pandemic accompanied by deaths. Then it comes out: "They had the opportunity to save life; they made the vaccine, they put it in the refrigerator. . . ." That translates to "they did nothing." And worse "they didn't even recommend an immunization campaign to the Secretary."

When it came to the ACIP, whose first task was to ponder manufacture, Sencer did not insist on drawing Alexander out, much less encourage Goldfield, and the March 10 meeting ended with the issue of what happened after manufacture blurred. The minutes of the meeting state: "It was, therefore, agreed that the production of vaccine must proceed and that a plan for vaccine administration be developed."

Everybody present we have talked to says the same. That is as far as they got. Sencer himself called it for us:

> I went into the [ACIP] meeting with an open mind . . . We met all morning . . . By 2:00 or 2:30 a consensus had emerged . . . Stallones summed it up the best: *First,* there was evidence of a new strain with man-to-man transmission. *Second,* always before when a new strain was found there was a subsequent pandemic. And *third,* for the first time, there was both the knowledge and the time to provide for mass immunization. So, he said, "if we believe in preventive medicine we have no choice." I asked the committee to sleep on it and let us phone them the next day to make sure they still felt the same way, which we did—and they did.

Sencer and his staff turned promptly to the practical effects of the consensus. This had never been considered ACIP business. Governmental consultation, legislation, budgeting, contracting and the like were not its charge. Implementation was Sencer's business. One ACIP member who stayed over for a day and called upon some senior CDC officials, commented to us: "I found them all busy with planning and mostly unable to talk to me."

Sencer himself went to work with one aide and wrote a nine-page paper, known to all and sundry as his "action-memorandum." In the process, he recalls, he made up his own mind precisely what the Federal government should do. His paper was designed at once to say it and to sell it.

In form this memorandum was addressed to David Mathews, Secretary of HEW, from Dr. Theodore Cooper, the Assistant Secretary for Health, Sencer's boss. In fact it was to go on up from Mathews to the Office of Management and Budget (OMB), to the Domestic Council, to the White House, to President Ford, as *the* decision paper in the case. It was written for that purpose and it served so. Thus it has a special place in our decision-making story. . . .

Sencer began his memo with "Facts":

1. In February 1976 a new strain of influenza virus. . . .

2. The virus is antigenically related to the [one] implicated as the cause of the 1918–19 pandemic which killed 450,000 people—more than 400 of every 100,000 Americans.
3. The entire U.S. population under the age of 50 is probably susceptible to this new strain.

   . . .

6. Severe epidemics or pandemics of influenza recur at approximately 10 year intervals. . . . In 1968–69. . . .
7. A vaccine . . . can be developed before the next flu season; however, the production of large quantities would require extraordinary efforts by drug manufacturers.

CDC officials present and past, Sencer included, have complained to us about the overemphasis on 1918 at the Secretary's level and the White House. Here is where it began.

Sencer turned next to "Assumptions":

1. Although there has been only one outbreak . . . [there is] a strong possibility that this country will experience widespread [swine] influenza in 1976–77. . . . major antigenic shift . . . population almost universally under 50 is susceptible . . . ingredients for a pandemic.
2. . . . Routine actions would have to be supplemented.
3. The situation is one of "go or no go." . . . there is barely enough time. . . . A decision must be made now.
4. There is no medical epidemiologic basis for excluding any part of the population . . . *i.e.,* everyone can catch it and don't count on "herd effect." . . . it is assumed . . . socially and politically unacceptable to *plan* for less than 100 percent coverage. Therefore . . . any recommendation for action must be directed toward the goal of immunizing 213 million people in three months. . . .

Sencer still is seething about Ford and Cooper who were soon to make exaggerated pledges of vaccine for everybody. But the drafters of their statements followed his lead.

The Sencer memorandum then got down to recommendations, offering four options of a common sort in government, three framed to be rejected by the reader, with the fourth the one desired by the writer. First was "do nothing," followed by a set of "pros" and "cons." Among the cons:

- The Administration can tolerate unnecessary health expenditures better than unnecessary death and illness.
- In all likelihood Congress will act on its own initiative.

Second was "minimum response." This must have had some staff support in CDC. It proposed making vaccine for all, the government committed to buy part, whether used or not (for Federal beneficiaries in Medicare, Medicaid, Veterans Administration and Department of Defense), the other part available commercially, and everyone exhorted to get shots through normal channels. This was relatively cheap and also easy in administrative terms, nothing unprecedented about it (except numbers of doses and dollars). But among the "cons":

- There is little assurance that vaccine manufacturers will undertake the . . . massive production effort . . . required. . . .
- . . . the poor, the near poor and the aging usually get left out. . . .
- Probably only about half the population would be immunized.

Third was a "government program," federal and state, without private physicians, and fourth was a "combined approach" which added a role for the private sector.

The fourth option was recommended. It envisaged Federal purchase of vaccine for everybody, production by the private manufacturers, field trials through NIAID, licensing by BoB, planning through the states, immunization through a mix of public-private services and surveillance through CDC. The estimated cost was $134 million, $100 million for vaccine, the rest for operations and surveillance or research. Administratively, as Sencer warned, this was a leap

into the dark, "no precedents, nor mechanisms in place," and a heroic response to a dire possibility.

Sencer, in so recommending, may have played the hero in his own mind; if so he was but the first who did. Mathews, Cooper and Ford, among others, would follow.

In retrospect, this action-memorandum reads as though it were deliberately designed to force a favorable response from a beset Administration that could not afford to turn it down and then to have it leak. The memorandum certainly had that effect, but CDC associates doubt Sencer was deliberate. They think him "a physician with a conscience." They think he simply meant to make the strongest case he could.

However that may be, Sencer rolled the felt need to do "something" into one decision: manufacture, planning, immunizing and surveillance all together, and tied the whole to Meyer's deadline for the manufacturers, those egg supplies. On their account the deadline was two weeks away, "go or no go."

Cooper Endorses

Sencer's paper was completed March 13 and he took it to Washington. On Monday morning, March 15, he met Secretary Mathews in an emergency session. This had been arranged by Cooper's deputy, Dr. James Dickson, who attended and brought Meyer. Cooper was in Cairo, keeping a long-planned engagement, but Dickson had his proxy; Cooper and Sencer had talked on the phone the week before (and Cooper had arranged to be reached, if wanted, through White House facilities).

Mathews had been in office only since the previous August. A gracious man and graceful, he had left the Presidency of the University of Alabama where he had deep roots (and to which he would return) for a Department where he was almost unknown. Seven months had scarcely changed that; he remained but a name to most of Cooper's people. Moreover they were unaware that by his own account to us he had brought with him a deep feeling for preventive medicine. He thinks that he and they were philosophically in tune. From what they tell us most of them would find the thought surprising.

Before seeing Sencer, the Secretary held his daily staff meeting. Dickson filled in for Cooper. Mathews' custom was to go around the circle of his operating chiefs and principal staff officers. When Dickson's turn came he described the swine flu problem much as Sencer's paper had done: "strong possibility." The meeting dissolved then and there in stories of 1918. As one participant explained to us, "We understood it might not happen . . . but lots of us had tales to tell about what it might be like if it did. . . ."

The meeting with Sencer followed. Sencer pushed Mathews hard. He did not rely on his paper (who does?), he enlarged upon it. He had been bracing for this meeting and apparently worried about it. In PHS, Mathews was often called "the phantom," all too readily dismissed as uninformed, uninterested, and worse, uninfluential at such crucial places as the OMB. Sencer was in budgetary trouble and he had been for some years. President Nixon's New Federalists—still more James Lynn, Ford's Budget Director—liked discretionary funds for states and maximum reliance upon private medicine. CDC believed in limiting discretion to assure results. Also it drew sustenance from categorical grants and wanted more of them. Under the Republicans both OMB and planning staffs at PHS had sought to hold back new departures and to trim the old. Revenue-sharing with the states plus Medicare and Medicaid, *not* project grants through CDC, had seemed to them the way to go.

Sencer's memorandum is expressive of his worries:

> Given this situation can we afford the administrative and programmatic inflexibility that would result from normal considerations about duplicative costs, third party reimbursements and Federal-State or public-private relationships and responsibilities? The magnitude of the challenge suggests that the Department must either be willing to take extraordinary steps or be willing to accept an approach to the problem that cannot succeed.

From what others tell us, Sencer pressed Mathews harder than he need have done. He evidently underestimated either the sheer force of his own message unadorned, or Mathews, or perhaps both. Dickson remembers:

> I presented the issue to Mathews. . . . He said to me, "What's the probability?" I said, "Unknown." From the look on Mathews' face when I said that, you could take it for granted that this decision was going to be made.

Mathews bears him out, commenting to us:

> The moment I heard Sencer and Dickson, I *knew* the "political system" would *have* to offer some response. No way out, unless they were far out from the center of scientific consensus (a small band of people in influenza). They weren't—although some of those people waffled later. So it was inevitable. . . .
>
> As for the *possibility* of another 1918 . . . one had to assume the *probability* greater than zero. If they say "unknown" that's the least they can mean. Well, that's enough for action if you know in time. You can't face the electorate later, if it eventuates, and say well, the probability was so low we decided not to try, just two or five percent, you know, so why spend the money. The "political system" should, perhaps, but *won't* react that way. . . . So again, it's inevitable.

Moreover, Mathews recalls favoring the substance, risk aside. Sencer, in his view, would have been wrong had he conceived Administration preferences for state and private medicine as tantamount to lack of faith in immunization programs. These Mathews remembers liking. He recalls thinking the addition of a flu program desirable even had the risk seemed far away.

Dickson recalls something more in Mathews' reaction:

> . . . politically impossible to say no, but more, it's what "unknown" conveyed to [Mathews] about the risk in human terms . . . lives. . . . It didn't seem to him remote at all.

Meyer, listening, watching, took relatively little part until late. This was not shyness, just prudence. He recalls some discomfort at Sencer's "hard sell" but never having met Mathews before, he was unsure of the ground-rules. As he put it to us:

> I felt uncomfortable about the firmness, absoluteness with which Sencer put the issue and the decision to the Secretary. Yet being a stranger to the Secretary I was hesitant about having rows with Sencer over tone.

Meyer remembers making two main points: The first was that with the uncertainty of a pandemic and likely reactions if none appeared, "everybody should be brought into the act. . . ." The second, in response to Mathews' inquiry, concerned safe manufacture of enough vaccine up to the proper standard: "a hell of a job" but it could be done.

The meeting ended on that note.

Then, or sometime after, Mathews heard of a new book, just out coincidentally, *Epidemic and Peace, 1918* by Alfred Crosby. Mathews promptly ordered copies and sent them to associates in HEW, the Budget and the White House. He also gave one to Ford.

Late in the morning of March 15, Mathews wrote a note to Lynn, the Director of the Budget:

> There is evidence there will be a major flu epidemic this coming fall. The indication is that we will see a return of the 1918 flu virus that is the most virulent form of flu. In 1918 a half million people died. The projections are that this virus will kill one million Americans in 1976.
>
> To have adequate protection, industry would have to be advised now in order to have time to prepare the some 200 million doses of vaccine required for mass inoculation. The decision will have to be made in the next week or so. We will have a recommendation on this matter since a supplemental appropriation will be required.

Note the escalation since the ACIP meeting five days earlier. There, except for the expectant Kilbourne, members tell us they had in their heads such likelihoods of epidemic spread as two or 20 percent, which translate into odds of 49:1 or 4:1 *against.* Nobody there explicitly equated spread with the severity of 1918. Kilbourne expected something relatively mild. Others may have thought the single figure in their mind applied quite separately to spread and to severity. A two percent chance of a two percent chance is exceedingly long odds. Sencer's memorandum then converts these (mostly unacknowledged) odds into "strong possibility" of a pandemic "antigenically related" to 1918; writing about spread he hints at severity, but never anywhere commits himself. Now Mathews, after their Monday meeting, equates spread with severity, converts the possible into the certain, "will," and with a doubled population he projects twice the casualties of fifty years ago. Had Sencer's case so moved him? Had he simply not thought it through? Or was he impressing his addressee, the Budget Director? Perhaps some of each.

Lynn already had heard something of this. So had his deputy, Paul O'Neill, the bright young man of OMB in Lyndon Johnson's time (beginning as a health programs examiner) who since had had a meteoric rise. O'Neill consulted with his colleague in the White House "deputies club," James Cavanaugh, soon to become deputy to Richard Cheney, the chief of staff.

Cavanaugh was then still Deputy Director of the Domestic Council, handling "operations" (which meant processing the day-to-day particulars). He formerly had been the health man on the Council's staff and liked to keep his hand in. His successor, Spencer Johnson, was brand new. A notable survivor, Cavanaugh had come to HEW in John Gardner's time, continued as a staffer under Robert Finch, been briefly Acting Assistant Secretary for Health and then had been "loaned" by Elliot Richardson to John Ehrlichman when the Domestic Council was first formed. There, remarkably, Cavanaugh remained and even flourished under Ford, while the Council's Director, James Cannon, Vice President Rockefeller's choice, dealt with policy issues in the longer run.

Cavanaugh already had the ball, more or less, Cooper having warned him before leaving town. Dickson sent the Sencer memorandum over and

Cavanaugh checked it out. The man with whom he chose to check was an old boss, Dr. Charles Edwards, Cooper's predecessor, now out of government. Edwards, hearing Cavanaugh's account, said, as the latter tells us, that from what he'd heard he'd go with Sencer, "the only possible course." Cooper, returning March 21, emphatically agreed. For Cavanaugh this sufficed. Johnson had inherited a duty to spy out the second and third echelons in HEW, although his acquaintance barely extended to Rockville, much less Atlanta. Cavanaugh saw no need to use him.

O'Neill, meanwhile, who had the final action since new money was involved, heard grumbling from his health examiners. Victor Zafra, the division chief, had read the *New York Times* of February 20 and had been waiting since for CDC to come in crying doom. He and his assistants deeply suspected a cooked-up job. Their relations with technicians inside PHS, however, were too strained or distant to give them a grip on anything like Alexander's worry (not at least in the short time available). So they wrapped their suspicions, instead, in classic budgetary guise, questioning the estimates. To quote from their internal memorandum:

PHS did not consider the possibility of reprogramming funds . . . we are not convinced that the $134 million estimate is a hard figure. . . . We think the figure could be trimmed down considerably using alternative assumptions and divisions of responsibility among the Federal and State governments and the private sector.

Tactically this could not help but fail by light of Sencer's urgency. O'Neill and Lynn saw that at once and although they too were suspicious—having Sencer in their sights—forebore to press the point. They did ask whether a new authorization was required to support appropriations; the examiners, along with Cooper's aides, said no (perhaps too flat an answer but accepted). Objections become harder still if nothing is needed but money.

Cavanaugh recalls pursuing other subjects, among them the idea of going for vaccine production right away while holding off a bit on

choosing among options for its distribution. He spoke with "somebody at HEW" and was told no: "jet spread." He did not argue. The thought occurred to others besides him. At some point in the week before decision, as he told us:

There was a discussion between the President and the Vice President, after some meeting or other, in which Rockefeller said maybe one should go over to the Pentagon and get hold of a logistics officer and figure out how to do inoculations [throughout the country] in two to four weeks, thus beating "jet spread." Those were the time limits we'd been given and we also had been told they were too *tight* for manageable mass-immunization. Rockefeller's attitude was "HEW just doesn't know how, but I'll bet the military do." The thought wasn't followed up.

In Ford's Administration, few of Rockefeller's were.

If Cavanaugh was serious about distinguishing immunization from production he did not press the point. The others around Ford whom we have seen heard nothing of it, did not think of it themselves, and doubt they would have liked it had they thought about it. O'Neill remarked to us:

As HEW presented the issue the time factor was key, not only to production—egg supplies—but to protection of the population before winter. Everybody by November. That's what Sencer was saying. So why decide twice? Commit now and be done with it. There isn't time at the White House to create *extra* decisions for the man to make. He's got plenty as it is.

Besides, Sencer was ready to press *his* case. If we held off on part of it how would the President look: Pennypincher? Trading lives for bucks? Indecisive? Can't make up his mind?

Besides the case was not now simply Sencer's. Cooper, returning, had made it his own. And Cooper was trusted in quarters where Sencer was suspect ("manipulative"), not least in the Domestic Council and the White House.

Cooper very often, as his aides report, mistrusted Sencer too. Sencer was 800 miles away and played his own game and had wherewithal to do it. This is a formula to drive a strong Assistant Secretary to distraction. Cooper certainly had strength and we gather was often distracted. A mercurial man, he was sometimes very angry. Yet here he showed himself an instant convert to Sencer's cause.

How did it come about that those two were together on this matter at this moment? The question is intriguing and important; the answer is elusive; we may not have fathomed its depths. But what we find is clear. First, Cooper respected Sencer's professional judgment, the more so on an issue outside his own specialty (he was trained as a cardiac surgeon). Second, Cooper had a personal agenda into which Sencer's proposals fit. As leader and trustee of Federal services for health (which is, we think, how Cooper saw himself) he had been seeking ways to raise the consciousness of private citizens—of voluntary agencies, of parents, of physicians—to *prevention* of diseases through immunization and other means. Now there were vaccines for many infectious diseases; later, perhaps, for neurological disorders, conceivably even cancers. An associate commented to us:

> Cooper had a strong sense of the importance of volunteer organizations and our dependence on them and the need to change and perfect them for the tasks ahead. . . . He wanted to move immediately onto a new footing, steadily supported by the voluntary groups and by parents all across the country—not subject to unpredictable shifts of government priorities. He was keen to increase comprehension of preventive medicine and support for it out there in the private sector where it could be shielded from those governmental ups and downs . . . those Nixon economy drives. . . .

Third, Cooper's father, a physician, had told him ghastly tales about 1918. He and Dickson, who also had a father with grim stories on the subject, traded recollections back and forth. The "worst case" possibility was vivid in the mind of the Assistant Secretary for Health.

Dickson mentioned to us:

> Cooper really feared 1918. Something happened in Hershey, Pennsylvania, that stuck in Cooper's mind. They'd had to call out the troops to bury people *en masse*—they died so fast.

So Cooper, from the time Sencer first talked to him in February, was prepared to take an activist approach, provided it had backing from the "scientific community," that is to say from the relevant experts. He wanted to be sure that anything from CDC was first reviewed by the ACIP, and had support from NIAID, BoB and *their* advisers. Not leaving everything to others, Cooper himself talked to Dr. Albert Sabin. The latter's live vaccine for polio (superseding in this country Dr. Jonas Salk's killed-virus vaccine) had been used in the last nationwide mass immunization, 100 million in two seasons, "half the number in twice the time" that Sencer was now seeking. Sabin was encouraging, as Cooper knew when Sencer phoned him to report affirmatively on the ACIP meeting. So Cooper left for Cairo confident he could support what Sencer came up with. When he returned he did.

Meanwhile, his colleagues had gone to the President.

Ford Announces

President Ford first heard of HEW's request for supplemental funds and all these entailed the afternoon of Monday, March 15, when Lynn, O'-Neill and Cavanaugh met with him on another project. Three days later Ford heard somewhat more from Mathews and agreed to have a full review the following week.

It was a busy time for all concerned, not least for Ford. Swine flu was by no means the biggest item on his agenda. Among other things, presidential primaries were underway. Ford narrowly defeated Ronald Reagan in New Hampshire and had picked up strength in the next four primaries, especially the March 9 battle in Florida, where Reagan had hoped for an upset.

On the same day, Ford had improved his position by telling Cheney to get rid of their lackluster campaign manager, Bo Callaway. But Ford's confidence was to be shaken by Reagan's surprise victory in North Carolina on Tuesday, March 23.

The day before the North Carolina primary, Lynn and O'Neill with Mathews, Cooper, Cheney, Cannon, Cavanaugh and Johnson met the President to review HEW's recommendation. From Lynn he got a packet in advance, including as was customary a summary paper with "talking points," questions for Mathews and Cooper. This was backed by Sencer's action-memorandum. In between was an OMB attachment labeled "Uncertainties Surrounding a Federal Mass Swine Influenza Immunization Program." Into this Lynn's aides had poured the hardest questions they could think of (or extract from other sources) on short notice. It was not a very arresting list. . . . Cooper made short work of it. Someone on Mathews' staff or Cooper's had prepared a swine flu flip chart. Ford made short work of that. As one of his auditors says he "blew up . . . waved it away," sensibly preferring discussion.

By all accounts the discussion ranged widely, covering at once the arguments for action, and a long list of drawbacks: The pandemic might not come and then the President would seem a spendthrift and alarmist, or a bumbler. If it came, the states and private sector might be overwhelmed, or seem so—"however well they did, it wouldn't be enough"—and he'd be blamed, again a bumbler. Or vaccine might not be ready soon enough. Uncertainty about the egg supply meant, ultimately, roosters. The Secretary of Agriculture had been reassuring: "The roosters of America are ready to do their duty. . . ." Still, yield per egg of vaccine might be less than was wanted. And so forth. As one participant recalls:

I told the President that this was a no-win position politically. There was no good to come of it as far as the election was concerned . . . if there were no pandemic a lot of people would have sore arms in October. If there were a pandemic, no matter how much we'd done it wouldn't be enough and he'd be roundly criticized.

Others tell us they said much the same, but one of them remembers thinking (and, he hopes, saying):

There is no way to go back on Sencer's memo. If we tried to do that, it would leak. That memo's a gun to our head.

Among the things Ford was *not* warned about were six: trouble with serious side effects, with children's dosages, with liability insurance, with expert opinion, with PHS public relations, and with his own credibility. On the contrary, the vaccine was presumed both safe and efficacious; insurance was not known to be a problem; experts were pronounced on board; Cooper and Sencer could cope with the press. And while the venture's cost to Ford in public terms was aired nobody raised the opposite, the burden to the program of *his* sponsorship amidst a problematic fight for the Republican nomination.

These six are the drawbacks that in fact would give the effort the bad name it has today among attentive publics. Some of them may not have been foreseeable, as most of Ford's aides tell us now. For what it may be worth, we tend to disagree. At least it can be said that signs of each were somewhere to be seen had staffers penetrated far enough. But with agendas of their own, or sitting on the sidelines, or beset by other work, they didn't.

Hearing what he heard, Ford saw the issue simply. Politics had no part in it. As he recalled when we saw him:

I think you ought to gamble on the side of caution. I would always rather be ahead of the curve than behind it. I had a lot of confidence in Ted Cooper and Dave Mathews. They had kept me informed from the time this was discovered. Now Ted Cooper was advocating an early start on immunization, as fast as we could go, especially in children and old people. So that was what we ought to do, unless there were some major technical objection.

This agrees with what others remember. Some may have been pleased that what was right to do was also politic, one-upping Reagan: Here would be the *President,* decisive for the public good. Others though were worried by the public risks Ford ran in longer terms. Mathews recalled for us:

> I told him that I knew it was a no-win situation for him, and that it wasn't necessary for him to make the announcement—I said I would do it if he wished me to.

Two of Ford's aides had talked of this, but Mathews was a weak reed in their eyes and anyway, "we thought he'd punted." Besides the President seemed quite content, some even thought him eager, to announce a swine flu program as his own and urge public support of it. He evidently thought then, and still does, that this was his plain duty: "If you want to get 216 million people immunized this requires the imprimatur of the White House." Like Mathews, Cooper, Sencer, Ford may also have had a refreshing sense of doing a direct, uncomplicated, decently heroic deed.

So Matthews' offer was not pursued. Cooper tells us that *he* would have been glad, even then, to make the announcement himself. The same can be said of Sencer, who wishes they had simply let him walk the supplemental up to the House Appropriations Committee and announce it there. Nothing like that was suggested to Ford by Cooper or anyone else.

The meeting of March 22 did not end with a final decision. Instead the President decided to postpone decision until he had heard the views of experts in the field outside the government, the scientific community personified. O'Neill, who pressed the point, remembered in our interview:

> I really felt strongly that the President should meet a representative group of "scientists" in advance. In private conversations we had found no discernible dissent. . . . The President, of necessity, had to rely very heavily on their scientific judgment. . . . I thought they ought to be willing to commit themselves publicly.

Ford himself seems to have seen still more in this, not only shoring up his credibility but genuinely reaching for advice. Like Mathews before him he had been told that a swine flu pan-

demic, shades of 1918, was "possible," but that the probability remained "unknown." (Cooper refused to put any numbers on it, although once he offered "one to 99.") If those words meant what Ford took them to mean, justifying an unprecedented Federal action, he wanted to be sure the experts felt the same, or know if some did not, and why, and wanted to hear it from them at first hand. Lacking a science adviser (the post was in abeyance then), he asked, as he recalls, that the "best" scientists (along with experts on such things as manufacturing) be brought together with him two days hence. Others recall his asking for "a full spectrum" of scientific views. Either way, he ended this first meeting on that note.

Cavanaugh undertook to assemble the required experts in consultation with Cooper, who consulted in turn with Sencer and Meyer, among others. The list of expert invitees as they contrived it included Kilbourne, Stallones, Dr. Frederick Davenport (a noted virologist), Maurice Hilleman (the respected head of Merck virology labs), and as a crowning touch *both* Salk and Sabin. These two were outside the ACIP circle—which to Cavanaugh assured a spectrum—and were inveterate opponents, personally and professionally. To Cavanaugh this meant that if there were clay feet on Sencer's program, Salk would be the man to find them (Sabin having indicated his support). If they agreed, despite their enmity, this should assure the President the "best support available." They, at any rate, were by far the best *known* to press and public.

Alexander was not on the list. Cavanaugh did not know him. The others, juggling numbers, did not propose him.

No members of Congress were on the list either. Several were due to be informed by phone, but no one proposed to have them in the meeting. The Senate sub-committee chairman most interested, Edward Kennedy, had been lambasting Ford for a retreat on health insurance. No one proposed Kennedy; if not him, nobody. Besides, in retrospect at least, the aides with whom we've spoken are convinced it would have seemed either "political" or "weak" for Ford to have brought in the opposition to share *his* decision.

On March 24, at 3:30 p.m., Ford met his scientists and some others from the states, the AMA and so forth, in the Cabinet Room. He was accompanied by a full complement of aides and HEW officials. Sencer opened with a briefing. The President then turned to Salk who strongly urged mass immunization. In back rows aides sighed with relief. Salk recalled for us:

> When the President asked for comment I made the points that influenza was indeed an important disease, and that the program was an opportunity to educate the public and to justify further research. . . . I don't think I then said but I certainly thought of it as a great opportunity to fill part of the "immunity gap" [between antigens in our environment and populations without antibodies]. We should close the gap whenever we can. Here was a chance. . . . That's what I saw in the program, so of course I supported it.

Sabin followed Salk, then Hilleman, and then the President asked others to chime in. He went around the table seeking views as if he really wanted them, which indeed he did. His respondents saw that and it gratified them but it also puzzled them. Summoned to the White House on short notice, many for the first time, ushered into a large, formal meeting, watching Ford call first on one and then another, most of those we've interviewed took it to be "programmed," a "stage set" and they, "players" . . . "the decision taken" . . . "we were used."

Indeed it had been programmed, oddly enough twice. Stallones recalled for us a call from Sencer, the night before, to tell him when to speak and what the President would ask. The "talking points" Ford got from Johnson were, however, different in detail. Sencer evidently had to vie for programming with the Domestic Council.

At some point in the meeting, Ford asked for a show of hands on whether to proceed. All hands went up. He then asked whether there were any dissents or objections on the other side. A long silence ensued. One of the experts present tells us now:

> Later, I regretted not having spoken up and said, "Mr. President, this may not be proper for me to say, but I believe we should not go

ahead with immunization until we are sure this is a real threat."

However that may be, it wasn't said.

Earnestly in his mind, though *pro forma* to his listeners, the President then observed that he would be glad to talk to anyone who had doubts for his ear alone. He would suspend the meeting and would wait a few moments in the Oval Office. So he did.

While waiting, Ford reviewed with Cavanaugh and others the announcement he would make and when to make it. If done at once, it could but strengthen the impression of a "programmed" meeting (so, in fact, it did). But if delayed, the television news that night and then the morning papers might be filled with separate interviews from leaky scientists. One of Ford's advisers said to us in retrospect:

> . . . the net result might be a speculative spate of new stories and editorials which either scared people or presented them with the impression of an imminent national emergency or made it look as though the President couldn't make up his mind.

Or the press might charge him with deliberate stalling to create a media event. And Ford himself, remembering the moment, added in his talk with us: "If you've got unanimity, you'd better *go* with it. . . ."

So he went. He stopped by the Cabinet Room, collared both Sabin and Salk, waved good-bye to the others, and continued to the Press Room, over the old swimming pool, with its facilities for instant briefing. Then and there with Salk and Sabin flanking him, he announced his decision:

> I have been advised that there is a very real possibility that unless we take effective counteractions, there could be an epidemic of this dangerous disease next fall and winter here in the United States.
>
> Let me state clearly at this time: no one knows exactly how serious this threat could be. Nevertheless, we cannot afford to take a chance with the health of our nation. Accordingly, I am today announcing the following actions.

. . . I am asking the Congress to appropriate $135 million, prior to their April recess, for the production of sufficient vaccine to inoculate every man, woman, and child in the United States.

Sabin spoke up also. Mathews and Cooper then took questions.

The reporters were relatively well-prepared. To Cavanaugh's chagrin a "Fact Sheet" for the briefing had arrived while Ford was still consulting in the Cabinet Room. Simultaneously, a group of White House aides had called the subcommittee chairmen and some others on the Hill to give them advance warning. Word of this began to trickle back. And two days earlier, John Cochran of NBC News had scooped his confreres with a story on the Monday meeting. They had been boning up on swine flu since.

Cochran, who had Alabama ties, got wind on Sunday night that Mathews had a White House meeting the next day, and pulled its purpose out of sources in the Secretary's Office. He then got it confirmed, still more reluctantly, from White House aides who feared it would be played "sensationally" in a way to preempt Ford or scare the public. When NBC ran a straightforward, circumspect account instead, they were relieved.

Cochran and Robert Pierpoint of CBS, among others, thereupon proceeded to the question they, as White House correspondents, had to ask: was this political? Those two went about seeking answers differently. In reportorial terms, one way seems as good as the other. Cochran ranged across the list of Ford's political advisers, covering them thoroughly, we believe, from top to bottom without finding an enthusiast among them. This made a lasting impression. He was ready, thereafter, to assume the politicians felt compelled to do the bidding of the experts. Pierpoint, hearing that his bureau in Atlanta had some input, called and got an earful. A local CBS man had been following the story. With his interest heightened by the coverage on NBC he had called sources inside CDC, professional sources, experts, and been told on *deep* background that, given present evidence, nationwide immunization was unjustified, "a crazy program," or words to that effect. Sencer's advocacy they attributed to obscure pressure on him from above, to some

"political" motive he, for reasons unknown, could not resist. Doctors often use the term "political" for anything that isn't "scientific." To the CBS reporters, and especially to Pierpoint, it could have only one meaning in this case. He was so exercised that he persuaded his superiors to put his findings in the same story as Ford's announcement of March 24. The Cronkite show that night had Pierpoint saying:

Some experts seriously question whether it is logistically possible to inoculate two hundred million Americans by next fall. But beyond that, some doctors and public health officials have told CBS News that they believe that such a massive program is premature and unwise, that there is not enough proof of the need for it, and it won't prevent more common types of flu. But because President Ford and others are endorsing the program, those who oppose it privately are afraid to say so in public.

A day later all three networks aired dissent from open sources, mainly Dr. Sidney Wolfe, a frequent critic of the public health establishment. But the critics Pierpoint mentioned were the ones who left a mark at CBS. For him, for his bureau chief in Washington and for at least some of the Cronkite show's producers, Ford's program was forever suspect: dubious in expert eyes, hence probably political. As one of them put it to us:

It was a rotten program, rotten to the core. We thought it was politically inspired . . . it certainly was awful in technical terms . . . unwarranted . . . unnecessary. That impression came straight from CDC. We didn't get onto Wolfe until later.

It might be that the President himself had been imposed upon. Pierpoint liked Cavanaugh and thought him a good citizen. As both remember, Pierpoint called to tell him (without revealing sources) that there was dissenting medical opinion *in* the government. Cavanaugh was startled, having heard none, nor had Cooper, nor had Mathews. Sencer had reported unanimity from the ACIP, polled on the phone, and so had

Meyer from polling a panel of his own. Sencer's polling may have been a bit contrived; one member told us he remembers hearing that an all-out program was required for congressional approval, another that the White House was insisting on immunization. Cavanaugh knew nothing of such details. Besides there was no going back; the thing was done.

Chapter 7 Review Questions

1. How would you define *professionalism?* Do you agree with Mosher's definition? In what ways might you expand on his meaning of the term? Is there a difference between public-sector and private-sector professionals?

2. Compare this case study with some of the previous cases. What were some examples of public professionals in these cases? Where did they derive their sources of influence? Who were "the professional elites"? How did they exercise influence?

3. What are the differences among staff professionals, line professionals, professional elites, administrative professionals, and emerging professionals? Were any of these types of professionals found in this case?

4. According to Mosher, where are "the key zones of potential tension and conflict in agencies"? Were these tensions exemplified in any of the previous case studies?

5. Do you agree with Mosher's conclusion: "For better or worse—or better *and* worse—much of our government is now in the hands of professionals (including scientists)"? Explain why you agree or disagree. Cite some of the problems that may be associated with professionals' control of government.

6. What mechanisms are essential for ensuring that professionals act wisely and in the public interest? Do you agree with Mosher that higher education offers the best route for securing responsible professional actions? Or are there other checks and safeguards that you consider more powerful tools for maintaining professional accountability to the public interest?

Key Terms

professional associations

professional elites

professional career patterns

professional accreditation

established professions

emergent professions

public service professionals

general professions

supporting line professions

staff professions

administrative professions

key zones of potential tension

Suggestions for Further Reading

The best book on this subject remains Frederick C. Mosher, *Democracy and the Public Service,* Second Edition (New York: Oxford University Press, 1982), for which the first Louis Brownlow Memorial Book Prize was awarded. Also useful as a companion volume is Frederick C. Mosher and Richard J. Stillman II, eds., *Professions in Government* (New Brunswick, N.J.: Transaction Books, 1982).

Now somewhat dated but nevertheless well worth examining are Corinne L. Gilb, *Hidden Hierarchies: The Professions and Government* (New York: Harper & Row, 1966); Howard M. Vollmer and Donald Mills, *Professionalization* (New York: Prentice-Hall, 1966); Burton J. Bledstein, *The Culture of Professionalism* (New York: W. W. Norton, 1976); Guy Benueniste, *The Politics of Expertise,* Second Edition (San Francisco: Boyd & Fraser, 1977); the entire issue of *Daedalus,* 92 (1963), which was devoted to "The Professions," edited by Kenneth S. Lynn; and Brian Chapman, *The Profession of Government* (London: Allen & Unwin, 1959). Students of this topic would do well to study selectively several of the outstanding books on individual professional groups within government such as Samuel P. Huntington, *The Soldier and The State* (Cambridge, Mass.: Harvard University Press, 1957); Morris Janowitz, *The Professional Soldier* (Glencoe, Ill.: Free Press, 1960); John E. Harr, *The Professional Diplomat* (Princeton, N.J.: Princeton University Press, 1969); Richard J. Stillman II, *The Rise of the City Manager* (Albuquerque: University of New Mexico Press, 1974); and Don Price, *The Scientific Estate* (Cambridge, Mass.: Harvard University Press, 1965).

In recent years there have been some fine studies dealing with the relationship between professionals and elected or appointed officials: Hugh Heclo, *A Government of Strangers* (Washington, D.C.: Brookings Institution, 1977); Thomas P. Murphy, Donald E. Nuechterlein, and Ronald Stupak, *Inside Bureaucracy* (Boulder, Colo.: Westview Press, 1978); John W. Macy, Bruce Adams, and J. Jackson Walter, eds., *America's Unelected Government* (Washington, D.C.: National Academy of Public Administration, 1983); Frederick C. Mosher, *A Tale of Two Agencies* (Baton Rouge, La: Louisiana State University Press, 1984); as well as several of the articles that appeared in the bicentennial issue of the *Public Administration Review,* "The American Constitution and the Administrative State" (January/February 1987), edited by Richard J. Stillman II, see particularly, Chester A. Newland, "Public Executives: Imperium Sacerdotium, Collegium? Bicentennial Leadership Challenges"; and James P. Pfiffner, "Political Appointees and Career Executives: The Democracy—Bureaucracy Nexus in the Third Century"; as well as Edie N. Goldenberg, "The Permanent Government in an Era of Retrenchment and Redirection," in Lester M. Salamon and Michael S. Lund, eds., *The Reagan Presidency and the Governing of America* (Washington, D.C.: The Urban Institute Press, 1985).

Despite the apparent power and influence of professional groups over the formulation of public policy, there continues a striking dearth of interest in overall assessments of this topic on the part of students of public administration except for pieces such as Richard Schott, "Public Administration as a Profession: Problems and Prospects," *Public Administration Review,* 36 (May/June 1976), pp. 253–259, and York Wilbern, "Professionalism and the Public Service: Too Little or Too Much?" *Public Administration Review,* 14 (Winter 1954), pp. 15–21.

PART
TWO

THE MULTIPLE FUNCTIONS OF PUBLIC ADMINISTRATORS: THEIR MAJOR ACTIVITIES, RESPONSIBILITIES, AND ROLES

Public administrators must fulfill many functions, often simultaneously. Part Two focuses on several of the important activities performed by public administrators—decision making, administrative communications, management, personnel motivation, budgeting, and implementation. The extent, scope, and capability with which administrators perform these functions vary widely from administrator to administrator, from job to job, and from locale to locale. However, it is safe to say these six functions are considered some of the most critical activities that public administrators must perform if they are to succeed—indeed survive—in their jobs.

As in Part One of this book, in Part Two, chapter by chapter, a single concept is discussed in a reading and its relevance is illustrated in a case study. Although the six major roles of administrators are individually discussed in the following chapters, it should be emphasized that the reality of the administrative processes frequently forces public administrators to assume all these responsibilities at the same time; this makes their work much more complex, less neatly compartmentalized or clear-cut than these individual chapters may suggest. The significant functional concepts discussed in Part Two include:

Chapter 8 *Decision Making: The Concept of Incremental Public Choice* How are decisions made in the public sector and why do public administrators frequently feel as if they are "flying by the seat of their pants"?

Chapter 9 *Administrative Communications: The Concept of Information Networks* How does the flow of communications inside organizations influence the way decisions are made and how well (or how poorly) administrators perform their work?

Chapter 10 *Executive Management: The Concept of the Uniqueness of Public Management* What is a successful management practice for public administrators to adopt? Why is public management significantly different from business management?

Chapter 11 *Personnel Motivation: Theory X and Theory Y* Why is personnel motivation so significant to organizational performance and productivity? How can public administrators most effectively motivate their employees?

Chapter 12 *Public Budgeting: The Concept of Budgeting as Political Compromise and Strategy* What is the nature of the budgetary process in government? Why is a knowledge of budgeting so fundamental to administrative survival?

Chapter 13 *Implementation: The Concept of Optimal Conditions for Effectively Accomplishing Objectives* What is the best way for administrators to get their jobs done effectively, timely, efficiently, correctly, and responsibly?

Decision Making: The Concept of Incremental Public Choice

"A wise policy-maker consequently expects that his policies will achieve only part of what he hopes and at the same time will produce unanticipated consequences he would have preferred to avoid. If he proceeds through a succession *of incremental changes, he avoids serious lasting mistakes. . . ."*

Charles E. Lindblom

READING 8

Introduction

Few concepts are debated in administration more frequently than decision making—how decisions are made; whom they are made by; why they are decided on in the first place; and what impact they have once the choice is made. Gallons of ink have been spilled in academic journals debating whether or not decision making is an art or a science, how best to construct a decision-making model, or how to arrive at the most rational (or optimal) choice. One point emerges from these seemingly endless discussions: the process by which individuals and groups determine a correct course of action from among various alternatives is one of the central functions of an administrator and thus deserves careful consideration by students of public administration.

What is the decision-making function? On one level, we all use decision making daily in confronting a myriad of personal choices, such as when to get up in the morning and what clothes to wear. On the larger and more complicated level of public administration, however, the decisional process involves vital community or societal choices—where to build a new school, when to negotiate an arms limitation treaty, or how to organize a new federal program for poverty relief. The process of choice runs the length and breadth of public administration and involves 4, 40, 400, or 4,000 steps, depending on the complexity and range of variables presented by the problem at hand.

Charles E. Lindblom (1917–   ), a Yale economist and long-time scholar of public policy issues, furnishes an important conceptual understanding of governmental decision making in his essay, "The Science of 'Muddling Through.'" Lindblom, unlike most economists, has seriously thought about the relationships between economics and politics for many years, an interest evident in his earliest writings with Robert A. Dahl in *Politics, Economics and Welfare* (1953), as well as in his more recent book, *Politics and Markets* (1977). In an effort to realistically analyze the way governmental decisions are made, at the heart of Lindblom's brilliant studies is a model of decision making that he succinctly outlines in the following essay.

Based on earlier writings by Chester Barnard and Herbert Simon, Lindblom's central thesis is that there are two distinct varieties of decision making. One he calls the rational-comprehensive or root method, and the second, the successive limited comparisons or branch method. The first method is found in the classic texts on administration, and the latter is the "real" way decisions are arrived at in government. In the traditional *rational-comprehensive* or *root method* an administrator confronts a given objective, such as reducing poverty by a certain amount. The decision maker, in choosing the best policy to pursue, rationally ranks all the relevant values (or advantages) in attaining this objective, such as improving the health of the poor, reducing crime, improving property values, and eliminating illiteracy. He or she then formulates as many possible alternatives to achieve the stated objective—e.g., a guaranteed income plan, direct government subsidies, higher welfare payments, or work-relief programs—and selects from among the options the *best* alternative that serves to maximize the ranked list of values. This approach to decision making is *rational,* because the alternatives and values are logically selected and weighed in relative importance. It is also *comprehensive,* for all the alternatives and values are taken into account by the policy maker.

What *actually* occurs in administrative decision making, argues Professor Lindblom, is quite another process, namely, the *successive limited comparisons* or *branch method.* An objective is established—reducing poverty by a set amount, for example—but in public discussions this objective quickly becomes compromised. It may soon be mixed up with other goals such as educating minority students or providing work relief for the jobless. Administrators tend to overlook or avoid many of the social values that could be derived from their program, concentrating instead on those that they consider immediately relevant. In selecting the appropriate course of action, administrators outline not a broad range of possibilities, but only a few incremental steps that experience tells them are feasible. Furthermore, in practice, policy makers do not rationally select the optimal program that satisfies a clearly delineated list of values. To the contrary, under the successive limited comparisons method, contends Lindblom, public administrators pragmatically select from among the immediate choices at hand the most suitable compromise that satisfies the groups and individuals concerned with the program.

Lindblom sees the first approach, the root method, as wrongly assuming that administrators making decisions have unlimited amounts of time and resources available to them. "It assumes intellectual capacities and sources of information that simply do not exist and it is even more absurd as an approach to policy when the time and money that can be allocated to a policy problem is limited as is always the case." Second, the root method holds that there are always clear-cut values on which all interested parties agree. In fact, argues Lindblom, in a democratic society where members of Congress, agencies, and interest groups are in continual disagreement over the relative importance of program objectives, policy makers cannot begin to rank explicitly the values derived from any program. There are simply too many groups with too many unknown values. The weight given to their relative importance depends ultimately on personal perspectives. "Even when an administrator resolves to follow his own values as a criterion for decisions, he will often not know how to rank them when they conflict with one another as they usually do." Third, the root method assumes that ends and means in policy choices are distinct, when in fact they are frequently intertwined. Selection of a goal to be accomplished often cannot easily be separated from the means by which it is achieved. For instance, the objective of slum clearance is intrinsically associated with the removal of residents from the neighborhood and the other methods employed to achieve the goal, such as the clearing of buildings. Means and ends often become hopelessly confused in public policy choices. Finally, says Lindblom, the choice of a given course of action depends ultimately not on whether it maximizes the intended values (even if the values could be identified and ranked), but rather on whether or not it serves as a compromise acceptable to all parties concerned. "If agreement directly on policy as a test for the 'best' policy seems a poor substitute for testing the policy against its objectives, it ought to be remembered that objectives themselves have no ultimate validity other than they are agreed upon. . . . Agreement on policy thus becomes the only practicable test of the policy's correctness," argues Lindblom.

Lindblom's view of the reality of administrative decision making contains five characteristics. First, it is *incremental,* for small steps are always taken to achieve objectives, not broad leaps and bounds. Second, it is *noncomprehensive.* In other words, because policy makers' resources are always limited, they cannot take into consideration the full range of policy choices available to them at any given moment nor can they possibly understand the full effects of their decisions or all of the values derived from any alternative they select. Third, the branch technique of decision making involves *successive comparisons* because policy is never made once and for all, but is made and remade endlessly by small chains of comparisons between narrow choices. Fourth, in practice, decision making *suffices* rather than maximizes from among the available options. "A wise policy maker completely expects that his policies will achieve only part of what he hopes and at the same time will produce unanticipated consequences he would have preferred to avoid." Finally, Lindblom's picture of governmental decision making rests on a *pluralist* conception of the public sector, in which many contending interest groups compete for influence over policy issues, continually forcing the administrator, as the person in the middle, to secure agreement among the competing parties. The political arts of compromise thus become a major part of decisional methods.

There are two advantages of the branch method, asserts Lindblom, the first being that "if he proceeds through a succession of small incremental changes, the administrator therefore has the advantage of avoiding serious lasting mistakes" as well as permitting easy alterations should the wrong course be pursued. The second benefit of incrementalism is that it fits "hand and glove" with the American political system, which operates chiefly by means of gradual changes, rarely by dramatic shifts in public policies. "Non-incremental policy proposals are therefore typically not only politically irrelevant but also unpredictable in their policy consequences," writes Lindblom. The branch method allows for the art of compromise that American politics demand and produces the gradual changes that American tradition generally favors.

However, from the perspective of the "outside expert" or the academic problem solver, Lindblom points out, this approach seems "unscientific and unsystematic." Indeed, administrators may appear as if they were flying "by the seat of their pants," although in fact the outside theorists do not grasp that administrators are "often practicing a systematic method" of successive limited comparisons. Yet, as Lindblom admits, ". . . sometimes decision makers are pursuing neither a theoretical approach nor successive comparisons nor any systematic method."

Lindblom's approach to governmental decision making, which for some may be too descriptive and not sufficiently prescriptive, debunks the classic view of how public choices are made, substituting an incremental model that is peculiarly a product and extension of economic theory of choice (subsequently, much of the language used in decisional theory—words like "optimizing" and "maximizing"—is derived from economics). Kenneth Arrow, Thomas Schelling, Herbert Simon, Edward Banfield, and Robert Dahl are among the major contemporary economists and political scientists who have pioneered the incremental view of decision making in the post-World War II era. Lindblom has fully developed this idea into an elaborate working model in the following article, "The Science of 'Muddling Through.'"

As you read this selection, keep the following questions in mind:

Is Lindblom too pessimistic about the ability of administrators to make profound choices that will significantly alter or reshape their external environment?

What do you see as the benefits and disadvantages of the branch method and are there any remedies for its defects?

How does Lindblom's concept square with any of the previous case studies, such as Case Study 7, "The Swine Flu Affair"? Was the "Swine Flu" decision made incrementally? Why or why not?

Does Lindblom's "muddling through" idea apply in normal governmental decisions involving simple issues as well as in such catastrophes as "The Swine Flu Affair"? What decisional methods might have averted the unfortunate choices made in the "Swine Flu" case?

Do you agree with Lindblom that "the branch method compared to other decisional models often looks far superior," particularly from the perspective of the practitioner?

CHARLES E. LINDBLOM

The Science of "Muddling Through"

Suppose an administrator is given responsibility for formulating policy with respect to inflation. He might start by trying to list all related values in order of importance, e.g., full employment, reasonable business profit, protection of small savings, prevention of a stock market crash. Then all possible policy outcomes could be rated as more or less efficient in attaining a maximum of these values. This would of course require a prodigious inquiry into values held by members of society and an equally prodigious set of calculations on how much of each value is equal to how much of each other value. He could then proceed to outline all possible policy alternatives. In a third step, he would undertake systematic comparison of his multitude of alternatives to determine which attains the greatest amount of values.

In comparing policies, he would take advantage of any theory available that generalized about classes of policies. In considering inflation, for example, he would compare all policies in the light of the theory of prices. Since no alternatives are beyond his investigation, he would consider strict central control and the abolition of all prices and markets on the one hand and elimination of all public controls with reliance completely on the free market on the other, both in the light of whatever theoretical generalizations he could find on such hypothetical economies.

Finally, he would try to make the choice that would in fact maximize his values.

An alternative line of attack would be to set as his principal objective, either explicitly or without conscious thought, the relatively simple goal of keeping prices level. This objective might be compromised or complicated by only a few other goals, such as full employment. He would in fact disregard most other social values as beyond his present interest, and he would for the moment not even attempt to rank the few values that he regarded as immediately relevant. Were he pressed, he would quickly admit that he was ignoring many related values and many possible important consequences of his policies.

As a second step, he would outline those relatively few policy alternatives that occurred to him. He would then compare them. In comparing his limited number of alternatives, most of them familiar from past controversies, he would not ordinarily find a body of theory precise enough to carry him through a comparison of their respective consequences. Instead he would rely heavily on the record of past experience with small policy steps to predict the consequences of similar steps extended into the future.

Moreover, he would find that the policy alternatives combined objectives or values in different ways. For example, one policy might offer price level stability at the cost of some risk of unemployment; another might offer less price stability but also less risk of unemployment. Hence, the next step in his approach—the final selection—would combine into one the choice among values and the choice among instruments for reaching values. It would not, as in the first method of policy-making, approximate a more mechanical process of choosing the means that best satisfied goals that were previously clarified and ranked. Because practitioners of the second approach expect to achieve their goals only partially, they would expect to repeat endlessly the sequence just described, as conditions and aspirations changed and as accuracy of prediction improved.

Reprinted with permission from *Public Administration Review,* © 1959 by The American Society for Public Administration, 1120 G Street, N.W., Suite 500, Washington D.C. All rights reserved.

By Root or by Branch

For complex problems, the first of these two approaches is of course impossible. Although such an approach can be described, it cannot be practiced except for relatively simple problems and even then only in a somewhat modified form. It assumes intellectual capacities and sources of information that men simply do not possess, and it is even more absurd as an approach to policy when the time and money that can be allocated to a policy problem is limited, as is always the case. Of particular importance to public administrators is the fact that public agencies are in effect usually instructed not to practice the first method. That is to say, their prescribed functions and constraints—the politically or legally possible—restrict their attention to relatively few values and relatively few alternative policies among the countless alternatives that might be imagined. It is the second method that is practiced.

Curiously, however, the literatures of decision making, policy formulation, planning, and public administration formalize the first approach rather than the second, leaving public administrators who handle complex decisions in the position of practicing what few preach. For emphasis I run some risk of overstatement. True enough, the literature is well aware of limits on man's capacities and of the inevitability that policies will be approached in some such style as the second. But attempts to formalize rational policy formulation—to lay out explicitly the necessary steps in the process—usually describe the first approach and not the second.[1]

The common tendency to describe policy formulation even for complex problems as though it followed the first approach has been strengthened by the attention given to, and successes

enjoyed by, operations research, statistical decision theory, and systems analysis. The hallmarks of these procedures, typical of the first approach, are clarity of objective, explicitness of evaluation, a high degree of comprehensiveness of overview, and, wherever possible, quantification of values for mathematical analysis. But these advanced procedures remain largely the appropriate techniques of relatively small-scale problem-solving where the total number of variables to be considered is small and value problems restricted. Charles Hitch, head of the Economics Division of RAND Corporation, one of the leading centers for application of these techniques, has written:

> I would make the empirical generalization from my experience at RAND and elsewhere that operations research is the art of suboptimizing, i.e., of solving some lower-level problems, and that difficulties increase and our special competence diminishes by an order of magnitude with every level of decision making we attempt to ascend. The sort of simple explicit model which operations researchers are so proficient in using can certainly reflect most of the significant factors influencing traffic control on the George Washington Bridge, but the proportion of the relevant reality which we can represent by any such model or models in studying, say, a major foreign-policy decision, appears to be almost trivial.[2]

Accordingly, I propose in this paper to clarify and formalize the second method, much ne-

---

[1] James G. March and Herbert A. Simon similarly characterized the literature. They also take some important steps, as have Simon's recent articles, to describe a less heroic model of policy-making. See *Organizations* (John Wiley and Sons, 1958), p. 137.

[2] "Operations Research and National Planning—A Dissent," 5 *Operations Research* 718 (October, 1957). Hitch's dissent is from particular points made in the article to which his paper is a reply; his claim that operations research is for low-level problems is widely accepted.

For examples of the kind of problems to which operations research is applied, see C. W. Churchman, R. L. Ackoff and E. L. Arnoff, *Introduction to Operations Research* (John Wiley and Sons, 1957); and J. F. McCloskey and J. M. Coppinger (eds.), *Operations Research for Management*, Vol. II (The Johns Hopkins Press, 1956).

glected in the literature. This might be described as the method of *successive limited comparisons.* I will contrast it with the first approach, which might be called the rational-comprehensive method.[3] More impressionistically and briefly— and therefore generally used in this article— they could be characterized as the branch method and root method, the former continually building out from the current situation, step-to-step and by small degrees; the latter starting from fundamentals anew each time, building on the past only as experience is embodied in a theory, and always prepared to start completely from the ground up.

Let us put the characteristics of the two methods side by side in simplest terms.

Rational-Comprehensive (Root)

1a. Clarification of values or objectives distinct from and usually prerequisite to empirical analysis of alternative policies.
2a. Policy-formulation is therefore approached through means-end analysis: First the ends are isolated, then the means to achieve them are sought.
3a. The test of a "good" policy is that it can be shown to be the most appropriate means to desired ends.
4a. Analysis is comprehensive; every important relevant factor is taken into account.
5a. Theory is often heavily relied upon.

Successive Limited Comparisons (Branch)

1b. Selection of value goals and empirical analysis of the needed action are not distinct from one another but are closely intertwined.

2b. Since means and ends are not distinct, means-end analysis is often inappropriate or limited.
3b. The test of a "good" policy is typically that various analysts find themselves directly agreeing on a policy (without their agreeing that it is the most appropriate means to an agreed objective).
4b. Analysis is drastically limited:
   i) Important possible outcomes are neglected.
   ii) Important alternative potential policies are neglected.
   iii) Important affected values are neglected.
5b. A succession of comparisons greatly reduces or eliminates reliance on theory.

Assuming that the root method is familiar and understandable, we proceed directly to clarification of its alternative by contrast. In explaining the second, we shall be describing how most administrators do in fact approach complex questions, for the root method, the "best" way as a blueprint or model, is in fact not workable for complex policy questions, and administrators are forced to use the method of successive limited comparisons.

Intertwining Evaluation and Empirical Analysis (1b)

The quickest way to understand how values are handled in the method of successive limited comparisons is to see how the root method often breaks down in *its* handling of values or objectives. The idea that values should be clarified, and in advance of the examination of alternative policies, is appealing. But what happens when we attempt it for complex social problems? The first difficulty is that on many critical values or objectives, citizens disagree, congressmen disagree, and public administrators disagree. Even where a fairly specific objective is prescribed for

---

[3] I am assuming that administrators often make policy and advise in the making of policy and am treating decision-making and policy-making as synonymous for purposes of this paper.

the administrator, there remains considerable room for disagreement on sub-objectives. Consider, for example, the conflict with respect to locating public housing, described in Meyerson and Banfield's study of the Chicago Housing Authority[4]—disagreement which occurred despite the clear objective of providing a certain number of public housing units in the city. Similarly conflicting are objectives in highway location, traffic control, minimum wage administration, development of tourist facilities in national parks, or insect control.

Administrators cannot escape these conflicts by ascertaining the majority's preference, for preferences have not been registered on most issues; indeed, there often *are* no preferences in the absence of public discussion sufficient to bring an issue to the attention of the electorate. Furthermore, there is a question of whether intensity of feeling should be considered as well as the number of persons preferring each alternative. By the impossibility of doing otherwise, administrators often are reduced to deciding policy without clarifying objectives first.

Even when an administrator resolves to follow his own values as a criterion for decisions, he often will not know how to rank them when they conflict with one another, as they usually do. Suppose, for example, that an administrator must relocate tenants living in tenements scheduled for destruction. One objective is to empty the buildings fairly promptly, another is to find suitable accommodation for persons displaced, another is to avoid friction with residents in other areas in which a large influx would be unwelcome, another is to deal with all concerned through persuasion if possible, and so on.

How does one state even to himself the relative importance of these partially conflicting values? A simple ranking of them is not enough; one needs ideally to know how much of one value is worth sacrificing for some of another value. The answer is that typically the administrator chooses—and must choose—directly among policies in which these values are combined in different ways. He cannot first clarify his values and then choose among policies.

A more subtle third point underlies both the first two. Social objectives do not always have the same relative values. One objective may be highly prized in one circumstance, another in another circumstance. If, for example, an administrator values highly both the dispatch with which his agency can carry through its projects *and* good public relations, it matters little which of the two possibly conflicting values he favors in some abstract or general sense. Policy questions arise in forms which put to administrators such a question as: Given the degree to which we are or are not already achieving the values of dispatch and the values of good public relations, is it worth sacrificing a little speed for a happier clientele, or is it better to risk offending the clientele so that we can get on with our work? The answer to such a question varies with circumstances.

The value problem is, as the example shows, always a problem of adjustments at a margin. But there is no practicable way to state marginal objectives or values except in terms of particular policies. That one value is preferred to another in one decision situation does not mean that it will be preferred in another decision situation in which it can be had only at great sacrifice of another value. Attempts to rank or order values in general and abstract terms so that they do not shift from decision to decision end up by ignoring the relevant marginal preferences. The significance of this third point thus goes very far. Even if all administrators had at hand an agreed set of values, objectives, and constraints, and an agreed ranking of these values, objectives, and constraints, their marginal values in actual choice situations would be impossible to formulate.

Unable consequently to formulate the relevant values first and then choose among policies to achieve them, administrators must choose directly among alternative policies that offer

[4]Martin Meyerson and Edward C. Banfield, *Politics, Planning and the Public Interest* (The Free Press, 1955).

different marginal combinations of values. Somewhat paradoxically, the only practicable way to disclose one's relevant marginal values even to oneself is to describe the policy one chooses to achieve them. Except roughly and vaguely, I know of no way to describe—or even to understand—what my relative evaluations are for, say, freedom and security, speed and accuracy in governmental decisions, or low taxes and better schools than to describe my preferences among specific policy choices that might be made between the alternatives in each of the pairs.

In summary, two aspects of the process by which values are actually handled can be distinguished. The first is clear: evaluation and empirical analysis are intertwined; that is, one chooses among values and among policies at one and the same time. Put a little more elaborately, one simultaneously chooses a policy to attain certain objectives and chooses the objectives themselves. The second aspect is related but distinct: the administrator focuses his attention on marginal or incremental values. Whether he is aware of it or not, he does not find general formulations of objectives very helpful and in fact makes specific marginal or incremental comparisons. Two policies, X and Y, confront him. Both promise the same degree of attainment of objectives *a, b, c, d,* and *e.* But X promises him somewhat more of *f* than does Y, while Y promises him somewhat more of *g* than does X. In choosing between them, he is in fact offered the alternative of a marginal or incremental amount of *f* at the expense of a marginal or incremental amount of *g.* The only values that are relevant to his choice are these increments by which the two policies differ; and, when he finally chooses between the two marginal values, he does so by making a choice between policies.[5]

As to whether the attempt to clarify objectives in advance of policy selection is more or

less rational than the close intertwining of marginal evaluation and empirical analysis, the principal difference established is that for complex problems the first is impossible and irrelevant, and the second is both possible and relevant. The second is possible because the administrator need not try to analyze any values except the values by which alternative policies differ and need not be concerned with them except as they differ marginally. His need for information on values or objectives is drastically reduced as compared with the root method; and his capacity for grasping, comprehending, and relating values to one another is not strained beyond the breaking point.

Relations Between Means and Ends (2b)

Decision-making is ordinarily formalized as a means-ends relationship: means are conceived to be evaluated and chosen in the light of ends finally selected independently of and prior to the choice of means. This is the means-ends relationship of the root method. But it follows from all that has just been said that such a means-ends relationship is possible only to the extent that values are agreed upon, are reconcilable, and are stable at the margin. Typically, therefore, such a means-ends relationship is absent from the branch method, where means and ends are simultaneously chosen.

Yet any departure from the means-ends relationship of the root method will strike some readers as inconceivable. For it will appear to them that only in such a relationship is it possible to determine whether one policy choice is better or worse than another. How can an administrator know whether he has made a wise or foolish decision if he is without prior values or objectives by which to judge his decisions? The answer to this question calls up the third distinctive difference between root and branch methods: how to decide the best policy.

---

[5]The line of argument is, of course, an extension of the theory of market choice, especially the theory of consumer choice, to public policy choices.

The Test of "Good" Policy (3b)

In the root method, a decision is "correct," "good," or "rational" if it can be shown to attain some specified objective, where the objective can be specified without simply describing the decision itself. Where objectives are defined only through the marginal or incremental approach to values described above, it is still sometimes possible to test whether a policy does in fact attain the desired objectives; but a precise statement of the objectives takes the form of a description of the policy chosen or some alternative to it. To show that a policy is mistaken one cannot offer an abstract argument that important objectives are not achieved; one must instead argue that another policy is more to be preferred.

So far, the departure from customary ways of looking at problem-solving is not troublesome, for many administrators will be quick to agree that the most effective discussion of the correctness of policy does take the form of comparison with other policies that might have been chosen. But what of the situation in which administrators cannot agree on values or objectives, either abstractly or in marginal terms? What then is the test of "good" policy? For the root method, there is no test. Agreement on objectives failing, there is no standard of "correctness." For the method of successive limited comparisons, the test is agreement on policy itself, which remains possible even when agreement on values is not.

It has been suggested that continuing agreement in Congress on the desirability of extending old age insurance stems from liberal desires to strengthen the welfare programs of the federal government and from conservative desires to reduce union demands for private pension plans. If so, this is an excellent demonstration of the ease with which individuals of different ideologies often can agree on concrete policy.

Labor mediators report a similar phenomenon: the contestants cannot agree on criteria for settling their disputes but can agree on specific proposals. Similarly, when one administrator's objective turns out to be another's means, they often can agree on policy.

Agreement on policy thus becomes the only practicable test of the policy's correctness. And for one administrator to seek to win the other over to agreement on ends as well would accomplish nothing and create quite unnecessary controversy.

If agreement directly on policy as a test for "best" policy seems a poor substitute for testing the policy against its objectives, it ought to be remembered that objectives themselves have no ultimate validity other than they are agreed upon. Hence agreement is the test of "best" policy in both methods. But where the root method requires agreement on what elements in the decision constitute objectives and on which of these objectives should be sought, the branch method falls back on agreement wherever it can be found.

In an important sense, therefore, it is not irrational for an administrator to defend a policy as good without being able to specify what it is good for.

Non-Comprehensive Analysis (4b)

Ideally, rational-comprehensive analysis leaves out nothing important. But it is impossible to take everything important into consideration unless "important" is so narrowly defined that analysis is in fact quite limited. Limits on human intellectual capacities and on available information set definite limits to man's capacity to be comprehensive. In actual fact, therefore, no one can practice the rational-comprehensive method for really complex problems, and every administrator faced with a sufficiently complex problem must find ways drastically to simplify.

An administrator assisting in the formulation of agricultural economic policy cannot in the first place be competent on all possible policies. He cannot even comprehend one policy entirely. In planning a soil bank program, he cannot successfully anticipate the impact of higher or lower farm income on, say, urbanization—the possible consequent loosening of family ties, possible consequent eventual need for revisions in social security and further implications for tax problems arising out of new federal responsibilities for social security and municipal responsibilities for urban services. Nor, to follow another line of repercussions, can he work through the soil bank program's effects on prices for agricultural products in foreign markets and consequent implications for foreign relations, including those arising out of economic rivalry between the United States and the U.S.S.R.

In the method of successive limited comparisons, simplification is systematically achieved in two principal ways. First, it is achieved through limitation of policy comparisons to those policies that differ in relatively small degree from policies presently in effect. Such a limitation immediately reduces the number of alternatives to be investigated and also drastically simplifies the character of the investigation of each. For it is not necessary to undertake fundamental inquiry into an alternative and its consequences; it is necessary only to study those respects in which the proposed alternative and its consequences differ from the status quo. The empirical comparison of marginal differences among alternative policies that differ only marginally is, of course, a counterpart to the incremental or marginal comparison of values discussed above.[6]

Relevance as Well as Realism

It is a matter of common observation that in Western democracies public administrators and policy analysts in general do largely limit their analyses to incremental or marginal differences in policies that are chosen to differ only incrementally. They do not do so, however, solely because they desperately need some way to simplify their problems; they also do so in order to be relevant. Democracies change their policies almost entirely through incremental adjustments. Policy does not move in leaps and bounds.

The incremental character of political change in the United States has often been remarked. The two major political parties agree on fundamentals; they offer alternative policies to the voters only on relatively small points of difference. Both parties favor full employment, but they define it somewhat differently; both favor the development of water power resources, but in slightly different ways; and both favor unemployment compensation, but not the same level of benefits. Similarly, shifts of policy within a party take place largely through a series of relatively small changes, as can be seen in their only gradual acceptance of the idea of governmental responsibility for support of the unemployed, a change in party positions beginning in the early 30's and culminating in a sense in the Employment Act of 1946.

Party behavior is in turn rooted in public attitudes, and political theorists cannot conceive of democracy's surviving in the United States in the absence of fundamental agreement on potentially disruptive issues, with consequent limitation of policy debates to relatively small differences in policy.

Since the policies ignored by the administrator are politically impossible and so irrelevant, the simplification of analysis achieved by con-

---

[6]A more precise definition of incremental policies and a discussion of whether a change that appears "small" to one observer might be seen differently by another is to be found

in my "Policy Analysis," 48 *American Economic Review* 298 (June, 1958).

centrating on policies that differ only incrementally is not a capricious kind of simplification. In addition, it can be argued that, given the limits on knowledge within which policy-makers are confined, simplifying by limiting the focus to small variations from present policy makes the most of available knowledge. Because policies being considered are like present and past policies, the administrator can obtain information and claim some insight. Non-incremental policy proposals are therefore typically not only politically irrelevant but also unpredictable in their consequences.

The second method of simplification of analysis is the practice of ignoring important possible consequences of possible policies, as well as the values attached to the neglected consequences. If this appears to disclose a shocking shortcoming of successive limited comparisons, it can be replied that, even if the exclusions are random, policies may nevertheless be more intelligently formulated than through futile attempts to achieve a comprehensiveness beyond human capacity. Actually, however, the exclusions, seeming arbitrary or random from one point of view, need be neither.

Achieving a Degree of Comprehensiveness

Suppose that each value neglected by one policy-making agency were a major concern of at least one other agency. In that case, a helpful division of labor would be achieved, and no agency need find its task beyond its capacities. The shortcomings of such a system would be that one agency might destroy a value either before another agency could be activated to safeguard it or in spite of another agency's efforts. But the possibility that important values may be lost is present in any form of organization, even where agencies attempt to comprehend in planning more than is humanly possible.

The virtue of such a hypothetical division of labor is that every important interest or value

has its watchdog. And these watchdogs can protect the interests in their jurisdiction in two quite different ways: first, by redressing damages done by other agencies; and, second, by anticipating and heading off injury before it occurs.

In a society like that of the United States in which individuals are free to combine to pursue almost any possible common interest they might have and in which government agencies are sensitive to the pressures of these groups, the system described is approximated. Almost every interest has its watchdog. Without claiming that every interest has a sufficiently powerful watchdog, it can be argued that our system often can assure a more comprehensive regard for the values of the whole society than any attempt at intellectual comprehensiveness.

In the United States, for example, no part of government attempts a comprehensive overview of policy on income distribution. A policy nevertheless evolves, and one responding to a wide variety of interests. A process of mutual adjustment among farm groups, labor unions, municipalities and school boards, tax authorities, and government agencies with responsibilities in the fields of housing, health, highways, national parks, fire, and police accomplishes a distribution of income in which particular income problems neglected at one point in the decision processes become central at another point.

Mutual adjustment is more pervasive than the explicit forms it takes in negotiation between groups; it persists through the mutual impacts of groups upon each other even where they are not in communication. For all the imperfections and latent dangers in this ubiquitous process of mutual adjustment, it will often accomplish an adaptation of policies to a wider range of interests than could be done by one group centrally.

Note, too, how the incremental pattern of policy-making fits with the multiple pressure pattern. For when decisions are only incremental—closely related to known policies, it is easier for one group to anticipate the kind of moves another might make and easier too for it to make correction for injury already accomplished.[7]

Even partisanship and narrowness, to use pejorative terms, will sometimes be assets to rational decision-making, for they can doubly insure that what one agency neglects, another will not; they specialize personnel to distinct points of view. The claim is valid that effective rational coordination of the federal administration, if possible to achieve at all, would require an agreed set of values[8]—if "rational" is defined as the practice of the root method of decision-making. But a high degree of administrative coordination occurs as each agency adjusts its policies to the concerns of the other agencies in the process of fragmented decision-making I have just described.

For all the apparent shortcomings of the incremental approach to policy alternatives with its arbitrary exclusion coupled with fragmentation, when compared to the root method, the branch method often looks far superior. In the root method, the inevitable exclusion of factors is accidental, unsystematic, and not defensible by any argument so far developed, while in the branch method the exclusions are deliberate, systematic, and defensible. Ideally, of course, the root method does not exclude; in practice it must.

Nor does the branch method necessarily neglect long-run considerations and objectives. It is clear that important values must be omitted in considering policy, and sometimes the only way long-run objectives can be given adequate attention is through the neglect of short-run consideration. But the values omitted can be either long-run or short-run.

[7]The link between the practice of the method of successive limited comparisons and mutual adjustment of interests in a highly fragmented decision-making process adds a new facet to pluralist theories of government and administration.
[8]Herbert Simon, Donald W. Smithburg, and Victor A. Thompson, *Public Administration* (Alfred A. Knopf, 1950), p. 434.

Succession of Comparisons (5b)

The final distinctive element in the branch method is that the comparisons, together with the policy choice, proceed in a chronological series. Policy is not made once and for all; it is made and remade endlessly. Policy-making is a process of successive approximation to some desired objectives in which what is desired itself continues to change under reconsideration.

Making policy is at best a very rough process. Neither social scientists, nor politicians, nor public administrators yet know enough about the social world to avoid repeated error in predicting the consequences of policy moves. A wise policy-maker consequently expects that his policies will achieve only part of what he hopes and at the same time will produce unanticipated consequences he would have preferred to avoid. If he proceeds through a *succession* of incremental changes, he avoids serious lasting mistakes in several ways.

In the first place, past sequences of policy steps have given him knowledge about the probable consequences of further similar steps. Second, he need not attempt big jumps toward his goals that would require predictions beyond his or anyone else's knowledge, because he never expects his policy to be a final resolution of a problem. His decision is only one step, one that if successful can quickly be followed by another. Third, he is in effect able to test his previous predictions as he moves on to each further step. Lastly, he often can remedy a past error fairly quickly—more quickly than if policy proceeded through more distinct steps widely spaced in time.

Compare this comparative analysis of incremental changes with the aspiration to employ theory in the root method. Man cannot think without classifying, without subsuming one experience under a more general category of experiences. The attempt to push categorization as far as possible and to find general propositions which can be applied to specific situations is what I refer to with the word "theory." Where root analysis often leans heavily on theory in this sense, the branch method does not.

The assumption of root analysis is that theory is the most systematic and economical way to bring relevant knowledge to bear on a specific problem. Granting the assumption, an unhappy fact is that we do not have adequate theory to apply to problems in any policy area, although theory is more adequate in some areas—monetary policy, for example—than in others. Comparative analysis, as in the branch method, is sometimes a systematic alternative to theory.

Suppose an administrator must choose among a small group of policies that differ only incrementally from each other and from present policy. He might aspire to "understand" each of the alternatives—for example, to know all the consequences of each aspect of each policy. If so, he would indeed require theory. In fact, however, he would usually decide that, *for policy-making purposes,* he need know, as explained above, only the consequences of each of those aspects of the policies in which they differed from one another. For this much more modest aspiration, he requires no theory (although it might be helpful, if available), for he can proceed to isolate probable differences by examining the differences in consequences associated with past differences in policies, a feasible program because he can take his observations from a long sequence of incremental changes.

For example, without a more comprehensive social theory about juvenile delinquency than scholars have yet produced, one cannot possibly understand the ways in which a variety of public policies—say on education, housing, recreation, employment, race relations, and policing—might encourage or discourage delinquency. And one needs such an understanding if he undertakes the comprehensive overview of the problem prescribed in the models of the root method. If, however, one merely wants to mobilize knowledge sufficient to assist in a choice among a small group of similar policies—alternative policies on juvenile court procedures, for example—he can do so by comparative analysis of the results of similar past policy moves.

Theorists and Practitioners

This difference explains—in some cases at least—why the administrator often feels that the outside expert or academic problem-solver is sometimes not helpful and why they in turn often urge more theory on him. And it explains why an administrator often feels more confident when "flying by the seat of his pants" than when following the advice of theorists. Theorists often ask the administrator to go the long way round to the solution of his problems, in effect ask him to follow the best canons of the scientific method, when the administrator knows the best available theory will work less well than more modest incremental comparisons. Theorists do not realize that the administrator is often in fact practicing a systematic method. It would be foolish to push this explanation too far, for sometimes practical decision-makers are pursuing neither a theoretical approach nor successive comparisons, nor any other systematic method.

It may be worth emphasizing that theory is sometimes of extremely limited helpfulness in policy-making for at least two rather different reasons. It is greedy for facts; it can be constructed only through a great collection of observations. And it is typically insufficiently precise for application to a policy process that moves through small changes. In contrast, the comparative method both economizes on the need for facts and directs the analyst's attention to just those facts that are relevant to the fine choices faced by the decision-maker.

With respect to precision of theory, economic theory serves as an example. It predicts that an economy without money or prices would in certain specified ways misallocate resources, but this finding pertains to an alternative far removed from the kind of policies on which administrators need help. On the other hand, it is not precise enough to predict the consequences of policies restricting business mergers, and this is the kind of issue on which the administrators need help. Only in relatively restricted areas does economic theory achieve sufficient precision to go far in resolving policy questions; its helpfulness in policy-making is always so limited that it requires supplementation through comparative analysis.

Successive Comparison as a System

Successive limited comparison is, then, indeed a method or system; it is not a failure of method for which administrators ought to apologize. None the less, its imperfections, which have not been explored in this paper, are many. For example, the method is without a built-in safeguard for all relevant values, and it also may lead the decision-maker to overlook excellent policies for no other reason than that they are not suggested by the chain of successive policy steps leading up to the present. Hence, it ought to be said that under this method, as well as under some of the most sophisticated variants of the root method—operations research, for example—policies will continue to be as foolish as they are wise.

Why then bother to describe the method in all the above detail? Because it is in fact a common method of policy formulation, and is, for complex problems, the principal reliance of administrators as well as of other policy analysts.[9]

And because it will be superior to any other decision-making method available for complex problems in many circumstances, certainly superior to a futile attempt at super-human comprehensiveness. The reaction of the public administrator to the exposition of method doubtless will be less a discovery of a new method than a better acquaintance with an old. But by becoming more conscious of their practice of this method, administrators might practice it with more skill and know when to extend or constrict its use. (That they sometimes practice it effectively and sometimes not may explain the extremes of opinion on "muddling through," which is both praised as a highly sophisticated form of problem-solving and denounced as no method at all. For I suspect that in so far as there is a system in what is known as "muddling through," this method is it.)

One of the noteworthy incidental consequences of clarification of the method is the light it throws on the suspicion an administrator sometimes entertains that a consultant or adviser is not speaking relevantly and responsibly when in fact by all ordinary objective evidence he is. The trouble lies in the fact that most of us approach policy problems within a framework given by our view of a chain of successive policy choices made up to the present. One's thinking about appropriate policies with respect, say, to urban traffic control is greatly influenced by one's knowledge of the incremental steps taken up to the present. An administrator enjoys an intimate knowledge of his past sequences that "outsiders" do not share, and his thinking and that of

---

[9] Elsewhere I have explored this same method of policy formulation as practiced by academic analysts of policy ("Policy Analysis," 48 *American Economic Review* 298 [June, 1958]). Although it has been here presented as a method for public administrators, it is no less necessary to analysts more removed from immediate policy questions, despite their tendencies to describe their own analytical efforts as though they were the rational-comprehensive method with an especially heavy use of theory. Similarly, this same

method is inevitably resorted to in personal problem-solving, where means and ends are sometimes impossible to separate, where aspirations or objectives undergo constant development, and where drastic simplification of the complexity of the real world is urgent if problems are to be solved in the time that can be given to them. To an economist accustomed to dealing with the marginal or incremental concept in market processes, the central idea in the method is that both evaluation and empirical analysis are incremental. Accordingly I have referred to the method elsewhere as "the incremental method."

the "outsider" will consequently be different in ways that may puzzle both. Both may appear to be talking intelligently, yet each may find the other unsatisfactory. The relevance of the policy chain of succession is even more clear when an American tries to discuss, say, antitrust policy with a Swiss, for the chains of policy in the two countries are strikingly different and the two individuals consequently have organized their knowledge in quite different ways.

If this phenomenon is a barrier to communication, an understanding of it promises an enrichment of intellectual interaction in policy formulation. Once the source of difference is understood, it will sometimes be stimulating for an administrator to seek out a policy analyst whose recent experience is with a policy chain different from his own.

This raises again a question only briefly discussed above on the merits of like-mindedness among government administrators. While much of organization theory argues the virtues of common values and agreed organizational objectives, for complex problems in which the root method is inapplicable, agencies will want among their own personnel two types of diversification: administrators whose thinking is organized by reference to policy chains other than those familiar to most members of the organization and, even more commonly, administrators whose professional or personal values or interests create diversity of view (perhaps coming from different specialties, social classes, geographical areas) so that, even within a single agency, decision-making can be fragmented and parts of the agency can serve as watchdogs for other parts.

CASE STUDY 8

Introduction

No American public official has faced a more difficult and complex question than Henry L. Stimson, secretary of war from 1940 to 1945 and the man chiefly responsible for the overall direction of the United States atomic energy program from its inception in the early 1940s. His recommendations to the new president, Harry S. Truman, who assumed office in April 1945 following President Roosevelt's unexpected death, were critical in this nation's decision to drop two atomic bombs on Nagasaki and Hiroshima in August 1945, bringing devastation to those two industrial cities, death to more than 100,000 Japanese civilians, and a rapid end to World War II. Although this kind of decision was unique, never having been made before or since, Stimson's account does serve as an appropriate case study for understanding how important, complicated administrative decisions are arrived at within government. His strikingly objective, first-person essay outlines how various individuals, groups, and forces within the government shaped the choices concerning the use of the nuclear bomb and leads us to appreciate the human dilemmas arising from the technical innovations of science. It shows how such innovations frequently add enormous moral and ethical complexities to administrative choices in government.

In reading Stimson's essay, it is certainly difficult to lay aside the ultimate moral issues—whether or not the atomic bomb should have been built in the first place or later used against the Japanese. From the vantage point of public administration, however, the story offers several unique insights into the decisional processes of American government and raises a number of profound questions about the way public choices are determined.

As you read this selection, keep the following questions in mind:

How did Stimson perceive the alternatives to using the atomic bomb? On what sources did he primarily rely for factual information in arriving at his decision?

Pay particular attention to the constant "air of uncertainty" that hung over policy makers in this case—no one really knew if the atomic bomb would work until it was dropped on Japan. Was this air of uncertainty as apparent in previous case studies? In particular, how did this uncertainty influence the choices of the decision makers?

Does the case study support or contradict Lindblom's "incremental" model of governmental decision making?

What does the story say about Mosher's concept, discussed in Chapter 7, regarding the influence of professionals as key decision makers within government? Who were the professionals in this case?

What were some of the difficulties in the relationship between the professionals and the politicians in this case study? Also, were there conflicts between professionals? If so, over what issues and how were these differences resolved?

HENRY L. STIMSON

The Decision to Use the Atomic Bomb

It was the fall of 1941 that the question of atomic energy was first brought directly to my attention. At that time President Roosevelt appointed a committee consisting of Vice President Wallace, General Marshall, Dr. Vannevar Bush, Dr. James B. Conant, and myself. The function of this committee was to advise the President on questions of policy relating to the study of nuclear fission which was then proceeding both in this country and in Great Britain. For nearly four years thereafter I was directly connected with all major decisions of policy on the development and use of atomic energy, and from May 1, 1943, until my resignation as Secretary of War on September 21, 1945, I was directly responsible to the

President for the administration of the entire undertaking; my chief advisers in this period were General Marshall, Dr. Bush, Dr. Conant, and Major General Leslie R. Groves, the officer in charge of the project. At the same time I was the President's senior adviser on the military employment of atomic energy.

The policy adopted and steadily pursued by President Roosevelt and his advisers was a simple one. It was to spare no effort in securing the earliest possible successful development of an atomic weapon. The reasons for this policy were equally simple. The original experimental achievement of atomic fission had occurred in Germany in 1938, and it was known that the Germans had continued their experiments. In 1941 and 1942 they were believed to be ahead of us, and it was vital that they should not be the first to bring atomic weapons into the field of battle. Furthermore, if we should be the first to develop the weapon, we should have a great new instrument for shortening the war and minimizing destruction. At no time, from 1941 to 1945, did I ever hear it suggested by the President, or by any other responsible member of the government, that atomic energy should not be used in the war. All of us of course understood the terrible responsibility involved in our attempt to unlock the doors to such a devastating weapon; President Roosevelt particularly spoke to me many times of his own awareness of the catastrophic potentialities of our work. But we were at war, and the work must be done. I therefore emphasize that it was our common objective, throughout the war, to be the first to produce an atomic weapon and use it. The possible atomic weapon was considered to be a new and tremendously powerful explosive, as legitimate as any other of the deadly explosive weapons of modern war. The entire purpose was the production of a military weapon; on no other ground could the wartime expenditure of so much time and money have been justified. The exact circumstances in which that weapon might be used were unknown to any of us until the middle of 1945, and when that time came, as we shall presently see, the military use of atomic energy was connected with larger questions of national policy.

The extraordinary story of the successful development of the atomic bomb has been well told elsewhere. As time went on it became clear that the weapon would not be available in time for use in the European Theater, and the war against Germany was successfully ended by the use of what are now called conventional means. But in the spring of 1945 it became evident that the climax of our prolonged atomic effort was at hand. By the nature of atomic chain reactions, it was impossible to state with certainty that we had succeeded until a bomb had actually exploded in a full-scale experiment; nevertheless it was considered exceedingly probable that we should by midsummer have successfully detonated the first atomic bomb. This was to be done at the Alamogordo Reservation in New Mexico. It was thus time for detailed consideration of our future plans. What had begun as a well-founded hope was now developing into a reality.

On March 15, 1945 I had my last talk with President Roosevelt. My diary record of this conversation gives a fairly clear picture of the state of our thinking at that time. I have removed the name of the distinguished public servant who was fearful lest the Manhattan (atomic) project be "a lemon"; it was an opinion common among those not fully informed.

The President . . . had suggested that I come over to lunch today. . . . First I took up with him a memorandum which he sent to me from —— who had been alarmed at the rumors of extravagance in the Manhattan project. —— suggested that it might become disastrous and he suggested that we get a body of "outside" scientists to pass upon the project because rumors are going around that Vannevar Bush and Jim Conant have sold the President a lemon on the subject and ought to be checked up on. It was rather a jittery and nervous memorandum and rather silly, and I was prepared for it and I gave the President a list of the scientists who were actually engaged on it to show the very high standing of them and it comprised four Nobel Prize men, and also how practically every physicist of standing was engaged with us in the project. Then I outlined to him the future of it and when it was likely to come off and told him how important it was to get ready. I went over with him the two schools of thought that exist in respect to the future control after the war of this project, in case it is successful, one of them being the secret close-in attempted control of the project by those who control it now, and the other being the international control based upon freedom both of science and of access. I told him that those things must be settled before the first projectile is used and that he must be ready with a statement to come out to the people on it just as soon as that is done. He agreed to that. . . .

This conversation covered the three aspects of the question which were then uppermost in our minds. First, it was always necessary to suppress a lingering doubt that any such titanic undertaking could be successful. Second, we must consider the implications of success in terms of its long-range postwar effect. Third, we must face the problem that would be presented at the time of our first use of the weapon, for with that first use there must be some public statement.

I did not see Franklin Roosevelt again. The next time I went to the White House to discuss atomic energy was April 25, 1945, and I went to explain the nature of the problem to a man whose only previous knowledge of our activities was that of a Senator who had loyally accepted our assurance that the matter must be kept a secret from him. Now he was President and Commander-in-Chief, and the final responsibility in this as in so many other matters must be his. President Truman accepted this responsibility with the same fine spirit that Senator Truman had shown before in accepting our refusal to inform him.

I discussed with him the whole history of the project. We had with us General Groves, who explained in detail the progress which had been made and the probable future course of the work. I also discussed with President Truman the broader aspects of the subject, and the memorandum which I used in this discussion is again a fair sample of the state of our thinking at the time.

Memorandum Discussed with President Truman April 25, 1945

1. Within four months we shall in all probability have completed the most terrible weapon ever known in human history, one bomb of which could destroy a whole city.
2. Although we have shared its development with the U.K., physically the U.S. is at present in the position of controlling the resources with which to construct and use it and no other nation could reach this position for some years.
3. Nevertheless it is practically certain that we could not remain in this position indefinitely.
   a. Various segments of its discovery and production are widely known among many scientists in many countries, although few scientists are now acquainted with the whole process which we have developed.
   b. Although its construction under present methods requires great scientific and industrial effort and raw materials, which are temporarily mainly within the possession and knowledge of U.S. and U.K., it is extremely probable that much easier and cheaper methods of production will be discovered by scientists in the future, together with the use of materials of much wider distribution. As a result, it is extremely probable that the future will make it possible for atomic bombs to be constructed by smaller nations or even groups, or at least by a larger nation in a much shorter time.
4. As a result, it is indicated that the future may see a time when such a weapon may be constructed in secret and used suddenly and effectively with devastating power by a wilful nation or group against an unsuspecting nation or group of much greater size and material power. With its aid even a very powerful unsuspecting nation might be conquered within a very few days by a very much smaller one. . . .
5. The world in its present state of moral advancement compared with its technical development would be eventually at the mercy of such a weapon. In other words, modern civilization might be completely destroyed.
6. To approach any world peace organization of any pattern now likely to be considered, without an appreciation by the leaders of our country of the power of this new weapon, would seem to be unrealistic. No system of control heretofore considered would be adequate to control this menace. Both inside any particular country and between the nations of the world, the control of this weapon will undoubtedly be a matter of the greatest difficulty and would involve such thoroughgoing rights of inspection and internal controls as we have never heretofore contemplated.
7. Furthermore, in the light of our present position with reference to this weapon, the question of sharing it with other nations and, if so shared, upon what terms, becomes a primary question of our foreign relations. Also our

leadership in the war and in the development of this weapon has placed a certain moral responsibility upon us which we cannot shirk without very serious responsibility for any disaster to civilization which it would further.

8. On the other hand, if the problem of the proper use of this weapon can be solved, we would have the opportunity to bring the world into a pattern in which the peace of the world and our civilization can be saved.

9. As stated in General Groves' report, steps are under way looking towards the establishment of a select committee of particular qualifications for recommending action to the executive and legislative branches of our government when secrecy is no longer in full effect. The committee would also recommend the actions to be taken by the War Department prior to that time in anticipation of the postwar problems. All recommendations would of course be first submitted to the President.

The next step in our preparations was the appointment of the committee referred to in paragraph (9) above. This committee, which was known as the Interim Committee, was charged with the function of advising the President on the various questions raised by our apparently imminent success in developing an atomic weapon. I was its chairman, but the principal labor of guiding its extended deliberations fell to George L. Harrison, who acted as chairman in my absence. It will be useful to consider the work of the committee in some detail. Its members were the following, in addition to Mr. Harrison and myself:

James F. Byrnes (then a private citizen) as personal representative of the President.

Ralph A. Bard, Under Secretary of the Navy.

William L. Clayton, Assistant Secretary of State.

Dr. Vannevar Bush, Director, Office of Scientific Research and Development, and president of the Carnegie Institution of Washington.

Dr. Karl T. Compton, Chief of the Office of Field Service in the Office of Scientific Research and Development, and president of the Massachusetts Institute of Technology.

Dr. James B. Conant, Chairman of the National Defense Research Committee, and president of Harvard University.

The discussions of the committee ranged over the whole field of atomic energy, in its political, military, and scientific aspects. That part of its work which particularly concerns us here relates to its recommendations for the use of atomic energy against Japan, but it should be borne in mind that these recommendations were not made in a vacuum. The committee's work included the drafting of the statements which were published immediately after the first bombs were dropped, the drafting of a bill for the domestic control of atomic energy, and recommendations looking toward the international control of atomic energy. The Interim Committee was assisted in its work by a Scientific Panel whose members were the following: Dr. A. H. Compton, Dr. Enrico Fermi, Dr. E. O. Lawrence, and Dr. J. R. Oppenheimer. All four were nuclear physicists of the first rank; all four had held positions of great importance in the atomic project from its inception. At a meeting with the Interim Committee and the Scientific Panel on May 31, 1945 I urged all those present to feel free to express themselves on any phase of the subject, scientific or political. Both General Marshall and I at this meeting expressed the view that atomic energy could not be considered simply in terms of military weapons but must also be considered in terms of a new relationship of man to the universe.

On June 1, after its discussions with the Scientific Panel, the Interim Committee unanimously adopted the following recommendations:

1. The bomb should be used against Japan as soon as possible.
2. It should be used on a dual target—that is, a military installation or war plant surrounded by or adjacent to houses and other buildings most susceptible to damage, and

3. It should be used without prior warning [of the nature of the weapon]. One member of the committee, Mr. Bard, later changed his view and dissented from recommendation (3).

In reaching these conclusions the Interim Committee carefully considered such alternatives as a detailed advance warning or a demonstration in some uninhabited area. Both of these suggestions were discarded as impractical. They were not regarded as likely to be effective in compelling a surrender of Japan, and both of them involved serious risks. Even the New Mexico test would not give final proof that any given bomb was certain to explode when dropped from an airplane. Quite apart from the generally unfamiliar nature of atomic explosives, there was the whole problem of exploding a bomb at a predetermined height in the air by a complicated mechanism which could not be tested in the static test of New Mexico. Nothing would have been more damaging to our effort to obtain surrender than a warning or a demonstration followed by a dud—and this was a real possibility. Furthermore, we had no bombs to waste. It was vital that a sufficient effect be quickly obtained with the few we had.

The Interim Committee and the Scientific Panel also served as a channel through which suggestions from other scientists working on the atomic project were forwarded to me and to the President. Among the suggestions thus forwarded was one memorandum which questioned using the bomb at all against the enemy. On June 16, 1945, after consideration of that memorandum, the Scientific Panel made a report, from which I quote the following paragraphs:

The opinions of our scientific colleagues on the initial use of these weapons are not unanimous: they range from the proposal of a purely technical demonstration to that of the military application best designed to induce surrender. Those who advocate a purely technical demonstration would wish to outlaw the use of atomic weapons, and have feared that if we use the weapons now our position in future negotiations will be prejudiced. Others emphasize the opportunity of saving American lives by immediate military use, and believe that such use will improve the international prospects, in that they are more concerned with the prevention of war than with the elimination of this special weapon. We find ourselves closer to these latter views; *we can propose no technical demonstration likely to bring an end to the war; we see no acceptable alternative to direct military use.* [Italics are Stimson's]

With regard to these general aspects of the use of atomic energy, it is clear that we, as scientific men, have no proprietary rights. It is true that we are among the few citizens who have had occasion to give thoughtful consideration to these problems during the past few years. We have, however, no claim to special competence in solving the political, social, and military problems which are presented by the advent of atomic power.

The foregoing discussion presents the reasoning of the Interim Committee and its advisers. I have discussed the work of these gentlemen at length in order to make it clear that we sought the best advice that we could find. The committee's function was, of course, entirely advisory. The ultimate responsibility for the recommendation to the President rested upon me, and I have no desire to veil it. The conclusions of the committee were similar to my own, although I reached mine independently. I felt that to extract a genuine surrender from the Emperor and his military advisers, they must be administered a tremendous shock which would carry convincing proof of our power to destroy the Empire. Such an effective shock would save many times the number of lives, both American and Japanese, that it would cost.

The facts upon which my reasoning was based and steps taken to carry it out now follow.

U.S. Policy toward Japan in July 1945

The principal political, social, and military objective of the United States in the summer of 1945 was the prompt and complete surrender of

Japan. Only the complete destruction of her military power could open the way to lasting peace.

Japan, in July 1945, had been seriously weakened by our increasingly violent attacks. It was known to us that she had gone so far as to make tentative proposals to the Soviet government, hoping to use the Russians as mediators in a negotiated peace. These vague proposals contemplated the retention by Japan of important conquered areas and were therefore not considered seriously. There was as yet no indication of any weakening in the Japanese determination to fight rather than accept unconditional surrender. If she should persist in her fight to the end, she had still a great military force.

In the middle of July 1945, the intelligence section of the War Department General Staff estimated Japanese military strength as follows: in the home islands, slightly under 2,000,000; in Korea, Manchuria, China proper, and Formosa, slightly over 2,000,000; in French Indo-China, Thailand, and Burma, over 200,000; in the East Indies area, including the Philippines, over 500,000; in the by-passed Pacific islands, over 100,000. The total strength of the Japanese Army was estimated at about 5,000,000 men. These estimates later proved to be in very close agreement with official Japanese figures.

The Japanese Army was in much better condition than the Japanese Navy and Air Force. The Navy had practically ceased to exist except as a harrying force against an invasion fleet. The Air Force had been reduced mainly to reliance upon Kamikaze, or suicide, attacks. These latter, however, had already inflicted serious damage on our seagoing forces, and their possible effectiveness in a last ditch fight was a matter of real concern to our naval leaders.

As we understood it in July, there was a very strong possibility that the Japanese government might determine upon resistance to the end, in all the areas of the Far East under its control. In such an event the Allies would be faced with the enormous task of destroying an armed force of five million men and five thousand suicide aircraft, belonging to a race which had already amply demonstrated its ability to fight literally to the death.

The strategic plans of our armed forces for the defeat of Japan, as they stood in July, had been prepared without reliance upon the atomic bomb, which had not yet been tested in New Mexico. We were planning an intensified sea and air blockade, and greatly intensified strategic air bombing, through the summer and early fall, to be followed on November 1 by an invasion of the southern island of Kyushu. This would be followed in turn by an invasion of the main island of Honshu in the spring of 1946. The total U.S. military and naval force involved in this grand design was of the order of 5,000,000 men; if all those indirectly concerned are included, it was larger still.

We estimated that if we should be forced to carry this plan to its conclusion, the major fighting would not end until the latter part of 1946, at the earliest. I was informed that such operations might be expected to cost over a million casualties, to American forces alone. Additional large losses might be expected among our allies, and, of course, if our campaign were successful and if we could judge by previous experience, enemy casualties would be much larger than our own.

It was already clear in July that even before the invasion we should be able to inflict enormously severe damage on the Japanese homeland by the combined application of "conventional" sea and air power. The critical question was whether this kind of action would induce surrender. It therefore became necessary to consider very carefully the probable state of mind of the enemy, and to assess with accuracy the line of conduct which might end his will to resist.

With these considerations in mind, I wrote a memorandum for the President, on July 2, which I believe fairly represents the thinking of the American government as it finally took shape in action. This memorandum was prepared after discussion and general agreement with Joseph C. Grew, Acting Secretary of State, and Secretary of the Navy Forrestal, and when I discussed it with the President, he expressed his general approval.

Memorandum from the President, Proposed Program for Japan, July 2, 1945

1. The plans of operation up to and including the first landing have been authorized and the preparations for the operation are now actually going on. This situation was accepted by all members of your conference on Monday, June 18.
2. There is reason to believe that the operation for the occupation of Japan following the landing may be a very long, costly, and arduous struggle on our part. The terrain, much of which I have visited several times, has left the impression on my memory of being one which would be susceptible to a last ditch defense such as has been made on Iwo Jima and Okinawa and which of course is very much larger than either of those two areas. According to my recollection it will be much more unfavorable with regard to tank maneuvering than either the Philippines or Germany.
3. If we once land on one of the main islands and begin a forceful occupation of Japan, we shall probably have cast the die of last ditch resistance. The Japanese are highly patriotic and certainly susceptible to calls for fanatical resistance to repel an invasion. Once started in actual invasion, we shall in my opinion have to go through with an even more bitter finish fight than in Germany. We shall incur the losses incident to such a war and we shall have to leave the Japanese islands even more thoroughly destroyed than was the case with Germany. This would be due both to the difference in the Japanese and German personal character and the differences in the size and character of the terrain through which the operations will take place.
4. A question then comes: Is there any alternative to such a forceful occupation of Japan which will secure for us the equivalent of an unconditional surrender of her forces and a permanent destruction of her power again to strike an aggressive blow at the "peace of the Pacific"? I am inclined to think that there is enough such chance to make it well worthwhile our giving them a warning of what is to come and a definite opportunity to capitulate. As above suggested, it should be tried before the actual forceful occupation of the homeland islands is begun and furthermore the warning should be given in ample time to permit a national reaction to set in.

We have the following enormously favorable factors on our side—factors much weightier than those we had against Germany:

Japan has no allies.

Her navy is nearly destroyed and she is vulnerable to a surface and underwater blockade which can deprive her of sufficient food and supplies for her population.

She is terribly vulnerable to our concentrated air attack upon her crowded cities, industrial and food resources.

She has against her not only the Anglo-American forces but the rising forces of China and the ominous threat of Russia.

We have inexhaustible and untouched industrial resources to bring to bear against her diminishing potential.

We have great moral superiority through being the victim of her first sneak attack.

The problem is to translate these advantages into prompt and economical achievement of our objectives. I believe Japan *is* susceptible to reason in such a crisis to a much greater extent than is indicated by our current press and other current comment. Japan is not a nation composed wholly of mad fanatics of an entirely different mentality from ours. On the contrary, she has within the past century shown herself to possess extremely intelligent people, capable in an unprecedentedly short time of adopting not only the complicated technique of Occidental civilization but to a substantial extent their culture and their political and social ideas. Her advance in all these respects during the short period of sixty or seventy years has been one of the most astounding feats of national progress in history—a leap from the isolated feudalism of centuries into the position of one of the six or seven great powers of the world. She has not only built up powerful armies and navies. She has maintained an honest and effective national finance and respected position in many of the sciences in which we pride ourselves. Prior to the forcible seizure of power over her government by the fanatical military group in 1931, she had for ten years lived a reasonably responsible and respectable international life.

My own opinion is in her favor on the two points involved in this question:

a. I think the Japanese nation has the mental intelligence and versatile capacity in such a crisis to recognize the folly of a fight to the finish and to accept the proffer of what will amount to an unconditional surrender; and

b. I think she has within her population enough liberal leaders (although now submerged by the terrorists) to be depended upon for her reconstruction as a responsible member of the family of nations. I think she is better in this last respect than Germany was. Her liberals yielded only at the point of the pistol and, so far as I am aware, their liberal attitude has not been personally subverted in the way which was so general in Germany.

On the other hand, I think that the attempt to exterminate her armies and her population by gunfire or other means will tend to produce a fusion of race solidity and antipathy which has no analogy in the case of Germany. We have a national interest in creating, if possible, a condition wherein the Japanese nation may live as a peaceful and useful member of the future Pacific community.

5. It is therefore my conclusion that a carefully timed warning be given to Japan by the chief representatives of the United States, Great Britain, China, and, if then a belligerent, Russia by calling upon Japan to surrender and permit the occupation of her country in order to insure its complete demilitarization for the sake of the future peace.

This warning should contain the following elements:

The varied and overwhelming character of the force we are about to bring to bear on the islands.

The inevitability and completeness of the destruction which the full application of this force will entail.

The determination of the Allies to destroy permanently all authority and influence of those who have deceived and misled the country into embarking on world conquest.

The determination of the Allies to limit Japanese sovereignty to her main islands and to render them powerless to mount and support another war.

The disavowal of any attempt to extirpate the Japanese as a race or to destroy them as a nation.

A statement of our readiness, once her economy is purged of its militaristic influence, to permit the Japanese to maintain such industries, particularly of a light consumer character, as offer no threat of aggression against their neighbors, but which can produce a sustaining economy, and provide a reasonable standard of living. The statement should indicate our willingness, for this purpose, to give Japan trade access to external raw materials, but no longer any control over the sources of supply outside her main islands. It should also indicate our willingness, in accordance with our now established foreign trade policy, in due course to enter into mutually advantageous trade relations with her.

The withdrawal from their country as soon as the above objectives of the Allies are accomplished, and as soon as there has been established a peacefully inclined government, of a character representative of the masses of the Japanese people. I personally think that if in saying this we should add that we do not exclude a constitutional monarchy under her present dynasty, it would substantially add to the chances of acceptance.

6. Success of course will depend on the potency of the warning which we give her. She has an extremely sensitive national pride and, as we are now seeing every day, when actually locked with the enemy will fight to the very death. For that reason the warning must be tendered before the actual invasion has occurred and while the impending destruction, though clear beyond peradventure, has not yet reduced her to fanatical despair. If Russia is a part of the threat, the Russian attack, if actual, must not have progressed too far. Our own bombing should be confined to military objectives as far as possible.

It is important to emphasize the double character of the suggested warning. It was designed to promise destruction if Japan resisted, and hope, if she surrendered.

It will be noted that the atomic bomb is not mentioned in this memorandum. On grounds of secrecy the bomb was never mentioned except when absolutely necessary, and furthermore, it had not yet been tested. It was of course well forward in our minds, as the memorandum was written and discussed, that the bomb would be the best possible sanction if our warning were rejected.

The Use of the Bomb

The adoption of the policy outlined in the memorandum of July 2 was a decision of high politics; once it was accepted by the President, the position of the atomic bomb in our planning became quite clear. I find that I stated in my diary, as early as June 19, that "the last chance warning . . . must be given before an actual landing of the ground forces in Japan, and fortunately the plans provide for enough time to bring in the sanctions to our warning in the shape of heavy ordinary bombing attack and an attack of S-1." S-1 was a code name for the atomic bomb.

There was much discussion in Washington about the timing of the warning to Japan. The controlling factor in the end was the date already set for the Potsdam meeting of the Big Three. It was President Truman's decision that such a warning should be solemnly issued by the U.S. and the U.K. from this meeting, with the concurrence of the head of the Chinese government, so that it would be plain that *all* of Japan's principal enemies were in entire unity. This was done, in the Potsdam ultimatum of July 26, which very closely followed the above memorandum of July 2, with the exception that it made no mention of the Japanese Emperor.

On July 28 the Premier of Japan, Suzuki, rejected the Potsdam ultimatum by announcing that it was "unworthy of public notice." In the face of this rejection we could only proceed to demonstrate that the ultimatum had meant exactly what it said when it stated that if the Japanese continued the war, "the full application of our military power, backed by our resolve, will mean the inevitable and complete destruction of the Japanese armed forces and just as inevitably the utter devastation of the Japanese homeland."

For such a purpose the atomic bomb was an eminently suitable weapon. The New Mexico test occurred while we were at Potsdam, on July 16. It was immediately clear that the power of the bomb measured up to our highest estimates. We had developed a weapon of such a revolutionary character that its use against the enemy might well be expected to produce exactly the kind of shock on the Japanese ruling oligarchy which we desired, strengthening the position of those who wished peace, and weakening that of the military party.

Because of the importance of the atomic mission against Japan, the detailed plans were brought to me by the military staff for approval. With President Truman's warm support I struck off the list of suggested targets the city of Kyoto. Although it was a target of considerable military importance, it had been the ancient capital of Japan and was a shrine of Japanese art and culture. We determined that it should be spared. I approved four other targets including the cities of Hiroshima and Nagasaki.

Hiroshima was bombed on August 6, and

Nagasaki on August 9. These two cities were active working parts of the Japanese war effort. One was an army center; the other was naval and industrial. Hiroshima was the headquarters of the Japanese Army defending southern Japan and was a major military storage and assembly point. Nagasaki was a major seaport and it contained several large industrial plants of great wartime importance. We believed that our attacks had struck cities which must certainly be important to the Japanese military leaders, both Army and Navy, and we waited for a result. We waited one day.

Many accounts have been written about the Japanese surrender. After a prolonged Japanese cabinet session in which the deadlock was broken by the Emperor himself, the offer to surrender was made on August 10. It was based on the Potsdam terms, with a reservation concerning the sovereignty of the Emperor. While the Allied reply made no promises other than those already given, it implicitly recognized the Emperor's position by prescribing that his power must be subject to the orders of the Allied Supreme Commander. These terms were accepted on August 14 by the Japanese, and the instrument of surrender was formally signed on September 2, in Tokyo Bay. Our great objective was thus achieved, and all the evidence I have seen indicates that the controlling factor in the final Japanese decision to accept our terms of surrender was the atomic bomb.

The two atomic bombs which we had dropped were the only ones we had ready, and our rate of production at the time was very small. Had the war continued until the projected invasion on November 1, additional fire raids of B-29's would have been more destructive of life and property than the very limited number of atomic raids which we could have executed in the same period. But the atomic bomb was more than a weapon of terrible destruction; it was a psychological weapon. In March 1945 our Air Force had launched its first great incendiary raid on the Tokyo area. In this raid more damage was done and more casualties were inflicted than was the case at Hiroshima. Hundreds of bombers took part and hundreds of tons of incendiaries were dropped. Similar successive raids

burned out a great part of the urban area of Japan, but the Japanese fought on. On August 6 one B-29 dropped a single atomic bomb on Hiroshima. Three days later a second bomb was dropped on Nagasaki and the war was over. So far as the Japanese could know, our ability to execute atomic attacks, if necessary by many planes at a time, was unlimited. As Dr. Karl Compton has said, "it was not one atomic bomb, or two, which brought surrender; it was the experience of what an atomic bomb will actually do to a community, *plus the dread of many more,* that was effective."

The bomb thus served exactly the purpose we intended. The peace party was able to take the path of surrender, and the whole weight of the Emperor's prestige was exerted in favor of peace. When the Emperor ordered surrender, and the small but dangerous group of fanatics who opposed him were brought under control, the Japanese became so subdued that the great undertaking of occupation and disarmament was completed with unprecedented ease.

A Personal Summary

In the foregoing pages I have tried to give an accurate account of my own personal observations of the circumstances which led up to the use of the atomic bomb and the reasons which underlay our use of it. To me they have always seemed compelling and clear, and I cannot see how any person vested with such responsibilities as mine could have taken any other course or given any other advice to his chiefs.

Two great nations were approaching contact in a fight to a finish which would begin on November 1, 1945. Our enemy, Japan, commanded forces of somewhat over 5,000,000 armed men. Men of these armies had already inflicted upon us, in our breakthrough of the outer perimeter of their defenses, over 300,000 battle casualties. Enemy armies still unbeaten had the strength to cost us a million more. *As long as the Japanese government refused to surrender,* we should be forced to take and hold the ground, and smash the Japanese ground armies, by close-in fighting of the same desperate and costly kind that we had faced in the Pacific islands for nearly four years.

In the light of the formidable problem which thus confronted us, I felt that every possible step should be taken to compel a surrender of the homelands, and a withdrawal of all Japanese troops from the Asiatic mainland and from other positions, before we had commenced an invasion. We held two cards to assist us in such an effort. One was the traditional veneration in which the Japanese Emperor was held by his subjects and the power which was thus vested in him over his loyal troops. It was for this reason that I suggested in my memorandum of July 2 that his dynasty should be continued. The second card was the use of the atomic bomb in the manner best calculated to persuade that Emperor and the counselors about him to submit to our demand for what was essentially unconditional surrender, placing his immense power over his people and his troops subject to our orders.

In order to end the war in the shortest possible time and to avoid the enormous losses of human life which otherwise confronted us, I felt that we must use the Emperor as our instrument to command and compel his people to cease fighting and subject themselves to our authority through him, and that to accomplish this we must give him and his controlling advisers a compelling reason to accede to our demands. This reason furthermore must be of such a nature that his people could understand his decision. The bomb seemed to me to furnish a unique instrument for that purpose.

My chief purpose was to end the war in victory with the least possible cost in the lives of the men in the armies which I had helped to raise. In the light of the alternatives which, on a fair estimate, were open to us I believe that no man, in our position and subject to our responsibilities, holding in his hands a weapon of such possibilities for accomplishing this purpose and saving those lives, could have failed to use it and afterwards looked his countrymen in the face.

As I read over what I have written, I am aware that much of it, in this year of peace, may have a harsh and unfeeling sound. It would perhaps be possible to say the same things and say them more gently. But I do not think it would be wise. As I look back over the five years of my service as Secretary of War, I see too many stern and heartrending decisions to be willing to pretend that war is anything else than what it is. The face of war is the face of death; death is an inevitable part of every order that a wartime leader gives. The decision to use the atomic bomb was a decision that brought death to over a hundred thousand Japanese. No explanation can change that fact and I do not wish to gloss it over. But this deliberate, premeditated destruction was our least abhorrent choice. The destruction of Hiroshima and Nagasaki put an end to the Japanese war. It stopped the fire raids, and the strangling blockade; it ended the ghastly specter of a clash of great land armies.

In this last great action of the Second World War we were given final proof that war is death. War in the twentieth century has grown steadily more barbarous, more destructive, more debased in all its aspects. Now, with the release of atomic energy, man's ability to destroy himself is very nearly complete. The bombs dropped on Hiroshima and Nagasaki ended a war. They also made it wholly clear that we must never have another war. This is the lesson men and leaders everywhere must learn, and I believe that when they learn it they will find a way to lasting peace. There is no other choice.

Chapter 8 Review Questions

1. What are the key differences between the *root* and *branch* methods of decision making? Summarize the advantages and disadvantages of each method.
2. Does the case study, "The Decision to Use the Atomic Bomb," exemplify the root or branch method of decision making? Explain your reasons for selecting one or the other method by citing examples from the case.

3. How does the case point up the influence of professionals in the decisional process? Which professionals in this case influenced its outcome? In what ways did they impact on the decisional processes? Does the case support Mosher's concept of the professional state discussed in the previous chapter? If so, how?

4. Compare this case about the atomic bomb with the previous case, "The Swine Flu Affair." Discuss the major differences in the way these two critical national decisions were reached. In particular, consider the number and kinds of people who became involved in the decisional processes, the care and manner by which the options for administrative action were presented and considered, the factors forcing the final decision, and the overall effectiveness of the decisional processes.

5. On the basis of your comparative appraisal of the two cases, can you generalize about how proper timing as well as the general historic time period play important roles in the way these or other public decisions are reached?

6. Also on the basis of your comparison of the two cases, why does who gets involved in the decisional process (or who is left out) play such a critical role in the quality and kind of decisions that are made in government?

Key Terms

incremental decision making	rational comprehensive analysis
root method	policy alternatives
branch method	maximization of values
clarification of objectives	empirical analysis
intertwining ends and means	policy outcomes
successive limited comparisons	ranking objectives

Suggestions for Further Reading

Making good, correct, and efficient decisions in the public interest has been a major concern of public administration literature since the early, "conscious" development of the field. In particular, the writings of Frederick Taylor and his followers about scientific management examined methods of rational decision making in organizations at the lower levels of industrial or business hierarchies. However, the post-World War II writings of Herbert Simon, especially his *Administrative Behavior: The Study of Decision Making Processes in Administrative Organization* (New York: Macmillan, 1947), shifted the focus of administrative thinking to *the decision* as the central focus of study and analysis. The enormous impact of this book (for which Simon won the Nobel Prize in 1978), as well as his other writings on public administration, make it worthy of careful attention by students of the field even today.

Other important writings on this topic include Charles E. Lindblom, *The Intelligence of Democracy: Decision Making Through Mutual Adjustment* (New York: Free Press, 1965), and his book co-authored with David Braybooke, *A Strategy of Decision* (New York: Free Press, 1963). For criticisms of the Simon–

Lindblom incrementalist approach see Yehezkel Dror, "Muddling Through—Science or Inertia?" *Public Administration Review,* 24 (September 1964), pp. 154–157, and Amitai Etzioni, "Mixed Scanning: A Third Approach to Decision Making," *Public Administration Review,* 27 (December 1967), pp. 385–392. The debate over incrementalism is hardly over, for an entire symposium in the *Public Administration Review,* 39 (November/December 1979) was devoted to its pros and cons. Pay particular attention to the articles by Charles E. Lindblom, "Still Muddling, Not Yet Through" (pp. 511–516); Camille Cates, "Beyond Muddling" (pp. 527–531); and Bruce Adams, "The Limitations of Muddling Through" (pp. 545–552); plus Amitai Eztioni, "Mixed Scanning Revisited," *Public Administration Review* 46 (January/February 1986), pp. 8–14. By contrast, Aaron Wildavsky, "Toward a Radical Incrementalism" in Alfred DeGrazia, *Congress: The First Branch of Government* (Washington, D.C.: American Enterprise Institute, 1966) pushes the incremental concept about as far as possible; whereas Paul R. Schulman, "Nonincremental Policy Making: Notes Toward an Alternative Paradigm," *American Political Science Review* 69 (December 1975), presents possibly the most searching critique of the incremental model.

Since the 1960s numerous decision models other than incrementalism have been proposed with various degrees of success. The most prominent include the *systems model* as represented in Fremont J. Lyden and Ernest G. Miller, eds., *Planning Programming-Budgeting: A Systems Approach to Management* (Chicago: Markham Publishing Co., 1968); *games theory* as outlined in Thomas C. Schelling, *The Strategy of Conflict* (Cambridge, Mass.: Harvard University Press, 1963); the *bureaucratic model* as represented in Graham T. Allison, *Essence of Decision: Explaining the Cuban Missile Crisis* (Boston: Little, Brown, 1971); *cost-benefit* as found in Edward M. Gramlich, *Benefit-Cost Analysis of Government Programs* (Englewood Cliffs, N.J.: Prentice-Hall, 1981); *personal judgment* approach of Harvey Sherman, *It All Depends* (University, Ala.: University of Alabama Press, 1966); as well as the *Policy analysis method* as discussed in William N. Dunn, *Public Policy Analysis: An Introduction* (Englewood Cliffs, N.J.: Prentice-Hall, 1981). These books only scratch the surface of a vast, complex area of decision-making study. You would be well advised to read the current issues of such journals as *Public Administration Review, Administrative Science Quarterly, Journal of Policy Analysis and Management, Public Management,* or *Harvard Business Review* for up-to-date perspectives on decision-making methodology. For two survey textbooks that outline a broad range of public sector quantitative decision techniques, see Michael J. White et al., *Managing Public Systems: Analytic Techniques for Public Administration* (No. Scituate, Mass.: Duxbury Press, 1981); and Richard D. Bingham and Marcus E. Ethridge, eds., *Reaching Decisions in Public Policy and Administration* (New York: Longman, 1982). For an up-to-date scholarly review of various decision-making approaches and where we stand today regarding their application to government, read George W. Downs and Patrick D. Larkey, *The Search for Government Efficiency: From Hubris to Helplessness* (New York: Random House, 1986); James G. March, "Theories of Choice and Decision Making," *Society* 20 (1982); and Michael Murray, *Decisions: A Comparative Analysis* (New York: Longman, 1986).

Administrative Communications: The Concept of Information Networks

"Blockages in the communications system constitute one of the most serious problems in public administration. They may occur in any one of the three steps in the communication process: initiation, transmission, or reception."

H. Simon, D. Smithburg, and V. Thompson

Introduction

In arriving at even the most routine policy decisions, the typical public administrator is a prisoner of a seemingly endless communications network that defines the problem at hand and the possible alternatives. Administrators are normally pressed from many sides with informational and data sources flowing into their offices from their superiors, subordinates, other agencies, citizen groups, and the general public. Sometimes the information arrives through routine formal channels; at other times it wells up or trickles down to the administrator via unsolicited routes. Whatever the source, the public decision maker must selectively sort out this information, and, in turn, dispense a substantial quantity of information to people within and outside the organizational structure; this is done by memoranda, reports, conferences, phone conversations, and informal encounters that touch off a new chain of communications and decisions by others. Like a telephone switchboard, a policy maker's office acts as a nerve center where the lines of communications cross and are connected and where information is received, processed, stored, assembled, analyzed, and dispensed.

Our conceptual understanding of the importance and complexity of the communications links within public organizations and their critical role in administrative decisions depends to a large extent on the work of Herbert A. Simon (1916–   ). In collaboration with Donald Smithburg and Victor Thompson, Simon wrote the text *Public Administration* (1950); this work, drawing on Simon's earlier writing, *Administrative Behavior* (1947), for which Simon won the Nobel Prize for economics in 1978, offered one of the first integrated behavioral interpretations of public administration. By introducing ideas from sociology, psychology, and political science, Simon and his associates sought to discover "a realistic behavioral description of the process of administration," emphasizing its informal human dynamics.

At the root of public administration, according to Simon, Smithburg, and Thompson, were continual conflicts among contending groups that resulted from such internal pressures as empire-building tendencies, differing individual backgrounds, and varying group identifications, as well as such external pressures as competing interest groups, members of Congress, and other agency heads struggling for scarce resources and influence. Similar to Norton Long's conception of the political power contest surrounding administrative activities (discussed in Chapter 4), the authors envision administrators as people "in the middle of continual conflict" whose actions and activities demand a considerable effort directed toward conflict resolution and compromise. As they write, "public administrators, and particularly those responsible for directions of unitary organizations, are themselves initiators and transformers of policy, brokers, if you like, who seek to bring about agreement between the program goals of government agencies and the goals and values of groups that possess political power." In short, "the greatest distinction between public administration and other administration is . . . to be found in the political character of public administration."

Decisions within this political setting can never be wholly rational but rather, the authors contend, are of a "bounded rational" nature. That is to say, instead of insisting on an "optimal solution," the public policy maker must be satisfied with what is "good enough," or as Lindblom suggests more simply in Chapter 8, must "muddle through." The prime ends of a public administrator's efforts are decisions that are not "maximizing" but "sufficing," that have as their goals not efficiency but achieving agreement, compromise, and ultimately survival.

One of the major vehicles for achieving coordination and compromise, in the view of Simon, Smithburg, and Thompson, is the communications network, which they define as the "process whereby decisional premises are transmitted from one member of an organization to another." The communications network acts principally as an integrating device for bringing together frequently conflicting elements of an organization in order to secure cooperative group effort. Three steps are involved in the communications process: first, "someone must initiate the communication"; second, "the command must be transmitted from its source to its destination"; and third, "communications must make its impact upon the recipient." The information travels in two ways: (1) the formal or planned channels such as memoranda, reports, and written communications; and (2) the unplanned or informal ways such as face-to-face contacts, conferences, or phone calls to friends. Simon, Smithburg, and Thompson place considerable emphasis on the informal lines of communications that many refer to as "the grapevine." "In most organizations, the greater part of the information that is used in decision-making is informally transmitted," they observe.

The central problems in communications are the blockages that occur: "Blockages in the communication system constitute one of the most serious problems in public administration. They may occur in any one of the three steps in the communications process: initiation, transmission, or reception. Those who have information may fail to tell those who need the information as a basis of action;

those who should transmit the information may fail to do so; those who receive the information may be unwilling or unable to assimilate it."

Seven critical types of communications blockages in public organizations are enumerated by the authors, the first being, simply, *barriers of language.* Words are frequently misinterpreted or understood differently as messages pass from one individual to another within organizations. Second, *frames of reference* differ so that the perception of information varies among individuals. Personal "mental sets" thus often prevent accurate comprehension of the problem at hand. Third, *status distance* can block communications because as information moves upward or downward through the various hierarchical levels of an organization "a considerable filtering and distorting" occurs. Fourth, *geographical distance* impedes the communications process; a far-flung department with many field offices spread over the nation or the world has great difficulty in ensuring prompt and accurate information exchange among its component units. Fifth, *self-protection* of the individual who reports actions plays a role in the informational links. Often "information that will evoke a favorable reaction will be played up; the mistakes and the fumbles tend to be glossed over." Sometimes the deception is conscious and at other times unconscious, but this activity always serves to distort objective reality. Sixth, *the pressures of work* tend to leave important matters overlooked or unreported. Finally, the *censorship* inherent in many governmental activities such as foreign intelligence or military operations limits the accurate flow of information within many public agencies.

These characteristic psychological and institutional communication blockages, suggest Simon, Smithburg, and Thompson, raise the vital question of "where a particular decision can best be made." Selection of the appropriate place for decision making directly depends on how effectively and easily information can be transmitted from its source to a decisional center, and how effectively and easily the decision can be transmitted from the decision maker to the point where action will occur. For instance, a military hierarchy could grant to individual company commanders the authority for deciding on the use of tactical nuclear weapons. This action would reduce the "time costs" associated with communicating to higher headquarters in the event of possible enemy attack and thus would allow for extreme military flexibility at lower echelons, but "local option" in this case might very well increase other costs, such as the likelihood of a nuclear accident. On the other hand, if authority for using these weapons had to be cleared, say, by the president of the United States and by other major Allied powers, the risk of accident might very well be reduced but the time costs of gaining consent to use these weapons from many sources might make a decision so cumbersome and lengthy that there would be no opportunity for swift retaliatory response. As Simon, Smithburg, and Thompson point out, "Ease or difficulty of communications may sometimes be a central consideration in determining how far down the administrative line the function of making a particular decision should be located." The authors thus view the communications process not only as determining the outcome of particular decisions but as a prime influence on the structure of decision making within organizations. Extreme decentralization may achieve flexibility and initiative at the local level but may exact costs in terms of uniformity and control of response; vice versa, extreme centralization may produce maximum oversight but may reduce organizational responsiveness. Ultimately, the costs associated with delegating such decisional authority within an organizational hierarchy are always relative and are determined by the values and objectives of the organization. In the following selection from Simon, Smithburg, and Thompson's *Public Administration,* many of the enduring and difficult dilemmas of communications within public organizations are outlined.

As you read this selection, keep the following questions in mind:

Can you think of any additional blockages to administrative communications other than those outlined by the authors? For instance, reflect on any communications barriers that might have been apparent to you in the previous cases, "The Swine Flu Affair" or "The Decision to Use the Atomic Bomb."

Is it possible to trace the *formal* network of communications in an organization? The *informal* network? What factors would create or determine a formal informational network? For example, what impact have computers had in recent years?

Can you draw from this essay generalizations concerning the communications process as a means for establishing executive authority and control over an organization? How does fragmentation of executive authority occur in public organizations and how can communications be used effectively "to cure" this problem (think about the first case, "The Blast in Centralia No. 5")?

Finally, consider the following essay in relation to Norton Long's concept of administrative power—do administrative communications influence the patterns of administrative power? How did communications influence the outcomes in the case study in Chapter three, "Dumping $2.6 Million on Bakersfield"?

HERBERT A. SIMON, DONALD W. SMITHBURG, AND VICTOR A. THOMPSON

The Communication Process

The American disaster at Pearl Harbor is one of the dramatic examples in modern times of the possible consequences of failure of an organization communication system. Quite apart from the question of who or what was to "blame" for Pearl Harbor, a large part of the military dam-

From *Public Administration* by Herbert A. Simon, Donald W. Smithburg, and Victor A. Thompson. Copyright 1950 by Herbert A. Simon, Donald W. Smithburg, and Victor A. Thompson. Reprinted by permission.

age inflicted by the Japanese undoubtedly could have been avoided if two serious breaks in the military communication system had not occurred. The first was the failure to secure proper top-level attention to the intercepted "Winds" message that gave warning an attack was impending. The second was the failure to communicate to the military commander in Hawaii information accidentally obtained from the radar system by an enlisted man that unidentified planes were approaching Pearl Harbor.

Less dramatic, but of equal importance, is the role that communication plays in the day-to-day work of every organization. Without communication, not even the first steps can be taken toward human cooperation, and it is impossible to speak about organizational problems without speaking about communication, or at least taking it for granted.

This process, which is central to all organizational behavior, can be illustrated with the example of a policeman operating a patrol car. He is told to patrol in a particular patrol area; he is provided with a manual of regulations and approved procedures; when he reports for duty in the morning, he may receive specific instructions of things to watch for during the day. He may be given a list of license numbers of recently stolen automobiles and perhaps a description of a fugitive. As he patrols his beat, a call may come to him from the police radio informing him of a store burglary to investigate.

The patrolman, in turn, becomes a source of communications that influence other organization members. His report on the burglary investigation is turned over to the investigations division where it becomes the basis of further activity by a detective. Certain data from this report are recorded by a clerk and are later summarized for the weekly report that goes to the chief of police. Information contained in this weekly report may lead to a redistribution of patrol areas to equalize work loads. Meanwhile, other data from the report have gone into the pawnshop file where they are used by other detectives who systematically survey local pawnshops for stolen goods.

Communication and Organization Structure

By tracing these and other communications from source to destination, we discover a rich and complex network of channels through which orders and information flow. Viewing the communication process from a point in an organization where a decision is to be made, the process has a twofold aspect: communications must flow to the decision center to provide the basis for decision, and the decision must be communicated from the decision center in order to influence other members of the organization whose cooperation must be secured to carry out the decision.

The question of where in the organization a particular decision can best be made will depend in considerable part upon how effectively and easily information can be transmitted from its source to a decision center, and how effectively and easily the decision can be transmitted to the point where action will take place. The decision of a social worker in a public welfare agency in granting or refusing an application for assistance illustrates how these factors enter into the picture. The principal facts and values that have to be brought to bear on this decision are: (1) the economic and social facts of the applicant's situation; (2) accepted principles of casework; and (3) the eligibility regulations and casework policies of the agency. The first set of facts is obtained by interviewing the applicant, by correspondence, and by field investigation. The second set of considerations is derived from the education and training of the social worker and his supervisors. Policies governing the third set of considerations are largely established by the legislative body and the top administrative levels of the agency and communicated downward.

If the decision on the application is to be

made by the social worker himself, these three sets of considerations must be communicated to him. The costs of communication here are the time cost of his own investigational activities, the costs of training him adequately in the accepted principles of casework, and the costs of indoctrinating him in agency policies by formal training, instructions, discussion with his supervisor, or otherwise. Once he has made the decision, it must be communicated to the applicant—a relatively simple step—and certain reports on his action must be transmitted to his superiors for supervisory and control purposes.

On the other hand, the decision on the application might be placed in the hands of the casework supervisor, rather than the social worker. This might shorten the communication chain required to bring agency policy to bear on the decision and the chain that reports on the action would have to travel. Further, if the social workers were relieved of this decision, they would probably not need to be as thoroughly trained in casework as if they made the decisions themselves—training efforts could be concentrated on the supervisors. However, in other respects new costs of communication would be incurred. It would be necessary to communicate from social worker to supervisor all the circumstances of the applicant's situation—a very voluminous reporting job and an almost impossible one if intangible impressions received by the social worker in the interview are to be communicated. Moreover, there would be an extra step in communicating the decision on the application to the applicant via the social worker.

Ease or difficulty of communication may sometimes be a central consideration in determining how far down the administrative line the function of making a particular decision should be located (or, as it is usually put, "how far authority should be delegated"). Delegation increases the difficulty of communicating organization policies that are decided at the top and reports from the decision center to the top that are required to determine compliance with pol-

icy. Delegation may also involve greater training costs by multiplying the number of persons who have to be competent to make a particular decision. Delegation usually reduces the difficulty of communicating to the decision center information about the particular situation in question, and usually reduces the difficulty of communicating the decision to the point where it is placed into operation. All these factors were illustrated in the previous example.

Steps in the Communication Process

In the study of communication processes it is convenient to distinguish three steps:

1. Someone must initiate the communication. If the communication is a monthly report, someone must be assigned the task of preparing the report. Many of the most important communications originate outside the organization, or in special "intelligence" units of the organization. Examples of the first would be a fire alarm, a phone call to the police department, or the filing of a patent application or a workman's compensation claim. Examples of the second would be the reports of military reconnaisance aircraft, an information report by an embassy to the State Department on developments abroad, or a compilation of employment statistics by the U.S. Department of Labor.
2. The communication must be transmitted from its source to its destination.
3. The communication must make its impact upon the recipient. The communication has not really been "communicated" when it reaches the desk of the recipient, but only when it reaches his mind. There is a potential gap here 'twixt cup and lip. It will receive attention in later portions of this chapter.

We shall see that costs and difficulties of communication may be encountered at each of these three stages of the process. Before we proceed to a detailed analysis of these costs and difficulties, however, it is necessary to describe in somewhat greater detail the elements that go to make up an organization communication system.

Elements of the Communication System

Roughly, organizational communications fall in two categories: planned or "formal" communications and unplanned or "informal" communications. Every organization has some formal arrangements whereby knowledge can be transmitted to those who need it. But this formal transmission of information is supplemented by a great deal of communication that springs from the willingness, indeed, the eagerness, of employees to share information with one another even when such transmission is not formally authorized, and even when it is forbidden.

Formal Communication

The administrative manual of a large organization often specifies who may write officially to whom; who must report to whom and on what occasions; who shall see memoranda on particular subjects; who shall give out information on specified subjects. This attempt to plan and to channel communications can be seen in perhaps its most elaborate form in the armed services, where extremely intricate patterns of communication are incorporated into formal rules and where channels are rigidly enforced.

Where the work of an organization consists of processing applications or claims, the written procedures will usually specify in considerable detail just how the application is to be routed, what information is to be entered on it at each step, and what work is to be performed. Similarly, the form, content, and responsibility for preparation of accounting records is almost always formally determined.

Informal Communications

. . . The growth of an informal communication system . . . supplements the formal, prescribed system. For example, the unit chief who wants advance information as to whether it is going to be easy or difficult to secure a budget increase for the coming year may find that a friend who is assistant to the bureau chief can give him the desired information long before any formal bulletin flows down through the established channels.

Method of Informal Communication   The ways in which information is disseminated informally are many. Jones, Smith, and Goldberg who work in different sections lunch together. Each has connections with various parts of the organization, and they swap information. Mrs. Johnson belongs to the same lodge auxiliary as the wife of Mr. Alexander who is administrative assistant to the bureau chief. Mrs. Johnson gets some information which she transmits to her husband who, in turn, passes it on to his section.

But informal communication is not only the inevitable, if somewhat illicit, shop talk and gossip. It includes any kind of information outside the specified channels. Nor is it always easy to define what is meant by "channels"—normally these include communications along the lines of formal authority, or along lines that have been explicitly authorized by the formal hierarchy. In most organizations, the greater part of the information that is used in decision-making is informally transmitted.

Barriers to Effective Communication

The amount of misunderstanding in the world caused by failure of people to communicate effectively with each other can hardly be exaggerated. Words are tenuous. The failure of human plans and aspirations are all too often bitterly recalled in terms like "if it could have been gotten across," or "if I had said it this way rather than that, he might have understood."

Blockages in the communication system constitute one of the most serious problems in public administration. They may occur in any one of three steps in the communications process: initiation, transmission, or reception. Those who have information may fail to tell those who need the information as a basis of action; those who should transmit the information may fail to do so; those who receive the information may be unwilling or unable to assimilate it.

The Barrier of Language

Among the barriers to effective communication one of the most serious is the use of language that is not understandable to the recipient. In a society as specialized as ours there are literally hundreds of different languages which cluster around the various specialties. Many words quite understandable to a physician are Greek to the layman. Many words quite understandable to the skilled machinist are incomprehensible to the doctor. The vocabulary shared by all Americans is meager indeed.

Not only is the shared vocabulary meager, but the words that are shared often mean different things to different people. Philosophers like Ogden and Richards and Carnap have shown how many traps in philosophy have at their base a faulty use of language. At a more popular level, students of semantics have also shown us that many so-called problems are really pseudo-problems which, when correctly formulated, disappear.

Within administration, the written communication is likely to be even more plagued by language difficulties than the oral communication. Most persons in face-to-face contacts try to speak in terms that will be understood by the listener—and if they do not, they will soon be aware of the fact. They can repeat the communication in different terms. They can explain what they "really mean." The author of a written

communication has no such an opportunity to assess his audience or to gauge the degree to which his words are being understood.

Frame of Reference

Very often the communication process is impeded because those giving, transmitting, or receiving the communication have a "mental set" that prevents accurate perception of the problem. The stimuli that fall on a person's eyes and ears are screened, filtered, and modified by the nervous system before they even reach consciousness—and memory makes further selections of the things it will retain and the things it will forget. This selecting process is an important reason why our judgments of people are so often wrong. If we have a favorable impression of a man, we are likely to remember the good things about him that come to our attention and to forget, discount, or explain away the bad things. Only a series of several vivid, undesirable impressions is likely to change our initial estimate of him.

Status Distance

Communication between persons distant in scalar status most often takes place through a chain of intermediaries. When there is contact between individuals of different status, communication from the superior to the subordinate generally takes place more easily than communication from the subordinate to the superior. If communication were not difficult between persons of widely different status, organizations would not feel the need, as they so often do, to install suggestion boxes that permit low-level employees to bring their ideas to the attention of top executives. And experience with formal suggestion systems shows that even this device is often inadequate to lower the barrier of status difference.

Status differences exert a considerable filtering and distorting influence upon communication—both upward and downward. Upward communication is hampered by the need of pleasing those in authority. Good news gets told. Bad news often does not. The story of Haround al Raschid, the caliph who put on beggar's clothes and went out among his people to hear what they really thought, is the story of the isolation of every high status executive. Most executives are very effectively insulated from the operating levels of the organization. For a number of reasons, pleasant matters are more apt to get communicated upwards than information about mistakes. Subordinates do not want to call attention to their mistakes, nor do they want the executive to think that they can't handle their own difficulties without turning to him. They want to tell him the things he would like to hear. Hence, things usually look rosier at the top than they really are. . . .

Geographical Distance

One of the most striking and far-reaching phenomena of our era has been the tremendous extension of the mechanical techniques of communication. Changes in the technology of communication have changed both the structure and the problems of administrative organizations. Probably more than any other single factor, the improvement of the means of communication has had a centralizing effect upon administration—centralizing in the sense that a field officer can now be supervised in much greater detail than was previously possible.

Far-flung organizations can now be within hour-to-hour communication with their headquarters. This has enabled central offices to keep a far tighter check rein upon the activities of their agents in the field. Ambassadors who formerly had broad discretion to act in their negotiations with other nations, now can and must constantly check their views with a central office. The operations of widely dispersed field offices can come under the constant scrutiny of central headquarters.

Even where geographical dispersion is not wide, such as in modern police and fire departments, the effect of instantaneous communica-

tion has changed the whole pattern of their operations. It has made possible a greater efficiency and greater specialization. The radio police car can be summoned rapidly to an area of trouble. The work of the fire department can be directed rapidly and efficiently.

Inadequacy of Techniques But modern communication techniques have not completely overcome the problems of communicating at a distance, and, in addition, they have added new problems of their own. Communication by letter, wire, or telephone, although it may be rapid, is no effective substitute for the face-to-face interchange. As Latham has pointed out:

> Impediments to the free exchange of thought are difficult enough to overcome in the same city, building, or even room. They become even more difficult with the increase of distance between the central office and the field. In the same environment, geographical, social, and professional, the common milieu sometimes gives many clues to understanding which precise words could not have spelled out. This element is missing in communications at a distance.[1]

The difficulties of communication at a distance, even with modern means, are several. Oral communication by telephone, while the closest counterpart to face-to-face conference, is by no means a perfect substitute. It is costly, and mechanically imperfect over great distances, and the important overtones of oral communication that are ordinarily conveyed by facial expression and gesture are missing.

Written communication is an even less adequate substitute for the conference. Even in verbal content, a two-page single-spaced letter is the equivalent of only ten minutes' conversation. A division head, with offices adjacent to those of his bureau chief, might confer with his

---

[1]Earl Latham, *The Federal Field Service* (Chicago: Public Administration Service, 1947), pp. 8–9.

superior individually and in conference a half hour or an hour daily. To communicate the same material in writing would require an interchange of six to twelve single-spaced pages a day. Even then, the letter is much less likely to convey exact ideas than is a conversation, where misunderstanding can be detected and corrected immediately, questions raised, and so forth.

Insufficient Communication Moreover, daily personal contact stimulates communication. A man may think to pass on to his superior or subordinate over a luncheon table a piece of information that it would not occur to him to put down in a letter. Where there is geographical separation, the person at each end of the communication line finds it difficult to visualize and keep constantly in mind the needs for information at the other end of the line. A constant complaint of field offices is that they learn from the daily newspapers or from clients things that should have been communicated to them from the central office.

Consider, for example, the problem of communicating a change in rent control regulations. Such a change will probably be publicly announced by the central office at a press conference and instantly transmitted in more or less complete form by newspaper wire services throughout the country. Washington representatives of real estate groups will also advise their local clients of the new regulation, often by telegraph or telephone. To prevent premature disclosure of the regulations, the central office may be reluctant to send them in advance to local field offices, with the result that these field offices may be bombarded by questions from tenants and landlords before they have had any detailed information on the new regulations from the central office. This pattern repeated itself again and again in wartime regulatory programs and was a continual source of friction between central and field offices.

Excessive Communication Paradoxically, field offices often complain that they receive too many communications at the same time that they complain that they are insufficiently informed on new developments. The attempt of the central office to supervise closely the operations in the field often results in a steady flow of procedural regulations, instructions, bulletins, and whatnot to the field offices. If too much of this material is trivial, detailed, or unadapted to local problems—and the field office will often feel that it is—it may remain unread, undigested, and ineffective. This problem is not one of geographical separation alone, but applies generally to organization communications.

Self-protection of the Initiator

We have already pointed out that most persons find it difficult to tell about actions that they believe would put them in a bad light. It is much easier to secure reports about overtime than it is to get reports on the number of times the workers reported late or took extra time for lunch. Furthermore, the ordinary work code demanding loyalty to work groups also prevents the communication of information that would seem to reflect upon one's friends or upon the organization of which one is a part. In consequence, reports flowing upward in the organization, such as reports to Congress, the President, or the public, tend to be "sugar-coated." Information that will evoke a favorable reaction will be played up; the mistakes and the fumbles tend to be glossed over. Information going downward is equally suspect. A casual reading of any house organ will reveal how carefully the higher executives and their actions are "explained" to employees in a way that will show the wisdom of their decisions and their benevolence toward those who occupy the lower levels. In part, this deception is conscious. In part, it is unconscious. These upward and downward distortions make an actual and objective view of the organization difficult to obtain.

Pressure of Other Work

A person in an ordinary work situation is normally pressed for time. He must establish a system of priorities as to the various demands made upon him. In such circumstances he is likely to respond to the pressures of the immediate work situation while giving lower priority to the more abstract demands of communicating with others. Furthermore, the constant demand for information concerning the details of his work often meets with unspoken resentment because it seems to reflect upon his integrity. If he does not know why he is asked for specific types of information, he is likely to conjure up ideas that the "head office" will use the information against him or that the request has no purpose—that it is mere make-work.

Similarly, the central office is likely to take an authoritarian view of the communication process and resent the constant inquiries from those lower in the hierarchy or the field. It, too, is likely to slough off the job of communication and to regard it as less important than the task of setting policy. Thus, in many agencies the task of communication is thought of as something basically clerical—a mere stenographic transmittal of decisions. Communication is likely to be shunted into the background.

Deliberate Restrictions upon Communication

One problem of much government communication is to see that it reaches those who should have the information and yet to prevent it from reaching those who would use it in an undesirable way. There is always disagreement between those individuals who believe that the public should have information concerning every aspect of government policy and policy formulation—particularly those in the press whose business is the dissemination of information—and those in government service who would argue that the compromises which are essential in the formation of public policy would not be possible if every move had to be carried on in the relentless glare of publicity.

Whether or not to have publicity is not a new problem. The founding fathers determined that the only possible way in which agreement could be reached on a new constitution was to conduct the deliberations without continuous publicity. To prevent the publication of the deliberations they even went so far as to establish a guard for the aged, brilliant, but garrulous Benjamin Franklin to see that his disclosures in the neighborhood taverns would not jeopardize the goals of the convention.

CASE STUDY 9

Introduction

In the foregoing discussion of the concept of administrative communications, Simon, Smithburg, and Thompson illustrated with the story of Pearl Harbor the dramatic importance of effective administrative communications. The Japanese attack caught the American military off-guard largely because of two serious breakdowns in communications: the failure to secure top-level attention to the intercepted "Winds Message," and the failure to communicate to the local base commander the early radar warnings of the approaching enemy aircraft. Both information gaps in military communications had immediate, drastic consequences for American national defense.

In the following case study, the lessons regarding the importance of accurate and timely information are drawn from a more recent wartime situation—Vietnam. This story takes place far from the battlefield—for the most part, inside Central Intelligence Agency (CIA) headquarters near Washington, D.C.—and involves information important for planning the course of the war, estimates of enemy Vietcong (VC) troop strength.

This well-written, compelling story is told in the first person by the principal player, Sam Adams, a mid-level CIA analyst who early in the course of the Vietnam War began to study VC defection statistics. By seriously examining for the first time samples of captured enemy documents in early 1966, Adams made the startling, but relatively simple, deduction that official U.S. data on VC troops were grossly understated. Rather, the real figures on VC troops were at least twice as high as official estimates (at that time, 270,000 personnel).

When he first discovered these serious statistical errors, Adams initially expected his revelations to earn both praise and support from his superiors because it seemed to him that the size of the enemy opposition had a primary, if not the major, role in shaping the overall nature, direction, and level of American response to the Vietnam conflict. What follows in Adams's own words is the unusual but fascinating tale of how his government agency (the CIA) coped with information that it clearly preferred not to hear. Akin to the fable of the messenger who lost his head because he brought bad news to the king, Adams found himself ignored, ridiculed, and ostracized by his superiors, a treatment that in the end forced his resignation from the CIA.

Although part of the story involves how information on enemy troop strength was collected, much of Adams's account focuses on the receptivity, or the lack of receptivity, to new but unwanted information, and the variety of complex "organizational defense mechanisms" that are raised as barriers against data that run counter to ingrained institutional doctrines. The severe career and personal penalties meted out to an individual like Adams who unflinchingly dared to tell the truth to his superiors, and the promotional rewards that accrue to those who "get along and go along" with the system, are poignant lessons for those who think that communicating truth to the powerful in government agencies may be either easy or simple.

As you read this selection, keep the following questions in mind:

How did Adams arrive at his estimates of VC troop strength? Do you think he used a reasonable and valid approach in gathering this information?

Was the significance of the data, in your opinion, as important as he claimed? Explain why or why not.

What strategies did Adams use to get his information to the top-level war policy planners? Who were his allies and enemies in this effort to gain access to the top-level planners?

What defense mechanisms did the organization utilize to protect itself from Adams's unwanted statistics?

How did history repeat itself with regard to Adams's information about the Cambodian war?

If you had been Sam Adams, would you have altered your strategies in speaking the truth to your superiors in any way?

On the basis of this case or from your own experience, can you generalize about organizational receptivity to new and perhaps unwelcome information?

How did Simon, Smithburg, and Thompson classify the type or types of barriers to administrative communications that is evidenced in this case? Do you think the authors placed sufficient emphasis on the type(s) of communications barriers? If not, how might you rewrite their discussion of administrative communications to give the problem encountered by Adams adequate attention?

SAM ADAMS

Vietnam Cover-Up: Playing War with Numbers

In late 1965, well after the United States had committed ground troops to Vietnam, the CIA assigned me to study the Vietcong. Despite the almost 200,000 American troops and the advanced state of warfare in South Vietnam, I was the first intelligence analyst in Washington to be given the full-time job of researching our South Vietnamese enemies. Incredible as it now seems, I remained the only analyst with this assignment until just before the Tet offensive of 1968.

At CIA headquarters in 1965 nobody was studying the enemy systematically, the principal effort being geared to a daily publication called the "Sitrep" (Vietnam Situation Report), which concerned itself with news about the activities of South Vietnamese politicians and the location of Vietcong units. The Sitrep analysts used the latest cables from Saigon, and tended to neglect information that didn't fit their objectives. The Johnson Administration was already wondering how long the Vietcong could stick it out, and since this seemed too complicated a question for the Sitrep to answer, the CIA's research department assigned it to me. I was told to find out the state of enemy morale.

Good News and Bad News

I looked upon the new job as something of a promotion. Although I had graduated from Harvard in 1955, I didn't join the Agency until 1963,

and I had been fortunate in my first assignment as an analyst of the Congo rebellion. My daily and weekly reports earned the praise of my superiors, and the Vietcong study was given to me by way of reward, encouraging me in my ambition to make a career within the CIA.

Without guidance and not knowing what else to do, I began to tinker with the VC defector statistics, trying to figure out such things as where the defectors came from, what jobs they had, and why they had wanted to quit. In short order I read through the collection of weekly reports, and so I asked for a ticket to Vietnam to see what other evidence was available over there. In mid-January 1966, I arrived in Saigon to take up a desk in the U.S. Embassy. After a couple of weeks, the CIA station chief (everyone called him "Jorgy") heard I was in the building adding and subtracting the number of defectors. He called me into his office. "Those statistics aren't worth a damn," he said. "No numbers in Vietnam are, and, besides, you'll never learn anything sitting around Saigon." He told me I ought to go to the field and start reading captured documents. I followed Jorgy's advice.

The captured documents suggested a phenomenon that seemed incredible to me. Not only were the VC taking extremely heavy casualties, but large numbers of them were deserting. I got together two sets of captured papers concerning desertion. The first set consisted of enemy unit rosters, which would say, for example, that in a certain seventy-seven-man outfit, only sixty men were "present for duty." Of the seventeen absent, two were down with malaria, two were at training school, and thirteen had deserted.

The other documents were directives from various VC headquarters telling subordinates to do something about the growing desertion rate. "Christ Almighty," they all seemed to say. "These AWOLs are getting out of hand. Far too many of our boys are going over the hill."

I soon collected a respectable stack of rosters, some of them from large units, and I began to extrapolate. I set up an equation which went like this: If A, B, and C units (the ones for which I had documents) had so many deserters in such and such a period of time, then the number of deserters per year for the whole VC Army was X. No matter how I arranged the equation, X always turned out to be a very big number. I could never get it below 50,000. Once I even got it up to 100,000.

The significance of this finding in 1966 was immense. At that time our official estimate of the strength of the enemy was 270,000. We were killing, capturing, and wounding VC at a rate of almost 150,000 a year. If to these casualties you added 50,000 to 100,000 deserters—well, it was hard to see how a 270,000-man army could last more than a year or two longer.

I returned in May to tell everyone the good news. No one at CIA headquarters had paid much attention to VC deserters because captured documents were almost entirely neglected. The finding created a big stir. Adm. William F. Raborn, Jr., then director of the CIA, called me in to brief him and his deputies about the Vietcong's AWOL problem. Right after the briefing, I was told that the Agency's chief of research, R. Jack Smith, had called me *"the* outstanding analyst" in the research directorate.

But there were also skeptics, particularly among the CIA's old Vietnam hands, who had long since learned that good news was often illusory. To be on the safe side, the Agency formed what was called a "Vietcong morale team" and sent it to Saigon to see if the news was really true. The team consisted of myself, acting as a "consultant," and four Agency psychiatrists, who presumably understood things like morale.

The psychiatrists had no better idea than I'd had, when I started out, how to plumb the Vietcong mind. One of the psychiatrists said, "We'll never get Ho Chi Minh to lie still on a leather couch, so we better think up something else quick." They decided to ask the CIA men in the

provinces what *they* thought about enemy morale. After a month or so of doing this, the psychiatrists went back to Washington convinced that, by and large, Vietcong spirits were in good shape. I went back with suitcases full of captured documents that supported my thesis about the Vietcong desertion rate.

But I was getting uneasy. I trusted the opinion of the CIA men in the field who had told the psychiatrists of the Vietcong's resilience. The South Vietnamese government was in one of its periodic states of collapse, and somehow it seemed unlikely that the Vietcong would be falling apart at the same time. I began to suspect that something was wrong with my prediction that the VC were headed for imminent trouble. On reexamining the logic that had led me to the prediction, I saw that it was based on three main premises. Premise number one was that the Vietcong were suffering very heavy casualties. Although I'd heard all the stories about exaggerated reporting, I tended not to believe them, because the heavy losses were also reflected in the documents. Premise two was my finding that the enemy army had a high desertion rate. Again, I believed the documents. Premise three was that both the casualties and the deserters came out of an enemy force of 270,000. An old Vietnam hand, George Allen, had already told me that this number was suspect.

In July, I went to my supervisor and told him I thought there might be something radically wrong with our estimate of enemy strength, or, in military jargon, the order of battle. "Maybe the 270,000 number is too low," I said. "Can I take a closer look at it?" He said it was okay with him just so long as I handed in an occasional item for the Sitrep. This seemed fair enough, and so I began to put together a file of captured documents.

The documents in those days were arranged in "bulletins," and by mid-August I had collected more than 600 of them. Each bulletin contained several sheets of paper with summaries in English of the information in the papers taken by American military units. On the afternoon of August 19, 1966, a Friday, Bulletin 689 reached my desk on the CIA's fifth floor. It contained a report put out by the Vietcong headquarters in Binh Dinh province, to the effect that the guerrilla-militia in the province numbered just over

50,000. I looked for our own intelligence figures for Binh Dinh in the order of battle and found the number 4,500.

"My God," I thought, "that's not even a tenth of what the VC say."

In a state of nervous excitement, I began searching through my file of bulletins for other discrepancies. Almost the next document I looked at, the one for Phu Yen province, showed 11,000 guerrilla-militia. In the official order of battle we had listed 1,400, an eighth of the Vietcong estimate. I almost shouted from my desk, "There goes the whole damn order of battle!"

Unable to contain my excitement, I began walking around the office, telling anybody who would listen about the enormity of the oversight and the implications of it for our conduct of the war. That weekend I returned to the office, and on both Saturday and Sunday I searched through the entire collection of 600-odd bulletins and found further proof of a gross underestimate of the strength of the enemy we had been fighting for almost two years. When I arrived in the office on Monday a colleague of mine brought me a document of a year earlier which he thought might interest me. It was from Vietcong headquarters in South Vietnam, and it showed that in early 1965 the VC had about 200,000 guerrilla-militia in the south, and that they were planning to build up to 300,000 by the end of the year. Once again, I checked the official order of battle. It listed a figure of exactly 103,573 guerrilla-militia—in other words, half as many as the Vietcong said they had in early 1965, and a third as many as they planned to have by 1966.[1]

No Official Comment

That afternoon, August 22, I wrote a memorandum suggesting that the overall order of battle estimate of 270,000 might be 200,000 men too low. Supporting it with references to numerous bulletins, I sent it up to the seventh floor, and then waited anxiously for the response. I imagined all kinds of sudden and dramatic telephone calls. "Mr. Adams, come brief the director." "The President's got to be told about this, and you'd better be able to defend those numbers." I wasn't sure what would happen, but I was sure it would be significant, because I knew this was the biggest intelligence find of the war—by far. It was important because the planners running the war in those days used statistics as a basis for everything they did, and the most important figure of all was the size of the enemy army— that order of battle number, 270,000. All our other intelligence estimates were tied to the order of battle: how much rice the VC ate, how much ammunition they shot off, and so forth. If the Vietcong Army suddenly doubled in size, our whole statistical system would collapse. We'd be fighting a war twice as big as the one we thought we were fighting. We already had about 350,000 soldiers in Vietnam, and everyone was talking about "force ratios." Some experts maintained that in a guerrilla war our side had to outnumber the enemy by a ratio of 10 to 1; others said 5 to 1; the most optimistic said 3 to 1. But even if we used the 3 to 1 ratio, the addition of 200,000 men to the enemy order of battle meant that somebody had to find an extra 600,000 troops for our side. This would put President Johnson in a very tight fix—either quit the war or send more soldiers. Once he was informed of the actual enemy strength, it seemed inconceivable that he could continue with the existing force levels. I envisioned the President calling the director on the carpet, asking him why this information hadn't been found out before.

Nothing happened. No phone calls from anybody. On Wednesday I still thought there must have been some terrible mistake; on Thursday I thought the news might have been so important that people were still trying to decide what to do with it. Instead, on Friday, the memorandum dropped back in my in-box. There was no comment on it at all—no request for amplification, no question about my numbers, nothing, just a routine slip attached showing that the entire CIA hierarchy had read it.

I was aghast. Here I had come up with 200,000 additional enemy troops, and the CIA hadn't even bothered to ask me about it, let alone tell

---

[1] A document was later captured which showed the Vietcong not only reached but exceeded their quota. Dated April 1966, it put the number of guerrilla-militia at 330,000.

anybody else. I got rather angry and wrote a second memorandum, attaching even more references to other documents. Among these was a report from the Vietcong high command showing that the VC controlled not 3 million people (as in our official estimate) but 6 million (their estimate). I thought that this helped to explain the origins of the extra 200,000 guerrilla-militia, and also that it was an extraordinary piece of news in its own right. A memorandum from my office—the office of Current Intelligence—ordinarily would be read, edited, and distributed within a few days to the White House, the Pentagon, and the State Department. It's a routine procedure, but once again I found myself sitting around waiting for a response, getting angrier and angrier. After about a week I went up to the seventh floor to find out what had happened to my memo. I found it in a safe, in a manila folder marked "Indefinite Hold."

I went back down to the fifth floor, and wrote still another memo, referencing even more documents. This time I didn't send it up, as I had the others, through regular channels. Instead, I carried it upstairs with the intention of giving it to somebody who would comment on it. When I reached the office of the Asia-Africa area chief, Waldo Duberstein, he looked at me and said: "It's that Goddamn memo again. Adams, stop being such a prima donna." In the next office, an official said that the order of battle was General Westmoreland's concern, and we had no business intruding. This made me even angrier. "We're all in the same government," I said. "If there's discrepancy this big, it doesn't matter who points it out. This is no joke. We're in a war with these guys." My remarks were dismissed as rhetorical, bombastic, and irrelevant.

On the ninth of September, eighteen days after I'd written the first memo, the CIA agreed to let a version of it out of the building, but with very strange restrictions. It was to be called a "draft working paper," meaning that it lacked official status; it was issued in only 25 copies, instead of the usual run of over 200; it could go to "working-level types" only—analysts and staff people—but not to anyone in a policy-making position—to no one, for example, on the National Security Council. One copy

went to Saigon, care of Westmoreland's Order of Battle Section, carried by an official who worked in the Pentagon for the Defense Intelligence Agency.

By this time I was so angry and exhausted that I decided to take two weeks off to simmer down. This was useless. I spent the whole vacation thinking about the order of battle. When I returned to the Agency, I found that it came out monthly and was divided into four parts, as follows:

Communist regulars	About 110,000
	(it varied by month)
Guerrilla-militia	Exactly 103,573
Service troops	Exactly 18,553
Political cadres	Exactly 39,175
	That is 271,301
	or about 270,000

The only category that ever changed was "Communist regulars" (uniformed soldiers in the Vietcong Army). In the last two years, this figure had more than doubled. The numbers for the other three categories had remained precisely the same, even to the last digit. There was only one conclusion: no one had even looked at them! I decided to do so right away, and to find out where the numbers came from and whom they were describing.

I began by collecting more documents on the guerrilla-militia. These were "the soldiers in black pajamas" the press kept talking about; lightly armed in some areas, armed to the teeth in others, they planted most of the VC's mines and booby traps. This was important, I discovered, because in the Da Nang area, for example, mines and booby traps caused about two-thirds of all the casualties suffered by U.S. Marines.

I also found where the number 103,573 came from. The South Vietnamese had thought it up in 1964; American Intelligence had accepted it without question, and hadn't checked it since. "Can you believe it?" I said to a fellow analyst. "Here we are in the middle of a guerrilla war, and we haven't even bothered to count the number of guerrillas."

The service troops were harder to locate. The order of battle made it clear that these VC soldiers were comparable to specialists in the American Army—ordnance sergeants, quartermasters, medics, engineers, and so forth. But despite repeated phone calls to the Pentagon, to U.S. Army headquarters, and to the office of the Joint Chiefs of Staff, I couldn't find anyone who knew where or when we'd hit upon the number 18,553. Again I began collecting VC documents, and within a week or so had come to the astonishing conclusion that our official estimate for service troops was at least two years old and five times too low—it should not have been 18,553, but more like 100,000. In the process I discovered a whole new category of soldiers known as "assault youths" who weren't in the order of battle at all.

I also drew a blank at the Pentagon regarding political cadres, so I started asking CIA analysts who these cadres might be. One analyst said they belonged to something called the "infrastructure," but he wasn't quite sure what it was. Finally, George Allen, who seemed to know more about the VC than anyone else, said the "infrastructure" included Communist party members and armed police and people like that, and that there was a study around which showed how the 39,175 number had been arrived at. I eventually found a copy on a shelf in the CIA archives. Unopened, it had never been looked at before. The study had been published in Saigon in 1965, and one glance showed it was full of holes. Among other things, it left out all the VC cadres serving in the countryside—where most of them were.

By December 1966 I had concluded that the number of Vietcong in South Vietnam, instead of being 270,000, was more like 600,000, or over twice the official estimate.[2] The higher number made many things about the Vietnam war fall into place. It explained, for instance, how the Vietcong Army could have so many deserters and casualties and still remain effective.

[2]This was broken down as follows: Communist regulars, about 100,000; guerrilla-militia, about 300,000; service troops, about 100,000; political cadres, about 100,000.

Nobody Listens

Mind you, during all this time I didn't keep this information secret—just the opposite. I not only told everyone in the Agency who'd listen, I also wrote a continuous sequence of memorandums, none of which provoked the least response. I'd write a memo, document it with footnotes, and send it up to the seventh floor. A week would pass, and then the paper would return to my in-box: no comment, only the same old buck slip showing that everyone upstairs had read it.

By this time I was so angry and so discouraged with the research directorate that I began looking for another job within the CIA, preferably in a section that had some use for real numbers. I still believed that all this indifference to unwelcome information afflicted only part of the bureaucracy, that it was not something characteristic of the entire Agency. Through George Allen I met George Carver, a man on the staff of Richard Helms, the new CIA director, who had the title "special assistant for Vietnamese affairs." Carver told me that I was "on the right track" with the numbers, and he seemed an independent-minded man who could circumvent the bureaucratic timidities of the research directorate. At the time I had great hopes of Carver because, partly as a result of his efforts, word of my memorandums had reached the White House. Cables were passing back and forth between Saigon and Washington, and it had become fairly common knowledge that something was very wrong with the enemy strength estimates.

In mid-January 1967, Gen. Earle Wheeler, chairman of the Joint Chiefs of Staff, called for an order-of-battle conference to be held in Honolulu. The idea was to assemble all the analysts from the military, the CIA, and the Defense Intelligence Agency in the hope that they might reach a consensus on the numbers. I went to Honolulu as part of the CIA delegation. I didn't trust the military and, frankly, I expected them to pull a fast one and lie about the numbers. What happened instead was that the head of Westmoreland's Order of Battle Section, Col. Gains B. Hawkins, got up right at the beginning of the conference and said, "You know, there's a lot more of these little bastards out there than we thought there were." He and his analysts then raised the estimate of enemy strength in each category of the order of battle; instead of the 103,573 guerrilla-militia, for example, they'd come up with 198,000. Hawkins's remarks were unofficial, but nevertheless, I figured, "the fight's over. They're reading the same documents that I am, and everybody's beginning to use real numbers."

I couldn't have been more wrong.

After a study trip to Vietnam, I returned to Washington in May 1967, to find a new CIA report to Secretary of Defense Robert McNamara called something like "Whither Vietnam?" Its section on the Vietcong Army listed all the discredited official figures, adding up to 270,000. Dumbfounded, I rushed into George Carver's office and got permission to correct the numbers. Instead of my own total of 600,000, I used 500,000, which was more in line with what Colonel Hawkins had said in Honolulu. Even so, one of the chief deputies of the research directorate, Drexel Godfrey, called me up to say that the directorate couldn't use 500,000 because "it wasn't official." I said: "That's the silliest thing I've ever heard. We're going to use real numbers for a change." Much to my satisfaction and relief, George Carver supported my figures. For the first time in the history of the Vietnam war a CIA paper challenging the previous estimates went directly to McNamara. Once again I said to myself: "The battle's won; virtue triumphs." Once again, I was wrong.

Soon after, I attended the annual meeting of the Board of National Estimates on Vietnam. Held in a windowless room on the CIA's seventh floor, a room furnished with leather chairs, blackboards, maps, and a large conference table, the meeting comprised the whole of the intelligence community, about forty people representing the CIA, the Defense Intelligence Agency, the Army, the Navy, the Air Force, and the State Department. Ordinarily the meeting lasted about a week, its purpose being to come to a community-wide agreement about the progress of the war. This particular consensus required the better part of six months.

The procedure of these estimates requires the CIA to submit the first draft, and then everyone else argues his group's position. If one of the services violently disagrees, it is allowed to take exception in a footnote to the report. The CIA's first draft used the same 500,000 number that had gone to McNamara in May. None of us expected what followed.

George Fowler from DIA, the same man who'd carried my guerrilla memo to Saigon in September 1966, got up and explained he was speaking for the entire military. "Gentlemen, we cannot agree to this estimate as currently written. What we object to are the numbers. We feel we should continue with the official order of battle." I almost fell off my chair. The official OB figure at that time, June 1967, was still 270,000, with all the old components, including 103,573 guerrilla-militia.

In disbelief I hurried downstairs to tell my boss, George Carver, of the deception. He was reassuring. "Now, Sam," he said, "don't you worry. It's time to bite the bullet. You go on back up there and do the best you can." For the next two-and-a-half months, armed with stacks of documents, I argued with the military over the numbers. By the end of August, they no longer insisted on the official order of battle figures, but would not raise them above 300,000. The CIA numbers remained at about 500,000. The meetings recessed for a few weeks at the end of the month, and I left Washington with my wife, Eleanor, to visit her parents in Alabama. No sooner had we arrived at their house when the phone rang. It was George Carver. "Sam, come back up. We're going to Saigon to thrash out the numbers."

I was a little cynical. "We won't sell out, will we?"

"No, no, we're going to bite the bullet," he said.

Army Estimate

We went to Saigon in early September to yet another order-of-battle meeting, this one convened in the austere conference room in Westmoreland's headquarters. Among the officers supporting Westmoreland were Gen. Philip Davidson, head of intelligence (the military calls it G-2); General Sidle, head of press relations ("What the dickens is he doing at an OB conference?" I thought); Colonel Morris, one of Davidson's aides; Col. Danny Graham, head of the G-2 Estimates Staff; and of course, Col. Gains B. Hawkins, chief of the G-2 Order of Battle Section. There were also numerous lieutenant colonels, majors, and captains, all equipped with maps, charts, files, and pointers.

The military dominated the first day of the conference. A major gave a lecture on the VC's low morale. I kept my mouth shut on the subject, even though I knew their documents showed a dwindling VC desertion rate. Another officer gave a talk full of complicated statistics which proved the Vietcong were running out of men. It was based on something called the crossover memo which had been put together by Colonel Graham's staff. On the second day we got down to business—the numbers.

It was suspicious from the start. Every time I'd argue one category up, the military would drop another category down by the same amount. Then there was the little piece of paper put on everybody's desk saying that the military would agree to count more of one type of VC if we'd agree to eliminate another type of VC. Finally, there was the argument over a subcategory called the district-level service troops.

I stood up to present the CIA's case. I said that I had estimated that there were about seventy-five service soldiers in each of the VC's districts, explaining that I had averaged the numbers in a sample of twenty-eight documents. I briefly reviewed the evidence and asked whether there were any questions.

"I have a question," said General Davidson. "You mean to tell me that you only have twenty-eight documents?"

"Yes sir," I said. "That's all I could find."

"Well, I've been in the intelligence business for many years, and if you're trying to sell me a number on the basis of that small a sample, you might as well pack up and go home." As I resumed my seat, Davidson's aide, Colonel Morris, turned around and said, "Adams, you're full of shit."

A lieutenant colonel then got up to present the military's side of the case. He had counted about twenty service soldiers per district, he said, and then he went on to describe how a district was organized. When he asked for questions, I said, "How many documents are in your sample?"

He looked as if somebody had kicked him in the stomach. Instead of answering the question, he repeated his description of how the VC organized a district.

Then George Carver interrupted him. "Come, come, Colonel," he said. "You're not answering the question. General Davidson has just taken Mr. Adams to task for having only twenty-eight documents in his sample. It's a perfectly legitimate question. How many have you in yours?"

In a very low voice, the lieutenant colonel said, "One." I looked over at General Davidson and Colonel Morris to see whether they'd denounce the lieutenant colonel for having such a small sample. Both of them were looking at the ceiling.

"Colonel," I continued, "may I see your document?" He didn't have it, he said, and, besides, it wasn't a document, it was a POW report.

Well, I asked, could he please try and remember who the twenty service soldiers were? He ticked them off. I kept count. The total was forty.

"Colonel," I said, "you have forty soldiers here, not twenty. How did you get from forty to twenty?"

"We scaled down the evidence," he replied.

"Scaled down the evidence?"

"Yes," he said. "We cut out the hangers-on."

"And how do you determine what a hanger-on is?"

"Civilians, for example."

Now, I knew that civilians sometimes worked alongside VC service troops, but normally the rosters listed them separately. So I waited until the next coffee break to ask Colonel Hawkins how he'd "scale down" the service troops in a document I had. It concerned Long Dat District in the southern half of South Vietnam, and its 111 service troops were broken down by components. We went over each one. Of the twenty in the medical component, Hawkins would count three, of the twelve in the ordnance section, he'd count two, and so forth, until Long Dat's 111 service soldiers were down to just over forty. There was no indication in the document that any of those dropped were civilians.

As we were driving back from the conference that day, an Army officer in the car with us explained what the real trouble was: "You know, our basic problem is that we've been told to keep our numbers under 300,000."

Later, after retiring from the Army, Colonel Hawkins confirmed that this was basically the case. At the start of the conference, he'd been told to stay below a certain number. He could no longer remember what it was, but he recalled that the person who gave it to him was Colonel Morris, the officer who had told me I was "full of shit."

The Saigon conference was in its third day, when we received a cable from Helms that, for all its euphemisms, gave us no choice but to accept the military's numbers. We did so, and the conference concluded that the size of the Vietcong force in South Vietnam was 299,000. We accomplished this by simply marching certain categories of Vietcong out of the order of battle, and by using the military's "scaled-down" numbers.

I left the conference extremely angry. Another member of the CIA contingent, William Hyland (now head of intelligence at the Department of State), tried to explain. "Sam, don't take it so hard. You know what the political climate is. If you think they'd accept the higher numbers, you're living in a dream world." Shortly after the conference ended, another category was frog-marched out of the estimate, which dropped from 299,000 to 248,000.

I returned to Washington, and in October I went once again in front of the Board of National Estimates, by this time reduced to only its CIA members. I told them exactly what had happened at the conference—how the number had been scaled down, which types of Vietcong had left the order of battle, and even about the affair of Long Dat District. They were sympathetic.

"Sam, it makes my blood boil to see the military cooking the books," one of the board members said. Another asked, "Sam, have we gone beyond the bounds of reasonable dishonesty?" And I said, "Sir, we went past them last August." Nonetheless, the board sent the estimate

forward for the director's signature, with the numbers unchanged. I was told there was no other choice because Helms had committed the CIA to the military's numbers.

"But that's crazy," I said. "The numbers were faked." I made one last try. My memorandum was nine pages long. The first eight pages told how the numbers had got that way. The ninth page accused the military of lying. If we accepted their numbers, I argued, we would not only be dishonest and cowardly, we would be stupid. I handed the memo to George Carver to give to the director, and sent copies to everyone I could think of in the research branch. Although I was the only CIA analyst working on the subject at the time, nobody replied. Two days later Helms signed the estimate, along with its doctored numbers.

That was that. I went into Carver's office and quit Helms's staff. He looked embarrassed when I told him why I was doing so, but he said there was nothing he could do. I thanked him for all he had done in the earlier part of the year and for his attempt at trying to deal with real rather than imaginary numbers. I thought of leaving the CIA, but I still retained some faith in the Agency, and I knew that I was the only person in the government arguing for higher numbers with accurate evidence. I told Carver that the research directorate had formed a VC branch, in which, I said, I hoped to find somebody who would listen to me.

Facing Facts

In November General Westmoreland returned to Washington and held a press conference. "The enemy is running out of men," he said. He based this on the fabricated numbers, and on Colonel Graham's crossover memo. In early December, the CIA sent McNamara another "Whither Vietnam?" memo. It had the doctored numbers, but this time I was forbidden to change them. It was the same story with Helm's New York briefing to Congress. Wrong numbers, no changes allowed. When I heard that Colonel Hawkins, whom I still liked and admired, had been reassigned to Fort Holabird in Baltimore, I went to see him to find out what he really thought about the order of battle. "Those were the worst three months in my life," he said, referring to July, August, and September, and he offered to do anything he could to help. When he had been asked to lower the estimates, he said, he had retained as many of the frontline VC troops as possible. For several hours we went over the order of battle. We had few disagreements, but I began to see for the first time that the Communist regulars, the only category I'd never looked at, were also seriously understated—perhaps by as many as 50,000 men. No one was interested, because adding 50,000 troops would have forced a reopening of the issue of numbers, which everyone thought was settled. On January 29, 1968, I began the laborious job of transferring my files from Carver's office to the newly formed Vietcong branch.

The next day the VC launched the Tet offensive. Carver's office was chaos. There were so many separate attacks that someone was assigned full time to stick red pins in the map of South Vietnam just to keep track of them. Within a week's time it was clear that the scale of the Tet offensive was the biggest surprise to American intelligence since Pearl Harbor. As I read the cables coming in, I experienced both anger and a sort of grim satisfaction. There was just no way they could have pulled it off with only 248,000 men, and the cables were beginning to show which units had taken part. Many had never been in the order of battle at all; others had been taken out or scaled down. I made a collection of these units, which I showed Carver. Two weeks later, the CIA agreed to re-open the order-of-battle controversy.

Suddenly I was asked to revise and extend the memorandums that I had been attempting to submit for the past eighteen months. People began to congratulate me, to slap me on the back and say what a fine intelligence analyst I was. The Agency's chief of research, R. Jack Smith, who had once called me "*the* outstanding analyst" in the CIA but who had ignored all my reporting on the Vietcong, came down from the seventh floor to shake my hand. "We're glad to have you back," he said. "You know more about Vietnam than you did about the Congo." All of this disgusted me, and I accepted the compli-

ments without comment. What was the purpose of intelligence, I thought, if not to warn people, to tell them what to expect? As many as 10,000 American soldiers had been killed in the Tet offensive because the generals had played politics with the numbers, and here I was being congratulated by the people who had agreed to the fiction.

In February the Agency accepted my analysis, and in April another order-of-battle conference was convened at CIA headquarters. Westmoreland's delegation, headed by Colonel Graham (now a lieutenant general and head of the Defense Intelligence Agency) continued to argue for the lower numbers. But from that point forward the White House stopped using the military estimate and relied on the CIA estimate of 600,000 Vietcong.

All along I had wondered whether the White House had had anything to do with fixing the estimates. The military wanted to keep them low in order to display the "light at the end of the tunnel," but it had long since occurred to me that maybe the generals were under pressure from the politicians. Carver had told me a number of times that he had mentioned my OB figures to Walt Rostow of the White House. But even now I don't know whether Rostow ordered the falsification, or whether he was merely reluctant to face unpleasant facts. Accepting the higher numbers forced the same old decision: pack up or send a lot more troops.

On the evening of March 31, the question of the White House role became, in a way, irrelevant. President Johnson made his announcement that he wasn't going to run again. Whoever the next President was, I felt, needed to be told about the sorry state of American intelligence so that he could do something about it. The next morning, April 1, I went to the CIA inspector general's office and said: "Gentlemen, I've come here to file a complaint, and it involves both the research department and the director. I want to make sure that the next administration finds out what's gone on down here." On May 28 I filed formal charges and asked that they be sent to "appropriate members of the White House staff" and to the President's Foreign Intelligence Advisory Board. I also requested an investigation by the CIA inspector general. Helms responded by telling the inspector general to start an investigation. This took two months. The director then appointed a high-level review board to go over the inspector general's report. The review board was on its way to taking another two months when I went to the general counsel's office and talked to a Mr. Ueberhorst. I said, "Mr. Ueberhorst, I wrote a report for the White House about three months ago complaining about the CIA management, and I've been getting the run-around ever since. What I want is some legal advice. Would I be breaking any laws if I took my memo and carried it over to the White House myself?" A few days later, on September 20, 1968, the executive director of the CIA, the number-three man in the hierarchy, called me to his office: "Mr. Adams, we think well of you, but Mr. Helms says he doesn't want your memo to leave the building." I took notes of the conversation, so my reproduction of it is almost verbatim. "This is not a legal problem but a practical one of your future within the CIA," I was told. "Because if you take that memo to the White House, it will be at your own peril, and even if you get what you want by doing so, your usefulness to the Agency will thereafter be nil." The executive director carried on this conversation for thirty-five minutes. I copied it all out until he said, "Do you have anything to say, Mr. Adams?" "Yes sir," I said, "I think I'll take this right on over to the White House, and please tell the director of my intention." I wrote a memorandum of the conversation, and sent it back up to the executive director's office with a covering letter saying, "I hope I'm quoting you correctly; please tell me if I'm not."

A short while later he called me back to his office and said, "I'm afraid there's been a misunderstanding, because the last thing in the world the director wanted to do was threaten. He has decided that this thing can go forward."

I waited until after the Presidential election. Nixon won, and the next day I called the seventh floor to ask if it was now okay to send on my memo to the White House. On November 8, 1968, Mr. Helms summoned me to his office. The first thing he said to me was "Don't take notes." To the best of my recollection, the conversation then proceeded along the following lines. He asked what was bothering me; did I think

my supervisors were treating me unfairly, or weren't they promoting me fast enough? No, I said. My problem was that he caved in on the numbers right before Tet. I enlarged on the theme for about ten minutes. He listened without expression, and when I was done he asked what I would have had him do—take on the whole military? I said, that under the circumstances, that was the only thing he could have done; the military's numbers were faked. He then told me that I didn't know what things were like, that we could have told the White House that there were a million more Vietcong out there, and it wouldn't have made the slightest bit of difference in our policy. I said that we weren't the ones to decide about policy; all we should do was to send up the right numbers and let them worry. He asked me who I wanted to see, and I said that I had requested appropriate members of the White House staff and the President's Foreign Intelligence Advisory Board in my memo, but, frankly, I didn't know who the appropriate members were. He asked whether Gen. Maxwell Taylor and Walt Rostow would be all right. I told him that was not only acceptable, it was generous, and he said he would arrange the appointments for me.

With that I was sent around to see the deputy directors. The chief of research, R. Jack Smith, asked me what the matter was, and I told him the same things I had told Helms. The Vietnam war, he said, was an extraordinarily complex affair, and the size of the enemy army was only—his exact words—"a small but significant byway of the problem." His deputy, Edward Procter, now the CIA's chief of research, remarked, "Mr. Adams, the real problem is you. You ought to look into yourself."

Permission Denied

After making these rounds, I wrote letters to Rostow and Taylor, telling them who I was and asking that they include a member of Nixon's staff in any talks we had about the CIA's shortcomings. I forwarded the letters, through channels, to the director's office, asking his permission to send them on. Permission was denied, and that was the last I ever heard about meeting with Mr. Rostow and General Taylor.

In early December I did manage to see the executive secretary of the President's Foreign Intelligence Advisory Board, J. Patrick Coyne. He told me that a few days earlier Helms had sent over my memo, that some members of PFIAB had read it, and that they were asking me to enlarge on my views and to make any recommendations I thought were in order. Coyne encouraged me to write a full report, and in the following weeks I put together a thirty-five-page paper explaining why I had brought charges. A few days after Nixon's inauguration, in January 1969, I sent the paper to Helms's office with a request for permission to send it to the White House. Permission was denied in a letter from the deputy director, Adm. Rufus Taylor, who informed me that the CIA was a team, and that if I didn't want to accept the team's decision, then I should resign.

There I was—with nobody from Nixon's staff having heard of any of this. It was far from clear whether Nixon intended to retain the President's Foreign Intelligence Advisory Board. J. Patrick Coyne said he didn't know. He also said he didn't intend to press for the release of the thirty-five page report. I thought I had been had.

For the first time in my career, I decided to leave official channels. This had never occurred to me before, not even when Helms had authorized the doctored numbers in the month before Tet. I had met a man named John Court, a member of the incoming staff of the National Security Council, and through him I hoped for a measure of redress. I gave him my memorandum and explained its import—including Westmoreland's deceptions before Tet—and asked him to pass it around so that at least the new administration might know what had gone on at the CIA and could take any action it thought necessary. Three weeks later Court told me that the memo had gotten around, all right, but the decision had been made not to do anything about it.

So I gave up. If the White House wasn't interested, there didn't seem to be any other place I could go. I felt I'd done as much as I possibly could do, and that was that.

Once again I thought about quitting the Agency. But again I decided not to, even though

my career was pretty much in ruins. Not only had the deputy director just suggested that I resign, but I was now working under all kinds of new restrictions. I was no longer permitted to go to Vietnam. After the order-of-battle conference in Saigon in September 1967, Westmoreland's headquarters had informed the CIA station chief that I was persona non grata, and that they didn't want me on any military installations throughout the country. In CIA headquarters I was more or less confined to quarters, since I was no longer asked to attend any meetings at which outsiders were present. I was even told to cut back on the lectures I was giving about the VC to CIA case officers bound for Vietnam.[3]

I suppose what kept me from quitting this time was that I loved the job. The numbers business was going along fairly well, or so I thought, and I was becoming increasingly fascinated with what struck me as another disturbing question. Why was it that the Vietcong always seemed to know what we were up to, while we could never find out about them except through captured documents? At the time of the Tet offensive, for example, the CIA had only a single agent in the enemy's midst, and he was low-level.

At about this time, Robert Klein joined the VC branch. He had just graduated from college, and I thought him one of the brightest and most delightful people I had ever met. We began batting back and forth the question of why the VC always knew what was going to happen next. Having written a study on the Vietcong secret police in 1967, I already knew that the Communists had a fairly large and sophisticated espionage system. But I had no idea *how* large, and, besides, there were several other enemy organizations in addition to the secret police that had infiltrated the Saigon government. Klein and I began to sort them out. The biggest one, we found, was called the Military Proselytizing Directorate, which concentrated on recruiting

---

[3]In mid-1968 I had discovered that Agency officers sent to Vietnam received a total of only one hour's instruction on the organization and methods of operation of the Vietcong. Disturbed that they should be sent up against so formidable a foe with so little training, I had by the end of the year increased the hours from one to twenty-four. I gave most of the lectures myself.

agents in the South Vietnamese Army and National Police. By May 1969 we felt things were beginning to fall into place, but we still hadn't answered the fundamental question of how many agents the VC had in the South Vietnamese government. I decided to do the obvious thing, which was to start looking in the captured documents for references to spies. Klein and I each got a big stack of documents, and we began going through them, one by one. Within two weeks we had references to more than 1,000 VC agents. "Jesus Christ!" I said to Klein. "A thousand agents! And before Tet the CIA only had one." Furthermore, it was clear from the documents that the thousand we'd found were only the tip of a very big iceberg.

Right away I went off to tell everybody the bad news. I had begun to take a perverse pleasure in my role as the man in opposition at the Agency. The first person I spoke to was the head of the Vietnam branch of the CIA Clandestine Services. I said, "Hey, a guy called Klein and I just turned up references to over 1,000 VC agents, and from the looks of the documents the overall number might run into the tens of thousands." He said, "For God's sake, don't open that Pandora's box. We have enough troubles as it is."

The next place I tried to reach was the Board of National Estimates, which was just convening its annual meeting on the Vietnam draft. Because of the trouble I'd made the year before, and because the meeting included outsiders, I wasn't allowed to attend. By now, Klein and I had come to the very tentative conclusion, based mostly on extrapolations from documents, that the Military Proselytizing Directorate alone had 20,000 agents in the South Vietnamese Army and government. This made it by far the biggest agent network in the history of espionage, and I was curious to know whether this was known in Saigon. I prompted a friend of mine to ask the CIA's Saigon station chief—back in Washington to give another briefing I wasn't allowed to attend—just how many Vietcong agents there were in the South Vietnamese Army. The station chief (a new one; Jorgy had long since moved) was taken aback at the question. He'd never considered it before. He said, "Well, the South Vietnamese Military Security Service has about 300

suspects under consideration. I think that about covers it." If Klein and I were anywhere near right with our estimate of 20,000, that made the station chief's figure too low by at least 6,000 percent.

New Discoveries

Deciding that we didn't yet know enough to make an issue of the matter, Klein and I went back to plugging the documents. The more we read, the wilder the story became. With a great deal of help from the CIA counterintelligence staff, we eventually found that Vietcong agents were running the government's National Police in the northern part of the country, that for many years the VC had controlled the counterintelligence branch of the South Vietnamese Military Security Service (which may explain why the station chief's estimate was so low), and that in several areas of Vietnam, the VC were in charge of our own Phoenix Program. Scarcely a day passed without a new discovery. The most dramatic of them concerned a Vietcong agent posing as a South Vietnamese ordnance sergeant in Da Nang. The document said that the agent had been responsible for setting off explosions at the American air base in April 1969, and destroying 40,000 tons of ammunition worth $100 million. The explosions were so big that they attracted a Congressional investigation, but the military managed to pass them off as having been started accidentally by a grass fire.

The problem with all these reports was not that they were hidden, but that they'd never been gathered and analyzed before in a systematic manner. Although CIA men in the field were aware of VC agents, Washington had failed to study the extent of the Vietcong network.

This is exactly what Klein and I attempted in the fall of 1969. By this time we had concluded that the total number of VC agents in the South Vietnamese Army and government was in the neighborhood of 30,000. While we admitted that the agents were a mixed bag—most of them were low-level personnel hedging their bets—we nonetheless arrived at an extremely bleak overall conclusion. That was that the agents were so numerous, so easy to recruit, and so hard to catch that their existence "called into question the basic loyalty of the South Vietnamese government and armed forces." This, in turn, brought up questions about the ultimate chances for success of our new policy of turning the war over to the Vietnamese.

In late November Klein and I had just about finished the first draft of our study when we were told that *under no circumstances* was it to leave CIA headquarters, and that, specifically, it shouldn't go to John Court of the White House staff. Meanwhile, however, I had called Court a number of times, telling him that the study existed, and that it suggested that Vietnamization probably wouldn't work. For the next two-and-a-half months, Court called the CIA front office asking for a draft of our memo on agents. Each time he was turned down.

Finally, in mid-February 1970, Court came over to the VC branch, and asked if he could have a copy of the agent memorandum. I told him he couldn't, but that I supposed it was okay if he looked at it at a nearby desk. By closing time Court had disappeared, along with the memo. I phoned him the next morning at the Executive Office Building and asked him if he had it. "Yes, I took it. Is that okay?" he said. It wasn't okay, and shortly after informing my superiors I received a letter of reprimand for releasing the memo to an "outsider." (Court, who worked for the White House, was the "outsider.") All copies of the study within the CIA—several were around being reviewed—were recalled to the Vietcong branch and put in a safe. Klein was removed from working on agents, and told that if he didn't "shape up," he'd be fired.

The research department and perhaps even Helms (I don't know) apparently were appalled by the agent's memo reaching the White House. It was embarrassing for the CIA, since we'd never let anything like that out before. To suddenly say, oh, by the way, our ally, the South Vietnamese government, is crawling with spies, might lead someone to think that maybe the Agency should have noticed them sooner. We'd been in the war, after all, for almost six years.

Court later wrote a précis of the memo and gave it to Kissinger. Kissinger gave it to Nixon. Shortly thereafter, the White House sent a direc-

tive to Helms which said, in effect: "Okay, Helms, get that damn agent paper out of the safe drawer." Some months later, the Agency coughed it up, almost intact.

Meanwhile, Klein quit. I tried to talk him out of it, but he decided to go to graduate school. He did so in September 1970, but not before leaving a letter of resignation with the CIA inspector general. Klein's letter told the complete story of the agent study, concluding with his opinion that the White House would never have learned about the Communist spies had it not been for John Court's sticky fingers.

By now my fortunes had sunk to a low ebb. For the first time in seven years, I was given an unfavorable fitness report. I was rated "marginal" at conducting research; I had lost my "balance and objectivity" on the war, and worst of all, I was the cause of the "discontent leading to the recent resignation" of Klein. For these shortcomings I was being reassigned to a position where I would be "less directly involved in research on the war." This meant I had to leave the Vietcong branch and join a small historical staff, where I was to take up the relatively innocuous job of writing a history of the Cambodian rebels.

Once again, I considered resigning from the CIA, but the job still had me hooked, and ever since the coup that deposed Sihanouk in March 1970 I had been wondering what was going on in Cambodia. Within a few weeks of that coup, the Communist army had begun to disappear from the southern half of South Vietnam for service next door, and I was curious to find out what it was up to. When I reported to the historical staff, I began, as usual, to collect documents. This was my main occupation for almost the next five months. I knew so little about Cambodia that I was fairly indiscriminate, and therefore grabbed just about everything I could find. By late April 1971, I had gathered several thousand reports, and had divided them into broad categories, such as "military" and "political." In early May, I began to go through the "military" reports.

One of the first of these was an interrogation report of a Vietcong staff officer who had surrendered in Cambodia in late 1970. The staff officer said he belonged to a Cambodian Communist regional command with a code name I'd never heard of: C-40. Apparently C-40 had several units attached to it, including regiments, and I'd never heard of any of these, either. And, it seemed, the units were mostly composed of Khmers, of whom C-40 had a total of 18,000. Now that appeared to me to be an awful lot of Khmer soldiers just for one area, so I decided to check it against our Cambodian order of battle. Within a month I made a startling discovery: there was *no* order of battle. All I could find was a little sheet of paper estimating the size of the Khmer Communist Army at 5,000 to 10,000 men. This sheet of paper, with exactly the same numbers, had been kicking around since early 1970.

It was the same story as our Vietcong estimate of 1966, only worse. In Vietnam we had neglected to look at three of the four parts of the Vietcong Army; in Cambodia we hadn't looked at the Khmer Communist Army at all. It later turned out that the 5,000-to-10,000 figure was based on numbers put together by a sergeant in the Royal Cambodian Army in 1969.

From then on, it was easy. Right in the same room with me was every single intelligence report on the Khmer rebels that had ever come in. Straightaway I found what the VC Army had been doing in Cambodia since Sihanouk's fall: it had put together the largest and best advisory structure in the Indochina war. Within two weeks I had discovered thirteen regiments, several dozen battalions, and a great many companies and platoons. Using exactly the same methods that I'd used on the Vietcong estimate before Tet (only now the methods were more refined), I came to the conclusion that the size of the Cambodian Communist Army was not 5,000 to 10,-000 but more like 100,000 to 150,000. In other words, the U.S. government's official estimate was between ten and thirty times too low.

My memo was ready in early June, and this time I gave a copy to John Court of the White House the day before I turned it in at the Agency. This proved to have been a wise move, because when I turned it in I was told, "Under no circumstances does this go out of the room." It was the best order-of-battle paper I'd ever done. It has about 120 footnotes, referencing about twice that many intelligence reports, and it was solid as a rock.

A week later I was taken off the Khmer Communist Army and forbidden to work on numbers anymore. A junior analyst began reworking my memo with instructions to hold the figure below 30,000. The analyst puzzled over this for several months, and at last settled on the same method the military had used in lowering the Vietcong estimate before Tet. He marched two whole categories out of the order of battle and "scaled down" what was left. In November 1971, he wrote up a memo placing the size of the Khmer Communist Army at 15,000 to 30,000 men. The CIA published the memo, and that number became the U.S. government's official estimate.

More Distortions

The present official estimate of the Khmer rebels—65,000—derives from the earlier one. It is just as absurd. Until very recently the Royal Cambodian Army was estimated at over 200,000 men. We are therefore asked to believe that the insurgents, who control four-fifths of Cambodia's land and most of its people, are outnumbered by the ratio of 3 to 1. In fact, if we count *all* the rebel soldiers, including those dropped or omitted from the official estimate, the Khmer Rebel Army is probably larger than the government's—perhaps by a considerable margin.

The trouble with this kind of underestimate is not simply a miscalculation of numbers. It also distorts the meaning of the war. In Cambodia, as in the rest of Southeast Asia, the struggle is for allegiance, and the severest test of loyalty has to do with who can persuade the largest number of peasants to pick up a gun. When American intelligence downgrades the strength of the enemy army, it ignores the Communist success at organizing and recruiting people. This is why the Communists call the struggle a "people's war" and why the government found it difficult to understand.

I spent the rest of 1971 and a large part of 1972 trying to get the CIA to raise the Cambodian estimate. It was useless. The Agency was busy with other matters, and I became increasingly discouraged. The Cambodian affair seemed to me to be a repeat of the Vietnam one, the same people made the same mistakes, in precisely the same ways, and everybody was allowed to conceal his duplicity. In the fall of 1972 I decided to make one last attempt at bringing the shoddiness of American intelligence to the attention of someone, anyone who could do anything about it.

Between October 1972 and January 1973 I approached the U.S. Army inspector general, the CIA inspector general, and the Congress—all to no avail. To the Army inspector general I delivered a memorandum setting forth the details of what had happened to the VC estimate before Tet. I mentioned the possibility of General Westmoreland's complicity, which might have implicated him in three violations of the Uniform Code of Military Justice. The memorandum asked for an investigation, but the inspector general explained that I was in the wrong jurisdiction. Of the CIA inspector general I requested an investigation of the Cambodian estimates, but he adopted the device of neglecting to answer his mail, and no inquiry took place. In a last desperate measure—desperate because my friends at the CIA assured me that Congressional watchdog committees were a joke—I even appealed to Congress. To committees in both the House and Senate that watch over the CIA I sent a thirteen-page memorandum with names, dates, numbers, and a sequence of events. A staff assistant to the Senate Armed Services Committee thought it an interesting document, but he doubted that the Intelligence Subcommittee would take it up because it hadn't met in over a year and a half. Lucien Nedzi, the chief superintendent of the CIA in the House, also thought the document "pertinent," but he observed that the forthcoming elections obliged him to concern himself primarily with the question of busing. When I telephoned his office in late November, after the elections had come and gone, his administrative assistant told me, in effect, "Don't call us; we'll call you."

By mid-January 1973 I had reached the end of the road. I happened to read a newspaper account of Daniel Ellsberg's trial in Los Angeles, and I noticed that the government was alleging that Ellsberg had injured the national security by releasing estimates of the enemy force in Vi-

The Moral of the Tale

Readers interested in the question of integrity in American government might take note of three successful bureaucrats mentioned in this chronicle. All of them acknowledged or abetted the counterfeiting of military intelligence, and all of them have risen to high places within their respective apparats. Lt. Gen. Daniel Graham, who helped to lower the U.S. Army's estimate of Vietcong strength, is now the head of the Defense Intelligence Agency; Edward Procter, who steadfastly ignored accurate intelligence, is now chief of the CIA research directorate; and William Hyland, who conceded the impossibility of contesting a political fiction, is now the head of State Department Intelligence. Their collective docility might also interest readers concerned with questions of national security.

—Sam Adams

etnam. I looked, and damned if they weren't from the same order of battle which the military had doctored back in 1967. Imagine! Hanging a man for leaking faked numbers! In late February I went to Los Angeles to testify at the trial and told the story of how the numbers got to be so wrong. When I returned to Washington in March, the CIA once again threatened to fire me. I complained and, as usual, the Agency backed down. After a decent interval, I quit.

One last word. Some day, when everybody has returned to his senses, I hope to go back to the CIA as an analyst. I like the work.

Editor's Note *In January 1982, CBS Television ran a controversial documentary entitled, "Missing or Uncounting of the Enemy in Vietnam," based largely on the writings of and interviews with Sam Adams, the author of this case study. The program caused an unprecedented amount of discussion and criticism and led to a $120 mil-*

lion libel suit against CBS by General William C. Westmoreland, the commander of U.S. Army forces in Vietnam during the height of the conflict, who was cast as the major villain in the report. During the course of the ensuing debate over the program (Westmoreland eventually dropped his suit against CBS), an unusual "confession" appeared in print, "Vietnam Anguish: Being Ordered to Lie," Washington Post (November 14, 1982), p. C1+, by Lt. Col. Gains Hawkins. Beginning in February 1966, Hawkins had served for 18 months in Vietnam in military intelligence and during much of that time was charged with preparing the "Order of Battle," which essentially outlined the nature and strength of the enemy forces. In short, Hawkins was Adams's counterpart within the military in Vietnam, the man on the scene who generated the enemy troop estimates for Westmoreland.

According to Hawkins, when he arrived at his new post he went to work analyzing the numbers of enemy troops and soon had developed figures showing upwards of 500,000 enemy forces, roughly twice the amount of the figures then being used. As Hawkins writes: "When I briefed General Westmoreland on our new figures, he expressed surprise. He voiced concern about the major increase in the irregular forces and political cadres that we had found. He expressed concern about possible public reaction to the new figures—that they might lead people to think we had made no progress in the war. The general did not accept the new numbers."

"I then reduced them, quite arbitrarily, and returned to General Westmoreland to brief him on my second, lower count. But he rejected it as well."

Adams's story, now over a decade old, remains controversial, but is in large part probably correct as presented here.

Chapter 9 Review Questions

1. What are the differences between formal and informal channels of communications? Why do public administrators have to be concerned with the informal lines of communications as well as with the formal lines? How does one find out about the formal and informal lines of communications in an organization?

2. Were there both formal and informal methods of communications illustrated in the case, "Vietnam Cover-Up"? If so, what were some of the examples of each? Which were the most important in creating the dilemmas that Sam Adams faced in obtaining and communicating his critical information to the top-level policy planners within the CIA?

3. What types of communication blockages discussed in the Simon, Smithburg, and Thompson reading were illustrated in the Adams case? What strategies did Adams devise in circumventing these blockages? In your estimation, did Adams exhaust all the available routes to get his message to the top-level policy makers?

4. What does the "Vietnam Cover-Up" case study tell us about the interrelationships between organizational norms and values and an organization's receptivity to open communications? Specifically, how did the CIA's doctrine toward the Vietnam War help to create major communications barriers? In your view, what can be done to prevent this problem from recurring?

5. How do communications systems make or break an administrator's ability to control and direct the policies of his or her organization? As an administrator, what techniques would you utilize to ensure that the information you receive

is accurate, timely, and *not* distorted by preconceived personal or institutional biases?

6. Can you generalize about the moral dilemmas facing an individual like Adams who works for a public organization and strongly values truthfulness in performing his work? What potential risks does this sort of individual face within the organization given the possibility of censorship of communications? What choices might influence an employee's decision to stay and fight for reforming the system from within—for what he or she values as the truth—versus quitting and going public with the information? Can you identify your own ethical standards that would determine at what point you might be forced to resign in protest over a similar type of issue?

Key Terms

formal communications
informal communications
deliberate restrictions on
   communication

language barriers
status differences
geographic differences

Suggestions for Further Reading

The importance placed on communications processes in shaping governmental and organizational decisions was largely the result of several seminal works. These writings of the following key theorists should be studied with some care: Chester Barnard, *The Functions of the Executive* (Cambridge, Mass.: Harvard University Press, 1938); Herbert Simon, *Administrative Behavior: A Study of Decision-Making Processes in Administrative Organization* (New York: Macmillan, 1947); Karl W. Deutsch, *The Nerves of Government* (New York: Free Press, 1950); Norbert Weiner, *Cybernetics: Or Control and Communication in the Animal and the Machine* (New York: John Wiley & Sons, 1948); and Harlan Cleveland, *The Knowledge Executive: Leadership in an Information Society* (New York: E. P. Dutton, 1985), presents a current, lively study of this topic from a leadership perspective.

For more pragmatic works on the subject, review Herbert Kaufman in collaboration with Michael Couzens, *Administrative Feedback: Monitoring Subordinates' Behavior* (Washington, D.C.: The Brookings Institution, 1973); Lyman W. Porter and Kathleen H. Roberts, "Communications in Organizations," in Marvin Dunette, ed., *Handbook of Industrial and Organizational Psychology* (Chicago: Rand McNally, 1976), pp. 1527–1551; Lyman W. Porter, "Communications: Structure and Process," in Harold L. Fromkin and John L. Sherwood, eds., *Integrating the Organization* (New York: Free Press, 1974), pp. 237–240; and George C. Edwards III, "Problems in Bureaucratic Communications;" Herbert Kaufman, "Red Tape;" and Francis E. Rourke, "Executive Secrecy," in Francis E. Rourke, ed., *Bureaucratic Power in National Policy Making,* Fourth Edition

(Boston: Little, Brown, 1986). The best new practical textbooks on this topic are Fred Knight and Harold B. Horn, *Telecommunications* (Washington, D.C.: International City Management Association, 1982); and David S. Arnold, Christine S. Becker, and Elizabeth K. Kellar, *Effective Communication: Getting the Message Across* (Washington, D.C.: International City Management Association, 1983).

Certainly during the last decade or so the computer revolution has rocked the field of administrative communications, as it will no doubt continue to do. For informative works on this topic, see Michael A. Arbib, *Computers and the Cybernetic Society* (New York: Academic Press, 1977); H. Dominic Covvey, *Computer Consciousness: Surviving the Automated 80s* (Reading, Mass.: Addison-Wesley, 1980); James Martin, *Telematic Society,* Second Edition (Englewood Cliffs, N.J.: Prentice-Hall, 1981); and Bruce W. Arden, ed., *What Can Be Automated?* (Cambridge, Mass.: M.I.T. Press, 1980). For recent works involving computer security and privacy matters, see E. B. Fernandez, *Database Security and Integrity* (Reading, Mass.: Addison-Wesley, 1981); John R. Talbot, *Management Guide to Computer Security* (New York: John Wiley & Sons, 1981); and James N. Danziger, Kenneth L. Kraemer, and William H. Dutton, *Computers and Politics* (New York: Columbia University Press, 1982).

The crisis of war can illuminate problems of administrative communications with unusual clarity. For some excellent examples, see Gordon W. Prange, *At Dawn We Slept: The Untold Story of Pearl Harbor* (New York: McGraw-Hill, 1981); E. B. Potter, *Battle for Leyte Gulf: Command and Communications* (Syracuse, N.Y.: Inter-University Case No. 126); and John W. Spanier, *The Truman-MacArthur Controversy and the Korean War* (Cambridge, Mass.: Harvard University Press, 1959).

The current studies on communications as related to the world of public administration tend to be highly specialized, focusing on such topics as "The Freedom of Information Act" and "Management Information Systems" as reflected in two recent *Public Administration Review* symposia: Barry Bozeman and Stuart Bretschneider, eds., "Public Management Information Systems," *Public Administration Review* special issue, 46 (November 1986), and Lotte E. Feinberg and Harold C. Relyea, "Symposium: Toward a Government Information Policy—FOI at 20", *Public Administration Review* 46 (November/December 1986).

Executive Management: The Concept of the Uniqueness of Public Management

"The debate between the assimilators and the differentiators, like the dispute between proponents of convergence and divergence between the U.S. and the Soviet Union, reminds me of the old argument about whether the glass is half full or half empty. I conclude that public and private management are at least as different as they are similar, and that the differences are more important than the similarities."

Graham T. Allison, Jr.

READING 10

Introduction

Writings on public management are a comparatively new phenomena; in fact, they are peculiarly products of this century because large-scale formal organizations, both public and private, are modern in origin and existence. Humanity's dependence on massive organizations that span the continent and the globe is therefore recent hence, the comprehensive, detailed analysis of these institutions is also new to scholarly interest. The flood of modern literature analyzing the nature, behavior, and ideal methods for constructing viable human institutions and internal personal relationships has been prompted in part by the need to establish and construct these organizations in ways that effectively cope with problems of the present age.

The central dilemma in studying modern organizations and their management lies in the proper theoretical perspective. As Dwight Waldo reminds us, studying organization is akin to the fable of the blind men and the elephant. "Each of the blind men . . . touched with his hands a different part of the elephant, and as a result there was among them a radical difference of opinion as to the nature of the beast."[1]

[1]Dwight Waldo, *Ideas and Issues in Public Administration* (New York: McGraw-Hill, 1953), p. 64.

A principal cause of the considerable divergence of opinion about organizations thus stems from the specialized vantage points from which observers come to examine human institutions. The economist has a different view than the philosopher, so also the insider versus the outsider and the worker versus the manager. These ideas are not right or wrong; rather, a number of approaches exist for reaching the truth about complex formal organizations. In studying organizations, material that is valid or useful to one individual may not seem so to another.

For one reason or another, very often *one* theoretical perspective in America tends to dominate our understanding of what constitutes good or appropriate public sector organizational practices, namely business perspectives. Not infrequently do we read about political candidates or their appointees promising, "I can make government more businesslike!" or citing as their reason for holding high public office "a successful track-record as a manager in private enterprise." Editorial writers, civic association speakers, and media pundits often echo these refrains in favor of applying entepreneurial talent to public enterprises. Popular opinion generally supports the viewpoint that if only public administrators would simply manage their affairs like business, government—and maybe even the entire country—would run a lot better.

The tendency to identify good management in government with good business management is common even in serious public administration literature. Indeed, discussions of business management methods dominated much of the early development of the conscious study of public administration at the beginning of the twentieth century. Frederick W. Taylor and his business-oriented scientific management concepts served as the core of much of the field of public administration prior to World War II. The Brownlow Committee Report (1937), which some scholars believe was the highwater mark of the influence of public administration thinking on government, largely mirrored the business organization practices of the day. In many respects, this strong influence of business practices on government continues today through such imported private sector techniques as performance budgets, cost-benefit analysis, cost-accounting procedures, performance appraisals, management by objective, zero-based budgeting, and so on. Indeed, you only need to think about the names of major governmental processes and institutions to appreciate the enormous influence of what Waldo calls "our business civilization"—there are government corporations, city managers, efficiency ratings, the contracting out for services, chief administrative officers, and county executives.

Yet, despite the deep-rooted and continuing enthusiasm—on both the popular and the scholarly levels—to make government more business-like, the fundamental issue remains unanswered: is government like business? Can the public sector, in fact, be run like the private sector? Indeed, it is a critical question for the field as a whole, for if public and private management are the same in scope, purpose, and process, why do we have the separate field of public administration and, therefore, public administrators? Why not simply teach and practice "administration" without distinguishing between "public" and "private"? This issue goes to the heart of the intellectual discipline and the professional practice of our field. In many ways, this issue has been a dilemma since the inception of public administration and is of continuing interest to many scholars and practitioners today.

Graham T. Allison, Jr. (1941–   ), currently dean of the John F. Kennedy School of Government at Harvard University and author of several important books in the field such as *The Essence of Decision* (1971), reflected on this question before a major symposium on public management research agendas sponsored by the Office of Personnel Management. In the following essay, Allison summarizes his remarks on this subject. He takes off on a frequently quoted "law" from the late political scientist Wallace Sayre, which maintains that public and private management are fundamentally alike in all unimportant respects. Allison probes this law from several standpoints: first, by the *personal impressions* of managers who have seen both sides of the fence, for example, John Dunlop; second, by *scholarly surveys* of the literature comparing both public and private management practices and activities; and third, by an *operational perspective* of two actual administrators in action—Doug Costle at the EPA and Roy Chapin at American Motors.

By looking at this issue from a number of angles, Allison is able to draw these important conclusions: (1) while the need for increased governmental efficiency is real, "the notion that there is any significant body of private management practices and skills that can be transferred directly to public management . . . is wrong"; (2) while "performance in many public management positions can be improved substantially," an improvement will not come "from massive borrowing of specific private management skills and understandings"; (3) while it is possible to learn from experiences in public or private settings, "the effort to develop public management as a field of knowledge should start from the problems faced by practicing public managers." Worthy of careful attention, too, are the lists at the end of Allison's essay that outline the specific strategies he sees as necessary for the development of both the professional practice and the academic dimensions of public management.

As you read this selection, keep the following questions in mind:

What essential arguments does Allison put forward in favor of the uniqueness of public management? How does Allison arrive at his conclusions? Do you agree or disagree with Allison's argument and his reasoning?

What model for public management does Allison propose? What are its elements? How does he support its value?

What are the implications of his argument—namely, the uniqueness thesis—for teaching, practice, and scholarship in the field of public management?

GRAHAM T. ALLISON, JR.

Public and Private Management: Are They Fundamentally Alike in All Unimportant Respects?

My subtitle puts Wallace Sayre's oft quoted "law" as a question. Sayre had spent some years in Ithaca helping plan Cornell's new School of Business and Public Administration. He left for Columbia with this aphorism: public and private management are fundamentally alike in all unimportant respects.

Sayre based his conclusion on years of personal observation of governments, a keen ear for what his colleagues at Cornell (and earlier at OPA) said about business, and a careful review of the literature and data comparing public and private management. Of the latter there was virtually none. Hence, Sayre's provocative "law" was actually an open invitation to research.

Unfortunately, in the 50 years since Sayre's pronouncement, the data base for systematic comparison of public and private management has improved little. Consequently . . . I, in effect, take up Sayre's invitation to *speculate* about similarities and differences among public and private management in ways that suggest significant opportunities for systematic investigation. . . .

Framing the Issue: What Is Public Management?

What is the meaning of the term "management" as it appears in Office of *Management* and Budget, or Office of Personnel *Management?* Is "management" different from, broader or narrower than "administration"? Should we distinguish between management, leadership, entrepreneurship, administration, policy making, and implementation?

Who are "public managers"? Mayors, governors, and presidents? City managers, secretaries, and commissioners? Bureau chiefs? Office directors? Legislators? Judges?

Recent studies of OPM and OMB shed some light on these questions. OPM's major study of the "Current Status of Public Management Research" completed in May 1978 by Selma Mushkin of Georgetown's Public Service Laboratory starts with this question. The Mushkin report notes the definition of "public management" employed by the Interagency Study Committee on Policy Management Assistance in its 1975 report to OMB. That study identified the following core elements:

1. *Policy Management*   The identification of needs, analysis of options, selection of programs, and allocation of resources on a jurisdiction-wide basis.
2. *Resource Management*   The establishment of basic administrative support systems, such as budgeting, financial management, procurement and supply, and personnel management.
3. *Program Management*   The implementation of policy or daily operation of agencies carrying out policy along functional lines (education, law enforcement, etc.).[1]

Reprinted from pp. 27–38 of *Setting Public Management Research Agendas: Integrating the Sponsor, Producer and User.* Washington, D.C.: Office of Personnel Management. OPM Document 127–53–1. February 1980.

[1]Selma J. Mushkin, Frank H. Sandifer and Sally Familton. *Current Status of Public Management: Research Conducted*

The Mushkin report rejects this definition in favor of an "alternative list of public management elements." These elements are:

- Personnel Management (other than work force planning and collective bargaining and labor management relations)
- Work Force Planning
- Collective Bargaining and Labor Management Relations
- Productivity and Performance Measurement
- Organization/Reorganization
- Financial Management (including the management of intergovernmental relations)
- Evaluation Research, and Program and Management Audit.[2]

Such terminological tangles seriously hamper the development of public management as a field of knowledge. In our efforts to discuss public management curriculum at Harvard, I have been struck by how differently people use these terms, how strongly many individuals feel about some distinction they believe is marked by a difference between one word and another, and consequently, how large a barrier terminology is to convergent discussion. These verbal obstacles virtually prohibit conversation that is both brief and constructive among individuals who have not developed a common language or a mutual understanding of each other's use of terms. . . .

This terminological thicket reflects a more fundamental conceptual confusion. There exists no over-arching framework that orders the domain. In an effort to get a grip on the phenomena—the buzzing, blooming confusion of people in jobs performing tasks that produce results—both practitioners and observers have strained to find distinctions that facilitate their work. The attempts in the early decades of this century to draw a sharp line between "policy" and "administration," like more recent efforts

to mark a similar divide between "policy making" and "implementation," reflect a common search for a simplification that allows one to put the value-laden issues of politics to one side (who gets what, when, and how), and focus on the more limited issue of how to perform tasks more efficiently.[3] But can anyone really deny that the "how" substantially affects the "who," the "what," and the "when"? The basic categories now prevalent in discussions of public management—strategy, personnel management, financial management, and control—are mostly derived from a business context in which executives manage hierarchies. The fit of these concepts to the problems that confront public managers is not clear.

Finally, there exists no ready data on what public managers do. Instead, the academic literature, such as it is, mostly consists of speculation tied to bits and pieces of evidence about the tail or the trunk or other manifestation of the proverbial elephant.[4] In contrast to the literally thousands of cases describing problems faced by private managers and their practice in solving these problems, case research from the perspective of a public manager is just beginning. . . .[5]

[3]Though frequently identified as the author who established the complete separation between "policy" and "administration," Woodrow Wilson has in fact been unjustly accused. "It is the object of administrative study to discover, first, what government can properly and successfully do, and, secondly, how it can do these proper things with the utmost possible efficiency . . ." (Wilson, "The Study of Public Administration," published as an essay in 1888 and reprinted in *Political Science Quarterly,* December 1941, p. 481.) For another statement of the same point, see Brooks Adams, *The Theory of Social Revolutions* (Macmillan 1913), pp. 207–208.

[4]See Dwight Waldo, "Organization Theory: Revisiting the Elephant," *PAR,* (November-December 1978). Reviewing the growing volume of books and articles on organization theory, Waldo notes that "growth in the volume of the literature is not to be equated with growth in knowledge."

[5]See *Cases in Public Policy and Management,* Spring 1979 of the Intercollegiate Case Clearing House for a bibliography containing descriptions of 577 cases by 366 individuals from 79 institutions. Current casework builds on and expands earlier efforts of the Inter-University Case Program. See, for example, Harold Stein, ed., *Public Administration*

---

by or Supported by Federal Agencies (Public Services Laboratory, Georgetown University, 1978). p. 10.

[2]*Ibid.,* p. 11.

But the paucity of data on the phenomena inhibits systematic empirical research on similarities and differences between public and private management, leaving the field to a mixture of reflection on personal experience and speculation.

For the purpose of this presentation, I will follow Webster and use the term management to mean the organization and direction of resources to achieve a desired result. I will focus on *general managers,* that is, individuals charged with managing a whole organization or multifunctional sub-unit. I will be interested in the general manager's full responsibilities, both *inside* his organization in integrating the diverse contributions of specialized sub-units of the organization to achieve results, and *outside* his organization in relating his organization and its product to external constituencies. I will begin with the simplifying assumption that managers of traditional government organizations are public managers, and managers of traditional private businesses, private managers. Lest the discussion fall victim to the fallacy of misplaced abstraction, I will take the Director of EPA and the Chief Executive Officer of American Motors as, respectively, public and private managers. Thus, our central question can be put concretely: in what ways are the jobs and responsibilities of Doug Costle as Director of EPA similar to and different from those of Roy Chapin as Chief Executive Officer of American Motors?

Similarities: How Are Public and Private Management Alike?

At one level of abstraction, it is possible to identify a set of general management functions. The most famous such list appeared in Gulick and

Urwick's classic *Papers in the Science of Administration.*[6] Gulick summarized the work of the chief executive in the acronym POSDCORB. The letters stand for:

- Planning
- Organizing
- Staffing
- Directing
- Coordinating
- Reporting
- Budgeting

With various additions, amendments, and refinements, similar lists of general management functions can be found through the management literature from Barnard to Drucker.[7]

I shall resist here my natural academic instinct to join the intramural debate among proponents of various lists and distinctions. Instead, I simply offer one composite list (see Table 10.1) that attempts to incorporate the major functions that have been identified for general managers, whether public or private.

These common functions of management are not isolated and discrete, but rather integral components separated here for purposes of analysis. The character and relative significance of the various functions differ from one time to another in the history of any organization, and between one organization and another. But whether in a public or private setting, the challenge for the general manager is to integrate all these elements so as to achieve results.

[6]Luther Gulick and Al Urwick, eds., *Papers in the Science of Public Administration* (Institute of Public Administration, 1937).

[7]See, for example, Chester I. Barnard, *The Functions of the Executive* (Harvard University Press, 1938), and Peter F. Drucker, *Management: Tasks, Responsibilities, Practices* (Harper and Row, 1974). Barnard's recognition of human relations added an important dimension neglected in earlier lists.

and Policy Development: A Case Book (Harcourt, Brace, and World, 1952), and Edwin A. Bock and Alan K. Campbell, eds., *Case Studies in American Government* (Prentice-Hall, 1962).

Table 10.1   Functions of General Management

Strategy

1. **Establishing objectives and priorities** for the organization (on the basis of forecasts of the external environment and the organization's capacities).
2. **Devising operational plans** to achieve these objectives.

Managing internal components

3. **Organizing and staffing:** In organizing the manager establishes structure (units and positions with assigned authority and responsibilities) and procedures (for coordinating activity and taking action); in staffing he tries to fit the right persons in the key jobs.*
4. **Directing personnel and the personnel management system:** The capacity of the organization is embodied primarily in its members and their skills and knowledge; the personnel management system recruits, selects, socializes, trains, rewards, punishes, and exits the organization's human capital, which constitutes the organization's capacity to act to achieve its goals and to respond to specific directions from management.
5. **Controlling performance:** Various management information systems—including operating and capital budgets, accounts, reports and statistical systems, performance appraisals, and product evaluation—assist management in making decisions and in measuring progress towards objectives.

Managing external constituencies

6. **Dealing with "external" units** of the organization subject to some common authority: Most general managers must deal with general managers of other units within the larger organization—above, laterally, and below—to achieve their unit's objectives.
7. **Dealing with independent organizations:** Agencies from other branches or levels of government, interest groups, and private enterprises that can importantly affect the organization's ability to achieve its objectives.
8. **Dealing with the press and public** whose action or approval or acquiescence is required.

*Organization and staffing are frequently separated in such lists, but because of the interaction between the two, they are combined here. See Graham Allison and Peter Szanton, *Remaking Foreign Policy* (Basic Books, 1976), p. 14.

Differences: How Are Public and Private Management Different?

While there is a level of generality at which management is management, whether public or private, functions that bear identical labels take on rather different meaning in public and private settings. As Larry Lynn has pointed out, one powerful piece of evidence in the debate between those who emphasize "similarities" and those who underline "differences" is the nearly unanimous conclusion of individuals who have been general managers in both business and government. Consider the reflections of George Shultz (former Director of OMB, Secretary of Labor, Secretary of the Treasury; now President of Bechtel), Donald Rumsfeld (former congressman, Director of OEO, Director of the Cost of Living Council, White House Chief of Staff, and Secretary of Defense; now President of GD Searle and Company), Michael Blumenthal (former Chairman and Chief Executive Officer of Bendix, Secretary of the Treasury, and now Vice Chairman of Burrows), Roy Ash (former President of Litton Industries, Director of OMB; now President of Addressograph), Lyman Hamilton (former Budget Officer in BOB, High Commissioner of Okinawa, Division Chief in the World Bank and President of ITT), and George Romney (former President of American Motors, Governor of Michigan and Secretary of Housing and Urban Development).[8] All judge public management different from private management—and harder!

[8]See, for example, "A Businessman in a Political Jungle," *Fortune* (April 1964); "Candid Reflections of a Businessman in Washington," *Fortune* (January 29, 1979); "A Politician Turned Executive," *Fortune* (September 10, 1979); and "The Ambitions Interface," *Harvard Business Review* (November–December, 1979) for the views of Romney, Blumenthal, Rumsfeld, and Shultz, respectively.

Three Orthogonal Lists of Differences

My review of these recollections, as well as the thoughts of academics, has identified three interesting, orthogonal lists that summarize the current state of the field: one by John Dunlop; one major *Public Administration Review* survey of the literature comparing public and private organizations by Hal Rainey, Robert Backoff and Charles Levine; and one by Richard E. Neustadt prepared for the National Academy of Public Administration's Panel on Presidential Management.

John T. Dunlop's "impressionistic comparison of government management and private business" yields the following contrasts.[9]

1. Time Perspective Government managers tend to have relatively short time horizons dictated by political necessities and the political calendar, while private managers appear to take a longer time perspective oriented toward market developments, technological innovation and investment, and organization building.

2. Duration The length of service of politically appointed top government managers is relatively short, averaging no more than 18 months recently for assistant secretaries, while private managers have a longer tenure both in the same position and in the same enterprise. A recognized element of private business management is the responsibility to train a successor or several possible candidates while the concept is largely alien to public management since fostering a successor is perceived to be dangerous.

3. Measurement of Performance There is little if any agreement on the standards and measurement of performance to appraise a government manager, while various tests of performance—financial return, market share,

performance measures for executive compensation—are well established in private business and often made explicit for a particular managerial position during a specific period ahead.

4. Personnel Constraints In government there are two layers of managerial officials that are at times hostile to one another: the civil service (or now the executive system) and the political appointees. Unionization of government employees exists among relatively high-level personnel in the hierarchy and includes a number of supervisory personnel. Civil service, union contract provisions, and other regulations complicate the recruitment, hiring, transfer, and layoff or discharge of personnel to achieve managerial objectives or preferences. By comparison, private business managements have considerably greater latitude, even under collective bargaining, in the management of subordinates. They have much more authority to direct the employees of their organization. Government personnel policy and administration are more under the control of staff (including civil service staff outside an agency) compared to the private sector in which personnel are much more subject to line responsibility.

5. Equity and Efficiency In governmental management great emphasis tends to be placed on providing equity among different constituencies, while in private business management relatively greater stress is placed upon efficiency and competitive performance.

6. Public Processes Versus Private Processes Governmental management tends to be exposed to public scrutiny and to be more open, while private business management is more private and its processes more internal and less exposed to public review.

7. Role of Press and Media Governmental management must contend regularly with the press and media; its decisions are often anticipated by the press. Private decisions are less

[9]John T. Dunlop, "Public Management," draft of an unpublished paper and proposal, Summer 1979.

often reported in the press, and the press has a much smaller impact on the substance and timing of decisions.

8. Persuasion and Direction

In government, managers often seek to mediate decisions in response to a wide variety of pressures and must often put together a coalition of inside and outside groups to survive. By contrast, private management proceeds much more by direction or the issuance of orders to subordinates by superior managers with little risk of contradiction. Governmental managers tend to regard themselves as responsive to many superiors while private managers look more to one higher authority.

9. Legislative and Judicial Impact

Governmental managers are often subject to close scrutiny by legislative oversight groups or even judicial orders in ways that are quite uncommon in private business management. Such scrutiny often materially constrains executive and administrative freedom to act.

10. Bottom Line

Governmental managers rarely have a clear bottom line, while that of a private business manager is profit, market performance, and survival.

The *Public Administration Review*'s major review article comparing public and private organizations, Rainey, Backoff and Levine, attempts to summarize the major points of consensus in the literature on similarities and differences among public and private organizations.[10]

Third, Richard E. Neustadt, in a fashion close to Dunlop's, notes six major differences between Presidents of the United States and Chief Executive Officers of major corporations.[11]

1. Time-Horizon

The private chief begins by looking forward a decade, or thereabouts, his likely span barring extraordinary troubles. The first-term President looks forward four years at most, with the fourth (and now even the third) year dominated by campaigning for reelection. (What second-termers look toward we scarcely know, having seen but one such term completed in the past quarter century.)

2. Authority

over the enterprise. Subject to concurrence from the Board of Directors which appointed and can fire him, the private executive sets organization goals, shifts structures, procedure, and personnel to suit, monitors results, reviews key operational decisions, deals with key outsiders, and brings along his Board. Save for the deep but narrow sphere of military movements, a President's authority in these respects is shared with well-placed members of Congress (or their staffs); case by case, they may have more explicit authority than he does (contrast authorizations and appropriations with the "take-care" clause). As for "bringing along the Board," neither the Congressmen with whom he shares power or the primary and general electorates which "hired" him have either a Board's duties or a broad view of the enterprise precisely matching his.

3. Career System

The model corporation is a true career system, something like the Forest Service after initial entry. In normal times the chief himself is chosen from within, or he is chosen from another firm in the same industry. He draws department heads et al. from among those with whom he's worked, or whom he knows in comparable companies. He and his principal associates will be familiar with each other's roles—indeed he probably has had a number of them—and also usually with one another's operating styles, personalities, idiosyncrasies. Contrast the President who rarely has had much experience "downtown," probably knows little of most roles there (much of what he knows will turn out wrong), and less of most associates whom he appoints there, willy nilly, to

[10]Hal G. Rainey, Robert W. Backoff, and Charles N. Levine, "Comparing Public and Private Organizations," *Public Administration Review* (March–April, 1976).

[11]Richard E. Neustadt, "American Presidents and Corporate Executives," a paper prepared for a meeting of the National Academy of Public Administration's Panel on Presidential Management, October 7–8, 1979.

fill places by Inauguration Day. Nor are they likely to know one another well, coming as they do from "everywhere" and headed as most are toward oblivion.

4. *Media Relations* The private executive represents his firm and speaks for it publicly in exceptional circumstances; he and his associates judge the exceptions. Those aside, he neither sees the press nor gives its members access to internal operations, least of all in his own office, save to make a point deliberately for public-relations purposes. The President, by contrast, is routinely on display, continuously dealing with the White House press and with the wider circle of political reporters, commentators, columnists. He needs them in his business, day by day, nothing exceptional about it, and they need him in theirs: the TV Network News programs lead off with him some nights each week. They and the President are as mutually dependent as he and Congressmen (or more so). Comparatively speaking, these relations overshadow most administrative ones much of the time for him.

5. *Performance Measurement* The private executive expects to be judged, and in turn to judge subordinates, by profitability, however the firm measures it (a major strategic choice). In practice, his Board may use more subjective measures; so may he, but at risk to morale and good order. The relative virtue of profit, of "the bottom line" is its legitimacy, its general acceptance in the business world by all concerned. Never mind its technical utility in given cases, its apparent "objectivity," hence "fairness," has enormous social usefulness: a myth that all can live by. For a President there is no counterpart (except *in extremis* the "smoking gun" to justify impeachment). The general public seems to judge a President, at least in part, by what its members think is happening to them, in their own lives; Congressmen, officials, interest groups appear to judge by what they guess, at given times, he can do for or to their causes. Members of the press interpret both of these and spread a simplified criterion affecting both, the

legislative box-score, a standard of the press's own devising. The White House denigrates them all except when it does well.

6. *Implementation* The corporate chief, supposedly, does more than choose a strategy and set a course of policy; he also is supposed to oversee what happens after, how in fact intentions turn into results, or if they don't to take corrective action, monitoring through his information system, acting, and if need be, through his personnel system. A President, by contrast, while himself responsible for budgetary proposals, too, in many spheres of policy, appears ill-placed and ill-equipped to monitor what agencies of states, of cities, corporations, unions, foreign governments are up to or to change personnel in charge. Yet these are very often the executants of "his" programs. Apart from defense and diplomacy the federal government does two things in the main: it issues and applies regulations and it awards grants in aid. Where these are discretionary, choice usually is vested by statute in a Senate-confirmed official well outside the White House. Monitoring is his function, not the President's except at second-hand. And final action is the function of the subjects of the rules and funds; they mostly are not federal personnel at all. In defense, the arsenals and shipyards are gone; weaponry comes from the private sector. In foreign affairs it is the *other* governments whose actions we would influence. From implementors like these a President is far removed most of the time. He intervenes, if at all, on a crash basis, not through organizational incentives.

Underlying these lists' sharpest distinctions between public and private management is a fundamental *constitutional difference.* In business, the functions of general management are centralized in a single individual: the Chief Executive Officer. The goal is authority commensurate with responsibility. In contrast, in the U.S. government, the functions of general management are constitutionally spread among competing institutions: the executive, two houses of

Congress, and the courts. The constitutional goal was "not to promote efficiency but to preclude the exercise of arbitrary power," as Justice Brandeis observed. Indeed, as *The Federalist Papers* make starkly clear, the aim was to create incentives to compete: "the great security against a gradual concentration of the several powers in the same branch, consists in giving those who administer each branch the constitutional means and personal motives to resist encroachment of the others. Ambition must be made to counteract ambition."[12] Thus, the general management functions concentrated in the CEO of a private business are, by constitutional design, spread in the public sector among a number of competing institutions and thus shared by a number of individuals whose ambitions are set against one another. For most areas of public policy today, these individuals include at the federal level the chief elected official, the chief appointed executive, the chief career official, and several congressional chieftains. Since most public services are actually delivered by state and local governments, with independent sources of authority, this means a further array of individuals at these levels.

An Operational Perspective: How Are the Jobs and Responsibilities of Doug Costle, Director of EPA, and Roy Chapin, CEO of American Motors, Similar and Different?

If organizations could be separated neatly into two homogeneous piles, one public and one private, the task of identifying similarities and differences between managers of these enterprises would be relatively easy. In fact, as

Dunlop has pointed out, "the real world of management is composed of distributions, rather than single undifferentiated forms, and there is an increasing variety of hybrids." Thus for each major attribute of organizations, specific entities can be located on a spectrum. On most dimensions, organizations classified as "predominantly public" and those "predominantly private" overlap.[13] Private business organizations vary enormously among themselves in size, in management structure and philosophy, and in the constraints under which they operate. For example, forms of ownership and types of managerial control may be somewhat unrelated. Compare a family-held enterprise, for instance, with a public utility and a decentralized conglomerate, a Bechtel with ATT and Textron. Similarly, there are vast differences in management of governmental organizations. Compare the Government Printing Office or TVA or the Police Department of a small town with the Department of Energy or the Department of Health and Human Services. These distributions and varieties should encourage penetrating comparisons within both business and governmental organizations, as well as contrasts and comparisons across these broad categories, a point to which we shall return in considering directions for research.

Absent a major research effort, it may nonetheless be worthwhile to examine the jobs and responsibilities of two specific managers, neither polar extremes, but one clearly public, the other private. For this purpose, and primarily because of the availability of cases that describe the problems and opportunities each confronted, consider Doug Costle, Administrator of EPA, and Roy Chapin, CEO of American Motors.[14]

---

[12]*The Federalist Papers.* No. 51. The word "department" has been translated as "branch," which was its meaning in the original papers.

[13]Failure to recognize the fact of distributions has led some observers to leap from one instance of similarity between public and private to general propositions about similarities between public and private institutions or management. See, for example, Michael Murray, "Comparing Public and Private Management: An Exploratory Essay," *Public Administration Review* (July–August, 1975).

[14]These examples are taken from Bruce Scott, "American Motors Corporation" (Intercollegiate Case Clearing House #9-364-001); Charles B. Weigle with the collaboration of

Doug Costle, Administrator of EPA, January 1977

The mission of EPA is prescribed by laws creating the agency and authorizing its major programs. That mission is "to control and abate pollution in the areas of air, water, solid wastes, noise, radiation, and toxic substances. EPA's mandate is to mount an integrated, coordinated attack on environmental pollution in cooperation with state and local governments."[15]

EPA's organizational structure follows from its legislative mandates to control particular pollutants in specific environments: air and water, solid wastes, noise, radiation, pesticides and chemicals. As the new Administrator, Costle inherited the Ford Administration's proposed budget for EPA of $802 million for federal 1978 with a ceiling of 9,698 agency positions.

The setting into which Costle stepped is difficult to summarize briefly. As Costle characterized it:

- "Outside there is a confusion on the part of the public in terms of what this agency is all about: what it is doing, where it is going."
- "The most serious constraint on EPA is the inherent complexity in the state of our knowledge, which is constantly changing."
- "Too often, acting under extreme deadlines mandated by Congress, EPA has announced regulations, only to find out that they knew very little about the problem. The central problem is the inherent complexity of the job that the agency has been asked to do and the

fact that what it is asked to do changes from day to day."
- "There are very difficult internal management issues not amenable to a quick solution: the skills mix problem within the agency; a research program with laboratory facilities scattered all over the country and cemented in place, largely by political alliances on the Hill that would frustrate efforts to pull together a coherent research program."
- "In terms of EPA's original mandate in the bulk pollutants we may be hitting the asymptotic part of the curve in terms of incremental clean-up costs. You have clearly conflicting national goals: energy and environment, for example."

Costle judged his six major tasks at the outset to be:

- assembling a top management team (six assistant administrators and some 25 office heads);
- addressing EPA's legislative agenda (EPA's basic legislative charter—the Clean Air Act and the Clean Water Act—were being rewritten as he took office; the pesticides program was up for reauthorization also in 1977);
- establishing EPA's role in the Carter Administration (aware that the Administration would face hard tradeoffs between the environment and energy, energy regulations and the economy, EPA regulations of toxic substances and the regulations of FDA, CSPS, and OSHA, Costle identified the need to build relations with the other key players and to enhance EPA's standing);
- building ties to constituent groups (both because of their role in legislating the agency's mandate and in successful implementation of EPA's programs);
- making specific policy decisions (for example, whether to grant or deny a permit for the Seabrook Nuclear Generating Plant cooling system. Or how the Toxic Substance Control Act, enacted in October 1976, would be im-

C. Roland Christensen, "American Motors Corporation II" (Intercollegiate Case Clearing House #6-372-350); Thomas R. Hitchner and Jacob Lew under the supervision of Philip B. Heymann and Stephen B. Hitchner, "Douglas Costle and the EPA (A)" (Kennedy School of Government Case #C94-78-216); and Jacob Lew and Stephen B. Hitchner, "Douglas Costle and the EPA (B)" (Kennedy School of Government Case #C96-78-217). For an earlier exploration of a similar comparison, see Joseph Bower, "Effective Public Management," *Harvard Business Review* (March–April, 1977).

[15]U.S. Government Manual, 1978/1979, 507.

plemented; this act gave EPA new responsibilities for regulating the manufacture, distribution, and use of chemical substances so as to prevent unreasonable risks to health and the environment. Whether EPA would require chemical manufacturers to provide some minimum information on various substances, or require much stricter reporting requirements for the 1,000 chemical substances already known to be hazardous, or require companies to report all chemicals, and on what timetable, had to be decided and the regulations issued);

- rationalizing the internal organization of the agency (EPA's extreme decentralization to the regions and its limited technical expertise).

No easy job.

Roy Chapin and American Motors, January 1977

In January 1967, in an atmosphere of crisis, Roy Chapin was appointed Chairman and Chief Executive Officer of American Motors (and William Luneburg, President and Chief Operating Officer). In the four previous years, AMC unit sales had fallen 37 percent and market share from over six percent to under three percent. Dollar volume in 1967 was off 42 percent from the all-time high of 1963 and earnings showed a net loss of $76 million on sales of $656 million. Columnists began writing obituaries for AMC. *Newsweek* characterized AMC as "a flabby dispirited company, a product solid enough but styled with about as much flair as corrective shoes, and a public image that melted down to one unshakeable label: loser." Said Chapin: "We were driving with one foot on the accelerator and one foot on the brake. We didn't know where the hell we were."

Chapin announced to his stockholders at the outset that "we plan to direct ourselves most specifically to those areas of the market where we can be fully effective. We are not going to attempt to be all things to all people, but to concentrate on those areas of consumer needs we can meet better than anyone else." As he recalled: "There were problems early in 1967 which demanded immediate attention, and which accounted for much of our time for several months. Nevertheless, we began planning beyond them, establishing objectives, programs and timetables through 1972. Whatever happened in the short run, we had to prove ourselves in the marketplace in the long run."

Chapin's immediate problems were five:

- The company was virtually out of cash and an immediate supplemental bank loan of $20 million was essential.
- Car inventories—company owned and dealer owned—had reached unprecedented levels. The solution to this glut took five months and could be accomplished only by a series of plant shutdowns in January 1967.
- Sales of the Rambler American series had stagnated and inventories were accumulating; a dramatic merchandising move was concocted and implemented in February, dropping the price tag on the American to a position midway between the VW and competitive smaller U.S. compacts, by both cutting the price to dealers and trimming dealer discounts from 21 percent to 17 percent.
- Administrative and commercial expenses were judged too high and thus a vigorous cost reduction program was initiated that trimmed $15 million during the first year. Manufacturing and purchasing costs were also trimmed significantly to approach the most effective levels in the industry.
- The company's public image had deteriorated; the press was pessimistic and much of the financial community had written it off. To counteract this, numerous formal and informal meetings were held with bankers, investment firms, government officials, and the press.

As Chapin recalls "with the immediate fires put out, we could put in place the pieces of a corporate growth plan—a definition of a way of life in the auto industry for American Motors. We felt that our reason for being, which would enable us not just to survive but to grow, lay in bringing a different approach to the auto market—in picking our spots and then being innovative and aggressive." The new corporate growth plan included a dramatic change in the approach to the market to establish a "youthful image" for the company (by bringing out new sporty models like the Javelin and by entering the racing field), "changing the product line from one end to the other" by 1972, acquiring Kaiser Jeep (selling the company's non-transportation assets and concentrating on specialized transportation, including Jeep, a company that had lost money in each of the preceding five years, but that Chapin believed could be turned around by substantial cost reductions and economies of scale in manufacturing, purchasing, and administration).

Chapin succeeded: for the year ending September 30, 1971, AMC earned $10.2 million on sales of $1.2 billion.

Recalling the list of general management functions in Table 10.1, which similarities and differences appear salient and important?

Strategy

Both Chapin and Costle had to establish objectives and priorities and to devise operational plans. In business, "corporate strategy is the pattern of major objectives, purposes, or goals and essential policies and plans for achieving these goals, stated in such a way as to define what business the company is in or is to be in and the kind of company it is or is to be."[16] In reshaping the strategy of AMC and concentrating on particular segments of the transportation

market, Chapin had to consult his Board and had to arrange financing. But the control was substantially his.

How much choice did Costle have at EPA as to the "business it is or is to be in" or the kind of agency "it is or is to be"? These major strategic choices emerged from the legislative process which mandated whether he should be in the business of controlling pesticides or toxic substances and if so on what timetable, and occasionally, even what level of particulate per million units he was required to control. The relative role of the President, other members of the Administration (including White House staff, Congressional relations, and other agency heads), the EPA Administrator, Congressional committee chairmen, and external groups in establishing the broad strategy of the agency constitutes an interesting question.

Managing Internal Components

For both Costle and Chapin, staffing was key. As Donald Rumsfeld has observed "the single, most important task of the chief executive is to select the right people. I've seen terrible organization charts in both government and business that were made to work well by good people. I've seen beautifully charted organizations that didn't work very well because they had the wrong people."[17]

The leeway of the two executives in organizing and staffing were considerably different, however. Chapin closed down plants, moved key managers, hired and fired, virtually at will. As Michael Blumenthal has written about Treasury, "if you wish to make substantive changes, policy changes, and the Department's employees don't like what you're doing, they have ways of frustrating you or stopping you that do not exist in private industry. The main method they have is Congress. If I say I want to shut

[16]Kenneth R. Andrews, *The Concept of Corporate Strategy* (Dow Jones-Irwin, 1971), p. 28.

[17]"A Politician-Turned-Executive," *Fortune* (September 10, 1979), p. 92.

down a particular unit or transfer the function of one area to another, there are ways of going to Congress and in fact using friends in the Congress to block the move. They can also use the press to try to stop you. If I at Bendix wished to transfer a division from Ann Arbor to Detroit because I figured out that we could save money that way, as long as I could do it decently and carefully, it's of no lasting interest to the press. The press can't stop me. They may write about it in the local paper, but that's about it."[18]

For Costle, the basic structure of the agency was set by law. The labs, their location, and most of their personnel were fixed. Though he could recruit his key subordinates, again restrictions like the conflict of interest law and the prospect of a Senate confirmation fight led him to drop his first choice for the Assistant Administrator for Research and Development, since he had worked for a major chemical company. While Costle could resort to changes in the process for developing policy or regulations in order to circumvent key office directors whose views he did not share, for example, Eric Stork, the Deputy Assistant Administrator in charge of Mobile Source Air Program, such maneuvers took considerable time, provoked extensive infighting, and delayed significantly the development of Costle's program.

In the direction of personnel and management of the personnel system, Chapin exercised considerable authority. While the United Auto Workers limited his authority over workers, at the management level he assigned people and reassigned responsibility consistent with his general plan. While others may have felt that his decisions to close down particular plants or to drop a particular product were mistaken, they complied. As George Schultz has observed: "One of the first lessons I learned in moving from government to business is that in business you must be very careful when you tell someone who is working for you to do something because

the probability is high that he or she will do it."[19]

Costle faced a civil service system designed to prevent spoils as much as to promote productivity. The Civil Service Commission exercised much of the responsibility for the personnel function in his agency. Civil service rules severely restricted his discretion, took long periods to exhaust, and often required complex maneuvering in a specific case to achieve any results. Equal opportunity rules and their administration provided yet another network of procedural and substantive inhibitions. In retrospect, Costle found the civil service system a much larger constraint on his actions and demand on his time than he had anticipated.

In controlling performance, Chapin was able to use measures like profit and market share, to decompose those objectives to sub-objectives for lower levels of the organization and to measure the performance of managers of particular models, areas, divisions. Cost accounting rules permitted him to compare plants within AMC and to compare AMC's purchases, production, and even administration with the best practice in the industry.

Managing External Constituencies

As Chief Executive Officer, Chapin had to deal only with the Board. For Costle, within the executive branch but beyond his agency lay many actors critical to the achievement of his agency's objectives: the President and the White House, Energy, Interior, the Council on Environmental Quality, OMB. Actions each could take, either independently or after a process of consultation in which they disagreed with him, could frustrate his agency's achievement of its assigned mission. Consequently, he spent considerable time building his agency's reputation and capital for interagency disputes.

Dealing with independent external organi-

[18]"Candid Reflections of a Businessman in Washington." *Fortune* (January 29, 1979), p. 39.

[19]"The Abrasive Interface," *Harvard Business Review* (November–December 1979), p. 95.

zations was a necessary and even larger part of Costle's job. Since his agency's mission, strategy, authorizations, and appropriations emerged from the process of legislation, attention to Congressional committees, and Congressmen, and Congressmen's staff, and people who affect Congressmen and Congressional staffers rose to the top of Costle's agenda. In the first year, top level EPA officials appeared over 140 times before some 60 different committees and subcommittees.

Chapin's ability to achieve AMC's objectives could also be affected by independent external organizations: competitors, government (the Clean Air Act that was passed in 1970), consumer groups (recall Ralph Nader), and even suppliers of oil. More than most private managers, Chapin had to deal with the press in attempting to change the image of AMC. Such occasions were primarily at Chapin's initiative, and around events that Chapin's public affairs office orchestrated, for example, the announcement of a new racing car. Chapin also managed a marketing effort to persuade consumers that their tastes could best be satisfied by AMC products.

Costle's work was suffused by the press: in the daily working of the organization, in the perception by key publics of the agency and thus the agency's influence with relevant parties, and even in the setting of the agenda of issues to which the agency had to respond.

For Chapin, the bottom line was profit, market share, and the long-term competitive position of AMC. For Costle, what are the equivalent performance measures? Blumenthal answers by exaggerating the difference between appearance and reality: "At Bendix, it was the reality of the situation that in the end determined whether we succeeded or not. In the crudest sense, this meant the bottom line. You can dress up profits only for so long—if you're not successful, it's going to be clear. In government there is no bottom line, and that is why you can be successful if you appear to be successful—though, of course, appearance is not

the only ingredient of success."[20] Rumsfeld says: "In business, you're pretty much judged by results. I don't think the American people judge government officials this way. . . . In government, too often you're measured by how much you seem to care, how hard you seem to try— things that do not necessarily improve the human condition. . . . It's a lot easier for a President to get into something and end up with a few days of good public reaction than it is to follow through, to pursue policies to a point where they have a beneficial effect on human lives."[21] As George Shultz says: "In government and politics, recognition and therefore incentives go to those who formulate policy and maneuver legislative compromise. By sharp contrast, the kudos and incentives in business go to the persons who can get something done. It is execution that counts. Who can get the plant built, who can bring home the sales contract, who can carry out the financing, and so on."[22]

This casual comparison of one public and one private manager suggests what could be done—if the issue of comparisons were pursued systematically, horizontally across organizations and at various levels within organizations. While much can be learned by examining the chief executive officers of organizations, still more promising should be comparisons among the much larger numbers of middle managers. If one compared, for example, a Regional Administrator of EPA and an AMC division chief, or two Comptrollers, or equivalent plant managers, some functions would appear more similar, and other differences would stand out. The major barrier to such comparisons is the lack of cases describing problems and practices of middle-level managers.[23] This should be a high priority in further research.

[20]*Fortune* (January 29, 1979), p. 36.

[21]*Fortune* (September 10, 1979), p. 90.

[22]*Harvard Business Review* (November–December 1979), p. 95.

[23]The cases developed by Boston University's Public Management Program offer a promising start in this direction.

The differences noted in this comparison, for example, in the personnel area, have already changed with the Civil Service Reform Act of 1978 and the creation of the Senior Executive Service. Significant changes have also occurred in the automobile industry: under current circumstances, the CEO of Chrysler may seem much more like the Administrator of EPA. More precise comparison of different levels of management in both organizations, for example, accounting procedures used by Chapin to cut costs significantly as compared to equivalent procedures for judging the costs of EPA mandated pollution control devices, would be instructive.

Implications for Research on Public Management

The debate between the assimilators and the differentiators, like the dispute between proponents of convergence and divergence between the U.S. and the Soviet Union reminds me of the old argument about whether the glass is half full or half empty. I conclude that public and private management are at least as different as they are similar, and that the differences are more important than the similarities. From this review of the "state of the art," such as it is, I draw a number of lessons for research on public management. I will try to state them in a way that is both succinct and provocative:

- First, the demand for performance from government and efficiency in government is both real and right. The perception that government's performance lags private business performance is also correct. But the notion that there is any significant body of private management practices and skills that can be transferred directly to public management tasks in a way that produces significant improvements is wrong.
- Second, performance in many public management positions can be improved substantially, perhaps by an order of magnitude.

That improvement will come not, however, from massive borrowing of specific private management skills and understandings. Instead, it will come, as it did in the history of private management, from an articulation of the general management function and a self-consciousness about the general public management point of view. The single lesson of private management most instructive to public management is the prospect of substantial improvement through recognition of and consciousness about the public management function.

Alfred Chandler's prize winning study, *The Visible Hand: The Managerial Revolution in American Business,* [24] describes the emergence of professional management in business. Through the 19th century most American businesses were run by individuals who performed management functions but had no self-consciousness about their management responsibilities. With the articulation of the general management perspective and the refinement of general management practices, by the 1920s, American businesses had become competitive in the management function. Individuals capable at management and self-conscious about their management tasks—setting objectives, establishing priorities, and driving the organization to results—entered firms and industries previously run by family entrepreneurs or ordinary employees and brought about dramatic increases in product. Business schools emerged to document better and worse practice, largely through the case method, to suggest improvements, and to refine specific management instruments. Important advances were made in technique. But the great leaps forward in productivity stemmed from the articulation of the general management point of view and the self-consciousness of managers about their function. (Analogously, at a

[24] Alfred Chandler, *The Visible Hand: The Managerial Revolution in American Business,* Belknap Press of Harvard University Press, 1977.

lower level, the articulation of the salesman's role and task, together with the skills and values of salesmanship made it possible for individuals with moderate talents at sales to increase their level of sales tenfold.)

The routes by which people reach general management positions in government do not assure that they will have consciousness or competence in management. As a wise observer of government managers has written, "One of the difficult problems of schools of public affairs is to overcome the old-fashioned belief—still held by many otherwise sophisticated people—that the skills of management are simply the application of 'common sense' by any intelligent and broadly educated person to the management problems which are presented to him. It is demonstrable that many intelligent and broadly educated people who are generally credited with a good deal of 'common sense' make very poor managers. The skills of effective management require a good deal of uncommon sense and uncommon knowledge."[25] I believe that the most significant aspect of the Civil Service Reform Act of 1978 is the creation of the Senior Executive Service: the explicit identification of general managers in government. The challenge now is to assist people who occupy general management positions in actually becoming general managers.

- Third, careful review of private management rules of thumb that can be adapted to public management contexts will pay off. The 80-20 rule—80 percent of the benefits of most production processes come from the first 20 percent of effort—does have wide application, for example, in EPA efforts to reduce bulk pollutants.
- Fourth, Chandler documents the proposition that the categories and criteria for identifying costs, or calculating present value, or mea-

suring the value added to intermediate products are not "natural." They are invented: creations of intelligence harnessed to operational tasks. While there are some particular accounting categories and rules, for example, for costing intermediate products, that may be directly transferable to public sector problems, the larger lesson is that dedicated attention to specific management functions can, as in the history of business, create for public sector managers accounting categories, and rules, and measures that cannot now be imagined.[26]

- Fifth, it is possible to learn from experience. What skills, attributes, and practices do competent managers exhibit and less successful managers lack? This is an empirical question that can be investigated in a straight-forward manner. As Yogi Berra noted: "You can observe a lot just by watching."
- Sixth, the effort to develop public management as a field of knowledge should start from problems faced by practicing public managers. The preferences of professors for theorizing reflects deep-seated incentives of the academy that can be overcome only by careful institutional design.

In the light of these lessons, I believe one strategy for the development of public management should include:

- *Developing a significant number of cases on public management problems and practices.* Cases should describe typical problems faced by public managers. Cases should attend not only to top-level managers but to middle and lower-level managers. The dearth of cases at this level makes this a high priority for development. Cases should examine both general functions of management and specific organizational tasks, for example, hiring and firing. Public management cases should concentrate on the job of the manager running his unit.

[25]Rufus Miles, "The Search for Identity of Graduate Schools of Public Affairs," *Public Administration Review* (November 1967).

[26]Chandler, *op. cit.,* pp. 277–279.

- *Analyzing cases to identify better and worse practice.* Scientists search for "critical experiments." Students of public management should seek to identify "critical experiences" that new public managers could live through vicariously and learn from. Because of the availability of information, academics tend to focus on failures. But teaching people what not to do is not necessarily the best way to help them learn to be *doers.* By analyzing relative successes, it will be possible to extract rules of thumb, crutches, and concepts, for example, Chase's "law": wherever the product of a public organization has not been monitored in a way that ties performance to reward, the introduction of an effective monitoring system will yield a 50 percent improvement in that product in the short run. GAO's handbooks on evaluation techniques and summaries suggest what can be done.

- *Promoting systematic comparative research:* management positions in a single agency over time; similar management positions among several public agencies; public management levels within a single agency; similar management functions, for example, budgeting or management information systems, among agencies; managers across public and private organizations; and even cross-nationally. The data for this comparative research would be produced by the case development effort and would complement the large-scale

development of cases on private management that is ongoing.

- *Linking to the training of public managers.* Intellectual development of the field of public management should be tightly linked to the training of public managers, including individuals already in positions of significant responsibility. Successful practice will appear in government, not in the university. University-based documentation of better and worse practice, and refinement of that practice, should start from problems of managers on the line. The intellectual effort required to develop the field of public management and the resources required to support this level of effort are most likely to be assembled if research and training are vitally linked. The new Senior Executive Service presents a major opportunity to do this.

The strategy outlined here is certainly not the only strategy for research in public management. Given the needs for effective public management, I believe that a *major* research effort should be mounted and that it should pursue a number of complementary strategies. Given where we start, I see no danger of over-attention to, or over-investment in the effort required in the immediate future.

Any resemblance between my preferred strategy and that of at least one school of government is not purely coincidental.

CASE STUDY 10

Introduction

The launch of Mission 51-L, the Space Shuttle *Challenger,* was postponed three times and "scrubbed" once from the planned date of January 22, 1986. The first postponement was announced on December 23, 1985, because of the late launch of Mission 61-C. Heavy work requirements moved the launch date back to January 25 and then to January 26. The "weather window" on January 26 suddenly deteriorated so that once again the launch was delayed until January 27. Strong crosswinds at the Kennedy Space Center runway, where the launch was to take place on January 27, forced a cancellation at 12:36 P.M., and the *Challenger* flight was rescheduled for January 28. The intense media coverage of the event, coupled with the "backup" that the delay of Mission 51-L was causing on other work at Kennedy, made everyone eager for 51-L to fly.

The weather for January 28 was forecast as clear but cold, with temperatures dropping to the low twenties overnight. Another "no-go" situation nearly occurred in the early morning hours of January 28 due to the rain and low ceilings at Casablanca, the alternative abort site, but the site was shifted to Dakar, Senegal. At 6:18 A.M. the crew awoke, ate, and were suited up. By 8:36 A.M. the seven-member crew of Commander Francis R. (Dick) Scobee, Pilot Michael J. Smith, Mission Specialist One Ellison S. Onizuka, Mission Specialist Two Judith A. Resnik, Mission Specialist Three Ronald E. McNair, Payload Specialist One S. Christa McAuliffe, and Payload Specialist Two Gregory B. Jarvis were strapped in their seats.

The flight of *Challenger* began at 11:38 A.M. and ended 73 seconds later. Before a worldwide television audience of an estimated eighty million people, the *Challenger* exploded in a fireball of hydrogen and oxygen propellants, destroying the rocket and the space shuttle and killing all of the crew members. The immediate cause of the accident, in the words of the Presidential Commission on the Space Shuttle Accident (the Rogers Report): "the Commission concluded that the cause of the Challenger accident was the failure of the pressure seal in the aft field joint of the right solid rocket motor. The failure was due to a faulty design unacceptably sensitive to a number of factors. These factors were the effects of temperature, physical dimensions, the character of the materials, the effects of reusability processing and the reaction of the joint to dynamic loading." In plain language, a small, washer-like seal in the rocket, called an O-ring, failed to function correctly in the extreme cold and caused the accident.

Almost six months before the *Challenger* accident, July 31, 1985, Roger Boisjoly, a junior engineer working for the solid booster manufacturer, Morton Thiokol, had prepared the following memo for Bob Lund, Thiokol's Vice President of Engineering. The memo was co-signed by Boisjoly's immediate superior, Arnie Thompson. Boisjoly headed a Thiokol task force to study the solid rocket seal problems.

> This letter is written to ensure that management is fully aware of the seriousness of the current O-ring erosion problem in the SRM [Solid Rocket Motor] joints from an engineering standpoint. The mistakenly accepted position on the joint problem was to fly without fear of failure and to run a series of design evaluations which would ultimately lead to a solution or at least a significant reduction of the erosion problem. This position is now drastically changed as a result of the SRM-16-A [a number designation for this particular rocket motor] nozzle joint erosion which eroded a secondary O-ring, with the primary O-ring never sealing. If the same scenario should occur in a field joint [between booster segments] (and it could) then it is a jump ball as to the success or failure of the joint. . . . The result would be a catastrophe of the highest order—loss of human life. An unofficial team (a memo defining the team and its purpose was never published) with leader was formed on 19 July 1985 and was tasked with solving the problem for both the short and the long term. This unofficial team is essentially nonexistent at this time. In my opinion, the team must be officially given the responsibility and the authority to execute the work that needs to be done on a non-interference basis (full-time assignment until completed). It is my honest and very real fear that if we do not take immediate action to dedicate a team to solve the problem, with the field joint having the number

one priority, then we stand in jeopardy of losing a flight, along with all the launch pad facilities.

There was concern by others at Thiokol and NASA over the erosion of the seals on the solid rockets, but most believed that the problem was being worked on, in a slow and careful manner, to the official satisfaction of those senior managers who were responsible for the shuttle program. Thus in no sense was the shuttle's launch considered unsafe. The O-ring joint was considered susceptible to what space engineers refer to as "single point failure," but management also believed that the backup seal would work and thus the launch would proceed in a satisfactory manner. However, to Boisjoly the official view became a growing concern. To him, cold temperatures at launch time would slow down "the actuation time" of the rubber-like material, which would mean that the secondary O-ring might not function if the primary ring failed.

In the following excerpts from the Rogers Report (taken to a large extent from direct testimony of the key NASA and Thiokol engineers and executives involved with the seal problem), the reader is treated to a rare inside look at the incredibly complex managerial processes concerned with the launch of 51-L and the failure of those processes to detect and remedy the seal problem before the launch. The opening section outlines the various levels involved in the Shuttle Flight Readiness Review, which is a carefully planned set of procedures designed to insure the readiness of all components for space flight. It involves technical experts at the Johnson Space Flight Center in Houston, Texas (headquarters for NASA's Shuttle Program); the Kennedy Space Center in Florida (where the flight originated); NASA's Marshall Space Flight Center in Huntsville, Alabama, the lead center in charge of the solid rockets; and Morton Thiokol's Wasatch Division in Utah, the prime contractor responsible for building the *Challenger*'s boosters.

As you read this case, think specifically about why Boisjoly's concerns over the seals never reached the top NASA management:

Who were these top NASA managers, and why were they not fully "in charge"?

Why did Thiokol's senior managers approve the launch even though they knew of the O-ring problem?

Overall, does this case support Allison's arguments about the uniqueness of public management? How so?

The Space Shuttle *Challenger* Accident

The Shuttle Flight Readiness Review is a carefully planned, step-by-step activity, established

Excerpts from the *Report of the Presidential Commission on the Space Shuttle* Challenger *Accident* (Washington, D.C.: U.S. Government Printing Office, June 6, 1986), chapter 5, pp. 82–103. Footnotes deleted.

by NASA program directive SPO-PD 710.5A, designed to certify the readiness of all components of the Space Shuttle assembly. The process is focused upon the Level I Flight Readiness Review, held approximately two weeks before a launch. The Level I review is a conference chaired by the NASA Associate Administrator

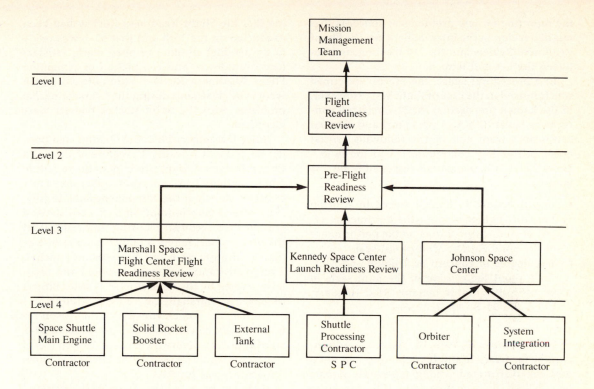

for Space Flight and supported by the NASA Chief Engineer, the Program Manager, the center directors and project managers from Johnson, Marshall and Kennedy, along with senior contractor representatives.

The formal portion of the process is initiated by directive from the Associate Administrator for Space Flight. The directive outlines the schedule for the Level I Flight Readiness Review and for the steps that precede it. The process begins at Level IV with the contractors formally certifying—in writing—the flight readiness of the elements for which they are responsible. Certification is made to the appropriate Level III NASA project managers at Johnson and Marshall. Additionally, at Marshall the review is followed by a presentation directly to the Center Director. At Kennedy the Level III review, chaired by the Center Director, verifies readiness of the launch support elements.

The next step in the process is the Certification of Flight Readiness to the Level II Program Manager at Johnson. In this review each Space Shuttle program element endorses that it has satisfactorily completed the manufacture, as-

sembly, test and checkout of the pertinent element, including the contractors' certification that design and performance are up to standard. The Flight Readiness Review process culminates in the Level I review.

In the initial notice of the review, the Level I directive establishes a Mission Management Team for the particular mission. The team assumes responsibility for each Shuttle's readiness for a period commencing 48 hours before launch and continuing through post-landing crew egress and the safing of the Orbiter. On call throughout the entire period, the Mission Management Team supports the Associate Administrator for Space Flight and the Program Manager.

A structured Mission Management Team meeting—called L-1—is held 24 hours, or one day, prior to each scheduled launch. Its agenda includes closeout of any open work, a closeout of any Flight Readiness Review action items, a discussion of new or continuing anomalies, and an updated briefing on anticipated weather conditions at the launch site and at the abort landing sites in different parts of the world. It is standard practice of Level I and II officials to encourage the reporting of new problems or concerns that might develop in the interval between the Flight Readiness Review and the L-1 meeting, and between the L-1 and launch.

In a procedural sense, the process described was followed in the case of flight 51-L. However, in the launch preparation for 51-L relevant concerns of Level III NASA personnel and element contractors were not, in the following crucial areas, adequately communicated to the NASA Level I and II management responsible for the launch:

• The objections to launch voiced by Morton Thiokol engineers about the detrimental effect of cold temperatures on the performance of the Solid Rocket Motor joint seal.
• The degree of concern of Thiokol and Marshall about the erosion of the joint seals in prior Shuttle flights, notably 51-C (January, 1985) and 51-B (April, 1985).

On December 13, 1985, the Associate Administrator for Space flight, Jesse Moore, sent out a message distributed among NASA Headquarters, NASA field centers, and U.S. Air Force units, that scheduled the Flight Readiness Review for January 15, 1986, and prescribed the dates for the other steps in the standard procedure.

The message was followed by directives from James A. (Gene) Thomas, Deputy Director of Launch and Landing Operations at Kennedy on January 2, 1986; by the National Space Transportation System Program Manager, Arnold Aldrich, on January 3; by William R. Lucas, the Marshall Center Director, on January 7; and by the Marshall Shuttle Projects Office on January 8. Each of these implementing directives prescribed for Level III the preparatory steps for the Flight Readiness Review.

The Flight Readiness Review was held, as scheduled, on January 15. On the following day, Aldrich issued the schedule for the combined Level I/Mission Management Team meetings; he also announced plans for the Mission Management Team meetings continuing throughout the mission and included the schedule for the L-1 review.

On January 23, Moore issued a directive stating that the Flight Readiness Review had been conducted on the 15th and that 51-L was ready to fly pending closeout of open work, satisfactory countdown, and completion of remaining Flight Readiness Review action items, which were to be closed out during the L-1 meeting. No problems with the Solid Rocket Booster were identified.

Since December, 1982, the O-rings had been designated a "Criticality 1" feature of the Solid Rocket Booster design, a term denoting a failure point—without back-up—that could cause a loss of life or vehicle if the component fails. In July, 1985, after a nozzle joint on STS 51-B showed erosion of a secondary O-ring, indicating that the primary seal failed, a launch constraint was placed on flight 51-F and subsequent launches. These constraints had been imposed and regularly waived by the Solid Rocket Booster Project Manager at Marshall, Lawrence B. Mulloy.

Neither the launch constraint, the reason for it, or the six consecutive waivers prior to 51-L were known to Moore (Level I) or Aldrich (Level II) or Thomas at the time of the Flight Readiness Review process for 51-L.

It should be noted that there were other and independent paths of system reporting that were designed to bring forward information about the Solid Rocket Booster joint anomalies. One path was the task force of Thiokol engineers and Marshall engineers who had been conducting subscale pressure tests at Wasatch during 1985, a source of documented rising concern and frustration on the part of some of the Thiokol participants and a few of the Marshall participants. But Level II was not in the line of reporting for this activity. Another path was the examination at each Flight Readiness Review of evidence of earlier flight anomalies. For 51-L, the data presented in this latter path, while it reached Levels I and II, never referred to either test anomalies or flight anomalies with O-rings.

In any event, no mention of the O-ring problems in the Solid Rocket Booster joint appeared in the Certification of Flight Readiness, signed for Thiokol on January 9, 1986, by Joseph Kilminster, for the Solid Rocket Booster set designated BI026.

Similarly, no mention appeared in the certification endorsement, signed on January 15,

1986, by Kilminster and by Mulloy, No mention appears in several inches of paper comprising the entire chain of readiness reviews for 51-L.

In the 51-L readiness reviews, it appears that neither Thiokol management nor the Marshall Level III project managers believed that the O-ring blow-by and erosion risk was critical. The testimony and contemporary correspondence show that Level III believed there was ample margin to fly with O-ring erosion, provided the leak check was performed at 200 pounds per square inch.

Following the January 15 Flight Readiness Review each element of the Shuttle was certified as flight-ready.

The L-1 Mission Management Team meeting took place as scheduled at 11:00 A.M. Eastern Standard Time January 25. No technical issues appeared at this meeting or in the documentation and all Flight Readiness Review actions were reported closed out.

Mr. Mulloy testified as follows regarding the Flight Readiness Review record about O-ring concerns.

Chairman Rogers: . . . Why wasn't that a cause for concern on the part of the whole NASA organization?

Mr. Mulloy: It was cause for concern, sir.

Chairman Rogers: Who did you tell about this?

Mr. Mulloy: Everyone, sir.

Chairman Rogers: And they all knew about it at the time of 51-L?

Mr. Mulloy: Yes, sir. You will find in the Flight Readiness Review record that went all the way to the L-1 review.

It is disturbing to the Commission that contrary to the testimony of the Solid Rocket Booster Project Manager, the seriousness of concern was not conveyed in Flight Readiness Review to Level I and the 51-L readiness review was silent.

The only remaining issue facing the Mission Management Team at the L-1 review was the approaching cold front, with forecasts of rain showers and temperatures in the mid-sixties. There had also been heavy rain since 51-L had been rolled out to the launch pad, approximately seven inches compared with the 2.5 inches that would have been normal for that season and length of exposure (35 days).

At 12:36 P.M. on the 27th, the Mission Management Team scrubbed the launch for that day due to high cross winds at the launch site. In the accompanying discussion that ran for about half an hour, all appropriate personnel were polled as to the feasibility of a launch within 24 hours. Participants were requested to identify any constraints. This meeting, aimed at launch at 9:38 A.M. on January 28, produced no constraints or concerns about the performance of the Solid Rocket Boosters.

At 2:00 P.M. on the 27th, the Mission Management Team met again. At that time, the weather was expected to clear, but it appeared that temperatures would be in the low twenties for about 11 hours. Issues were raised with regard to the cold weather effects on the launch facility, including the water drains, the eye wash and shower water, fire suppression system, and overpressure water trays. It was decided to activate heaters in the Orbiter, but no concerns were expressed about the O-rings in the Solid Rocket Boosters. The decision was to proceed with the countdown and with fueling, but all members of the team were asked to review the situation and call if any problems arose.

At approximately 2:30 P.M. EST, at Thiokol's Wasatch plant, Robert Ebeling, after learning of the predicted low temperature for launch, convened a meeting with Roger Boisjoly and with other Thiokol engineers. . . . Ebeling was concerned about predicted cold temperatures at Kennedy Space Center. In a post-accident interview, Mr. Ebeling recalled the substance of the meeting.

The meeting lasted one hour, but the conclusion of that meeting was Engineering—especially Arnie, Roger Boisjoly, Brian Russell, myself, Jerry Burns, they come to mind—were very adamant about their concerns on this lower temperature, because we were way below our data base and we were way below what we qualified for.

Later in the afternoon on the same day, Allan McDonald—Thiokol's liaison for the Solid Rocket Booster project at Kennedy Space Center—received a telephone call from Ebeling, expressing concern about the performance of the Solid Rocket Booster field joints at low temperatures. During testimony before the Commission on February 27, McDonald recounted that conversation:

Mr. McDonald: Well, I had first become aware of the concern of the low temperatures that were projected for the Cape, it was late in the afternoon of the 27th. I was at Carver Kennedy's house. He is a vice president of, as I mentioned, our space operations center at the Cape, and supports the stacking of the SRMs [Solid Rocket Motors].

And I had a call from Bob Ebeling. He is the manager of our ignition system and final assembly, and he worked for me as program manager at Thiokol in Utah. And he called me and said that they had just received some word earlier that the weatherman was projecting temperatures as low as 18 degrees Fahrenheit some time in the early morning hours of the 28th, and that they had some meetings with some of the engineering people and had some concerns about the O-rings getting to those kinds of temperatures.

And he wanted to make me aware of that and also wanted to get some more updated and better information on what the actual temperature was going to be depicted, so that they could make some calculations on what they expected the real temperature the O-rings may see. . . .

I told him that I would get that temperature data for him and call him back. Carver Kennedy then, when I hung up, called the launch operations center to get the predicted temperatures from pad B, as well as what the temperature history had been during the day up until that time.

. . . He obtained those temperatures from the launch operations center, and they basically said that they felt it was going to get near freezing or freezing before midnight. It would get as low as 22 degrees as a minimum in the early morning hours, probably around 6:00 o'clock, and that they were predicting a temperature of about 26 degrees at the intended time, about 9:38 the next morning.

I took that data and called back to the plant and sent it to Bob Ebeling and relayed that to him, and told him he ought to use this temperature data for his predictions, but I thought this was very serious and to make sure that he had the vice president, engineering, involved in this and all of his people; that I wanted them to put together some calculations and a presentation of material.

Chairman Rogers: Who's the Vice President, Engineering?

Mr. McDonald: Mr. Bob Lund is our Vice President, Engineering, at our Morton Thiokol facility in Utah.

To make sure he was involved in this, and that this decision should be an engineering decision, not a program management decision. And I told him that I would like him to make sure they prepared some charts and were in a position to recommend the launch temperature and to have the rationale for supporting that launch temperature.

I then hung up and I called Mr. Mulloy. He was staying at the Holiday Inn in Merritt Island and they couldn't reach him, and so I called Cecil Houston—Cecil Houston is the resident manager for the Marshall Space Flight Center office at KSC [Kennedy Space Center]—and told him about our concerns with the low temperatures and the potential problem with the O-rings.

And he said that he would set up a teleconference. He had a four-wire system next to his office. His office is right across from the VAB [Vehicle Assembly Building] in the trailer complex C over there. And he would set up a four-wire teleconference involving the engineering people at Marshall Space Flight Center at Huntsville, our people back at Thiokol in Utah; and that I should come down to his office and participate at Kennedy from there, and that he would get back with me and let me know when that time would be.

Editor's Note: The following is an account of the important teleconference set up to discuss the seal issue: a three-way phone call between Florida, Huntsville, and the Thiokol plant in Utah at 8:45 P.M., the night before the launch of Mission 51-L. Thiokol engineers in Utah telefaxed data charts hurriedly to managers in

Florida and Huntsville to back up their points. Listening in on the conference call in Florida were Allan McDonald and two key figures from the NASA Marshall Center: Larry Mulloy, who headed the solid rocket project at Marshall, and his boss, Stanley Reinartz, who headed the entire Shuttle Project Office. Listening in Huntsville were Reinartz's deputy Jud Lovingood and George Hardy, Marshall's Deputy Director for Science and Engineering. In Utah Thiokol's managers and engineers who listened or talked included: Roger Boisjoly and his supervisor, Arnie Thompson; Bob Lund, Vice President for Engineering; Joe Kilminster, manager of shuttle projects; and Jerry Mason, Senior Thiokol Vice President. Here Boisjoly explains his deep concern about next day's launch, given the low temperatures.

Mr. Boisjoly: I expressed deep concern about launching at low temperature. I presented . . . [a] chart that summarized the primary concerns, and that was the chart that I pulled right out of the Washington presentation without changing one word of it because it was still applicable, and it addresses the highest concern of the field joint in both the ignition transient condition and the steady state condition, and it really sets down the rationale for why we were continuing to fly. Basically, if erosion penetrates the primary O-ring seal, there is a higher probability of no secondary seal capability in the steady state condition. And I had two sub-bullets under that which stated bench testing showed O-ring not capable of maintaining contact with metal parts, gap, opening rate to maximum operating pressure. I had another bullet which stated bench testing showed capability to maintain O-ring contact during initial phase (0 to 170 milliseconds of transient). That was my comfort basis of continuing to fly under normal circumstances, normal being within the data base we had.

I emphasized, when I presented that chart about the changing of the timing function of the O-ring as it attempted to seal. I was concerned that we may go from that first beginning region into that intermediate region, from 0 to 170 being the first region, and 170 to 330 being the intermediate region where we didn't have a high probability of sealing or seating.

I then presented [a second chart] with added concerns related to the timing function. And basically on that chart, I started off talking about a lower temperature than current data base results in changing the primary O-ring sealing timing function, and I discussed the SRM-15 [Flight 51-C, January, 1985] observations, namely, the 15A [Left SRM, Flight 51-C] motor had 80 degrees arc black grease between the O-rings, and make no mistake about it, when I say black, I mean black just like coal. It was jet black. And SRM-15B [Right SRM, Flight 51-C] had a 110 degree arc of black grease between the O-rings. We would have low O-ring squeeze due to low temperature which I calculated earlier in the day. We should have higher O-ring Shore hardness. . . .

Now, that would be harder. And what that material really is, it would be likened to trying to shove a brick into a crack versus a sponge. That is a good analogy for purposes of this discussion. I also mentioned that thicker grease, as a result of lower temperatures, would have a higher viscosity. It wouldn't be as slick and slippery as it would be at room temperature. And so it would be a little bit more difficult to move across it.

We would have higher O-ring pressure actuation time, in my opinion, and that is what I presented. . . . These are the sum and substance of what I just presented. If action time increases, then the threshold of secondary seal pressurization capability is approached. That was my fear. If the threshold is reached, then secondary seal may not be capable of being pressurized, and that was the bottom line of everything that had been presented up to that point.

Chairman Rogers: Did anybody take issue with you?

Mr. Boisjoly: Well, I am coming to that. I also showed a chart of the joint with an exaggerated cross section to show the seal lifted off, which has been shown to everybody. I was asked, yes, at that point in time I was asked to quantify my concerns, and I said I couldn't. I couldn't quantify it. I had no data to quantify it, but I did say I knew that it was away from goodness in the current data base. Someone on the net commented that we had soot blow-by on SRM-22 [Flight 61-A, October, 1985] which was launched at 75 degrees. I don't remember who made the comment, but that is where the first comment came in about the disparity between my conclusion and the observed data because SRM-22 [Flight 61-A, October, 1985] had blow-by at essentially a room temperature launch.

I then said that SRM-15 [Flight 51-C, January, 1985] had much more blow-by indication and that it was indeed telling us that lower temperature was a factor. This was supported by inspection of flown hardware by myself. I was asked again for data to support my claim, and I said I have none other than what is being presented, and I had been trying to get resilience data, Arnie and I both, since last October, and that statement was mentioned on the net.

Others in the room presented their charts, and the main telecon session concluded with Bob Lund, who is our Vice President of Engineering, presenting his conclusions and recommendations charts which were based on our data input up to that point. Listeners on the telecon were not pleased with the conclusions and the recommendations.

Chairman Rogers: What was the conclusion?

Mr. Boisjoly: The conclusion was we should not fly outside of our data base, which was 53 degrees. Those were the conclusions. And we were quite pleased because we knew in advance, having participated in the preparation, what the conclusions were, and we felt very comfortable with that.

Mr. Acheson: Who presented that conclusion?

Mr. Boisjoly: Mr. Bob Lund. He had prepared those charts. He had input from other people. He had actually physically prepared the charts. It was about that time that Mr. Hardy from Marshall was asked what he thought about the MTI [Morton Thiokol] recommendation, and he said he was appalled at the MTI decision. Mr. Hardy was also asked about launching, and he said no, not if the contractor recommended not launching, he would not go against the contractor and launch.

There was a short discussion that ensued about temperature not being a discriminator between SRM-15 [Flight 51-C] and SRM-22 [Flight

61-A], and shortly after, I believe it was Mr. Kilminster asked if—excuse me. I'm getting confused here. Mr. Kilminster was asked by NASA if he would launch, and he said no because the engineering recommendation was not to launch.

Then MTI management then asked for a five-minute caucus. I'm not sure exactly who asked for that, but it was asked in such a manner that I remember it was asked for, a five-minute caucus, which we put on—the line on mute and went off-line with the rest of the net.

Chairman Rogers: Mr. Boisjoly, at the time that you made the—that Thiokol made the recommendation not to launch, was that the unanimous recommendation as far as you knew?

Mr. Boisjoly: Yes. I have to make something clear. I have been distressed by the things that have been appearing in the paper and things that have been said in general, and there was never one positive, pro-launch statement ever made by anybody. There have been some feelings since then that folks have expressed that they would support the decision, but there was not one positive statement for launch ever made in that room.

Mr. McDonald's testimony:

Mr. McDonald: I arrived at the Kennedy Space Center at about 8:15 [P.M.], and when I arrived there at the Kennedy Space Center the others that had already arrived were Larry Mulloy, who was there—he is the manager, the project manager for the SRB for Marshall. Stan Reinartz was there and he is the manager of the Shuttle Project Office. He's Larry Mulloy's boss.

Cecil Houston was there, the resident manager for Marshall. And Jack Buchanan was there. He happens to be our manager, Morton Thiokol's manager of our launch support services office at Kennedy.

The telecon hadn't started yet. It came on the network shortly after I got there. . . .

Chairman Rogers: Was it essentially a telephone conference or was there actually a network of pictures?

Mr. McDonald: It was a telephone conference. . . .

But I will relay . . . what I heard at the conference as best I can. The teleconference started I guess close to 9:00 o'clock and, even though all the charts weren't there, we were told to begin and that Morton Thiokol should take the lead and go through the charts that they had sent to both centers.

The charts were presented by the engineering people from Thiokol, in fact by the people that had made those particular charts. Some of them were typed, some of them were handwritten. And they discussed their concerns with the low temperatures relative to the possible effects on the O-rings, primarily the timing function to seal the O-rings.

They presented a history of some of the data that we had accumulated both in static test and in flight tests relative to temperatures and the performance of the O-rings, and reviewed the history of all of our erosion studies of the O-rings, in the field joints, any blow-by of the primary O-ring with soot or products of combustion or decomposition that we had noted, and the performance of the secondary O-rings.

And there was an exchange amongst the technical people on that data as to what it meant. . . . But the real exchange never really came until the conclusions and recommendations came in.

At that point in time, our vice president, Mr. Bob Lund, presented those charts and he presented the charts on the conclusions and recommendations. And the bottom line was that the engineering people would not recommend a launch below 53 degrees Fahrenheit. The basis for that recommendation was primarily our concern with the launch that had occurred about a year earlier, in January of 1985, I believe it was 51-C.

Mr. Mulloy's testimony:

Editor's Note: *Lawrence B. Mulloy was at Kennedy at the time but headed the Solid Rocket Booster Project at Marshall.*

Mr. Mulloy: That telecon was a little late starting. It was intended to be set up at 8:15 . . . and the telecon was begun at 8:45.

And Thiokol will then present to you today the data that they presented to us in that telecon.

I will not do that. The bottom line of that, though, initially was that Thiokol engineering, Bob Lund, who is the Vice President and Director of Engineering, who is here today, recommended that 51-L not be launched if the O-ring temperatures predicted at launch time would be lower than any previous launch, and that was 53 degrees.

Dr. Walker [Rogers Commission Member]: May I ask a question? I wish you would distinguish between the predicted bulk temperatures and the O-ring temperatures. In fact, as I understand it, you really don't have any official O-ring temperature prediction in your models, and it seems that the assumption has been that the O-ring temperature is the same as the bulk temperature, which we know is not the case.

Mr. Mulloy: You will see, sir, in the Thiokol presentation today that that is not the case. This was a specific calculation of what the O-ring temperature was on the day of the January 1985 launch. It is not the bulk temperature of the propellant, nor is it the ambient temperature of the air.

It was Thiokol's calculation of what the lowest temperature an O-ring had seen in previous flights, and the engineering recommendation was that we should not move outside of that experience base.

I asked Joe Kilminster, who is the program manager for the booster program at Thiokol, what his recommendation was, because he is the gentleman that I get my recommendations from in the program office. He stated that, based on that engineering recommendation, that he could not recommend launch.

At that point I restated, as I have testified to, the rationale that was essentially documented in the 1982 Critical Items List, that stated that the rationale had been that we were flying with a simplex joint seal. And you will see in the Thiokol presentation that the context of their presentation is that the primary ring, with the reduced temperatures and reduced resiliency, may not function as a primary seal and we would be relying on secondary.

And without getting into their rationale and getting ahead, the point, the bottom line, is that we were continuing—the assessment was, my assessment at that time was, that we would have an effective simplex seal, based upon the engineering data that Thiokol had presented, and that none of those engineering data seemed to change that basic rationale.

Stan Reinartz then asked George Hardy, the Deputy Director of Science and Engineering at Marshall, what his opinion was. George stated that he agreed that the engineering data did not seem to change this basic rationale, but also stated on the telecon that he certainly would not recommend launching if Thiokol did not.

At that time Joe Kilminster requested a five minute off-net caucus, and that caucus lasted approximately 30 minutes.

The teleconference was recessed at approximately 10:30 P.M. Eastern Standard Time. The off-net caucus of Thiokol personnel started and continued for about 30 minutes at the Wasatch office. The major issues, according to the testimony of Jerry Mason, Senior Vice President for Wasatch Operations, were the effect of temperature upon the O-rings and the history of erosion of the O-rings:

Mr. Mason: Now, in the caucus we revisited all of our previous discussions, and the important things that came out of that was that, as we had recognized, we did have the possibility that the primary O-ring might be slower to move into the seating position and that was our concern, and that is what we had focused on originally.

The fact that we couldn't show direct correlation with the O-ring temperature was discussed, but we still felt that there was some concern about it being colder.

We then recognized that, if the primary did move more slowly, that we could get some blow-by and erosion on the primary. But we had pointed out to us in that caucus a point that had not come across clearly in our earlier discussions, and that is that we had run tests where we deliberately cut large pieces out of the O-rings to see what the threshold of sealing was, and we found we could go to 125 thousandths of a cut out of the O-ring and it would still seal.

Approximately 10 engineers participated in the caucus, along with Mason, Kilminster, C. G.

Wiggins (Vice President, Space Division), and Lund. Arnold Thompson and Boisjoly voiced very strong objections to launch, and the suggestion in their testimony was that Lund was also reluctant to launch:

Mr. Boisjoly: Okay, the caucus started by Mr. Mason stating a management decision was necessary. Those of us who opposed the launch continued to speak out, and I am specifically speaking of Mr. Thompson and myself because in my recollection he and I were the only ones that vigorously continued to oppose the launch. And we were attempting to go back and rereview and try to make clear what we were trying to get across, and we couldn't understand why it was going to be reversed. So we spoke out and tried to explain once again the effects of low temperature. Arnie actually got up from his position which was down the table, and walked up the table and put a quarter pad down in front of the table, in front of the management folks, and tried to sketch out once again what his concern was with the joint, and when he realized he wasn't getting through, he just stopped.

I tried one more time with the photos. I grabbed the photos, and I went up and discussed the photos once again and tried to make the point that it was my opinion from actual observations that temperature was indeed a discriminator and we should not ignore the physical evidence that we had observed.

And again, I brought up the point that SRM-15 [Flight 51-C, January, 1985] had a 110 degree arc of black grease while SRM-22 [Flight 61-A, October, 1985] had a relatively different amount, which was less and wasn't quite as black. I also stopped when it was apparent that I couldn't get anybody to listen.

Dr. Walker: At this point did anyone else speak up in favor of the launch?

Mr. Boisjoly: No, sir. No one said anything, in my recollection, nobody said a word. It was then being discussed amongst the management folks. After Arnie and I had our last say, Mr. Mason said we have to make a management decision. He turned to Bob Lund and asked him to take off his engineering hat and put on his management hat. From this point on, management formulated the points to base their decision on. There was never one comment in favor, as I have said, of launching by any engineer or other nonmanagement person in the room before or after the caucus. I was not even asked to participate in giving any input to the final decision charts.

I went back on the net with the final charts or final chart, which was the rationale for launching, and that was presented by Mr. Kilminster. It was hand written on a notepad, and he read from that notepad. I did not agree with some of the statements that were being made to support the decision. I was never asked nor polled, and it was clearly a management decision from that point.

I must emphasize, I had my say, and I never [would] take [away] any management right to take the input of an engineer and then make a decision based upon that input, and I truly believe that. I have worked at a lot of companies, and that has been done from time to time, and I truly believe that, and so there was no point in me doing anything any further than I had already attempted to do.

I did not see the final version of the chart until the next day. I just heard it read. I left the room feeling badly defeated, but I felt I really did all I could to stop the launch.

I felt personally that management was under a lot of pressure to launch and that they made a very tough decision, but I didn't agree with it.

One of my colleagues that was in the meeting summed it up best. This was a meeting where the determination was to launch, and it was up to us to prove beyond a shadow of a doubt that it was not safe to do so. This is in total reverse to what the position usually is in a preflight conversation or a flight readiness review. It is usually exactly opposite that.

Dr. Walker: Do you know the source of the pressure on management that you alluded to?

Mr. Boisjoly: Well, the comments made over the [net] is what I felt. I can't speak for them, but I felt it—I felt the tone of the meeting exactly as I summed up, that we were being put in a position to prove that we should not launch rather than being put in the position and prove that we had enough data to launch. And I felt that very real.

Dr. Walker: These were the comments from the NASA people at Marshall and at Kennedy Space Center?

Mr. Boisjoly: Yes.

Dr. Feynman [Rogers Commission member]: I take it you were trying to find proof that the seal would fail?

Mr. Boisjoly: Yes.

Dr. Feynman: And of course, you didn't, you couldn't, because five of them didn't, and if you had proved that they would have all failed, you would have found yourself incorrect because five of them didn't fail.

Mr. Boisjoly: That is right. I was very concerned that the cold temperatures would change that timing and put us in another regime, and that was the whole basis of my fighting that night.

As appears from the foregoing, after the discussion between Morton Thiokol management and the engineers, a final management review was conducted by Mason, Lund, Kilminster, and Wiggins. Lund and Mason recall this review as an unemotional, rational discussion of the engineering facts as they knew them at that time; differences of opinion as to the impact of those facts, however, had to be resolved as a judgment call and therefore a management decision. The testimony of Lund taken by Commission staff investigators is as follows:

Mr. Lund: We tried to have the telecon, as I remember it was about 6:00 o'clock [MST], but we didn't quite get things in order, and we started transmitting charts down to Marshall around 6:00 or 6:30 [MST], something like that, and we were making charts in real time and seeing the data, and we were discussing them with the Marshall folks who went along.

We finally got the—all the charts in, and when we got all the charts in I stood at the board and tried to draw the conclusions that we had out of the charts that had been presented, and we came up with a conclusions chart and said that we didn't feel like it was a wise thing to fly.

Question: What were some of the conclusions?

Mr. Lund: I had better look at the chart.

Well, we were concerned the temperature was going to be lower than the 50 or the 53 that had flown the previous January, and we had experienced some blow-by, and so we were concerned about that, and although the erosion on the O-rings, and it wasn't critical, that, you know, there had obviously been some little puff go through. It had been caught.

There was no real extensive erosion of that O-ring, so it wasn't a major concern, but we said, gee, you know, we just don't know how much further we can go below the 51 or 53 degrees or whatever it was. So we were concerned with the unknown. And we presented that to Marshall, and that rationale was rejected. They said that they didn't accept that rationale, and they would like us to consider some other thoughts that they had had.

. . . Mr. Mulloy said he did not accept that, and Mr. Hardy said he was appalled that we would make such a recommendation. And that made me ponder of what I'd missed, and so we said, what did we miss, and Mr. Mulloy said, well, I would like you to consider these other thoughts that we have had down here. And he presented a very strong and forthright rationale of what they thought was going on in that joint and how they thought that the thing was happening, and they said, we'd like you to consider that when they had some thoughts that we had not considered.

. . . So after the discussion with Mr. Mulloy, and he presented that, we said, well, let's ponder that a little bit, so we went off-line to talk about what we—

Question: Who requested to go off-line?

Mr. Lund: I guess it was Joe Kilminster. . . .

And so we went off line on the telecon . . . so we could have a roundtable discussion here.

Question: Who were the management people that were there?

Mr. Lund: Jerry Mason, Cal Wiggins, Joe, I, manager of engineering design, the manager of applied mechanics. . . .

Before the Commission on February 25, 1986, Mr. Lund testified as follows regarding why he changed his position on launching Challenger during the management caucus when he was asked by Mr. Mason "To take off his engineering hat and put on his management hat":

Chairman Rogers: How do you explain the fact that you seemed to change your mind when you changed your hat?

Mr. Lund: I guess we have got to go back a little further in the conversation than that. We have dealt with Marshall for a long time and have always been in the position of defending our position to make sure that we were ready to fly, and I guess I didn't realize until after that meeting and after several days that we had absolutely changed our position from what we had been before. But that evening I guess I had never had those kinds of things come from the people at Marshall. We had to prove to them that we weren't ready, and so we got ourselves in the thought process that we were trying to find some way to prove to them it wouldn't work, and we were unable to do that. We couldn't prove absolutely that that motor wouldn't work.

Chairman Rogers: In other words, you honestly believed that you had a duty to prove that it would not work?

Mr. Lund: Well, that is kind of the mode we got ourselves into that evening. It seems like we have always been in the opposite mode. I should have detected that, but I did not, but the roles kind of switched. . . .

Editor's Note: *Joe Kilminster, Thiokol's Vice President for the Space Booster Program, whose signature went on the Thiokol recommendation to launch, said that he had come away from the teleconference unconvinced that temperature would be a factor in the seal failure, and that even if there was erosion due to the cold weather, there was still enough margin of safety to permit the launch of 51-L.*

Chairman Rogers: Mr. Kilminster, can you attempt to explain to the Commission why—I guess you changed your mind, too, didn't you?

Mr. Kilminster: Yes sir, based on the discussion that we had and the rationale that we developed. . . .

Chairman Rogers: . . . Did you have the feeling that the burden of proof was on you to show that it wasn't safe [to launch]?

Mr. Kilminster: No, I think we were asked to re-look at the data, which we did. . . .

Chairman Rogers: . . .Mr. Kilminster, did you have any feeling of pressure being put on you by NASA, or were you just calmly re-assessing?

Mr. Kilminster: I felt that the pressure that was put on us was to go back and look at the data, look at the detailed information that had been presented to see if there was something that we were seeing that we were not representing on the phone.

Chairman Rogers: You didn't feel that they were trying to get you to change your mind?

Mr. Kilminster: I did not feel a significant amount of pressure in that regard.

Editor's Note: At Marshall, George Hardy, Deputy Director of Science and Engineering, listened in and participated in the teleconference but "clearly interpreted this [discussion] as a somewhat positive statement of supporting rationale for launch."

Mr. Hardy: At the teleconference on the evening of January 27, 1986, Thiokol engineering personnel in Utah reviewed charts that had been data-faxed to Huntsville and KSC participants just prior to the beginning of the conference. Now, I am not going to repeat a lot of what you have already heard, but I will give you some of my views on the whole matter.

The presentations were professional in nature. There were numerous questions and answers. There was a discussion of various data and points raised by individuals at Thiokol or at Marshall or at Kennedy. I think it was a rather full discussion. There were some 14 charts presented, and as has been mentioned earlier, we spent about two, two and a half hours reviewing this. To my knowledge, anyone who desired to make a point, ask a question or express a view was in no way restrained from doing so.

As others have mentioned, I have heard this particular teleconference characterized as a heated discussion. I acknowledge that there

were penetrating questions that were asked, I think, from both, from all people involved. There were various points of view and an interpretation of the data that was exchanged. The discussion was not, in my view, uncharacteristic of discussions on many flight readiness issues on many previous occasions. Thiokol engineering concluded their presentation with recommendation that the launch time be determined consistent with flight experience to date, and that is the launch with the O-ring temperatures at or greater than 53 degrees Fahrenheit.

Mr. Kilminster at Thiokol stated . . . to the best of my recollection, that with that engineering assessment, he recommended we not launch on Tuesday morning as scheduled. After some short discussion, Mr. Mulloy at KSC summarized his assessment of the data and his rationale with that data, and I think he has testified to that.

Mr. Reinartz, who was at KSC, asked me for comment, and I stated I was somewhat appalled, and that was referring specifically to some of the data or the interpretation of some of the data that Thiokol had presented with respect to its influence on the joint seal performance relative to the issue under discussion, which specifically was the possibility that the primary seal may take longer to actuate and therefore to blow by the primary seal. The blow-by of the primary seal may be longer, and I am going to elaborate on that a little further in this statement.

Then I went on to say that I supported the assessment of data presented essentially as summarized by Mr. Mulloy, but I would not recommend launch over Thiokol's objections.

Somewhere about this time, Mr. Kilminster at Utah stated that he wanted to go off the loop to caucus for about five minutes. I believe at this point Mr. McDonald, the senior Thiokol representative at KSC for this launch suggested to Mr. Kilminster that he consider a point that I think I had made earlier, that the secondary O-ring is in the proper position to seal if blow-by of the primary O-ring occurred.

I clearly interpreted this as a somewhat positive statement of supporting rationale for launch. . . . The status of the caucus by Thiokol lasted some 30, 35 minutes. At Huntsville during this Thiokol caucus, we continued to discuss the data presented. We were off the loop, we were on mute. We were around a table in small groups. It was not an organized type discussion. But I did take that opportunity to discuss my assessment and understanding of the data with several of my key advisors, and none of us had any disagreement or differences in our interpretation of what we believed the data was telling us with regard to the primary issue at hand.

When Thiokol came back on line, Mr. Kilminster reviewed rationale that supported proceeding with the launch and so recommended.

Mr. Reinartz asked if anyone in the loop had a different position or disagreed or something to that effect, with the Thiokol recommendation as presented by Mr. Kilminster. There were no dissenting responses.

The telecon was terminated shortly after, and I have no knowledge of any subsequent events or discussions between personnel at KSC or at Thiokol on this matter.

At about 5:00 A.M. on January 28, a discussion took place among Messrs. Mulloy, Lucas, and Reinartz in which Mulloy reported to Lucas only that there had been a discussion with Thiokol over their concerns about temperature effects on the O-rings, and that it had been resolved in favor of launch. The following testimony of Mr. Mulloy and Dr. Lucas recounts that discussion.

General Kutyna [Rogers Commission member]: . . . Larry, let me follow through on that, and I am kind of aware of the launch decision process, and you said you made the decision at your level on this thing.

If this were an airplane, an airliner, and I just had a two-hour argument with Boeing on whether the wing was going to fall off or not, I think I would tell the pilot, at least mention it.

Why didn't we escalate a decision of this importance?

Mr. Mulloy: I did, sir.

General Kutyna: You did?

Mr. Mulloy: Yes, sir.

General Kutyna: Tell me what levels above you.

Mr. Mulloy: As I stated earlier, Mr. Reinartz, who is my manager, was at the meeting, and on

the morning, about 5:00 o'clock in the operations support room where we all were I informed Dr. Lucas of the content of the discussion.

General Kutyna: But this is not in the launch decision chain.

Mr. Mulloy: No, sir. Mr. Reinartz is in the launch decision chain, though.

General Kutyna: And is he the highest level in that chain?

Mr. Mulloy: No. Normally it would go from me to Mr. Reinartz to Mr. Aldrich to Mr. Moore.

Dr. Lucas' testimony is as follows:

Chairman Rogers: Would you please tell the Commission when you first heard about the problem of the O-rings and the seals insofar as it involves launch 51-L? And I don't want you to go way back, but go back to when you first heard. I guess it was on January 27th, was it?

Dr. Lucas [Marshall Center Director]: Yes, sir. It was on the early evening of the 27th, I think about 7:00 P.M., when I was in my motel room along with Mr. Kingsbury. And about that time, Mr. Reinartz and Mr. Mulloy came to my room and told me that they had heard that some members of Thiokol had raised a concern about the performance of the Solid Rocket Boosters in the low temperature that was anticipated for the next day, specifically on the seals, and that they were going out to the Kennedy Space Center to engage in a telecon with the appropriate engineers back at Marshall Space Flight Center in Huntsville and with corresponding people back at the Wasatch division of Thiokol in Utah.

And we discussed it a few moments and I said, fine, keep me informed, let me know what happens.

Chairman Rogers: And when was the next time you heard something about that?

Dr. Lucas: The next time was about 5:00 A.M. on the following morning, when I went to the Kennedy Space Center and went to the launch control center. I immediately saw Mr. Reinartz and Mr. Mulloy and asked them how the matter of the previous evening was dispositioned.

Chairman Rogers: You had heard nothing at all in between?

Dr. Lucas: No, sir.

Chairman Rogers: So from 8:00 o'clock that evening until 5:00 o'clock in the morning, you had not heard a thing?

Dr. Lucas: It was about 7:00, I believe, sir. But for that period of time, I heard nothing in the interim. . . .

Chairman Rogers: . . . And you heard Mr. Reinartz say he didn't think he had to notify you, or did he notify you?

Dr. Lucas: He told me, as I testified, when I went into the control room, that an issue had been resolved, that there were some people at Thiokol who had a concern about the weather, that that had been discussed very thoroughly by the Thiokol people and by the Marshall Space Flight Center people, and it had been concluded agreeably that there was no problem, that he had a recommendation by Thiokol to launch and our most knowledgeable people and engineering talent agreed with that. So from my perspective, I didn't have—I didn't see that as an issue.

Chairman Rogers: And if you had known that Thiokol engineers almost to a man opposed the flight, would that have changed your view?

Dr. Lucas: I'm certain that it would.

Chairman Rogers: So your testimony is the same as Mr. Hardy's. Had he known, he would not have recommended the flight be launched on that day.

Dr. Lucas: I didn't make a recommendation one way or the other. But had I known that, I would have then interposed an objection, yes.

Chairman Rogers: I gather you didn't tell Mr. Aldrich or Mr. Moore what Mr. Reinartz had told you?

Dr. Lucas: No, sir. . . .

It is clear that crucial information about the O-ring damage in prior flights and about the Thiokol engineers' argument with the NASA telecon participants never reached Jesse Moore or Arnold Aldrich, the Levels I and II program officials, or J. A. (Gene) Thomas, the Launch Director for 51-L. The testimony of Aldrich describes this failure of the communication system very aptly:

Dr. Feynman: . . . have you collected your thoughts yet on what you think is the cause—I wouldn't call it of the accident but the lack of communication which we have seen and which everybody is worried about from one level to another?. . .

Mr. Aldrich [Shuttle Program Director in Houston]: Well, there were two specific breakdowns at least, in my impression, about that situation. One is the situation that occurred the night before the launch and leading up to the launch where there was a significant review that has been characterized in a number of ways before the Commission and the Commission's Subpanels and the fact that that was not passed forward.

And I can only conclude what has been reported, and that is that the people responsible for that work in the Solid Rocket Booster project at Marshall believed that the concern was not of a significance that would be required to be brought forward because clearly the program requirements specify that critical problems should be brought forward to Level II and not only to Level II but through myself to Level I.

The second breakdown in communications, however, and one that I personally am concerned about is the situation of the variety of reviews that were conducted last summer between the NASA Headquarters Organization and the Marshall Organization on the same technical area and the fact that that was not brought through my office in either direction— that is, it was not worked through—by the NASA Headquarters Organization nor when the Marshall Organization brought these concerns to be reported were we involved.

And I believe that is a critical breakdown in process and I think it is also against the documented reporting channels that the program is supposed to operate to.

Now, it in fact did occur in that matter. In fact, there is a third area of concern to me in the way

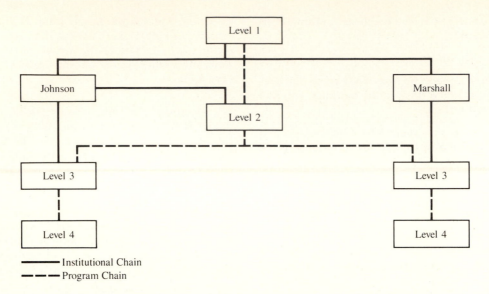

Level 1: The associate administrator for Space Flight. Oversees budgets for Johnson, Marshall, and
          Kennedy. Responsible for policy, budgetary, and top-level technical matters for Shuttle program.
Level 2: Manager, National Space Transportation Program. Responsible for Shuttle program baseline
          and requirements. Provides technical oversight on behalf of Level 1.
Level 3: Program managers for Orbiter, Solid Rocket Booster, External Tank and Space Shuttle Main
          Engine. Responsible for development, testing, and delivery of hardware to launch site.
Level 4: Contractors for Shuttle elements. Responsible for design and production of hardware.

the program has operated. There is yet one other way that could have come to me, given a different program structure. I'm sure you've had it reported to you as it has been reported to me that in August or I think or at least at some time late in the summer or early fall the Marshall SRB project went forward to procure some additional Solid Rocket Motor casings to be machined and new configurations for testing of the joints.

Now it turns out that the budget for that kind of work does not come through my Level II office. It is worked directly between the Marshall Center in NASA Headquarters and there again had I been responsible for the budget for that sort of work, it would have to come through me, and it would have been clear that something was going on here that I ought to know about.

And so there are three areas of breakdown, and I haven't exactly answered your question. But I have explained it in the way that I best know it and—well, I can say a fourth thing.

There was some discussion earlier about the amount of material that was or was not reported

on O-ring erosion in the FRRs [Flight Readiness Reviews] and I researched the FRR back reports and also the flight anomaly reports that were forwarded to my center—to my office—by the SRB [Solid Rocket Booster] project and as was indicated, there is a treatment of the Solid Rocket Motor O-ring erosion, I believe, for the STS 41-C FRR, which quantifies it and indicates some limited amount of concern.

The next time that is mentioned, I believe it is the STS 51-E, FRR in January 1985 or early in February, and that indicates, again, a reference to it but refers back to the 41-C as the only technical data.

And then from there forward the comment on O-ring erosion only is that there was another instance and it is not of concern.

Clearly the amount of reporting in the FRR is of concern to me, but in parallel with that, each of the flight anomalies in the STS program are required to be logged and reviewed by each of the projects and then submitted through the Level II system for formal close-out.

And in looking back and reviewing the anomaly close-outs that were submitted to Level II from the SRB project, you find that O-ring erosion was not considered to be an anomaly and, therefore, it was not logged and, therefore, there are not anomaly reports that progress from one flight to the other.

Yet, that is another way that that information could have flagged the system, and the system is set up to use that technique for flagging.

But if the erosion is classified as not an anomaly, it then is in some other category and the system did not force it in that direction. None of those are very focused answers, but they were all factors.

The Commission Chairman, Mr. Rogers, asked four key officials about their knowledge of the Thiokol objections to launch.

Chairman Rogers: . . . By way of a question, could I ask, did any of you gentlemen prior to launch know about the objections of Thiokol to the launch?

Mr. Smith [Kennedy Space Center Director]: I did not.

Mr. Thomas [Launch Director]: No, sir.

Mr. Aldrich [Shuttle Program Director]: I did not.

Mr. Moore [Associate Administrator for Space Flight]: I did not.

Additionally, in further testimony, J. A. (Gene) Thomas commented on the launch.

Mr. Hotz [Rogers Commission member]: . . . Mr. Thomas, you are familiar with the testimony that this Commission has taken in the last several days on the relationship of temperature to the seals in the Solid Rocket Booster?

Mr. Thomas: Yes, sir, I have been here all week.

Mr. Hotz: Is this the type of information that you feel that you should have as Launch Director to make a launch decision?

Mr. Thomas: If you refer to the fact that the temperature according to the Launch Commit Criteria should have been 53 degrees, as has been testified, rather than 31, yes, I expect that to be in the LCC. That is a controlling document that we use in most cases to make a decision for launch.

Mr. Hotz: But you are not really very happy about not having had this information before the launch?

Mr. Thomas: No, sir. I can assure you that if we had had that information, we wouldn't have launched if it hadn't been 53 degrees.

Chapter 10 Review Questions

1. Briefly, what arguments does Allison put forward to underscore the uniqueness of public management in comparison with business management? Do you agree with his reasoning? Why or why not?

2. Despite Allison's thesis, there is a repeated public demand—evidenced in the popular press and in political campaigns—that government *should* become more business-like. In your opinion, what are the sources and causes of this repeated public outcry? Specifically, would the space shuttle accident have been prevented if NASA management had been "more business-like"? Or would that not have "cured" the O-ring problems?

3. Why were the top managers on Levels I and II of the *Challenger* flight apparently not informed about the critical O-ring problem? Why did the interpretations of the O-ring problem *as a critical problem* differ between

junior engineers like Boisjoly and Thompson and more senior managers like Lund and Kilminster?

4. Whom do *you* consider at fault for *Challenger*'s unsolved problems—the major contractor, Morton Thiokol; the top NASA management at Marshall Space Flight Center or the Johnson Space Flight Center; those at the launch site at the Kennedy Center; or someone else? How would you assign responsibility for the accident?

5. If you were charged with constructing a better management system that would prevent such accidents from occurring in the future, what would you recommend?

6. Does this case study support Allison's argument about the uniqueness of public management in contrast to private business management practices? Explain why or why not.

Key Terms

Sayre's "law"

common management functions

measurement of performance

personnel constraints on
   public managers

career systems

media relations

terminological tangles

time perspectives of managers

equity and efficiency values

managing internal components

managing external components

implementation strategies

Suggestions for Further Reading

Much of the earliest literature on management in this century focused on the role of line managers in business, for example, Henri Fayol, *General and Industrial Management,* translated by Constance Storrs (London: Pitman, 1949); or Frederick W. Taylor, *Scientific Management* (New York: Harper and Row, 1911). Their emphasis on the values of efficiency, rationality, and clear lines of hierarchy was carried over into the public sector by such authors as Henry Bruere, W. F. Willoughby, Frederick Cleveland, Luther Gulick, and others, who pioneered the development of management techniques in the public sector prior to World War II. For a good collection of the works of these writers, see Frederick C. Mosher, *Basic Literature of American Public Administration, 1787–1950* (New York: Holmes and Meier, 1981).

A book that should be read in its entirety is Chester I. Barnard, *The Functions of the Executive* (Cambridge, Mass.: Harvard University Press, 1938), because Barnard stands in marked contrast to the pre-World War II scientific management theorists and because he made an enormous impact on other postwar writers like Herbert Simon, writers who decisively reshaped our whole view of this field. William B. Wolf, *The Basic Barnard* (Ithaca, N.Y.: Institute of Labor Relations,

Cornell University, 1974) offers the best available commentary on Barnard's life and work.

Postwar management thought is aptly described by Harold Koontz as "the management theory jungle," i.e., it is divided into multiple schools and perspectives. To sample some of these diverse points of view, read C. West Churchman, *The Systems Approach* (New York: Dell Publishing, 1968), or Bertram M. Gross, *The Managing of Organizations* (New York: Free Press, 1964), for the *systems approach;* read Harry Levinson, *The Exceptional Executive: A Psychological Conception* (Cambridge, Mass.: Harvard University Press, 1968), or Rensis Likert, *The Human Organization: Its Management and Value* (New York: McGraw-Hill, 1967), for the *human behavioral school;* refer to the several hundred cases available through the Harvard Business School that were instrumental in pioneering the methodology of the *case method;* for the *policy emphasis,* see Paul Appleby, *Policy and Administration* (University, Ala.: University of Alabama Press, 1949); and the *decision school* of management is well represented in books by Charles E. Lindblom and Herbert A. Simon, Donald W. Smithburg, and Victor A. Thompson (discussed in Chapters 8 and 9).

Where are we today in public management thought? Again, no consensus prevails. The older schools are still very influential. But unquestionably the economic pressures of the 1980s have brought about a new outpouring of ideas on efficiency and cutback management, which are reflected in the practical efficiency-oriented writings of Elizabeth Kellar, *Managing with Less* (Washington, D.C.: International City Management Association, 1979), and Mark W. Huddleston, *The Public Administration Workbook* (New York: Longman, 1987). The new world of the *knowledge manager* is vividly portrayed in Harlan Cleveland, *The Knowledge Executive* (New York: E. P. Dutton, 1985). A more specialized focus on peculiar management problems associated with various levels of government is found in Brian W. Rapp and Frank M. Patitucci, *Managing Local Government for Improved Performance: A Practical Approach* (Boulder, Colo.: Westview Press, 1977); Martha W. Weinberg, *Managing the State* (Cambridge, Mass.: M.I.T. Press, 1977); or, on the federal level, Laurence E. Lynn, Jr., *Managing the Public's Business* (New York: Basic Books, 1981). There are numerous books on management in specialized policy fields like defense, law enforcement, health care, and others. The *effective leadership trait* perspective is emphasized in such recent business-oriented books as Leonard Sayles, *Leadership* (New York: McGraw-Hill, 1979), and John P. Kotter, *The General Manager* (New York: Free Press, 1982). Humanistic management still remains a vital concern of *new public administration* writers, such as H. George Frederickson, *New Public Administration* (University, Ala.: University of Alabama Press, 1980), and Michael Harmon, *Action Theory for Public Administration* (New York: Longman, 1981). On the opposite side, quantitative, *efficiency-oriented* management is also apparent and popular, as found in Michael J. White et al., *Managing Public Systems: Analytic Techniques for Public Administration* (No. Scituate, Mass.: Duxbury Press, 1981). *Comparative approaches* also find favor, as in Joseph Bowers, *The Two Faces of Management* (Boston: Houghton Mifflin, 1983), and Donald F.

Kettl, *Government by Proxy* (Washington, D.C.: Congressional Quarterly Press, 1988).

For excellent articles that provide a realistic picture of the recent problems and prospects in public management, see Stephen K. Bailey, "Improving Federal Governance," *Public Administration Review,* 40 (November/December 1980), pp. 548–553; Frederick C. Mosher, "The Changing Responsibilities and Tactics of the Federal Government," *Public Administration Review,* 40 (November/December 1980), pp. 541–548; Herbert Kaufman, "Fear of Bureaucracy: A Raging Pandemic," *Public Administration Review,* 40 (January/February 1981), pp. 1–9; James L. Sundquist, "The Crisis of Competence," in Joseph A. Pechman, ed., *Setting National Priorities: Agenda for the 1980s* (Washington, D.C.: The Brookings Institution, 1980); Richard J. Stillman II, "Local Public Management in Transition," *Public Management,* 64 (May 1982), pp. 2–9; Chester Newland, "Public Executives: Imperium, Sacerdotium, Collegium? Bicentennial Leadership Challenges," *Public Administration Review,* 47 (January/February 1987), pp. 45–56, and in the same issue, James D. Carroll, "Public Administration in the Third Century of the Constitution: Supply-Side Management, Privatization or Public Investment?" pp. 106–114; and Charles H. Levine, "The Federal Government in the Year 2000," *Public Administration Review,* 46 (May/June 1986), pp. 191–206.

CHAPTER 11

Personnel Motivation: Theory X and Theory Y

"Management by direction and control—whether implemented with the hard, the soft, or the firm but fair approach—fails under today's conditions to provide effective motivation of human efforts toward organizational objectives. It fails because direction and control are useless methods of motivating people whose physiological and safety needs are reasonably satisfied and whose social, egoistic, and self-fulfillment needs are predominant."

Douglas McGregor

READING 11

Introduction

The emphasis on contemporary research in personnel relations has resulted in an impressive subfield of public administration that deals with the many ramifications of the individual in public organizations. Today most scholars and practitioners of public administration are aware that the handling of personnel issues can be one critical key to the successful management of any public agency.

Chapter 6 explored how our important understanding of the role of the informal group within organizations began. Though concerned primarily with business organizations, Elton Mayo's discoveries in the field of human relations at Western Electric in the 1920s expanded the traditional theories of public administration by showing how critical an impact the human group has on the management process.

However, early researchers in the personnel field tended to accept the basic goals of increased efficiency in organizational activities and actually sought ways by which management could obtain greater productivity from workers. Initially, monotony, alienation, and worker fatigue frequently were problems focused on in personnel studies. These studies often recommended a restructuring of the formal or procedural aspects of the institution as the means of control.

The more contemporary, second-generation personnel specialists like Chris Argyris, Warren Bennis, Rensis Likert, and Douglas McGregor have continued to stress the significance of the problems of the individual in organizations, but frequently with less concern about organizational performance and more careful attention toward helping to achieve worker satisfaction and personal growth on the job. Such writers have de-emphasized traditional administrative goals such as efficiency, and instead have shown a greater interest in support of individual values and a humanistic environment within organizations.

One of the leading proponents of this school of humanistic thought was the late Douglas McGregor (1906–1964), a Harvard-trained social psychologist, former president of Antioch College, and professor of industrial management at the Massachusetts Institute of Technology, who throughout much of his writings argued for an alternative philosophy regarding the personnel responsibilities of managers. McGregor criticized the traditional theory of personnel management—which he called Theory X—under which the manager was seen as an active agent for motivating people, "controlling their actions, modifying their behavior to fit the needs of the organization." Proponents of Theory X took a pessimistic view of human nature, portraying people as self-centered, gullible, resistant to change, and reluctant to work.

McGregor's critique of Theory X is based on Abraham Maslow's hierarchy of human needs (discussed at length in McGregor's essay). "The philosophy of management by direction and control—*regardless of whether it is hard or soft*—is inadequate to motivate because the human needs on which this approach relies are today unimportant motivators of behavior. Direction and control are essentially useless in motivating people whose important needs are social and egoistic." McGregor saw the necessity for managers to shift from Theory X—management by direction and control—to Theory Y or "the process primarily of creating opportunities, releasing potential, removing obstacles, encouraging growth, providing guidance." The goal then becomes the creation of a humanistic environment where "people can achieve their own goals best by directing their own efforts toward organizational objectives." Job enlargement, delegation of authority, decentralized responsibilities, and participatory management are several methods by which McGregor thought Theory Y could be practically implemented in organizations. In essence, McGregor searched for ways to create a healthy organization by allowing for maximum growth of human potential. He sought to achieve this through a realistic understanding of human motivation and a fostering of a democratic organizational environment conducive to the development of individual capabilities.

As you read this selection, keep the following questions in mind:

Are McGregor's ideas, primarily oriented toward private business, readily applicable to public organizations? Specifically, can the growth of human potential be *the* central value of public organizations, or might other goals such as representativeness, public service, and efficiency have priorities as well in public enterprises?

Do McGregor's Theory X and Theory Y really differ decisively in terms of their ultimate goals? That is to say, although the traditional and modern personnel management theories may differ in the means whereby their ends are attained, are the final goals of Theory X and Theory Y basically identical, i.e., increased organizational performance?

Does Maslow's theory of a hierarchy of human needs as described in the McGregor selection seem a valid theoretical basis for supporting Theory Y? From your own observations, can Maslow's concept be proven or disproven?

How does McGregor's concept compare with the work of Barnard, Mayo and others involving "informal groups" as described in Chapter 6 or the Simon–Smithburg–Thompson piece in Chapter 9?

DOUGLAS McGREGOR

The Human Side of Enterprise

It has become trite to say that the most significant developments of the next quarter century will take place not in the physical but in the social sciences, that industry—the economic organ of society—has the fundamental know-how to utilize physical science and technology for the material benefit of mankind, and that we must now learn how to utilize the social sciences to make our human organizations truly effective.

Many people agree in principle with such statements; but so far they represent a pious hope—and little else. Consider with me, if you will, something of what may be involved when we attempt to transform the hope into reality.

Let me begin with an analogy. A quarter century ago basic conceptions of the nature of matter and energy had changed profoundly from what they had been since Newton's time. The physical scientists were persuaded that under proper conditions new and hitherto unimagined sources of energy could be made available to mankind.

We know what has happened since then. First came the bomb. Then, during the past decade, have come many other attempts to exploit these scientific discoveries—some successful, some not.

From "The Human Side of Enterprise" by Douglas McGregor. In *Leadership and Motivation, Essays of Douglas McGregor*, edited by Bennis and Schein, 1966, The MIT Press, pp. 3–20.

The point of my analogy, however, is that the application of theory in this field is a slow and costly matter. We expect it always to be thus. No one is impatient with the scientist because he cannot tell industry how to build a simple, cheap, all-purpose source of atomic energy today. That it will take at least another decade and the investment of billions of dollars to achieve results which are economically competitive with present sources of power is understood and accepted.

It is transparently pretentious to suggest any *direct* similarity between the developments in the physical sciences leading to the harnessing of atomic energy and potential developments in the social sciences. Nevertheless, the analogy is not as absurd as it might appear to be at first glance.

To a lesser degree, and in a much more tentative fashion, we are in a position in the social sciences today like that of the physical sciences with respect to atomic energy in the thirties. We know that past conceptions of the nature of man are inadequate and in many ways incorrect. We are becoming quite certain that, under proper conditions, unimagined resources of creative human energy could become available within the organizational setting.

We cannot tell industrial management how to apply this new knowledge in simple, economic ways. We know it will require years of exploration, much costly development research, and a substantial amount of creative imagination on the part of management to discover how to apply this growing knowledge to the organization of human effort in industry.

May I ask that you keep this analogy in mind—overdrawn and pretentious though it may be—as a framework for what I have to say. . . .

Management's Task: Conventional View

The conventional conception of management's task in harnessing human energy to organizational requirements can be stated broadly in terms of three propositions. In order to avoid the complications introduced by a label, I shall call this set of propositions "Theory X":

1. Management is responsible for organizing the elements of productive enterprise—money, materials, equipment, people—in the interest of economic ends.
2. With respect to people, this is a process of directing their efforts, motivating them, controlling their actions, modifying their behavior to fit the needs of the organization.
3. Without this active intervention by management, people would be passive—even resistant—to organizational needs. They must therefore be persuaded, rewarded, punished, controlled—their activities must be directed. This is management's task—in managing subordinate managers or workers. We often sum it up by saying that management consists of getting things done through other people.

Behind this conventional theory there are several additional beliefs—less explicit, but widespread:

4. The average man is by nature indolent—he works as little as possible.

5. He lacks ambition, dislikes responsibility, prefers to be led.
6. He is inherently self-centered, indifferent to organizational needs.
7. He is by nature resistant to change.
8. He is gullible, not very bright, the ready dupe of the charlatan and the demagogue.

The human side of economic enterprise today is fashioned from propositions and beliefs such as these. Conventional organization structures, managerial policies, practices, and programs reflect these assumptions.

In accomplishing its task—with these assumptions as guides—management has conceived of a range of possibilities between two extremes.

The Hard or the Soft Approach?

At one extreme, management can be "hard" or "strong." The methods for directing behavior involve coercion and threat (usually disguised), close supervision, tight controls over behavior. At the other extreme, management can be "soft" or "weak." The methods for directing behavior involve being permissive, satisfying people's demands, achieving harmony. Then they will be tractable, accept direction.

This range has been fairly completely explored during the past half century, and management has learned some things from the exploration. There are difficulties in the "hard" approach. Force breeds counter-forces: restriction of output, antagonism, militant unionism, subtle but effective sabotage of management objectives. This approach is especially difficult during times of full employment.

There are also difficulties in the "soft" approach. It leads frequently to the abdication of management—to harmony, perhaps, but to indifferent performance. People take advantage of the soft approach. They continually expect more, but they give less and less.

Currently, the popular theme is "firm but fair." This is an attempt to gain the advantages of both the hard and the soft approaches. It is reminiscent of Teddy Roosevelt's "speak softly and carry a big stick."

Is the Conventional View Correct?

The findings which are beginning to emerge from the social sciences challenge this whole set of beliefs about man and human nature and about the task of management. The evidence is far from conclusive, certainly, but it is suggestive. It comes from the laboratory, the clinic, the schoolroom, the home, and even to a limited extent from industry itself.

The social scientist does not deny that human behavior in industrial organization today is approximately what management perceives it to be. He has, in fact, observed it and studied it fairly extensively. But he is pretty sure that this behavior is *not* a consequence of man's inherent nature. It is a consequence rather of the nature of industrial organizations, of management philosophy, policy, and practice. The conventional approach of Theory X is based on mistaken notions of what is cause and what is effect.

"Well," you ask, "what then is the *true* nature of man? What evidence leads the social scientist to deny what is obvious?" And, if I am not mistaken, you are also thinking, "Tell me—simply, and without a lot of scientific verbiage—what you think you know that is so unusual. Give me—without a lot of intellectual claptrap and theoretical nonsense—some practical ideas which will enable me to improve the situation in my organization. And remember, I'm faced with increasing costs and narrowing profit margins. I want proof that such ideas won't result simply in new and costly human relations frills.

I want practical results, and I want them now."

If these are your wishes, you are going to be disappointed. Such requests can no more be met by the social scientist today than could comparable ones with respect to atomic energy be met by the physicist fifteen years ago. I can, however, indicate a few of the reasons for asserting that conventional assumptions about the human side of enterprise are inadequate. And I can suggest—tentatively—some of the propositions that will comprise a more adequate theory of the management of people. The magnitude of the task that confronts us will then, I think, be apparent.

Perhaps the best way to indicate why the conventional approach of management is inadequate is to consider the subject of motivation. In discussing this subject I will draw heavily on the work of my colleague, Abraham Maslow of Brandeis University. His is the most fruitful approach I know. Naturally, what I have to say will be overgeneralized and will ignore important qualifications. In the time at our disposal, this is inevitable.

Physiological and Safety Needs

Man is a wanting animal—as soon as one of his needs is satisfied, another appears in its place. This process is unending. It continues from birth to death.

Man's needs are organized in a series of levels—a hierarchy of importance. At the lowest level, but preeminent in importance when they are thwarted, are his physiological needs. Man lives by bread alone, when there is no bread. Unless the circumstances are unusual, his needs for love, for status, for recognition are inoperative when his stomach has been empty for a while. But when he eats regularly and adequately, hunger ceases to be an important need. The sated man has hunger only in the sense that a full bottle has emptiness. The same is true of the other physiological needs of man—for rest, exercise, shelter, protection from the elements.

A satisfied need is not a motivator of behavior! This is a fact of profound significance. It is a fact which is regularly ignored in the conventional approach to the management of people. I shall return to it later. For the moment, one example will make my point. Consider your own need for air. Except as you are deprived of it, it has no appreciable motivating effect upon your behavior.

When the physiological needs are reasonably satisfied, needs at the next higher level begin to dominate man's behavior—to motivate him. These are called safety needs. They are needs for protection against danger, threat, deprivation. Some people mistakenly refer to these as needs for security. However, unless man is in a dependent relationship where he fears arbitrary deprivation, he does not demand security. The need is for the "fairest possible break." When he is confident of this, he is more than willing to take risks. But when he feels threatened or dependent, his greatest need is for guarantees, for protection, for security.

The fact needs little emphasis that since every industrial employee is in a dependent relationship, safety needs may assume considerable importance. Arbitrary management actions, behavior which arouses uncertainty with respect to continued employment or which reflects favoritism or discrimination, unpredictable administration of policy—these can be powerful motivators of the safety needs in the employment relationship *at every level* from worker to vice president.

Social Needs

When man's physiological needs are satisfied and he is no longer fearful about his physical welfare, his social needs become important motivators of his behavior—for belonging, for association, for acceptance by his fellows, for giving and receiving friendship and love.

Management knows today of the existence of these needs, but it often assumes quite wrongly that they represent a threat to the organization. Many studies have demonstrated that the tightly knit, cohesive work group may, under proper conditions, be far more effective than an equal number of separate individuals in achieving organizational goals.

Yet management, fearing group hostility to its own objectives, often goes to considerable lengths to control and direct human efforts in ways that are inimical to the natural "groupiness" of human beings. When man's social needs—and perhaps his safety needs, too—are thus thwarted, he behaves in ways which tend to defeat organizational objectives. He becomes resistant, antagonistic, uncooperative. But this behavior is a consequence, not a cause.

Ego Needs

Above the social needs—in the sense that they do not become motivators until lower needs are reasonably satisfied—are the needs of greatest significance to management and to man himself. They are the egoistic needs, and they are of two kinds:

1. Those needs that relate to one's self-esteem—needs for self-confidence, for independence, for achievement, for competence, for knowledge.
2. Those needs that relate to one's reputation—needs for status, for recognition, for appreciation, for the deserved respect of one's fellows.

Unlike the lower needs, these are rarely satisfied; man seeks indefinitely for more satisfaction of these needs once they have become important to him. But they do not appear in any significant way until physiological, safety, and social needs are all reasonably satisfied.

The typical industrial organization offers few opportunities for the satisfaction of these egoistic needs to people at lower levels in the hierarchy. The conventional methods of organizing work, particularly in mass production industries, give little heed to these aspects of human motivation. If the practices of scientific management were deliberately calculated to thwart these needs—which, of course, they are not—they could hardly accomplish this purpose better than they do.

Self-fulfillment Needs

Finally—a capstone, as it were, on the hierarchy of man's needs—there are what we may call the needs for self-fulfillment. These are the needs for realizing one's own potentialities, for continued self-development, for being creative in the broadest sense of that term.

It is clear that the conditions of modern life give only limited opportunity for these relatively weak needs to obtain expression. The deprivation most people experience with respect to other lower-level needs diverts their energies into the struggle to satisfy *those* needs, and the needs for self-fulfillment remain dormant.

Now, briefly, a few general comments about motivation:

We recognize readily enough that a man suffering from a severe dietary deficiency is sick. The deprivation of physiological needs has behavioral consequences. The same is true—although less well recognized—of deprivation of higher-level needs. The man whose needs for safety, association, independence, or status are thwarted is sick just as surely as is he who has rickets. And his sickness will be mistaken if we attribute his resultant passivity, his hostility, his refusal to accept responsibility to his inherent "human nature." These forms of behavior are *symptoms* of illness—of deprivation of his social and egoistic needs.

The man whose lower-level needs are satisfied is not motivated to satisfy those needs any longer. For practical purposes they exist no longer. (Remember my point about your need for air.) Management often asks, "Why aren't people more productive? We pay good wages, provide good working conditions, have excellent fringe benefits and steady employment. Yet people do not seem to be willing to put forth more than minimum effort."

The fact that management has provided for these physiological and safety needs has shifted the motivational emphasis to the social and perhaps to the egoistic needs. Unless there are opportunities *at work* to satisfy these higher-level needs, people will be deprived; and their behavior will reflect this deprivation. Under such conditions, if management continues to focus its attention on physiological needs, its efforts are bound to be ineffective.

People *will* make insistent demands for more money under these conditions. It becomes more important than ever to buy the material goods and services which can provide limited satisfaction of the thwarted needs. Although money has only limited value in satisfying many higher-level needs, it can become the focus of interest if it is the *only* means available.

The Carrot and Stick Approach

The carrot and stick theory of motivation (like Newtonian physical theory) works reasonably well under certain circumstances. The *means* for satisfying man's physiological and (within limits) his safety needs can be provided or withheld by management. Employment itself is such a means, and so are wages, working conditions, and benefits. By these means the individual can be controlled so long as he is struggling for subsistence. Man lives for bread alone when there is no bread.

But the carrot and stick theory does not work at all once man has reached an adequate subsistence level and is motivated primarily by higher needs. Management cannot provide a man with self-respect, or with the respect of his fellows, or with the satisfaction of needs for self-fulfillment. It can create conditions such that he is encouraged and enabled to seek such satisfactions *for himself,* or it can thwart him by failing to create those conditions.

But this creation of conditions is not "control." It is not a good device for directing behavior. And so management finds itself in an odd position. The high standard of living created by our modern technological knowhow provides quite adequately for the satisfaction of physiological and safety needs. The only significant exception is where management practices have not created confidence in a "fair break"—and thus where safety needs are thwarted. But by making possible the satisfaction of low-level needs, management has deprived itself of the ability to use as motivators the devices on which conventional theory has taught it to rely—rewards, promises, incentives, or threats and other coercive devices.

Neither Hard nor Soft

The philosophy of management by direction and control—*regardless of whether it is hard or soft*—is inadequate to motivate because the human needs on which this approach relies are today unimportant motivators of behavior. Direction and control are essentially useless in motivating people whose important needs are social and egoistic. Both the hard and the soft approach fail today because they are simply irrelevant to the situation.

People, deprived of opportunities to satisfy at work the needs which are now important to them, behave exactly as we might predict—with indolence, passivity, resistance to change, lack of responsibility, willingness to follow the demagogue, unreasonable demands for economic benefits. It would seem that we are caught in a web of our own weaving.

In summary, then, of these comments about motivation:

Management by direction and control—whether implemented with the hard, the soft, or the firm but fair approach—fails under today's conditions to provide effective motivation of human efforts toward organizational objectives. It fails because direction and control are useless methods of motivating people whose physiological and safety needs are reasonably satisfied and whose social, egoistic, and self-fulfillment needs are predominant.

For these and many other reasons, we require a different theory of the task of managing people based on more adequate assumptions about human nature and human motivation. I am going to be so bold as to suggest the broad dimensions of such a theory. Call it "Theory Y," if you will.

1. Management is responsible for organizing the elements of productive enterprise—money, materials, equipment, people—in the interest of economic ends.
2. People are *not* by nature passive or resistant to organizational needs. They have become so as a result of experience in organizations.
3. The motivation, the potential for development, the capacity for assuming responsibility, the readiness to direct behavior toward organizational goals are all present in people. Management does not put them there. It is a responsibility of management to make it possible for people to recognize and develop these human characteristics for themselves.
4. The essential task of management is to arrange organizational conditions and methods of operation so that people can achieve their own goals *best* by directing *their own* efforts toward organizational objectives.

This is a process primarily of creating opportunities, releasing potential, removing obstacles, encouraging growth, providing guidance. It is what Peter Drucker has called "management by objectives" in contrast to "management by control."

And I hasten to add that it does *not* involve the abdication of management, the absence of leadership, the lowering of standards, or the other characteristics usually associated with the "soft" approach under Theory X. Much on the contrary. It is no more possible to create an organization today which will be a fully effective application of this theory than it was to build an atomic power plant in 1945. There are many formidable obstacles to overcome.

Some Difficulties

The conditions imposed by conventional organization theory and by the approach of scientific management for the past half century have tied men to limited jobs which do not utilize their capabilities, have discouraged the acceptance of responsibility, have encouraged passivity, have eliminated meaning from work. Man's habits, attitudes, expectations—his whole conception of membership in an industrial organization— have been conditioned by his experience under these circumstances. Change in the direction of Theory Y will be slow, and it will require extensive modification of the attitudes of management and workers alike.

People today are accustomed to being directed, manipulated, controlled in industrial organizations and to finding satisfaction for their social, egoistic, and self-fulfillment needs away from the job. This is true of much of management as well as of workers. Genuine "industrial citizenship"—to borrow again a term from Drucker—is a remote and unrealistic idea, the meaning of which has not even been considered by most members of industrial organizations.

Another way of saying this is that Theory X places exclusive reliance upon external control of human behavior, while Theory Y relies heavily on self-control and self-direction. It is worth noting that this difference is the difference between treating people as children and treating them as mature adults. After generations of the former, we cannot expect to shift to the latter overnight.

Before we are overwhelmed by the obstacles, let us remember that the application of theory is always slow. Progress is usually achieved in small steps.

Consider with me a few innovative ideas which are entirely consistent with Theory Y and which are today being applied with some success:

Decentralization and Delegation

These are ways of freeing people from the too-close control of conventional organization, giving them a degree of freedom to direct their own activities, to assume responsibility, and, importantly, to satisfy their egoistic needs. In this connection, the flat organization of Sears, Roebuck and Company provides an interesting example. It forces "management by objectives" since it enlarges the number of people reporting to a manager until he cannot direct and control them in the conventional manner.

Job Enlargement

This concept, pioneered by I.B.M. and Detroit Edison, is quite consistent with Theory Y. It encourages the acceptance of responsibility at the bottom of the organization; it provides opportunities for satisfying social and egoistic needs. In fact, the reorganization of work at the factory level offers one of the more challenging opportunities for innovation consistent with Theory Y. The studies by A.T.M. Wilson and his associates of British coal mining and Indian textile manufacture have added appreciably to our understanding of work organization. Moreover, the economic and psychological results achieved by this work have been substantial.

Participation and Consultative Management

Under proper conditions these results provide encouragement to people to direct their creative energies toward organizational objectives, give them some voice in decisions that affect them, provide significant opportunities for the satisfaction of social and egoistic needs. I need only mention the Scanlon Plan as the outstanding embodiment of these ideas in practice.

The not infrequent failure of such ideas as these to work as well as expected is often attributable to the fact that a management has "bought the idea" but applied it within the framework of Theory X and its assumptions.

Delegation is not an effective way of exercising management by control. Participation becomes a farce when it is applied as a sales gimmick or a device for kidding people into thinking they are important. Only the management that has confidence in human capacities and is itself directed toward organizational objectives rather than toward the preservation of personal power can grasp the implications of this emerging theory. Such management will find and apply successfully other innovative ideas as we move slowly toward the full implementation of a theory like Y.

Before I stop, let me mention one other practical application of Theory Y which—while still highly tentative—may well have important consequences. This has to do with performance appraisal within the ranks of management. Even a cursory examination of conventional programs of performance appraisal will reveal how completely consistent they are with Theory X. In fact, most such programs tend to treat the individual as though he were a product under inspection on the assembly line.

Take the typical plan: substitute "product" for "subordinate being appraised," substitute "inspector" for "superior making the appraisal," substitute "rework" for "training or development," and, except for the attributes being judged, the human appraisal process will be virtually indistinguishable from the product inspection process.

A few companies—among them General Mills, Ansul Chemical, and General Electric—have been experimenting with approaches which involve the individual in setting "targets" or objectives *for himself* and in a *self-*evaluation of performance semi-annually or annually. Of course, the superior plays an important leadership role in this process—one, in fact, which demands substantially more competence than the conventional approach. The role is, however, considerably more congenial to many managers than the role of "judge" or "inspector" which is forced upon them by conventional performance. Above all, the individual is encouraged to take a greater responsibility for planning and appraising his own contribution to organizational objectives; and the accompanying effects on egoistic and self-fulfillment needs are substantial. This approach to performance appraisal represents one more innovative idea being explored by a few managements who are moving toward the implementation of Theory Y.

And now I am back where I began. I share the belief that we could realize substantial improvements in the effectiveness of industrial organizations during the next decade or two. Moreover, I believe the social sciences can contribute much to such developments. We are only beginning to grasp the implications of the growing body of knowledge in these fields. But if this conviction is to become a reality instead of a pious hope, we will need to view the process much as we view the process of releasing the energy of the atom for constructive human ends—as a slow, costly, sometimes discouraging approach toward a goal which would seem to many to be quite unrealistic.

The ingenuity and the perseverance of industrial management in the pursuit of economic ends have changed many scientific and techno-logical dreams into commonplace realities. It is now becoming clear that the application of these same talents to the human side of enterprise will not only enhance substantially these materialis-tic achievements but will bring us one step closer to "the good society." Shall we get on with the job?

Introduction

McGregor's Theory Y characterized a lifetime of thought and work described by Warren Bennis and Caroline McGregor in a collection of McGregor's essays edited after his death as an effort toward "bringing together a creative working truth towards a new consensus."[1] Few public administrators would deny the importance or worth of McGregor's idealistic *new consensus* as expressed in Theory Y, though no doubt many would question whether it could ever be achieved in practice. In short, many would ask: is this concept useful for the working public administrator, or is it another "pie-in-the-sky" theory by an academician?

The following story, "The Curious Case of the Indicted Meat Inspectors," by Peter Schuck, a professor of law at Yale University, provides a unique way of testing the utility of McGregor's Theory X and Theory Y for the public sector, using the demanding situation of a federal meat inspector's job. Reminiscent of the insightful moral issues raised by Case Study 1, "The Blast in Centralia No. 5," the following case tells the story of low-level USDA federal meat inspectors who were indicted by the U.S. Department of Justice for accepting "things of value" from certain Boston-based meat processing companies. To gain a proper perspective on their ensuing trial, the author takes the reader behind the scenes to glimpse the daily frustrations confronting an average USDA meat inspector: the highly un-pleasant working conditions, the confusing legal maze of regulations that they are repeatedly asked to enforce, the lack of support or direction from their superiors at the Department of Agriculture, and their woefully inadequate pay combined with continuous offers of "cumshaw" by the very businesses they are asked to regulate.

As you read the case, you may wonder why anyone would want to perform this line of work—under working conditions that are considerably beyond anything McGregor describes as Theory X—even though the work of USDA meat inspectors is clearly vital and necessary to the health and well-being of the general public. And perhaps here is the central irony underscored by the author: that the inspec-tor's job, although vital to the public, is given neither the public recognition nor the remuneration it deserves (ultimately leading to the meat inspectors' vulnera-bility to federal indictments for what turned out to be very minor infractions of the law).

Moreover, at the same time the meat inspectors went to jail, the businesses they

[1]Warren Bennis and Caroline McGregor, eds., *The Professional Manager, Essays by Douglas McGregor* (New York: McGraw-Hill, 1967), p. 196.

were regulating got off scot-free even though those businesses had offered bribes to the meat inspectors in the first place. Yet, the tale is not just another case of justice denied; on a deeper level it perhaps accurately portrays the demanding, often conflicting, cross-pressures under which many public employees must work day in and day out—frequently enforcing a myriad of complex laws which at any time they can be asked to account for by their immediate supervisor, the general public, or even a court of law.

As you read this selection, keep the following questions in mind:

McGregor's Theory Y assumes that employees' potential growth is the main or *only* goal of their employment. In this case study, what were the employers' and employees' main goals? Was personal growth their prime goal?

Given the facts in this case study, could McGregor's Theory Y have been applied to this type of public activity to improve the employment conditions in this case? Discuss why or why not.

If you could redesign the federal meat inspector's job, what reforms would you advocate to enhance its prestige, performance, and effectiveness?

Specifically, what measures would you recommend to keep the inspectors out of jail in the future?

PETER SCHUCK

The Curious Case of the Indicted Meat Inspectors

At seven o'clock on the morning of October 8, 1971, Edmund Wywiorski arrived for work at a meat-processing plant in Boston. He entered the plant, waving casually to employees inside the gate, and headed for the U.S. Government office at the rear of the building. As he walked slowly past the long, silent lines of processing machinery being hosed down for another day's work, Wywiorski's thoughts oscillated between his first morning as a U.S. Department of Agriculture meat inspector back in 1929, and the jubilee day, now less than two years off, when he would reach sixty-five and retire. He smiled to himself as he walked, trying to imagine how many carcasses he must have inspected in those forty-two

years. The old man, unaccustomed to such flights of fancy, broke off the effort as he approached the office door. Glancing at the other inspectors already inside, he knew immediately that something was up.

For most federal meat inspectors, as for Edmund Wywiorski, theirs is a career, a life's work. More than perhaps any other federal career job, however, meat inspection is a grueling, exacting enterprise. Of all blue-collar work in our society, only that of the policeman on the beat begins to compare with meat inspection for the rigor of the intellectual, physical, social, and psychological demands on the job.

The meat inspector works under extremely unpleasant, if not nauseating, conditions. Most meat-processing plants are old, hot, noisy, and noisome. The constant sight and smell of rent flesh, blood, entrails, and offal are sensuous assaults to which the inspector may grow accustomed, but never immune. Twelve-hour work

Reprinted with permission from Harper's Magazine, September 1972. © 1972 by Peter Schuck. Peter Schuck teaches at Yale Law School and was Deputy Assistant Secretary for Planning and Evaluation at HEW in 1977 and 1978.

days are common. The inspector must often cover many "houses" in a circuit, traveling from plant to plant at some distance and at odd hours.

What the meat inspector must endure is nothing compared to what he must know. Many inspectors now start at a GS-5 level, earning less than $7,400 per year, yet they cannot perform a day's work without routinely applying vast knowledge of food chemistry, bacteriology, animal pathology, sampling techniques, food-processing machinery and technology, plant construction, and industrial hygiene. The regulations, guidelines, and directives the inspector must follow and enforce are so numerous, intricate, and technical that they seem like the bureaucratic equivalent of Mission Control at Cape Kennedy. There are detailed regulations specifying the nature and condition of the salt solutions that may be used on wetting cloths applied to dressed carcasses. There are extensive instructions pertaining to packaging, labeling, and transportation of inspected products. Section 310.10 of the Manual of Meat Inspection Procedures sets forth in fifteen single-spaced pages the requirements for the "routine" (other than final inspection) postmortem inspection of every carcass. A typical excerpt follows:

> *Examination of the liver should include opening the large bile duct. This should be done very carefully as cutting through the duct into the liver tissue will interfere with the detection of the small lancet liver fluke. The incision should extend at least an inch through the bile duct dorsally and in the other direction as far as possible. The beef liver should be palpated on the entire parietal surface and within the area of the renal impression. Palpation should be accomplished by exerting sufficient pressure with the hands and fingers to be able to detect deep abscesses or cysts within the liver. . . .*

The complex regulations and instructions nevertheless leave the inspector with an irreducible residue of discretion within which he is empowered to impose grave sanctions against the processor, including closing down the plant. In part, this discretion derives from the inability of law to reconcile fully the imperatives of uniformity and diversity. The point at which a "remote product contamination," i.e., a dirty rail, becomes a "direct product contamination," i.e., a very dirty rail, is obviously a matter of degree, and the regulations concede as much. Yet the latter may justify the inspector's closing down production until the condition is remedied, while the former ordinarily will not.

But the inspector's discretion goes well beyond this. It is a commonplace in the industry, denied only by official USDA spokesmen, that if all meat-inspection regulations were enforced to the letter, no meat processor in America would be open for business. This fact, probably common to all regulated industries, says as much about an agency's tendency to overregulate as about an industry's unwillingness to comply with the law, yet the net result is the same: the inspector is not expected to enforce strictly every rule, *but rather to decide which rules are worth enforcing at all.* In this process, USDA offers no official guidance, for it feels obliged, like all public agencies, to maintain the myth that all rules are rigidly enforced. Unofficially, the inspector is admonished by his USDA superiors to "use common sense," to do his job in a "reasonable way."

Ironically this amalgam of discretion—conferred by law, custom, and necessity—represents to the inspector not power but impotence. For he is obliged to exercise this discretion in a fluid, political context in which he is a pawn of those interests—the processor, its employees, and USDA—with the greatest stake in that exercise. The inspector is the focus, but not the locus, of responsibility.

Most meat processors (or packers) operate on a narrow margin of profitability. In a fiercely competitive industry the incentives to cut costs are practically irresistible. Watered hams, fatty sausages, chicken ingredients instead of beef—these are but a few of the stratagems of the resourceful, cost-conscious packer. A 1 percent increase in the weight of poultry from added water, for example, has been estimated to cost consumers $32 million per year; government studies show excessive watering to be a routine practice. Violations of sanitation and construction standards are also profitable to the packer.

There is every reason to delay compliance as long as possible and only one reason to comply at all—the threat that the inspector will stop production until the offending condition is remedied.

To forestall this threat, the packer relies upon a mixed strategy with the inspector, offering the carrot and wielding the stick. The carrots available to the packer are many, and perhaps the most significant is overtime. Since an inspector may earn thousands of dollars annually in overtime to supplement his meager USDA salary, availability of this perquisite is of crucial importance. The packer decides each day how long the plant will operate and bears the cost of all inspectors required beyond the normal eight hours. Inspectors insist that the subtle offer and withholding of overtime is a mainstay of the system of rewards and punishments by which they are encouraged to be "reasonable."

Another carrot is the gift or favor. Many items are necessary to the inspector's work—boots for the wet floors, freezer coats, pens, office supplies—yet USDA refuses to supply some of them, and scrimps on others. Some packer gifts seem animated by simple goodwill, the oil that lubricates the interactions of people working closely together in the plant day in and day out. A bag of doughnuts for the night shift, a Thanksgiving turkey, a bottle of Scotch at Christmas—these are routinely given to plant employees, and the inspectors are often included. Other gratuities grow naturally out of specific work situations. According to one inspector, "when you have to work overtime, the packer may send out for beer and sandwiches. If you insist on paying, they tell you to go out and get it yourself. It is to the packer's interest to have you eat on the job, so the line can keep running."

To the inspector, a gift of meat is even less suspect. The packer who throws away literally hundreds of pounds of edible product daily for one reason or another—and deducts it as a business expense—does not seem particularly insidious when he asks the inspector, "Need anything for Sunday dinner, Doc?" An inspector observing policemen, firemen, politicians, representatives of veterans groups, hospitals, and other charitable organizations, as well as the packer

employees with whom he works, leaving the plant laden with free meat, is hard put to rationalize why he alone should refuse the proffered gift.

The practice is called "cumshaw"—accepting small amounts of product for one's own use at home. Inspectors argue that the pressure to conform to the practice begins from the first day on the job, and comes almost as much from other inspectors as from packers. "We are weaned on the tradition. The old-timers always say, 'It isn't a good inspector who pays for his Sunday dinner.' They tell you that everybody else does it and has always done it, that it has nothing to do with doing your duty, and that if you don't take it, someone else will. I figure the job is hard enough without having the other inspectors suspicious of you." There are unwritten ground rules, moral strictures transmitted from inspector to inspector, and these too are impressed on the new recruit: "Don't accept more meat than your family can use"; "Don't solicit the meat from the packer"; and by far the most important, "Don't let cumshaw influence your judgment or the way you do your job."

To the inspector this distinction between accepting a gratuity and accepting a bribe is clear and morally based. The general federal bribery statutes recognize this distinction and reinforce this morality by making it a crime for a public official to receive anything of value "in return for . . . being influenced in his performance of any official act . . .," or "for or because of any official act performed or to be performed by him."

The inspector readily acknowledges that what appears to be a gift may become a bribe—if it is large enough, takes certain forms, or is given under certain circumstances—but to him, the critical factor is always whether the gratuity induces him not to enforce the regulations in the normal manner. "Sure I'll accept bundles of meat to take home for my family," says one, echoing the sentiments of many. "But that doesn't affect my decisions in the plant one iota, and the packer knows that. The fact of the matter is that if you get on a high horse and *refuse* to take a bundle, it makes it much more difficult to get the job done. Everyone becomes edgy and suspicious. Enforcing the regulations requires reasonableness, cooperation, and flexibility, as USDA is always telling us. If the packer, his employees, or the other inspectors think I look down on them, they are not going to cooperate with me. How can it be morally wrong to do something that hurts nobody and helps me get the job done?"

In addition to the normal urge to self-justification, then, much in the meat inspector's daily life—the pressures of his work routine, temptations by the packer, the job socialization process, the traditions of the industry, the conventional morality of his fellow inspectors, the general bribery statute, and the imperatives of "getting the job done"—tells him that he may accept small gratuities from the packer with a clear conscience. Section 622 of the Wholesome Meat Act, however, tells him something very different. Where the packers are concerned, this section conforms to the traditional ethic—a packer commits a felony in giving something of value to an inspector *only if* it is given "with intent to influence said inspector . . . in the discharge of any duty. . . ." A convicted packer does not forfeit the right to engage in the meat business. The inspector, on the other hand, commits a felony if he receives *anything* of value "given with any purpose or intent whatsoever." And a convicted inspector, in addition to bearing normal criminal penalties, "shall . . . be summarily discharged from office."

The rationale for this double standard is obscure. Federal employees must be held to a high standard of conduct, to be sure, but should it be any higher than that applicable to a packer extensively regulated and certified to do interstate business by USDA? Should one party to an illegal transaction be regarded as guiltless while another is branded a felon? On October 8, 1971, these questions suddenly lost their academic quality.

The Department of Agriculture: A Case of Nonsupport

Ed Wywiorski, seeing the other inspectors huddled over a newspaper, quickly entered the office and looked at the banner headline in the *Boston Globe:* 40 MEAT INSPECTORS INDICTED IN HUB. A stunned silence lay over the inspectors, each gripped by a private terror. Minutes later, the office phone began its relentless ringing as wives, children, and friends called to ask if it could really be true. Wywiorski cannot recall what he did for the rest of the day or how he made his way back to his West Roxbury home, but his wife recalls that he arrived "in a trance" clutching a notice from USDA suspending him from duty until further notice, effective immediately. "Ed has literally been in a state of shock ever since that day," his wife confides, "and I don't think he will ever get over it."

Later that day, Herbert Travers, then the United States Attorney for Massachusetts and the man who had obtained the grand jury indictments, held a televised press conference in Boston to announce the indictment and suspension of the inspectors, the largest group of federal employees ever indicted at one time, and to assure the public that no impure food had resulted from the inspectors' crimes. The indictments received extensive publicity in the national media, featuring the remark of a USDA spokesman that "We're expecting the worst scandal since meat inspection became mandatory in 1907." Shortly after the indictments became public, the governor appointed Travers to a Superior Court judgeship.

Several days after he was suspended, Wywiorski and thirty-nine other inspectors, almost two-thirds of the inspectors in the Boston circuit, were arraigned in federal court in Boston under indictments charging some of them with having accepted "things of value," some of them with having accepted bribes, and some of them with having done both. In addition, some were charged with having conspired with certain individuals to defraud the U.S. Government of the full value of their services. Many inspectors were not served with their indictments by the Government until they were arraigned. Judge Charles Wyzanski chastised the prosecutors for finding time to be on TV but not to serve the indictments. The inspectors pleaded not guilty. None had any prior criminal record.

On October 22, the inspectors were summoned to the USDA office in Boston. Each was handed a written advance notice of a proposal to suspend him from duty without pay "until the outcome of the proceedings resulting from the indictment is known." The notice gave them forty-eight hours to respond. USDA refused to give them more time to obtain counsel and prepare their responses, although the forty-eight hours covered a holiday weekend, and Civil Service regulations entitle the employee to "all the time he actually needs to prepare and submit his answer." Five inspectors obtained a federal court order extending their time to respond until November 5. Despite oral assurances by USDA officials that *all* of the inspectors could have the additional time, USDA suspended the other thirty-five inspectors on November 1. This was done by identical form letters, although the inspectors were charged with vastly different crimes, ranging from receiving "a handful of screws" to accepting a bribe of thousands of dollars. Even before the suspensions, USDA had already begun filling the suspended inspectors' positions with permanent replacements.

The inspectors then appealed their suspensions to the Civil Service Commission and USDA, contending that to suspend them before they had even been tried, much less convicted, was illegal, and that USDA had not complied with the procedural requirements for suspension. Twenty-six of the cases are still pending before the Commission. In six other cases, the Commission's Appeals Examiner ordered immediate reinstatement pending trial.

USDA has appealed five of these reinstatement decisions to the Commission's Board of Appeals and Review and refuses to reinstate the inspectors pending the outcome. USDA failed to appeal the case of inspector Frank Cavaleri, yet it refused to reinstate him for seven weeks, and then immediately served him with another notice of suspension. Seven inspectors appealed their suspensions within USDA and won, but USDA rejected the decision of its own hearing examiner as "unacceptable" and appealed to the Commission, refusing reinstatement in the meanwhile.

One union official, surveying the fruits of

these hard-won administrative "victories," lamented, "USDA decided from the very beginning to throw these men to the wolves, and it is not going to let due process of law stand in its way." As a result, the inspectors have received no salary since October, and most have been unable to find any work while under indictment. Lack of income, coupled with high legal expenses, has driven all into debt and many to the point of utter financial ruin.

To an old-timer like Ed Wywiorski, who has spent two-thirds of his sixty-three years in USDA, the indifference of the Department to his plight has been profoundly dispiriting. After so many years, he had come to think of the Department possessively and metaphorically: it was "his" Department, it had nurtured him to manhood, it had trained him in a respected career, and it would provide for him in his old age. Now, it seemed, it had suddenly turned on him, almost rushing to condemn him before he had a chance to defend himself.

Many of the younger inspectors, however, see in the situation a confirmation of USDA's true allegiances. To them, the Department is simply a bureaucracy, cold and morally neutral, but possessed of an unerring instinct for political survival. One inspector puts it this way: "Look, we are probably the only regulatory officials who are required to go out among the regulated to do our job. We don't just visit them periodically, we just about marry them. Day after day, night after night, we are in the lion's den alone with the lion. How are we supposed to get along? USDA doesn't tell us. How are we supposed to resist the barrage of threats and temptations the packers constantly direct at us? USDA doesn't tell us. USDA *does* tell us to use our ingenuity to do our job, to use our common sense—but that's not very helpful when you're in the lion's den."

Every inspector has dozens of anecdotes about the failure of USDA supervisors to back him up in disputes with plant management. This pattern of nonsupport is clearly woven in the public records of USDA and outside investigative bodies. The conflict arises from the fact that the inspector, in the words of one old-timer, is "a shock absorber between USDA and the packer. If you tag too many violations, your supervisor will frequently say you are being too antagonistic and rigid. Then when you let some minor violations go, such as allowing 4 percent milk powder in a sausage instead of 3.5 percent, and the supervisor catches them, he blames it on you, not the packer."

Santa Mancina, the top USDA official in the Boston area, readily concedes that most inspector complaints about packer pressures are legitimate. "The packers up here are resistant as hell. I met with their trade association in an effort to communicate. They continually tried to pressure us. Hell, they threatened to go to Washington and cut our appropriations if we didn't play it their way. The packers, of course, complain about the inspectors, but I tend to believe the inspectors most of the time."

USDA files, only recently made public after a Freedom of Information Act suit, are filled with instances of vicious physical and verbal attacks on inspectors by packers or their employees. These assaults, criminal under the Wholesome Meat Act, elicit from USDA little more than gentle reproach and an exhortation to the packer to read the Act. The Act authorizes USDA to withdraw inspection permanently from serious or persistent violators, yet USDA has never invoked that authority. Reports by the General Accounting Office, the investigatory arm of Congress, repeatedly document the low morale of the inspection corps, attributing this in large part to USDA's failure to back up its inspectors.

USDA takes a rigidly legalistic position against the gratuity system while at the same time appearing to ignore—and even contribute to—the vortex of pressures and incentives that nourish this system. Once every year, USDA supervisors meet with inspectors to go over the regulations prohibiting acceptance of things of value from packers. According to many inspectors and supervisors, this is a very tongue-in-cheek affair. "The best analogy I can think of," says one, "is in the Army when they read you the Articles of War or instructions on how to respond to brainwashing. It is all very make-believe, and no one, least of all the supervisors, takes it seriously. If you press them about how to apply these lofty principles in the real world

of the plant, they say, 'Oh, it's okay to take a cup of coffee or an occasional meal from the packer.' If you ask how they reconcile that with the regulations, they tell you, 'Use your common sense.' We leave that meeting thinking small gifts are okay so long as they don't affect the way we do our jobs."

USDA enforces these regulations against inspectors with a passion rarely found in its dealings with unregenerate packers. Consider the case of inspector Harry Topol, thirteen years an inspector and a recipient of the USDA Certificate of Merit in 1968 "for sustained superior performance in carrying out assigned responsibilities." One Saturday morning in July 1969, Topol, on duty at a new assignment in Boston, received a telephone call from his brother-in-law, Salvatore Cina, who said he needed about ten pounds of frankfurters, salami, and bologna for a barbecue that afternoon. Cina asked Topol to put in the order for him, and said he would pick the meat up at the plant before closing. The plant closed before Cina arrived, so Topol filled out a purchase slip and took the meat from the order clerk, arranging to pay Monday since no cashier was on duty. On Topol's way out, a USDA supervisor saw the package, stopped him, and ordered him to return the meat. Topol complied and proceeded to forget about the matter.

Three months later, Topol received a letter from USDA charging him with violation of the regulation and proposing that he be fired. Astonished, Topol requested a hearing and received one—before a circuit supervisor in the meat-inspection program. The supervisor recommended that Topol be fired on the ground that he had purchased meat from a plant that had no retail outlet, despite the uncontradicted testimony of at least four individuals that they routinely walked into the plant off the street and bought meat.

Topol appealed and finally obtained a hearing before an official not connected with the meat-inspection program, who found that the plant did sell to the public and that all charges should be dismissed. The resourceful Director of Personnel, however, while accepting these findings, managed to have the last word. Topol had obtained credit for the purchase until Monday, he ruled, "a personal accommodation which was out of the ordinary." He suspended Topol for four weeks without pay. Two weeks after his suspension, Topol suffered a heart attack. Shortly thereafter, his wife had a nervous breakdown that her physician attributed to the strain of the yearlong ordeal.

The Department of Justice: "It Is More Blessed to Give than to Receive"

In April 1972, Ed Wywiorski's trial began. He had been indicted on eight counts of receiving meat, "a thing of value," in 1967 and 1968. Six of the counts alleged the receipt of a quantity "unknown to the Grand Jury," the seventh stated a quantity of "eight pounds, more or less," and the eighth cited a quantity of "twenty-one pounds and two ounces, more or less." Before trial, the prosecution conceded that Wywiorski had been indicted on three counts he could not possibly have committed, having been on vacation or at different locations at the times alleged. Judge Andrew Caffrey permitted James Krasnoo, the young Assistant U.S. Attorney prosecuting the inspector cases, to drop these counts over the objection of Arnold Felton, Wywiorski's attorney, who argued that the jury should be able to see the kind of evidence on which the prosecution's case rested. A fourth count was dismissed on a technicality.

Krasnoo then offered Felton a deal. "Wywiorski's only a little fish in a big pond," Krasnoo told Felton. "If he pleads guilty before trial, I'll recommend two years probation to the judge." Felton relayed this offer to his client. Wywiorski decided to stand trial on charges of having received four bundles of meat from Jack Satter, Baldwin Vincent Scalesse, and John McNeil. Satter and Scalesse were and are executives of Colonial Provision Company, and McNeil had been a quality-control man with Colonial.

The only damaging witness against Wywiorski was McNeil. He testified that he had no independent memory of transactions with Wywiorski but that when he worked at Colo-

nial he had given bundles of meat to inspectors on behalf of Colonial and had made notations on rack cards for each transaction, usually including the initials of the inspector, the date, and the amount of meat given. He had saved these cards, and he produced four bearing the notation "EdWy."

At the end of the first day of trial, Felton was confronted with an agonizing decision. Reviewing his thought processes, Felton says, "Wywiorski is an old, ineffectual, harmless guy, what people call a 'nebbish.' He would have made a terrible witness, Krasnoo would have made mincemeat of him. I decided he should plead guilty if we could get a favorable disposition." Felton called Krasnoo to ask if his offer to recommend probation on a guilty plea was still open. Krasnoo replied, "Tauro [the new U.S. Attorney] insists that we add on a $2,000 fine as a penalty for your having gone to trial." Wywiorski then called his wife from Felton's office. "I'm going to throw in the towel," he told her. "At least this way, I won't go to jail." Felton, Wywiorski, and Krasnoo then signed a form statement reciting that the determination as to a sentence recommendation "is *always* made after a verdict of Guilty or a Guilty plea has been entered, and *not before*. . . . Any statement relating to a recommendation by an Assistant U.S. Attorney made before a determination of guilt can only refer to his recommendation to be made to the U.S. Attorney, and does not refer to any recommendation to be made to the Court." The statement goes on to say that the final decision on sentence is that of the judge alone. The next day, Wywiorski entered a plea of guilty. Thus the trial ended before Felton could introduce evidence that on March 30, 1967, precisely the period during which McNeil said Wywiorski received meat, Wywiorski reported to his supervisor in writing that he had caught McNeil making entries of reports of laboratory results in official USDA folders without an inspector being present. The report concluded that McNeil left "in an annoyed and resentful manner."

On May 10, Wywiorski appeared before Judge Caffrey for sentencing. Caffrey told Wywiorski that before accepting his guilty plea and sentencing him, he wished to be satisfied that Wywiorski had in fact committed the crimes for which he was admitting guilt. Wywiorski stated that he had not. A surprised Caffrey reminded him that he could not accept a guilty plea unless he was actually guilty. Wywiorski again denied guilt. Caffrey suggested a short recess to resolve the confusion, during which Felton explained that Wywiorski could not plead guilty without admitting guilt, and that if he did not plead guilty, the deal with Krasnoo would be off. When court resumed, Caffrey once again asked Wywiorski if he was guilty. Wywiorski muttered that he had given McNeil the keys to his car (where McNeil had said the meat was probably placed). Caffrey then asked Krasnoo for his sentence recommendation, and Krasnoo responded with the agreed-upon recommendation. Judge Caffrey proceeded to sentence Wywiorski to one year in prison and a $1,000 fine.

Mrs. Wywiorski recalls the scene. "When the judge pronounced his sentence on Ed, even Krasnoo seemed stunned. Ed was in a trance. He had never for one moment believed that he would go to jail. All he had talked about was retirement, an end to the pressures in the plant. When the U.S. Marshals dragged him away, he still did not seem to know what had hit him. He is a totally broken man. And all this over four bundles of meat."

Wywiorski is now serving his prison sentence.

As of June 1, eight Boston meat inspectors had reached trial and had either been convicted or pleaded guilty. All six who have been sentenced so far have received prison sentences, ranging up to three years. The "bigger fish"—other line inspectors, two subcircuit supervisors, and a circuit supervisor, some of whom are accused of accepting money as well as meat—are still to come.

Krasnoo scoffs at the suggestion that the sentences have been unduly harsh. In his view, the inspectors have not been dealt with harshly enough: "These were public officials invested with a high public trust." (To the inspectors, this view is bitterly ironic. "For years," says one, "we've been pieces of shit, lowly GS-5s and 7s, barely noticed, barely lower middle class. Now,

all of a sudden, we are exalted public officials charged with weighty responsibilities and moral leadership.") The young prosecutor told one lawyer that the inspectors were damned lucky that he wasn't prosecuting their wives, who he felt must have had knowledge of their crimes.

Most of the forty inspectors, like Wywiorski, were indicted on the testimony of McNeil, and to a lesser extent Scalesse and Satter, before a federal grand jury first convened in early 1970. The prosecution's case at trial was and is based almost entirely upon the same evidence.

One of the intriguing questions that haunt these trials is why McNeil, who left Colonial in June 1967 to become a USDA inspector, and who is all too familiar with the gratuity system, decided to go before the grand jury and incriminate the inspectors. There is some evidence—based on McNeil's frequently expressed hostility toward Colonial, and on his threats to sue Colonial for compensation for injuries sustained by him and his wife while in Colonial's employ—that he thought his revelations would result in prosecutions not of the inspectors but of the "biggest fish" of all: Colonial Provision Company. Such an expectation would be a natural one, of course, for McNeil's testimony is at least as damaging to Colonial, a company with annual sales of over $50 million, as to a bunch of low-level inspectors, many of whom were charged with receiving small quantities of meat. And while the inspectors could be effectively disciplined administratively—by loss of pay, discharge, or otherwise—Colonial could be punished only by prosecution and public obloquy.

If McNeil's intention was to damage Colonial, he has utterly failed to do so. The Department of Justice has actually contrived the meat-inspection prosecutions in such a way that Colonial has managed to emerge unscathed. That has not been easy to do, given the admissions of McNeil, Scalesse, and Satter that they routinely gave meat, money, and other things of value to numerous inspectors; that McNeil, at Colonial's behest, doctored samples, illegally gained access to the USDA retention cage, and chose dummy samples; that Scalesse lied to the grand jury in at least three sessions; that Satter lied to the grand jury and had tried to bring political pressure to bear from Washington against zealous inspectors. But the ingenuity of a political Department of Justice is not to be underestimated.

According to the Justice Department's own evidence, employees of Colonial and six other Boston area packers routinely and systematically gave meat, money, and other things of value to the forty inspectors on behalf of the packers. *Yet none of these packers or their employees has been, or probably ever will be, indicted for these transactions.* The reason is simple: after lying to the grand jury, Satter and Scalesse finally claimed the Fifth Amendment, refusing to answer further questions. The Department then granted them immunity from prosecution in order to induce them to testify against the inspectors.

When asked why the U.S. Attorney decided to grant immunity from prosecution to Colonial and six other packers and their employees, but not to the inspectors, prosecutor Krasnoo gave three reasons:

1. "I would never grant immunity to a witness who lied before the grand jury." Yet Scalesse and Satter admittedly lied to the grand jury on several occasions prior to being granted immunity.
2. "The inspectors failed to cooperate by giving evidence to the grand jury." But the packer witnesses also failed to cooperate, until they were offered immunity, and there is every reason to believe that the inspectors would have cooperated had *they* been offered immunity. Well before the indictments were issued, at least one attorney representing a group of inspectors told Krasnoo his clients would "sing like canaries" in return for immunity. The offer was refused. To the inspectors, it was clear from their first appearance before the grand jury that they were the targets of the investigation.
3. "I know of no inspector who took the Fifth, so we couldn't offer them immunity." This is incorrect. A number of inspectors took the Fifth, as Krasnoo should certainly have known.

The real reasons that the Department of Justice pursued the minnows while protecting the whales probably lie elsewhere. As one former prosecutor put it: "From the Department's point of view, this was a smart prosecutive decision. By giving immunity to a relatively small number of influential packers who dealt with a relatively large number of inspectors, they could get a large number of convictions, a lot of publicity, and not step on any important toes. If they had prosecuted the packers, they would have had to prove 'intent to influence.' This way, the judge simply charges the jury that in order to convict, they need only find that the inspectors received anything of value. Since McNeil gets up with his cards and says they received, these are very easy cases to win."

The solicitude of the Department of Justice for Colonial, however, goes far beyond immunizing it from prosecution. For the Department has managed to draft indictments against the inspectors, containing well over 2,000 counts, most of which involve gratuities given by key Colonial personnel, without ever mentioning Colonial by name. The same is true of the six other immunized packing companies. The indictments recite that things of value were given, and conspiracies entered into with the defendants, by certain named individuals—Satter, Scalesse, and McNeil in most cases—but they are not identified as employees or agents of Colonial. For all the public knows or *could* know from the indictments, Colonial and the other immunized packers have been pure as the driven snow. Since the mass media have confined their attention entirely to the indictments and the sentences, there has been virtually no coverage of the trials, at which the involvement of Colonial and other packers is brought out.

The Department, to be sure, has secured indictments against three small packers, none of them involved with the forty inspectors. Only one case has been tried, and the outcome is most intriguing and bizarre. As the result of an FBI plant and the use of marked money, inspector Robert Gaff had apparently been caught red-handed immediately after receiving money from a packer, Waters & Litchfield Co. On October 29, 1971, Gaff pleaded guilty to four counts of receiving things of value from two packers. He was sentenced to serve a six-month sentence (half that meted out to Wywiorski for accepting four bundles of meat). After Gaff completed his term and left prison, Waters & Litchfield was brought to trial in April. The Department of Justice, in a most extraordinary and inexplicable maneuver, *waived a jury,* knowing full well that a jury, particularly with the price of meat on their minds, would be far more likely to convict than a judge would be. Then Gaff took the stand as the prosecution's main witness, and his testimony—testimony that had supported his plea of guilty and the grand jury indictment of Waters & Litchfield—was so garbled that the judge directed a verdict of not guilty. So the Department's record remains clean as a hound's tooth: no packers convicted.

Other aspects of the meat-inspector cases also raise the question of whether the lady holding the Scales of Justice in front of the Department's headquarters is actually peeking from under her blindfold. On the day the indictments were returned against the inspectors, Herbert Travers, the then U.S. Attorney, took the extraordinary step in a case of this sort of applying for the issuance of bench warrants for the immediate arrest of the inspectors. This procedure was highly unusual because no inspector had a prior criminal record (this is a condition of being a USDA inspector), and they were obviously unlikely to flee. Travers had arranged for federal agents to sweep through the meat districts and make a dramatic and well-publicized mass arrest and incarceration of the inspectors. The judge, seeing no justification for arrests, refused to issue the warrants.

When the indictments were announced in October to an attentive press, many of the counts against the inspectors were so trivial as to lend comic relief to an otherwise relentlessly depressing affair. One inspector indicted for receiving "a thing of value, to wit, a handful of screws," quipped, "I wouldn't mind if I had a big hand, but how many screws can I get in this?" Another inspector was indicted for receiving "a spiritual bouquet," a third for receiving a light bulb. Other "things of value" forming the basis for individual counts were half a can of shoe polish, "the picking up of one photograph," and a car wash. One inspector was charged with accepting a ride home for his daughter from a packer employee.

Many of the counts were not simply trivial, they were demonstrably mistaken. Frank Cavaleri, for example, was indicted on six counts, four of which occurred at times when he was not even working for the Government. Most inspectors had at least some counts of this order of accuracy. After all of the publicity and hoopla had been generated, of course, these counts were dropped by the U.S. Attorney's office, often over the objections of defense counsel who wished the jury to learn how casual the Department had been in securing indictments. The proliferation of counts had another purpose too. As one ex-prosecutor explained, "They threw indictments around like confetti to inundate the inspectors. Then Krasnoo could offer to drop most of the counts in exchange for a plea of guilty. Krasnoo was giving up nothing that was worth anything, of course, but to the inspectors, the offer must have seemed generous."

The Department of Justice has employed other questionable tactics. The indictments contain a large number of counts for accepting bribes—in which there is necessarily an allegation of intent to influence the inspector's official actions—as well as counts of simply receiving things of value, which include no such allegation. *Yet there has been no evidence that inspectors were bribed, and much evidence that they were not.* First, packer employees have admitted at the trials that the inspectors did their jobs and did not relax their application of the regulations. Second, Travers and Krasnoo have both stated publicly that the public has not been exposed to deficient meat products as a result of the indicted transactions. Third, Krasnoo has dropped all bribery counts before trial; he concedes that he has proved only the receipt of things of value by inspectors. Nevertheless, despite requests by defense attorneys not to do so, Krasnoo has used the term "bribery" in summations to the jury on a number of occasions.

The Department, in conjunction with the courts, also consistently penalizes those inspectors who invoke their right to go to trial. This practice is not unique to these cases, of course, but the result is not less unjust for being common. Inspector Hugh McDonald was indicted on 183 counts of receiving money, meat, and liquor; 163 counts were dropped before trial. Then Krasnoo induced him to plead guilty to nine counts of receiving meat and liquor, dropping the others. Krasnoo made no sentence recommendation to the judge. McDonald received one year in prison and a $1,000 suspended fine. Inspector Richard H. Murphy was indicted on 157 counts of receiving money and meat, 147 of which were dropped before trial. Krasnoo offered to make no sentence recommendation if Murphy pleaded guilty. Murphy insisted on going to trial and was convicted on ten counts of receiving money. Krasnoo then recommended a sentence of four years in prison, with a $4,000 suspended fine. Murphy received three years in prison and a $1,000 fine.

It is inconceivable that Murphy would have received so severe a sentence if he, like McDonald several weeks before, had pleaded guilty instead of invoking his right to put the Government to its proof in a trial. As Krasnoo well knows, Murphy's example has not been lost on the thirty-three inspectors still awaiting trial. "I have a strong case," says one "but look at the risk I run by going to trial before jurors angry about the high cost of meat. I will have to plead guilty to avoid paying 'the Murphy premium.' "

With the Department of Justice at the bargaining table, negotiation for guilty pleas can be a nasty business. In the case of one married inspector, the prosecution threatened to show that he had had sexual relations with a female employee of the packer. The Internal Revenue Service, presumably with the connivance of the Department of Justice, has conducted tax audits on a number of inspectors in an effort to show that they were living beyond their means, evidence that would assist the prosecution's case. The IRS, after securing records and cooperation from the attorney for several inspectors, has refused either to return the records or to issue a ruling, thus enhancing the bargaining power of the Justice Department in negotiating with the inspectors for guilty pleas.

The Boston meat-inspector cases raise disturbing questions. A steady stream of inspectors are now entering prison, their careers and reputations irretrievably lost, their families plunged into unspeakable despair. Yet within a mile of the federal courthouse, Colonial Provision Company flourishes, processing millions of pounds of meat daily; Jack Satter drives his Cadillac to his new job as president of Colonial, and Vinnie Scalesse has been promoted to head of a Colonial subsidiary. These admitted perjurers and the other packers who admittedly gave things of value to the inspectors continue to do business as before. John McNeil continues as a USDA inspector, sometimes training new inspectors in their duties, despite having admitted doctoring and switching USDA samples as a Colonial employee and having been a key link in a chain of illegality. The public continues to subsidize this system in several ways—in higher meat prices, reflecting the costs of gratuities, and in higher taxes, reflecting the packers' practice of deducting these gratuities as part of their operational "shrinkage." It is likely, in addition, that the public is getting an inferior product for its money. "How much rigorous inspection do you think is going on today at Colonial or these other houses?" one inspector asks. "These packers bought insurance against strict inspection. How do you think the inspector is going to behave knowing that he can be prosecuted simply on the word of the packer he is supposed to regulate and that the packer will not be touched?"

A society truly concerned about crime must concern itself with those social systems—like the meat plant—in which crime seems to make sense to otherwise moral men. "Cumshaw" is such a system, and it flourishes. While some of its practitioners have been punished, the most powerful have not. For the latter, at least, the system has paid handsome dividends.

Chapter 11 Review Questions

1. In your own words, can you describe McGregor's Theory X and Theory Y? Why do McGregor's Theories X and Y rest on the assumptions of Maslow's hierarchy of human needs? What is Maslow's hierarchy of human needs? From your experience, is such a hierarchy a valid idea?

2. What were the conflicting cross-pressures faced by the federal meat inspectors in their line of work? How did their work environment leave them vulnerable to possible federal indictments? Would you characterize their work situation as Theory X? Or something else?

3. Why did the public demand a higher level of ethics from the meat inspectors than from the meat packers? What were the causes and results of this double standard of public expectations as it affected the public employees? In your opinion, is this double standard typical?

4. Do you think the application of McGregor's Theory Y could have improved the meat inspectors' employment conditions and ultimately prevented their indictment? Would McGregor's Theory Y have been applicable in this case study? Explain why or why not. Specifically, why do the multiple responsibilities of most public employees make it more difficult to adopt McGregor's Theory Y? What were the multiple public responsibilities of the meat inspectors?

5. In human terms, what was the ultimate impact of the working environment on the lives of meat inspectors? Was their working environment healthy or destructive to human growth and development? Was there any possibility of improving their work environment? If so, how and in what direction?

6. In light of the foregoing case study, do you think McGregor's ideas are generally applicable to public sector organizations? Or, are they useful mainly in private business? Can you sum up what conditions might allow for the successful application of Theory Y? Under what conditions may it not be applicable?

Key Terms

Theory X	hierarchy of needs
Theory Y	physiological and safety needs
hard versus soft management	ego needs
job enrichment	needs of self-fulfillment
participatory management	management by objectives
decentralization of control	consultative management

Suggestions for Further Reading

Public personnel administration is a field of enormous complexity, specialization, and rapid change, and, therefore, looking at several basic introductory texts is necessary for a good overview: O. Glenn Stahl, *Public Personnel Administration,* Eighth Edition (New York: Harper & Row, 1983); Jonathan Beck, *Managing People in Public Agencies* (Boston: Little, Brown, 1984); Gilbert B. Siegel and Robert C. Myrtle, *Public Personnel Administration: Concepts and Practices* (Boston: Houghton Mifflin, 1985); and Steven H. Hays and T. Zane Reeves, *Personnel Management in the Public Sector* (Boston: Allyn and Bacon, 1984); To supplement these introductions, students should further examine the basic *framing* documents of public personnel, such as the Civil Service Act of 1883, the Hatch Acts, the Civil Service Reform Act of 1978, as well as several others contained in Frederick C. Mosher, ed., *Basic Documents of American Public Administration: 1776–1950* (New York: Holmes and Meier, 1976), and Richard J. Stillman II, ed., *Basic Documents of American Public Administration: Since 1950* (New York: Holmes and Meier, 1982).

For the best history of the American civil service system, see Paul Van Riper, *History of U.S. Civil Service* (New York: Harper & Row, 1958). For an insightful view of personnel practices at the local level, read Frank J. Thompson, *Personnel Policy in the City: The Politics of Jobs in Oakland* (Berkeley, Calif.: University of California Press, 1975); and for a view of its operation at the federal level, see Frederick C. Mosher, *Democracy and the Public Service,* Second Edition (New York: Oxford University Press, 1982); William I. Bacchus, *Staffing for Foreign Affairs* (Princeton: Princeton University Press, 1983); or Hugh Heclo, *A Government of Strangers: Executive Politics in Washington* (Washington, D.C.: The Brookings Institution, 1977). Articles contained in the two volumes of the "classics" series on personnel give readers a useful overview of the scope, diversity, and complexity of this field: Thomas H. Patten, Jr., ed., *Classics of Personnel Management* (Chicago: Moore Publishing Co., 1979), and Frank J. Thompson, *Classics of Public Personnel Policy* (Chicago: Moore Publishing Co., 1979).

Among the recent articles on federal personnel, some of the more interesting ones include Benton G. Moeller, "What Ever Happened to the Federal Personnel System," *International Personnel Management,* 9 (Spring 1982), pp. 1–8.; Bernard Rosen, "Uncertainty in the Senior Executive Service," *Public Administration Review,* 41 (March/April 1981), pp. 203–207; Norton E. Long, "S.E.S. and the Public Interest," *Public Administration Review,* 41 (May/June 1981), pp. 305–312; as well as the entire symposium on "The Public Service as an Institution," edited by Eugene B. McGregor, Jr., which contains several fine short essays on the subject, in *Public Administration Review,* 42 (July/August 1982), pp. 304–320.

For a set of comprehensive essays that explain the "state-of-the-art-of-public personnel administration," see Jack Rabin, et al., eds., *Handbook on Public Personnel Administration and Labor Relations* (New York: Marcel Dekker, 1983), as well as several of the essays contained in Frederick S. Lane, ed., *Current Issues in Public Administration*, Third Edition (New York: St. Martin's Press, 1986). One would also do well to skim current issues of *Public Administration Review, Harvard Business Review, Public Personnel Management, The Bureaucrat,* and *Public Management* for recent and fast-changing trends in the field of personnel.

Japanese personnel motivation techniques have recently gained wide popularity in the United States; for a balanced introduction to the subject, read William Ouchi, *Theory Z: How American Business Can Meet the Japanese Challenge* (New York: Avon Books, 1982). "Revitalization" themes also are broadly popular in the public service as reflected today by Robert B. Denhardt, et al., eds., *The Revitalization of the Public Service* (Columbia, Mo.: University of Missouri and Lincoln University, Extension Publications, 1987).

CHAPTER 12

Public Budgeting: The Concept of Budgeting as Political Compromise and Strategy

"If organizations are viewed as political coalitions, budgets are mechanisms through which subunits bargain over conflicting goals, make side-payments, and try to motivate one another to accomplish their objectives."

Aaron Wildavsky

READING 12

Introduction

Budgets serve many important functions in government. In one sense, budgets are contracts annually agreed on by the executive and legislative branches that allow executive agencies and departments to raise and spend public funds in specified ways for the coming fiscal year (normally running in state and local governments from July 1 to June 30; recently changed at the federal level by the Congressional Budget Act of 1974 to end on September 30 and to begin October 1 each year). A budget imposes a mutual set of legal obligations between the elected and appointed officers of public organizations with regard to taxation and expenditure policies. A budget is, therefore, a legal contract that provides a vehicle for fiscal controls over subordinate units of government by the politically elected representatives of the people.

Budgets have other purposes as well: they can be planning devices used to translate presently scarce fiscal and human resources in the public sector into future governmental goals and programs. In this respect, budgets are vital instruments for directing what tasks government will perform and how human talent in society and public monies will be used.

Budgets are also forces for internal coordination and efficiency in public administration. Budget formulations annually impose choices concerning how public programs should be undertaken, interrelated, and measured in terms of their value, effectiveness, and worth to the general public. Related to the concept of budgets as a coordinating device is the idea that budgets are economic documents. In this role federal budgets are tools of fiscal policy, for they stimulate or slow down national economic growth through increased or decreased taxation or revenue expenditures. Finally, budgets can also be viewed as political documents, reflecting through the allocation of funds the ultimate desires, interests, and power of various groups within the body politic as expressed by elected legislative bodies. In setting up an annual budget, various political participants engage in log rolling, compromises, and bargains to create a document that by and large mirrors the current priorities of the locality, state, or nation. The quality and quantity of government that the citizenry desires and will support at any given time is expressed by the budget.

Our conceptual understanding of these roles of the budget in modern government is comparatively new, being chiefly a twentieth-century phenomenon. In large part, our instituting formal budget documents began in the Progressive Era, when public budgets were developed as vehicles for governmental reform, to produce improved economy and efficiency in the public sector, and as instruments for imposing greater control over public spending. Many of these ideas and concepts were borrowed from the experience and practices of business management.

Although there remains today a strong emphasis on the earlier notions of budgets as vehicles for imposing control, economy, and efficiency in government, a prominent current view of the role of budgets—and a perspective frequently held by political scientists, budgeting specialists, and public administration practitioners—is a political one: budgets are principally governed by considerations of compromise, strategy, and bargaining. Aaron Wildavsky (1930–   ), a University of California at Berkeley political scientist and a well-known pioneer in budgetary theory and analysis, ably presents this political view in the following selection. He visualizes budgets less as a tool of public management and much more as a part of the general social decision-making process in which various participants—clientele groups, agencies, departments, the Office of Management and Budget, the president, the Council of Economic Advisors, Congress, and congressional subcommittees—combine to determine "who gets what, where, when, and how."

Wildavsky describes a process whereby all the participants in budgeting are under tremendous time pressures to deal with an enormous number of political, fiscal, and social calculations. He argues that: (1) although decisions are complex, they are simplified in order to deal with available choices quickly; (2) decisions are calculated on the basis of last year's budget allocations with attention given primarily to incremental increases or decreases over the previous year; (3) decisions are weighted in favor of the *fair share* concept, by which each participant is awarded a fair share of the total budget increases or decreases; (4) decisions are influenced by the roles assumed by each of the major participants—e.g., the agencies acting as the advocates for increases, the budget bureau serving as the major "cost cutter," and the legislators acting as "the final arbitrators"; (5) because final choices are related to how budget programs are perceived and evaluated by the various actors in the budget-making struggle, the form of presentation of budgets is often as important as the substance; and (6) budget decisions are rarely made without a careful eye on their impact on any agency's supporting clientele groups.

As you read this selection, keep the following questions in mind:

How does Wildavsky's understanding of the budgetary decision-making process compare with Charles Lindblom's earlier account of the administrative decision-making process (see Chapter 8)?

What are some of the difficulties with Wildavsky's political, or incremental, view of the budgetary process? For example, are all the participants in the budgeting process necessarily equal or are some better equipped for controlling the outcome of the contest? If the latter is true, does this cause an inequitable distribution of public monies?

What reforms in the process might ensure that budgetary decisions would always reward the widest possible public interest as opposed to the special interests?

Does Wildavsky see much difference between public and private business budgets?

How does his view of budgets relate to Norton Long's conception of administrative power as outlined in Chapter 4?

AARON WILDAVSKY

Budgeting as a Political Process

Budgets are predictions. They attempt to specify connections between words and numbers on the budget documents and future human behavior. Whether or not the behavior intended by the authors of the budget actually takes place is a question of empirical observation rather than one of definition. The budget of the Brazilian government, for example, has long been known as "a great lie" (Alionar Baleeiro, reported by Frank Sherwood), with little if any connection between what is spent for various purposes and what is contained in the formal document. Nor is there any necessary connection between the budgets of Soviet[1] and American[2] industrial firms and the expenditures they make or the actions they take.

Budgeting is concerned with the translation of financial resources into human purposes. Since funds are limited, a budget may become a

[1]Berliner, Joseph S., *Factory and Manager in the U.S.S.R.* (Cambridge, Mass.: Harvard University Press, 1957).

[2]Argyris, Chris, *The Impact of Budgets on People* (New York: Controllership Foundation, 1952); Sord, Bernhard H., and Glenn A. Welsch, *Business Budgeting: A Survey of Management Planning and Control Practices* (New York: Controllership Foundation, 1958).

mechanism for allocating resources. If emphasis is placed on receiving the largest returns for a given sum of money, or on obtaining the desired objectives at the lowest cost, a budget may become an instrument for pursuing efficiency.[3] A proposed budget may represent an organization's expectations; it may contain the amounts which the organization expects to spend. A budget may also reflect organizational aspirations; it may contain figures the organization hopes to receive under favorable conditions. Since the amounts requested often have an effect on the amounts received, budget proposals are often strategies. The total sum of money and its distribution among various activities may be designed to have a favorable impact in support of an organization's goals. As each participant acts on the budget he receives information on the preferences of others and communicates his own desires through the choices he makes. Here a budget emerges as a network of communications in which information is being continuously generated and fed back to the participants. Once enacted a budget becomes a precedent; the fact that something has been done before vastly increases the chances that it will be done again.[4]

For all purposes we shall conceive of budgets as attempts to allocate financial resources through political processes. If politics is regarded as conflict over whose preferences are to prevail in the determination of policy, then the budget records the outcomes of this struggle. If one asks who gets what the (public or private) organization has to give, then the answers for a moment in time are recorded in the budget. If organizations are viewed as political coalitions,[5] budgets are mechanisms through which subunits bargain over conflicting goals, make side-

payments, and try to motivate one another to accomplish their objectives.

Viewed in this light, the study of budgeting offers a useful perspective from which to analyze the making of policy. The opportunities for comparison are ample, the outcomes are specific and quantifiable, and the troublesome problem of a unit of analysis with which to test hypotheses—there is no real agreement on what a decision consists of—is solved by the very nature of the transactions in budgeting. Although a major effort has been made to collect budgetary material from many different countries, levels of government, and private firms, the results have only been fragmentary at best. Very little is available in any language on how budgeting is actually carried on. From Stourm's classic work on the budget (1889) to the present day, virtually the entire literature on budgeting has been normative in tone and content.[6] Yet the glimpses we do get of budgetary behavior in different systems suggest that there may be profound uniformities underlying the seeming diversities of form and structure.

Budgetary Calculations

Decisions depend upon calculation of which alternatives to consider and to choose. Calculation involves determination of how problems are identified, get broken down into manageable dimensions, and are related to one another, and how choices are made as to what is relevant and who shall be taken into account. A major clue toward understanding budgeting is the extraordinary complexity of the calculations involved.

[3]Smithies, Arthur, *The Budgetary Process in the United States* (New York: McGraw-Hill, 1955).

[4]Wildavsky, Aaron B., *Politics of the Budgetary Process* (Boston: Little, Brown, 1964).

[5]Cyert, Richard M., and James G. March, *A Behavioral Theory of the Firm* (Englewood Cliffs, N.J.: Prentice-Hall, 1963).

[6]Smithies; Burkhead, Jesse, *Government Budgeting* (New York: Wiley, 1956); Buck, A. E., *Public Budgeting: A Discussion of Budgetary Practice in the National, State, and Local Governments of the United States* (New York: Harper, 1929); Buck, A. E., *The Budget in Governments of Today* (New York: Macmillan, 1934); Willoughby, William F., *The Movement for Budgetary Reform in the United States* (New York: Appleton, 1918); Willoughby, William F., *The National Budget System* (Baltimore: Johns Hopkins Press, 1927).

In any large organization there are a huge number of items to be considered, many of which are of considerable technical difficulty. Yet there is little or no theory in most areas of policy which would enable practitioners to predict the consequences of alternative moves and the probability of their occurring.[7] Man's ability to calculate is severely limited; time is always in short supply; and the number of matters which can be encompassed in one mind at the same time is quite small.[8] Nor has anyone solved the imposing problem of the interpersonal comparison of utilities. Outside of the political process, there is no agreed upon way of comparing and evaluating the merits of different programs for different people whose preferences vary in kind and in intensity.

Simplification

Participants in budgeting deal with their overwhelming burdens by adopting aids to calculation. They simplify in order to get by. They make small moves, let experience accumulate, and use the feedback from their decisions to gauge the consequences. They use actions on simpler matters they understand as indices to complex concerns. They attempt to judge the capacity of the men in charge of programs even if they cannot appraise the policies directly. They may institute across-the-board ("meat axe") cuts to reduce expenditures, relying on outcries from affected agencies and interest groups to let them know if they have gone too far.[9] Hospital boards in Great Britain, unable to determine what costs should be in an absolute sense, rely on comparisons with comparable institutions. County councils keep close track of expenditures in only a few major areas to cut

down on the bulk of overspending. The timing of new starts on projects is used as a simplifying device for regulating total expenditures. Another way local authorities keep spending within limits is through the practice of "rate rationing," or allowing committees so many pence or shillings of each pound of income.[10] Industrial firms use the percentage of total industry sales or some percentage of earnings on assets employed before taxes in setting budgetary goals. Many organizations use the number of personnel as strategic control points in limiting expenditures.[11] Constraints are actively sought as in the common practice of isolating "prunable" items when looking for places to cut the budget.[12]

Incremental Method

By far the most important aid to calculation is the incremental method. Budgets are almost never actively reviewed as a whole in the sense of considering at once the value of all existing programs as compared with all possible alternatives. Instead, this year's budget is based on last year's budget, with special attention given to a narrow range of increases or decreases. The greatest part of any budget is a product of previous decisions. Long-range commitments have been made. There are mandatory programs whose expenses must be met. Powerful political support makes the inclusion of other activities inevitable. Consequently, officials concerned with budgeting restrict their attention to items and programs they can do something about—a few new programs and possible cuts in old ones.

When a British Treasury official warns in 1911 against "the habit of regarding each year's estimate as the starting-point for the next....,"[13] one can be sure that the practice has become

[7]Braybrooke, David, and Charles E. Lindblom, *A Strategy of Decision: Policy Evaluation as a Social Process* (New York: Free Press, 1963).

[8]Simon, Herbert A., *Models of Man: Social and Rational: Mathematical Essays on Rational Human Behavior in a Social Setting* (New York: Wiley, 1957).

[9]Wildavsky, pp. 1–13.

[10]Royal Institute of Public Administration, *Budgeting in Public Authorities* (New York: Macmillan, 1959).

[11]Sord and Welsch.

[12]Royal Institute, pp. 115–116.

[13]Higgs, Henry, *The Financial System of the United Kingdom* (London: Macmillan, 1914), pp. 135–136.

well established. Both the practice and the complaints continue unabated in Great Britain.[14] Incremental budgetary calculations can be found in such different places as Canadian provinces[15] and Michigan cities (where a sample budgetary guideline to department heads reads, "Budgets should be for the same level of service as the current year unless a variation is previously approved. . . ."[16]

Expectations of Participants

Incremental calculations proceed from an existing base. By "base" we refer to commonly held expectations among participants in budgeting that programs will be carried out at close to the going level of expenditures. The base of a budget, therefore, refers to accepted parts of programs that will not normally be subjected to intensive scrutiny. Since many organizational units compete for funds, there is a tendency for the central authority to include all of them in the benefits or deprivations to be distributed. Participants in budgeting often refer to expectations regarding their fair share of increases and decreases.[17] Argyris[18] quotes a supervisor as observing that employees had a well-developed notion of a fair output. In talking about the Philadelphia capital budget, Brown and Gilbert[19] observe that every department got a share because projects were considered partly as contributions toward keeping the departments going. The widespread sharing of deeply held

expectations concerning the organization's base and its fair share of funds provides a powerful (though informal) means of coordination and stability in budgetary systems which appear to lack comprehensive calculations proceeding from a hierarchical center.

Coordination and Supervision

The most powerful coordinating mechanisms in budgeting undoubtedly stem from the role orientations adopted by the major participants. Roles (the expectations of behavior attached to institutional positions) are parts of the division of labor. They are calculating mechanisms. In American national government, the administrative agencies act as advocates of increased expenditure, the Bureau of the Budget acts as presidential servant with a cutting bias, the House Appropriations Committee functions as a guardian of the Treasury, and the Senate Appropriations Committee serves as an appeals court to which agencies carry their disagreement with House action. The roles fit in with one another and set up a stable pattern of mutual expectations, which markedly reduces the burden of calculation for the participants. The agencies need not consider in great detail how their requests will affect the president's over-all program; they know that such criteria will be introduced by the Budget Bureau. Since the agencies can be depended upon to advance all the programs for which there is prospect of support, the Budget Bureau and the appropriations committees can concentrate respectively on fitting them into the president's program or paring them down. If the agencies suddenly reversed roles and sold themselves short, the entire pattern of mutual expectations would be upset, leaving the participants without a firm anchor in a sea of complexity. For if agencies refuse to be advocates, congressmen would not only have to choose among the margins of the best programs placed before them, they would

[14]Mitchell, Ronald J., *State Finance: The Theory and Practice of Public Finance in the United Kingdom* (London: Pitman, 1935); Royal Institute.

[15]McLeod, T. H., "Budgeting Provincial Expenditure" in Institute of Public Administration of Canada, Annual Conference, Fifth, *Proceedings* (Toronto: The Institute, 1953), pp. 11–19.

[16]Kressbach, Thomas W., *The Michigan City Manager in Budgetary Proceedings* (Ann Arbor: Michigan Municipal League, 1962), p. 41.

[17]Wildavsky, pp. 16–18.

[18]Argyris, p. 16.

[19]Brown, William H., Jr., and C. E. Gilbert, *Planning Municipal Investment: A Case Study of Philadelphia* (Philadelphia: University of Pennsylvania Press, 1961).

also have to discover what these good programs might be. Indeed, the Senate Appropriations Committee depends upon agency advocacy to cut its burden of calculation; if the agencies refused to carry appeals from House cuts, the senators would have to do much more work than their busy schedules permit.[20]

A writer on Canadian budgeting[21] refers to the tendency for an administrator to become "an enthusiastic advocate" of increased funds for his policies. When disagreements over departmental budgets arise, as they frequently do in private firms, the controller and the departmental representatives come to a meeting armed to the teeth to defend their respective positions.[22] The same interministerial battles go on in Great Britain,[23] the Netherlands,[24] and the Soviet Union, where "serious clashes" arise when ministries and republics ask for greater funds to fulfill their plans.[25]

In a discussion which deserves to be better known, W. Drees[26] points out that agency heads can defend the interests of their sectors because it is so difficult for them to relate their modest part in total expenditures to the over-all budgetary situation. Anything they could save through a spirit of forbearance would be too small a portion of the total to make the sacrifice worthwhile. From their point of view, total expenditures are irrelevant.

The role of guardian or defender of the treasury apparently did not come naturally. In the early days of public finance in France, "Financiers appropriated to themselves without restraint the spoils of the nation, and used for their own profit the funds intended for the Treasury; the only restraint lay in the fact that when their plundering exceeded the measure of tolerance they were hanged. It was a summary procedure of control *a posteriori*. . . ."[27] It took centuries to develop a finance minister like Louis Thiers, whose definition of his role included that "ferocity . . . needed to defend the Treasury."[28] The members of the U.S. House Appropriations Committee consider themselves guardians of the Treasury who take pride in the high degree of frequency with which they reduce estimates.[29] They reconcile this role with the defense of constituency interests by cutting estimates to satisfy one role and generally increasing amounts over the previous year to satisfy the other.

Among the legislatures of the world, however, guardianship appears to be quite rare. Drees[30] reports that in the Netherlands the legislative specialists concerned with finance, by advocating higher appropriations, defend the interests of the policy areas over which they have jurisdiction to a degree overriding party lines. Much the same thing happened in France during the Fourth Republic.[31] It may be that guardianship depends, first, on appropriations committees that have continuing power to affect outcomes—a rare occurrence in the modern world—and, second, on the development of cultural values and legislative mores that support an insistent financial check on the bureaucracy. Legislative committees in nations like Mexico, where virtually complete budgetary power is in the hands of the president, who heads the single

[20]Wildavsky.

[21]Ward, Norman, *The Public Purse* (Toronto: University of Toronto Press, 1962), p. 165.

[22]Argyris, p. 9.

[23]Brittain, Herbert, *The British Budgetary System* (New York: Macmillan, 1959), pp. 216–217.

[24]Drees, Willem, *On the Level of Government Expenditure in the Netherlands after the War* (Leiden: Stenfert Kroese, 1955), pp. 61–71.

[25]Davies, Robert W., *The Development of the Soviet Budgetary System* (Cambridge: Cambridge University Press, 1958), p. 184.

[26]Drees, pp. 61–71.

[27]Stourm, René, *The Budget* (New York: Appleton, 1917), p. 536.

[28]*Ibid.*, p. 69.

[29]Fenno, Richard F., "The House Appropriations Committee as a Political System: The Problem of Integration," *American Political Science Review* (1962) 56:310–324.

[30]Drees.

[31]Williams, Philip M., *Crisis and Compromise: Politics in the Fourth Republic,* 3rd ed. (Hamden, Conn.: Shoe String Press, 1964).

great party,[32] or Great Britain, where party responsibility overwhelms parliamentary initiative,[33] are hardly in a position to develop a role of guardianship.

Budgetary Goals

Possessing the greatest expertise and the largest numbers, working in the closest proximity to their policy problems and clientele groups, desirous of expanding their horizons, administrative agencies generate action through advocacy. But how much shall they ask for? Life would be simple if they could just estimate the costs of their ever-expanding needs and submit the total as their request. But if they ask for amounts much larger than the appropriating bodies believe are reasonable, the credibility of the agencies will suffer a drastic decline. In such circumstances, the reviewing organs are likely to apply a "measure of unrealism,"[34] with the result that the agency gets much less than it might have with a more moderate request. So the first decision rule is: Do not come in too high. Yet the agencies must also not come in too low, for the assumption is that if agency advocates do not ask for funds they do not need them. Since the budgetary situation is always tight, terribly tight, or impossibly tight, reviewing bodies are likely to accept a low request with thanks and not inquire too closely into the rationale. Given the distribution of roles, cuts must be expected and allowances made.

The agency decision rule might therefore read: Come in a little high (padding), but not too high (loss of confidence). But how high is too high? What agency heads do is to evaluate signals from the environment—last year's experience, legislative votes, executive policy statements, actions of clientele groups, reports from the field—and come up with an asking price somewhat higher than they expect to get.[35] In Michigan cities, for example, city managers sound out councilmen to determine what will go or get by in their budgets.[36] Departments and local authorities in Great Britain commonly make assessments "of how much spending is likely to be acceptable to the governing body."[37] After first determining what the mayor, finance director, councilmen, and other key participants will "die for," together with other projects which "cannot be moved," the men in charge of Philadelphia's capital budget let other projects by if they seem sound and if the request is not too far out of line.[38]

The Bureau of the Budget in the United States takes on the assigned role of helping the president realize his goals when it can discover what they are supposed to be. This role is performed with a cutting bias, however, simply because the agencies normally push so hard in asking for funds. The bureau helps the president by making his preferences more widely known throughout the executive branch so that those who would like to go along have a chance to find out what is required of them. Since Congress usually cuts the president's budget, Bureau figures tend to be the most the agencies can get, especially when the items are not of such paramount importance as to justify intensive scrutiny by Congress. Yet the power of the purse remains actively with Congress. If the Budget Bureau continually recommended figures which were blatantly disregarded by Congress, the agencies would soon learn to pay less and less attention to the president's budget. As a result, the Bureau follows consistent congressional action;[39] it can be shown empirically that Bureau recommendations tend to follow congressional actions over a large number of cases.

---

[32]Scott, Robert E., "Budget Making in Mexico," *Inter-American Economic Affairs* (1955) 9:3–20.

[33]Brittain.

[34]Royal Institute, p. 245.

[35]Wildavsky, pp. 21–32.

[36]Kressbach, p. 5.

[37]Royal Institute, p. 57.

[38]Brown and Gilbert, pp. 71–88.

[39]Wildavsky, pp. 4–42.

In deciding how much money to recommend for specific purposes, the House Appropriations Committee breaks down into large autonomous subcommittees in which the norm of reciprocity is carefully followed.[40] Specialization is carried further as subcommittee members develop limited areas of competence and jurisdiction. Budgeting is both incremental and fragmented as the committees deal with adjustments to the historical base of each agency. Sequential decision making is the rule as problems are first attacked in the jurisdiction in which they appear and then followed step-by-step as they manifest themselves elsewhere.[41] The subcommittee members treat budgeting as a process of making marginal monetary adjustments to existing programs, rather than as a mechanism for reconsidering basic policy choices every year.[42] Fragmentation and specialization are further increased through the appeals functions of the Senate Appropriations Committee, which deals with what has become (through House action) a fragment of a fragment. When the actions of subcommittees conflict, coordination may be achieved by repeated attacks on the problem or through reference to the House and Senate as a whole when the appropriations committees go beyond the informal zone of indifference set up by the more intense preferences of the membership. When one thinks of all the participants who are continually engaged in taking others into account, it is clear that a great many adjustments are made in the light of what others are likely to do.

Budgetary Strategies

Having decided how much to ask for, agencies engage in strategic planning to secure their budgetary goals. Strategies are the links between the goals of the agencies and their perceptions of the kinds of actions which their political environment will make efficacious. Budget officers in the U.S. national government uniformly believe that being a good politician—cultivating an active clientele, developing the confidence of other officials (particularly of the appropriations subcommittees), and using skill in following strategies that exploit opportunities—is more important in obtaining funds than demonstration of efficiency. Agencies seek to cultivate a clientele that will help them to expand and that will express satisfaction to other public officials. Top agency officials soon come to learn that the appropriations committees are very powerful; their recommendations are accepted approximately 90 per cent of the time.[43] Since budgetary calculations are so complex, the legislators must take a good deal on faith. Hence their demand that agency budget officers demonstrate a high degree of integrity. If the appropriations committees believe that they have been misled, they can do grave damage to the career of the offending budgeting officer and to the prospects of the agency he represents. While doing a decent job may be a necessary condition for success, the importance of clientele and confidence are so great that all agencies employ these strategies.[44]

In addition to these ubiquitous strategies there are contingent strategies which depend upon time, circumstance, and place. In defending the base, for example, cuts may be made in the most popular programs so that a public outcry results in restoration of the funds. The base may be increased within existing programs by shifting funds between categories.[45] Substantial additions to the base may come about through proposing new programs to meet crises and through campaigns involving large doses of advertising and salesmanship.[46] The dependence of these strategies on the incremental, increase-de-

[40]Fenno.

[41]Wildavsky, pp. 56–64.

[42]Fenno.

[43]Fenno.

[44]Wildavsky, pp. 65–98.

[45]Kressbach, p. 51; Stourm, p. 348.

[46]Wildavsky, pp. 101–123.

crease type of budgetary calculation is evident. By helping determine the ways in which programs are perceived and evaluated, the forms of budgetary presentation may assume considerable importance.

One major strategy deserves separate attention—the division of expenditures into capital and expense budgets. In practice, as Mosher says, "The Capital budget is a catalogue of prospective budgets for which money may be borrowed. . . ."[47] The attempted distinction between capital assets with future returns and ordinary expenditures soon breaks down under the pressure of avoiding tax increases or the appearance of deficits by borrowing for items designated in the capital budget.[48] The ideological emphasis on the size and growth of the deficit in the United States makes it likely that the introduction of a capital budget would permit substantially greater expenditures as apparent deficits become converted into formal surpluses.

Organizations wish to maintain themselves in their environment. For governmental agencies this can be taken to mean maintenance of political support from clientele groups and other governmental participants. We expect that policies are chosen not only because of any intrinsic merit but also because they add to, or at least do not seriously detract from, the necessary political support. The heads of agencies can expect to lose internal control, to be fired, to see their policies overturned, or even to find their organization dismembered if their recommendations are continually disapproved. They therefore seek to maintain a reasonable record of success (to guard their professional reputation, as Richard Neustadt puts it) in order to maintain the confidence of the key people in and out of their agency. Thus, they are compelled to

consider the probable actions of others differently situated who have a say in determining their income. These notions may be tested by observing how agency requests vary with the treatment they receive from the Budget Bureau and Congress.

Suppose that we wish to explain the level of appropriations which agencies request of Congress through the Bureau of the Budget and the amounts which Congress provides through appropriations laws. The goals of the participants may be conceived of as constraints which are represented by the role orientations adopted by members of the appropriations committees and by top agency officials. Moreover, we know that budgetary calculations are incremental. Thus, it becomes possible to create in symbolic form, as linear, stochastic differences equations, a series of simple decision rules embodying the relationships we expect to find. Given the availability of appropriations laws and of Budget Bureau requests for individual agencies, the decision rules can be tested for their fit in accommodating the times series comprising fifteen or twenty years' figures.

In the simplest form, for example, a decision rule might be that the funds requested by an agency in a particular year are a direct function of its appropriation in the previous years up to a normally distributed random error. A second decision rule might make allowance for the difference between what the agency asked for and actually received from Congress in the previous year. Should an agency decide to pad its request to make up for a cut, should it decide to insist on the worth of its programs despite congressional action—strategies such as these can be represented as separate decision rules. Davis, Dempster, and Wildavsky[49] are now able to show that basic parts of the federal budgetary process can be precisely described by a small number of relatively simple decision rules.

[47]Mosher, Frederick C., "Fiscal Planning and Budgeting in New York City" in New York State—New York City Fiscal Relations Committee, *A Report to the Governor of the State of New York and the Mayor of the City of New York* (New York: The Committee, 1956), p. 69.

[48]Burkhead, pp. 182ff; Mosher, p. 70; Sundelson, Jacob W., *Budgetary Methods in National and State Governments* (Albany: Lyon, 1938), pp. 146–198.

[49]Davis, Otto, M. A. H. Dempster, and Aaron Wildavsky, A Theory of the Budgetary Process, unpublished manuscript, 1966.

Budgets of Firms

Treatment of budgets as political instruments is justified not only in governmental activities but also in industrial enterprises. A more political phenomenon than budgeting in Soviet industrial firms has not been invented. Rewards to managers depend on meeting production quotas assigned in economic plans. But the supplies, skilled labor, and financial resources are often lacking. The first consequence is that the quota is not set from above but becomes the subject of bargaining as the managers seek to convince the ministries that quotas should be as low as possible. The managers find it prudent not to exceed their quota hugely, for in that case next year's quota will be raised beyond attainment. The second consequence is that production is not rationalized to yield the greatest output at the lowest cost but is geared instead to meeting specific incentives. Heavy nails, for example, are overproduced because quotas are figured by weight. Maintenance may be slighted in favor of huge effort for a short period in order to meet the quota. Funds are hidden in order to provide slack that can be used to pay "pushers" to expedite the arrival of supplies. The list of essentially deceitful practices to give the appearance of fulfilling the quota is seemingly endless: producing the wrong assortment of products, transferring current costs to capital accounts, shuffling accounts to pay for one item with funds designated for another, declaring unfinished goods finished, lowering the quality of goods, and so on.[50] The point is that the budgetary system arranges incentives so that managers cannot succeed with lawful practices. Communist China reveals the same pattern.[51] When similar incentives are set up in American industrial firms similar practices result, from running machines into the ground, to "bleeding the line,"

to meeting a monthly quota by doctoring the accounts.[52]

As in the Soviet Union, American firms often use budgets not to reflect or project reality but to drive managers and workers toward increased production. Indeed, some firms base their budgets on historical experience plus an added factor for increased performance.[53] Budgets are conceived of as forms of pressure on inherently lazy people so that (to paraphrase Mao Tse-tung) the more the pressure, the better the budget. Inevitably, managers and workers begin to perceive budgets as "perpetual needlers." In some cases this type of budget leads to discouragement because it is apparent that whatever the effort, the budget quota will be increased. Since accounting takes place by subunits in the firm, it is not surprising that fierce negotiations occur to assign costs among them. As a result, top officials find it necessary to engage in campaigns to sell budgets to the units. Otherwise, sabotage is likely.[54] While some attention has been given to human relations in budgeting[55] only Stedry[56] has attempted to explore the essential motivational problems of budgeting within a political, institutional framework. Yet without an understanding of the impact of different goals and incentive systems on human activity, reliable statements about the likely consequences of budget documents can hardly be made.

Intensive study of budgetary behavior has just begun. Despite the relative paucity of comparative data, patterns of behavior appear to be remarkably consistent across private and public organizations[57] and national and state boundaries. After the appearance of monographs on different budgetary systems in various environ-

[50]Berliner.

[51]Hsia, Ronald, *Economic Planning in Communist China* (New York: Institute of Pacific Relations, International Secretariat, 1955); Li, Chomin, *Economic Development of Communist China: An Appraisal of the First Five Years of Industrialization* (Berkeley: University of California Press, 1959).

[52]Jasinsky, Frank, "Use and Misuse of Efficiency Controls," *Harvard Business Review,* 34 (1956) no. 4:107.

[53]Axelson, Charles F., "What Makes Budgeting So Obnoxious?" *Business Budgeting,* 11 (1963), no. 5:22–27.

[54]Sord and Welsch, pp. 140–150.

[55]Bebling, Arnold A., "A Look at Budgets and People," *Business Budgeting,* 10 (1961), no. 2:16.

[56]Stedry, Andrew C., *Budget Control and Cost Behavior* (Englewood Cliffs, N.J.: Prentice-Hall, 1960).

[57]Wildavsky.

ments, it should be possible to create a small number of budgetary models specifying the elements of the organization coalition, the distribution of roles among the principal actors, the most prevalent aids to calculation, the strategies which appear as responses to types of incentives, and the outcomes to be expected in terms of amounts requested and received. Computer simulation may be used to test the effect of shocks to the budgetary systems. The study of budgeting as a political phenomenon in an organizational context may then become a major aid in the comparative analysis of governmental policy.

CASE STUDY 12

Introduction

Wildavsky's essay offers several stimulating insights into how budgetary decisions are reached in the public sector. His essay unravels many of the political complexities of public budgetary goals, bargaining, and strategy. Wildavsky's thesis also emphasizes that budgetary decision making is a seamless web of choices concerned not only with fiscal aspects of allocating public monies but with the fabric of democratic society.

In recent years, however, the Wildavsky incremental model of budgeting has been challenged by some who argue that the 1980s—the era of fiscal austerity and cutbacks—have made *bottom-up* (or incremental) budgeting obsolete. Both Barry Bozeman and Jeffrey Straussman, for example, argue that the bottom-up budgetary process is based on assumptions that are no longer valid, like the importance of a stable "uncutable base" from which negotiations proceed for the next fiscal year; the prime importance of negotiating strategies to agencies developing the overall budget; the critical importance of a strong, growing economy; the importance of stable groups of players in the budget game that accept only their fair share of the budget increases; and finally, the importance of compartmentalized budget-making practices, in which one set of players does not invade another's territory as they formulate the overall budget that the Congress and the president ratify afterward.[1]

Instead, Bozeman and Straussman argue, in the 1980s we have entered *top-down* budget making, a far cry from the Wildavsky model: the base is now "cutable" because of the pressures of external economic reality; the president through the Office of Management and Budget (OMB) exerts strong, overall top-down control in formulating the executive budget (at the local level, from state governors or city mayors); the instability of external events, crises, and the general environment decisively shape public budgets from "the outside-in" rather than from the "inside-out," as the incrementalist model suggests; and the old notion of compartmentalizing budget making or keeping it in-house by dealing only with known players, with known strategies and trade offs, is no longer apparent.

Are budgets of the 1980s fashioned from the top-down or the bottom-up?

---

[1]Barry Bozeman and Jeffrey Straussman, "Shrinking Budgets and Shrinking Budgetary Theory," *Public Administration Review,* 42 (Nov./Dec. 1982), pp. 509–515.

In the following case study by Irene S. Rubin, a political scientist at Northern Illinois University, we find out what happens inside one public agency, The Employment and Training Administration (ETA), when it sustains massive budget cuts in its principal program, The Comprehensive Employment and Training Act (CETA), which it was responsible for administering. The author carefully outlines the background of this federal program, sources of its declining political support, methods the Reagan administration used to cut its budget, responses of the agency to these cutbacks, and results of these reductions in monies and personnel for the overall program management and performance.

As you read this case, think about the following questions:

Does this case support Wildavsky's incremental or "bottom-up" budgetary concept? Or does it support Bozeman and Straussman's non-incremental "top-down" style of budget making? Which concept do you believe best describes current budgetary practices?

How did the president and OMB develop their strategies to inflict massive cuts in the CETA program? Why did Congress support these cuts? How did the agency (ETA) respond, and why were its defensive strategies largely ineffective? What "gamesmanship strategies" did they use to defend the Agency? Could their defenses have been devised any better, in your opinion?

What impact(s) did these cuts have on the CETA program, its management, its performance, and service delivery? How did the agency cope in surprisingly innovative ways with these reductions? Why did the high degree of uncertainty make "coping" so difficult for ETA?

What is your overall assessment of how ETA handled these cutbacks? Where might the agency have improved on its methods of handling the personnel and budgetary reductions?

IRENE S. RUBIN

The Employment and Training Administration
Budget Cuts by the President and Congress

The Employment and Training Administration (ETA), a major agency in the Department of Labor, was responsible for a number of programs, including the Comprehensive Employment and Training Act (CETA), unemployment insurance, employment services (job placement), veterans employment programs and apprentice-ship training. The ETA had a marked social service bias. Many of its programs were targeted to the poor; training, counseling, and job placement were seen as a way of reducing poverty. The programs were also designed to aid the unemployed. For example, Public Service Employment, a CETA program, provided the unemployed with work in public sector organizations. Other programs in CETA were designed to help particular classes of hard-to-employ people, such as housewives suddenly thrust into the marketplace, or youths from central cities who lacked skills and had no experience to offer employers.

The ETA generally did not provide services directly to the public but funded programs that were staffed by other levels of government. For example, the employment service is funded by the federal government but run by the state governments. CETA was a block grant program awarded to "prime sponsors" who were usually city governments or consortia of local governments. The prime sponsors contracted with private industry for training the unemployed and often ran Public Service Employment programs themselves.

The CETA program expanded rapidly for several years, increasing much faster in program dollars than in staff at headquarters. Given the complexity of the ETA's mission, the range of programs offered, the complexity of the arrangements for service delivery, and the relatively small staff to supervise all this activity, it is not surprising that the ETA gained a reputation in some quarters for being poorly managed and "flying by the seat of its pants."[1]

During the Reagan administration, the Employment and Training Administration experienced massive program cuts as well as extensive cuts in its administrative budget. The CETA program was due to expire in 1982, and though it seemed likely that some kind of program would be authorized to take its place, until the new legislation was passed, it was unclear how big the replacement program would be, how much administrative burden it would place on the central office, and how many people would be required to run it.

The ETA thus wrestled with both budget cuts and uncertainty. However, . . . the ETA was not confronted by a gap between the administration's intent and congressional action or inaction. Congress sided with the administration and sharply curtailed the ETA's budget. Later, Congress passed a reauthorization of the CETA program (the new bill was called the Job Training Partnership Act) that addressed many of the administration's concerns. The ETA case, then, is one in which the president both cut the agency and redesigned programs with the consent of Congress. . . .

Background

Agency Loss of Political Support

The Employment and Training Administration experienced a loss of political support over several years that led to continuous erosion of personnel levels and eventual budget reductions. In the mid 1970s there were a few well-publicized cases in which local officials ignored CETA regulations, creating scandals. These scandals created the impression that the agency was poorly managed.

For example, one involved the widespread practice in which city officials abused the Public Service Employment funds. Some cities reportedly fired their own employees to reduce payroll costs and then hired them back under grant funds as PSE employees because they were unemployed.[2] This practice was called "fiscal substitution." In essence, cities were substituting grant money for regular revenue.

There was also considerable publicity about improper expenditures by CETA sponsors and subcontractors. The result was several hundred million dollars of audit exceptions. An audit exception is a query by an auditor. It may mean that some data are unclear, a problem easily resolved, or it may indicate underlying and systematic management problems. Regardless of how many of the audit exceptions were cleared away, the number of dollars involved gave the impression of gross mismanagement.

In 1978, Congress acted to amend the CETA authorization act in an effort to reduce the number of abuses. The amendments were intended

[1]Robert Hunter, "Labor," in *Mandate for Leadership,* ed. Charles L. Heatherly (Washington: Heritage Foundation, 1981), p. 476.

[2]See, for example, "Detroit Allowed Funding for Hiring," *New York Times,* 13 April 1976, p. 11, which describes the Detroit case. The Department of Labor reportedly allowed Detroit to rehire laid-off employees, although the city violated regulations.

to "increase its targeting toward the poor, eliminate fiscal substitution by recipient jurisdictions, increase the amount of emphasis on transition to unsubsidized jobs, and reduce the levels of fraud and abuse."[3]

These improvements did not raise the political support levels of the agency, however, especially with respect to Public Service Employment. The new restrictions were adopted by local governments, but they made the program much less attractive to local officials. As a result, the program lost the support of much of its urban clientele. In fact, when Congress gradually cut back the program's funding, there was little protest. The coup de grâce in the president's March 1981 proposed budget reductions was only the culmination of a decline in support and funding of several years' duration.

The Reagan administration opposed CETA on ideological grounds, arguing that training should be separated from any kind of support payment. The combination of work training and payment made the program too much like a welfare program, and the public service aspect of the program was creating meaningless and dead-end jobs for PSE trainees, who were being trained for permanent jobs in the public sector that they might never fill, instead of jobs in the private sector. Finally, the politically conservative Heritage Foundation found the whole ETA badly run and recommended a total overhaul in administration:

> The Employment and Training Administration is currently one of the poorest managed, confused and directionless agencies in the government. The agency pursues three sometimes contradictory missions—social, economic, and political—and constantly shifts direction in response to the changing whims of Congress. It is an agency that flies by the seat of its pants, and does even that poorly.

Major changes are required in the legislation that provides the agency its mandate; in the agency's administrative personnel (from top to bottom) and in its management techniques.[4]

Erosion of Personnel and Funding

Over time, the result of the loss of political support was a loss of personnel positions and funding, eventuating in the loss of programs in ETA. The reductions in personnel began in 1977, when the official staffing ceiling was at 3831 permanent positions. By 1979, this had dropped to 3562. In 1980, the ceiling was down to 3185, and in 1981, there was an additional drop, to 3126. As of June of 1982, the agency-reported ceiling was 2750, while the official OMB ceiling for 1982 was 2557.[5]

Informants in the budget office at the ETA reported that these personnel reductions would continue in 1983 and 1984. They reported that the agency was expected to reduce another three hundred positions in 1983 or possibly spread out the drop over two years. The formal OMB-reported ceilings asked for a reduction of another three hundred positions in 1983 and an additional two hundred in 1984.

The continuing drop in personnel reflects both budget reductions and program changes. In the Omnibus Reconciliation Act of 1981, the Public Service Employees program was completely terminated, while other CETA programs were drastically cut back. Budget authority for CETA (budget authority is the legally mandated spending limit for the program) was reduced about 53 percent, and actual outlays for 1982 were reduced about 40 percent.[6]

[3]John William Ellwood, ed., *Reductions in U.S. Domestic Spending: How They Affect State and Local Government* (New Brunswick, N.J.: Transaction Books, 1982), p. 213. The authors cite the Congressional Budget Office, "An Analysis of President Reagan's Budget Revisions for Fiscal Year 1982," March 1981, pp. A-49.

[4]Hunter, "Labor," p. 476.

[5]The OMB-mandated personnel ceilings are taken from the U.S. Budget, appendix; the agency-reported ceilings are from personnel figures at ETA.

[6]These percentage reductions are computed by comparing 1982 authorizations and outlays with the Congressional Budget Office (CBO) estimates of how much it would cost in 1982 to provide the level of services provided in 1981. This calculation tends to make cuts look larger than if 1982 figures were just compared with 1981 figures, but comparisons based on "constant service levels" are more realistic and meaningful.

It was not long after the omnibus reconciliation of 1981 that the president asked for a second round of budget cuts for the 1982 budget. In September 1982 he asked for an additional 12 percent budget cut for all agencies. This cut was concentrated primarily in salaries and expenses; that is, there would be a reduction in the cost of administering federal programs rather than in the size of payments to individuals or to state and local governments. Along with the requested 12 percent budget cut, the president called for a reduction of seventy-five thousand civilian employees over a two-year period. It was clear that he expected much of his budget cut to result in personnel reductions and layoffs.

Congress approved almost all of the additional 12 percent cut that the president requested for the Employment and Training Administration. It cut the Employment Training program an additional 10 percent after the omnibus reconciliation. Further, the Congressional Budget Office (CBO) estimated that for the following fiscal years, 1983 and 1984, the funding outlays would continue to drop, assuming the program was reauthorized (which it was).[7]

Although the president's personnel reduction targets called for about 6–6.5 percent across-the-board personnel cuts, the Department of Labor was reportedly cut about 10 percent in personnel levels. The ETA initially took the heaviest brunt of the cuts, with early proposals for personnel reductions running as high as 38 percent, or about twelve hundred jobs. After extensive negotiation, the final reduction in force was reduced to about five hundred employees in the ETA, which was closer to a 15 percent reduction in staffing levels. Given the size of the budget cuts, these layoffs, as great as they were, were proportionally moderate.[8]

After all this budget struggle, the CETA program was reauthorized, as the Job Training Partnership Act. This new law solved some of the difficulties that the Heritage Foundation had pointed out in its evaluation of the CETA program. The new law decentralized much of the program control and oversight to the state governments as part of the president's overall decentralization strategy. The expectation was that as the state governments took control over the program, there would be less and less work at headquarters, and the size of the staff would continue to shrink.

The Sources of the Cuts

As the preceding account suggests, the ETA was cut back at several different times and in several different ways. On each occasion both the president and Congress played a role, although at each point one or the other may have been dominant. These relative roles can be illustrated by a more detailed examination of the sources of budget reductions in 1982.

The Omnibus Reconciliation

The major program cuts in the ETA occurred in the congressionally passed omnibus reconciliation. Although Congress cut the budget, the omnibus reconciliation was seen as the result of presidential policy. An assistant secretary for the Department of Labor described the origin of the ETA cutbacks in the following terms:

> There was a policy to terminate Employment and Training activities. It was a high-level decision, political, and made very early. Presumably, the decision flowed from the "man-

[7]For CBO estimates, see Ellwood, *Reductions in U.S. Domestic Spending*, p. 215. Using the previous year's actual appropriation as the basis for calculation, there was a 50 percent program funding reduction for CETA in 1982. See the U.S. Budget for 1983 and 1984, appendix.

[8]There was considerable pressure against the administration's proposal to cut more positions from the ETA because of evidence that the agency was already seriously understaffed and hence unable to monitor grantees adequately. For example, even the conservative Heritage Foundation reported in the spring of 1981 that the ETA might have been

cut back too far. The Human Resources Committee recommended overriding the president's recommendation in the spring of 1981, even before the president's second request for cuts, when reductions in ETA were expected to be considerably less severe than they eventually were. See Senate Committee on Appropriations, *Departments of Labor, Health and Human Services, Education and Human Services, Education and Related Agencies Appropriations, Fiscal Year 1982: Hearings*, 97th Cong., 1st sess., Part 1, 1981, p. 620.

date," if you want to talk of such things, of the 1980 elections.

The omnibus reconciliation of 1981 was described as originating with and being controlled by the administration:

It was a top-down process. [Budget Director] Stockman and OMB determined where, quickly, and I might say, efficiently. There was not a lot of appeal [from their decision]. Cabinet officers were in sync with the philosophy; it was not a normal policy review. It was almost done by fiat.

When asked to compare the roles of Congress and the president, the assistant secretary described how the reconciliation process was used to bypass the Department of Labor's traditional support in Congress:

The House struggled over the issues a little, but the president kept winning. The committee chair, Gus Hawkins, is a traditional, liberal L.A. Democrat. He could not bring himself and the committee to make the changes required by the budget resolution, and they got "rolled over," beaten. It was Gramm-Latta [the OMB-initiated Gramm-Latta amendment.] And Stockman negotiated with the appropriate coalitions.

We did not go through the process of legislative changes. If we had relied on that [process]—subcommittees, hearings, etc., [the drastic cuts and program changes] probably would not have happened. Liberal Democrats controlled the Education and Labor Committee [but they were bypassed].

One of the features of the budget process is that it forces action by Congress around the traditional budget process. The reconciliation bill [1981] made all kinds of changes that the traditional workings would not allow. It couldn't have been done as swiftly without the Budget Reform Act [1974] and the vehicle of reconciliation.

To summarize, the president and OMB dominated and directed the omnibus reconciliation of 1981. The "new" congressional budget process

(which was passed in 1974) allowed the president and OMB to bypass the traditional linkages between congressional committees and executive branch agencies.

The President's September Call for 12 Percent Reductions

The omnibus reconciliation in July 1981 was orchestrated by the president and the Office of Management and Budget, but it was executed by Congress. Theoretically, the president's September call for an additional 12 percent cut could have been handled in a similar way, but in fact the administration did not wait for Congress to act before it took action to implement the new round of cuts.

Considerably before Congress had taken final action on the 1982 budget, the ETA was told it would have to take the 12 percent cut. Because the cut was so large and because it was targeted to salaries and expenses (administrative costs), the ETA was forced to take immediate action to plan reductions in force. Since officials at the department level insisted that the ETA balance its budget, the proposed shortfall could not be ignored or even delayed. The agency was informed by departmental officials that it should accept the worst-case scenario for planning purposes. On 19 October 1981, before the battle between the president and Congress over the 1982 budget had been resolved, the assistant secretary for the ETA issued a general notice of anticipated reductions in force.[9]

The preparation for the reduction in force had to begin before Congress had acted on the budget because, first, Congress was passing continuing resolutions rather than a complete budget and, second, the agency needed to carry out the reduction in force in the first quarter of the year in order to save enough money. A reduction in force late in the fiscal year does not save very much money; firing an employee in the last month of the fiscal year would save only one month's salary. To save the same amount of money in the last month as would result from

[9]Memo to all national-office ETA employees from Albert Angrisani, assistant secretary of labor, "General Notice of Reduction in Force," 19 October 1981.

firing one person in the first month, twelve people would have to be fired.

Since preparations for a reduction in force take about three months and the effective date for the reduction was 31 December (the end of the first fiscal quarter), the preparation had to begin by early October. The agency was well along in implementing the president's budget request *before* Congress voted on that request.

Funding the Salary Increases

The third source of deficits for the 1982 fiscal year was the congressionally mandated salary increases. Congress voted during the continuing resolutions to allow salary increases for federal employees but did not include the cost of the increase in the continuing resolution. The result was that each agency had to decide whether it would fund the salary increase by further cutting the agency's expenditures (particularly personnel) or whether it would later request a supplemental appropriation from Congress to cover the increase. Congress had to act on each request separately and might grant it to some agencies and not to others.

If the ETA assumed that the administration would allow it to request a supplemental appropriation and that Congress would grant it, only to find out later in the fiscal year that these assumptions were wrong, the agency would have to find millions of dollars late in the year to cover the salary increases. Although, as noted, late reduction in force does not save much money, a furlough saves the same amount of money whenever it occurs, and everyone can participate in it. Thus if the agency had to save money late in the year, it would have to run a massive furlough.

Administrators at the ETA took the risk and asked for permission to apply for a supplemental appropriation. Officials at the departmental level approved the ETA's request. In case they did not get the supplemental appropriation, ETA officials planned a furlough, but this was cancelled just before it was to begin, when Congress granted the request.

The issue of the salary supplements involved both the administration and Congress, since the administration had to allow the agency to re-quest a supplemental appropriation and Congress had to grant the request. But the dominant role in this financial problem was played by Congress, which, fearing that the president would veto its continuing resolutions because of the total cost, passed a resolution calling for salary increases without including their cost in the resolution.

To summarize, the budget reductions were directed primarily by the administration rather than Congress, even though Congress did eventually approve the devastating budget cuts. Congress was responsible for only one of the three cuts that occurred in the 1982 budget, and that one occurred because the Congress was trying to resist the president's pressure to cut and feared a presidential veto. Later, the one cut that Congress initiated was reversed when the supplemental appropriation was granted. But although Congress did not generally direct or determine the cuts, neither did it oppose those made by the president. At least during the budget cycle for fiscal year 1982, the president had enough control over Congress to cut back the ETA's programs, budget, and personnel.

The President Versus the Agency

President Reagan and OMB Director David Stockman had little trouble getting Congress to go along with budget cuts for fiscal year 1982. And when Congress lagged behind the administration's schedule, the administration took action on its own. But how did the agency respond? Had the president taken sufficient control of the department to prevent a major rebellion? Was the ETA able to reach Congress or interest groups with a protest? Were any of the cuts overturned? Did the agency disobey any of the president's cutback directives?

The President's Control over the Agency

One way of judging the degree to which the president controlled the agency is to determine whether officials at the top policy-making levels of the department were presidential nominees and, if so, whether they followed the president's policy for cutting back the agency.

Both the secretary and the assistant secretary for the ETA, two key positions for the agency, were loyal to the president. There was no indication that the secretary opposed any of the cuts, and the assistant secretary carried out OMB's policies to the fullest extent possible. The assistant secretary for administration, however, was a holdover from the Carter administration and a career official. Thus, since President Reagan did not initially select all the assistant secretaries for the Department of Labor, his political control was not complete.

The assistant secretary for administration did leave office (voluntarily) after the initial cutback period, but while he was in the assistant secretary position, he helped to maintain norms of impartial (nonpolitical) administration of the department. He did not specifically oppose or resist the president's policies; rather, he consistently advocated positions that would keep the appearance of politics out of administration.

It is not clear that the president's initially incomplete control of the policy level of the Department of Labor harmed his effort to cut back the agency. The ETA was cut back successfully and avoided the appearance of using the reduction in force for political purposes.

A second way that the president can take control of an agency is to cause a reorganization in which those most responsive to his policies are promoted into a leadership group, while program loyalists are demoted from policy-making positions. Though the ETA is not an extreme example, it exhibited some elements of this pattern.

When the agency reorganized, it reduced the number of GS-14 positions and demoted the incumbents of those positions. Because a number of GS-15 positions had been eliminated during the reduction in force, the combined effect of the reduction in force and the reorganization was to reduce the number of middle-level managerial slots and hence the number of middle-level managers. Since GS-14s and 15s are high-level civil service positions that normally involve policy-making responsibilities, the outcome was to weaken the ability of program loyalists to determine policy. Circumstantial evidence suggests that this outcome might have been the result of a conscious decision, since the administration later informally announced a policy of reducing the number of middle-level managers.[10]

Regardless of how the purpose of the reorganization is interpreted, it is clear that an invisible line was drawn around the top policy-making group and that, by comparison with the Carter administration, contact between it and ordinary employees was reduced. The labor union which had participated in management decision making found itself outside the decision-making group and seldom consulted for advice. Other employees complained that the assistant secretary for the ETA seldom came to the building in which the ETA was located, and one speculated that the top administrators did not want to get to know them because that might make it more difficult to terminate their jobs.

To summarize, although the agency was not overwhelmingly politicized, and the reduction in force was not used to fire program loyalists or retain those more responsive to presidential policy initiatives, the president had a firm control over the top level of the Department of Labor and, in particular, over the assistant secretary who supervised the ETA. Decision making was concentrated in a policy-making elite at the top of the organization, and career civil servants who had had a role in decision making during the Carter years were excluded.

Given the level of administrative control over the agency, there was not an enormous amount the agency could do to protect itself against cuts. The ETA was not in a position to rouse its constituents to fight for threatened programs either

---

[10]"U.S. to Cut 40,000 Middle-Level Bosses" *Chicago Tribune*, 17 November 1983. The article quoted a White House spokesman to the effect that the Reagan administration planned to eliminate forty thousand middle-level management government jobs by forcing federal agencies to abolish or downgrade senior positions when they were vacated. The spokesman indicated the incumbents of those positions would not be demoted or fired but that the positions would be eliminated taken when they became vacant. Though the stated policy involved reduction by attrition, departmental officials could have been overzealous in carrying out this policy, or they could have received another, less formal communication to the effect that reductions in force or reorganizations could be used to force out incumbents.

within the administration or in Congress. CETA, and the Public Service Employment program in particular, did not have many friends inside or outside Congress. Its traditional supporters in Congress were outvoted and outmaneuvered by OMB and the president.

Though program administrators at the ETA sensed that their major avenues of response were cut off, they did not simply accept whatever cuts were assigned to them. The agency tried to delay or reverse the initial cuts in the spring of 1981, offering to meet a 2 percent cut by cutting back two programs that were highly popular on Capitol Hill. The hope was that Congress would reject the proposal, and the agency would escape that round of cuts.

One of these programs was the Veterans' Employment Service. The matter came up at Senate Budget Hearings, where the strategy was questioned and explained. Senator Burdick asked Secretary Donovan, "Why would the Department of Labor propose this reduction since Congress so strongly disagreed with this proposal two years ago, and in fact included language in the appropriations bill which mandated the Department of Labor to retain these positions?" Mr. Zuck, assistant secretary for administration, answered, "Obviously, if we were not faced with the need to make the budget reductions, that may not be the approach we would have taken, but every program in the department obviously was subject to being reviewed to determine whether or not some possible reductions could be made."[11]

In the end, the agency's strategy did not work. All it achieved was a short delay. Congress did reject the cut, as the agency intended, and the Office of Management and Budget restored the positions which the ETA had offered to cut. However, OMB did not restore the funding for those positions in the 1982 budget. In essence, it told the agency to take the cuts elsewhere.

Other than that effort, there were no reported attempts to avoid or reverse budget cuts.

[11]Senate Committee on Appropriations, *Departments of Labor, Health and Human Services, Education and Related Agencies Appropriations, Fiscal Year 1982: Hearings,* 97th Cong., 1st sess., 1981, Part 1, p. 555.

Managerial strategies focused on carrying out the required reduction in force in an equitable and cost-effective manner. In particular, administrators in the ETA sought to minimize the number of personnel separated through reduction in force. They also sought to minimize the damage done by the reduction by shifting people around and returning them to their previous positions, but all this was done without a hint of defiance or resistance.

Minimizing the Number of Personnel to Be Terminated

The response of a number of ETA career officials (civil servants) was to accept the cuts as either inevitable or necessary or both. Within that acceptance, however, was a belief that reductions in staffing levels should continue to be by attrition, as they had been since 1977. Reductions in force should be avoided, but if they could not, the number of people involved should be kept to a minimum.

Since departmental officials prevented the agency from running a dollar deficit, there was no possibility of spreading out the time for personnel reductions so that attrition could carry more of the burden of reducing the work force. One of the alternatives left to the agency was to reduce the nonpersonnel operating costs as much as possible.

Administrative costs were the major target of President Reagan's proposed 12 percent reductions in September of 1981. Since salaries and expenses are lumped together in the federal budget as administrative costs, a reduction in nonpersonnel administrative costs (operating expenses) would minimize the need to cut staff. These items included travel, printing, space rental, and other overhead items.

Cutting the operating budget presented a formidable task, one that challenged the managerial capacity of the agency. The cost of items like printing and rent had recently doubled, with no allowance from OMB for the increases in cost. In effect, OMB's action forced the agencies to cut their budgets in these operating lines by about 50 percent. On top of that, the ETA tried to squeeze additional savings to reduce the need for personnel cuts.

One budget official in the ETA described the process of putting together the salaries and expense budget for 1982. He said, "It was like a puzzle, with known quantities and estimates of unknown quantities to fit in. It was difficult because of the restrictions on the agency." He explained that the nonpersonal service items in the salaries and expense budget were pared "to reduce the number of people to be RIFfed." Then once the number of people who had to be separated was established, the costs for the reduction in force had to be estimated, and further cuts had to be made to produce enough funds to carry out the reduction.

In addition to trying to squeeze more money out of the expense budget, agency officials tried to minimize the number of layoffs by requesting supplemental appropriations from Congress. As suggested earlier, this strategy required the cooperation of the assistant secretary for the ETA, who eventually endorsed it. The Office of Management and Budget sent a signal of possible support for a smaller reduction in force. The assistant secretary accepted this signal as an indicator of the administration's policy and went along with the ETA's requests for supplemental appropriations. The planned number of jobs to be eliminated was thereby reduced from twelve hundred to five hundred.

The signal sent by OMB was a reduction in the size of the drop in personnel ceilings for the ETA. In October 1981, OMB issued the new personnel ceilings for ETA, at the level of 2750 positions. That was a drop of only 500 positions. The budget cuts required a drop of 1200 positions. Normally, if budget cuts are greater than ceiling reductions, the cuts determine the size of the reduction in force. The amount of money available to pay for salaries is a limiting factor. In this case, however, the ETA chose to use the ceiling level for a guide instead of the budget cut. The reasoning was that the smaller-than-expected ceiling reduction indicated that OMB supported a smaller reduction in force and that it might support ETA's request for supplemental funds. This argument was accepted by the assistant secretary. Why OMB relented on the personnel ceiling was never explained.

The ETA put in two requests for supplemental appropriations, one to cover the salary increase, one to reduce the deficits resulting from the higher staffing ceiling. Between the two supplemental requests, the ETA asked Congress for about $14 million. If Congress did not come through for the agency, the shortfall would require thirty–forty days of furlough. The impact would be a substantial salary reduction for all employees, to avoid terminating the employment of an additional seven hundred employees.

For many months the agency did not hear from Congress on its requests. In April and May of 1982, furlough notices were sent to employees. Congress did pass the supplemental appropriations in time to prevent the furloughs, however. To this extent, then, the ETA strategy was successful.

Keeping the Reductions in Force Nonpolitical

The career officials at the ETA, in cooperation with the assistant secretary for administration, strove to keep the reduction in force free from political manipulation. The ETA administration succeeded in running a neutral RIF, by the rules, but it is not clear whether the president and his appointees were trying to use the RIF politically. Hence it is not clear how much defiance of the administration was involved in these tactics.

In order to understand what the agency did to prevent politicization of the reduction-in-force regulations, the reader needs to know a bit about how the regulations can be used for political or personal purposes. The regulations that were in effect until the fall of 1983 left much room for administrative discretion. (The changes introduced in the fall of 1983 have only added to that discretion.)

For example, administrators could hold out some positions from the reduction in force, not allowing affected employees to bump into them or retreat into them. Those employees might then be laid off. After the reduction in force, the positions which were held out could be filled by selecting favorites in the organization or by recruiting from the outside.

A second technique—one not formally advocated by the Office of Personnel Management, but not strictly illegal—was to separate and demote more people than necessary based on finances and then after the reduction in force to repromote or rehire those that were favorites.

A third technique was to define the competitive levels (the groups of people with similar skills) narrowly, so that there were only one or two or three people in a given competitive level. When that happened, if a position was eliminated, the administrator could be fairly certain who in that competitive level would be affected and who would lose their jobs. If competitive levels were broad, then bumping was likely to be extensive, and predicting the impacts on individuals could be difficult, if not impossible.

A related technique was to run practice sessions, or dry runs, of the reduction in force. In this technique, managers made recommendations for the original positions to be eliminated and then watched for the outcomes of the simulations to see who would finally be separated from employment. If managers did not like the outcomes, they could choose a different "seed," or position, to eliminate and see who would be affected by the resulting chain of bumping and retreating.

The great discretion allowed by the rules required the secretaries of the departments to specify how decisions ought to be made. In the Department of Labor, the assistant secretary for administration drew up a list of rules for running the reduction in force, many of which were designed to prevent the kind of tactics mentioned above.[12] The assistant secretary set up an appeals procedures within the Department of Labor on whether the RIF was run according to the regulations. He received no procedural appeals from the ETA.

It is also clear that the ETA had no intention of overfiring and then hiring back. Much of its goal in designing the reduction in force was to reduce the number of people involved. The agency separated many fewer people than initially indicated by budget constraints. Moreover, managers anticipated further reductions in staffing over the next two years, making it difficult to hire anyone back.

Nevertheless there were some accusations

that the discretion was abused. The unions complained about the practice of running reductions in force on a trial basis, but agency managers argued that the trial runs very seldom led to any changes, because managers were usually not convinced that choosing another "seed" would produce a better outcome. Managers reported that they used the technique to prevent employees with absolutely indispensable skills from being separated from employment. Employees did not seem to feel that the criteria for selection of individuals to lay off were political; even the union did not charge that the choice of whom to separate had been based on political loyalties.

A second area in which questions were raised about the way discretion was used was in the merit evaluations. Civil service procedures allowed four years of seniority to be granted for outstanding performance ratings. Beginning in 1980, the top-level managers were to be rated in performance, while other employees could be evaluated if the agency wished. The system was implemented in 1981, and the evaluations of senior staff were completed just before the reduction in force. The rest of the employees were not evaluated before the RIF (because they had not been covered by the system for ninety days) and so had no possibility of receiving additional seniority.

The proximity between the performance evaluations and the RIFs put enormous pressure on managers to use the evaluations to protect selected employees from the danger of RIF. A much larger number of people were in fact judged outstanding in 1981 under the new system than in 1980 under the old system.[13] This change suggested some manipulation of the system.

In response to a wave of union protest, the evaluations were reviewed by support staff, office directors, and the assistant secretary and pronounced generally defensible. Reportedly, the evaluation system was less abused in the ETA than in sister agencies.

Not only were the merit evaluations sustained on review, but analysis of high ratings

[12]Memo for agency heads from Alfred Zuck, assistant secretary for administration and management, "Reduction-in-Force Decisions," 4 November 1981.

[13]The numbers involved were provided to me by the union local at ETA.

shows that they did not reflect attempts to protect some individuals so much as they reflected rater bias. Some bosses simply gave higher ratings to all their employees than others did. There was great variation from office to office. This is a weakness in the evaluation system and does not reflect a political use of the reduction-in-force procedures.

To summarize, presidential control over the ETA was substantial. The agency had little interest-group support to manipulate and was unable to reverse major cuts or program changes. The ETA tried a classic budget maneuver with Congress, offering programs to satisfy a budget cut that Congress would not accept, but the effort backfired when OMB restored the positions but not the funding in the 1982 budget. Thwarted in external strategies, the agency focused on reducing the size and maintaining the political neutrality of the reduction in force, tactics the administration accepted.

Though the Office of Management and Budget backed off from its worst-case scenario and allowed the ETA to ask for supplemental appropriations from Congress, the administration enhanced its control over the agency. Many of the agency's middle-level managerial positions were eliminated during the RIF and in the reorganization that followed. This action may have been part of a general strategy to create a politically loyal cadre at the top of the department and to remove program loyalists from policy-making positions.

Cutbacks and Management

The entire cutback process, including budget cuts, reductions in force, and reorganization, imposed new managerial complexity on the agency, absorbed time and attention, and lowered morale. Some of the managerial impacts were temporary, while others were longer lasting.

Budget Cuts

The budget cuts affected not just the programs in the states and cities but also the management of the agency itself. The uncertainty imposed by

the president's budget battle with Congress was reflected in the budgetary process at the ETA. The president's targeting of administrative costs guaranteed that internal agency management would be affected. In addition to difficulties in the budgetary process created by uncertainty and reductions in force, the budget cuts created bottlenecks.

The uncertainty in the congressional budget process combined with the financial complexity of running a reduction in force to create a chaotic situation in the budget office. RIFs are financially complex because it is difficult to estimate both savings and expenses.

One budget officer at the ETA described the budget process as it was supposed to work and as it actually occurred in the fall of 1981:

> We normally prepare a budget estimate in August. The salaries and expenditure budget depend on the decisions of the assistant secretary, who makes decisions on staffing and on program areas. [Given that we had no decisions from the assistant secretary] we could not do anything. It should take four–five weeks to do a salaries and expense budget. We complete it, and it is submitted for departmental review, and then it goes to OMB. We get it back at the end of September. We change it, to reconcile it [with comments received] and print it for the president's budget in January. [Last year] we did a budget each month practically—one in August, one in September, one in October, and one in December. All told, there were five or more revisions of the budget. Probably all agencies did the same thing.

The fact that the salaries and expense budget changed so many times understates the impact of uncertainty, because each budget was treated as a puzzle, with some knowns from which the unknowns had to be deduced. When the size of the budget cut was announced, the budget officers had to decide where the money was to come from. They first cut the nonpersonnel lines, as far as they could, to determine how much they would have to save by reductions in force and/or furloughs. They then estimated the number of positions that would have to be cut to yield the necessary dollar savings. Then the costs of the RIFs had to be estimated by figuring severance payments, lump sum payments for unused leave, and expected unemployment payments. That amount had to be made up by more separations or by furloughs, in a repeated process.

The budget process had to be carried out in August after the omnibus reconciliation, when the first budget figure for cuts was "known," and then had to be repeated in September, after the president's request for an additional 12 percent cut. These were the figures that led to estimates that over twelve hundred people would be laid off. Then OMB reduced the personnel ceiling by five hundred, and five hundred became the operating number for position reductions. Estimates from savings from a reduction in force of this size had to be made in order to come up with the appropriate figures for a request to Congress for a supplemental appropriation and to estimate the size of the furlough if Congress did not approve the request. Uncertainty about the supplemental appropriations lasted into July of 1982.

In addition to affecting the budget process, the cuts also affected routine administration. Because of the desire to squeeze every possible cent out of the nonpersonnel budget items, many routine operating expenditures were severely reduced. The agency lost two floors of space, which caused employees to move all over the remaining floors. The amount of chaos is not hard to imagine, as files were temporarily inaccessible and telephone numbers changed quickly, with no provision for forwarding calls. It became difficult to know who was employed, let alone how to reach them.

Travel was cut back to the point of making it difficult to monitor what was occurring in the field. The travel constraints also affected morale. Employees were not only unable to carry out their normal responsibilities, but they were trapped in Washington, in the middle of reductions in force, watching their programs and agency shrink and, in some cases, disappear. As soon as possible after the reduction in force, the freeze on travel was lifted in an effort to improve morale, but other cost constraints remained in place.

Another item that was cut that had implica-

tions for management was the incentive system for outstanding performance. The incentive system was intended to identify outstanding workers and gave them a financial bonus. When money to fund the system was withdrawn to help limit the size of the reduction in force, the effect was to substitute for a positive incentive system a negative one based on the fear of job loss.

Reductions in Force and Reorganization

The managerial problems caused by budget cuts were as nothing compared with the problems introduced by the reductions in force. Each phase of a reduction—the preparation, implementation, and recovery—introduces its own managerial difficulties.

The preparation of a reduction in force is an extremely time-consuming task. It normally takes about three months of work by the entire personnel office, plus considerable time on the part of the office managers. The office directors must review the position descriptions for every position in their offices in order to match people to jobs. Employees have to update their work histories to demonstrate what jobs they had done and what work they can do.

The personnel office has to draw up competitive levels—that is, clusters of jobs with similar skills—and has to prepare retention registers, which list employees according to their rights to claim available jobs. When the office directors pick the initial positions to eliminate, the personnel office must prepare individual letters to affected employees, telling them whether they have been separated from employment or whether they are eligible for another position. That means that for each affected person a total search must be made of other jobs for which the person is eligible.

The letters informing employees that they have been separated include calculations of severance benefits and lump sum payments. When the RIF is actually administered, many of the letters must be amended. Sometimes amendments are required because of mistakes, but more often changes occur because new positions come open or people who have been offered alternative jobs refuse them. Thus the personnel office must be able to calculate retention rights and severance benefits immediately, as new people are affected during the reduction in force.

Besides the overwhelming mechanics of a reduction in force, there are other tasks associated with the preparation for it. For example, as already mentioned, as the ETA managers decided to do trial runs, to see who would be affected in the end if a particular position was eliminated. Also managers had to be trained in how to inform employees of their rights and how to deliver the reduction-in-force letters. The employees themselves were trained in the RIF process so that they would know what was happening, what the rules were, and what the managers could and could not do for them.

In addition to the normal activities associated with the management and mechanics of RIF, the procedure was made more complex by the changing size of the planned reduction. The choice of twelve hundred positions to eliminate had already been determined and the people involved decided on when the reduction to five hundred was announced; thus the agency had to prepare the reduction in force again with fewer positions. The agency contract with the union specified that the union would be informed two months in advance of a reduction as to the job series and location of cuts, which put additional time pressure on the already hasty RIF.

The ETA official in charge of running the reduction in force described the process that went on:

I called the office managers in and explained to them the need for speed, and asked them how to allocate the position reductions. There was some turf protecting and fussing. They recommended that I just prorate the cuts. I went along. Some of the managers opposed my decision. My boss [the assistant secretary of ETA] said a few offices should be protected. There should be lesser cuts in unemployment compensation and some national program accounts. I didn't agree, but . . . the rest was across the board. Twelve hundred positions. By December 31.

As soon as the RIF for twelve hundred was prepared, the five hundred figure was accepted, and the reduction in the number of positions to be eliminated was prorated. The official in charge of the RIFs described this phase:

Quick! Back to the drawing board. Prorate the reductions. Then share the information with the unions. And then put out the RIF notices. There was no time to fuss around. There was *tremendous stress.* Seven hundred people's jobs. Keep them, or drop them. [Seven hundred was the difference in size between the first estimated reduction in force and the second and actual RIF.]

Because the agency had focused on reducing the number of employees to be affected by the reduction and tried to run a RIF that conformed to the letter and intent of the civil service regulations, little attention was paid to trying to rig the reduction to minimize its impact on program management. As a result, employees were bumped all over the organization, and nearly every office was affected in some way. Old work groups were broken up, and new people unfamiliar with the work were bumped in.

Though considerable attention was given to the technical qualifications of employees for their new jobs, there was no attempt to match jobs to personalities. Thus some programs lost the people who were necessary to get programs started, and even though they were sometimes replaced, the new people could not necessarily carry out the project. For example, office automation was halted after word processing equipment had been purchased, because the person who had been responsible for getting employees to adopt word processing had been transferred, and the replacement reportedly did not have either the personality or the skills to sell a new technology.

Another aspect of the RIF implementation that affected the agency management had to do with the seniority of employees. Because the agency had been cutting back personnel levels since 1977, there were few employees with low seniority. That meant that employees with many years' experience in the agency were likely to be separated from employment because there was no one below them to bump. For those who did bump, especially for those who were able to retreat to former positions, the demotions tended to be very severe. The result was that managers were sometimes demoted to clerical positions while maintaining their old salary. The effect on both morale and productivity was dramatic and negative, while savings were minimal. (According to the RIF rules then in effect, the salary stayed with an official who was downgraded in a reduction in force for a period of two years.) The greater the demotion, the greater the loss of productivity, as highly trained, highly paid employees did work that less experienced, less well-paid employees could have done.

Because the RIF had been run with more attention to political neutrality and position preservation and less attention to managerial damage, the initial outcome was that people were scattered all over the organization, assignments were interrupted, and people were working in jobs well below their skill levels. Estimates were that between one hundred and fifty-two hundred people in the central office were shifted to new jobs and new supervisors. Very few offices were untouched. As a result, the activity level during the recovery period was almost as intense as in the period before the RIF.

There are a number of ways of recovering from this chaos, some formal, some less formal. Two bosses can swap employees back to their old positions, or an employee can be reassigned to another job in the same unit in which he is currently working. Employees can be detailed or formally loaned to another unit, usually to the unit they worked in before the reduction in force. The purpose of all the shifting around is to reassemble work teams to finish projects that were interrupted or to regain someone whose skills or knowledge was deemed crucial to the unit.

Not only may people be shifted back to their old positions, but those who were demoted can be repromoted in one of two ways. If the position they have been demoted to is part of a career ladder, they can be immediately promoted up the top of that ladder by their new supervisor. Or if a position opens up between the new low position and the old higher one, the demoted person may compete for the new opening. There

is a requirement that demoted employees be considered for these positions, but there is no requirement that they be hired for them. A demoted person has a stronger right of consideration if a vacancy occurs at the level he or she occupied before the reduction in force.

At the ETA, the recovery period began immediately after the RIF, when the freeze on reassignments was lifted. People were traded "like baseball cards." "We traded supervisors, secretaries, etc." Sometimes "you got a turkey" bumped into your office, but "you could not get rid of those, even two for one." "There was some detailing." "One way to accommodate to the RIF was to get people back. Most of the high performers are [now] where they want to be." "We pushed here and there, exchanged lists at all hours of the day." The personnel office reported that there had been between thirty and forty repromotions between January and August of 1982 out of about two hundred demotions.

The personnel office director described the recovery phase in detail:

> The RIF was ETA-wide. The agency had no control over who moved from office to office. Some people may have been key—two managers would negotiate for Mr. X; the result could be a reassignment, temporarily or permanently. Some were detailed. Managers did their own swaps. As long as the two people being swapped are at the same grade level, it's O.K. After the RIF, we could go back to business as usual. There were between fifteen and twenty-five reassignments after the RIF. There were between fifty and seventy-five details, for a period of thirty, sixty or ninety days, as a transition device. Repromotions were allowed beginning three weeks after the RIF; there have been twenty-eight of them so far in the national office [as of July 1982].

Agency Impacts

Although the personnel director reported that the agency returned to business as usual after the RIF, in several ways the return was not immediate. For example, the freeze on promotions was maintained after the RIF, with the exception of repromotions. And there were problems of managing an operation with people only minimally familiar with their jobs. The recovery period, with all the swapping of personnel, was proceeding well when the reorganization began, which was followed by a second RIF and a round of demotions. The chaos was thus kept going for several more months.

One informant described the continuing chaos after the reduction in force:

Clearly there is a continuing impact of the shifting. That doesn't seem to stop. The RIF was over in December, but in April we had a headquarters reorganization. We also lost two floors of space and crowded everyone into the remaining space. We tried to fit the reorganization that was coming, but people couldn't report to their new supervisors. It's about done now. . . . Our boss likes to juggle the organization around a little. It's perceived as totally unorganized, and it's disruptive.

Another factor which slowed down the recovery was that repromotion of all demoted personnel dragged after a brisk start. The problem was that so many GS-14 and 15 positions had been eliminated during the RIF and reorganization that there were not enough positions remaining at that level to accommodate all the demoted employees.

Moreover, the threat of further RIFs and demotions remained, since the agency was basically watching over the transition to block grants run by the states. The agency was gradually reducing its own workload. Thus employees were never able to completely recover from the shock of budget cuts and reductions in force. Although the agency was able to overcome much of the immediate negative impact, it took many months. Eight months after the RIF and some three or four months after the reorganization, several managers expressed the view that the agency had sufficiently recovered to take on a new mission, if the RIF and reorganization did not become recurring events.

Adding the three months of preparation to the eight months of recovery, it took the agency nearly a year to return to a reasonable working level. Because the RIF and reorganization took so much time and effort, many other essential program activities were temporarily set aside. In particular, the agency had difficulty carrying out monitoring activities. As one administrator described it:

The agency shut itself down. Those demand things we had to do, we did. But other things, such as assist in the management of programs, we didn't do. I asked the regional administrators about the impact [of the reduction in force.] When regional administrators resumed work in January, they found some messes. For example, a big city prime sponsor had spent money on wrong items. If there had been monitoring, it would not have happened. You have to dig. The city owed us money and paid us back. There was also staff turnover among the grantees: we didn't know the new staff. The CETA system was also RIFting. They tried to reinvent what they had already done. One of the things that bothered me about the RIF was that all my discussions with the regional administrators were about the RIF, not about the program.

Even after the recovery period was over, some employees reported a continuing effect on morale. "We get our work done," reported one employee, "but we get it done more slowly."

Besides some of the short-term effects on the organization of the reductions in budget and staffing levels, the cutback process at the ETA had some broader, longer-term effects. One of the most important of these was the evolution of the relationship between management and labor. The unions, accustomed to a cooperative relationship focused on work satisfaction and the quality of work life, found that management had ceased to consult with them and rejected the results of their research. Because of the break in communications with management, the unions gradually retreated to the more formal posture imposed on them. They became more concerned with contract rights and the defense of those rights.

One union representative reported,

The union strategy has been to outmanage management. I am less inclined now to try to convince managers and more inclined to state a position. I used to try to help them find a way. Now I am saying, 'It's crazy.' It's given me an ulcer. I don't trust the assistant secretary, and I don't think the employees do. He hasn't met with the employees. He hardly comes here. We are losing the cooperative relationship. There is no more romance. We are playing by the book. It's a shame. Management loses more than the employees.

A second change that occurred during the cutback period is that many managers who felt they could gradually win over the new administration found that they could not. As a result, they began gradually detaching themselves. Although they did not defy orders or try to delay, they became more frank about indicating where particular decisions had been made. The union leaders reported that many managers had become more sympathetic to the union, sharing information with them in a way that did not used to occur. One informant reported, "They [the program managers] have more allegiance with the union than with the administration."

Even more important than the tendency to detach themselves from decisions they had to implement was the psychological isolation of middle-level managers who opposed the administration's plans for the agency:

Some managers now are very afraid. Those who are vocal are being isolated. Another layer is being put on top of them, or they are being transferred. There has been some attempt to squeeze some of those with twenty plus years of service, so they can bring in new people. They put the person in a job they know he can't do and let him fail and give him a poor evaluation.

Another long-term impact on the agency was felt by high-seniority employees who were demoted:

We had an upward mobility program. Those women are now back to typing. Work ethic values are destroyed. That is not effective resource management. Management says the RIF procedures do not provide the opportunity to do otherwise. They may be right, but it can be helped now, and there is no effort to do so. With no expectation of growth or movement, it's frustrating and difficult. I don't know if we will ever recover from that.

For employees, as noted previously, a negative incentive system was substituted for a positive one. The positive incentives included a financial bonus for outstanding performance, the satisfaction of working to benefit the lives of the unemployed and poor, and the general quality of work life. The financial bonus was temporarily eliminated. Agency leadership downplayed the importance of the quality of work life. Some employees came to fear being put into jobs they could not perform and receiving poor job-performance evaluations. They feared that political criteria might be used for reductions in force, and they feared to take a stand lest they be "shelved" (removed from policy positions) or fired. Whether or not these fears were justified, some employees believed they were.

Finally, the reduction in force further depleted the ranks of younger people and female managers. The younger people were disproportionately affected because of the importance of seniority in the calculation of retention rights; women managers were affected by both seniority rules and veterans' preference. Often women have been in their managerial positions for a shorter period than men, and because they normally do not have military service, veterans (mostly males) are more likely to be retained. The outcome for the agency of the RIF regulations is an older, less varied, and less vital work force. This impact on the agency will probably last for years.

Summary and Conclusions

Cutbacks at the ETA were designed and dictated by the president and the Office of Management and Budget. Congress generally went along with the president. Individual congressional supporters of the program were bypassed in the reconciliation process when they were unwilling to make cuts in accordance with instructions. The Office of Management and Budget successfully lobbied the right people in Congress to get its measures passed. When Congress did not act quickly enough, the administration moved on its own.

The ETA had few resources with which to fight the cuts. It did not have sufficient interest-group or popular support to reverse the cuts either in Congress or in the administration. Both the secretary and the assistant secretary of the ETA supported the president's policies. Accepting the inevitable, the agency took the cuts with good grace. It made only one effort to enlist congressional support to reverse a minor cut; Congress did reverse the cut, but the OMB forced the agency to take the same size cuts in ways more acceptable to Congress.

Rather than spending its energy fighting the cuts, the agency tried to minimize the size of the reduction in force. This it succeeded it doing, after obtaining administration support.

The cuts caused considerable damage to the agency's management. The speed, severity, and targeting of the president's cuts virtually guaranteed that they would necessitate reductions in force. The reduction procedure, even when followed to the letter, created continuing disruption for many months. The union was alienated and forced into a combative role, women were disproportionately threatened by demotions,

and some managers withdrew some of their effort and loyalty from the administration. They were not in open rebellion, but they were cut adrift, and their efforts were not fully tapped.

It took the ETA nearly a year to recover an adequate level of functioning. The CETA program was redesigned by the administration in reauthorization legislation, but there is no indication that the new program (the Job Training Partnership Act) will improve management at the federal level. The new program should, however, reduce the responsibilities of the Washington office by shifting responsibility for program management to the states.

In sum, although the agency was pared down, it was not stabilized at a smaller size with less fat and better management. Despite the administration's goal of improved management and the elimination of waste, it seemed to pay little attention to managerial problems. The cuts and reorganization were not designed to solve these problems. The president and OMB focused more on terminating programs and bypassing the agency by giving new programs to the state governments to administer. OMB may have shown some sensitivity to managerial need in paring back the size of the proposed personnel reductions. Agency managers in Washington did what they could to recover from the reduction in force and reorganization with a system of informal and formal swapping and repromotions to keep work teams together.

Chapter 12 Review Questions

1. Why does Wildavsky argue that public budgets are always made incrementally? What are the advantages and disadvantages of this method? Why is last year's base so critical to preparing this year's public budget?

2. What are the assumptions behind the Wildavsky incrementalist budget-making model? Are they valid for the 1980s? Overall, does the case study support Wildavsky's bottom-up incremental model? Explain your position.

3. According to Wildavsky, what are the key strategies or roles of some of the major players in the budgetary process, for instance, the agency heads, the Budget Office, and the legislature and its appropriations committees? Which players are the most influential in determining the way budgets are prepared? Why are their roles so predictable?

4. What were some of the key strategies or roles of the major players in the case

study, for instance, the president, the Office of Management and Budget (OMB), and the Congress? How would you assess the effectiveness or ineffectiveness of each of these key players' budgetary strategies as outlined in the case study? What were the major elements that led to the resolution of the issues in the case? In your opinion, was the outcome a fair and just one?

5. Rethink Mosher's "The Professional State" (Chapter 7). What roles (if any) did professionals play in the budget-making process in the case study? On the basis of this case, can you generalize about the impact of professionals on public budget making? Why did Wildavsky say that "guarding their professional reputations" is an important element influencing the future outcomes of budgetary decisions? Was there any evidence of this behavior on the part of professionals in the case study?

6. Does Wildavsky see any differences between budgeting in government organizations and private business firms? What are some of the key differences and similarities between private and public budget making? On the basis of your own experiences, do you agree with Wildavsky's position?

Key Terms

budgetary strategies	expectation of participants
budgetary calculation	line-item budgets
simplification devices	OMB (formerly BOB)
incremental method	Appropiations Committee
coordination mechanisms	padding
spending advocates versus	budgets of firms
Treasury guardians	professional reputations
budgetary role orientations	performance budgets
capital budgets versus	top-down versus bottom-up budget
operating budgets	making

Suggestions for Further Reading

An excellent way to increase your understanding of budgets is to obtain a current city, county, state, or federal budget (usually the summary document provides all the important information) and read it carefully. Most summaries are written so that the layperson can understand their major contents and proposals. Also, now that public budgets are frequently the subjects of front-page headlines, read the major news coverage devoted to them, particularly in leading newspapers like the *New York Times, Washington Post, Christian Science Monitor, Los Angeles Times, St. Louis Post Dispatch,* and *Wall Street Journal,* as well as in news magazines like *Time* and *Newsweek.* The best up-to-date, scholarly survey of budgetary subjects is found in a new, thoughtfully edited journal, *Public Budgeting and Finance.* Each issue contains insightful articles by some of the leading experts in the field; the journal is published by Transaction Books, New Brunswick, New Jersey. Also do not neglect studying current issues of the *Public Administration*

Review as well as the annual volumes of *Setting National Priorities* published by the Brookings Institution, Washington, D.C.

Although they become dated quickly, introductory texts also offer a useful overview. See Robert D. Lee, Jr., and Ronald W. Johnson, *Public Budgeting Systems,* Third Edition (Baltimore: University Park Press, 1982); J. Richard Aronson and Eli Schwartz, *Management Policies in Local Government Finance* (Washington, D.C.: International City Management Association, 1981); John L. Mikesell, *Fiscal Administration: Analysis and Applications for the Public Sector* (Chicago: Dorsey Press, 1986); Fremont J. Lyden and Marc Lindenberg, *Public Budgeting in Theory and Practice* (New York: Longman, 1983); Robert H. Haveman and Julius Margolis, *Public Expenditures and Policy Analysis*, Third Edition (Boston: Houghton Mifflin, 1983); John Wanat, *Introduction to Budgeting* (Belmont, Calif.: Wadsworth, 1978); and Aaron Wildavsky, *The Politics of the Budgetary Process,* Fourth Edition (Boston: Little, Brown, 1984). For an outstanding historic collection of several of the best essays written on public budgeting, see Allen Schick, *Perspectives on Budgeting* (Washington, D.C.: American Society for Public Administration, 1980). A handy, free guidebook that explains the difficult and arcane jargon of budgeting is *A Glossary of Terms Used in the Federal Budget Process* (Washington, D.C.: General Accounting Office, 1977).

Undoubtedly the most profound impact on federal budgetary practices in recent years was made by the enactment of the 1974 Congressional Budget Reform Act, which is examined in several scholarly books, including Allen Schick, *Congress and Money* (Washington, D.C.: The Urban Institute, 1980); Dennis S. Ippolito, *Congressional Spending* (Ithaca, N.Y.: Cornell University Press, 1981); Lance T. LeLoup, *The Fiscal Congress* (Westport, Conn.: Greenwood Press, 1980); Rudolph G. Penner, ed., *The Congressional Budget Process After Five Years* (Washington, D.C.: American Enterprise Institute, 1981); and James P. Pfiffner, *The President, the Budget, and Congress* (Boulder, Colo.: Westview Press, 1979). For two thoughtful case studies of federal budgetary politics in the 1980s, read Paul Light, *Artful Work: The Politics of Social Security Reform* (New York: Random House, 1985); and Irene S. Rubin, *Shrinking the Federal Government* (New York: Longman, 1985); and for an excellent look at where we are today with the application of various budgetary systems, see George W. Downs and Patrick D. Larkey, *The Search for Government Efficiency* (New York: Random House, 1986), especially Chapters 4 and 5, as well as two insightful essays in the *Public Administration Review* 44 (March/April 1984): Hardy Wickwar, "Budgets One and Many," pp. 99–102, and Naomi Caiden, "The New Rules of the Federal Budget Game," pp. 109–117.

For two practical, "how-to" books on budgeting, refer to Edward A. Leham, *Simplified Government Budgeting* (Chicago, Ill.: Municipal Finance Officers Association, 1981), and Richard J. Stillman II, *Results-oriented Budgeting for Local Public Managers* (Columbia, S.C.: Institute of Governmental Research, University of South Carolina, 1982).

A remarkable inside look at modern federal budgeting is William Greider, *The Education of David Stockman and Other Americans* (New York: Dutton, 1981). Also read David Stockman's autobiography, *The Triumph of Politics: The Inside Story of the Reagan Revolution* (New York: Harper & Row, 1986).

Implementation: The Concept of Optimal Conditions for Effectively Accomplishing Objectives

"Legislators and other policy formulators can go a long way toward assuring effective policy implementation if they see that a statute incorporates sound theory, provides precise and clearly ranked objectives, and structures the implementation process in a wide number of ways so as to maximize the probability of target group compliance. In addition, they can take positive steps to appoint skillful and supportive implementing officials, to provide adequate appropriations and to monitor carefully the behavior of implementing agencies through the long implementation process, and to be aware of the effects of changing socioeconomic conditions. . . ."

Paul Sabatier and Daniel Mazmanian

READING 13

Introduction

From the very beginning of its conscious development as a field of study, public administration has stressed the importance of "good," "correct," "timely," and "efficient" execution of public objectives. Sound implementation was and perhaps still is "the bottom line" of what the administrative enterprise is all about. As Woodrow Wilson wrote in "The Study of Administration," the first American essay on public administration in 1887, "The broad plans of government action are not administration; the detailed execution of such plans is administration."[1]

Although "detailed execution" may well have always been the central preoccupation of public administrators, the last two decades have witnessed an impressive emergence and growth of scholarship directed specifically at exploring this subject. Indeed, by the 1980s implementation scholarship had become a distinct and separate subfield of public administration, political science, and policy studies. Implementation scholarship now boasts its own considerable array of professional journals and dedicated scholars, as well as sizable conferences oriented toward

[1] Woodrow Wilson, "The Study of Administration," *Political Science Quarterly,* 2 (June 1887), p. 197.

discussing various intellectual viewpoints and new methodologies related to this subject.

Much of the original impetus to develop a conscious subfield of study concerning implementation came from what many perceived as the apparent failure of the Great Society Programs. In the mid-1960s President Lyndon B. Johnson succeeded in pushing through Congress in a relatively short period a vast range of new types of social programs designed to alleviate major social problems (such as hunger, delinquency, poverty, unemployment, racial discrimination and urban decay) as well as other prominent social concerns of the day and aimed at building "The Great Society." As Robert T. Nakamura and Frank Smallwood write, "It was not long before disillusionment began to set in as it became apparent that it might be easier to 'legitimize' social policy by passing ambiguous legislation than to carry out such policy by means of effective program implementation."[2]

By the late 1960s and early 1970s students of public affairs began questioning the value of passing so many laws creating new social programs without paying adequate attention to whether or not these laws were effectively implemented or carried out at all. Theodore Lowi, in his *The End of Liberalism* (1969), popularized this attack on the broad expansion of governmental activities, which, he argued, had eroded clear standards for administrative accountability and consequently had led to a crisis of public authority over the role and purposes of government in society. As public programs grew into more and more abstract and complex activities, according to Lowi, "it became more difficult to set precise legislative guidelines for execution of public policy."[3] It also opened up government programs to chaotic pluralistic competition. Lowi termed this phenomenon *interest group liberalism.* His solution was to return to a more simplified structure in which Congress and the president make precise laws and the courts formulate strict judicial standards to guide administrative actions, thereby reducing administrative discretion to a minimum. Hence, implementation would become little if any problem for administrators because their choices would be restricted and their direction from policy makers would be well defined and specific.

Meanwhile, other scholars were by then also busily pointing out that the Great Society Programs were not working as planned. Several case studies appeared at this time making much the same point—namely, that the Great Society Social Programs, for various reasons, were not or could not be effectively implemented—such as Martha Derthick's *New Towns In-Town*[4] and Daniel P. Moynihan's *Maximum Feasible Misunderstanding.*[5] Jeffrey Pressman and Aaron Wildavsky's *Implementation* (1973)[6] especially sparked much of the serious academic

[2] Robert T. Nakamura and Frank Smallwood, *The Politics of Policy Implementation* (New York: St. Martin's Press, 1980), p. 11.

[3] Theodore J. Lowi, *The End of Liberalism* (New York: W.W. Norton, 1969), p. 127.

[4] Martha Derthick, *New Towns In-Town* (Washington, D.C.: Urban Institute, 1972).

[5] Daniel P. Moynihan, *Maximum Feasible Misunderstanding* (New York: Free Press, 1970).

[6] Jeffrey L. Pressman and Aaron B. Wildavsky, *Implementation* (Berkeley: University of California Press, 1973).

interest in this topic. Pressman and Wildavsky wrote what was essentially a case
study of the Economic Development Administration's effort in the late 1960s to
provide jobs for the "hard-core" unemployed in Oakland, California. Their case
turned out to be a study in how not to get things done in government. At the end
of their book they offered a prescriptive list of warnings about what should *not*
be done to accomplish public policy objectives: "Implementation should not be
divorced from policy"; "Designers of policy [should] consider the direct means
of achieving their ends"; "Continuity of leadership is important"; "Simplicity in
policies is much to be desired"; and so on.

After the appearance of the Pressman and Wildavsky book, Erwin C. Hargrove of the Urban Institute called implementation "the missing link" in social
theory, and soon an impressive array of new methodological approaches began
to search for "the missing link."[7] Several of the more prominent implementation
theories that have been put forward during the past decade include the following:

Implementation as a linear process: Donald S. Van Meter and Carl E. Van
Horn, in an essay entitled, "The Policy Implementation Process: A Conceptual
Framework," which appeared in *Administration and Society* (1975), argue that
implementation involves a linear process composed of six variables that link
policy with performance: standards and objectives; resources; interorganizational communications and enforcement activities; characteristics of the implementing agencies; economic, social, and political conditions; and the disposition of the implementers.[8] Presumably relationships or changes in any one of
these inputs ultimately, according to the authors, can influence the successful
performance of the policy objectives.

Implementation as politics of mutual adaptation: In a study of several federal
programs by Milbrey McLaughlin in 1975 for the Rand Corporation, the
writer concludes, "The amount of interest, commitment and support evidenced by the principle actors had a major influence on the prospects for
success."[9] In other words, the political support from the top, according to
McLaughlin, was the key to success or failure of program implementation.

Implementation as gamesmanship: Eugene Bardach's *Implementation Game*
(1977), as the book's title indicates, sees the subject essentially as a
"game," "where bargaining, persuasion, and maneuvering under conditions
of uncertainty occur"[10] in order to exercise control of outcomes. For Bardach, implementation therefore involves all the arts of gamesmanship:
learning the rules of the game, devising tactics and strategy, controlling

---

[7]Edwin C. Hargrove, *The Missing Link* (Washington, D.C.: Urban Institute, 1975).

[8]Donald S. Van Meter and Carl E. Van Horn, "The Policy Implementation Process: A Conceptual
Framework," *Administration and Society,* 6, no. 4 (February 1975), p. 449.

[9]Milbrey McLaughlin, "Implementation as Mutual Adaptation," in Walter Williams and Richard
Elmore (eds.), *Social Program Implementation* (New York: Academic Press, 1976), pp. 167–180.

[10]Eugene Bardach, *The Implementation Game* (Cambridge, Mass.: M.I.T. Press, 1977), p. 56.

the flow of communications, and dealing with crises and uncertain situations as they arise.

Implementation as a circular policy leadership process: By contrast, Robert T. Nakamura and Frank Smallwood perceive implementation as a circular process intricately involved within the entire public policy-making process. In their book *The Politics of Policy Implementation* (1980), the authors argue, "Implementation is but one part of this [policy] process and is inextricably related to, and interdependent with, the other parts."[11] For Nakamura and Smallwood the critical element linking implementation to the rest of the policy process is leadership, which, in their words, is necessary "to coordinate activities in all three environments" (policy formulation, implementation and evaluation) in order to achieve program goals.

Implementation as contingency theory: Ernest R. Alexander, by contrast, in "From Idea to Action," in *Administration and Society* (1985), develops a contingency model of policy implementation.[12] He views implementation as a complex "continuing interactive process," one that involves interactions with the environment, stimulus, policy, programs, and outcomes—all very much depending on the specific content, elements, and timing of these interactions.

Implementation as interorganizational relationships: In *Public Administration Review* (1984), Laurence J. O'Toole, Jr., and Robert S. Montjoy, drawing on a large sample of GAO cases, focus on interorganizational linkages as a means for facilitating program implementation.[13] They argue against the commonly held notion that the more organizations involved with programmatic implementation, the more chances for delay and nonimplementation result. O'Toole and Montjoy discover "that with certain structures of interdependence, the chances of implementation are increased." Much of their essay outlines the specific types of these organizational interdependencies that serve to enhance program implementation.

Implementation as case analysis: As with the Pressman and Wildavsky book (cited earlier), case studies of a single implementation situation remain a popular approach to understanding this subject. They seek to draw specific "lessons" about right—or wrong—approaches to accomplishing public policies within a specific policy field. Charles S. Bullock III and Charles M. Lamb's *Implementation of Civil Rights Policy* (1986) presents a highly sophisticated case analysis of this sort.[14] It analyzes in depth five cases in the civil rights field

[11]Nakamura and Smallwood, *Politics,* p. 21.

[12]Ernest R. Alexander, "From Idea to Action: Notes for a Contingency Theory of the Policy Implementation Process," *Administration and Society,* 16, no. 4 (February 1985), pp. 403–425.

[13]Laurence J. O'Toole, Jr., and Robert S. Montjoy, "Interorganizational Policy Implementation: A Theoretical Perspective," *Public Administration Review,* 34, no. 6 (Nov./Dec. 1984), pp. 491–503.

[14]Charles S. Bullock III and Charles M. Lamb, *Implementation of Civil Rights Policy* (Monterey, Calif.: Brooks/Cole Publishing, 1986).

and draws conclusions about the significance of ten specific variables involving the effective implementation of civil rights policies. The authors conclude that five variables in particular are critical for successful policy implementation: federal involvement, specific agency standards, agency commitment, support from superiors, and favorable cost/benefit ratios.

Today the debate among scholars continues over what constitutes the appropriate conceptual framework to best comprehend the implementation of public policy. It remains hardly a settled matter, with theories and counter-theories being put forward at a brisk pace. Certainly, as yet, scholars have not agreed on any *one* model to explain public implementation processes or how models work in government. Nevertheless, it would be worthwhile to look closely at one of the more prominent approaches to this topic to help clarify and understand this topic more thoroughly. The following conceptual framework for viewing implementation by two California-based policy analysts, Paul Sabatier and Daniel Mazmanian, "The Conditions of Effective Implementation: A Guide to Accomplishing Policy Objectives," reflects one of the major influential—not to mention controversial—approaches to appear in recent years. In their essay, Sabatier and Mazmanian try to forecast what conditions promote or prevent policy implementation. They argue that the likelihood of implementation is enhanced by the existence of a favorable or "optimal" set of conditions. Conversely, in their view, implementation is impeded or prevented when some or all of these conditions do not exist. Much of their essay is spent elaborating on precisely what they consider the five essential conditions "that can go a long way toward assuring effective policy implementation if they are met." The writers also point out at the end of their essay how implementation can take place under less than ideal or "suboptimal conditions."

As you read this selection, keep the following questions in mind:

What assumptions do the authors make in building their conceptual model of optimal conditions for implementation? Do they assume, for example, that implementation activities take place in an open, democratic, and pluralistic society? One governed by laws? Or what? How do such assumptions shape the concept they put forward?

What implications does their model have for practicing public administrators? Can they use it successfully to predict when conditions are "ripe" for implementing programs or *how* to implement programs?

Are the two authors optimistic about the possibilities of shaping conditions to allow for successful implementation of public policies?

Would their ideas have proved useful for the policy makers and administrators designing a program in any of the previous case studies you have read in this text, such as "Dumping $2.6 Million on Bakersfield" or "The Swine Flu Affair"? How so?

PAUL SABATIER AND DANIEL MAZMANIAN

The Conditions of Effective Implementation

A Guide to Accomplishing Policy Objectives

. . . It is our contention that a statute or other major policy decision seeking a substantial departure from the status quo will achieve its objectives under the following set of conditions:

1. The program is based on a sound theory relating changes in target group behavior to the achievement of the desired end-state (objectives).
2. The statute (or other basic policy decision) contains unambiguous policy directives and structures the implementation process so as to maximize the likelihood that target groups will perform as desired.
3. The leaders of the implementing agencies possess substantial managerial and political skill and are committed to statutory goals.
4. The program is actively supported by organized constituency groups and by a few key legislators (or the chief executive) throughout the implementation process, with the courts being neutral or supportive.
5. The relative priority of statutory objectives is not significantly undermined over time by the emergence of conflicting public policies or by changes in relevant socioeconomic conditions that undermine the statute's "technical" theory or political support.

The conceptual framework underlying this set of conditions . . . is based upon a (proto) theory of public agencies that views them as bureaucracies with multiple goals that are in constant interaction with interest (constituency) groups,

other agencies, and legislative (and executive) sovereigns in their policy subsystem.

Before elaborating on each of these conditions, we should note that obtaining target group compliance is obviously much more difficult in some situations than in others. The greater the difficulty, the greater the legal and political resources that must be marshalled if compliance is to be achieved. In the terms of our framework, the required "strength" (or degree of bias) of the last four conditions is a function of several factors, including the amount of change required in target group behavior, the orientation of target groups toward the mandated change, and the diversity in proscribed activities of target groups. In other words, the greater the mandated change, the more opposed the target groups, and the more diverse their proscribed activities, the greater must be the degree of statutory structuring, the skill of implementing officials, the support from constituency groups and sovereigns, and the stability in socioeconomic conditions if statutory objectives are to be attained. Within this context, the set of five conditions should always be sufficient to achieve policy objectives. Moreover, each condition is probably necessary if the change sought is substantial and requires five to ten years of effort; in easier situations, however, it may be possible to omit one of the last three conditions.

Condition 1: The program is based on a sound theory relating changes in target group behavior to the achievement of the desired end-state (objectives).

Most basic policy decisions are based upon an underlying causal theory that can be divided into two components—the first relating achievement of the desired end-state(s) back to changes in target group behavior, the second specifying the means by which target group compliance can be obtained. Both the "technical" and the "compliance" components must be valid for the policy objective(s) to be attained.

At this point, we are concerned only with the former ("technical") component, as the remaining four conditions in our framework relate primarily to the latter. In particular, we wish to emphasize that target group compliance—and the costs involved in obtaining it—may be wasted if not correctly linked to the desired end-state. For example, the "technical" component of the theory underlying the 1970 Clean Air Amendments relates air quality levels back to emissions from various stationary and mobile sources (the target groups). It assumes that human activities are the major source of air pollutants and that pollutant emissions from various sources within an air basin can be related, via diffusion models, to air quality levels at specific locations. To the extent that nonhuman sources, such as volcanoes, constitute a major emission source or that little is known about pollutant interaction and transport in the atmosphere, target group compliance with legally prescribed emission levels will not achieve air quality objectives (or will do so only very inefficiently). Moreover, the administrative and other costs involved in obtaining compliance are likely to be resented—with a corresponding decline in political support for the program—to the extent that promised improvements in air quality are not at least approximated. In short, an invalid technical component has both direct and indirect effects on the (non)achievement of policy objectives.

We should note, however, that there are some programs for which target group compliance can be interpreted as *the* policy objective. In such instances, the absence of any explicit attempt to link target group behavior to some subsequent end-state means that the first of our five conditions would not apply (as the underlying "technical" component deals directly with that linkage). For example, the goal of desegregation policy in the South could be construed as the elimination of dual schools—in which case the compliance of local target groups (school boards) would be tantamount to successful implementation. Insofar, however, as the goal of desegregation was not simply the elimination of dual schools but also the improvement of black children's reading scores, the "technical" assumption that unified schools improve reading scores would have to be valid for the policy objective to be attained.

Condition 2: The statute (or other basic policy decision) contains unambiguous policy directives and structures the implementation process so as to maximize the likelihood that target groups will perform as desired.

This is the condition most under the control of policy formulators (such as legislators). Unfortunately, its importance has often been overlooked by behaviorally oriented social scientists. For these reasons, we will briefly examine its constituent parts.

(a) The policy objectives are precise and clearly ranked, both internally (within the specific statute) and in the overall program of implementing agencies. Statutory objectives that are precise and clearly ranked in importance serve as an indispensable aid in program evaluation, as unambiguous directives to implementing officials, and as a resource available to supporters of those objectives both inside and outside the implementing agencies. For example, implementing officials confronted with objections to their programs can sympathize with the aggrieved party but nevertheless respond that they are only following the legislature's instructions. Clear objectives can also serve as a resource to actors outside the implementing institutions who perceive discrepancies between agency outputs and those objectives (particularly if the statute also provides them formal access to the

implementation process, such as via citizen suit provisions).

While the desirability of unambiguous policy directives within a given statute is normally understood, it is also important that a statute assigned for implementation to an existing agency clearly indicate the relative priority that the new directives are to play in the totality of the agency's programs. If this is not done, the new directives are likely to undergo considerable delay and be accorded low priority as they struggle for incorporation into the agency's operating procedures.

(b) The financial resources provided to the implementing agencies are sufficient to hire the staff and conduct the technical analyses involved in the development of regulations, the administration of permit/service delivery programs, and the monitoring of target group compliance. Although this condition is fairly obvious, ascertaining what constitutes "sufficient" resources presents enormous difficulties in practice. As a general rule, however, a threshold level of funding is necessary for there to be any possibility of achieving statutory objectives, and the level of funding above this threshold is (up to some saturation point) proportional to the probability of achieving those objectives. Financial resources are perhaps particularly problematic in labor-intensive service delivery programs and in regulatory programs with a high scientific or technological component, where implementing agencies often lack the funds to engage in the research and development necessary to examine critically the information presented by target groups and, in some cases, to develop alternative technologies.

(c) Implementation is assigned to agencies supportive of statutory objectives that will give the new program high priority. Any new program requires implementing officials who are not merely neutral but also sufficiently committed and persistent to develop new regulations and standard operating procedures and

to enforce them in the face of resistance from target groups and from public officials reluctant to make the mandated changes.

Thus it is extremely important that implementation be assigned to agencies whose policy orientation is consistent with the statute and which will accord the new program high priority. This is most likely when a new agency is created with a clear mandate after an extensive political struggle, as the program will necessarily be its highest priority and the creation of new positions opens the door to a vast infusion of statutory supporters. Alternatively, implementation can be assigned to a prestigious existing agency that considers the new mandate compatible with its traditional orientation and is looking for new programs. In addition to selecting generally supportive agencies, a statute can sometimes stipulate that top implementing officials be selected from social sectors that generally support the legislation's objectives. Even if this cannot be done through legislation, legislative supporters can often play a critical role in the appointment of non-civil-service personnel within the implementing agencies.

In practice, however, the choice of implementing agencies and officials is often severely constrained. In many policy areas (such as education) there is little option but to assign implementation to existing agencies that may well be hostile or whose personnel may be so preoccupied with existing programs that any new mandate tends to get lost in the shuffle. In addition, most positions within any governmental agency are occupied by career civil servants who are often resistant to changes in existing procedures and programs and only moderately susceptible to the sanctions and inducements available to political appointees. In fact, the generally limited ability of policy formulators to assign implementation to agency officials committed to its objectives probably lies behind many cases of suboptimal correspondence of policy outputs with statutory objectives.

(d) The statute (or other basic policy decision) provides substantial hierarchical integration within and among implementing agencies by minimizing the number of veto/clearance points and by providing supporters of statutory objectives with inducements and sanctions sufficient to assure acquiescence among those with a potential veto. Surely one of the dominant themes in the implementation literature is the difficulty of obtaining coordinated action within any given agency and among the numerous semiautonomous agencies involved in most implementation efforts. The problem is particularly acute in federal statutes that rely on state and local agencies for carrying out the details of program delivery and for which some field-level implementors and/or target groups display considerable resistance toward statutory directives. Thus one of the most important attributes of any statute (or other basic policy decision) is the extent to which it hierarchically integrates the implementing agencies. To the extent the system is only loosely integrated, there will be considerable variation in the degree of behavioral compliance among implementing officials and target groups—as each responds to the incentives for modification within its local setting—and thus a distinctly suboptimal attainment of statutory objectives.

The degree of hierarchical integration among implementing agencies is determined by the number of veto/clearance points involved in the attainment of statutory objectives and the extent to which supporters of statutory objectives are provided with inducements and sanctions sufficient to assure acquiescence among those with a potential veto. Veto/clearance points involve those occasions in which an actor has the capacity (quite apart from the question of legal authority) to impede the achievement of statutory objectives. Resistance from specific veto points can be overcome, however, if the statute provides sufficient sanctions and/or inducements to convince role occupants (whether implementing officials or target groups) to alter their behavior. In short, if these sanctions and inducements are great enough, the number of veto points can delay—but probably never ultimately impede—behavioral compliance by target groups. In practice, however, the compliance incentives are usually sufficiently modest that the number of veto/clearance points becomes extremely important. As a result, the most direct route to a statutory objective—such as a negative income tax to provide a minimum income—is often preferable to complex programs administered by numerous semiautonomous bureaucracies.

(e) The decision rules of implementing agencies are supportive of statutory objectives. In addition to providing unambiguous objectives, generally supportive implementing officials, few veto points, and adequate incentive for compliance, a statute (or other basic policy decision) can further bias the implementation process by stipulating the formal decision rules of the implementing agencies. The decisions of implementing agencies are likely to be consistent with statutory objectives to the extent, for example, that the burden of proof in permit/licensing cases is placed on the applicant and that agency officials are required to make findings fully consistent with statutory objectives. In addition, a statute can assign authority to make final decisions within implementing institutions to those subunits most likely to support statutory objectives. Finally, when multimembered commissions are involved, the statute can stipulate the majority required for specific actions. In the case of regulatory agencies that operate primarily through the granting of permits or licenses, decision rules that make the granting of a permit contingent upon substantial consensus, such as a two-thirds majority, are obviously conducive to stringent regulation.

(f) The statute (or other basic policy decision) provides ample opportunity for constituency (interest) groups and sovereigns supportive

of statutory objectives to intervene in the implementation process through, for example, liberal rules of standing to agency and judicial proceedings and requirements for periodic evaluation of the performance of implementing agencies and target groups. While a statute can take steps to assure that implementing officials are generally supportive of statutory objectives and that the decision process involving implementing agencies and target groups contains few veto points, adequate incentives for compliance, and supportive formal rules, we nevertheless contend that implementing officials cannot necessarily be trusted to act in a manner consistent with statutory objectives. What is also required is constant oversight and intervention from supportive constituency groups and legislative (and executive) sovereigns.

A statute (or other basic policy decision) can take a number of steps to maximize the probability of such intervention. First, it can require opportunities for public input at numerous stages in the decision process of implementing agencies and even require that the agencies take positive steps to assure the participation of unorganized potential beneficiaries. Second, it can provide for liberal rules of standing to appeal agency decisions to the courts. For example, the citizen suit provisions of the 1970 Clean Air Amendments have been used on several occasions to compel the U.S. Environmental Protection Agency to carry out statutorily mandated provisions that it had failed, for one reason or another, to do. Third, requirements for periodic reporting of agency performance to legislative and executive sovereigns and for evaluation studies by prestigious independent organizations (such as the National Academy of Sciences) are conducive to external oversight of the implementing agencies and probably to the achievement of statutory objectives.

In sum, a carefully formulated statute (or other basic policy decision) should be seen as a means by which legislators and other policy formulators can structure the entire implementation process and maximize the probability that the policy outputs of the implementing agencies and the behavior of target groups (whether outside or inside those agencies) will be consistent with statutory objectives. This requires, first, that they develop unambiguous policy objectives and incorporate a valid technical theory linking target group compliance with the desired impacts. In order to maximize the probability of such compliance, they should then assign implementation to supportive agencies, provide implementing officials with adequate financial resources, hierarchically integrate the implementation process through minimizing veto points and providing sufficient incentives to overcome resistance, bias the formal decision rules of implementing agencies, and provide opportunities for outsiders to participate in the implementation process and to evaluate accurately agency (and target group) performance.

But a statute, no matter how well it structures implementation, is not a sufficient condition for assuring target group compliance with its objectives. Assuring sufficient compliance to actually achieve those objectives normally takes at least three to five, and often ten to twenty, years. During this period, there are constant pressures for even supportive agency officials to lose their commitment, for supportive constituency groups and sovereigns to fail to maintain active political support, and for the entire process to be gradually undermined by changing socioeconomic forces. In short, while a statute can go a long way toward assuring successful implementation, there are additional conditions that must be fulfilled if its objectives are to be attained.

Condition 3: The leaders of the implementing agencies possess substantial managerial and political skill and are committed to statutory objectives.

As already indicated, legislators and other

policy formulators can take a number of important steps—both in the drafting of a statute and in the subsequent appointment of non-civil-service personnel—to increase substantially the probability that the leaders of implementing agencies will be supportive of statutory objectives. In practice, however, statutory levers are often somewhat limited (except where creation of a new agency is feasible), and the process of appointing political executives is heavily dependent upon the wishes of the chief executive and important legislators—several of whom may well not be committed to implementation of the basic policy decision. In short, the support of top implementing officials is sufficiently important and problematic to warrant being highlighted as a separate condition for successful implementation.

Moreover, policy support is essentially useless if not accompanied by political and managerial skill in utilizing available resources. Political skill involves the ability to develop good working relationships with sovereigns in the agency's subsystem, to convince opponents and target groups that they are being treated fairly, to mobilize support among latent supportive constituencies, to present the agency's case adroitly through the mass media, and so forth. Managerial skill involves developing adequate controls so that the program is not subject to charges of fiscal mismanagement, maintaining high morale among agency personnel, and managing internal dissent in such a way that dissidents are convinced they have received a fair hearing.

Finally, there is some evidence that maintaining high morale, commitment, and perhaps even skill becomes increasingly difficult over time. Innovative policy initiatives often attract committed and skillful executives to implementing institutions, particularly in the case of new agencies. But such people generally become burned out and disillusioned with bureaucratic routine after a few years, to be replaced by officials much more interested in personal security and organizational maintenance than in taking risks to attain policy goals.

Condition 4: The program is actively supported by organized constituency groups and by a few key legislators (or the chief executive) throughout the implementation process, with the courts being neutral or supportive.

It is absolutely crucial to maintain active political support for the achievement of statutory objectives over the long course of implementation. If the first three conditions have been met, this essentially requires that sufficient support be maintained among legislative and executive sovereigns to provide the implementing agencies with the requisite financial resources annually, as well as assuring that the basic statute is not seriously undermined but instead modified to overcome implementation difficulties.

This seemingly rather simple requirement is, however, exceedingly difficult to accomplish, for a variety of reasons. First, the rather episodic issue-attention span of the general public and the mass media tends to undermine diffuse political support for any particular program among both the public and legislators. Second, there is a general tendency for organized constituency support for a wide variety of programs—including environmental and consumer protection, as well as efforts to aid the poor—to decline over time, while opposition from target groups to the costs imposed on them remains constant or actually increases. This shift in the balance of constituency support for such programs gradually becomes reflected in a shift in support among members of the legislature as a whole and the committees in the relevant subsystem(s). Third, most legislators lack the staff resources and/or the incentives to monitor program implementation actively. The exception is constituent casework, which tends to be heavily skewed towards complaints. Without active political support from a few key legislators, implementing officials supportive of the program find it difficult to overcome the constant drumbeat of constituent complaints, as well as the delay and resistance inherent in implementing any program requiring substantial behavioral change (except in those instances where target groups support such change).

Despite these difficulties, the necessary infusion of political support can be maintained if two factors are present. The first is the presence of a "fixer" (or fixers)—that is, an important legislator or executive official who controls resources important to other actors and who has the desire and the staff resources to closely monitor the implementation process, to intervene with agency officials on an almost continuous basis, and to protect the budget and the legal authority of the implementing agencies. Except in very unusual circumstances, however, any particular "fixer" is unlikely to occupy a crucial position and/or to maintain an interest throughout the long process of implementation. This brings us to the second, and ultimately the most important requirement, namely, the presence of an organized supportive constituency (interest) group that has the resources to monitor closely program implementation, to intervene actively in agency proceedings, to appeal adverse agency decisions to the courts and to the legislature, and to convince key legislators that the program merits their active support. For the paramount advantage of any organization over an individual is continuity. If the supportive constituency is present, "fixers" can generally be found and/or nurtured.

Programs involving intergovernmental relations, however, pose additional difficulties to the maintenance of political support. On the one hand, programs of intergovernmental "subordinates" (such as localities vis-à-vis states and the federal government) are often subject to revision and/or emasculation by superordinate units of government. Unless a program's representatives occupy important positions at the superordinate level, there is little that can be done to maintain its legal (and sometimes financial) integrity. Conversely, superordinate levels are usually confronted with substantial local variation in political support for program objectives and, consequently, in the compliance of local implementing officials with program directives. While such variation can, in principle, be overcome if the superordinate statute provides very substantial incentives for compliance and sufficient financial resources to enable superordinate officials essentially to replace local implementors, in practice the system is seldom structured to that degree, and thus superordinate officials are forced to bargain with recalcitrant local implementors. The result is greater sensitivity to local demands and generally a suboptimal achievement of statutory objectives.

The discussion thus far has focused on the need for political support among the legislative and executive sovereigns of implementing agencies. But one must not neglect the courts. In most cases, the contemporary deference of most federal and state courts to agency decision making means that they play a rather minor role in the implementation process except on procedural issues and to assure conformity with explicit statutory directives. But courts strongly opposed to a given statute have the authority to emasculate implementation through delay in enforcement proceedings, through repeatedly unfavorable statutory interpretations, and, in extreme cases, by declaring the statute unconstitutional. On the other hand, there have been some instances where courts have substantially strengthened programs through favorable rulings. Given the enormous potential role of the courts, we argue that successful implementation of statutory objectives requires that they be either neutral or supportive.

Condition 5: The relative priority of statutory objectives is not significantly undermined over time by the emergence of conflicting public policies or by changes in relevant socioeconomic conditions that undermine the statute's "technical" theory or political support.

Change is omnipresent in most contemporary societies, in part because most countries are immersed in an international system over which they have only modest control, in part because policy issues tend to be highly interrelated. Pollution control, for example, is linked to energy, to inflation and national monetary policy, to transportation, to public lands, and to numerous other issues. As a result of this continuous change, any particular policy decision is susceptible to an erosion of political support as other issues become relatively more important over time. Obvious examples would be the effect of the Vietnam War and inflation on many Great Society programs and the effect of the energy crisis and inflation on pollution control programs. Change can also be so extensive as essentially to undermine the technical assumptions upon which a policy is based, as when the migration of poor people from the South and Puerto Rico to northern industrial cities brought into serious question the ability of state and local governments to provide matching funds for welfare programs.

It is in responding to such changes that support for a particular program from key legislators, organized constituency groups, and implementing officials becomes crucial. If they are sensitive to the effects that changes in seemingly tangential policies and in technical assumptions can have on "their" program, they can take steps to see that these repercussions are addressed in any new legislation.

Policy Feedback and Evaluation

Thus far our attention has been focused on the extent to which implementing agencies and target groups act in a manner consistent with statutory objectives and ultimately on the extent to which those objectives are actually attained. In this respect we have mirrored the focus on formal goals of much of the literature on implementation assessment and program evaluation.

But if one is interested in the evolution of policy and particularly with the political feedback process, a much wider range of impacts (or outcomes) needs to be considered. Of particular importance are unintended impacts that affect political support for the program's objectives. For example, any assessment of the implementation of school desegregation policy should be concerned not only with the amount of desegregation achieved but also with the effect of desegregation on "white flight" and ultimately on the amount of political and financial support for the public schools. Moreover, there is some evidence that political feedback is based primarily upon perceived, rather than actual, impacts and that policy elites evaluate a program not in terms of the extent to which it achieves its legal mandate but rather in terms of its perceived conformity with their policy preferences.

The actual process of policy evaluation and feedback occurs continuously on an informal basis as the implementing agencies interact with concerned constituency groups, legislative (and executive) sovereigns, and the courts. At periodic intervals, however, the process normally becomes more formal and politically salient as attempts are made to revise substantially the basic statute. For example, major efforts to amend federal air pollution control law seem to occur every three to four years. Some of these revisions can be attributed to continued resistance from affected target groups, while others can be traced to significant changes in relevant social and economic conditions. Whatever the source of proposed changes, it is important that supporters of the original objectives provide for independent evaluation studies to accurately assess the actual impacts of the program. Such systematic evaluation serves both to correct imperfections in program design and performance and to counteract the tendency for complaints to dominate the informal feedback process.

Implementation Under Suboptimal Conditions

A frequently voiced criticism against both legislators and scholars is that they have been far more concerned with the passage of legislation than with its effective implementation. Over the past decade, however, a burgeoning interest in policy implementation and evaluation has occurred in the academic community. This has matched a corresponding shift of emphasis among legislators from the passage of major new policy initiatives to more effective implementation and oversight of existing programs. One of the principal purposes of this paper is to provide both communities an understanding of the conditions under which statutes (and other basic policy decisions) that seek to change the status quo can be effectively implemented—that is, can achieve their policy objectives.

Our discussion has shown that legislators and other policy formulators can go a long way toward assuring effective policy implementation if they see that a statute incorporates a sound technical theory, provides precise and clearly ranked objectives, and structures the implementation process in a wide number of ways so as to maximize the probability of target group compliance. In addition, they can take positive steps to appoint skillful and supportive implementing officials, to provide adequate appropriations and to monitor carefully the behavior of implementing agencies throughout the long implementation process, and to be aware of the effects of changing socio-economic conditions and of new legislation (even in supposedly unrelated areas) on the original statute.

In practice, of course, even those legislators and other policy formulators concerned with effective implementation operate under substantial constraints that make it extremely difficult for them to perform all these tasks. Valid technical theories may not be available. Imperfect information, goal conflict, and multiple vetoes in legislative bodies make it very difficult to pass legislation that incorporates unambiguous objectives and coherently structures the implementation process. Implementation must often be assigned to agencies that are not supportive of the policy objectives. Supportive interest groups and legislators with the resources to serve as "fixers" may not be available or may go on to other things over the long course of implementation.

Nevertheless, even under such suboptimal conditions, several steps can be taken at least to increase the probability of effective implementation.

1. If a valid "technical" theory linking target group behavior to policy objectives is not available or is clearly problematic, then the authors of the statute should make a conscious effort to incorporate in it a learning process through experimental projects, extensive research and development, evaluation studies, and an open decision process involving as many different inputs as possible.

2. If the legislature insists on passing legislation with only the most ambiguous policy directives, then supporters of different points of view can initiate litigation in the hopes of finding a court that will invalidate the law as an unconstitutional delegation of (legislative) authority. While not very promising, this strategy has been employed successfully at least once in a California case, with subsequent legislation providing much clearer guidance to the agency.

3. If implementation cannot be assigned to strongly supportive agencies, then it is absolutely crucial to provide for intervention by outsiders through citizen suit provisions, periodic reporting to sovereigns, evaluation studies by prestigious and relatively indepen-

dent outsiders, and perhaps special legislative oversight committees.

4. If there are no active supportive interest groups with the necessary resources to monitor implementation carefully, then identification and mobilization of such a group must be a major priority of supportive legislators and implementing officials—as any program is doomed in the long run without one. While it is occasionally possible to create new organizations from scratch, a more feasible strategy is to convince an existing organization with the requisite resources to expand its program to make program monitoring a major responsibility.

5. If a "fixer" is not readily available, then program supporters must make a major effort to find or develop one. This may involve convincing a competent new legislator to specialize in this area or convincing an existing legislator that constituents strongly support the program and thus require it being given higher priority. If legislators in the relevant committees having jurisdiction over the implementing agencies are apathetic (or, worse, hostile) toward the new program, then efforts should be made to reorganize committee jurisdictions or perhaps to create a special oversight committee with a program supporter as chairperson. Whatever the means, however, finding a "fixer" is of paramount importance for effective implementation.

In short, even if the conditions for effective implementation are not met at the time of the basic policy decision, policy formulators and other program supporters can still take a number of steps to approximate the ideal over time.

CASE STUDY 13

Introduction

As the foregoing essay by Paul Sabatier and Daniel Mazmanian indicates, serious scholars are spilling a lot of ink over the problems of public sector implementation. Theories about bureaucratic implementation, as a consequence, now abound in books and journals. But from the standpoint of the practicing public administrator on the firing line, how does the work actually get done? How are government objectives achieved in practice? What are the methods used and the problems administrators encounter in the implementation process? Does the theory of implementation square with its "real-life" practice from the standpoint of an administrator?

The following case study is a first-person, autobiographical account of a local administrator, Frank Durr, who headed an Office of Volunteer Services in a Florida community during late 1983 and early 1984. He suddenly confronted an urgent, seemingly overwhelming, life-threatening crisis. During Christmas 1983 an unexpected cold wave hit his town, and he quickly had to distribute food, clothing, and supplies to needy local migrant farm families whose lives were endangered by the devastating freeze. Frank Durr's objectives may have at first glance *seemed* simple and straightforward—i.e., take care of those in need quickly and compassionately. However, as you read through this insightful personal account of what happened in "The Florida Freeze," you will see that even the simplest administrative operations, such as providing local relief services, with the most obvious objectives—namely, quickly speeding supplies to the hungry and homeless—can become an incredibly complicated affair involving all sorts of unforeseen problems and pitfalls. In order to get his job accomplished, Durr had to simultaneously—and artfully—struggle with numerous difficult issues, personalities, and organizational dilemmas.

As you study this case, think about the following issues:

What were the chief problems Durr encountered during the implementation of this relief operation? How did he cope with them? From your perspective, was he successful at accomplishing his assignments? Why or why not?

How does this case study relate to the ideas about implementation in the foregoing reading by Sabatier and Mazmanian? Based on your analysis of the case, where might you amend or modify their views? Would you add or delete any points in their list of necessary "optimal" conditions for successful implementation of objectives?

Can you generalize, from the case study and the foregoing reading, about why implementation in the public sector can often become so complicated and frustrating to those involved?

FRANK R. DURR

The Florida Freeze

Freeze Strands Migrants with No Money, Food

Twenty-four year old Reba Mason clutched her 3 month old son as she watched two toddlers play barefoot on a cold floor. She was one of the 14 people in her family who had driven a bus from their home in Cullman, Ala. because they had heard jobs picking fruit and vegetables were plentiful. They arrived Dec. 23, two days before a freeze destroyed a large part of the crops they had planned to pick. Now, the bus was out of gas, they had spent their money, they could find no work, and they were down to about the last bottle of milk for the children.

With a cold drizzle falling outside, and no place for them to sleep but aboard the heatless bus, Reba Mason was getting desperate. Some of them are facing eviction notices, others are piling up in homes with their families or friends. Others are just staying out in the woods or in unheated trailers.

Tampa Tribune
(December 31, 1983)

An original essay written for this text and published by permission of the author, Dr. Frank R. Durr.

The headline told the story. On Christmas Eve 1983, a devastating freeze hit Hillsborough County, Florida, destroying not only 93 percent of the strawberry crop but also threatening to destroy the lives of thousands of migrant farmworkers whose very existence depended upon the harvesting of that crop.

On Friday, December 23, only hours before the freeze, the Plant City Service Center of the Department of Health and Rehabilitative Services (HRS), the Florida Agency responsible for the health and welfare of its citizens, was about to close its doors for the Christmas holiday. I had spent most of December developing resources for food, clothing, and toys which my office, the Office of Volunteer Services, collected and distributed to needy families in East and South Hillsborough County. Many of these families were from among the 10,000–15,000 farmworkers who annually migrated to the area to harvest the multimillion-dollar strawberry crop.

The community had been generous in its giving, and as I made my last-minute check of the remaining gifts to be distributed, I was ready to declare the 1983 Christmas campaign an unqualified success. My two lead volunteers and chief architects in the Christmas effort, Patricia Cox and Juan Morales, were all smiles as we loaded the last deliveries on Juan's truck. As we shook hands and exchanged holiday wishes, I congratulated myself on the recruitment of these two people. Pat, the director of Daystar, Inc., an arm of Catholic Social Services, was a woman who possessed extraordinary abilities to organize and polarize support for our program. Juan was equally valuable. His standing in the Hispanic community, both as its religious leader and as a former farmworker, facilitated the establishment of a valuable communication link between my office and the migrant camps. Juan not only knew the location of the camps but also had free access to them—an asset considering most migrant camps were off limits to outsiders, especially to HRS personnel. Now, heading toward home, I felt secure in the knowledge that we could enjoy the holiday with our respective families. Little did I know that Pat, Juan, and I would play a dominant role in a human drama that was about to unfold.

On Saturday night, December 24, a hard freeze lay on the fields of East Hillsborough County; temperatures dipped into the mid-teens and remained there for several hours, spreading devastation to all plant life. Migrant families and friends huddled together in tin shacks and lean-to frames struggling to keep warm. Without heat or blankets, they could only wait for the warmth of the coming day. Christmas Sunday brings no joy—only a little relief from the bitter cold. People and agencies that could offer aid and comfort to the migrants are closed and unaware of their plight. Monday, December 26, is also a legal holiday. Some farmworker self-help groups that are in touch with the migrants open their doors to offer whatever assistance they can, but they are quickly overwhelmed by the sheer numbers of those in need. In addition, there is a severe shortage of food and blankets, thereby compounding the frustration among those who want to help and those who patiently wait for it.

By late Monday, December 26, local television stations began to broadcast appeals for food and clothing by Benito Lopez, the popular leader of the Migrant Farmworker Association (MFA), an association representing most of the farm laborers in Hillsborough and surrounding counties. Lopez, a veteran of many labor wars, made a convincing appeal to local citizens to help the farmworkers. Lopez was a familiar face at the Plant City Center. I had met him on several occasions and was impressed by his sincerity and by the reverence his followers held for him. Whenever there was a problem between a farmworker and HRS, you could count on a visit from Lopez. A man approximately 35 years old, Lopez had the ability to still an audience merely by his presence. The Hispanic community held him in awe. He was the man that stood up to the United Farmworkers Union (UFW) when Chavez was preoccupied with workers in California, thereby causing a rift between the UFW and the local farmworkers; hence the formation of the MFA. Lopez had also endeared himself to the workers by winning pay increases for tomato pickers in South Florida, and he took an interest in parent groups and education programs benefiting migrant children. As a result of his activities, then Florida Governor Bob Graham appointed Lopez to a state council on farmworker affairs. Considering Lopez's personal qualities and reputation, I was not surprised to see him in front of the TV cameras.

On Tuesday, December 27, the first workday after the freeze, I arrived at my office early, fully expecting to see hundreds of migrants milling around in the parking lot. Instead, I found myself alone. At 7:30 A.M., I was the first person to enter the building. I immediately phoned Pat Cox and asked her to meet me at 9 A.M. in my office. A few minutes before Pat was due, I made a quick visit to the food stamp unit at the far corner of the Center. Again I was surprised to find the waiting room nearly vacant. I stayed only long enough to locate Millie Sparks, the Food Stamp Supervisor, and arrange a meeting with her for later in the day; I wanted to discuss the potential impact of the freeze and our ability to deal with a dramatic increase of applications should that occur. On my way back to the office, I passed Juan and was about to invite him to the meeting with Pat but resisted the temptation. It occurred to me that if Juan could remain detached from the agency, he would be of more value to both me and the migrants. We each trusted Juan; however, I thought that their trust in him might be greatly diminished if it were common knowledge that he was an HRS volunteer. Pat was in my office when I returned. We decided that our first priority would be to develop a short-range plan, one which could be implemented immediately based on resources readily available to us.

Simply stated, the plan called for an immediate inventory of our own supplies, development of a local support system for donations of food and clothing, a volunteer responsible for the collection and storage of supplies, and an informal system of accountability and control. Pat's job was to coordinate the plan within the community to include the recruitment of volunteers and resources; mine was to inventory our supplies, arrange for a distribution point, and develop an accountability and control system. We agreed to meet again in my office on Thursday, December 29.

My first decision was one concerning the need to monitor the activities of the food stamp operation. I decided to decentralize the activities. As long as they were able to keep up with the number of new applications, I would let them do that and thus would have more time to accumulate the items necessary to meet the emergency demands over an extended period. I believed that the longer the food stamp office was able to accommodate the immediate flow of applicants, the longer I would have to develop a viable emergency food program.

Another key individual in the Center that I wanted to coordinate my activities with was the Center manager, Kay Sharp. As a direct service supervisor (DSS) in the HRS hierarchy, she was responsible for two or more program units. For Kay, that meant that she supervised—among others—Millie Spark's activities in the food stamp program; and because Kay was the highest ranking staff member in the Center, she became its manager. Even though my position did not come under the supervision of Kay or any other person in the building, I still felt responsible to coordinate my activities with her. When I attempted to see Kay, her secretary advised me that she was on annual leave pending reassignment to another city. That meant that the Center would be without a permanent manager for at least four weeks: the position would need to be advertised for two weeks, after which the selection process would take place and finally the assignment. In these instances, the district administrator, our chief executive officer, would assign someone to fill the position on a temporary basis until a new DSS could be found.

One choice for the temporary assignment was Adele Pomroy, a person well known to me. In fact she was the one whom Kay had replaced and who had selected me for the volunteer coordinator's position that I now occupied. Pomroy had been promoted to a position of higher responsibility in district headquarters—affectionately called the "pink palace" because of the building's color. However, I remembered Pomroy rather unaffectionately. She had recently led a move to eliminate the volunteer coordinator positions throughout the district and replace us with more administrative staff in district headquarters. Although the move failed, there was still another reason for me to be concerned over Pomroy's assignment, however temporary; she was, in my view, the perfect bureaucrat. One reason I gave her that title was her apparent reluctance to make decisions unless she had the regulation or supporting document before her. Her favorite phrase— "Let's not turn over that rock now"—suggested that if she could not find an answer in the policy file she would rather not take the risk of making a decision. This decision-making concept disturbed me because if the devastation was as severe as expected—if the system was unable to accommodate massive numbers of farmworker applications—then Pomroy would be forced to manage in a reactive and totally new environment, one in which many rocks would be turned over before the ordeal was finished.

On Thursday, December 29, Pat and I met in my office to compare notes. She reported that we had enough food on hand to feed ten to fifteen families for two or three days. I briefed her on my decision to monitor and work closely with the food stamp office. Given Kay's impending departure and her potential replacement, Pomroy, I asked Pat to continue her efforts in the community to develop food resources and consider using her volunteers at Daystar as a back-up in the event we needed them. I wanted to complete as much of our planning as possible before Pomroy's arrival at the Center so that I could be in the position of advising her rather than taking her advice. As soon as Pat left, I revisited the food stamp office to check on the number of new applications received. Millie told me that the number was average for the season and that they were not experiencing any particular problems as far as applications were concerned. However, trouble of another sort had surfaced; several farmworkers who applied for assistance in recent days had received assistance in another state. In these instances, federal regulations permitted the local office to defer approval of those applications for up to 30 days. The intent of the regulation was to ensure that applicants did not receive two issuances of food stamps within the same period of authorization. As a result of the staff's exercising this option, some migrant families had filed a complaint with the Florida Rural Legal Service (FRLS), a farmworker advocacy group whose purpose is to safeguard farmworker's legal rights. In response to the complaints, the FRLS dispatched a representative to our office to investigate. According to food stamp workers, the attitude of the representative was wholly argumentative and hostile toward them. A finding of FRLS eventually charged our staff with bias toward the farmworkers. Lopez also visited the food stamp office to question Millie about the alleged bias. When the law was explained to him, Lopez left the building, apparently satisfied with the explanation.

The visits by FRLS and Lopez combined with an already large caseload only served to increase tension among food stamp personnel. The incidents were especially unsettling to Millie, who in Kay's absence had borne the brunt of dealing directly with both Lopez and the FRLS. I took the opportunity to pledge my support to Millie and shared with her my plan to accumulate as much food for emergency distribution as possible so that it would be available in the event her workers were unable to keep up with the demand for services. By this time, I was convinced that if we could acquire food in sufficient quantities to be available to farmworkers whenever it was needed, we could keep them satisfied, thereby substantially reducing the chances of a confrontation between food stamp personnel on one side and angry, disgruntled, frustrated, and desperate farmworkers on the other. Millie appreciated my thoughts and even offered to provide me a space for the distribution of food—an offer she was later to retract.

Beginning with the first weekend following the freeze, Friday, December 30, through Monday, January 2, the media began to pick up the tempo of its coverage of the migrants' plight. As the meetings became more frequent and larger, so did the criticism of local HRS food stamp policies and procedures. Leading the charge against us was Lopez. His name and his picture as leader of the Migrant Farmworker

Association were in every newspaper and his face on every channel complaining, threatening, and asking for help. There was no question about it; he was mad and he was going to do something about it. There was no doubt either that he was about to "flex his muscle" and that it would be aimed at the Plant City Service Center. The Center offered Lopez a perfect setting for airing all of his problems. It was easily accessible to the public and its entrance and exits all opened directly onto the parking lot. Its square structure located in the center of the property made it easy to surround the building with demonstrators, in addition to providing plenty of parking space. The city itself was small and had ample media coverage with three television stations representing the major networks and two additional independent stations. Last but not least, the city was in the heart of the strawberry industry, making it easy for Lopez to muster a huge number of farmworkers within a short period of time.

On Tuesday, January 3, Kay Sharp returned to the Center to clear her calendar and desk in preparation for her departure on the following Friday. Although Tuesday was rather a routine day at the Center, by Wednesday migrant workers began to gather in front of the food stamp office. First they came in small numbers but by the end of the week, twenty-five to thirty were always visible milling around in the parking lot.

Friday, January 6, the last official day for Sharp, was one of conflict and frustration for her. Throughout the day, Lopez and his MFA lieutenants and several HRS staff from District Headquarters in Tampa paraded in and out of her office. The purpose of Lopez's visit was to try to negotiate a method by which farmworkers could be processed for food stamp assistance without the normal waiting period of two to three days. All of these attempts were doomed to failure because no one at the district or state level had the authority to suspend prevailing regulations regarding the processing of food stamp applications. There were no emergency provisions built into the food stamp program. Any such changes would have to come directly from the governor's office in Tallahassee. By

day's end Sharp had to feel grateful that she could leave the Center forever.

On Monday, January 9, Pat called me early to tell me she had some exciting news. During the weekend, she had received an invitation to attend a meeting of the Greater Brandon Ministerial Association. The Association, composed of the religious leaders from the area, was scheduling a meeting for the coming Thursday to consider ways and means of aiding the migrant farmworkers. She also told me a woman from Governor Graham's office asked her for information on the farmworkers' situation. The governor was scheduled for a meeting with Lopez later in the month, and she wanted to know what the workers really wanted and needed so that she could brief the governor before the meeting. During the conversation, the aide asked Pat, "What happened to the grant that United Way got in December?" Neither of us had any knowledge of available money that could be used for freeze relief—let alone from United Way.

I was delighted that Pat, my lead volunteer, had established a contact within the governor's office and that there were some monies in the county that might be used for emergency relief. I encouraged Pat to develop and maintain her liaison with the caller in the event we became stalled as the result of some unforeseen obstacle.

On Tuesday, January 10, I went from my house directly to a meeting with Ed Folkes at the Regional Service Center in Tampa. Ed was the senior human services supervisor of the district's food stamp program and had the authority to alter staffing patterns in the district, including Plant City. I wanted to brief Ed on the latest developments in the farmworker crisis. Ed assured me that the district was addressing the problem and that he was assigning four workers from other food stamp offices to help out in Plant City. Still, I was not satisfied that he fully understood the urgency of the situation. Even with added staff, the time lag for expedited service would not substantially reduce the waiting time of three days. As a last resort, I warned Ed that the farmworker problem could become a "political firecracker" and that Lopez was about to report to the governor about our inability, or worse our unwillingness, to help his people. When I had finished my argument, I left his office believing that I had failed to convince him of the true gravity of the crisis.

My thoughts then turned to the meeting scheduled for Thursday, January 12. I decided to invite District Program Manager (DPM) Stephanie Watson to attend the meeting in my place. Her attendance would be an opportunity for the community to get first-hand answers and information from someone in a position to speak for the establishment. She advised me that she could not go to the meeting but suggested that I ask Lopez to call her. She wanted to tell him that the agency was forming a task force to deal with the farmworker problems. In my mind, the task force probably referred to the four workers that Ed was going to reassign. Nevertheless, I was pleased that she was interested in establishing a dialogue with Lopez, and it gave substance to any claims we might make that we intended to deal with the crisis. In addition, Watson had asked me to carry the message to Lopez. I saw this as establishing my credentials with both the district headquarters and Lopez as an active participant in the problem-solving process. I also viewed Watson's action as an invitation for direct access to her, a useful access point in the hierarchical chain to be used as it became necessary.

On Thursday, January 12, Pat and I were the first to arrive at the Ministerial Association meeting. I wanted to be there before anyone else so that I could get Lopez aside and arrange for his call to Watson before the meeting started. I was eager for him as well as the ministers to know that the agency was attempting to do something to alleviate the food stamp bottleneck. I sincerely wanted Lopez to feel that he could work in harmony with HRS so that together we could resolve the crisis. At the same time, I wanted district headquarters personnel to realize that Lopez was moderate, not a radical, as many of our staff thought of him. In actuality, I believed his commitment to the farmworker welfare forced us to become better workers and supervisors because he possessed the knowledge to seek the right answers.

My attempt to see Lopez before the meeting failed. He did not arrive until minutes after it began. We started with all those present introducing themselves and their organizations. As I was awaiting my turn, I noticed Juan enter the room with Lopez and two or three other farmworkers. When it became Lopez's turn, he took the opportunity to blast the Plant City Food Stamp Office, calling it "the worse food stamp office in the State." Suddenly, there were twelve pairs of eyes focused on me as I prepared to introduce myself to the group. Everyone knew that I represented HRS. As calmly as I could, I gave my name and organization, and then—instead of sitting down—I responded to Lopez's charge. I admitted that there was cause for complaint but the system needed time to adjust to an unexpected emergency. I explained the work of the task force and Watson's invitation for Lopez to call her directly. I used that as an example of our continuing effort to resolve both the real and perceived problems within the system. I was also quick to point out that our system of food stamp allocations was a federal one, totally controlled by and responsible to the U.S. Department of Agriculture, not our local office. My announcement of Watson's message could hardly be ignored by Lopez. He agreed to talk with her after the meeting.

The main item on the agenda concerned a grant that United Way wanted to allocate to farmworker relief. The exact amount was not specified but it was reported to be in the neighborhood of $30,000. The chairperson told the group that the association could use the money if the organizational representatives in attendance would authorize them to act on behalf of all. I had to abstain from voting but the measure was overwhelmingly approved by the other participants. We did not know it then, but another group would also receive funds from the grant, Lutheran Ministries of Florida (LMF), another friend of the Daystar program in Plant City.

After the meeting adjourned, Lopez and I walked to the nearest phone, where I got Watson on the line for him. The conversation lasted only a few minutes with Lopez listening most of the time. When he hung up, I asked him to identify some of the problems at the Plant City office, but he declined to do so. As I shook his hand to leave, Pat approached me waving a check for $600 given her by the ministers: money to be used to buy food and blankets for the farmworkers, illegal aliens included. The agency by law was prohibited from helping non-U.S. citizens but all Catholic social agencies—such as Daystar, Inc.—refused to make any distinction between legal and illegal farmworkers. The issue had not surfaced with us but it loomed in the future as a potential problem in the event anyone in HRS chose to make it one.

The question that it posed was this: would the agency be in violation of the law if we were to dispense food—purchased by grant monies—to needy farmworkers without regard to their legal status? Fortunately, when money was allocated, there were no legal barriers imposed relative to the citizenship of those who were in need of emergency aid.

When I returned to my office from the meeting, I learned that Pomroy had been officially designated to fill in at the Center until a replacement for Kay Sharp could be named. By this time, however, Pomroy no longer represented the threat to the volunteer program that she once had; between Sharp's departure and the announcement of Pomroy's assignment, I had developed a strong support system of my own. It included a solid relationship with Pomroy's supervisor, Watson, and an external communication net with the governor's office via Pat Cox. There was no doubt in my mind that if Pomroy were to attempt to short-circuit our efforts to provide emergency assistance to the farmworkers, I had plenty of power to overrule her. The only harm that she could do now was simply to get in our way.

One problem persisted, however: the fact that we did not have a suitable place to dispense food. My first choice, Daystar, was in the process of moving out of one location and looking for another. Remembering my conversation with Millie days earlier, I asked for one of her vacant rooms. Whereas, before, she seemed willing, now she refused me on the assumption that the room would be needed to house additional personnel to be assigned at some future date. This left me with only one alternative, a room that

was given to me to store toys during the Christmas campaign. However, even the use of this room could be denied me because I was only a tenant in the building. The room was large enough, but it was a considerable distance from the food stamp entrance.

Another disadvantage to its use resulted from its proximity to the Aid to Families with Dependent Children (AFDC) Unit. Traffic in and out of the room could create a disturbance for the AFDC workers. In the final analysis, we had no choice but to opt for that room.

In order to secure the room for my program, I put in a call to my immediate supervisor, Jean Frankel, at district headquarters in Tampa. Until now, Jean had remained in the background and I had chosen to keep it that way, not because she represented any threat to our plan, but because I wanted to remain in control of the volunteer effort and keep our work and its problems primarily a local issue. There was also the feeling that headquarters had decided to keep the problem in Plant City as far away from them as possible. They possibly did not want to risk a full confrontation with Lopez and his allies. Now, however, I was ready to involve Jean. I did not want her involved in the problem but rather in the solution, via support and approval of my activities. Jean concurred with my plan for the room but suggested that I make the request in writing, which I did. As the week ended, I was confident that I had done everything possible to ensure the success of our plan.

On Tuesday, January 17, I sent both Juan Morales and Pat Cox into the migrant camps with the mission of gathering information on the true condition of the farmworkers. The knowledge they gained proved invaluable to the volunteer program by giving me the advantage of first-hand intelligence. Once it became known in the community that I possessed this information, every representative of those who were trying to help, or even thinking about it, made it a point to call either Pat or me first. In effect, by the mere fact that we knew a little bit more than anyone else, we were soon propelled into a position of being the experts on the problem. On Friday, January 20, Pat called to tell me that Lutheran Ministries of Florida had been selected by United Way to administer the grant and that Daystar would represent LMF in Plant City. Our first share of money would amount to approximately $5,000 and Pat expected to be able to purchase the food within the next week or ten days. Later, in my office, Pat and I decided on our referral plan. We would use the regular HRS referral form that all of our workers were familiar with. I was satisfied that we had resolved the issue but then Pat told me that LMF required a form of its own, one that every applicant must complete in order to receive food. The form was actually a statement to be signed by the farmworker: "I personally declare that I do not have or receive food stamps to meet this need. Additionally, I declare that my income does not fall within guidelines."

As far as I was concerned, this statement made no sense at all. For example, how could the Lutherans expect the farmworkers, most of whom could not read or write English, to understand what they were signing? Another issue: how many will sign it just to get the food? I decided to remedy the situation by adding the Spanish translation underneath the English version. In my opinion, the form in its original state was worthless, and I was disappointed that LMF would produce such a document. Later, LMF overruled my revision, insisting that I stick to the original form, which I did. In the meantime, we made copies of the form and distributed them to food stamp workers with instructions that they give them to the applicants as soon as we received our first shipment of food. We did not know it at the time, but it would be another week before any proceeds of the grant would be in our hands.

On Friday, January 27, Daystar was given $1,000 to buy food. Pat came to my office about mid-morning with the news that she would have the food purchased and ready to distribute the following Monday. I suggested that she notify Millie about the start-up date so that she could alert her workers to begin giving out the referrals. Pat reported to me later that she had talked with Millie and advised her that Daystar would begin operations on Monday afternoon between the hours of 3:00 and 5:00 P.M. This conversation between Pat and Millie was impor-

tant because first Millie and then Pomroy would deny that it ever took place. Both of their denials were to result in an irreversible rift between Millie and Pomroy on one side and Pat on the other. For Pat, the denials amounted to calling her a liar.

On Monday, January 30, Juan picked up a load of food from the Jewel-T Warehouse in Tampa and brought it to the Center. As if by some mystical power, approximately 100 migrant farmworkers gathered in the parking lot in front of the food stamp office. Lopez was among those in the lot. He and his aides were handing out the LMF forms along with an explanation of their meaning. While Pat was still working to get everything ready for the 3 P.M. opening, Lopez approached her and asked if she could open sooner. Pat told him that she could but she would have to get Millie's approval first. She found Millie in the copy room and asked her if she had any objections to begin food distribution before 3 P.M. Millie gave her an approval to do so. When Pat informed Lopez of Millie's approval, he asked Pat if there was any way for the food stamp people to run the names of potential recipients through our computers. Lopez wanted to know who was or was not already approved for food stamp assistance. He wanted to ensure that only those who were not getting assistance would be eligible for the emergency food. Pat responded that it was an HRS matter, and that he must get Millie's approval.

Next, two events occurred perhaps simultaneously: an agitated Pomroy asked Pat if Millie knew in advance that the food would be distributed before 3 P.M. Of course, Pat informed her. Pomroy countered that Millie had just told her that she knew nothing about it. When Pat insisted that Millie knew, Pomroy left saying that she was going to hold a meeting. In the meantime, Lopez asked either Millie or her lead worker to check the names and social security numbers in the computer to determine who had received food stamps and who had not. His request was refused on the grounds that the computers were overheated because of the already heavy traffic on them. To prove the point, he was shown fans being used to cool the computer machines. But Lopez was adamant. He insisted, and when he was refused a second time, he asked to use the telephone. When this request was granted, he called someone in the governor's office. Whoever was on the other end of the line in Tallahassee asked to speak to the person in charge, whereupon Lopez handed the phone to Millie (or her assistant), who was then ordered to run the names. Much to his credit, only those who were in need received emergency food that day. According to Pat, Lopez confided in her that HRS staff under sufficient pressure would approve anyone for emergency assistance rather than risk a hassle.

I was not present during either of the aforementioned events, but when I returned home that evening, I received an unexpected call from Jean Frankel, my supervisor in district headquarters. When she asked me what was going on in Plant City, I had no idea of what she was alluding to. When I confessed my ignorance, she told me that Pomroy was "up in the air over Cox letting Lopez use the computers." I knew that those computer rooms were kept locked and that no one could get to a computer without the express approval of computer personnel or Millie. In any event, I knew that Pat could not and would not be able to authorize anyone's use of them. However, I promised to call Pat and make a report back to Jean. I immediately called Pat and she verified what I had already assumed—namely, that she was not the one who authorized Lopez's access to the computers.

Once we had settled that question, she related the events of Pomroy's meeting that evening. Lopez, who for some unknown reason attended the meeting, gave Pat a vote of confidence when he told Pomroy that he was very satisfied with the way she handled the emergency food operation. From then on, Pomroy refrained from any comment about the distribution of food. However, Lopez was not finished. He fired another salvo at Pomroy when he told her that he was going to "hit" the Ruskin Food Stamp Office in South Hillsborough County. On hearing this, Pomroy became visibly upset and asked Pat if the grant included Ruskin. Pat could not answer that question because United Way had not disclosed to us how the money was going to be divided. When I called Jean back, I

related Pat's account of the computer incident and followed it by telling her of Lopez's threat to move on the Ruskin office. I also told her that I thought Lopez was carrying on a war of nerves in an attempt to escalate the conflict but Plant City remained the primary focus of his efforts.

During Tuesday morning, January 31, Juan picked up another shipment of food and delivered it to the Center. Before it could be completely unloaded, problems began to surface. Several social workers in the AFDC unit complained to Pomroy that Juan was making too much noise. In addition, several hundred farmworkers gathered in the parking lot outside the food stamp office, presenting a possibility that there would be neither enough food for them nor enough time to distribute it. First, Pomroy asked Pat to keep the noise down, then she asked her if she would open at noon instead of 3 P.M. Pat agreed to try to do both, although she was of the opinion that the AFDC workers were complaining needlessly. Pat began dispensing food promptly at noon. As the day wore on, it became apparent that there was not enough time to feed all of the migrants. As soon as Pomroy realized this, she went to Pat and asked her to remain open until 5:50 P.M., an extra half hour, which Pat agreed to do.

Meanwhile, the food stamp workers and Millie were having their own problems. Whenever Lopez thought we were not processing applicants quickly enough, he would initiate a sit-down in the food stamp waiting room. When he was satisfied that we were being more responsive, he would call a halt to the demonstration. Those staff other than Millie's also felt the tension. Most feared for their own personal safety and that of their automobiles. By mid-afternoon, there were perhaps six or seven hundred farmworkers milling around in the Center's parking areas, some sitting on their own cars and trucks and others sitting on our cars and trucks. The whole building—inside and out—resembled a combat zone. It seemed to be a veritable tinderbox ready to ignite at the slightest provocation.

In the middle of all of the tension, Millie threatened to undermine the tenuous stand-off. Against the wishes of her supervisor, Pomroy, she refused to keep the food stamp office open past 5 P.M. Time after time, she told Pat that the distribution of food would not go beyond 5 P.M., definitely creating an unsettling situation at the Plant City Service Center. Of course, in the midst of this interoffice squabble was Pat. She wanted to stay open, not just past closing, but until all of the food was distributed. Before the day ended, reason did prevail. The office remained open until the food supply ran out. When the food was gone, the farmworkers dispersed; and after they dispersed, our workers went home.

The remainder of the week was slow in comparison to Tuesday, partly because our food supply did not arrive as scheduled and partly because crowds were smaller, probably because of the scarcity of food in our bins. However, Lopez was a constant visitor during the entire week. If Lopez was popular with the press before the freeze, now he was a celebrity. Everywhere he ventured, reporters and video cameras followed.

The first week of February was decidedly more quiet than the previous one; more food arrived but the need for it diminished, giving evidence that the farmworkers were beginning to receive help from other agencies such as the Salvation Army (a recipient of other grant monies as well). Pat continued to maintain a regular schedule at the Center from 3 to 5 P.M. During the week, she also received an additional $500 from her church, St. Clements Catholic Church in Plant City. She used the money to purchase blankets and with the help of Juan took them to the farmworkers in the migrant camps. When she returned to my office, she never failed to describe conditions she had witnessed. Homes were wooden-crate, plywood shelters with few if any windows. From inside, she could see daylight where the corners were nailed together; floors sagged beneath her weight. There was no insulation and no heat except from cooking units. Even so, the families were friendly and courteous; the children happy. Pat Cox's perspective on migrant camplife brought a new understanding and appreciation of a culture very few of us knew about. These were sobering revelations that added fuel to our determination to see our job finished even though it might involve an element of personal risk by bucking the estab-

lishment. In Pat's case, it meant putting up with Millie and Pomroy. On the positive side, her contacts with the governor's office were highly supportive and developed into a daily occurrence. And by Friday, February 10, another 35 families had received food.

On the following Monday, February 13, we received another shipment of food. This time Pat asked me to observe the unloading and give her my personal opinion of the noise level it generated. I thought that the whole affair was carried out with minimum effort and noise. The only disturbance that I noted came from the break room, where the AFDC unit was hosting a going-away party for one of the staff's friends.

On Tuesday, February 14, Pat received a call from someone at Hillsborough County Community Services asking her to manage a grant for farmworker relief. I learned later that Lopez had petitioned the governor for additional funds to help his people with back truck payments, rent, and utilities. Pat was elated. Now she saw an opportunity to jettison HRS and take over a new program in which she would be in complete charge. As for me, I knew that with Pat in charge, our clients—farmworkers and all—would receive fair, prompt, and equal treatment. Now it was Pomroy's turn to be furious. Pat coordinated her new program with every agency in the county—except HRS. Pomroy asked to be included, but Pat refused to allow her.

On Monday, February 27, Pat opened the county program, thus ending the farmworker crisis for HRS. Thereafter, all requests for emergency food were referred to Pat's program.

In retrospect, nearly everyone involved considered the experience a valuable one. Based on lessons learned, the agency developed a Farmworker Contingency Plan that can be implemented immediately on order of district headquarters. The plan provides for preapproved personnel reassignments and the temporary easing of regulations in crisis situations such as those created by the freeze. In May 1984, Pat Cox was selected as Volunteer of the Year for HRS. In addition, she received a special award from the Hillsborough County Commission. Juan Morales was cited by the president of the United States for his volunteer work with HRS during the Florida freeze. As for myself, I have developed a zeal for championing the cause of migrant children—a generation of Americans—whose future we cannot and must not abandon to chance. During the twentieth anniversary celebration of the Redlands Christian Migrant Association (RCMA), I was given the "Friend of Migrant Children" award.

Chapter 13 Review Questions

1. How do you define the word "implementation"? In what ways does "implementation" differ from "management" or "administration"? What are the similarities and differences among these terms?

2. Can you outline how the concept of implementation draws on other ideas concerning decision making, communications, politics, budgeting, public professional expertise, and the general environment that have been discussed earlier in this text? How does the concept of implementation both use and build on these other concepts?

3. Why has implementation become such a major concern for students and practitioners of public administration and public policy in recent decades? What was responsible for its development as a recent focus of scholarly research? Do you think there is a valid need for studying implementation in the public sector and, if so, why?

4. What are the essential elements of the implementation model that Sabatier and Mazmanian propose? What are its basic assumptions and utility for practicing public administrators? Can you define "optimal" and "suboptimal" conditions for implementation?

5. Were the conditions found in the case study, "The Florida Freeze," optimal or suboptimal? Where or how did these conditions for implementation apply—or fail to apply? Would you add any as being essential for effective implementation, or delete any? Or would you develop an entirely different implementation model based on your reading of this case?

6. Consider the key administrator in "The Florida Freeze," Frank Durr, and evaluate whether or not he was successful at implementing this program under crisis conditions. By what standards can we judge whether or not administrators are successful at the task of program implementation?

Key Terms

conditions for implementation
target group behavior
sound technical theory
unambiguous policy directives
sufficient/insufficient resources

veto points
policy feedback
performance evaluation
constituency intervention points
"fixers"

supportive/unsupportive agencies
hierarchical integration
precisely ranked objectives

optimal/suboptimal conditions
skillful/unskillful implementers
conflicting policy priorities

Suggestions for Further Reading

The book that started much of the contemporary theorizing about this subject is now in its second edition and is still well worth reading, Jeffrey L. Pressman and Aaron B. Wildavsky, *Implementation, Second Edition* (Berkeley, Calif.: University of California Press, 1978) as well as several of the case studies that criticized the implementation of Great Society programs and also stimulated early research in this field, especially Martha Derthick, *New Towns In-Town* (Washington, D.C.: Urban Institute, 1972); Daniel P. Moynihan, *Maximum Feasible Misunderstanding* (New York: Free Press, 1969); Stephan K. Bailey and Edith K. Mosher, *ESEA: The Office of Education Administers a Law* (Syracuse: Syracuse University Press, 1968) as well as Beryl A. Radin, *Implementation, Change and the Federal Bureaucracy* (New York: Teachers College Press, 1977).

Serious students of implementation theory should review carefully the major conceptual approaches cited in the introduction to this chapter as well as other important contributions such as: Martin Rein and Francine F. Rabinovitz, "Implementation: A Theoretical Perspective," in Walter D. Burnham and Martha W. Weinberg, eds., *American Politics and Public Policy* (Cambridge, Mass.: MIT Press, 1978) and also in the same book, Michael M. Lipsky, "Implementation on its Head"; Carl E. Van Horn, *Policy Implementation in the Federal System* (Lexington, Mass.: Lexington Books, 1979); A. Dunsire, *Implementation in Bureaucracy* (New York: St. Martin, 1979); Walter Williams, *The Implementation Perspective* (Berkeley, Calif.: University of California Press, 1980); J. S. Larson, *Why Government Programs Fail* (1980); Helen M. Ingram and Dean E. Mann, eds., *Why Policies Succeed or Fail* (Los Angeles: Sage, 1980); R. D. Behn, "Why Murphy was Right," *Policy Analysis* (Summer 1980); G. C. Edwards, *Implementing Public Policy* (Washington, D.C.: Congressional Quarterly Press, 1980); Susan Barrett and Colin Fudge, eds., *Policy and Action: Essays on Implementation of Public Policy* (London: Methuen, Inc., 1981); Dennis J. Palumbo and Marvin A. Harder, eds., *Implementing Public Policy* (Lexington, Mass.: Lexington Books, 1981); Daniel A. Mazmanian and Paul A. Sabatier, eds., *Effective Public Policy Implementation* (Lexington, Mass.: Lexington Books, 1982); B. Hjern and D. O. Porter, "Implementation Structure," *Organization Studies* (1981); Randall B. Ripley and Grace A. Franklin, *Bureaucracy and Policy Implementation* (Homewood, Ill.: Dorsey Press, 1982); Walter Williams, et al., *Studying Implementation: Methodological and Administrative Issues* (Chatham, N.J.: Chatham House, 1982), and B. Hjern and C. Hull, eds., "Implementation Beyond Hierarchy," Special Issue, *European Journal of Political Research.*

During the 1980s greater attention has been paid by scholars to careful case analyses of implementation within the context of particular policy fields such as: M. K. Marvel, "Implementation and Safety Regulation: Varieties of Federal and State Administration Under OSHA," *Administration and Society* (May 1982); S. L. Yafee, *Prohibitive Policy: Implementing the Federal Endangered Species Act* (Cambridge, Mass.: MIT Press, 1982); Donald C. Menzel, "Implementation of the Federal Surface Mining Control and Reclamation Act of 1977," *Public Administration Review* (March/April 1981); Dean E. Mann, ed., *Environmental Policy Implementation* (Lexington, Mass.: Lexington Books, 1982); Charles S. Bullock III and Charles M. Lamb, *Implementation of Civil Rights Policy* (Monterey, Calif.: Brooks/Cole, 1984); David L. Kirp and Donald N. Jensen, eds., *School Days, Rule Days* (Philadelphia, Pa.: Taylor & Francis, 1986); Gary C. Bryner, *Bureaucratic Discretion* (New York: Pergamon Press, 1987) and Donald F. Kettl, *Government by Proxy* (Washington, D.C.: Congressional Quarterly Press, 1988).

PART THREE

ENDURING AND UNRESOLVED RELATIONSHIPS: CENTRAL VALUE QUESTIONS, ISSUES, AND DILEMMAS OF CONTEMPORARY PUBLIC ADMINISTRATION

Part Three focuses on three key persistent and pressing relationships in the field of public administration today: the problems of political-administrative relationships; the public and the private sector; and ethics and the public service. All of these relational issues are new in the sense that they have come to the forefront of recent discussions and controversies in public administration. Yet, these issues have certainly been part of the problems and perplexities of public administration since its inception as an identifiable field of study after the turn of the twentieth century. Indeed, the topics of political-administrative relationships, the problems of ethics, and relationships between public and business administrations were central themes of the writings of many early administrative theorists, such as Woodrow Wilson, Frederick Taylor, Luther Gulick, Louis Brownlow, and Leonard White. No doubt one could even trace the origins of these topics back to the classic writings of Plato, Aristotle, Moses, and Pericles. But for a variety of reasons—the Reagan revolution, with its themes of privatization, concern about government performance, secrecy, the Iran-Contra scandal, public attacks on bureaucracy, and high taxes—we are witnessing the reemergence of these older issues as very real dilemmas for public administrators today. Readings and cases in Part Three therefore address these critical issues:

Chapter 14 *The Relationship Between Politics and Administration: The Concept of Issue Networks* What are the current trends and practices in political oversight and control of administration? What are the implications for public administration and the governance of America?

Chapter 15 *The Relationship Between the Public and Private Sectors: The Concept of Third-Party Government* What is the relationship between public and private sectors? How have new forms of public action through sharing government authority with a host of "third parties" affected performance of government? What are the advantages and disadvantages of using different tools to accomplish public policy goals? What does this "new reality" of public management practices mean for contemporary public administrators?

Chapter 16 *The Relationship Between Ethics and Public Service: The Concept of* *the Moral Ambiguities of Public Choice* How are ethical choices involved in contemporary decisions facing public servants? What is an appropriate conceptual model for understanding how ethical choices are involved in public administrators' choices? How can these choices be made in a more responsible manner?

CHAPTER 14

The Relationship Between Politics and Administration: The Concept of Issue Networks

"The iron triangle concept is not so much wrong as it is disastrously incomplete. And the conventional view is especially inappropriate for understanding changes in politics and administration during recent years. . . . Looking for the closed triangles of control, we tend to miss the fairly open networks of people that increasingly impinge upon government."

Hugh Heclo

READING 14

Introduction

Perhaps no issue has been more controversial or more discussed in public administration since its inception as a self-conscious field of study than the appropriate relationship between the politically elected representatives of the legislature and the permanent bureaucracy of the executive branch. Indeed, the first essay on the subject of public administration written in the United States, "The Study of Administration," prepared by a young political scientist named Woodrow Wilson in 1887, essentially wrestled with the problem of the proper relationship between these two spheres of government: politics and administration.[1] Wilson wrote his essay at a time when civil service reform had recently been instituted in the federal government (the Pendleton Act had been passed in 1883). Wilson sought to encourage the development of the newly established merit system and the emergence of a field of academic study—public administration—because in his words, "It is getting to be harder to run a constitution than to frame one." The new complexities of government—both in terms of widening popular participation of the citizenry in democratic government and the rising technological problems of organizing public programs—created, in Wilson's view, the urgent need for developing effective administrative services free from congressional "meddling."

Generally, the drift—both in terms of intellectual thought and institutional

[1] Woodrow Wilson, "The Study of Administration," *Political Science Quarterly,* 2 (June 1887), 197–222.

reform in the United States during the century after Wilson's writing—until the 1970s was toward a realization of the Wilsonian argument in favor of greater administrative independence from legislative oversight. War, international involvements, economic crises, and a host of other influences (including public administration theorists) supported the claims for administrative independence from detailed legislative control. In particular, as political scientist Allen Schick notes, three factors led to congressional acquiescence. The first factor was the massive growth in the size of government. "Big government weakened the ability of Congress to govern by controlling the details and it vested administration with more details over which to govern. In the face of bigness Congress could master the small things only by losing sight of the important issues." This was bolstered by the message of public administration theorists "that a legislature should not trespass on administrative matters inevitably registered on Congressional thinking about its appropriate role, especially because the theme was so attractively laced with the promise of order and efficiency in the public service and carried the warning that legislative intrusion would be injurious to good government."[2]

Nonpartisanship in foreign affairs also played a powerful role in checking congressional intrusion in executive affairs by conveying "the assurance that unchecked executive power would be applied benevolently in the national interest of the United States." Pluralism, a third factor in fostering congressional retreat, according to Schick, furthered administrative independence by the convincing certainty that wider administrative discretion over executive agencies would be in fact used "to provide benefits to powerful interests in society to the benefit of everyone."

In retrospect, perhaps these assumptions were naive, but they were generally accepted as truths until the early 1970s. Suddenly the abuses of Watergate, the disastrous consequences of Vietnam, the failure of numerous Great Society social programs, combined with an unusually high turnover of congressional seats, brought about a dramatic revival of congressional interest in the problems of the Congress's control over executive activities. A variety of new laws were enacted to achieve more control: for example, widening the requirement of Senate approval of presidential appointees to executive offices; creation of the Congressional Budget Office to act as a legislative fiscal watchdog; the passage of the Freedom of Information Act to provide Congress and the general public with greater access to executive activities; and the War Powers Resolution, which restricted presidential initiative in foreign military involvements.

Concomitant with the rise of congressional oversight in the 1960s and 1970s, it became fashionable to argue that governmental policies emerged from *iron triangles*—three-way interactions involving elected members of Congress, particularly key committee and subcommittee chairpersons; career bureaucrats, particularly agency heads or senior staffers; and special interest lobbies, particularly powerful lobbies in specialized fields like health, welfare, education, and defense. From this closed triad of interests, so the theory goes, governmental

[2]Allen Schick, "Congress and the 'Details' of Administration," *Public Administration Review,* 36 (Sept./Oct. 1976), pp. 516–528.

policies emerge by means of members of Congress writing and passing favorable legislation, bureaucrats implementing these congressional mandates in return for bigger budgets, and special-interest groups backing (with re-election monies and other support) the helpful members of Congress: In all, a tidy and closed relationship.

Is this how the political-administrative relationships in government actually work today? In the following essay Hugh Heclo (1944–   ), currently a professor of government at George Mason University, takes issue with the iron triangle conception of modern political-administrative relationships. He emphasizes, "The iron triangle concept is not so much wrong as it is disastrously incomplete." "Unfortunately," writes Heclo, "our standard political conceptions of power and control are not very well suited to the loose-jointed play of influence that is emerging in political administration. We tend to look for one group exerting dominance over another, for subgovernments that are strongly insulated from other outside forces in the environment, for policies that get 'produced' by a few 'makers.'" Instead, says Heclo, in "looking for the few who are powerful, we tend to overlook the many whose webs of influence provoke and guide the exercise of power. These webs, or what I will call 'issue networks,' are particularly relevant to the highly intricate and confusing welfare policies that have been undertaken in recent years."

Note that in Heclo's view of the *issue networks,* unlike the iron triangle concept, which assumed a small identifiable circle of participants, the participants are largely shifting, fluid, and anonymous. In fact, he writes, "it is almost impossible to say where a network leaves off and its environment begins." Whereas iron triangles are seen as relatively stable groups that coalesce around narrow policy issues, Heclo's issue networks are dispersed and numerous players move in and out of the transitory networks, without anyone being clearly in control over programs or policies. Although the "iron triangles at their roots had economic gain as an interest of all parties concerned," Heclo believes "any direct material interest is often secondary to intellectual or emotional commitment involving issue networks." Passion, ideas, and moral dedication replace, to a significant degree, material and economic gain from policy involvement.

The profound influence of the rise of these issue networks on government is manifold, Heclo thinks, especially in adding new layers of complexity to government. First, networks keep issues, potentially simple to solve, complex instead, primarily in order to gain power and influence by virtue of their own specialized expertise. Second, rather than fostering knowledge and consensus, issue networks push for argument, division, and contention to "maintain the purity of their viewpoints," which in turn sustain support from their natural but narrow public constituencies. Third, issue networks spawn true believers who become zealots for narrow interests rather than seekers of broad mandates of consensus, support, and confidence for public programs. Finally, rather than pushing for closure of debate, issue networks thrive by keeping arguments boiling and disagreements brewing. They survive by talking, debating, and arguing the alternatives, and not by finding common grounds for agreement and getting down to making things happen.

As you read this selection, keep the following questions in mind:

How does Heclo's issue network concept differ from the notion of iron triangles as the basis for political-administrative relationships?

What examples does Heclo give to support his new conceptualization of this relationship?

Do you find his arguments reasonable and correct on the basis of your experience or your reading of the case studies in this text?

What impact does the rise of issue networks have on democratic government in general and public administration in particular?

What new roles must public administrators assume, given the growth of issue networks today? Specifically, in your opinion, how can an administrator prepare or be trained for assuming these new roles?

HUGH HECLO

Issue Networks and the Executive Establishment

The connection between politics and administration arouses remarkably little interest in the United States. The presidency is considered more glamorous, Congress more intriguing, elections more exciting, and interest groups more troublesome. General levels of public interest can be gauged by the burst of indifference that usually greets the announcement of a new President's cabinet or rumors of a political appointee's resignation. Unless there is some White House "tie-in" or scandal (preferably both), news stories about presidential appointments are usually treated by the media as routine filler material.

This lack of interest in political administration is rarely found in other democratic countries, and it has not always prevailed in the United States. In most nations the ups and downs of political executives are taken as vital signs of the health of a government, indeed of its survival. In the United States, the nineteenth-century turmoil over one type of connection between politics and administration—party spoils—frequently overwhelmed any notion of presidential leadership. Anyone reading the history of those troubled decades is likely to be struck by the way in which political administration in Washington registered many of the deeper strains in American society at large. It is a curious switch that appointments to the bureaucracy should loom so large in the history of the nineteenth century, when the federal government did little, and be so completely discounted in the twentieth century, when government tries to do so much.

Political administration in Washington continues to register strains in American politics and society, although in ways more subtle than the nineteenth-century spoils scramble between Federalists and Democrats, Pro- and Anti-tariff forces, Nationalists and States-Righters, and so on. Unlike many other countries, the United States has never created a high level, government-wide civil service. Neither has it been fa-

Excerpted with permission from Anthony King, ed., *The New Political System.* Washington, D.C.: American Enterprise Institute for Public Policy Research, 1978, pp. 87–124.

vored with a political structure that automatically produces a stock of experienced political manpower for top executive positions in government.[1] How then does political administration in Washington work? More to the point, how might the expanding role of government be changing the connection between administration and politics?

Received opinion on this subject suggests that we already know the answers. Control is said to be vested in an informal but enduring series of "iron triangles" linking executive bureaus, congressional committees, and interest group clienteles with a stake in particular programs. A President or presidential appointee may occasionally try to muscle in, but few people doubt the capacity of these subgovernments to thwart outsiders in the long run.

Based largely on early studies of agricultural, water, and public works policies, the iron triangle concept is not so much wrong as it is disastrously incomplete.[2] And the conventional view is especially inappropriate for understanding changes in politics and administration during recent years. Preoccupied with trying to find the few truly powerful actors, observers tend to overlook the power and influence that arise out of the configurations through which leading policy makers move and do business with each other. Looking for the closed triangles of control, we tend to miss the fairly open networks of people that increasingly impinge upon government.

To do justice to the subject would require a major study of the Washington community and the combined inspiration of a Leonard White and a James Young. Tolerating a fair bit of injustice, one can sketch a few of the factors that seem to be at work. The first is growth in the sheer mass of government activity and associated expectations. The second is the peculiar, loose-jointed play of influence that is accompanying this growth. Related to these two is the third: the layering and specialization that have overtaken the government work force, not least the political leadership of the bureaucracy.

All of this vastly complicates the job of presidential appointees both in controlling their own actions and in managing the bureaucracy. But there is much more at stake than the troubles faced by people in government. There is the deeper problem of connecting what politicians, officials, and their fellow travelers are doing in Washington with what the public at large can understand and accept. It is on this point that political administration registers some of the larger strains of American politics and society, much as it did in the nineteenth century. For what it shows is a dissolving of organized politics and a politicizing of organizational life throughout the nation. . . .

Unfortunately, our standard political conceptions of power and control are not very well suited to the loose-jointed play of influence that is emerging in political administration. We tend to look for one group exerting dominance over another, for subgovernments that are strongly insulated from other outside forces in the environment, for policies that get "produced" by a few "makers." Seeing former government officials opening law firms or joining a new trade association, we naturally think of ways in which they are trying to conquer and control particular pieces of government machinery.

Obviously questions of power are still important. But for a host of policy initiatives undertaken in the last twenty years it is all but impossible to identify clearly who the dominant actors are. Who is controlling those actions that go to make up our national policy on abortions, or on income redistribution, or consumer protection, or energy? Looking for the few who are powerful, we tend to overlook the many whose webs of influence provoke and guide the exercise of power. These webs, or what I will call "issue

[1]Hugh Heclo, *A Government of Strangers: Executive Politics in Washington* (Washington, D.C.: Brookings Institution, 1977).

[2]Perhaps the most widely cited interpretations are J. Leiper Freeman, *The Political Process* (New York: Random House, 1965); and Douglass Cater, *Power in Washington* (New York: Vintage, 1964).

networks," are particularly relevant to the highly intricate and confusing welfare policies that have been undertaken in recent years.

The notion of iron triangles and subgovernments presumes small circles of participants who have succeeded in becoming largely autonomous. Issue networks, on the other hand, comprise a large number of participants with quite variable degrees of mutual commitment or of dependence on others in their environment; in fact it is almost impossible to say where a network leaves off and its environment begins. Iron triangles and subgovernments suggest a stable set of participants coalesced to control fairly narrow public programs which are in the direct economic interest of each party to the alliance. Issue networks are almost the reverse image in each respect. Participants move in and out of the networks constantly. Rather than groups united in dominance over a program, no one, as far as one can tell, is in control of the policies and issues. Any direct material interest is often secondary to intellectual or emotional commitment. Network members reinforce each other's sense of issues as their interests, rather than (as standard political or economic models would have it) interests defining positions on issues.

Issue networks operate at many levels, from the vocal minority who turn up at local planning commission hearings to the renowned professor who is quietly telephoned by the White House to give a quick "reading" on some participant or policy. The price of buying into one or another issue network is watching, reading, talking about, and trying to act on particular policy problems. Powerful interest groups can be found represented in networks but so too can individuals in or out of government who have a reputation for being knowledgeable. Particular professions may be prominent, but the true experts in the networks are those who are issue-skilled (that is, well informed about the ins and outs of a particular policy debate) regardless of formal professional training. More than mere technical experts, network people are policy activists who know each other through the issues.

Those who emerge to positions of wider leadership are policy politicians—experts in using experts, victuallers of knowledge in a world hungry for right decisions.

In the old days—when the primary problem of government was assumed to be doing what was right, rather than knowing what was right—policy knowledge could be contained in the slim adages of public administration. Public executives, it was thought, needed to know how to execute. They needed power commensurate with their responsibility. Nowadays, of course, political administrators do not execute but are involved in making highly important decisions on society's behalf, and they must mobilize policy intermediaries to deliver the goods. Knowing what is right becomes crucial, and since no one knows that for sure, going through the process of dealing with those who are judged knowledgeable (or at least continuously concerned) becomes even more crucial. Instead of power commensurate with responsibility, issue networks seek influence commensurate with their understanding of the various, complex social choices being made. Of course some participants would like nothing better than complete power over the issues in question. Others seem to want little more than the security that comes with being well informed. As the executive of one new group moving to Washington put it, "We didn't come here to change the world; we came to minimize our surprises."[3]

Whatever the participants' motivation, it is the issue network that ties together what would otherwise be the contradictory tendencies of, on the one hand, more widespread organizational participation in public policy and, on the other, more narrow technocratic specialization in complex modern policies. Such networks need to be distinguished from three other more familiar terms used in connection with political administration. An issue network is a shared-

[3]Steven V. Roberts, "Trade Associations Flocking to Capital as U.S. Role Rises," *New York Times,* March 4, 1978, p. 44.

knowledge group having to do with some aspect (or, as defined by the network, some problem) of public policy. It is therefore more well-defined than, first, a shared-attention group or "public"; those in the networks are likely to have a common base of information and understanding of how one knows about policy and identifies its problems. But knowledge does not necessarily produce agreement. Issue networks may or may not, therefore, be mobilized into, second, a shared-action group (creating a coalition) or, third, a shared-belief group (becoming a conventional interest organization). Increasingly, it is through networks of people who regard each other as knowledgeable, or at least as needing to be answered, that public policy issues tend to be refined, evidence debated, and alternative options worked out—though rarely in any controlled, well-organized way.

What does an issue network look like? It is difficult to say precisely, for at any given time only one part of a network may be active and through time the various connections may intensify or fade among the policy intermediaries and the executive and congressional bureaucracies. For example, there is no single health policy network but various sets of people knowledgeable and concerned about cost-control mechanisms, insurance techniques, nutritional programs, prepaid plans, and so on. At one time, those expert in designing a nationwide insurance system may seem to be operating in relative isolation, until it becomes clear that previous efforts to control costs have already created precedents that have to be accommodated in any new system, or that the issue of federal funding for abortions has laid land mines in the path of any workable plan.

The debate on energy policy is rich in examples of the kaleidoscopic interaction of changing issue networks. The Carter administration's initial proposal was worked out among experts who were closely tied in to conservation-minded networks. Soon it became clear that those concerned with macroeconomic policies had been largely bypassed in the planning, and last-minute amendments were made in the proposal presented to Congress, a fact that was not lost on the networks of leading economists and economic correspondents. Once congressional consideration began, it quickly became evident that attempts to define the energy debate in terms of a classic confrontation between big oil companies and consumer interests were doomed. More and more policy watchers joined in the debate, bringing to it their own concerns and analyses: tax reformers, nuclear power specialists, civil rights groups interested in more jobs; the list soon grew beyond the wildest dreams of the original energy policy planners. The problem, it became clear, was that no one could quickly turn the many networks of knowledgeable people into a shared-action coalition, much less into a single, shared-attitude group believing it faced the moral equivalent of war. Or, if it was a war, it was a Vietnam-type quagmire.

It would be foolish to suggest that the clouds of issue networks that have accompanied expanding national policies are set to replace the more familiar politics of subgovernments in Washington. What they are doing is to overlay the once stable political reference points with new forces that complicate calculations, decrease predictability, and impose considerable strains on those charged with government leadership. The overlay of networks and issue politics not only confronts but also seeps down into the formerly well-established politics of particular policies and programs. Social security, which for a generation had been quietly managed by a small circle of insiders, becomes controversial and politicized. The Army Corps of Engineers, once the picturebook example of control by subgovernments, is dragged into the brawl on environmental politics. The once quiet "traffic safety establishment" finds its own safety permanently endangered by the consumer movement. Confrontation between networks and iron triangles in the Social and Rehabilitation Service, the disintegration of the mighty politics of the Public Health Service and its corps—the list could be extended into a chronicle of American national government during the last generation. The point is that a somewhat new and difficult dynamic is being played out in the world of politics and administration. It is not what has been feared for so long: that technocrats and other people in white coats will expropriate the policy process. If there is to be any expropriation, it is likely to be by the policy activists, those who care deeply about a set of issues and are determined to shape the fabric of public policy accordingly. . . .

The Executive Leadership Problem

Washington has always relied on informal means of producing political leaders in government. This is no less true now than in the days when party spoils ruled presidential appointments. It is the informal mechanisms that have changed. No doubt some of the increasing emphasis on educational credentials, professional specialization, and technical facility merely reflects changes in society at large. But it is also important to recognize that government activity has itself been changing the informal mechanisms that produce political administrators. Accumulating policy commitments have become crucial forces affecting the kind of executive leadership that emerges. E. E. Schattschneider put it better when he observed that "new policies create new politics."[4]

For many years now the list of issues on the public agenda has grown more dense as new policy concerns have been added and few dropped. Administratively, this has proliferated the number of policy intermediaries. Politically, it has mobilized more and more groups of people who feel they have a stake, a determined stake, in this or that issue of public policy. These changes are in turn encouraging further specialization of the government's work force and bureaucratic layering in its political leadership. However, the term "political" needs to be used carefully. Modern officials responsible for making the connection between politics and administration bear little resemblance to the party politicians who once filled patronage jobs. Rather, today's political executive is likely to be a person knowledgeable about the substance of particular issues and adept at moving among the networks of people who are intensely concerned about them.

What are the implications for American government and politics? The verdict cannot be one-sided, if only because political management of the bureaucracy serves a number of diverse purposes. At least three important advantages can be found in the emerging system.

First, the reliance on issue networks and policy politicians is obviously consistent with some of the larger changes in society. Ordinary voters are apparently less constrained by party identification and more attracted to an issue-based style of politics. Party organizations are said to have fallen into a state of decay and to have become less capable of supplying enough highly qualified executive manpower. If government is committed to intervening in more complex, specialized areas, it is useful to draw upon the experts and policy specialists for the public management of these programs. Moreover, the congruence between an executive leadership and an electorate that are both uninterested in party politics may help stabilize a rapidly changing society. Since no one really knows how to solve the policy puzzles, policy politicians have the important quality of being disposable without any serious political ramifications (unless of course there are major symbolic implications, as in President Nixon's firing of Attorney General Elliot Richardson).

Within government, the operation of issue networks may have a second advantage in that they link Congress and the executive branch in ways that political parties no longer can. For many years, reformers have sought to revive the idea of party discipline as a means of spanning

[4]E. E. Schattschneider, *Politics, Pressures and the Tariff* (Hamden: Archon, 1963), p. 288 (originally published 1935).

the distance between the two branches and turning their natural competition to useful purposes. But as the troubled dealings of recent Democratic Presidents with their majorities in Congress have indicated, political parties tend to be a weak bridge.

Meanwhile, the linkages of technocracy between the branches are indeliberately growing. The congressional bureaucracy that has blossomed in Washington during the last generation is in many ways like the political bureaucracy in the executive branch. In general, the new breed of congressional staffer is not a legislative crony or beneficiary of patronage favors. Personal loyalty to the congressman is still paramount, but the new-style legislative bureaucrat is likely to be someone skilled in dealing with certain complex policy issues, possibly with credentials as a policy analyst, but certainly an expert in using other experts and their networks.

None of this means an absence of conflict between President and Congress. Policy technicians in the two branches are still working for different sets of clients with different interests. The point is that the growth of specialized policy networks tends to perform the same useful services that it was once hoped a disciplined national party system would perform. Sharing policy knowledge, the networks provide a minimum common framework for political debate and decision in the two branches. For example, on energy policy, regardless of one's position on gas deregulation or incentives to producers, the policy technocracy has established a common language for discussing the issues, a shared grammar for identifying the major points of contention, a mutually familiar rhetoric of argumentation. Whether in Congress or the executive branch or somewhere outside, the "movers and shakers" in energy policy (as in health insurance, welfare reform, strategic arms limitation, occupational safety, and a host of other policy areas) tend to share an analytic repertoire for coping with the issues. Like experienced party politicians of earlier times, policy politicians in the knowledge

networks may not agree; but they understand each other's way of looking at the world and arguing about policy choices.

A third advantage is the increased maneuvering room offered to political executives by the loose-jointed play of influence. If appointees were ambassadors from clearly defined interest groups and professions, or if policy were monopolized in iron triangles, then the chances for executive leadership in the bureaucracy would be small. In fact, however, the proliferation of administrative middlemen and networks of policy watchers offers new strategic resources for public managers. These are mainly opportunities to split and recombine the many sources of support and opposition that exist on policy issues. Of course, there are limits on how far a political executive can go in shopping for a constituency, but the general tendency over time has been to extend those limits. A secretary of labor will obviously pay close attention to what the AFL-CIO has to say, but there are many other voices to hear, not only in the union movement but also minority groups interested in jobs, state and local officials administering the department's programs, consumer groups worried about wage-push inflation, employees faced with unsafe working conditions, and so on. By the same token, former Secretary of Transportation William Coleman found new room for maneuver on the problem of landings by supersonic planes when he opened up the setpiece debate between pro- and anti-Concorde groups to a wider play of influence through public hearings. Clearly the richness of issue politics demands a high degree of skill to contain expectations and manage the natural dissatisfaction that comes from courting some groups rather than others. But at least it is a game that can be affected by skill, rather than one that is predetermined by immutable forces.

These three advantages are substantial. But before we embrace the rule of policy politicians and their networks, it is worth considering the threats they pose for American government. Issue networks may be good at influencing policy, but can they govern? Should they?

414 Chapter 14 / The Relationship Between Politics and Administration

The first and foremost problem is the old one of democratic legitimacy. Weaknesses in executive leadership below the level of the President have never really been due to interest groups, party politics, or Congress. The primary problem has always been the lack of any democratically based power. Political executives get their popular mandate to do anything in the bureaucracy secondhand, from either an elected chief executive or Congress. The emerging system of political technocrats makes this democratic weakness much more severe. The more closely political administrators become identified with the various specialized policy networks, the farther they become separated from the ordinary citizen. Political executives can maneuver among the already mobilized issue networks and may occasionally do a little mobilizing of their own. But this is not the same thing as creating a broad base of public understanding and support for national policies. The typical presidential appointee will travel to any number of conferences, make speeches to the membership of one association after another, but almost never will he or she have to see or listen to an ordinary member of the public. The trouble is that only a small minority of citizens, even of those who are seriously attentive to public affairs, are likely to be mobilized in the various networks.[5] Those who are not policy activists depend on the ability of government institutions to act on their behalf.

If the problem were merely an information gap between policy experts and the bulk of the population, then more communication might help. Yet instead of garnering support for policy choices, more communication from the issue networks tends to produce an "everything causes cancer" syndrome among ordinary citizens. Policy forensics among the networks yield more experts making more sophisticated claims

and counterclaims to the point that the nonspecialist becomes inclined to concede everything and believe nothing that he hears. The ongoing debates on energy policy, health crises, or arms limitation are rich in examples of public skepticism about what "they," the abstruse policy experts, are doing and saying. While the highly knowledgeable have been playing a larger role in government, the proportion of the general public concluding that those running the government don't seem to know what they are doing has risen rather steadily.[6] Likewise, the more government has tried to help, the more feelings of public helplessness have grown.

No doubt many factors and events are linked to these changing public attitudes. The point is that the increasing prominence of issue networks is bound to aggravate problems of legitimacy and public disenchantment. Policy activists have little desire to recognize an unpleasant fact: that their influential systems for knowledgeable policy making tend to make democratic politics more difficult. There are at least four reasons.

Complexity

Democratic political competition is based on the idea of trying to simplify complexity into a few, broadly intelligible choices. The various issue networks, on the other hand, have a stake in searching out complexity in what might seem

[5]An interesting recent case study showing the complexity of trying to generalize about who is "mobilizable" is James N. Rosenau, *Citizenship Between Elections* (New York: The Free Press, 1974).

[6]Since 1964 the Institute for Social Research at the University of Michigan has asked the question, "Do you feel that almost all of the people running the government are smart people, or do you think that quite a few of them don't seem to know what they are doing?" The proportions choosing the latter view have been 28 percent (1964), 38 percent (1968), 45 percent (1970), 42 percent (1972), 47 percent (1974), and 52 percent (1976). For similar findings on public feelings of lack of control over the policy process, see U.S. Congress, Senate, Subcommittee on Intergovernmental Relations of the Committee on Government Operations, *Confidence and Concern: Citizens View American Government,* committee print, 93d Cong., 1st sess., 1973, pt. 1, p. 30. For a more complete discussion of recent trends see the two articles by Arthur H. Miller and Jack Citrin in the *American Political Science Review* (September 1974).

simple. Those who deal with particular policy issues over the years recognize that policy objectives are usually vague and results difficult to measure. Actions relevant to one policy goal can frequently be shown to be inconsistent with others. To gain a reputation as a knowledgeable participant, one must juggle all of these complexities and demand that other technocrats in the issue networks do the same.

Consensus

A major aim in democratic politics is, after open argument, to arrive at some workable consensus of views. Whether by trading off one issue against another or by combining related issues, the goal is agreement. Policy activists may commend this democratic purpose in theory, but what their issue networks actually provide is a way of processing dissension. The aim is good policy—the right outcome on the issue. Since what that means is disputable among knowledgeable people, the desire for agreement must often take second place to one's understanding of the issue. Trade-offs or combinations—say, right-to-life groups with nuclear-arms-control people; environmentalists and consumerists; civil liberties groups and anti-gun controllers—represent a kind of impurity for many of the newly proliferating groups. In general there are few imperatives pushing for political consensus among the issue networks and many rewards for those who become practiced in the techniques of informed skepticism about different positions.

Confidence

Democratic politics presumes a kind of psychological asymmetry between leaders and followers. Those competing for leadership positions are expected to be sure of themselves and of what is to be done, while those led are expected to have a certain amount of detachment and dubiety in choosing how to give their consent to be governed. Politicians are supposed to take

credit for successes, to avoid any appearance of failure, and to fix blame clearly on their opponents; voters weigh these claims and come to tentative judgments, pending the next competition among the leaders.

The emerging policy networks tend to reverse the situation. Activists mobilized around the policy issues are the true believers. To survive, the newer breed of leaders, or policy politicians, must become well versed in the complex, highly disputed substance of the issues. A certain tentativeness comes naturally as ostensible leaders try to spread themselves across the issues. Taking credit shows a lack of understanding of how intricate policies work and may antagonize those who really have been zealously pushing the issue. Spreading blame threatens others in the established networks and may raise expectations that new leadership can guarantee a better policy result. Vagueness about what is to be done allows policy problems to be dealt with as they develop and in accord with the intensity of opinion among policy specialists at that time. None of this is likely to warm the average citizen's confidence in his leaders. The new breed of policy politicians are cool precisely because the issue networks are hot.

Closure

Part of the genius of democratic politics is its ability to find a nonviolent decision-rule (by voting) for ending debate in favor of action. All the incentives in the policy technocracy work against such decisive closure. New studies and findings can always be brought to bear. The biggest rewards in these highly intellectual groups go to those who successfully challenge accepted wisdom. The networks thrive by continuously weighing alternative courses of action on particular policies, not by suspending disbelief and accepting that something must be done.

For all of these reasons, what is good for policy making (in the sense of involving well-informed people and rigorous analysts) may be bad for democratic politics. The emerging policy technocracy tends, as Henry Aaron has said of social science research, to "corrode any simple faiths around which political coalitions ordinarily are built."[7] Should we be content with simple faiths? Perhaps not; but the great danger is that the emerging world of issue politics and policy experts will turn John Stuart Mill's argument about the connection between liberty and popular government on its head. More informed argument about policy choices may produce more incomprehensibility. More policy intermediaries may widen participation among activists but deepen suspicions among unorganized nonspecialists. There may be more group involvement and less democratic legitimacy, more knowledge and more Know-Nothingism. Activists are likely to remain unsatisfied with, and nonactivists uncommitted to, what government is doing. Superficially this cancelling of forces might seem to assure a conservative tilt away from new, expansionary government policies. However, in terms of undermining a democratic identification of ordinary citizens with their government, the tendencies are profoundly radical.

A second difficulty with the issue networks is the problem that they create for the President as ostensible chief of the executive establishment. The emerging policy technocracy puts presidential appointees outside of the chief executive's reach in a way that narrowly focused iron triangles rarely can. At the end of the day, constituents of these triangles can at least be bought off by giving them some of the material advantages that they crave. But for issue activists it is likely to be a question of policy choices that are right or wrong. In this situation, more analysis and staff expertise—far from helping—may only hinder the President in playing an independent political leadership role. The influence of the policy technicians and their networks permeates everything the White House may want to do. Without their expertise there are no option papers, no detailed data and elaborate assessments to stand up against the onslaught of the issue experts in Congress and outside. Of course a President can replace a political executive, but that is probably merely to substitute one incumbent of the relevant policy network for another.

It is, therefore, no accident that President Carter found himself with a cabinet almost none of whom were either his longstanding political backers or leaders of his party. Few if any of his personal retinue could have passed through the reputational screens of the networks to be named, for example, a secretary of labor or defense. Moreover, anyone known to be close to the President and placed in an operating position in the bureaucracy puts himself, and through him the President, in an extremely vulnerable position. Of the three cabinet members who were President Carter's own men, one, Andrew Young, was under extreme pressure to resign in the first several months. Another Carter associate, Bert Lance, was successfully forced to resign after six months, and the third, Griffin Bell, was given particularly tough treatment during his confirmation hearings and was being pressured to resign after only a year in office. The emerging system of political administration tends to produce executive arrangements in which the President's power stakes are on the line almost everywhere in terms of policy, whereas almost nowhere is anyone on the line for him personally.

Where does all this leave the President as a politician and as an executive of executives? In an impossible position. The problem of connecting politics and administration currently places any President in a classic no-win predicament. If he attempts to use personal loyalists as agency and department heads, he will be accused of politicizing the bureaucracy and will most likely put his executives in an untenable position for dealing with their organizations and the related networks. If he tries to create a countervailing

[7]Henry J. Aaron, *Politics and the Professors* (Washington, D.C.: Brookings Institution, 1978), p. 159.

source of policy expertise at the center, he will be accused of aggrandizing the Imperial Presidency and may hopelessly bureaucratize the White House's operations. If he relies on some benighted idea of collective cabinet government and on departmental executives for leadership in the bureaucracy (as Carter did in his first term), then the President does more than risk abdicating his own leadership responsibilities as the only elected executive in the national government; he is bound to become a creature of the issue networks and the policy specialists. It would be pleasant to think that there is a neat way out of this trilemma, but there is not.

Finally, there are disturbing questions surrounding the accountability of a political technocracy. The real problem is not that policy specialists specialize but that, by the nature of public office, they must generalize. Whatever an influential political executive does is done with all the collective authority of government and in the name of the public at large. It is not difficult to imagine situations in which policies make excellent sense within the cloisters of the expert issue watchers and yet are nonsense or worse seen from the viewpoint of ordinary people, the kinds of people political executives rarely meet. Since political executives themselves never need to pass muster with the electorate, the main source of democratic accountability must lie with the President and Congress. Given the President's problems and Congress's own burgeoning bureaucracy of policy specialists, the prospects for a democratically responsible executive establishment are poor at best.

Perhaps we need not worry. A case could be made that all we are seeing is a temporary commotion stirred up by a generation of reformist policies. In time the policy process may reenter a period of detumescence as the new groups and networks subside into the familiar triangulations of power.

However, a stronger case can be made that the changes will endure. In the first place, sufficient policy-making forces have now converged in Washington that it is unlikely that we will see a return to the familiar cycle of federal quiescence and policy experimentation by state governments. The central government, surrounded by networks of policy specialists, probably now has the capacity for taking continual policy initiatives. In the second place, there seems to be no way of braking, much less reversing, policy expectations generated by the compensatory mentality. To cut back on commitments undertaken in the last generation would itself be a major act of redistribution and could be expected to yield even more turmoil in the policy process. Once it becomes accepted that relative rather than absolute deprivation is what matters, the crusaders can always be counted upon to be in business.

A third reason why our politics and administration may never be the same lies in the very fact that so many policies have already been accumulated. Having to make policy in an environment already crowded with public commitments and programs increases the odds of multiple, indirect impacts of one policy on another, of one perspective set in tension with another, of one group and then another being mobilized. This sort of complexity and unpredictability creates a hostile setting for any return to traditional interest group politics.

Imagine trying to govern in a situation where the short-term political resources you need are stacked around a changing series of discrete issues, and where people overseeing these issues have nothing to prevent their pressing claims beyond any resources that they can offer in return. Imagine too that the more they do so, the more you lose understanding and support from public backers who have the long-term resources that you need. Whipsawed between cynics and true believers, policy would always tend to evolve to levels of insolubility. It is not easy for a society to politicize itself and at the same time depoliticize government leadership. But we in the United States may be managing to do just this.

CASE STUDY 14

Introduction

Eighteen American Warplanes set out from Lakenheath Air Base in England . . . April 14, 1986, to begin a 14-hour, 5,400-mile round-trip flight to Tripoli, Libya. It is now clear that nine of those Air Force F–111's had an unprecedented peacetime mission. Their targets: Col. Muammar el-Qaddafi and his family.

So begins Seymour M. Hersh's fascinating story of the Reagan administration's abortive attempt to kill Libyan leader Colonel Qaddafi. Ultimately, as Hersh describes, although the plot failed because of some curious unforeseen mishaps, this event raises disturbing issues about the way American foreign policy is administered as well as its effective oversight by politically responsible officials.

Seymour Hersh, a senior *New York Times* investigative reporter, not only carefully reconstructs the facts surrounding this failed assassination attempt, which might well have brought America into a full-scale Middle Eastern war, but also takes the reader behind the scenes into the shadowy, little-understood world of covert operations and high-level foreign policy intrigue involving a five-year effort "to get Qaddafi." The whole affair, which was shrouded in secrecy and involved numerous "players" at the White House, CIA, State Department, and Defense Department. They relied heavily on internal manipulation of data, "backchannels" to promote their plans, distribution of deceptive intelligence information, conscious withholding of other information (called "disinformation"), and questionable evidence of the terrorist bombing of a West Berlin discotheque to justify the attack. "They covered their tracks beautifully," Lt. Colonel Oliver North, a key National Security adviser who helped develop the plan is quoted as saying. "There was no executive order to kill."

Hersh's story relates cogently to the preceding selection by Hugh Heclo. What is the appropriate relationship between politics and administration, between political oversight and bureaucratic action, or between policy choice and policy implementation? Who *should* be in charge? Who should be accountable, and how?

Recall that much of Heclo's essay argues against the "iron triangle" notion as a realistic way for us to think about contemporary political-administrative relationships. Instead, Heclo posits a more complex concept, one he sees as a more realistic view of the problem, one that he terms *issue networks*.

As you read this case, think about what it says *generally* about Heclo's thesis from the standpoint of the following questions:

Where was administrative responsibility lodged in this case? To whom were "the pros" accountable *in theory* and *in practice?* Why were the lines of accountability and oversight not all that clear? Indeed, who were "the pros" and "the pols" in this story and how did their own identity confusion (i.e., whether or not they were professionals *or* politicians) help create these fundamental issues of accountability?

Why are communications so critical to effective political oversight? (You might review Chapter 9, which deals with communications.) How is it evidenced in this case? What particular tactics and strategies did the key players use to control communications to their own advantage and thus escape political oversight by Congress? Why were they permitted to do this? How can this situation be prevented in the future?

Does the term *issue networks* adequately describe the reality of political-administrative relationships in this case? Is the term *iron triangles* better? What term properly describes these relationships? Or, can you invent a new descriptive term to identify the political-administrative relationship in this case study?

As evidenced by this story, why is the problem of relating politics to administration so important and critical for us today? And yet, why is it so difficult to clarify either in theory or achieve in practice? What ideas or institutional practices might help solve this dilemma?

SEYMOUR M. HERSH

Target Qaddafi

Eighteen American warplanes set out from Lakenheath Air Base in England . . . April 14 [1986] to begin a 14-hour, 5,400-mile round-trip flight to Tripoli, Libya. It is now clear that nine of those Air Force F-111's had an unprecedented peacetime mission. Their targets: Col. Muammar el-Qaddafi and his family.

The mission, authorized by the White House, was to be the culmination of a five-year clandestine effort by the Reagan Administration to eliminate Qaddafi, who had been described a few days earlier by the President as the "mad dog of the Middle East."

Since early 1981, the Central Intelligence Agency had been encouraging and abetting Libyan exile groups and foreign governments, especially those of Egypt and France, in their efforts to stage a coup d'état—and kill, if necessary—the bizarre Libyan strongman. But Qaddafi, with his repeated threats to President Reagan and support of international terrorism, survived every confrontation and in the spring of 1986 continued to be solidly in control of Libya's 3 million citizens. Now the supersonic Air Force F-111's were ordered to accomplish what the C.I.A. could not. . . .

From *The New York Times Magazine* (February 22, 1987) pp. 17ff. Copyright © 1987 by the New York Times Company. Reprinted by permission.

The planners for the Libyan raid avoided the more formal White House Situation Room, where such meetings might be noticed by other staffers, and met instead in the office of former Navy Capt. Rodney B. McDaniel, the N.S.C.'s executive secretary. The small ad hoc group, formally known as the Crisis Pre-planning Group, included Army Lieut. Gen. John H. Moellering of the Joint Chiefs of Staff; Michael H. Armacost, Under Secretary of State for political affairs, and Richard L. Armitage, Assistant Secretary of Defense for international security affairs. Most of the planning documents and option papers on the bombing were assigned to a small subcommittee headed by North; this committee included Howard J. Teicher, the N.S.C.'s Near East specialist, and Capt. James R. Stark of the Navy, who was assigned to the N.S.C.'s office of political-military affairs.

For [Oliver] North, a Marine lieutenant colonel who had emerged by early 1985 as the ranking National Security Council operative on terrorism, the Libyan raid was a chance to begin a new phase in the American counterterrorism struggle—the direct use of military force. He had served as a member of Vice President Bush's Task Force on Combating Terrorism, whose report—made public last February—presciently summarized the pros and cons of the mission:

"Use of our well-trained and capable military forces offers an excellent chance of success if a military option can be implemented. Successful employment, however, depends on timely and refined intelligence and prompt positioning of forces. Counterterrorism missions are high-risk/high-gain operations which can have a severe negative impact on U.S. prestige if they fail."

At the time of the attack on Libya, North, [John] Poindexter [National Security Council Director] and Teicher had been deeply involved in the Administration's secret arms dealings with Iran for nearly a year; they also knew that funds from those dealings were being funneled from a Swiss bank account controlled by North to the Administration-backed contras fighting against the Sandinista Government in Nicaragua.

North has told associates that only he and a few colleagues worked on the targeting of Qaddafi and that they left no written record. " 'There was no executive order to kill and no administrative directive to go after Qaddafi,' " one former N.S.C. official quotes North as saying. "They've covered their tracks beautifully."

Even the official bombing orders supplied by the White House to the Pentagon did not cite as targets the tent where Qaddafi worked or his family home. Instead, North has told colleagues, the stated targets were the command-and-control center and administrative buildings of El-Azziziya Barracks in Tripoli, none of which were struck by bombs, as well as the military side of the Tripoli airport and a commando training site in the nearby port city of Sidi Bilal, which were hit by the other nine F-111's. Also mistakenly hit by one F-111 assigned to attack the barracks was a heavily populated residential area of Tripoli near the French Embassy.

The shielded orders explain a series of strong denials after the bombing, especially by State Department officials, when it became clear that Qaddafi's personal quarters had been a primary target. That, too, was part of the White House orchestration, officials acknowledge.

One well-informed Air Force intelligence officer says, "There's no question they were looking for Qaddafi. It was briefed that way. They were going to kill him." An Air Force pilot involved in highly classified special operations acknowledges that "the assassination was the big thing."

Senior Air Force officers confidently predicted prior to the raid that the nine aircraft assigned to the special mission had a 95 percent "P.K."—probable kill. Each of the nine F-111's carried four 2,000-pound bombs. The young pilots and weapons-systems officers, who sit side-by-side in the cockpit, were provided with reconnaissance photographs separately depicting, according to one Air Force intelligence officer, "where Qaddafi was and where his family was."

The mission was the first combat assignment for most of the fliers. Qaddafi's home and his camouflaged Bedouin tent, where he often worked throughout the night, were inside the grounds of El-Azziziya. The notion of targeting Qaddafi's family, according to an involved N.S.C. aide, originated with several senior C.I.A. officers, who claimed that in Bedouin culture Qaddafi would be diminished as a leader if he could not protect his home. One aide recalls a C.I.A. briefing in which it was argued that "if you really get at Qaddafi's house—and by extension, his family—you've destroyed an important connection for the people in terms of loyalty."

In charge of the mission was Col. Sam W. Westbrook 3d, a Rhodes scholar and 1963 Air Force Academy graduate who was subsequently promoted to brigadier general and reassigned in September to the prestigious post of Commandant of Cadets at the Academy. A special biography made available to recruiting officers for the Academy includes a typewritten addendum stating that Westbrook led the Libya raid and cautioning that he "is not cleared to address this subject under any circumstances."

Israeli intelligence, North has told associates, pinpointed Qaddafi's exact location during the long night of April 14, as the Air Force jets, bucking strong headwinds, flew around France, Portugal and Spain to the Mediterranean. The last fix on Qaddafi's location came at 11:15 P.M., Libyan time, two hours and 45 minutes before the first bombs fell. He was still at work in his tent.

In the hours following the raid, Qaddafi's status was not known, but inside the White House there was excitement, one N.S.C. staff aide recalls, upon initial reports that he had not been heard from. Teicher reacted to the belief that Qaddafi had been killed by excitedly telling colleagues: "I'll buy everybody lunch, and not at the Exchange," an inexpensive Friday night staff hangout.

Shortly afterward, a C.I.A. operative in Tripoli informed the agency that the Libyan leader had survived but was said to be shaken by the bombing and the injuries to his family. All eight of Qaddafi's children, as well as his wife, Safiya, were hospitalized, suffering from shock and various injuries. His 15-month-old adopted daughter, Hana, died several hours after the raid.

Poststrike infrared intelligence photographs showed that the bombs, guided by the F-111's sophisticated onboard laser system, left a line of craters that went past both Qaddafi's two-story stucco house and his tent. Newsmen reported that the bombs had damaged his tent and the porticoed family home.

The Air Force viewed Qaddafi's survival as a fluke. Two senior officers separately compare his escape with Hitler's in the assassination attempt led by Count Claus von Stauffenberg in 1944, and a four-star general, after describing in an interview the tight bomb pattern near Qaddafi's tent, says resignedly, "He must have been in the head."

Another well-informed Air Force officer says: "The fact is, they got into the exact target areas they had planned. It was an ironic set of circumstances that prevented Qaddafi from being killed. It was just an accident, a bad day." The officer is referring to the fact that the laser-guidance systems on four of the nine F-111's attacking Qaddafi's quarters malfunctioned prior to the attack. The pilots had to abort the mission before reaching the target, thus eliminating at least 16 more bombs that could have been dropped. The high-technology system that was to insure Qaddafi's death may have spared his life.

The C.I.A. already knew how difficult a target Qaddafi could be. In late 1981, according to a senior Government official, after Libyan forces returned from Chad, Qaddafi promoted the commander of his successful invasion to general and invited him to his desert headquarters. On the jeep ride, the new general pulled out a revolver and fired point-blank at Qaddafi.

The C.I.A. knew of the plot in advance, the official says, but was unable to learn for several days that the officer had missed and been shot to death by the Colonel's security guard, believed to be an East German. After the attempt, Qaddafi was not seen publicly for 40 days.

After the raid on Tripoli, any suggestion that the United States had specifically targeted Qaddafi and his family was brushed aside by senior Administration officials, who emphasized that the Government had no specific knowledge of Qaddafi's whereabouts that night.

Secretary of State George P. Shultz told newsmen, "We are not trying to go after Qaddafi as such, although we think he is a ruler that is better out of his country." One of the Air Force's goals, he said, was to "hit directly" at the guard around Qaddafi.

At a closed budget hearing before the House Appropriations defense subcommittee six days after the raid, Secretary of Defense Caspar W. Weinberger was questioned about the Air Force targeting by Democratic Representative Norman D. Dicks of Washington. "Mr. Secretary, you are a lawyer," Dicks said, according to a subsequently released manuscript. "Can you characterize this in any other way than an attempt to eliminate a foreign leader?"

"Oh, yes, Mr. Dicks, we sure can," Weinberger responded. "His living quarters is a loose term. This is a command-and-control building. His living quarters vary from night to night. He never spends two nights in the same place. His actual living quarters are a big Bedouin sort of tent. We are not targeting him individually."

When questioned for this article, Adm. William J. Crowe Jr., chairman of the Joint Chiefs of Staff, said through a spokesman that there had been what he termed "some loose talk" during planning sessions about "getting" Qaddafi, but, he went on, such targeting was "never part of the plan." The spokesman added, "There was a lot of bantering at these meetings," but Crowe and his aides "did not take the bravado seriously."

A Congressional aide who participated in classified briefings on the raid says he understood all along that the denials of Administration officials of any assassination plans were pro forma. "I found myself feeling somewhat ambivalent," he recalled, because of the Air Force's target—"you know, 'Scum of the earth.'"

A senior American foreign service officer on assignment in the Middle East at the time of the raid recalls having few illusions: "As abhorrent as we find that kind of mission, the Arabs don't. The first word I got was, 'You screwed it up again.' We missed."

Only one F-111 was reported missing during the attack and the overall operation was subsequently described by Weinberger as a complete success.

In private, however, there was acute disappointment in the White House and Pentagon, military officials say, because five of the nine F-111's had failed to engage their target—besides the four malfunctioning guidance systems, human error aboard another F-111 resulted in the bombing of the residential area, killing more than 100 people.

There was criticism from abroad, but the attack was strongly supported by the American public and Congress. A New York Times/CBS poll, taken the day after the raid, showed that 77 percent of those queried approved, although many voiced fear that it would lead to further terrorism.

One reason for the widespread support was a collective sense of revenge: the White House had repeatedly said prior to the attack that it had intercepted a series of communications, said to be "irrefutable" and a "smoking gun," which seemed to directly link Libya to the April 5 bombing of the La Belle discothèque in West Berlin, in which an American serviceman was killed and at least 50 others injured. There were also nearly 200 civilian casualties, including one death.

Many in the intelligence community believe that the Reagan Administration's obsession with Libya began shortly after the President's inauguration in 1981, and remained a constant preoccupation.

Director of Central Intelligence Casey and Secretary of State Alexander M. Haig Jr. took office prepared to move against Qaddafi, who had been utilizing a number of former C.I.A. operatives, most notably Edwin P. Wilson and Frank E. Terpil, to help set up terrorist training camps.

There were other reasons for American concern. Qaddafi was relentlessly anti-Israel, supported the most extreme factions in Syria and opposed the more moderate regimes of Jordan's King Hussein and Egypt's Anwar el-Sadat. There also were reports early in 1981 that Libya was attempting to become a nuclear power, and Qaddafi's often-stated ambition to set up a new federation of Arab and Moslem states in North Africa alarmed policy makers, especially after his successful invasion early in the year of Chad. One of the areas seized by Libyan forces was believed to be rich in uranium.

Qaddafi was further viewed as having close ties to the Soviet Union, a point repeatedly driven home in a 15-minute color movie that was prepared by the C.I.A. in 1981 for the President and key White House officials. It was clear early in the Administration, one former White House aide recalls, that the best way to get the President's attention was through visual means. The movie, which substituted for a written psychological profile of Qaddafi, the aide says, was meant "to show the nature of the beast. If you saw it, there's little doubt that he had to go."

Libya became a dominant topic of the Administration's secret deliberations on C.I.A. covert action. At senior staff meetings, one participant later recalled, Haig repeatedly referred to Qaddafi as a "cancer to be cut out."

In mid-1981, Haig put William P. Clark, the Deputy Secretary of State, in charge of a secret task force to look into the Qaddafi issue. The initial goal of the small group, which included a representative from the Department of Energy, was to evaluate economic sanctions, such as an embargo on Libyan oil purchases. Libya was then supplying about 10 percent of total American imports of crude oil, and an estimated 2,000 American citizens lived in Libya. Such planning was hampered by the fact that Libyan crude oil was of high quality and much in demand. Clark, whose confirmation hearings had been marked by controversy over his lack of knowledge about foreign affairs, turned to Robert C. (Bud) McFarlane, then the State Department counselor, for help.

One immediate step, taken early in 1981, was

to encourage Egypt and other moderate Arab states to continue their longstanding plotting against Qaddafi. In May, the State Department ordered the closing of the Libyan diplomatic mission in Washington and gave Libyan diplomats five days to leave the country.

There were reports in American newspapers, leaked by Government officials, suggesting that Libyan opposition to Qaddafi was growing and citing the defection of Mohammed Magaryef, a former Libyan Auditor General living in exile in London who would become the focal point of American, French and Egyptian efforts over the next four years to overthrow Qaddafi.

In August 1981, President Reagan approved a series of naval war games inside the so-called "line of death"—the 120-mile limit claimed by Libya in the Gulf of Sidra. As expected, the Libyan Air Force rose to the bait and Navy jets shot down two SU-22 warplanes about 60 miles off the Libyan coast.

Libya accused the United States of "international terrorism." According to an account later provided to the columnist Jack Anderson, an enraged Qaddafi, in a telephone call to Ethiopian leader Lieut. Col. Mengistu Haile Mariam after the planes were shot down, threatened to assassinate President Reagan.

One former Cabinet-level official, who served in a national security position in 1981, recalls that there was no question that the "only thing to do with Qaddafi was kill him. He belonged dead." However, White House and C.I.A. planning throughout much of 1981 was hampered, the former official says, by President Carter's 1978 executive order against assassinations. "The thought was to get a third party," the former official said—such as Egypt's President Sadat, who some in the White House believed was within a few days of moving against Qaddafi when he was assassinated on Oct. 6, 1981. On Oct. 7, Magaryef and other exiles formed a National Front for the Salvation of Libya, based in London, "to rid Libya and the world of the scourge of Qaddafi's regime."

In the weeks following Sadat's death, newspapers and television reported a barrage of Qaddafi death threats to Reagan and senior Administration officials. Secret Service protection was ordered for the President's three top aides,

Edwin Meese 3d, James A. Baker 3d and Michael K. Deaver, and security for senior Cabinet members, including Haig and Weinberger, was increased. Haig, at a news conference, told newsmen: "We do have repeated reports coming to us from reliable sources that Mr. Qaddafi has been funding, sponsoring, training, harboring terrorist groups, who conduct activities against the lives of American diplomats."

There were further reports that five Libyan-trained terrorists had arrived in the United States to assassinate the President and some of his aides. Mr. Reagan publicly endorsed those reports. "We have the evidence and he knows it," he told newsmen, referring to Qaddafi.

According to key sources, there was little doubt inside Clark's task force about who was responsible for the spate of anti-Qaddafi leaks—the C.I.A., with the support of the President, Haig and Clark. "This item stuck in my craw," one involved official recalls. "We came out with this big terrorist threat to the U.S. Government. The whole thing was a complete fabrication."

Casey began traveling regularly to the State Department to attend policy meetings of the Clark group. He was accompanied at first by his deputy, Vice Adm. Bobby R. Inman, a longtime intelligence officer who had served as director of the National Security Agency in the Carter Administration.

According to one participant, Casey claimed to have reports and intercepts directly linking Qaddafi to terrorist activities. "I listened to Casey's pitch and it was going for broke," the participant recalls. " 'We're going to take care of Qaddafi.' Everyone was very careful—no one uttered the word assassination—but the message was clear: 'This matter has to be resolved.' "

If Casey's intelligence was correct, the participant recalls, it threatened the day-to-day ability of American officials to travel internationally. Inman attended only one meeting, at which he said little.

The participant, experienced in intelligence matters, was struck by Inman's sudden disappearance and the lack of specificity in Casey's presentations. Privately, Inman confirmed to a task force member that there was no further specific intelligence on the Libyan "death threats."

A trip to N.S.A. headquarters was arranged for the member; there was nothing in the raw intercepts other than "broad mouthings" by Qaddafi, the official recalls.

During this time, the American intelligence community consistently reported that Iran and its religious leadership were far more involved than Libya in international terrorism. Qaddafi was known to have brutally murdered former Libyan officials, but he was not known to have acted on his many threats against Western political leaders. An intelligence official who has had direct access to communications intelligence reports says, "The stuff I saw did not make a substantial case that we had a threat. There was nothing to cause us to react as we have, saying Qaddafi is public enemy No. 1."

Inman soon resigned from the C.I.A. and Casey continued to handle the intelligence briefings to Clark on Libyan terrorism. Some task force members were convinced that Clark's aides, including McFarlane and Michael A. Ledeen, then a State Department consultant, were leaking Casey's reports. One task force official eventually concluded that Casey was in effect running an operation inside the American Government: "He was feeding the disinformation into the [intelligence] system so it would be seen as separate, independent reports" and taken seriously by other Government agencies.

There were reprisals planned if Qaddafi did strike. By the early 1980's, the Navy had completed elaborate contingency plans for the mining of Libyan harbors, and submarines bearing the mines were dispatched to the Mediterranean during training exercises. In late 1981, a White House official was sent to Lajes Air Base in the Azores, one N.S.C. aide recalls, to insure that it was secure in case an air raid against Libya was ordered. "When Haig was talking about the hit team," the aide recalled, "we were ready to bomb." None of Qaddafi's alleged threats materialized.

In January 1982, Clark succeeded Richard V. Allen as national security adviser and quickly named McFarlane as a deputy. McFarlane brought in Donald R. Fortier from the State Department's policy planning staff. The two had

worked together on defense issues as Congressional aides in the last days of the Carter Administration.

Later, Howard Teicher, another McFarlane protégé from the State Department, joined the staff. North, who had come to the White House on a temporary basis in the summer of 1981, was kept on. He would establish a close working relationship with McFarlane. "He accompanied McFarlane to meetings with the President and the Chairman of the Joint Chiefs that other N.S.C. staffers would not participate in," one of North's former colleagues recalls.

After a year and a half, Clark, who had a poor relationship with Nancy Reagan and the men who ran the White House staff, resigned. The President picked McFarlane as his successor, and McFarlane named Fortier and Vice Adm. John Poindexter as deputy assistants. Fortier was given the authority to delve into any N.S.C. activity, including covert action.

A critical step occurred in early 1984 when, after a series of political defeats on the contra-aid issue in Congress, President Reagan authorized McFarlane, one aide recalls, to get the contras funded "in any way you can." North subsequently wrote an internal memorandum outlining the shape of much of the future N.S.C. activities, calling for White House-led fund-raising efforts in the private community and among foreign governments. Meanwhile, Fortier, relying on raw intelligence, was beginning to argue that the Administration could make some policy moves toward Iran. The N.S.C. staff began to go operational.

Muammar El-Qaddafi again became an obsession in Washington after the June 1985 hijacking of an Athens-to-Rome Trans World Airlines flight by a group of Lebanese Shiite Moslems. One Navy diver on board was killed and 39 other Americans were held hostage for 17 days. There was no evidence linking the hijacking to Libya, but within the Reagan Administration feelings ran high that action must be taken, and striking against Iran and Syria wouldn't do. By July, the N.S.C. was secretly involved in conversations with Israeli officials over the possibility of trading American arms to Iran for hostages. And any attempt to target Syria would be strongly resisted by the Pentagon. Syria's superb antiaircraft defenses had shot down an American Navy fighter plane in 1983 and one navigator, Lieut. Robert O. Goodman Jr., had been captured. He was later released to the Rev. Jesse Jackson, one of the President's most severe critics.

The target was obvious. In July, McFarlane opened a high-level foreign policy meeting with the President by declaring that diplomatic and economic pressure had failed to curb Qaddafi's support for terrorism and much stronger measures had to be taken.

During the late summer and early fall, there was a series of White House meetings on Libya, under the supervision of Poindexter and Fortier. The two even made a secret visit to Egypt to coordinate possible joint military operations against Qaddafi.

By October, the President had formally authorized yet another C.I.A. covert operation to oust Qaddafi. But, according to a report in The Washington Post, the Administration was forced to have Secretary of State Shultz appear in secret before the House Select Committee on Intelligence in order to prevent a rare committee veto of the action. Committee members were said to have been concerned over a top-secret 1984 C.I.A. assessment concluding that it would be possible to call on "disaffected elements" in the Libyan military who could be "spurred to assassination attempts or to cooperate with the exiles against Qaddafi."

United States officials knew of at least two major French operations to assassinate or overthrow Qaddafi in 1984, both directed by the Direction de la Sécurité Extérieure, the French counterpart of the C.I.A. According to a participant, officials at the National Security Agency monitored cable traffic from C.I.A. headquarters to its station in Paris authorizing the sharing of highly sensitive intelligence, including satellite photographs and communications intercepts, in support of the operations. Teams of Libyan exiles were armed with Israeli and other third-party weaponry, brought to the Sudan for combat training and infiltrated through Tunisia into Libya.

Neither plot succeeded, although one, in May 1984, resulted in a pitched battle with Qaddafi loyalists near El-Azziziya Barracks. Libya later reported that 15 members of the exile group had been slain. Qaddafi emerged unscathed.

The secret White House planning escalated dramatically after terrorist bombings in airports in Vienna and Rome on Dec. 27, 1985, killed 20 people, five of them Americans.

Within days, the N.S.C.'s Crisis Pre-planning Group authorized contingency military planning that included possible B-52 bomber strikes on Libya from the United States, as well as F-111 attacks from England. Predictably, Qaddafi responded to published reports of American plans by warning that his nation would "harass American citizens in their own streets" if the bombers came.

Newsmen were told that the C.I.A. had found a strong Libyan connection to the airport attacks, although the Israelis publicly blamed them on a Palestinian terrorist faction led by Abu Nidal. A State Department special report, made public early in 1986, was unable to cite any direct connection between Libya and the airport incident. The sole link was that three of the passports used by the terrorists in Vienna had been traced to Libya. One had been lost in Libya by a Tunisian laborer eight years earlier and two had been seized by Libyan officials from Tunisians as they were expelled in mid-1985.

One involved White House aide believes that the basic decision to use military force was made at a high-level National Security Planning Group meeting on Jan. 6, 1986, in the emotional aftermath of the airport bombings. All of the key Administration officials attended, including the President, Shultz, Weinberger, Casey and Poindexter.

Reviewing his notes of the Jan. 6 meeting, a White House aide recalls that a decision was made to provoke Qaddafi by again sending the Navy and its warplanes on patrol in the Gulf of Sidra. Any Libyan response would be seized upon to justify bombing.

According to this N.S.C. aide, there was talk, inspired by a memorandum written by North, Teicher and Stark, of using one of the Navy's most accurate weapons, the Tomahawk missile, to attack targets in Libya. Libyan air defenses, the White House had been told, were excellent and would probably shoot down some American aircraft. The Tomahawk, a submarine-launched cruise missile with a range of 500 miles, is accurate at that distance to within one hundred feet of a target.

The next day, Jan. 7, [1986], the President, declaring that there was "irrefutable" evidence of Qaddafi's role in the airport attacks, announced economic sanctions against Libya, including a ban on direct import and export trade. The idea, advocated by Fortier, was "to get economic sanctions out of the way so the next time they could do more," one involved White House aide recalls. President Reagan, the aide adds, may not have been fully aware that he was being boxed in by an N.S.C. staff that wanted action. "We were making an end run on the President," the aide says.

But the President, although unwilling to stop the planning, continued to resist a military response pending a "smoking gun"—some evidence linking Qaddafi to the airport bombings.

Another of Mr. Reagan's concerns was that an attack on Libya must appear to be a just response. The Joint Chiefs were known to be reluctant to use force as a response to terrorism, and had been resisting White House staff entreaties to move a third aircraft carrier into the Mediterranean to buttress the two already on patrol. The Joint Chiefs had claimed that at least three carriers and their strike force would be needed if Libya responded to a bombing with its 500 fighter aircraft. Adding a third carrier to the task force, the Joint Chiefs explained, would disrupt the schedule of leaves for seamen and pilots. One White House aide recalls a tense meeting in which Richard Armitage of the Defense Department declared, "Cancel the leaves," only to have the Joint Chiefs insist that three carriers could not be on station until March.

Speaking at the National Defense University at Fort McNair in Washington on Jan. 15, George Shultz argued that the United States had a legal right to use military force against states that support terrorism. Under international law, he claimed, "a nation attacked by terrorists is per-

mitted to use force to prevent or pre-empt future attacks, to seize terrorists or to rescue its citizens, when no other means is available."

Shultz's statement was part of a carefully constructed scenario. In subsequent weeks, one White House official recalls, State Department lawyers began to prepare an extensive legal paper arguing, in part, that "in the context of military action what normally would be considered murder is not."

Two days after Shultz's speech, the President signed a secret executive order calling for contacts with Iran and waiving regulations blocking arms shipments there. Casey was instructed not to inform Congress, as the law provided, because of "security risks." The White House was careening down two dangerous paths.

Early in 1986, intelligence sources said, the National Reconnaissance Office, the secret group responsible for the procurement and deployment of America's intelligence and spy satellites, was ordered to move a signals intelligence satellite (SIGINT) from its orbit over Poland to North Africa, where it could carefully monitor Libyan communications.

Libyan diplomatic and intelligence traffic had long been a routine target of the N.S.A., whose field stations ring the globe; but beefed-up coverage was deemed necessary. Interception stations in England, Italy and Cyprus, among others, were ordered to monitor and record all communications out of Libya. In the N.S.A. this is known as "cast-iron" coverage. A high-priority special category (SPECAT) clearance was set up for the traffic, denying most N.S.A. interception stations access to the Libyan intelligence. A special procedure for immediately funneling the intercepts to the White House was established.

A third American aircraft carrier arrived in the Mediterranean in mid-March, and the three carriers and their 30-ship escort were sent on an "exercise" into the Gulf of Sidra. It was the largest penetration by the American fleet into the Libyan-claimed waters.

One involved N.S.C. aide acknowledges that Poindexter, who had succeeded McFarlane as national security adviser, and Fortier had determined that the Navy should respond to any loss of American life in the exercise by bombing five targets in Libya. As the Navy task force sailed toward Libya, the aide remembers, he overheard Fortier and General Moellering, the Joint Chiefs' delegate to the Crisis Pre-planning Group, disagree on tactics during a meeting in the N.S.C. crisis center. Fortier, the aide says, asked the general to outline the Navy's rules of engagement in case Libya responded. "Proportionality," the general said.

"They should be disproportionate," the aide heard Fortier sharply respond.

On March 25 and 26, the Sixth Fleet attacked four Libyan ships, destroying two of them. Navy aircraft also conducted two raids against a radar site on the Libyan coast. There were no American casualties and no Libyan counterattack. The White House, pressing the advantage, warned Qaddafi that any Libyan forces venturing more than 12 miles from shore—the international limit recognized by the United States—were subject to attack.

Qaddafi's failure to rise to the bait frustrated the N.S.C. staff. One senior State Department official acknowledges, "Everybody wanted to beat the hell out of Libya." Instead, the fleet was withdrawn after three days in the Gulf of Sidra, two days earlier than planned.

The basic question for N.S.C. aides remained: how to convince the reluctant President that bombing was essential. In late March, the N.S.A. intercepted a message from Tripoli to Libyan agents in East Berlin, Paris, Belgrade, Geneva, Rome and Madrid ordering them "to prepare to carry out the plan." Shortly before 8 P.M. on April 4, Washington time (April 5 in Germany), the La Belle disco in West Berlin was blown up. Fourteen hours later, the men in the White House had their "smoking gun."

By 10 A.M. on Saturday, April 5, the N.S.A. had intercepted, decoded, translated from Arabic and forwarded to the White House a cable from the Libyan People's Bureau in East Berlin to Tripoli stating, in essence, according to N.S.C. and State Department officials, that "We have something planned that will make you happy." A few hours later, a second message from East Berlin to Tripoli came across the top-secret computer terminals in the N.S.C. providing the exact time of the La Belle bombing and reporting that

"an event occurred. You will be pleased with the result."

The messages were rushed to the California White House, where the President was spending Easter. The decision to bomb was made that afternoon, one former White House official recalls: "The same people who wanted to have a show of force in late March could now do it in the context of terrorism." The President would no longer be, as one aide put it, "the inhibitor."

By Monday, Teicher had prepared a discussion paper for a talk at a high-level meeting on the proposed bombing; one key element, a firsthand source recalls, was a proposal that the intercepts should be declassified and made public in a Presidential speech. The idea, the White House official adds, was to again "make an end run on the President" and prevent any second thoughts.

The inevitable leaks came within hours. One State Department intelligence officer recalls, upon seeing the intercepts, "It was too good. I knew it would leak."

On April 7, Richard R. Burt, the Ambassador to West Germany, publicly linked the Libyans to the La Belle bombing. Interviewed on the "Today" show, Burt said, "There is very, very clear evidence that there is Libyan involvement."

Yet police officials in West Berlin repeatedly told newsmen that they knew of no evidence linking Libya to the discothèque bombing. One week after the attack, Manfred Ganschow, chief of the anti-terrorist police in Berlin, was quoted as having "rejected the assumption that suspicion is concentrated on Libyan culprits."

Christian Lochte, president of the Hamburg office of the Protection of the Constitution, a domestic intelligence unit, told a television interviewer five days after the bombing, "It is a fact that we do not have any hard evidence, let alone proof, to show the blame might unequivocally be placed on Libya. True, I cannot rule out that Libya, in some way, is responsible for the attack. But I must say that such hasty blame, regarding the two dreadful attacks at the end of the year on the Vienna and Rome airports, for which Libya had immediately been made responsible, did not prove to be correct."

A senior official in Bonn, interviewed last

month for this article, said that the West German Government continued to be "very critical and skeptical" of the American intelligence linking Libya to the La Belle bombing. The United States, he said, which has extremely close intelligence ties with West Germany, had made a tape of its intercepts available to German intelligence, with no change in Bonn's attitude.

Some White House officials had immediate doubts that the case against Libya was clear-cut. The messages had been delivered by the N.S.A. to the White House, as directed, without any analysis. There was nothing in any of them specifically linking Qaddafi to the La Belle bombing. What is more, the discothèque was known as a hangout for black soldiers, and the Libyans had never been known to target blacks or other minorities.

The normal procedure for SPECAT intelligence traffic from Libya is that it be processed and evaluated by the G-6 group at N.S.A. headquarters at Fort Meade, Md., before being relayed elsewhere. But the La Belle traffic was never forwarded to G-6. As of this month, the April 4 and 5 Libyan intercepts had not been seen by any of the G-6 experts on North Africa and the Middle East.

"The G-6 section branch and division chiefs didn't know why it was taken from them," says an N.S.A. official. "They were bureaucratically cut out and so they screamed and yelled."

Another experienced N.S.A. analyst notes: "There is no doubt that if you send raw data to the White House, that constitutes misuse because there's nobody there who's capable of interpreting it." N.S.A. officials had no choice if the White House asked for the intercepts, he says, but adds, "You screw it up every time when you do it—and especially when the raw traffic is translated into English from a language such as Arabic, that's not commonly known."

Yet another analyst points out that Qaddafi was known to have used personal couriers in the past—and not radio or telephone communication—in his many assassinations and assassination attempts.

A senior State Department official who was involved in the White House deliberations on the Libyan bombing insists that he and his colleagues were satisfied with the handling of the intercepts.

"There was nothing to suggest that it was not handled in good faith," he says. "The intercepts did not say La Belle disco was bombed. They never identified the site. But there was a history that the Libyans were going to mount an operation in Europe."

There was an atmosphere of cynicism and disarray within the National Security Council as it prepared to bomb Libya while supplying arms to Iran. Poindexter was being hailed in Newsweek as "a cool warrior" who "steadies the N.S.C." But privately, some security council officials say, he was feeling overwhelmed, and would soon be telling close associates that he wanted a transfer to the National Security Agency. By April, some N.S.C. insiders, and reportedly the President, knew that William Casey had started undergoing radiation treatment for prostate cancer; his illness was not made public until December. Donald Fortier also was extremely ill. He would die of liver cancer in August.

In the weeks preceding April 14, Oliver North has told associates, he became extremely active in the Libyan planning. The Joint Chiefs had decided on a two-pronged aerial attack, involving Navy units in the Mediterranean and the F-111's from England. But none of the military planners wanted to see American airmen shot down and paraded around Libya; and there was concern that the Navy's A-6 bombers would be vulnerable to antiaircraft fire. The F-111's not only flew much faster—they would hit the target going 9 miles a minute—but also had far superior electronic defense mechanisms to ward off enemy missiles.

The round-trip from England to Libya, over France, would be about seven hours, well within the F-111's limits. Admiral Crowe and the Joint Chiefs agreed that the F-111's would play the lead role in the attack, buttressed by 12 Navy A-6's, which were assigned to bomb an airfield and military barracks 400 miles east of Tripoli.

But North has told colleagues that he had doubts about the Air Force's mission, and they were heightened when the French refused to permit the F-111 overflight. The Air Force was now confronted with a difficult assignment against the strong headwinds of the Bay of Biscay.

According to an account given to colleagues, North, just prior to the bombing, made a series of suggestions at a high-level meeting attended by the President, Poindexter, Crowe and Gen. Charles A. Gabriel, the Air Force Chief of Staff. With the approval of Casey, North had already interceded with the Israelis to increase the intelligence available before the mission. Now he argued for using a covert Navy SEAL team, which would surface on the beach near Qaddafi's tent and residence and set up a laser beam that could guide the American bombs directly to the main targets. The attacking planes could then launch their bombs offshore—out of range of Libyan antiaircraft missiles—and be just as effective. The SEAL team, apparently at North's direction, had already been deployed to the Middle East.

But, North told colleagues, Crowe said no—that no one wanted to put Americans at risk.

North reportedly then raised the issue of using the Air Force's most-advanced fighter-bomber, the supersecret Stealth, said to be capable of avoiding enemy radar. The aircraft would be perfect to attack Qaddafi's personal quarters and tent; it could be ferried to the huge American naval base at Rota, Spain, and attack from there. Admiral Crowe again said no, explaining that the Stealth technology was too valuable to risk.

North told colleagues that he persisted in seeking alternatives, raising the possibility of attacking the Qaddafi quarters with a conventionally armed Tomahawk cruise missile fired from a submarine. Admiral Crowe, the report goes, responded that there were too few conventionally armed Tomahawks in the arsenal. North has claimed that he then raised the possibility of supplementing the bombing by mining and quarantining the harbors, saying he wanted "a far more sophisticated scenario to cover up the fact that the target was going to be an assassination."

The President sided with the Joint Chiefs Chairman, North told colleagues. At the close of the meeting, with the President out of hearing, North related, Crowe walked up to him, and nose to nose warned: "Young man, you'd better watch your step."

Through an aide, Crowe denies the encounter, saying that he "did not recall any discussion on substantive matters that he ever had" with North. "Nor does he recall any meetings with North except as a back-bench note taker" at White House meetings, the aide said. Furthermore, Crowe was quoted by an aide as saying, "He doesn't recall North having any input at all in the April raid."

In a nationally televised speech on April 14, President Reagan said the intelligence linking Libya to the La Belle bombing "is direct, it is precise, it is irrefutable. We have solid evidence about other attacks Qaddafi has planned." He described the Tripoli raid as a "series of strikes against the headquarters, terrorist facilities and military assets that support Muammar Qaddafi's subversive activities."

The President added: "We Americans are slow to anger. We always seek peaceful avenues before resorting to the use of force, and we did. We tried quiet diplomacy, public condemnation, economic sanctions and demonstrations of military force—and none succeeded."

According to one involved N.S.C. official, there was other language prepared for the President—a few paragraphs bracketed into the text in case the White House could confirm that Qaddafi had been killed. The message would echo an analysis prepared by Abraham D. Sofaer, the State Department legal adviser, claiming that the United States had the legal right "to strike back to prevent future attacks." The killing of Qaddafi, under that doctrine, was not retaliation nor was it in any way a crime.

But Qaddafi was not killed, and a White House official recounts an elaborate briefing a day or so after the raid at which the Air Force's failure to accomplish its mission was obvious. "The Navy people were at ease, confident," the aide recalls. "All had worked perfectly." The Navy's two main targets had been accurately attacked, with no loss. "The poor Air Force guy," recalls the aide. "He was defensive and polite. Talked about how the White House kept on changing signals."

The intelligence satellite that had been moved from Poland was ordered to remain over Libya, in the hope that the bombing would rally those military men opposed to Qaddafi and spark a revolt. "They honestly thought Qaddafi would fall or be overthrown," one National Security Agency official says, referring to the N.S.C, "and so they kept the bird up there."

There was no coup d'état—and there was one intelligence satellite missing over Eastern Europe in late April, when an explosion rocked one of the reactors at the Soviet nuclear power plant in Chernobyl, in the Ukraine. After another bureaucratic battle inside the intelligence community, one N.S.A. official recalls, the satellite was returned to its normal orbit above Poland, as the United States tried to unravel the extent of damage to the nuclear power plant and the scope of the fallout threat to Western Europe.

The White House's two-track policy toward Libya and Iran continued. In May, McFarlane, accompanied by North and Teicher, among others, traveled to Teheran bearing arms. A few weeks later, Poindexter routinely approved a proposal, strongly supported by Casey and Shultz, calling for another disinformation operation against Libya in the hopes of provoking Qaddafi. The C.I.A. triggered the renewed planning, one insider recalls, by reporting once again that "Qaddafi was on the ropes."

In September, there was a second visit by American officials to Iran, and continued arms trading. Within a month the policy—and the National Security Council—began to come apart. By early November, the Iran scandal was on the front pages. Its major casualty was the credibility of a popular President.

In the wake of that scandal, Oliver North would emerge in the public's perception as a unique and extraordinary player inside the National Security Council, a hard-charging risk-taker who was different from his colleagues. It is now apparent that North was but one of many at work in the White House who believed in force, stealth and operations behind the back of the citizenry and the Congress. He was not an aberration, but part of a White House team whose full scope of operations has yet to be unraveled.

North, along with Poindexter, Teicher and others, have left the Government. The much-reviled Colonel Qaddafi remains in power.

Chapter 14 Review Questions

1. How does Heclo conceptualize the current relationship between politics and administration? What are the basic elements of his *issue network* idea and how does the idea differ from the *iron triangle* notion of political-administrative relations?

2. Did you find this issue network concept evident in the foregoing case study? If so, in what ways? (Remember the Heclo essay argues that issue networks are principally involved in shaping welfare policies, not defense policies.)

3. In what ways does the issue network concept pose serious dilemmas for democratic government in general and public administration in particular?

4. Heclo primarily applied the issue network notion to the federal level of government. Is it possible to apply it to state and local levels, as well? Describe why or why not.

5. What implications does the issue network theory hold for the practical functions and training of public administrators? Does it essentially alter the types of jobs, tasks, and roles they perform?

6. On the basis of your analysis of the foregoing reading and case study, what general recommendations would you make to improve the relationships between administration and politics in America? Be sure to think carefully about the *value implications* of any new reform measures you may advocate.

Key Terms

politics-administration dichotomy

issue networks

iron triangles

policy makers

proliferation of interests

think tanks

technopols

trade and professional associations

public policy processes

issue specialization

issue watchers

single-issue organizations

presidential appointees

professional-bureaucratic complex

Suggestions for Further Reading

You would do well to compare and contrast Heclo's ideas with those of earlier theorists who argued for a clearer, more distinct separation of politics and administration (what is termed the political-administrative dichotomy), especially Woodrow Wilson, "The Study of Administration," *Political Science Quarterly,* 2 (June 1887), pp. 197–222; Frank J. Goodnow, *Politics and Administration* (New York: Macmillan, 1900); or the later writers who discovered the interest groups involved with administrative processes and gave roots to the iron triangle concept, particularly Paul Appleby, *Policy and Administration* (University, Ala.: University of Alabama Press, 1949); E. Pendelton Herring, *Public Administration and the Public Interest* (New York: Russell and Russell, 1936); and David B. Truman, *The Governmental Process* (New York: Alfred A. Knopf, 1951).

Today, of course, because of the sheer size, complexity, and power of American government, new and more complicated political-administrative relationships have arisen, described by several astute observers, including Hugh Heclo, *A Government of Strangers: Executive Politics in Washington* (Washington, D.C.: The Brookings Institution, 1977); Don K. Price, *The Scientific Estate* (Cambridge, Mass.: Harvard University Press, 1965); Frederick C. Mosher, *Democracy and the Public Service,* Second Edition (New York: Oxford University Press, 1982); Emmette S. Redford, *Democracy in the Administrative State* (New York: Oxford University Press, 1969); Francis E. Rourke, *Bureaucracy, Politics and Public Policy,* Third Edition (Boston: Little, Brown, 1984); Harold Seidman and Robert Gilmour, *Politics, Position and Power*, Fourth Edition (New York: Oxford University Press, 1986); Lawrence C. Dodd and Richard L. Schott, *Congress and the Administrative State* (New York: John Wiley & Sons, 1979); Louis Fisher, *The Politics of Shared Power: Congress and the Executive* (Washington, D.C.: Congressional Quarterly Press, 1981); and Herbert Kaufman, *The Administrative Behavior of Federal Bureau Chiefs* (Washington, D.C.: The Brookings Institution, 1981).

Both the *National Journal* and *Congressional Quarterly* serve to provide timely insiders' views of this topic. You should give particular attention to the writers who discuss the changes in the presidency, Congress, and interest groups that have decisively altered political-administrative relationships in recent years:

see Samuel Beer, ed., *The New American Political System* (Washington, D.C.: The American Enterprise Institute, 1979); Lawrence C. Dodd and Bruce I. Oppenheimer, *Congress Reconsidered,* Second Edition (Washington, D.C.: Congressional Quarterly Press, 1981); Randall B. Ripley and Grace A. Franklin, *Congress, The Bureaucracy and Public Policy* (Chicago: Dorsey Press, 1984); Norman J. Ornstein and Shirley Elder, *Interest Groups, Lobbying and Policymaking* (Washington, D.C.: Congressional Quarterly Press, 1978); and Harrison W. Fox, Jr., and Susan W. Hammond, *Congressional Staffs* (New York: Free Press, 1977).

Several excellent book-length case examinations of various policy fields provide further insights into this subject. See Robert J. Art, *The TFX Decision* (Boston: Little, Brown, 1968); Stephen Bailey and Edith K. Mosher, *ESEA: The Office of Education Administers a Law* (Syracuse, N.Y.: Syracuse University Press, 1968); A. Lee Fritschler, *Smoking and Politics* (Englewood Cliffs, N.J.: Prentice-Hall, 1975); Richard J. Stillman II, *The Integration of the Negro in the U.S. Armed Forces* (New York: Praeger Publishers, 1968); Daniel P. Moynihan, *The Politics of the Guaranteed Income* (New York: Random House, 1973); Milton D. Morris, *Immigration: The Beleaguered Bureaucracy* (Washington, D.C.: Brookings Institution, 1985); Charles L. Schultze, *The Politics and Economics of Public Spending* (Washington, D.C.: The Brookings Institution, 1968); I. M. Destler, *U.S. Foreign Economic Policy-Making* (Washington, D.C.: The Brookings Institution, 1978); Martha Derthick, *Policy-Making for Social Security* (Washington, D.C.: The Brookings Institution, 1978); Barbara J. Nelson, *Making an Issue of Child Abuse* (Chicago: University of Chicago Press, 1984); Paul Light, *Artful Work: The Politics of Social Security Reform* (New York: Random House, 1985) and Frederick C. Mosher, *A Tale of Two Agencies* (Baton Rouge, La.: Louisiana State University Press, 1984). For a good collection of essays, many dealing with various aspects of this topic, read Francis E. Rourke, *Bureaucratic Power in National Policy Making,* Fourth Edition (Boston: Little, Brown, 1986). See also several of the essays contained in the bicentennial issue of the *Public Administration Review* (January/February 1987), edited by Richard J. Stillman, II; particularly, Chester A. Newland, "Public Executives: Imperium, Sacerdotium, Collegium? Bicentennial Leadership Challenges"; James P. Pfiffner, "Political Appointees and Career Executives: The Democracy-Bureaucracy Nexus in the Third Century"; and James D. Carroll, "Public Administration in the Third Century of the Constitution: Supply-Side Management Privatization or Public Investment"; as well as several essays contained in new books published by the Urban Institute, Washington, D.C.: John L. Palmer, ed., *Perspectives on the Reagan Years* (1986); and Lester M. Salamon and Michael S. Lund, eds., *The Reagan Presidency and the Governing of America* (1985); plus G. Calvin MacKenzie, ed., *The In and Outers* (Baltimore: Johns Hopkins University Press, 1987); and James P. Pfiffner, *The Strategic Presidency* (Chicago: The Dorsey Press, 1988).

CHAPTER 15

The Relationship Between the Public and Private Sectors: The Concept of Third-Party Government

"The types of instruments [for taking public action] that are the easiest to implement may be the hardest to enact; conversely, the forms that are most likely to be enacted are also the most difficult to carry out."

Lester M. Salamon

READING 15

Introduction

There once was a time, as Frederick C. Mosher reminds us, when government "was responsible for and expended money for what it did by itself through its own personnel and facilities." Consequently, much of the public management lore, like that of private enterprise, according to Mosher, "was based upon the premise that efficiency rested upon the effective supervision and direction of its own operations." Rather, recent decades have witnessed "exploding responsibilities of the national government in virtually all functional fields and its carrying out of those responsibilities through, and interdependently with, non-federal institutions and individuals."[1]

Data tend to support Mosher's point. Although the federal budget between 1949 and 1986 grew over 25 times, from approximately $39 billion to $980 billion, payment for services of federal employees and goods that the federal government purchased directly rose as a percentage of the GNP from 8 percent in 1949 to 16 percent in 1953. Since that time, this figure has steadily declined to less than 7 percent today. In addition, two-thirds of these payments for "in-house" employees and services were spent in *defense-related purposes,* leaving 2.4 percent for civilian needs (compared with 2.8 percent in 1949). Except for the Korean War and Vietnam War eras, when the federal work force rose quickly and then declined sharply, the total number of civilian federal employees has remained roughly 3 million during the last 40 years (3.02 million in 1985). As a total

[1]Frederick C. Mosher, "The Changing Responsibilities and Tactics of the Federal Government," *Public Administration Review,* 40, no. 6 (Nov./Dec. 1980), p. 541.

As a total

percentage of the U.S. population, civilian and military employees grew from 25 per 1,000 in 1947, to 31 per 1,000 in 1957, to 37 per 1,000 in 1970, but has since declined steadily to 28 per 1,000 in 1985.

The conclusion that students of government and public administration draw from these data is that increasingly federal expenditures and responsibilities (and to a large extent state and local ones as well) are shifting dramatically in new directions. The traditional in-house performance of public activities by government has given way to five different types of government action. First, a substantial portion of this activity consists of *contracts and grants* to do the work of the public sector outside the formal bounds of public agencies through private businesses, universities, and nonprofit enterprises—even foreign governments. Much domestic research and many overseas public works projects are accomplished in this manner at numerous federal agencies like the National Aeronautics and Space Administration and the Agency for International Development. At the state and local levels, garbage collection, computer facilities, and many other such services are often handled through contractual arrangements. Increasingly, government is turning to "third parties" to accomplish much of its responsibilities and tasks. But there are other forms of indirect public action as well.

Second, a fast growing and very large portion of federal expenditures today goes to *direct transfer payments* to individuals. These direct benefits and reimbursements for individuals rose from 21 percent of the federal budget in 1954 to 46 percent in 1986. Most of these payments ($445.9 billion in 1986) go to individuals for income support through such programs as Social Security, Medicare, unemployment benefits, veterans benefits, and retirement programs.

Third, *aid to state and local governments,* although declining from a high of $109.7 billion in 1978 (in constant 1982 dollars) to $92.8 billion in 1986, accounts today for approximately 11 percent of federal budget outlays. Two-thirds of these monies in reality go to individuals through intergovernmental transfer payments to state and local governments that administer these programs in such fields as housing, Medicaid, nutrition, welfare, and education.

Fourth, *regulation* is yet another indirect route used to promote public action in recent years. Although regulatory power has been around for some time (since 1887 on the national level, when the federal government established the Interstate Commerce Commission to regulate railroads), it has been extended during the past two decades into new fields through the use of government contracts and state and local aid requirements. Federal regulations now apply to such areas as equal employment opportunity, environmental protection, energy conservation, occupational health and safety, and consumer protection.

Finally, in the 1980s, *tax incentives and loan guarantees* are used pervasively to promote various kinds of public actions in the name of the public interest. In general, they are used to provide incentives to people to do what government wants them to do without formal regulatory controls or direct governmental action. Tax credits, tax deductions, tax exemptions, and corporate loan guarantees are examples of such forms of indirect public action. Tax incentives and loan guarantees often seek to encourage or discourage public investment in certain economic fields such as home ownership, international trade, energy conservation, family farms, and small businesses.

In the following selection, "Rethinking Public Management: Third-Party Government and the Changing Forms of Government Action," Lester M. Salamon, a senior scholar at the Urban Institute in Washington, D.C., offers a penetrating examination of these new forms (some quite old, but until recently little used) of government action, which he terms "third-party government." In his view, many of these forms involve the pervasive sharing of governmental authority with a host of "third parties (hospitals, universities, states, cities, industrial corporations, etc.)" in order "to carry out its purposes." Salamon outlines the basic attributes of these new forms of government action, the ways they are reshaping the landscape of governmental operations, their impact on the changing role of public managers and management processes, as well as their profound implications for the character of democratic government.

In particular, Salamon points out three critical issues concerning the rise of third-party government: first, *accountability issues,* or questions involving whether or not third parties who exercise public authority in various ways will do so in a responsible manner in accordance with the public interest, as well as the desires of the general electorate and elected public officials; second, *issues of management,* or how traditional tools of management can be applied or adapted effectively to control and direct these new forms of government action; third, *policy coordination,* or how unity of purpose and organizational cooperation can be achieved through third-party government, which tends to promote the reverse—fragmentation of goals and competitive behavior.

Salamon's central thesis is that "each tool involves a finely balanced complex of institutional, procedural, political and economic relationships that substantially shape the character of the governmental action that results." "In other words," he writes, "the choice of the program tool is a political, not just an economic issue: it involves important questions of power and purpose as well as of equity and efficiency." Much of Salamon's thoughtful and thought-provoking essay deals with "the trade-offs" involving the use of each of the various forms of third-party action.

As you read this selection, keep the following questions in mind:

What does Salamon mean by the term *third-party government?*

Why does he argue that it is being used increasingly today to promote various types of public actions? What does this concept mean for the study of public administration as well as students entering this field?

What are the various categories Salamon sets up to evaluate the forms of third-party action, such as the "directness/indirectness dimension of third-party action," the "automatic/administered dimension," the "cash/in-kind dimension," or the "visibility/invisibility dimension"?

Do you agree with the central paradox that Salamon points to at the end of his essay: "that the types of instruments that are the easiest to implement may be the hardest to enact; conversely, the forms that are most likely to be enacted are also the most difficult to carry out"? Is there any way that you think this paradoxical problem can be resolved?

LESTER M. SALAMON

Rethinking Public Management: Third-Party Government and the Changing Forms of Government Action

I. The Rise of Third Party Government and the Changing Forms of Public Action

The Problem

The need for greater attention to the tools and techniques of public action should be apparent to anyone who has looked closely at recent trends in Federal government activity and operations. While political rhetoric and a considerable body of academic research continue to picture the Federal government as a rapidly expanding behemoth growing disproportionally in both scope and size relative to the rest of the society in order to handle a steadily growing range of responsibilities, in fact something considerably more complex has been underway. For, while the range of Federal responsibilities has indeed increased dramatically, the relative size of the Federal enterprise, in terms of both budget and employment, has paradoxically remained relatively stable. Between 1954 and

1979, for example, the rate of growth of the Federal budget just barely exceeded that of the Gross National Product (GNP), so that the budget's share of the GNP increased only from 19.4 to 20.9%. Even more important, the rate of growth of Federal civilian employment lagged far behind the real growth of the budget, so that the number of Federal employees per 1000 people in the population registered a decline during this 25-year period of more than 10%.

What accounts for this paradox of relatively stable budgets and declining employment despite substantial growth in responsibilities is the dramatic change that has occurred in the forms of Federal action. For one thing, a major proliferation has taken place in the tools of government action, as the Federal government has turned increasingly to a wide range of new, or newly expanded, devices, e.g., loans, loan guarantees, insurance, social regulation, government corporations, many of which do not appear in the budget. In the process, moreover, a significant transformation has taken place in the way the Federal government goes about its business—a shift from direct to indirect or "third-party" government, from a situation in which the Federal government ran its own programs to one in which it increasingly relies on a wide variety of "third parties"— states, cities, special districts, banks, hospitals,

From *Public Policy*, vol. 29, no. 3 (Summer 1981), pp. 255–275. Published by John Wiley and Sons, Inc. Copyright © 1981 by the President and Fellows of Harvard College and reprinted by their permission.

manufacturers, and others—to carry out its purposes.[1]

In both respects recent developments have clear historical antecedents. Yet the recent developments have been so substantial as to constitute a qualitative, and not just a quantitative, change.

Illustrative of this has been the transformation that has occurred in the *grant-in-aid* system, perhaps the classic instrument of what is here termed "third-party government." From its meager beginnings in the nineteenth century, the grant-in-aid device has mushroomed into a massive system of interorganizational action. More than 500 grant-in-aid programs are now on the books, making Federal resources available to state and local governments for everything from emergency medical services to the construction of the interstate highway system. Since 1955 alone, grant-in-aid funding has grown 26-fold, three times faster than the budget as a whole. By 1979, therefore, grants-in-aid accounted for about 17% of all Federal budget outlays, and over 40% of all domestic expenditures aside from direct income transfers like Social Security. What is more, the basic structure of the grant-in-aid system also changed markedly, with the introduction of new forms of grants (project grants, block grants, general revenue sharing) and a substantial proliferation in the numbers and types of entities—cities, counties, special districts, nonprofit corporations, etc.—that, along with the states, are now eligible for direct grant assistance.[2]

But the recent changes in the forms of Federal government action extend far beyond the transformation of the grant-in-aid system. Indeed, the grant-in-aid is now overshadowed by a host of other ingenious tools for carrying out the public's business—loans, loan guarantees, new forms of regulation, tax subsidies, government corporations, interest subsidies, insurance, and numerous others.

Since many of these latter tools are not reflected in Federal budget totals, they have attracted far less attention. Yet their scope and scale are massive and growing. In fiscal year 1979, for example, the Federal government made more than $130 billion in new *loan or loan guarantee* commitments for purposes as diverse as college education and crop supports. Federal *regulatory activities,* once primarily economic in focus, have now become major vehicles for the promotion of a wide array of health, safety, environmental, and social goals. Between 1970 and 1975 alone, seven new regulatory agencies were created, 30 major regulatory laws were enacted, and the number of pages published annually in the *Federal Register* tripled (Lilley and Miller, 1977). Various estimates place the cost of these regulatory activities at anywhere from $40 billion to $120 billion annually. Increased use has also been made of the tax code as an instrument of policy, as *tax deductions* have been provided to encourage the hiring of the unemployed, to stimulate energy conservation, and for a host of other reasons. By 1979 the estimated total value of these "tax subsidies" stood close to $150 billion, up from $40 billion a decade earlier.[3] Beyond this, a number of *government-sponsored enterprises* have been created—Conrail, Amtrak, the U.S. Railway Association, Comsat, the Government National Mortgage Association—and various policy

[1]For further explication of this point see: Salamon, L. M. "The Rise of Third-Party Government," *The Washington Post,* June 29, 1980.

[2]*Budget of the U.S. Government, Fiscal Year 1981, Special Analyses,* p. 254; U.S. Advisory Commission on Intergovernmental Relations (1977): *Categorical Grants: Their Role and Design,* Washington, DC: U.S. GPO, p. 25. Interestingly, the 1979 budget marks the first decline in the grant-in-aid share of the budget, and this downward trend is projected to continue. Thus the FY1982 budget estimates that grants-in-aid will account for only 14% of FY1982 outlays, compared to a high of 17.3% in FY1978. *Budget of the U.S. Government, Fiscal Year 1982, Special Analyses,* p. 252.

[3]*Budget of the U.S. Government, FY1981, Special Analysis G,* pp. 230–234; U.S. Congress Joint Economic Committee, *Federal Subsidy Programs* (1974), p. 5. These estimates reflect orders of magnitude only because of uncertainty over the interactions that exist among various tax provisions.

goals are also pursued through Federal underwriting of *insurance*. This latter activity alone now involves some $2 trillion in contingent liabilities for the Federal government.

The proliferation, expansion, and extension of these and other tools of Federal policy have substantially reshaped the landscape of Federal operations. In almost every policy sphere, Federal operations now involve a complex collage of widely assorted tools mobilizing a diverse collection of different types of actors to perform a host of different roles in frequently confusing combinations.

What is involved here, moreover, is not simply the contracting out of well-defined functions or the purchase of specified goods and services from outside suppliers. The characteristic feature of many of these new, or newly expanded, tools of action is that they involve the sharing of a far more basic governmental function: the exercise of discretion over the spending of Federal funds and the use of Federal authority. They thus continually place Federal officials in the uncomfortable position of being held responsible for programs they do not really control.

The $6–8 billion that Congress annually appropriates for employment and training assistance, for example, goes not to the Department of Labor, which is regularly held accountable for its wise use, but automatically to more than 450 locally organized "prime sponsors," which enjoy substantial discretion in selecting both the training and the trainees, and over which the Labor Department has only limited control. In the loan guarantee programs, many of the key decisions are left to private bankers, who process the applications and extend the credit that the Federal government then guarantees. Even in the procurement area important changes of the same sort have taken place, as the government has been forced to rely on outside suppliers not only to provide products and services that the government has conceived and designed, but, at least in the acquisition of major systems, to do much of the conception and design work as well (U.S. Commission on Government Procurement, 1972).

What makes this situation especially problematic, moreover, is that those who exercise authority on the Federal government's behalf in these programs frequently enjoy a substantial degree of autonomy from Federal control. State and local government agencies, for example, have their own source of independent political support, while many of the Federal government's private partners frequently find themselves in the fortuitous position of needing the Federal government less than the Federal government needs them. Instead of a hierarchical relationship between the Federal government and its agents, therefore, what frequently exists in practice is a far more complex bargaining relationship in which the Federal agency often has the weaker hand.

The Implications

This set of changes has profound implications for the character of democratic government and the management of public programs. In the first place, it raises serious questions of *accountability* because those who exercise public authority in these programs are only tangentially accountable to the elected officials who enact and oversee the programs. This is all the more troublesome, moreover, because many of the "third-party" implementers are especially touchy about the exercise of Federal oversight, creating pressures to restrict accountability to narrow, technical questions of fiscal control and administrative procedure and sidestep more value-laden issues of program results.

Closely related to these questions of accountability, moreover, are serious *issues of management*. In a word, many of these new forms of action render the traditional concerns of public administration and the traditional techniques of public management if not irrelevant, then at least far less germane. The "street-level bureaucrats"[4] in these forms of action are frequently

---

[4]The term "street-level bureaucrat" was used by Michael Lipsky to refer to the service providers who enjoy substan-

not public employees at all, but bankers and businessmen, hospital administrators, and corporate tax accountants. Under these circumstances, a body of knowledge that focuses on how to organize and operate a public agency, how to motivate and supervise public employees, has far less to say. What is needed instead is a far more complicated political economy of the tools of public action that clarifies the incentives of the non-Federal actors, helps inform choices about the appropriateness of different tools for different purposes, and provides guidance about how Federal managers can bargain more successfully to shape the behavior of the erstwhile allies on whom they are forced to depend. Under these circumstances, public management takes on a whole new dimension that the implementation literature has yet to acknowledge.

Finally, these changes in the forms of government action have important implications for the *coordination* of government activities. The problems the Federal government has recently been called upon to resolve—poverty, urban distress, environmental degradation, etc.—can rarely be solved through individual programs. To address them meaningfully requires the successful orchestration of a number of different activities. Yet the program structure that has evolved, by parceling varied chunks of authority among a number of different actors in ways that are barely visible, let alone subject to control, complicates the task of coordination and taxes the integrative institutions of government.

II. New Focus for Public Management Research

What these comments suggest is that the failures of public action about which so much has been written may result less from the incompetence or malfeasance of government managers

than from the tools we have required them to use and the curious ways we have required them to act. Under these circumstances, the improvement of government performance requires not simply better management, but a clearer understanding of the tools through which the government's business is performed.

It is the argument here that the development of such a systematic body of knowledge about the alternative tools of public action is the real "missing link" (Hargrove, 1975) in the theory and practice of public management. Filling in this missing link, however, will require a basic reorientation of existing research and the acceptance of a new unit of analysis that focuses on alternative tools of intervention rather than on individual programs or policies.

The Existing State of Knowledge

This is not the first time that attention has been called to the importance of examining the tools of government action. Almost 30 years ago Dahl and Lindblom (1953) observed that the proliferation of new techniques of social action had displaced the competition of ideologies in the Western world and represented "perhaps the greatest political revolution of our times."

If so, however, it has also been the least well examined such revolution. For, despite the impressive endorsement, the systematic study of the techniques of government action has hardly gotten off the ground. To be sure, some impressive work has been done in identifying Federal "subsidy" programs and calculating their costs and distributive effects.[5] What is more, some individual tools, like grants-in-aid, have been examined in depth (see, e.g., Elazar, 1962; Grodzins, 1966; Ingram, 1977; Monypenny, 1960; Nathan et al., 1975; Sanford, 1967; U.S. Advisory Commission on Intergovernmental Relations, 1977a, 1977b, 1978, 1979). But most tools have hardly been scrutinized at all, and

___

tial operational autonomy in the delivery of local police, welfare, educational and other services (see Lipsky, 1971).

[5]See, for example, U.S. Congress Joint Economic Committee, *Subsidy and Subsidy-Effect Programs of the U.S. Government,* 89th Cong., 1st Sess., Washington, DC: U.S. GPO, March 1965).

there has been a virtual absence of systematic comparative work analyzing different tools or examining the changing forms of action as a whole.[6]

As late as 1977, for example, the Congressional Budget Office found that no comparative data existed on default rates, risk factors, or other key features of Federal *loan guarantee programs,* even though these programs involved outstanding liabilities in excess of $300 billion (Peat et al., 1979). A special Interagency Council on Accident Compensation and Insurance reported just last year that it could not only not provide an accurate estimate of the contingent liabilities the Federal government has incurred through its various *insurance programs;* but also that it was not sure how many such programs exist.[7] Although *regulatory programs* have been examined more closely, much of this work has focused on the more traditional economic regulation rather than the newer "social" regulation. Moreover, some of the key operational features of regulatory programs, such as the relationships between Federal and state authorities, have been "little explored" (U.S. General Accounting Office, 1980). Indeed, it was not until 1978 that the first list of Federal regulatory programs was even compiled (U.S. General Accounting Office, 1978).

In short, whatever value there is in developing a systematic body of knowledge about the tools of public action—and the argument here is that it is great—that body of knowledge is still far from complete. As the U.S. Office of Management and Budget (1980) recently concluded after an intensive two-year study:

> . . . the relative effectiveness of different forms of assistance such as grants, loans, and

risk assumption for meeting different types of program objectives has not been systematically reviewed in the public literature. In light of the scope, magnitude, and importance of assistance as a tool of national leadership, much more needs to be known.

Lest the present call for more attention to the tools of government action go the way of the earlier one, therefore, it may be well to explore, at least in a preliminary way, how such an approach might be structured and what it would entail.

Central Premise

The central premise of the reorientation of implementation analysis that is suggested here is that different tools of government action have their own distinctive dynamics, their own "political economies," that affect the content of government action. This is so for much the same reasons that particular agencies and bureaus are now considered to have their own personalities and styles—because each instrument carries with it a substantial amount of "baggage" in the form of its own characteristic implementing institutions, standard operating procedures, types of expertise and professional cadre, products, degree of visibility, enactment and review processes, and relationships with other societal forces.

A loan guarantee program, for example, will typically involve reliance on local bankers, who tend to approach their responsibilities with a "risk minimization" perspective, who tend to resist nonfinancial criteria for program operation or evaluation, and who traditionally utilize conservative tests of soundness. In addition, such programs regularly escape review by executive branch or Congressional budget agencies, are most closely scrutinized, if at all, by the Treasury Department, are the province of the Banking Committees, not the Appropriations Committees, in the Congress, and are of special concern to the Federal Reserve and the financial

---

[6]One exception, which reviews the accountability problems resulting from increased public use of the private sector, is Smith (1975).

[7]U.S. Interagency Council on Accident Compensation and Insurance, "Partial Inventory of Current Federal Accident Compensation and Insurance Initiatives and Programs," mimeo (January 31, 1979).

community generally because of their potential implications for the allocation of credit in the economy.

It is reasonable to assume that these features systematically affect the operation of this type of program and that they are quite different from the comparable features affecting a grant-in-aid or tax incentive program. When Congress decided in the early 1930s to shift from a direct loan to a loan-guarantee form of program to cope with the urban housing problem, for example, it wittingly or unwittingly built into the nation's housing policy the prevailing perspectives of the bankers and realtors who help to operate the program locally. The result, as the Douglas Commission reported in 1968, was to confine benefits "almost exclusively to the middle class, and primarily only to the middle section of the middle class," while "the poor and those on the fringes of poverty have been almost completely excluded" on grounds that they were "bad credit risks and that the presence of Negroes tended to lower real estate values" (U.S. National Commission on Urban Problems, 1968).

In short, each tool involves a finely balanced complex of institutional, procedural, political, and economic relationships that substantially shape the character of the government action that results. By the same token, however, these features affect the likelihood that different tools will be enacted. In other words, the choice of program tool is a political, and not just an economic, issue: it involves important questions of power and purpose as well as of equity and efficiency.

Two questions thus form the core of the analysis of tools of government action that is suggested here:

(1) What consequences does the choice of tool of government action have for the effectiveness and operation of a government program?

(2) What factors influence the choice of program tools? In particular, to what extent are political or other administrative or symbolic reasons involved? Why are some tools chosen over others for particular purposes?

Basic Analytics

To answer these questions, it is necessary to begin with a clearer understanding of the major types of program tools, and the central differences among them. At a minimum, this requires a basic descriptive typology of program tools. Under current circumstances, however, even such a basic descriptive framework is unavailable. The *Catalog of Federal Domestic Assistance,* for example, lists 15 types of Federal assistance ranging from "Formula Grants" through "Dissemination of Technical Information." The catalog however, ignores many critical program tools, e.g., tax incentives, regulations, government-sponsored corporations. In addition, the catalog's groupings obscure many important distinctions (e.g., it groups "interest subsidies" under the general category of "Direct Payments for Specified Use" and fails to distinguish between price supports and social security payments).

Even more important than a descriptive framework, however, is the formulation of a more cross-cutting set of analytical categories in terms of which the various tools can be measured and assessed, and on the basis of which reasonable hypotheses, geared to the two questions above, can be generated and tested. Since this is the more difficult task, it may be useful to sketch out here in a purely suggestive way some of the major dimensions such an analytical framework might entail and some of the hypotheses it might support. Although the discussion here draws on literature where available, it should be clear that the intent is to stimulate further thinking rather than advance a definitive framework for the field. In this spirit, five dimensions of the tools of government action seem worthy of attention:

(1) The Directness/Indirectness Dimension:
The first such dimension concerns the extent of

reliance on nonfederal actors that a particular tool entails. Direct federal activities have long been suspect in American government, as much out of a philosophical hostility to concentrated governmental power as out of a concern about the rigidity and unresponsiveness supposed to accompany centralized operations. Recent research on the implementation of public programs suggests, however, that indirect forms of action have their own substantial drawbacks. Pressman and Wildavsky (1973) demonstrate convincingly, for example, that federal efforts to encourage economic development and employment in Oakland were frustrated by a form of action that vested critical responsibilities in a large number of federal and nonfederal actors, each of whom had his own priorities and perspectives that had to be reconciled anew at each of several dozen decision points that stood between program conception and completion. Similarly, Chase (1979) found that the most serious problems in implementing three social service programs in New York City all involved "some player or players in the implementation process whom the program manager does not control but whose cooperation or assistance is required." And Berman (1980) differentiates between the "macro-implementation" of a program and its "micro-implementation" to emphasize the looseness of the tie between the adoption of a policy and its actual operation by a largely autonomous local agent.

What is important about the use of indirect forms of action is not simply the administrative complexity of the resulting program structure, however. Of equal or greater importance is the incongruence that can arise between the goals of the federal government—as articulated, however imperfectly, in legislation, report language, or regulations—and the goals of the nonfederal implementing agents. This is clearly the case when the agent is a for-profit corporation. But it is equally true of state and local governments since different interests, different priorities, and different concerns find effective expression at different levels of government. Proposals to turn more decision-making power over to the states and localities thus involve more than questions of administrative efficiency; they also involve questions of program purpose and substance.

Taken together, these considerations suggest the following tentative hypothesis:

Hypothesis 1: The more indirect the form of government action—i.e., the more it places important discretionary authority in the hands of nonfederal actors, and the more the interests and goals of these actors diverge from those of the federal government—the more difficult will be the implementation of the resulting program and the less likely will the program be to achieve its goals.

To the extent that this hypothesis is true, it raises significant questions about why so much of federal action now relies upon basically indirect devices. The answer, it appears, is that the dictates of implementation frequently diverge from the imperatives of enactment. In the first place, the success of federal programs frequently depends on access to a resource under some third party's control. Delivering a degree of authority to this third party is often the only way to get the program the resources it needs. This is especially true in view of a second factor, the hostility of key producer and provider groups (including state and local governments) to federal competition in their fields. The price of political acquiescence in the establishment of a federal role, therefore, is frequently the acceptance by the federal government of a tool of action that cuts these third parties into a meaningful piece of the federal action. Finally, as already noted, the use of indirect devices has strong philosophical and ideological roots because the protection of the private sector from governmental intervention and the preservation of state and local autonomy are viewed as political values in their own right, worth protecting even at the cost of some sacrifice of administrative efficiency or national purpose. What this suggests is a companion hypothesis:

Hypothesis 2: The more direct the form of government action, the more likely it is to encounter political opposition.

(2) The Automatic/Administered Dimension: A second key dimension of different instruments of government action concerns the extent to which they rely on automatic, as opposed to administered, processes. An automatic process is one that utilizes existing structures and relationships (e.g., the tax structure or the price system) and requires a minimum of administrative decision-making. A tax credit automatically available to all firms investing in new plant or equipment, for example, would represent a largely automatic tool. A similar sum made available through grants on the basis of separately reviewed applications would represent a more highly administered tool.

Generally speaking, automatic tools are operationally more efficient since they involve less administrative oversight and transaction cost. They are also less disruptive of ongoing social processes, such as the price system and the market. This suggests the following hypothesis:

Hypothesis 3: The more automatic the tool of government action, the easier to manage, the fairer the operation, and the less disruptive the side effects.

Despite these hypothesized advantages, however, instruments that rely upon essentially automatic processes have significant drawbacks. For one thing, there is far less certainty that they will have the results intended, especially when they are attached to processes with far different purposes. A program that seeks to promote worker safety by levying higher disability insurance charges on companies with poor safety records rather than by imposing detailed safety regulations, for example, may continuously be in the position of doing too little too late. In addition, while promoting administrative efficiency, such tools sacrifice "tar-

get efficiency," the effective targeting of program benefits. A tax credit program aimed at encouraging additional productive investment in plant and equipment, for example, may end up delivering substantial benefits to firms that would have made these investments anyway, or freeing resources for forms of investment that are nonproductive and speculative. Those most concerned about the achievement of program objectives and the targeting of program resources may consequently be wary of tools that lack sufficient controls. These considerations thus suggest the following additional hypothesis:

Hypothesis 4: The more automatic the tool of government action, the less certain the achievement of program purposes, the greater the leakage of program benefits, and the more problematic the generation of needed political support.

(3) The Cash Versus In-Kind Dimension: In assistance-type programs in particular, important differences exist between programs that deliver their benefits in the form of cash and those that deliver them in kind. Cash-type programs reserve far more flexibility to recipients and are typically easier to administer. In-kind programs (e.g., food stamps, housing assistance), by tying benefits to a particular service or good, constrain recipient choices, often providing more of a particular good than a recipient would freely choose and thereby reducing the marginal value of the benefit to the recipient. This suggests the following hypothesis:

Hypothesis 5: Programs that utilize cash assistance are easier to manage and more highly valued by recipients than programs that provide assistance in kind.

While cash forms of assistance have attractions from the point of view of recipients, however, they have drawbacks from the point of view of building political support. In the first place, in-kind programs, by committing resources to the purchase of a particular good or service, can stimulate support from the producers of that good or service that would otherwise not exist. The food stamp program, for example, enjoys support from agricultural and farm interests that would not be forthcoming for a general, cash income-assistance program. Similarly, builder support for aid to the poor is much stronger for programs that tie such aid to the production of housing than for programs that make such assistance available in the form of cash. In the second place, in-kind assistance is more likely to go for the purpose intended than is outright cash. Those who make a case for assistance in terms of a particular need may therefore feel obliged to champion the delivery mechanism most certain to apply that assistance to that particular need. What these considerations suggest, therefore, is the following companion hypothesis:

Hypothesis 6: The greater the reliance on in-kind tools of action, the greater the prospects for political support.

(4) The Visibility-Invisibility Dimension:
Because of the structure of the budget and legislative processes, certain tools of government action are far less visible than others. Tax incentives, for example, are far less open to regular scrutiny than outright grants. "Entitlement" programs, which establish legal rights to program benefits independent of the budget, are far less closely scrutinized than programs that are subject to yearly control. In some cases, the costs of federal action are not even known. This is the case, for example, with regulatory actions, the true impact of which appears not in the federal budget, but in the balance sheets of the regulated industries. What this suggests is the following hypothesis:

Hypothesis 7: The less visible a tool of government action is in the regular budget process, the less subject it will be to overall management and control.

To the extent this hypothesis is correct, it follows that invisibility is a politically attractive attribute of a tool. Indeed, research by Boulding and Pfaff (1972) found that the less visible federal subsidies delivered most of their benefits to the better off while assistance to the poor came in far more visible forms. What this suggests is the following hypothesis:

Hypothesis 8: The less visible the costs of a tool, the more attractive the tool will be to those who will benefit from it. The more powerful the beneficiaries, therefore, the more likely they will be to receive whatever benefits they secure through less visible tools.

(5) Design Standards versus Performance Standards for Program Control:
Attention to the instruments of government action has implications not only for basic choices among different tools, but also for decisions about how different tools, once chosen, are managed. One of the central issues in this regard is the extent to which reliance is placed on performance standards as opposed to design standards in program operations. Design standards involve controls over detailed aspects of program operations: accounting procedures, fund transfers among different program accounts, personnel recruitment procedures, specific technological processes to adopt to reduce air pollution at particular types of sites. Performance standards, by contrast, specify desired outputs but leave to the discretion of program managers or their third-party agents the decisions about how to design activities to achieve these outputs. Students of social regulation have faulted much of the federal government's recent regulatory effort in precisely these terms, arguing that by placing too much stress on design specifications (e.g., the location and numbers of fire extinguishers in industrial plants) rather than on performance standards (the days lost through fires), these activities end up being far less efficient economically and far more cumbersome administratively than is necessary (Schultze, 1977). Similar observations have been made

about other programs where detailed restrictions are imposed on the mix of inputs (e.g., the ratio of welfare case workers to recipients) rather than focusing attention on outputs (e.g., the reduction of dependency) (Levine, 1972). What these findings suggest is the following hypothesis:

> Hypothesis 9: The more a form of government action uses performance standards instead of design regulations, the less cumbersome it is administratively and the more efficient is its use of resources.

Attractive as performance standards are, however, they are not without their problems. For one thing, program purposes are frequently kept deliberately vague in order to hold together the political coalition often required for passage. Moreover, programs often serve multiple purposes, and opinions can differ over the priorities to attach to each. In addition, the measurement of success and failure in terms of particular performance criteria can often be quite subjective, creating added possibilities for conflict and confusion, especially where responsibility for program decisions is split between federal authorities and their "third-party" agents. Finally, the use of performance standards involves greater uncertainty since results are not apparent for a considerable time and great opportunity exists for mistakes along the way. Those responsible for program oversight can therefore be expected to find such uncertainty exceedingly unattractive. Based on these considerations, therefore, the following hypothesis seems plausible:

> Hypothesis 10: The more a tool involves reliance on federally determined performance standards, the more likely it is to encounter political opposition and resistance from its administrators.

(6) Summary—The Public Management Paradox: Taken together, the hypotheses identified above suggest an important paradox that may lie at the heart of much of the recent disappointment with federal program performance. *Simply put, this paradox is that the types of instruments that are the easiest to implement may be the hardest to enact; conversely, the forms that are most likely to be enacted are also the most difficult to carry out.*

III. Conclusions and Implications

Whether the hypotheses outlined here are accepted or rejected, the discussion should demonstrate the character and range of issues that open up when the unit of analysis in implementation research is changed from the individual program to the generic tools of government action. These are not, moreover, simply theoretical issues. They are tangible questions that face decision-makers day-to-day as they decide whether to use a regulation, a tax credit, a grant, or a loan guarantee to encourage electric utilities to switch from oil- to coal-powered generators; or whether to build an economic development strategy on the basis of grants to local governments, loan guarantees through private banks, employment tax credits to business, or equity assistance to community development corporations.

Up to this point, these decisions have not been informed by any systematic understanding of the consequences that the choices of tools of government action have for the operations of public programs. As a result, the political pressures have not encountered any analytical counterpoise and have typically prevailed, often trapping program managers in no-win situations that are doomed from the start. For implementation researchers then to come along and declare programs a failure because of "poor management" or inattention to implementation is to add insult to injury and invite justifiable scorn.

What is needed instead is a usable body of knowledge about how different tools of government action work and how they can be adapted to different purposes. It is this body of knowledge that is the appropriate domain of implementation study. And it is this range of issues on which implementation research can finally cut its theoretical teeth.

Bibliography

Berman, P. (Spring 1978): "The Study of Macro and Micro Implementation of Social Policy," *Public Policy, 26*(2), 157.

Boulding, K. E., and Pfaff, M. (1972): *Redistribution to the Rich and the Poor: The Grants Economics of Income Distribution,* Belmont, CA: Wadsworth Publishing Co., pp. 2–4.

Chase, G. (Fall 1979): "Implementing a Human Services Program: How Hard Will It Be?" *Public Policy, 27*(4), 385–435.

Dahl, R., and Lindblom, C. E. (1953): *Politics, Economics and Welfare,* New York: Harper and Row, p. 8.

Drucker, P. (Winter 1969): "The Sickness of Government," *The Public Interest,* No. 14, 3–23.

Elazar, D.J. (1962): *American Partnership: Intergovernmental Cooperation in Nineteenth Century United States,* Chicago: Univ. Chicago P.

Grodzins, M. (1966): *The American System: A New View of Government in the United States,* Daniel Elazar, Ed., Chicago: Rand McNally Co.

Hargrove, E. (1975): *The Missing Link: The Study of the Implementation of Social Policy,* Washington, DC: The Urban Institute.

Ingram, H. (Fall 1977): "Policy Implementation through Bargaining: The Case of Federal Grants-in-Aid," *Public Policy, 25*(4), 498–526.

Lilley, W., III, and Miller, J. C., III (Spring 1977): "The New Social Regulation," *The Public Interest,* No. 47, 49–51.

Lipsky, M. (June 1971): "Street-Level Bureaucracy and the Analysis of Urban Reform," *Urban Affairs Quarterly, VI* (4), 391–409.

Monypenny, P. (March 1960): "Federal Grants-in-Aid to State Governments: A Political Analysis," *National Tax Journal, 13* (1), 1–16.

Nathan, R. P., et al., (1975): *Monitoring Revenue Sharing,* Washington, DC: The Brookings Institution.

Peat, Marwick, Mitchell & Co. (1979): "Loan Insurance and Loan Guarantee Programs: A Comparison of Current Practices and Procedures," in Congressional Budget Office, *Loan Guarantees: Current Concerns and Alternatives for Control.*

Pressman, J. L., and Wildavsky, A. (1973): *Implementation: How Great Expectations in Washington are Dashed in Oakland,* Berkeley: Univ. California P.

Salamon, L. M. (1980): "The Rise of Third-Party Government," *The Washington Post,* June 29.

Sanford, T. (1967): *Storm over the States,* New York: McGraw-Hill.

Schultze, C. (1977): *The Public Use of Private Interest,* Washington, DC: The Brookings Institution.

Smith, B. L. R., Ed. (1975): *The New Political Economy: The Public Use of the Private Sector,* New York: Wiley.

U.S. Advisory Commission on Intergovernmental Relations (1977a): *Block Grants: A Comparative Analysis (A-62),* Washington, DC: U.S. GPO.

U.S. Advisory Commission on Intergovernmental Relations (1977b): *The Intergovernmental Grant System as Seen By Local, State, and Federal Officials,* Washington, DC: U.S. GPO.

U.S. Advisory Commission on Intergovern-
mental Relations (1978): *Categorical Grants:
Their Role and Design,* Washington, DC: U.S.
GPO.

U.S. Advisory Commission on Intergovernmental Relations (February 1979): *A Catalog of Federal Grant-in-Aid Programs to State and Local
Governments: Grants Funded Feb. 78,* Washington, DC: U.S. GPO.

U.S. Commission on Government Procurement
(1972): *Report,* Washington, DC: U.S. GPO,
pp. 73–75.

U.S. General Accounting Office (1978): *Federal
Regulatory Programs and Activities,* Washington, DC: General Accounting Office.

U.S. General Accounting Office (January 1980):
*Economic Analysis of Alternative Program Ap-
proaches: Program Plan,* Washington, DC:
General Accounting Office.

U.S. National Commission on Urban Problems
(1968): *Building the American City,* Washington, DC: U.S. GPO, p. 100.

U.S. Office of Management and Budget (1980):
Managing Federal Assistance in the 1980s, p.
31.

CASE STUDY 15

Introduction

The Cornwall County school system recently spent over $50 million to build
new schools and other facilities but found it now lacked the custodial crews to
keep these buildings in good condition. What should be done? The new school
superintendent, John Lowell (a real person whose name has been changed) is
approached by ServiceMaster Corporation, a private nationwide custodial business, with a proposal to manage all the custodial functions and related personnel
on a contractual basis for the school system for the next five years. Maintenance
previously had been done "in house" by the Cornwall schools, but for various
reasons, outlined in the case, the ServiceMaster offer looked good to the new
superintendent.

Should the school system contract out its custodial services or continue to run
them itself? The following case, "The Cornwall County School District," by
David Kennedy and Robert Leone, focuses on Superintendent John Lowell's
choice concerning whether to ask the school board to approve the ServiceMaster
contract or improve the existing custodial arrangements. It presents the classic
decision faced by many public administrators today over whether or not to use
"third parties" to accomplish government purposes (in this case, keeping the
local schools clean) and, if so, how to go about pursuing those aims (in this case,
as the reader will soon see, whether or not to enter into this contract was *the*
formidable task). These decisions were complicated by local politics, economic
costs, uncertainties about ServiceMaster's past performance, the company's peculiar value orientation, and the lack of past local experiences with contracting
out custodial services.

As you read this case, think about the following questions:

What were the "pluses" and "minuses" for the Cornwall County school system to the ServiceMaster contract? On balance, do you think the contract was a good idea?

What were the chief sources of support for this idea? What were the sources of opposition?

What role does quality custodial service play in determining John Lowell's success or failure as an administrator? What were his motivations for pushing so hard for this idea? In your view, were these essentially selfish motivations?

In the end, do you think the school board was wrong in not supporting John Lowell's proposed contract with ServiceMaster? Why or why not?

What does this case say about the problems of determining the "costs" and "benefits" of using third-party government? Does this case change or challenge the concept of third-party government outlined in the preceding selection by Lester Salamon?

DAVID KENNEDY AND ROBERT LEONE

Cornwall County School District

Cornwall was a city of around 78,000 people, 185 miles east of the state capitol and—like much of the rest of the state—practiced a unique brand of politics noteworthy for its enthusiasm and open—if not brazen—patronage. Cornwall's political scene had long been dominated by the long-time residents of the close-knit community. "It's not a machine," said one politically active native. "But there are understandings." Some of those understandings—those involving the prerogatives of school board members—came to dominate a 1985 decision by the Cornwall County School Board to hire outside professionals to maintain the school district's buildings. The issues involved educational goals, economics, and, of course, local politics.

This case was written by David Kennedy and Robert Leone for use at the John Fitzgerald Kennedy School of Government, Harvard University. The locale, participants' names, and certain other details have been disguised; ServiceMaster Industries Incorporated, however, is a real firm and played the role described. The authors would like to express their gratitude to ServiceMaster for its encouragement in developing this case (1085). Copies of the Kennedy School cases are available from the Kennedy School Case Program Distribution Office. For information, call (617) 495-9523.

Cleanliness

Superintendent John Lowell had been concerned about the state of the system—38 schools with some 28,000 students—ever since he came from New York to work in the system in 1981. "I'd been doing site visits to the schools and seeing floors that had one coat of wax on them, or two coats of wax, that was rubbing off as soon as the kids tracked mud in," he said. "I got involved with telling them how to wax the floors when I got here. . . . I mean, not seminars, but to individual people where there were problems."

Some of the county's schools had really serious cleanliness problems. "One was extremely dirty," said Meredith Davies, who in early 1984 was transferred from her post as the district's business manager to a new executive position which included responsibility in areas as diverse as custodial supervision and political affairs.

When you first looked at the building in the administrative area, it didn't look that bad. Well, we started walking in the building, and the glass wasn't clean; it had graffiti on the walls that had not been removed, or attempted to be removed; you had the walk-off mats that had seldom been taken outside and dusted; the halls hadn't been dust-mopped in maybe two days. At any rate, it was dirty.

One school reportedly had rest rooms so horrendous that when they were finally attended to, urinals had to be cleaned with a chisel.

Not all of the district's schools suffered so. Terry Hand, principal of a 750-student junior high, was perfectly happy with the state of her seemingly spotless building and grounds. "I have, I guess, 29 individual restrooms over here, and they smell like the day they were built," she said.

They haven't repainted the halls in 13 years, and the halls look just like they were painted the week before. I think there's a lot of pride as far as the parents wanting to furnish the money that we need for the schools; I have a very active PTA, very, and we raise a lot of money. The students, I think, are very conscious of wanting a good school. I mean, I see kids just stop and pick up paper; the janitors do it, I do it, the teachers do it . . . we can go right now and there's a good possibility that you won't find one piece of paper all around.

Hand benefitted from a crew of four singularly dedicated janitors she had selected herself over the years. "My janitors cannot work harder than they're working," she said.

I mean, they're working every minute. They're supposed to have an hour for lunch. Never. I mean, there's not a day that any one of those janitors will take half an hour [for lunch]. Not a day. They're supposed to have a break in the morning and afternoons; they never, never, never take a break in the afternoon. They take their little break in the morning. One of them's supposed to come to work at, I think, 6:30. He's here before 5:00 in the morning.

Overall, though, said Davies, in too many schools "we did have problems. Not from the standpoint that we had little creepy crawly things on the floors, and the kids couldn't walk in the halls because of the dirt. It wasn't that bad, and I don't mean to imply that. We just had some problems."

One such problem, in Lowell's and Davies' view, was that there was no central management or training for cleaning staff. Although Davies recognized that the district needed custodial attention, and that it fell in her new bailiwick, she was somewhat at a loss for a solution. "I am far from an expert in janitorial services, believe me," she said. Custodians reported to the principals in their schools; the principals—on custodial affairs, at least—reported to, and got support from, nobody. "Some of our principals knew absolutely nothing about how to clean a school, or how to maintain a school," said Davies. "They couldn't really give directions to their custodians. They had no one to turn to to get directions." Nor were there any particular standards for either the staff's qualifications or the jobs they were supposed to do. "We had thirty-eight school sites," said Davies.

We had thirty-eight different crews, with thirty-eight different supervisors: those being the principals. We did not have any consistency. We did not have any standards of quality as far as the schools were concerned. We didn't have any controls over cleaning chemicals or supplies; they pretty much used whatever they wanted in any quantity they wanted. We simply hired people, gave them a mop and a bucket and said, "Here's a school; go to work."

The lack of training led to some serious performance problems. "One example we found," said Davies, "was a custodian buffing a hallway with a scrubbing pad on his buffing machine. Didn't know the difference; he *thought* he was shining it."

Principals' jobs in managing custodians weren't getting any easier, either. The state had experienced a high tech boom in the late 1970s and early 1980s. According to Lowell, the high tech firms were hiring not only engineers and technicians, but manual laborers as well. Custodial hiring suffered. "Anybody that walked in and applied, we had to take them," said Davies. "We had no one else available; they were all working with computer firms and defense contractors. We did not get the best caliber of employee."

Besides the problems with performance, Lowell, at least, had some philosophical differences with the status quo. He'd come in from outside the district with plans to make real educational improvements in Cornwall, and had already moved to teach students to read earlier, ensure that they did more homework, standardize performance testing across the county, cut allowed student absenteeism, and the like. He wanted principals to help him with that, and he was doubtful about the merits of their using time to manage cleaning staff. "I don't think principals know how to manage custodians," he said. "They ought to be leaders in instruction, but I don't expect them to be leaders in custodial areas also."

At the same time, the county's stakes in maintaining good, clean schools were rising. The economic boom had changed the area's long-stable character. The district undertook a $60 million building program: old buildings were refurbished or replaced, new schools were built, every high school got new recreational facilities. Pure pragmatism dictated taking some care with all this fresh plant. "When you invest $60 million into buildings, you want them to be maintained; you want them to stay clean," said Davies. "So we felt we had to do something."

Politics

There was more than pragmatism at work, however. The growth of the high tech industry in Cornwall had given rise to a sense that improving the quality of schools was important to the county's future. "Here were all these people coming from urban areas and saying, 'You mean that's the building my kid's going to go to school in?'" said school board member Paul Marshall. "It was hurting us economically."

The influx of "foreigners"—meaning from out of state—also caused some serious stresses. "The pressure that the system has received from the outside is profound. People said, 'Hey, look, we move our kids from an excellent educational system and we see no reason why we can't have the same here,'" said then-board president Andrew Busby.

The more that became evident, the more the board found itself looking at concerned people in the audience who were asking questions—and legitimate questions—and not getting answers. You could see the trend; people wanted to get involved. And that caused those people who would ordinarily not even think about wanting to be a member of a board like we have to come forward and put on their campaign shoes and to win a seat: and to be very concerned.

John Lowell himself was working in Cornwall in part because a high tech industry lobbying group had made it clear that it believed it was time for new blood in the system; Lowell was the first superintendent in the history of Cornwall to have been brought in from outside the district, much less from out of state. The newcomers, along with some members of the board, said Busby,

. . . felt that it was time to change, time to try and do something about the political situation we have in this part of the country, especially in this county. And luckily we were able to do that, to get a man from the outside, someone who was concerned about education and not what favors he or she could get out of the job. . . . But there were some awful ill feelings when that man was selected, because some board members felt it should be a local man.

The vote to hire Lowell was nine-five: a close vote in that community. Time dulled the controversy surrounding Lowell's appointment only marginally: four years after his appointment, Lowell was still being reminded by long-time board members that they had voted against him then and would do it again if given a chance. "If we held that vote today it'd still be 9-5," he said.

Some of Lowell's actions were guaranteed to prolong that controversy. The new superintendent, along with his supporters on the board, had instituted some changes which struck at the heart of the board's traditional political privileges. Board members, said Busby, had traditionally been accorded pretty much complete patronage powers within the system.

We've had a history of appointing principals and administrators in this county not necessarily on merit, or attitude, or performance ability, or on being pro-education, but on who you knew, and on how well you were in cahoots with the superintendent and board members. If you could get on the telephone and convince a majority of board members that you are powerful enough, nine times out of ten you were put in those positions. It could be kinfolks, could be a political bloc of votes out there that several board members needed, or some big political muckety-muck in the county who wanted that particular person. Just a mess.

Busby could speak in the past tense only because one of Lowell's first moves on coming in to Cornwall had been to set up a review committee distinct from the board to advise on academic—principals, administrators, and teachers—appointments. The influence of the board over those jobs was considerably diminished. "It used to be," said board veteran Nancy Olsen, "if you told a man you have a job, he had it; you know, they'd leave it up to the board member. But it's changed." Members still held sway, however, over non-academic jobs: bus drivers, maintenance workers, kitchen staff, and janitors. "Some of us on the board had a very bad time with schools in our districts," said Busby.

Just filthy, dirty conditions; that's all it was to it. And nine times out of ten I found that either the head janitor or the janitorial staff was people who got their jobs because of board members. And they had been there for quite some time, and just nobody, not even principals, could tell them what to do. . . . It was a dynasty that was set up, and you just didn't knock it. . . . They could get on a tele-

phone and run right back to that board member, and of course the board member would either be so bold as to get up in board meetings and complain about it, or put someone's head on the chopping block because of it, or go to some office and take somebody down a notch or two: which is of course entirely wrong, but not uncommon.

Options

Unfortunately, there seemed no easy and effective way to improve the situation. Meredith Davies had arranged for some of the district's cleaning supplies vendors to give workshops—on floor waxing techniques, for instance—to janitors who could go back to their schools and instruct their co-workers. That had helped some, but was hardly good enough. "I could get the wax people in one time, I could get the disinfectant company in one time, I could get the sweeping compound people in one time, but there was just no continuity in training or anything of that nature," Davies recalled. "So that did not seem to solve the problem."

The only other option seemed to be to hire a housekeeping firm which would simply take over and serve the district's janitorial needs. "They would come in and actually do the work," said Davies.

But then they would either leave—and we were back to square one—or they would stay. If they stayed then we had 117 custodians that we didn't need. Getting rid of our custodians was not acceptable to the board or the administration; that was not a good option for us at all. We didn't even pursue it. I was looking more for someone to come in and do training on how to wax a floor, how to use disinfectants, instruct on the chemicals end of it. We needed something that I could get into as well and have an ongoing monitoring system, and continuing education at different levels. We just had not found anything that would give us a total program, and in the meantime we were just kind of grasping at straws and doing more looking. . . .

ServiceMaster

Bob Little was looking, too; he was looking for Cornwall County, or something very much like it. Little was the regional sales representative for the educational division of ServiceMaster Industries, Inc., a management services firm headquartered in Downers Grove, Illinois, outside Chicago. The core of the company's business was a management program for plant operations and maintenance; energy; housekeeping; and laundry services for health care and educational institutions and industrial facilities. ServiceMaster estimated it provides one or more of these three services to fully 15% of U.S. hospitals. (As a separate operation, the company also provided cleaning services to the residential and commercial markets through a network of 3,000 franchises, which can be found in nearly any municipal yellow pages.) It had a distinctive way of doing business, providing management and technical support to improve the performance of non-ServiceMaster staff. In any given facility the firm would train, supervise, and provide a system of products, processes, and equipment to the custodians. The custodians remained on the school or hospital's payroll, and the school or hospital—formally, at any rate—made all hiring, firing and disciplinary decisions. ServiceMaster usually provided one or two full-time managers. Those managers instructed the staff in standardized cleaning procedures, held monthly workshops to promote such things as literacy and staff involvement in the hospital community, and made recommendations to hospital authorities about promotions and disciplinary actions. The managers in turn were backed up by a corporate staff which developed cleaning chemicals and tools—lightweight battery-powered vacuums, for instance—and work procedures to match, and helped develop and catalogue the monthly workshops.

ServiceMaster's energy and maintenance business followed the same general patterns and usually went hand-in-hand with custodial supervision. Rather than sending in people to do actual maintenance or energy-conservation work, ServiceMaster would survey a site and draw up a computerized preventive-maintenance schedule, or a roster of possible conservation actions along with their costs, benefits, and payoff times. Once the initial work was done the firm provided a computer link to Downers Grove, and issued, for instance, seasonal work schedules or assessed and monitored the economics of purchasing alternative boilers and air conditioners. Again, local people on the local payroll did all hands-on work. The development work in the areas of custodial, maintenance, and energy management was done by ServiceMaster, with each customer receiving any benefits of scale.

ServiceMaster had entered the educational market several years ago; it saw vast opportunities in selling its services to schools, be they local public institutions or colleges and universities. Seeing a wide-open field, Little had moved into the new sales force from a position selling the company's services to health care institutions. When he came calling, unannounced, on Superintendent Lowell in October 1984, he was on his first sweep through his new territory. He knew what he was looking for, though. "I had to set some goals and strategies," he said.

It was totally new for us [to work in education] and we were pioneering, really. As I looked at the state, we had 64 districts, and I said, I want to look at one of the larger districts, one in the top 10, and I want one of those top 10 districts to have a superintendent that is going to give some good tour and referral.

Cornwall County filled the bill nicely.

Little had no idea that Cornwall was having problems with its janitors; he saw it merely as a potentially good market for all three of ServiceMaster's management programs. He walked into the school board offices without an appointment on October 7 and got five minutes with Lowell. He told the superintendent that ServiceMaster provided contract management services for janitorial, maintenance, and energy conservation. Lowell was interested. "He really turned on to the custodial operation; maintenance was secondary from the word 'go,'" Little recalled, although the salesman continued to push, and Lowell to consider, all three areas. The superintendent introduced the salesman to Meredith Davies and a few days later Little returned for a conference with Lowell, Davies and the district's business manager. Lowell was torn. He liked what he knew so far about the firm, but the timing was not propitious. The high tech boom had gone flat, for reasons unexplained by industry analysts, and with it went the county's school budget growth. The district had stopped its $60 million building program at $45 million and was cutting back on physical education, art, guidance programs, clerical help and substitute teachers; everything, in short, not academically essential. The district was already spending $2,081,000 annually on custodial care. "I said," Lowell recalled,

> Bob, I'm interested, but we can't afford it; I said we're cutting back, we have no money. He said, would you be interested if I showed you on paper that we wouldn't cost you any money; that we might in fact save you money? I said, well, probably, but I doubt that you can do that, you know. And he says, well, we can make your force more efficient, we can tell you if you're overstaffed, we can help you develop your manpower.

Lowell, though intrigued, was skeptical, but he okayed a factfinding visit to a school district in an adjacent state where ServiceMaster was performing its full range of management functions. Little, Davies, and a highly respected principal, Carl Fisher, who'd been having serious trouble keeping his high school clean, made the trip. "I talked to the superintendent and I talked to some of the principals and some of the custodial staff . . ." said Fisher. "It was very impressive. . . . I was very pleased by what I heard the superintendent and the custodians say." "One of the things the principals told us," said Davies, "each one we talked to, was, 'I am no longer head custodian. I'm free to do other things.' They still have supervisory responsibility, because it's their building, but they don't have to deal with day-to-day management." They also said, according to Davies, that between custodial, maintenance, and energy economies they were saving some $230,000 annually.

Discussions continued back in Cornwall. The more Lowell heard about ServiceMaster's custodial operation, the more he liked it. "They told me they had a training program, they had incentives for career objectives, they had an award system," he said.

> These are things we could use for teachers, much less custodians. And here we were hiring a group of people that weren't well trained, weren't well educated, and we had no development program for them. And I thought, we could get all this for nothing? We ought to look at it.

The next step in looking at it was for ServiceMaster to bring in an engineering team to survey the county's schools to see what shape they were in from a janitorial, maintenance, and energy efficiency perspective, how many people would be needed to clean and service them, whether any special tools or supplies might be required, and the like. The survey would result in a status report to the county as well as serving as the data base ServiceMaster would use to draw up its contract proposal. Lowell told Little simply to proceed, but Little insisted that he be allowed to present the idea to the board and get their permission to go ahead. "That proved to be a good thing," said Lowell. "I didn't think it was a big deal, but you don't bring all these people in without the board's permission." The board didn't mind, and the survey began.

While ServiceMaster's engineers went through the system interviewing principals, checking boilers, and measuring floor areas, Little began a series of meetings with individual board members to explain the company's program and solicit their support. He learned some interesting things. Lowell had told him, Little said, "cost us a dollar and you won't get it." But the board members evidently weren't so adamant. "When I met with them one-on-one during the survey process, some of them stated that they realized a program like this was going to cost them money. So then I knew that we did have some board members who would vote 'yes,' even if it did." They acknowledged, he said, a need for custodial training and development. They asked whether there would be cutbacks or layoffs, to which he said they might have to cut back or add on, but that the board would retain hiring and firing control. Little understood how things worked in Cornwall. "The board gives a lot of latitude to John and Meredith," he said.

> Okay? Granted. But sometimes they don't. If it's a first cousin, if it's a whatever, they don't give any latitude at all. They'll call you and say, don't touch 'em. Fire anybody you want, but don't touch that one.

Only three days into the survey, as a result of his caucuses with board members, Little unilaterally withdrew ServiceMaster's bid for maintenance and energy management contracts and changed the status of the survey in those areas to that of "feasibility study." That study would not even be circulated to the board; only Lowell would see it. One motive, he said, was that even the early analysis indicated that the district's maintenance department, supervised by long-time district employee Cheryl Thompson, was understaffed by eight to ten people relative to the number his firm would want to do the job, and he didn't feel that the board was likely to spring for the extra salaries.

There was more to it, though. ServiceMaster's proposals to supervise custodial services in Cornwall County were, at least to Thompson, insult added to injury. The maintenance department handled bus, grounds, and physical plant upkeep with considerable success, and Thompson's strongest supporter on the school board, James Miller, had more than once suggested to the board that custodians be put under her control as well. The board had demurred, but Thompson still had ideas on the subject. "I want custodians to clean plus maintain," she said.

> I want to put one head janitor in every school, that would be working with me and the rest of the people in the department. Go and maintain those schools: mechanical, everything. Building itself; grounds if necessary.
> . . . I always told them you could get rid of

50% of the custodial staff and do more work than you're doing now. Make them work eight hours a day. Very simple. . . . See those guys, they work maybe two hours a day and sit on their cans the rest. . . . I believe in what ServiceMaster's doing, don't get me wrong. Like I said, I've been trying to do that for years. But it makes me feel bad because they won't let me do it. And it wouldn't have cost them a dime. To me, I'd be ashamed to say that I need ServiceMaster to come tell me how to run my business. I'd be embarrassed to do that.

There seemed, however, to be ample board support for the custodial services; Little's head-count, based on his conferences with board members—he met eventually with all but one, Harold Kirk, who declined to see him—told him the contract was virtually signed. To cap his sales process, Little, following standard ServiceMaster operating procedure for major sales, flew Lowell, Davies, and six board members (the president, vice president, and the board's four committee chairpeople) to Downers Grove to tour ServiceMaster's corporate headquarters. "What we found was a very, very interesting laboratory, a dedicated workforce, and a fascinating company philosophy," said Lowell. The company's standard tour brought visitors through an antiseptic cleaning products lab, complete with microcomputers and white-coated technicians, run by an articulate Ph.D. chemist. Test corridors were covered with different finishes to check quality and longevity; standardized black heel marks were applied and then removed under controlled conditions. The energy management section of the building was filled with humming mainframes and graphics plotters churning out time plots of energy use for institutions contracted with ServiceMaster. The company's vice president for education talked eagerly of literacy programs for workers, of a corporate commitment to filling 20% of new supervisory positions from the custodial ranks, of the challenge of managing and educating an often illiterate or non-English speaking workforce. "We were just impressed with their approach," said Lowell.

We talked a little bit about how they train people, and their commitment to people and their improvement, and I was impressed with the fact that they just had their act together. . . . Their products seemed great. So many things about the firm seemed first class.

To Lowell, the firm's religious orientation was an issue he wanted to think more about. Marion Wade, who founded the company in the 1940's, was committed to practicing biblical values in the marketplace. ServiceMaster's four corporate objectives, prominently displayed in its annual reports and throughout its corporate building, were "To honor God in all we do, To help people develop, To pursue excellence, and, To grow profitably." Open Bibles could be found in a number of executives' offices. The company's personnel even had a specialized vocabulary: ServiceMaster didn't "work for" or "hire out" to clients, as a typical contractor might; it "served" them; it didn't discipline recalcitrant janitors, but "counseled" them.

Lowell was wary. "I was skeptical about people who used God as a reason for what they are doing, you know," he said. "I asked my ServiceMaster hosts some pointed questions about their values. I asked them if there were any non-Christians in the corporation, and the answer was, yes." Lowell concluded that the firm's religious orientation was no hindrance. On balance, said Lowell, he and his party returned from Downers Grove, "very, very impressed: much more committed than I was before I left."

Meanwhile, the survey finished, Little had drawn up a work plan and a five-year, fixed price contract. The hopes for cost savings, or even a financial wash, were dashed. Having ServiceMaster on the job—meaning two full-time managers, plus a larger team for the transition, and most cleaning equipment and supplies— would cost Cornwall $74,685 annually over and above its current $2 million-plus budget. Moreover, ServiceMaster was going to do that job with thirteen fewer custodians than the current 117. The firm promised that attrition, rather than layoffs, would be allowed to control the reduction. This contract amount was fixed, however; it did not decline with the planned shrinking of

the workforce (and, if attrition didn't create the planned reduction by June 1986, the district would be responsible for the extra salaries until all thirteen were gone).

Even though he'd been adamant from the start that any program be cost-free to the district, Lowell was eager to sign. He felt that it wasn't desirable for the district to try to emulate ServiceMaster's program on its own. "We couldn't do it with our present manpower," he said. "We'd have to bring people on staff, and that would cost money. We'd be married to more positions, which I didn't want." He felt ServiceMaster's terms were reasonable, even advantageous.

We're going to have two full time people in this district, two full-time salaries; that's got to be worth sixty-five or seventy thousand right there, with their fringe package and everything. Plus the equipment they brought in, plus the chemicals. I don't think that's a bad price; I think that's a fair price for what we're getting, if we have a) cleaner schools and b) better morale among custodians and some career paths for custodians. Carefully trained custodians that have better attitudes about their work: it will have a hell of an effect. I think it will spill over into the classroom, even. The schools are cleaner, [then] teachers are happier. I just thought it made sense.

Lowell also had hopes that ServiceMaster's presence would improve—however obliquely— what he viewed as the negative effects of patronage politics in the district. "We made it very clear [to the board] that the management firm would not make hiring decisions, that they would be made through our office with their recommendations," he said.

But it was no secret that we expected a strong commitment from custodians for cleaner schools. We were going to give them the training and the equipment and the supplies they needed to get that standard up to where we wanted it. I personally felt that those who wanted to just have a cushy job, sit through to retirement, would be uncomfortable and would leave. I did feel that was one of the plusses: that would help us thin out our ranks.

Then-board president Busby supported ServiceMaster for, in part, the same reasons. "If you took a staff member at the central district office to do custodial management," he said,

> there would be some schools within this school district that they would be tied to politically: either with the principal or head janitor, or janitors on the staff, or kinfolks somewhere in the system. They would have to, sometimes, for political reasons, do a little dodge: go around the tree, so to speak. With ServiceMaster, there's no reason for that being done.
>
> It was my hope that the training that those people would instill in the janitorial staff, or the maintenance staff, or whomever in this district, could be done on the whole without looking back for any reason. And it seems to me that the janitorial staffs—no matter how politically oriented—if you tell them time and time again that they should be doing something a certain way, they're going to finally realize that that's the best way to do it, and they'll go ahead and do it. So that's where I was coming from.

Lowell, Davies, and Little made only one adjustment to the ServiceMaster proposal before it was submitted to the board: they suggested that ServiceMaster phase the start-up to fit the budget allocated for the current year. That meant that the board wouldn't have to approve any incremental cost until the next budget year. The contract was put on the board's—specifically, the Facilities Committee's—agenda for its December 5 meeting.

Which was almost the end of the story. Lowell, Davies, and Little thought they were in good shape with the board, but they weren't. "There was," said Little with some feeling, "a little politics." James Miller, who opposed ServiceMaster, chaired the committee. Vice-chair Rosalyn Harris was ill; Miller appointed Harold Kirk to fill her seat.

Kirk had recently talked with top managers at two local hospitals which had used—and then dismissed—ServiceMaster for custodial supervision. Both, he said, had told him that "they did have ServiceMaster at one time but decided it wasn't in their best interest, that they could do the job better themselves, by training people for their needs."

> One of the comments that both firms made to me was the fact that it's like buying a new broom. It sweeps clean when you first have it. They went on to say that ServiceMaster normally sends some of their top personnel on the job when they first sign the contract. And then, the first thing that you'll find out is that [those people] . . . disappeared from the job, and they had other [ServiceMaster] people that didn't know much more than what their own personnel knew.

Instead of hiring ServiceMaster, said Kirk, "I just felt it would be best to train our own people, and try to keep the work locally. We could have done just as well, I think, as far as cost is concerned; if we have too many people on the job then we could have eliminated some by attrition. But we're not going to be saving anything by eliminating people, because those salaries will go to ServiceMaster." Kirk put Bob Little on the podium and grilled him for forty-five minutes, then moved that the committee reject the contract on the basis that the $75,000 was not available. He suggested instead that when the funds were available, they be used to hire a new director of buildings and grounds. None of the other members seconded. Another member then moved that Lowell be instructed to investigate training facilities "to standardize custodial services in the system" and have a recommendation for the board in January or February. Again no second. "Andrew Busby, the president of the board, came over to Meredith Davies and said, 'We're going to lose it if we don't table it,'" recalled Little. "And Meredith said, 'Well, John and I don't want it tabled, but we don't want to lose it. So they tabled it.'" Following Busby's lead, two members moved to defer action on the contract for a month, and to use the time to try to negotiate a better contract. It wasn't quite that easy. First, Kirk made a substitute motion: to table the contract and reconsider it later "when funds are available." No second. *Then* the original motion—to defer and renegotiate—passed.

A full board meeting was scheduled for an hour after the committee adjourned. There was a way to try to vote ServiceMaster in during that meeting; the full board could decline, by majority vote, to recognize the committee minutes—thus voiding the deferral—and take up the question again. Both Lowell and Busby had to be willing to push the point, however.

Chapter 15 Review Questions

1. What is "third-party" government? What accounts for its recent growth? What effects does it have on public administration?

2. Do you agree with Lester Salamon that the rise of "third-party" government has changed the traditional techniques of public management? In what ways? How do such changes influence the tasks and responsibilities of public administrators and their educational preparation necessary to fulfill their career assignments in the future?

3. What are the implications of the growth of "third-party" government on democratic government in general? Do you believe overall it will have good or bad influences?

4. In the case study "Cornwall County School District," what key problems confronted the school superintendent, John Lowell, in determining whether or not to contract out custodial services to ServiceMaster? How did he go about making his choice? Was it, in your opinion, done fairly and impartially?

5. Much of the selection by Lester Salamon about "third-party" government was oriented toward the *federal level,* whereas the case study on Cornwall schools was about *local level* issues involving government contracts. Do you think Salamon's ideas can be applied properly to the local or state levels? Or do they have to be modified in some ways? If so, how?

6. Specifically, does the case support or contradict Salamon's belief that "the choice of program tool is a political, not just an economic, issue: it involves important questions of power and purpose as well as equity and efficiency"? Think back to Case 10, "The Space Shuttle *Challenger* Accident." How did the "contracting out" of the shuttle's work affect the "power and purpose" of NASA's programs? Did this federal contracting out situation essentially differ or pose much the same problems for public managers as evidenced in Case 15, "Cornwall County School District?"

Key Terms

third-party government
grant-in-aid system
loan guarantee
direct transfer payments

directness/indirectness dimension
automatic/administered dimension
cash/in-kind dimension
visibility/invisibility dimension

regulatory power   design standards/performance
tax incentives   standards
government insurance programs   public management paradox
loan incentives   "The Missing Link"
policy coordination   traditional management tools

Suggestions for Further Reading

The issue of using "third parties" to do the work of government tends to divide itself into those strongly favoring it and those equally opposed to it. The advocates include E. S. Savas, *Privatizing the Public Sector: How to Shrink* Government (Chatham, N.J.: Chatham House, 1982), as well as his *Alternatives for Delivering Public Services Toward Improved Performance* (Boulder, Colo.: Westview Press, 1977); Vincent Ostrom, *The Intellectual Crisis in American Public Administration,* revised edition (University, Ala.: The University of Alabama Press, 1974), as well as his and Elinor Ostrom's, "Public Choice: A Different Approach to the Study of Public Administration," *Public Administration Review,* 31 (March/April 1971), pp. 203–216. By contrast, critics of this approach include Donald F. Kettl, *Government by Proxy: [Mis?] Managing Federal Programs* (Washington, D.C.: Congressional Quarterly Press, 1988); Gordon Adams, *The Iron Triangle: The Politics of Defense Contracting* (New York: Council on Economic Priorities, 1981); Douglas W. Ayres, "Municipal Interfaces in the Third Sector: A Negative View," *Public Administration Review,* 35 (Oct./Sept. 1975), pp. 459–463; Charles Wolf, Jr., "A Theory of Non-Market Failures," *The Public Interest,* 55 (Spring 1979), pp. 114–133.

For a more balanced treatment of this topic, see Bruce L. R. Smith and D.C. Hague, eds., *The Dilemma of Accountability in Modern Government: Independence Versus Control* (New York: St. Martin's Press, 1971); Phillip J. Cooper, "Government Contracts in Public Administration," *Public Administration Review,* 50 (Sept./Oct. 1980), pp. 459–468; Clarence Danhof, *Government Contracting and Technological Change* (Washington, D.C.: The Brookings Institution, 1968); Ruth Hoogland DeHoog, *Contracting Out for Human Services* (New York: State University of New York Press, 1984); Donald Fisk, Herbert Kiesling, and Thomas Muller, *Private Provision of Public Services: An Overview* (Washington, D.C.: The Urban Institute, 1978); Frederick C. Mosher, "The Changing Responsibilities and Tactics of the Federal Government," *Public Administration Review,* 40 (Nov./Dec. 1980), pp. 541–547; Donald F. Kettl, "The Fourth Face of Federalism," *Public Administration Review,* 41 (May/June 1981) pp. 366–373; Charles E. Lindblom, *Politics and Markets* (New York: Basic Books, 1977); Ted Kolderie, "The Two Different Concepts of Privatization," *Public Administration Review,* 46 (July/August 1986), pp. 285–291; and James D. Carroll, "Public Administration in the Third Century of the Constitution: Supply Side Management, Privatization or Public Investment?" *Public Administration Review,* 47 (Jan./Feb. 1987) pp. 106–114.

The subject of regulation has been dealt with extensively and separately in a variety of new books—many also strongly "pro" or "con"—appearing in the 1980s: Michael S. Baram, *Alternatives to Regulation* (Lexington, Mass.: Lexington Books, 1981); George C. Eads and Michael Fix, *Relief or Reform? Reagan's Regulatory Dilemma* (Washington, D.C.: Urban Institute Press, 1984); A. Lee Fritschler, *Smoking and Politics,* Third Edition (Englewood Cliffs, N.J.: Prentice-Hall, 1983); Florence Heffron with Neil McFeeley, *The Administrative Regulatory Process* (White Plains, N.Y.: Longman, 1983); Robert E. Litan and William D. Nordhaus, *Reforming Federal Regulation* (New Haven, Conn.: Yale University Press, 1983); Kenneth J. Meier, *Regulation: Politics, Bureaucracy, and Economics* (New York: St. Martin's Press, 1985); Michael D. Reagan, *Regulation: The Politics of Policy* (Boston: Little, Brown, 1987); Michael Pertschuk, *Revolt Against Regulation* (Berkeley, Calif.: University of California Press, 1982); Robert W. Poole, Jr., *Instead of Regulation: Alternatives to Federal Regulatory Agencies* (Lexington, Mass.: Lexington Books, 1981); and James Q. Wilson, ed., *The Politics of Regulation* (New York: Basic Books, 1980).

The Relationship Between Ethics and Public Service: The Concept of the Moral Ambiguities of Public Choice

"There is no public decision whose moral effect can be gauged in terms of what game theorists refer to as a 'zero sum' result: a total victory for the right and a total defeat for the wrong. This ineluctable fact is not only because 'right' and 'wrong' are incapable of universally accepted definition. It is because an adequate response to any social evil contains the seeds of both predictable and unpredictable pathologies. . . . One mark of moral maturity is in the appreciation of the inevitability of untoward and often malignant effects of benign moral choices."

Stephen K. Bailey

READING 16

Introduction

Long before the Iran-Contra affair, leading thinkers in public administration recognized that the critical issues of government ultimately involved moral choices. The definitive policy decisions made by public officials often have at their base conflicting ethical issues, such as whether to give precedence to the public interest or to the narrower demands of profession, department, bureau, or clientele. The ambivalent position in which public officials often find themselves has led some sensitive administrative theorists like Chester Barnard to say that the chief qualification of an executive is the ability to resolve these competing ethical codes—legal, technical, personal, professional, and organizational codes. In Barnard's view, the strength and quality of an administrator lies in his or her capacity to deal effectively with the moral complexities of organizations without being broken by the imposed problems of choice: ". . . neither men of weak responsibility nor those of limited capability," writes Barnard, "can endure or carry the burden of many simultaneous obligations of different types. If they are 'overloaded' either ability, responsibility, or morality or all three will be destroyed.

Conversely, a condition of complex morality, great activity, and high responsibility cannot endure without commensurate ability."[1]

For Paul Appleby, another administrative theorist, the institutional arrangements in government provide the most effective safeguards for ensuring ethical administrative behavior. Appleby, in his book *Morality and Administration in Democratic Government,*[2] contends, however, that the traditional constitutional arrangements, such as checks and balances, federalism, or the Bill of Rights, do not supply this protection against immorality. Rather, two institutional safeguards are the best guarantees of administrative morality: (1) the ballot box, and (2) hierarchy. By means of the *ballot box* the electorate judges direct the performance of government at periodic intervals. Through *hierarchy* important decisions are forced upward in the administrative structure where they can receive broader, less technical, and more political review. Appleby equates the application of broad, disinterested, and political judgment with responsible and ethical administration.

In the following selection written as a memorial essay to Appleby, Stephen K. Bailey (1916–1982), a political science professor and former dean of the Maxwell School, draws on Appleby's writings to develop some further insights into the essential qualities of moral behavior in the public service. At the core of Bailey's essay is his emphasis on three moral qualities in public administration: "optimism, courage and fairness tempered by charity." *Optimism,* in the author's view, is the ability of a public servant to deal with morally ambiguous situations confidently and purposefully. *Courage* is the capacity to decide and act in the face of situations when inaction, indecision, or agreement with the popular trend would provide the easy solution. *Fairness tempered by charity* allows for the maintenance of standards of justice in decisions affecting the public interest.

Bailey emphasizes the high ethical content of most important public questions. He points out how the varied complexities of public service add enormous complications to moral behavior so that the resolution of public issues can never be black or white. The "best solution," writes Bailey, "rarely is without its costs. . . . And one mark of moral maturity is in the appreciation of the inevitability of untoward and often malignant effects of benign moral choices." A strain of pessimism appears in Bailey's writing, for he observes that public policies rarely lead to a total victory for the "right" and a total defeat for the "wrong." Indeed, policy solutions themselves often create new policy problems.

As you read this selection, keep the following questions in mind:

Does Bailey's essay, in your estimation, offer some valuable advice to practicing public servants?

---

[1]Chester I. Barnard, *The Functions of the Executive* (Cambridge, Mass.: Harvard University Press, 1938), p. 272.

[2]Paul H. Appleby, *Morality and Administration in Democratic Government* (Baton Rouge, La.: Louisiana State University Press, 1952).

Does Bailey provide some reasonable standards for ethical conduct in government?

Can you visualize how Bailey's ideas might be applied, for example, in any of the previous cases, such as "The Decision to Drop the Atomic Bomb" or "The Blast in Centralia No. 5"?

Does Bailey give enough credit to the importance of structure and procedure in maintaining ethical conduct in public administration?

STEPHEN K. BAILEY

Ethics and the Public Service

When Paul Appleby was asked to deliver the Edward Douglass White lectures at Louisiana State University in the Spring of 1951, he chose as his topic *Morality and Administration in Democratic Government.* He preferred the term "morality" because he did not wish to suggest his lectures were "either a treatment in the systematic terms of general philosophy or a 'code of administrative ethics'."[1] His attempt instead was to cast the light of his uncommon wisdom upon what he considered to be the central ethical and moral issues of the American public service. These issues centered upon the felicitous interaction of moral institutional arrangements and morally ambiguous man.

In some ways *Morality and Administration* is a disconcerting book. The essays are discontinuous. Each one is chocked with insight, but in the collection viewed as a whole, theoretical coherence and structure emerge implicitly rather than explicitly. Some inherently ambiguous terms like "responsibility" are clarified only by

context. The final chapter, "The Administrative Pattern," is not the logical fulfillment of the preceding chapters. It stands beside the other essays, not on top of them. Furthermore, in spite of the highly personal connotation of the word "morality," Appleby spent most of his time discussing the effect of the governmental system upon official morality rather than vice versa. He saw in the American governmental system a series of political and organizational devices for promoting ethical choices. The most serious threats to the "good society" came, in his estimation, not from the venality of individuals but from imperfections in institutional arrangements.

His normative model ran somewhat as follows: politics and hierarchy force public servants to refer private and special interests to higher and broader public interests. Politics does this through the discipline of the majority ballot which forces both political executives and legislators to insert a majoritarian calculus into the consideration of private claims. Hierarchy does it by placing in the hands of top officials both the responsibility and the necessity of homogenizing and moralizing the special interests inevitably represented by and through the lower echelons of organizational pyramids.[2]

Reprinted by permission from Roscoe C. Martin, ed., *Public Administration.* Syracuse, N.Y.: Syracuse University Press, 1965, pp. 283–298. Quotations from Paul H. Appleby, *Morality and Administration in Democratic Government.* Baton Rouge: Louisiana State University Press, 1952. Used by permission.

[1] Paul H. Appleby, *Morality and Administration in Democratic Government* (Baton Rouge: Louisiana State University Press, 1952), p. vii.

[2] The intellectual as distinct from the moral implications of hierarchy have been suggested by Kenneth Underwood in

Both politics and hierarchy are devices for assuring accountability to the public as a whole. The public makes its will known in a variety of ways and through a variety of channels, but its importance is largely in its potential rather than in its concrete expressions. "Its capacity to be, more than its being, is the crux of democratic reality."[3] Politics and hierarchy induce the public servant to search imaginatively for a public-will-to-be. In this search, the public servant is often a leader in the creation of a new public will, so he is in part accountable to what he in part creates. But in any case the basic morality of the system is in its forcing of unitary claims into the mill of pluralistic considerations.

The enemies of this normative model, then, are obvious: they are whatever disrupts politics and hierarchy. For whatever disrupts politics and hierarchy permits the settlement of public issues at too low a level of organization—at too private a level, at too specialized a level. As Madison saw in Federalist 10, bigness is the friend of freedom. But Appleby saw more clearly than Madison that bigness is freedom's friend only if administrative as well as legislative devices exist to ensure that policy decisions emerge out of the *complexity* of bigness rather than out of the simplicity of its constituent parts. The scatteration of power in the Congress, the virtual autonomy of certain bureaus and even lesser units in the executive branch, an undue encroachment of legal and other professional norms upon administrative discretion, the substitution of the expert for the generalist at the higher levels of general government, the awarding of statutory power at the bureau rather than at the department level, the atomized character of our political parties—these,

according to Appleby, are the effective enemies of morality in the governmental system. They are the symptoms of political pathology. "Our poorest governmental performances, both technically and morally," he wrote, "are generally associated with conditions in which a few citizens have very disproportionate influence."[4] He felt that "the degradation of democracy is in the failure to organize or in actual disintegration of political responsibility, yielding public interest to special influence."[5]

Here, then, is the grand design. Government is moral in so far as it induces public servants to relate the specific to the general, the private to the public, the precise interest to the inchoate moral judgment. Within this context, a moral public decision becomes one in which "the action conforms to the processes and symbols thus far developed for the general protection of political freedom as the agent of more general freedom; . . . leaves open the way for modification or reversal by public determination; . . . is taken within a hierarchy of controls in which responsibility for action may be readily identified by the public; . . . and embodies as contributions of leadership the concrete structuring of response to popularly felt needs, and not merely responses to the private and personal needs of leaders."[6]

It is no disparagement of Paul Appleby's contributions to a normative theory of democratic governance to point out that he dealt only intermittently and unsystematically with the moral problems of the individual public servant. The moral system intrigued him far more consistently than the moral actor. All of his books and essays contain brilliant flashes of insight into the moral dilemmas of individual executives, administrators, and legislators, but there emerges no *gestalt* of personal ethics in government. One can only wish that he had addressed himself to a systematic elaboration of the per-

---

his contention that "the policy-making executive is to be distinguished from the middle management-supervisor levels most basically in the excessively cognitive, abstract dimensions of his work." See his paper, "The New Ethic of Personal and Corporate Responsibility," presented at the Third Centennial Symposium on *The Responsible Individual,* April 8, 1964, University of Denver.

[3]Appleby, p. 35.

[4]*Ibid.,* p. 214.

[5]*Ibid.,* p. 211.

[6]*Ibid.,* p. 36.

sonal as well as the institutional aspects of public ethics. For the richness of his administrative experience and the sensitivity of his insight might have illuminated uniquely the continuing moral problems of those whose business it is to preserve and improve the American public service.

Perhaps, without undue pretention, this memorial essay can attempt to fashion a prolegomenon to a normative theory of personal ethics in the public service—building upon and elaborating some of the fragments which Appleby scattered throughout his writings and teaching.

Appleby's fragments suggest that personal ethics in the public service is compounded of mental attitudes and moral qualities. Both ingredients are essential. Virtue without understanding can be quite as disastrous as understanding without virtue.

The three essential mental attitudes are: (1) a recognition of the moral ambiguity of all men and of all public policies, (2) a recognition of the contextual forces which condition moral priorities in the public service, and (3) a recognition of the paradoxes of procedures. The essential moral qualities of the ethical public servant are: (1) optimism, (2) courage, and (3) fairness tempered by charity.

These mental attitudes and moral qualities are relevant to all public servants in every branch and at every level of government. They are as germane to judges and legislators as they are to executives and administrators. They are as essential to line officers as to staff officers. They apply to state and local officials as well as to national and international officials. They are needed in military, foreign, and other specialized services quite as much as they are needed in the career civil service and among political executives. They, of course, assume the virtue of probity and the institutional checks upon venality which Appleby has so brilliantly elaborated. They are the generic attitudes and qualities without which big democracy cannot meaningfully survive.

Mental Attitudes

The moral public servant must be aware of the moral ambiguity of all men (including himself) and of all public policies (including those recommended by him). Reinhold Niebuhr once stated this imperative in the following terms: "Man's capacity for justice makes democracy possible, but man's inclination to injustice makes democracy necessary."[7] American public ethics finds its historic roots in the superficially incompatible streams of Calvinism and Deism. The former emphasized a depravity which must be contained; the latter emphasized a goodness which must be discovered and released. The relevance of this moral dualism to modern governance is patent. Any law or any act of administrative discretion based upon the assumption that most men will not seek to maximize their own economic advantage when reporting assets for income tax purposes would be quite unworkable. But so would any law or any act of administrative discretion which assumed that most men would use any and every ruse to avoid paying taxes at all. Similarly, any administrative decision threatening the chances of reelection of a powerfully placed Congressman almost inevitably invokes counterforces which may be serious both for the decision-maker and for the program he or his agency espouses. But administrative decisions fashioned totally out of deference to private ambitions and personal interests can negate the very purposes of general government and can induce the righteous reaction of a voting public.

The fact is that there is no way of avoiding the introduction of personal and private interests into the calculus of public decisions. As James Harvey Robinson once wrote, "In all governmental policy there have been overwhelming elements of personal favoritism and private gain, which were not suitable for publi-

---

[7] *The Children of Light and the Children of Darkness* (New York: Scribners, 1944), p. xi of Foreword.

cation. This is owing to the fact that all governments are managed by human beings, who remain human beings even if they are called kings, diplomats, ministers, secretaries, or judges, or hold seats in august legislative bodies. No process has been discovered by which promotion to a position of public responsibility will do away with a man's interest in his own welfare, his partialities, race, and prejudices. Yet most books on government neglect these conditions; hence their unreality and futility."[8] The most frequently hidden agenda in the deliberations of public servants is the effect of substantive or procedural decisions upon the personal lives and fortunes of those deliberating. And yet the very call to serve a larger public often evokes a degree of selflessness and nobility on the part of public servants beyond the capacity of cynics to recognize or to believe. Man's feet may wallow in the bog of self-interest, but his eyes and ears are strangely attuned to calls from the mountaintop. As moral philosophy has insistently claimed, there is a fundamental moral distinction between the propositions "I want this because it serves my interest," and "I want this because it is right."

The fact that man is as much a rationalizing as a rational animal makes the problem of either proving or disproving disinterestedness a tricky and knotty business. "I support the decision before us because it is good for the public," may emerge as a rationalization of the less elevated but more highly motivational proposition: "I support the decision before us because it will help reelect me, or help in my chances for promotion, recognition, or increased status." But the latter may have emerged, in turn, from a superordinate proposition: "Only if I am reelected (or promoted) can I maximize my powers in the interests of the general citizenry." Unfortunately, no calipers exist for measuring the moral purity of human motivations.

But, in any case, few would deny the widespread moral hunger to justify actions on a wider and higher ground than personal self-interest. In fact, the paradox is that man's self-respect is in large part determined by this capacity to make himself and others believe that self is an inadequate referent for decisional morality. This capacity of man to transcend, to sublimate, and to transform narrowly vested compulsions is at the heart of all civilized morality. That this capacity is exercised imperfectly and intermittently is less astounding than the fact that it is exercised at all. Man's capacity for benevolent and disinterested behavior is both a wonder and a challenge to those who work below, beside, and above him. It is in recognition of this moral reality that Appleby wrote in one of his most eloquent statements that "the manner and means of supporting one's own convictions, including inventiveness in perceiving how high ground may be held, are one measure of skill in the administrative process."[9]

But appeal to high morality is usually insufficient. It is in appreciating the reality of self-interest that public servants find some of the strongest forces for motivating behavior—public and private. Normally speaking, if a public interest is to be orbited, it must have as a part of its propulsive fuel a number of special and particular interests. A large part of the art of public service is in the capacity to harness private and personal interests to public interest causes. Those who will not traffic in personal and private interests (if such interests are themselves within the law) to the point of engaging their support on behalf of causes in which both public and private interests are served are, in terms of moral temperament, unfit for public responsibility.

But there is a necessary moral corollary: a recognition of the morally ambivalent effect of all public policies. There is no public decision whose moral effect can be gauged in terms of what game theorists refer to as a "zero-sum"

[8] *The Human Comedy* (London: The Bodley Head, 1937), p. 232.

[9] Appleby, p. 222.

result: a total victory for the right and a total defeat for the wrong. This ineluctable fact is not only because "right" and "wrong" are incapable of universally accepted definition. It is because an adequate response to any social evil contains the seeds of both predictable and unpredictable pathologies. One can, in the framing of laws or decisions, attempt to anticipate and partly to mitigate the predictable pathologies (although this is rarely possible in any complete sense). But one mark of moral maturity is in the appreciation of the inevitability of untoward and often malignant effects of benign moral choices. An Egyptian once commented that the two most devastating things to have happened to modern Egypt were the Rockefeller Foundation and the Aswan Dam. By enhancing public health, the Rockefeller Foundation had upset the balance of nature with horrendous consequences for the relationship of population to food supplies; by slowing the Nile, the Aswan Dam had promoted the development of enervating parasites in the river. The consequence of the two factors was that more people lived longer in more misery.

The bittersweet character of all public policy needs little further elaboration: welfare policies may mitigate hunger but promote parasitic dependence; vacationing in forests open for public recreation may destroy fish, wildlife, and, through carelessness in the handling of fire, the forests themselves. Unilateral international action may achieve immediate results at the cost of weakening international instruments of conflict resolution. Half a loaf *may* be worse than no loaf at all. It also may be better in the long run but worse in the short run—and vice versa.

Awareness of these dilemmas and paradoxes can immobilize the sensitive policy-maker. That is one of the reasons why both optimism and courage are imperative moral qualities in the public service. At best, however, awareness of moral ambiguity creates a spirit of humility in the decision-maker and a willingness to defer to the views of others through compromise. Humility and a willingness to compromise are priceless attributes in the life-style of the generality of public servants in a free society. For they are the preconditions of those fruitful accommodations which resolve conflict and which allow the new to live tolerably with the old. Humility, however, must not be equated with obsequiousness, nor willingness to compromise with a weak affability. As Harold Nicolson once wrote, "It would be interesting to analyze how many false decisions, how many fatal misunderstandings have arisen from such pleasant qualities as shyness, consideration, affability or ordinary good manners. It would be a mistake . . . to concentrate too exclusively upon those weaknesses of human nature which impede the intelligent conduct of discussion. The difficulties of precise negotiation arise with almost equal frequency from the more amiable qualities of the human heart."[10]

Men and measures, then, are morally ambiguous. Even if this were not a basic truth about the human condition, however, moral judgments in the public service would be made difficult by the shifting sands of context. An awareness of the contextual conditions which affect the arranging of moral priorities is an essential mental attitude for the moral public servant.

The moral virtues of the Boy Scout oath are widely accepted in the United States. But, as Boy Scouts get older, they are faced time and again with the disturbing fact that contexts exist within which it is impossible to be both kind and truthful at the same time. Boy Scouts are trustworthy. But what if they are faced with competing and incompatible trusts (e.g., to guard the flag at the base and to succor a distant wounded companion)? Men should be loyal, but what if loyalties conflict?

To the morally sensitive public servant, the strains of establishing a general value framework for conducting the public business is nothing compared to the strains of re-sorting specific values in the light of changing contexts. The

[10]Quoted by James Reston, in *The New York Times,* April 11, 1957.

dilemmas here are genuine. If value priorities are shifted with every passing wind, the shifter will suffer from his developing reputation as an opportunist. If value priorities are never adjusted, the saints come marching in and viable democratic politics goes marching out. To be consistent enough to deserve ethical respect from revered colleagues and from oneself; to be pliable enough to survive within an organization and to succeed in effectuating moral purposes—this is the dilemma and the glory of the public service.

In general, the higher a person goes on the rungs of power and authority, the more wobbly the ethical ladder. It is not the function of the junior civil servant in a unit of a branch of a bureau to worry about congressional relations—except on specific mandate from above. But a bureau chief, an assistant secretary, undersecretary, or secretary of a department may find himself contextually conditioned to respond frequently to congressional forces whose effect it is to undermine the integrity of the hierarchical arrangements in the executive branch. The heroic proportions of the Presidency become clear when one recognizes that the winds are fiercest and most variable above the timber line. The very fact that the President has fewer moments in the day than there are critical problems to be solved, and that crises often emerge unheralded, means an unevenness in the application of his time and attention to adjusting or influencing the moral niceties of any single issue. Appleby understood this when he wrote, "On many matters he [the President] will appear rather neutral; beyond enumerating items in messages and budgets he can expend his time and energies on only a few things. On as many matters as possible he normally yields for the sake of larger concerns."[11] The crucial word is "yields." Put in another way, if the President had more time and staff assistance he would "yield" to far fewer private and petty claims than he presently supports tacitly or openly.

During the Kennedy administration, the President called together a small group of top legislators, cabinet officers, and executive office staff to advise him on whether he should support the extension of price supports for cotton. His staff reminded him of the bonanza which price supports gave to the biggest and wealthiest cotton farmers. Legislative and cabinet leaders reminded him that a Presidential veto on an important agricultural bill could mean forfeiting key and critical legislative support on subsequent domestic and international matters of overriding importance to the nation's security and welfare. The President agreed not to veto the bill, but the moral torment was there. According to one witness, he stared at the wall and mumbled to himself, "There is something wrong here. We are giving money to those who don't need it. If I am reelected in 1964, I'm going to turn this government upside down."

President Eisenhower was an honorable chief executive. Yet he publicly lied about the U-2 affair. The context was the crucial determinant.

If the heat in the ethical kitchen grows greater with each level of power, no public servant is immune from some heat—some concern with context. As Appleby has written, "A special favor, in administration even—as by a traffic policeman to a blind person or a cripple—would be regarded as a political good when it appears an act of equity compensating for underprivilege."[12]

There is not a moral vice which cannot be made into a relative good by context. There is not a moral virtue which cannot in peculiar circumstances have patently evil results. The mental attitude which appreciates this perversity can be led, of course, into a wasteland of ethical relativity. But this is by no means either inevitable or in the American culture even probable. Where this attitude tends to lead the ma-

[11]Appleby, p. 127.

[12]*Ibid.*, p. 65.

ture public servant is toward a deep respect for the inconstant forces which swirl around public offices, and toward a deeper understanding of the reasons why moral men sometimes appear to make unethical public decisions. An old American Indian proverb is relevant: "Do not scoff at your friend until you have walked three miles in his moccasins." Because it is not easy for any man to place himself empathetically in the arena or moral dilemmas faced by another man, charity is a difficult moral virtue to maintain with any constancy. But as we shall review more fully below, charity is an essential moral quality in the public service of a democracy.

The third mental attitude which the public servant of a free society must cultivate is a recognition of the paradoxes of procedures. Justice Frankfurter once wrote, "The history of American freedom is, in no small measure, the history of procedure."[13] Rules, standards, procedures exist, by and large, to promote fairness, openness, depth of analysis, and accountability in the conduct of the public's business. Those who frequently by-pass or short-cut established means are thereby attacking one aspect of that most precious legacy of the past: the rule of law. Official whim is the enemy of a civilized social order. Not only does it sow the seeds of anarchy in organization, it denies to a new idea the tempering which the heat of procedural gauntlets normally provides. John Mills' "market place" is of little utility if an idea is never allowed to enter the town at all.

But, alas, if procedures are the friend of deliberation and order, they are also at times the enemy of progress and dispatch. Furthermore, there are procedures and procedures. There are apt procedures and inept procedures. The only really bitter comments in *Morality and Administration* are reserved for those members of the legal profession who believe that administration should be circumscribed by precise legal norms, and that a series of administrative courts

should be the effective arbiters and sanctioners of administrative discretion.[14] And this, of course, is only one aspect of the problem. Juridic procedures aside, both administration and legislation are frequently encumbered by rules and clearances which limit both responsiveness and the accountability they were presumably designed to enhance. The Rules Committee of the House of Representatives is not only the guardian of orderly procedures, it is the graveyard of important social measures. The contract and personnel policies of many agencies—federal, state, and local—have frequently led to what Wallace Sayre has termed "the triumph of technique over purpose." Anyone who has been closely associated with reorganization studies and proposals knows that every shift in organization—in the structural means for accomplishing governmental ends—is pregnant with implications for the ends themselves. Only a two-dimensional mind can possibly entertain seriously the notion that the structural and procedural aspects of government are unrelated to competing philosophies of substantive purpose.

The public servant who cannot recognize the paradoxes of procedures will be trapped by them. For in the case of procedures, he who deviates frequently is subversive; he who never deviates at all is lost; and he who tinkers with procedures without an understanding of substantive consequence is foolish. Of all governmental roles, the administrative role is procedurally the most flexible. But even here procedural flexibility in the public interest is achieved only by the optimistic, the courageous, and the fair.

Moral Qualities

If mental attitudes related to the moral ambiguities, contextual priorities, and procedural paradoxes of public life are necessary prerequisites

---

[13]Felix Frankfurter, *Malinski v. New York,* 324, U.S. 401, 414, 1945.

[14]See especially Appleby, Chapter 4.

to ethical behavior on the part of public servants, they are insufficient to such behavior. Attitudes must be supported by moral qualities—by operating virtues. A list of all relevant virtues would be a long one: patience, honesty, loyalty, cheerfulness, courtesy, humility—where does one begin or stop? One begins beyond the obvious and ends where essentiality ends. In the American context, at least, the need for the virtue of honesty is too obvious to need elaboration. Although Appleby has a chapter on "Venality in Government," he properly dismisses the issue with a single sentence: "Crude wrong doing is not a major, general problem of our government." And he continues with the pregnant remark, "Further moral advance turns upon more complicated and elevated concerns."[15]

The three *essential* moral qualities in the public service are optimism, courage, and fairness tempered by charity.

Optimism is an inadequate term. It connotes euphoria, and public life deals harshly with the euphoric. But optimism is a better word than realism, for the latter dampens the fires of possibility. Optimism, to paraphrase Emerson, is the capacity to settle with some consistency on the "sunnier side of doubt." It is the quality which enables man to face ambiguity and paradox without becoming immobilized. It is essential to purposive as distinct from reactive behavior. Hannah Arendt once commented that the essence of politics was natality not mortality. Politics involves creative responses to the shifting conflicts and the gross discomfitures of mankind. Without optimism on the part of the public servants, the political function cannot be performed. There is no incentive to create policies to better the condition of mankind if the quality of human life is in fact unviable, and if mankind is in any case unworthy of the trouble.

Optimism has not been the religious, philo-sophical, or literary mood of the twentieth century. But in spite of a series of almost cataclysmic absurdities it has been the prevailing mood of science, education, and politics. It is the mood of the emerging nations; it is the mood of the space technologist; it is the mood of the urban renewer. Government without the leavening of optimistic public servants quickly becomes a cynical game of manipulation, personal aggrandizement, and parasitic security. The ultimate corruption of free government comes not from the hopelessly venal but from the persistently cynical. Institutional decadence has set in when the optimism of leadership becomes a ploy rather than an honest mood and a moral commitment. True optimism is not Mr. Micawber's passive assumption that something will turn up; true optimism is the affirmation of the worth of taking risks. It is not a belief in sure things; it is the capacity to see the possibilities for good in the uncertain, the ambiguous, the inscrutable.

Organic aging and the disappointments and disaffections of experience often deprive mature individuals of the physical and psychic vitality which in youth is a surrogate for optimism. That is why optimism as a moral virtue—as a life-style—is one of the rare treasures sought by all personnel prospectors whose responsibility it is to mine the common lodes for extraordinary leadership talent. Thus is true in all organizations; it is especially true in the public service. What else do we mean, when we speak disparagingly of "bureaucratic drones," than that they are those who have entered the gates of Dante's Hell and have "abandoned all hope"?

In the midst of World War II when crises were breaking out at every moment and from every quarter, an ancient White House clerk was caught by a frenetic Presidential aide whistling at his work. The aide asked, "My God, man, don't you know what's going on?" The clerk replied, "Young man, you would be terrified if you knew how little I cared." A sprinkling of such in the public service can be tolerated as droll. If a majority, or even a substantial

[15]Appleby, p. 56.

minority of public servants become jaded, however, especially at leadership levels, an ethical rot settles in, which ultimately destroys the capacity of a government to function effectively in the public interest.

The second essential moral quality needed in the public service is courage. Personal and public life are so shot through with ambiguities and paradoxes that timidity and withdrawal are quite natural and normal responses for those confronted with them. The only three friends of courage in the public service are ambition, a sense of duty, and a recognition that inaction may be quite as painful as action.

Courage in government and politics takes many forms. The late President John F. Kennedy sketched a series of profiles of one type of courage—abiding by principle in an unpopular cause. But most calls upon courage are less insistent and more pervasive. In public administration, for example, courage is needed to ensure that degree of impersonality without which friendship oozes into inequities and special favors. Appleby relates a relevant story about George Washington. Washington told a friend seeking an appointment: "You are welcome to my house; you are welcome to my heart. . . . My personal feelings have nothing to do with the present case. I am not George Washington, but President of the United States. As George Washington, I would do anything in my power for you. As President, I can do nothing."[16] Normally it takes less courage to deal impersonally with identifiable interest groups than with long-standing associates and colleagues upon whom one has depended over the years for affection and for professional and personal support. This is true in relationship to those inside as well as those outside the organization. Part of the loneliness of authority comes from the fact, again in the words of Paul Appleby, that "to a distinctly uncomfortable degree [the administrator] must

make work relationships impersonal."[17] Appleby was quick to see that impersonality invites the danger of arrogance, but he also saw that the courage to be impersonal in complicated organizational performance is generally valuable as far as the affected public is concerned. "Its tendency is to systematize fair dealing and to avoid whimsy and discrimination—in other words to provide a kind of administrative due process."[18]

The need for this kind of courage on a day-to-day basis is probably greater, and more difficult to conjure, in the legislative than in either the executive or the judicial branches of government.

A second area for consistent courage in the public service is to be found in the relationship of general administrators to experts and specialists. It takes quite as much courage to face down minority expert opinion as it does to face down the majority opinion of a clamoring crowd. In some ways it takes more, for relationships with experts are usually intimate in the decisional process, whereas relations with the crowd are often distant and indistinct. Both courage and wisdom are reflected in the words of Sir Winston Churchill: "I knew nothing about science, but I knew something about scientists, and had had much practice as a minister in handling things I did not understand."[19]

Perhaps on no issue of public ethics is Appleby more insistent than on the necessity of experts being kept in their proper place—subordinate to politicians and general administrators. "Perhaps," he wrote, "there is no single problem in public administration of moment equal to the reconciliation of the increasing dependence upon experts with an unending democratic reality."[20] The expert, whether professional, procedural, or programmatic, is essential to the proper functioning of a complex and highly technical social system. But the autonomous or

[16]*Ibid.*, p. 130.

[17]*Ibid.*, p. 221.

[18]*Ibid.*, p. 149.

[19]*Life,* February 28, 1949, p. 61.

[20]Appleby, p. 145.

disproportionate power of experts, and of the limited worlds they comprehend, is a constant threat to more general consideration of the public good.

During World War II, a 25-year-old civil servant in the soap division of O.P.A. found himself, because of the temporary absence of superiors, dealing directly with the president and legal staff of Lever Brothers. After a few minutes of confrontation the president of Lever Brothers turned scornfully to the government employee and asked, "Young man, what do you know about soap?" A strong voice replied, "Sir, I don't know much about soap, but I know a hell of a lot about price control."

This is the courage needed by a Budget Bureau examiner in dealing with the Pentagon; this is the courage needed by an Assistant Secretary of Health, Education, and Welfare in dealing with the Surgeon General; this is the courage needed by a transient mayor in dealing with a career engineer in the public works department; this is the courage needed by a Congressman faced with appraising the "expert" testimony of an important banker in his district.

Perhaps the most essential courage in the public service is the courage to decide. For if it is true that all policies have bittersweet consequences, decisions invariably produce hurt. President Eliot of Harvard once felt constrained to say that the prime requisite of an executive was his willingness to give pain. Much buck-passing in public life is the prudent consequence of the need for multiple clearances in large and complex institutions. But buck-passing which stems from lack of moral courage is the enemy of efficient and responsible government. The inner satisfactions which come from the courage to decide are substantial; but so are the slings and arrows which are invariably let loose by those who are aggrieved by each separate decision. The issues become especially acute in personnel decisions. Courage to fire, to demote, to withhold advancement, or to shift assignments against the wishes of the person involved,

is often the courage most needed and the most difficult to raise.

The third and perhaps most essential moral quality needed in the public service is fairness tempered with charity. The courage to be impersonal and disinterested is of no value unless it results in just and charitable actions and attitudes. Government in a free society is the authoritative allocator of values in terms of partly ineffable standards of justice and the public weal. It requires the approximation of moving targets partly camouflaged by the shadows of an unknowable future. The success or failure of policies bravely conceived to meet particular social evils is more frequently obscured than clarified by the passage of time. As R. G. Collingwood once pointed out, "The only thing that a shrewd and critical Greek like Herodotus would say about the divine power that ordains the course of history is that . . . it rejoices in upsetting and disturbing things."[21]

What remains through the disorder and unpredictability of history is the sense on the part of the public and of working colleagues that power for whatever ends was exercised fairly and compassionately. The deepest strain in our ethical heritage is "man's sense of injustice." The prophetic voices of the Old Testament repaired time and again to this immemorial standard. "Let Justice roll down like waters. . . ." Hesiod, speaking for generations of ancient Greeks, wrote "Fishes and beasts and fowls of the air devour one another. But to men Zeus has given justice. Beside Zeus on his throne Justice has her seat."[22] Justice was the only positive heritage of the Roman World. The establishment of justice follows directly behind the formation of union itself in the Preamble to the American Constitution.

But the moral imperative to be just—to be fair—is a limited virtue without charity. Abso-

[21]*The Idea of History* (Oxford: Clarendon Press, 1946), p. 22.
[22]Quoted in Edith Hamilton, *The Greek Way* (New York: W. W. Norton, 1930), p. 292.

lute justice presupposes omniscience and total disinterestedness. Public servants are always faced with making decisions based upon both imperfect information and the inarticulate insinuations of self-interest into the decisional calculus. Charity is the virtue which compensates for inadequate information and for the subtle importunities of self in the making of judgments designed to be fair. Charity is not a soft virtue. To the contrary, it involves the ultimate moral toughness. For its exercise involves the disciplining of self and the sublimation of persistent inner claims for personal recognition, power, and status. It is the principle above principle. In the idiom of the New Testament, it is the losing of self to find self. Its exercise makes of compromise not a sinister barter but a recognition of the dignity of competing claimants. It fortifies the persuasive rather than the coercive arts. It stimulates the visions of the good society without which government becomes a sullen defense of existing patterns of privilege.

The normative systems of politics and organization which Appleby elaborated in his writings are umbilically related to the mental attitudes and moral qualities of the individual moral actor in the public service. They nourish these attitudes and qualities. They condition and promote public morality. But the reverse is also true. Without proper mental attitudes and moral qualities on the part of the public servant, Appleby's normative systems could neither exist nor be meaningfully approximated.

The intermeshing of the mental attitudes and moral qualities of the individual moral actor with the institutional arrangements elaborated by Paul Appleby produces in effect a working definition of the public interest. Men of good will may disagree on what amalgam of commonly shared interests of the nation's several publics constitutes a *substantive* public interest. What this essay attempts to suggest is that normative, procedural, institutional, attitudinal, and moral standards do exist which preserve

and promote a public interest far more fundamental than any set of transient policies can possibly preserve or promote.

Bureaucracy and technology are the pervasive realities of modern civilization. Together they have made possible order, prosperity, and mobility in unprecedented magnitudes; but unfortunately they have demonstrated a perverse tendency to drain from man the blood of his essential humanity. The nobility of any society is especially encapsulated and made manifest to the world in the personal example of its public leaders and public servants. Perhaps, therefore, Appleby's writings about morality and government—no matter how wise and how provocative—were of less importance than the lessons of his example as a public servant. For in selecting the mental attitudes and moral qualities of the moral public servant, I have been guided far more by my memories of Paul Appleby than by my perusal of his writings. Appleby in his public career demonstrated an uncommon understanding of the moral ambiguities, the contextual priorities, and the paradoxes of procedures in ethical governance. Of all men of my acquaintance in public life, he was the most completely endowed in the moral qualities of optimism, courage, and fairness tempered by charity. While his wisdom illuminated everything he observed and experienced, his example shone even more brilliantly than his wisdom.

The Spanish philosopher Unamuno, thinking of Goethe's dying words, "Light, light, more light," declared passionately, "No! warmth, warmth, more warmth, for we die of cold, not of darkness. It is not the night that kills, but the frost."[23]

Without denigrating the richness of his intellectual contributions, Paul Appleby's charity of spirit was perhaps his fundamental contribution to ethics and the public service.

[23]Douglas V. Sheere, "The Golden Rule," in R. M. McIver, ed., *Great Expressions of Human Rights* (New York: Harper & Bros., 1950), p. 55.

CASE STUDY 16

Introduction

Today, we take air travel for granted. We routinely purchase tickets, check our bags at the terminal counter, go through the perfunctory security checks, step aboard the plane, and settle down to our favorite book, magazine, or movie. We are soon aloft at 30,000 feet, soaring at speeds in excess of 600 miles per hour. We give little thought to the entire experience of flying, comfortably assuming that we will arrive on time at our desired destination.

Statistics show that we have good reasons for taking all this safety, comfort, and speed for granted. In 1981 over 100,000 people were killed in highway accidents worldwide, yet not one life was lost among the 286 million airline passengers who flew during that year. Nevertheless, flying still requires a lot of faith— faith that the crew is well-trained, that the instruments work to perfection, that the airplane's structural design is sound enough to withstand the stresses and strains of jet-age speeds, that the ground crews prepare the plane correctly, that the weather reports are up-to-date and accurate, and that the myriad of regulations and details involved in modern flying are properly carried out. The hard, depressing fact remains that 3,461 people have died in U.S. airplane accidents since the start of the commercial jet age, and more than 10,000 deaths have been reported worldwide.

The following case study by Morton Hunt ranks along with Case Study 1, "The Blast in Centralia No. 5," as one of the very best articles ever written about public organizations and public officials. Like "The Blast in Centralia No. 5," this case depicts a major disaster caused by a failure in administrative procedures and human error. The two cases also underscore how matters of life and death often hinge on effective public administration and public administrators.

Hunt, a *New Yorker* writer, describes fairly and accurately the events leading to the crash of Lockheed Electra Flight 320, bound from Chicago to New York City on February 3, 1959, which killed 64 people. Not only does the author carefully recount the facts of the disaster, he also treats the reader to a rare, behind-the-scenes look at the immense difficulties faced by the Civil Aeronautics Board (CAB) investigators as they tried to uncover the reasons for the crash. Like a good detective story, clues are traced with care—many leading down blind alleys—until finally the truth emerges about the real causes of the accident.

Although the case gives us many insights into the routines and procedures of a government regulatory agency coping with a major commercial airline disaster, in the final analysis it furnishes an excellent picture of the moral demands and dimensions of a public manager's work. In this case, the public manager is Chief Investigator Joseph O. Fluet, who is under tremendous public pressure to produce the final CAB report on the official causes of the disaster rapidly. Fluet is also pressured for results favorable to two opposing parties—the airline pilots and the airline manufacturers—whose livelihoods and reputations depend on the final verdict of Fluet's investigations. Fluet's position as the man in the middle underscores several of the ethical and moral themes outlined by Stephen Bailey's foregoing essay.

As you read this selection, keep the following questions in mind:

How did Fluet organize the tasks of the investigation of the crash of Flight 320?

How did the investigators go about reaching their conclusions? What formidable obstacles and pressures did these men encounter from the pilot's union, the plane manufacturer, and the general public?

Was Fluet's job essentially like that of a businessman (refer to Chapter 15)? Or does the case support Bailey's arguments about the fundamental moral nature of public management?

Can you list the distinctive moral choices Fluet faced in his job?

MORTON HUNT

The Case of Flight 320

Like many other facets of present-day technology, the operation of passenger airplanes has developed so rapidly as to leave public understanding far behind. The average person still thinks about flying in rather primitive terms, and on a stormy winter night, hearing the drone of a plane somewhere in the turbid maelstrom above, he is apt to burrow deeper under the bedcovers and think pityingly of the poor souls aloft, as though they were battling for their lives in a wallowing schooner with its canvas in shreds, its mainmast splintered, and its seams leaking freely. The night of Tuesday, February 3, 1959, was just such a night over much of the northern part of the East Coast, and in particular over the New York City area. Muddy clouds hung low all evening, trailing still lower tatters of scud that wiped clammily across the ground; hour after hour, drizzle alternated with chill rain showers or stinging sleet. Patches of fog and mist filled the hollows of the suburbs and slithered across the city's rivers and bays. At LaGuardia Airport, a raw, fitful wind whipped freezing rain into the faces of those entering the terminal to catch a plane or to meet incoming passengers. In the chrome-and-plastic waiting room of American Airlines, a score of fidgety people were awaiting the delayed arrival of

Flight 320 from Chicago. According to schedule, it should have arrived at 11:05 P.M., but shortly before that time an airline agent had erased "11:05" from the board and chalked "11:40" in its place, and a little later he amended this to "11:55." Every now and then, someone would walk over to the windows and peer into the opaque ocean of air that somewhere contained the oncoming plane.

That night, the wind being generally from the southwest, planes coming in to LaGuardia approached from the northeast, letting down from their normal flight altitude over Westchester County and descending in a straight path over Larchmont, New Rochelle, Pelham Bay Park, and Clason Point, in the Bronx. At 11:50 P.M., just north of the Larchmont-Mamaroneck line, Frank Swenson, a thirty-seven-year-old assistant export manager of a pump and generator company, was about to enter his apartment house, near the Boston Post Road, when he heard a plane passing overhead. Because it seemed to be flying rather low, he paused to listen; he had noticed ice forming on the ground, and he wondered whether the unknown plane was in any trouble from ice forming on its wings. A minute or so later, in a house about three miles to the west at 31 Inverness Road, New Rochelle, Dr. Gerhart Schwarz, a forty-six-year-old radiologist, was awakened by a peculiar-sounding and apparently very low airplane; he rushed out onto his terrace and peered into the black skies, but could see nothing. Shortly afterward, Mrs. Julian Allen, a middle-aged housewife, heard a plane passing over her house, near Pelham Shore Road and Pelhamdale Avenue, just below the southern boundary of New Rochelle; it seemed to her that the engines were laboring and that the plane sounded as if it were "lacking in buoyancy." She wondered what was wrong, but the sound died away, and so did her moment of apprehension. Some four miles farther to the south, at about 11:54 P.M., Percy Tumber, a forty-nine-year-old greenskeeper at the Oakland Golf and Country Club, in Bayside, was riding in the back seat of a car headed down the Hutchinson River Parkway toward the Whitestone Bridge, when suddenly he was deafened and shaken by a torrent of strange high-pitched sound. Looking up through the car's back window, he saw a large plane directly overhead, skimming through the fringes of the cloud bottom, with the lights on the ground reflecting from its gleaming belly. It was making an unearthly whining sound, and it seemed to him to be no more than a hundred feet up; he had a disturbing certainty that something was very wrong.

There is little doubt that what at least some of these people were hearing was Flight 320, but the troubles they imputed to it existed principally in their own uninformed minds. Flight 320—a stubby-winged giant aluminum cylinder bearing the registry number N 6101A and named Flagship New York—was in perfect condition in the final minutes of a routine trip from Chicago. The plane, a type known to the trade as an L-188 and to the public as a Lockheed Electra, was brand-new, from its rounded crimson nose to its red rudder assembly, a hundred and four feet aft. Its air speed of a hundred and seventy-five knots was perfectly safe and proper for this part of the approach to LaGuardia (in full flight it cruised at close to four hundred miles an hour); its four Allison turboprop engines, far from laboring, were loafing along at fourteen hundred horsepower each (they could develop nearly four thousand horsepower each when necessary); and the queer, high-pitched sound heard by people on the ground was the normal but unfamiliar one caused by the turbines of the four engines spinning at 13,820 revolutions per minute and expelling great blasts of hot gases. As

protection against ice—which was not then forming on the plane, even though the ground was freezing—there was a hot-air system for the wings, a defrosting spray for the propeller blades, electric heaters for the Pitot tubes (through which air reaches the air-speed indicator), and a warning light on the pilot's panel to inform him of any buildup of ice on the front of the fuselage. The Electra at that time was the very latest type of plane to go into commercial service. It had been on the drawing boards and in the design laboratories at Lockheed for several years; in its subsequent testing phase, with maddening caution, the Civil Aeronautics Administration (later rechristened the Federal Aviation Agency), had spent nearly twenty thousand hours inspecting its parts and test-flying it, to make sure that every particle of it was up to federal requirements. On August 22, 1958, the C.A.A. had finally certified the Electra for passenger operations, and on December 5, 1958, American Airlines had received from Lockheed the first of thirty-five Electras it had ordered. A strike by American's pilots, lasting from December 19, 1958, through January 9, 1959, delayed the introduction of the Electra into standard operations, but on January 23rd, after the strike was settled, the New York-Chicago run of the Electras was inaugurated, and by the night of February 3rd the new American Airlines planes had made nearly two hundred uneventful trips between the two cities.

The three men in the cockpit of Flagship New York would have smiled tolerantly at the apprehensions of Mr. Swenson and the others. Captain Albert DeWitt, a strong-chinned man of fifty-nine whose dark hair and trim mustache made him look far younger than his age, was qualified to fly nine kinds of commercial airliners, and in the past three decades had spent 28,135 hours, or more than three years, off the ground. Twenty-five hundred hours of this had been "instrument time," in which he was sealed in by weather or darkness and unable to fly by direct observation. The co-pilot, Frank Hlavacek, and the flight engineer, Warren Cook—men in their thirties—had accumulated far less flying time than DeWitt, but by all current standards both were seasoned veterans. As the plane headed southwest over Westchester, Captain

DeWitt was at the wheel, Cook was monitoring a broad panel of dials and indicators that gave him a clinical picture not only of the health of the four engines but of all the mechanical and electrical systems of the plane, and Hlavacek, in the co-pilot's seat, was working the radio. On a control pedestal at his left hand were the tuning handles of three different radio receivers, and en route he had talked with federal air-traffic controllers and with American Airlines employees at Chicago's Midway Airport, at Idlewild, and at LaGuardia, reporting the plane's position and receiving weather news and verbal clearance.

To laymen, the night of February 3rd was a formless mixture of wind, sleet, and clouds; to the three crew members it was a neat pattern of narrow, interlacing radio beams. Each beam had a fixed direction and frequency, and was identified by a Morse-code signal given at regular intervals. Tuning his radios to the frequencies of these beams, Hlavacek could tell, by the sound he picked up and by the markings on an aeronautical chart in his lap, where the plane was at any moment. The LaGuardia radio beam, which Hlavacek had tuned in while the plane was still over the middle of New Jersey, emanated from an antenna located in an open lot in the Clason Point section of the lower Bronx, just 2.8 nautical miles across the East River from the airport. From that antenna, four spokes of steady tone on 209 kilocycles stretched out reassuringly into the storm. One, reaching almost forty miles toward Ridgefield, Connecticut, was in a direct line with LaGuardia's Runway 22, on which Flight 320 was to land. But far more precise than this beam was another one, on 109.9 megacycles, which originated in a tiny hut at the near end of Runway 22. This was called the "back-course" beam, to distinguish it from the standard, or front, beam, which guided planes coming in from the opposite direction. As soon as the Electra flew into the range of this precision beam, the electronic ears of the plane's I.L.S. (Instrument Landing System) radio equipment would automatically activate a dial on the instrument panel, its vertical needle moving to one side or the other, according to whether the plane was veering off in either direction from the straight path down the beam. And that was not all. As the plane moved down the LaGuardia beam over New Rochelle, it crossed a "fan marker," or highly localized transmitter, which directed a fan-shaped radio signal straight up into the air. As soon as the plane passed through this beam, a white light would show on the instrument panel, indicating that the runway lay 7.6 nautical miles ahead; when it passed over the LaGuardia radio-beam transmitter at Clason Point, the white light would show again, indicating that the runway was now 2.8 miles away and the plane could safely start its final descent. And, in addition to these electronic safeguards, Hlavacek was getting instructions by voice from LaGuardia. As a plane heads in for LaGuardia from Chicago, it enters the jurisdiction of the field's Approach Control officer somewhere over New Jersey; when it is on the final approach to the runway, it is transferred to Local Control. Hlavacek had been in the knowledgeable hands of Approach Control ever since passing over Jersey City. Altogether, a man feeling his way across his own bedroom in the dark could have been no more at home than Hlavacek and DeWitt were in the blackness of that winter night.

Unaware of all that was being done to get them in safe and sound, the sixty-eight passengers in the cabin buckled their seat belts and waited for the landing. By and large, they were successful professional people, travelling in pursuit of their careers. The group included, among others, a television producer; a public-relations executive; an authority on photosynthesis from the University of Illinois; a magazine editor; a lawyer from the Wall Street district; a Bell Telephone research engineer from New Jersey; four Protestant clergymen; a steel man, a valve man, a paper man, and a fat-and-oils man; several old men; several young women; a college senior; a boy of eight; and an eleven-month-old infant. The two stewardesses finished clearing away the remains of the snack served during the flight and then took seats in the lounge, belted themselves in, and waited for the touchdown.

Since 11:34 P.M., when Flight 320 passed over Jersey City, it had been in the charge of an Approach Control operator named John Grula, who was sitting before a radar screen in a dimly lit room in the tower above the LaGuardia Administration Building. (Like all other air-traffic-control personnel, Grula works for the Federal

Aviation Agency.) In response to his orders, the spot of light representing Flight 320 on his screen had obligingly crawled up toward the Tappan Zee Bridge of the New York State Thruway and had then begun a large, slow, counterclockwise circle over Rockland County, descending according to his instructions.

"Turn left now, heading three-six-zero for the LaGuardia back course," Grula said at 11:39.

"Roger," replied the voice of Hlavacek. "Turning left, three-six-zero." And the little spot of light began to inch around in a circle.

"Now, American Three-twenty," called Grula two minutes later, after shepherding a couple of other flights along, "turn left, heading two-seven-zero, two-seven-zero. . . . Barometric pressure now two-nine-seven-seven, two-nine-seven-seven."

Again Hlavacek acknowledged reception. Step by step, Grula swung the spot of light around in a complete circle while ordering it to lower altitudes; then he brought it eastward across upper Westchester, and finally swung it around to head southwest, until he could see, by its position on his screen, that it was coming into the narrow zone where it would pick up both the LaGuardia radio beam and the I.L.S. back-course beam. "American Three-twenty," he called at 11:48. "Cleared for a back-course approach to the airport. Turn right, heading two-one-zero, to intercept the LaGuardia back-course. When you do, take over and complete your approach."

A moment later, Hlavacek called back to say they were now on the I.L.S. back-course beam and were taking over, and another moment later he announced that they had just passed over the New Rochelle fan marker.

At this point, Flight 320 was ordered to switch its radio to 118.7 megacycles and report to Local Control. Fred Prawdzik, the F.A.A. employee in charge of Local Control, was sitting upstairs in the glassed-in tower room, looking out through the slanting windows toward Runway 22. At 11:53, he heard on his radio, "LaGuardia Tower, American Three-twenty. We're by New Rochelle." Prawdzik had only one other plane in his sector at the moment—a Northeast Airlines DC-3 several miles closer to the runway and in a position to land safely before the advent

of Flight 320—so he left the Electra's course unchanged. "American Three-twenty, LaGuardia Tower," he radioed. "Report the range station [the second marker, over Clason Point]. Straight in, Runway Two-two, wind south-southwest, seven." In another minute or two, Prawdzik saw two lights coming down out of the clouds over the East River as the DC-3 broke through and drifted toward the runway. Just then, Flight 320 announced that it was over the Clason Point transmitter, 2.8 miles from the end of the runway, and as soon as Prawdzik had seen the DC-3 roll down the runway and turn off, he called back. "American Three-twenty," he said. "Cleared to land straight in, Runway Two-two, wind south-southwest, eight."

"Three-tw—twenty," replied Hlavacek's voice at 11:55:27.

Prawdzik, knowing the position of the plane and the normal approach speed of an Electra, figured that it would break through the cloud ceiling in about half a minute and touch down about half a minute after that. He waited, watching attentively. Nothing appeared. He glanced at the sweep second hand of his clock, moving imperturbably around the dial; the half minute passed, then three-quarters, and then the minute, and still there was nothing to be seen but the runway lights and the haze-dimmed red lights of a gas tank across the river. Prawdzik pushed his microphone button. "American Three-twenty, LaGuardia Tower," he said. "Do you read?" He paused but there was no answer. He called again, peremptorily; there was no answer. He called a third time, a trifle stridently. There was no answer. On the assumption that the plane had missed the runway and was going around for a new approach, he told Flight 320 what altitude to climb to and then began calling the other controllers on his intercom and telling them, with some urgency, that he no longer knew 320's position. Within two or three minutes, the controllers had stopped all inbound and departing traffic at the field; every approaching plane would have to hold its position until Flight 320 was found. Prawdzik and the other controllers kept calling the plane, on several different frequencies, but without success. A radar scanner spotted an unidentified bright dot moving west from New Rochelle and thought it might be 320, but an Idlewild controller reported that it was a plane under his control. "Three-twenty," Prawdzik called again and again. "Come in. Do you read? Three-twenty, do you read?"

In the plane itself, when Hlavacek called La-Guardia to announce that they were over New Rochelle and, later on, over Clason Point, everything was in perfect order for the final approach. The landing gear and flaps were lowered, and after Clason Point was passed, DeWitt eased the power back to twelve hundred horsepower per engine, reduced the air speed to a hundred and forty knots, and established a gentle rate of descent. Flight Engineer Cook had his hands on the alternate set of throttles, ready to adjust them if there was any deviation from the power setting that the Captain had chosen. DeWitt was guiding the aircraft. Hlavacek was monitoring the flight instruments and outside conditions, and standing by to report them to DeWitt. Glancing at his altimeter, he called out, "Six hundred feet." From here on, he would call out the altitude every hundred feet; if DeWitt did not break out of the cloud ceiling at four hundred feet, he was required by federal air regulations to apply power, start climbing, and call the tower for new orders. All of a sudden, Hlavacek saw lights appear outside DeWitt's window. The next instant, there was a terrific concussion, a vast wash of water, and a blackness and coldness as of the end of time. Hlavacek was first aware of a tearing pain in his midriff, where his seat belt held him fast; then he noticed that he was underwater. He fumbled at his seat-belt buckle, somehow got it open, and was astonished to find himself floating straight upward and breaking the surface of the East River, off Riker's Island. Despite the darkness, he could see a segment of wing floating nearby, and he climbed onto it; there he sat, stupefied and infinitely bewildered, hearing all around him a babble of cries and screams.

Flight Engineer Cook heard the mighty sound of the plane hitting; then everything was pitch-black and he was underwater, his legs trapped against the control pedestal. After wriggling wildly and without hope for an endless span of frozen time, he came loose, floated up with a searing pain in his lungs, and burst into the night air near Hlavacek, who feebly pulled him onto the wing.

"Where is Al?" mumbled Hlavacek thickly, through a smashed jaw.

"I don't think he made it," Cook gasped.

In the cabin, everything had seemed to rip open all at once, and through huge rents in the fuselage the paralyzing cold salt water rushed in. Herbert Forman, a thirty-six-year-old engineer, had been dozing when he felt the impact; immediately, an incredible weight of water poured over him. He clawed free of his seat belt and trousers, flailed around a bit, and to his amazement found himself floating in a dark river, with faint lights visible in the distance. Nearby, he made out a dark shape and swam for it; it was the wing segment, and Hlavacek and Cook soon dragged him onto it. Seymour Kemach, a display salesman from Brooklyn, had been chatting in the lounge with one of the stewardesses; with the crash he blacked out for a second, and then came to his senses to find the broken cabin rapidly filling with water. In the darkness, he was aware of a tangle of seats, floating floor sections, and screaming people. Stumbling to the door, he yanked at it several times, finally got it open, and fought his way out, pulling with him a young boy and a couple of women. They all climbed into what seemed to be part of the tail assembly, which was floating nearby. Altogether, nine people got out of the wreck alive. One died the next day. Sixty-four were killed in the crash.

While Flight 320 was in the final minute of its journey, the tugboat H. Thomas Teti, Jr., was slowly hauling two empty barges down Riker's Island Channel in the East River. The lights of Runway 22 were about a mile ahead, but because of the rain and low-lying fog they could not be seen from the tug; the Teti was being steered by radar, with visual checks of channel markers and buoys when they were close enough at hand. In the pilothouse, Captain Samuel Nickerson, a spare, sombre man of fifty-seven, was talking with his co-captain, Everett Phelps, who had just come in to relieve him, when they were startled by a tremendous concussion off to starboard, toward Riker's Island. On deck, someone yelled "Plane wreck!," and Nickerson, who had long fretted about the lowness of the planes coming over this section of water in bad weather, responded with an immediate order. "Let go the scows!" he shouted, and deckhands scrambled out to cast off the hawsers. Nickerson called for full power and a hard turn to starboard, and threw on the searchlight. The tug, her light probing spongily through the fog, made for the scene of the crash, and after several minutes Nickerson and the deckhands began to see floating wreckage and the pale circles of desperate faces. For the next ten minutes, all was the ghastly confusion of a sea rescue at night. In the midst of it, the tug radioed the news to the Coast Guard, which soon notified the controllers at La-Guardia where their missing plane was. At ten minutes past midnight, a police launch appeared, but the rescue work had been done; nine survivors were aboard the Teti, and nothing else was visible but small scraps of wreckage. The Teti headed for a police dock at College Point, Queens, a mile from the airport. There the survivors—six passengers, plus Hlavacek, Cook, and a stewardess named Joan Zeller—were put ashore and taken by ambulance to Flushing Hospital or Queens General Hospital. Newspaper reporters kept asking what had happened. No one knew.

The task of finding out what happened was one of the duties assigned by Congress twenty-two years ago to the Civil Aeronautics Board, a small, independent federal agency whose province is the regulation of air-carrier routes, air-mail subsidies, and the cost of air travel, in addition to the investigation of all accidents involving civilian aircraft and the determination of their causes. On the night Flight 320 crashed, the C.A.B.'s chief investigator for the New York area was Joseph O. Fluet, a stocky, wavy-haired man of fifty-one who had been, successively, an airplane mechanic, a private pilot, the operator of a small-town airport, and a federal check pilot before coming to the C.A.B. in 1942. Fluet, whose broad shoulders and dented nose suggest an ex-boxer but whose manner is gentle and a bit professional, had gone to bed in his house, in Great Neck, shortly before midnight. A few minutes later, the phone rang. It was a flight controller at LaGuardia with the bad news. "Oh, good Lord!" Fluet said. "Any indication of difficulty during the flight? . . . None? . . . No word yet about survivors, I suppose? . . . All right, now tell me how the weather was at the time. . . . Did any flight land just before him? . . . Aha! Please send someone off to catch the crew of that DC-3 and tell them I want written statements about conditions during their approach and landing. I'll make the tower my headquarters until morning. O.K.? . . . I'm on my way." It was the beginning of his hundred-and-twenty-sixth air-crash investigation.

At the field, Fluet hurried up to the large glass-enclosed control room at the top of the tower, where a group of F.A.A. men and airport officials were waiting for him. His first action was to go to the west windows, facing Runway 22, and take notes on the ceiling and the visibility. Then he asked if anyone had ordered a check of the back-course transmitter, the main La-Guardia radio beam, the fan marker, and the controllers' radar. He had no particular reason to think that any of them had misled the plane, but some possibilities had to be investigated at once, the evidence being perishable; if any radio device had been malfunctioning, routine maintenance might fix it and leave no clue. An F.A.A. man said that technicians were already working on the job.

"Good," Fluet said. "Next, will one of you please phone the police and see if they can give us a list of all survivors and their whereabouts?" Another man volunteered to see to it. "Now," said Fluet, "who were on Approach Control and Local Control at the time?" Grula, Prawdzik, and several men who had been on alternate positions spoke up. Fluet led them over to a vacant desk and began to question them about whether Flight 320 had mentioned any mechanical troubles, obstreperous passengers, icing, or turbulence; then he queried them closely about the plane's conduct as seen on the radar screen. Grula said he thought that Flight 320 had been somewhat slow in responding to orders, but Prawdzik, who used no radar screen at the Local Control position, said that he had noticed nothing unusual on the radio, except that the copilot's voice had faltered a bit on the last transmission.

It was soon clear that the controllers could provide Fluet with no obvious clue to the cause of the accident. "I'd like each of you to make a full written statement," he said, "and I'd like to hear the tapes myself right now." (Controller-aircraft talk is continuously recorded at all major airports.) A few minutes later, he was seated in the F.A.A. supervisor's office, on the third floor of the Administration Building, listening to the playback and timing the intervals with a stop-watch. He heard nothing revealing or incriminating, but still he was making progress by exclusion; judging by the words and the sound of Hlavacek's voice, he could tentatively assume that the crash was not due to engine failure, a run-away propeller, fire, or structural failure—though the final elimination of these would have to wait upon examination of the wreckage. Similarly, he could temporarily rule out the idea of illness or asphyxiation of the crew. If it was not exactly a satisfying result, it was at least a beginning.

One obvious and indisputable fact was that the weather had been poor at the time, so Fluet's next stop was the Weather Bureau office, on the same floor of the building, where he catechized a meteorologist named James Dillon about the variability of the ceiling that evening, the extent of icing, the degree of turbulence near the surface, and the times of observed fog patches. The weather, he learned, had been terrible only from the layman's point of view, for the rain had never been heavy, the ceiling had hardly ever dropped below four hundred feet, and neither the icing nor the turbulence had been enough to disable even a small private plane, let alone a powerful, modern Electra. The only suspicious fact that emerged was that the barometer had been falling rapidly at the time, a condition that would have caused the plane's altimeters to read too high unless the crew had reset them before making the approach. A few minutes before landing time, Grula had told Hlavacek that the barometer read 29.77, and this was correct according to Dillon's records, but whether Hlavacek and DeWitt had properly reset their altimeters—a perfectly routine chore—would not be absolutely certain until the instrument panel was found.

Fluet next headed downstairs and along the corridors to the American Airlines flight-dispatch room. The atmosphere in the cluttered, brightly lit office was like that in an army command post where word has just arrived of a collapsed right flank. Losing no time, Fluet asked William H. Miller, American's regional operations officer, to get from Chicago the load manifest, flight plan, and passenger list of Flight 320, so he could look into the possibilities of overloading or dangerous cargo, unusual routing or flying conditions, persons on board who might be the object of sabotage, and so on. He also asked Miller to arrange for salvage operations as soon as possible, and instructed that word be passed to all interested parties that the C.A.B. would be conducting a full-scale investigation and that he would hold an organization meeting at 9 A.M. in the F.A.A. controller-training classroom on the third floor of the Administration Building.

At around 4 A.M., Fluet went back to the tower and got on the phone—to the police, who told him where the survivors were, to the hospitals (neither Cook nor Hlavacek was in any condition to talk), to an F.A.A. communications man (the radio and radar equipment had checked out satisfactorily), and, finally, to his superior, James Peyton, the chief of the C.A.B. accident-investigation division, in Washington, whom he asked for half a dozen expert assistants. Peyton promised to have the necessary investigators in New York by 9 A.M.

By 9 A.M., the controllers' training room at LaGuardia was overflowing. Fifty or sixty men had crowded in and were sitting on the chairs, the training desks, and the window sills. Fluet took a desk at the front of the room and called the meeting to order. There being no clear-cut indication of the cause of the crash, he said, it would be necessary to conduct a complete investigation, with a full complement of specialized teams.

The C.A.B., which has only about seven hundred employees, is one of the smallest of the federal agencies. (The F.A.A., which handles air-traffic control and pilot licensing and maintains the national network of air-navigation facilities, has some thirty thousand.) Moreover, of the seven hundred, only about sixty-five are actual investigators. But the C.A.B. has a powerful lever that multiplies its effectiveness—the self-defensiveness of everyone who might be implicated in a crash. The Air Line Pilots Association, eager to clear its members of blame in an accident, assiduously points out every imperfection in airline maintenance, the equipment of the plane, and so on. The airline, for its part, vigorously draws attention to the faults in such things as F.A.A. navigational facilities and the limits of aircraft design. And the F.A.A., the airport operator, the manufacturer of the airframe (the plane itself, not including the engines), and the makers of the propellers, the engines, and the instruments all have a position to defend. In investigating a crash, the C.A.B. sets up various technical teams on which each of the hostile groups is represented, and harnesses their mutual faultfinding into an effective investigative effort.

Fluet began by organizing the operations group, which would study the crew's flying records, their training on the Electra, the plane's flight plan, the evidence concerning the actual flight path, the evidence of witnesses and survivors, and the like. He named Joseph Zamuda, a C.A.B. investigator from Washington, chairman of the group, and then called for representatives from the F.A.A., American Airlines, the Lockheed Aircraft Corporation, the Air Line Pilots Association, and the Flight Engineers International Association. In a similar manner, he pieced together a structures group, to examine the wreckage for evidence of mechanical failure; a power-plant group, to conduct the post-mortem on engines and propellers; an instrument group, to study the instruments and radio devices; a weather group; and a group to collect reports of maintenance trouble with Electras in general and with American's Electras in particular. At the end of the session, Fluet again told them all that there was no ground for any one theory about the crash yet, and that every area deserved a thorough study.

Even as the organizational meeting was getting under way, the huge derrick barge Constitution, of the Merritt-Chapman & Scott Corporation, was being towed out to a police buoy marking the scene of the crash; from the position of the buoy, the C.A.B. men on board the Constitution could see that DeWitt had been considerably off course to the right. When the barge was finally anchored, an elderly, bespectacled diver named Gus Markelson was bolted into his helmet and dropped into the murky river. Steel cables were lowered to him, and after a long wait he surfaced and gave a signal to haul away. The crane took up the slack, and very slowly the long, lovely silver fuselage began to appear. To the men on the barge it looked almost intact, but a policeman in a launch on the far side of it shouted, "Christ! She's split down the middle like a broiled lobster!" Then the cables began to slide, and an instant later the huge shape slowly sank back into the water. By now the tide was flowing too swiftly for further work, and operations were halted until the next slack water, at about 7 P.M. Then Markelson went down again, under the glare of searchlights. This time, as the fuselage was being lifted clear, it broke in two, and the larger section fell back and sank at once. The rest—a piece about twenty feet long, which had been the body of the plane forward of the wings, but from which the whole cockpit had broken off—was slowly hoisted, swung over the deck, and lowered. There was nobody in it. The sleek, polished skin was ripped open, and all the seats had been torn loose.

So it went at every slack tide. In the opaque waters, Markelson groped his way about, not always sure what he had found and was sending up. Once it was an immense section of fuselage. Another time it was a piece of wing with two engines. Sometimes it was a tangle of electric wiring, or merely a twisted sheet of aluminum skin. And once in a while it was a seat with a passenger still buckled into it.

By Wednesday night, when Fluet had canvassed his field commanders for all they knew, and had gone home to get his first sleep in thirty-six hours, he had still developed no theory about the accident, but he had begun to reduce the area of uncertainty. He had acquired a considerable amount of negative information, not the least important of which was that the pilot and co-pilot of the Northeast Airlines DC-3 preceding Flight 320 had told Zamuda's operations group that there had been no icing and little turbulence; they had broken out of the cloud ceiling at four hundred feet and had made a routine landing in light rain, without difficulty. Even so, no more than five or ten per cent of the information Fluet wanted had so far been gathered, let alone evaluated. He had long since schooled himself not to think in terms of a tentative answer at an early stage, for fear of overlooking some inconspicuous but crucial item. "What I have to keep always in mind," he told a friend a few nights later, "is that sixty-five human beings died in that crash. Now, what is the objective? Not just concocting a plausible explanation but doing a real job of prevention. It mustn't happen again the same way. If I overlook anything—*Jesus!* The next one will be my fault. I *have* to keep my mind completely open." This attitude, widely cultivated among C.A.B. investigators, causes cases to drag on for weeks, and often for months, to the great annoyance of the public, certain congressmen, and lawyers ravenous for damages. In the end, however, the C.A.B. locates what it cautiously calls the "probable cause" in ninety-one per cent of its airline-accident cases. About half of these findings have resulted in specific "fixes"—perhaps a change in the control wiring of a runaway propeller, perhaps the strengthening of a tail member, perhaps a revision of some bit of approach procedure that had caused a near collision. Collectively, these fixes have been in large part responsible for the decrease in the airline death rate from 2.28 per hundred million passenger miles in 1939, to 1.6 in 1946, and to less than one from 1952 on.

Thursday morning, Zamuda phoned the Flushing Hospital and learned that Hlavacek was still in critical condition and was under heavy sedation. But at the Queens Central Hospital, doctors said that Flight Engineer Cook, despite a fractured breastbone and internal injuries, would be able to talk. Gathering his operations group and taking along a tape recorder, Zamuda led the way to Cook's bedside. Cook was flat on his back, feeble and pale, with his right cheek and chin bandaged and a drainage tube up his nose. Zamuda, a tall, casual, square-faced man who used to be a pilot, greeted Cook with solicitude, and the flight engineer smiled and replied in a weak, halting voice. Placing a microphone near Cook's head, Zamuda started by asking him about the plane's operating condition. Cook said that everything had been mechanically fine during the flight. He also said that until the very instant of the crash DeWitt had been controlling the plane not by means of the wheel and the rudder pedals but by operating the autopilot manually; that is, by

constantly resetting its controls, which then adjusted the plane's flight to his prescription. The investigators were mildly surprised; such a technique, though not forbidden, was rather unorthodox. Zamuda then asked Cook to describe the events of the final descent. Struggling against sedation and weakness, he answered, "Uh . . . we were cleared for the back-course approach. . . . We were right on it, and I was holding the power for Al. He said to keep it at one hundred and forty miles per hour—uh, *knots*, I mean one hundred and forty *knots*. I remember it was taking about twelve hundred horsepower per engine to maintain that, and I was concentrating on that, and I just happened to look up and then I saw Al's altimeter, and it was between zero and the hundred-foot mark on the drum—you know, the . . . and I was just going to yell, and we hit. If I had just seen . . ." The members of the group were electrified, and started hotly whispered side-discussions. The Electra was equipped with new precision altimeters, which indicated hundreds of feet by means of a hand that swung around a dial, and thousands of feet on a rotating drum that appeared through a little square window at the right side of the dial; the older type had three hands swinging around the dial—one for hundreds, one for thousands, and one for tens of thousands of feet. Cook said that he had seen an altitude of less than a hundred feet—yet he said that he'd read it off the drum, which had only thousand-foot marks on it.

Noticing the effects of his statement, Cook tried to clarify the matter. "The little drum," he said. "It was between zero and one hundred, and the big hand was about five hundred, I think it was. . . . Let me think. . . . I realized, just too late, if I'd hollered . . . We hit just then." He lapsed into silence. Zamuda brought him back to the details of the approach. The plane had been in cloud until the last second, Cook said, but everything had been in perfect order—flaps, gear, Pitot heat, engine power, and a score of other things.

"And you're sure the clock hand was at five?" asked one of the F.A.A. representatives.

Cook struggled to speak. "That's . . . and the clock read . . . I was looking right at it when we hit." A doctor bent over him for a moment, then stepped back. "The box was . . ." Cook mumbled. "The box was between zero and the . . . Was it? . . . Well, it was between zero and one on the drum and then the big hand was on five. We were right at five hundred feet when we hit, I'd say." He sighed and fell silent. After a few more questions, Zamuda thanked him and the group left.

It had been a peculiarly frustrating interview. Many a crash leaves no survivors to tell what they saw and heard. This time, a highly trained crewman had been in the cockpit and had survived the crash, yet he could tell the investigators of nothing that was wrong—except, of course, the altimeter reading, but what he had actually seen on the altimeter, and what it meant, was irritatingly uncertain.

As soon as Fluet learned of Cook's testimony about the altimeter, he decided to redouble his efforts to collect ground-witness testimony that might either support or rebut it. He set up an interview group under the leadership of a tall, hawk-nosed young C.A.B. man named Claude Schonberger. Edward E. Slattery, Jr., a veteran press officer of the C.A.B., ran an appeal for witnesses in the press and on the air, and within a day calls were pouring in. Schonberger and his team—one man from American Airlines, two from the Allison Division of General Motors, and one from the F.A.A.—travelled around the city and the suburbs from morning to night, taking down testimony both in longhand and on tape. In the end, when Schonberger's group plotted out the positions of the witnesses who had offered the most likely-sounding testimony, eight of them lay in a straight line approximating Flight 320's final back-course approach. All eight had thought the plane abnormally low, but only one had actually seen it clearly and could be considered a key witness. He was Percy Tumber, the greenskeeper. He estimated the altitude of the plane he had seen as about one hundred feet. What made his testimony important was that at that geographic point, in a normal approach, the plane should have been at eight hundred feet. Yet if what Tumber had seen was indeed the Electra, and if he had correctly estimated its altitude—and if the ceiling really was four hundred feet, as the Weather Bureau and the crew of the DC-3 had both said—why

had DeWitt and Hlavacek failed to see the ground and realize their situation in time? Schonberger's group had other testimony that might explain this puzzle, at least tentatively. Captain Nickerson, of the H. Thomas Teti, had said that because of rain and fog he could see markers and buoys only when they were hard by, and had not been able to spot survivors even with his searchlight until he was within two hundred feet of them. In other words, although the general weather profile showed a ceiling of four hundred feet, there may have been a small, localized patch of fog, low scud, and rain along the line of approach over the Bronx and the East River. It was therefore possible—though by no means proved—that Flight 320 had been abnormally low during its entire approach, and that the crew had not known this from outside evidence.

By now, all phases of Fluet's investigation had been organized and were proceeding simultaneously. Fluet brought the entire fifty-one-man investigative force together every other morning, so that each group chairman could brief everyone else on what his group had learned so far. Sometimes the different groups verified each other's findings; sometimes evidence by one group stimulated another group to try to prove the opposite. Schonberger's witness-interview group tended to feel that they had fairly well shown the plane to have been low all along, but Zamuda's operations group decided to concentrate on the opposite possibility; namely, that the plane had passed over Clason Point at the proper altitude and had descended too rapidly thereafter, because of DeWitt's relative unfamiliarity with the Electra's rate of sink and because of the weather complications.

What all the groups were waiting for was the recovery of the plane's cockpit, which Markelson had not yet been able to find, and while waiting, Zamuda and his men spent many hours studying DeWitt's long flying record. The Captain had never had an accident before, and his whole record was excellent. He had gone to ground school on the Electra for eighty-four and one-half hours, and had flown the plane itself a total of eleven hours and fifty-nine minutes in practice for his official F.A.A. flight check, which he passed on December 16, 1958. But in going through the entire file the operations group also found a couple of provocative items. By F.A.A. regulation, Electra pilots, until they had a hundred hours of time on the plane or a special exemption from their airline, were allowed to land only when the ceiling was higher and the visibility greater than required for other planes. Exemption from this restriction had been given to DeWitt by his airline after he had had only twelve and a half hours of scheduled operations in the Electra. Even more provocative was a flight-check report on him dated December 15, 1958, which noted that he had failed his I.L.S. procedure on the Electra that day. Lawrence E. McShane, an F.A.A. check pilot, had jotted down the comment that DeWitt had twice come in too high over the end of the runway. McShane advised him to practice for a couple of hours more; DeWitt did so, and passed his check the next day. But three days later the American Airlines pilots had gone on strike for almost a month. Conceivably, DeWitt could have been out of practice on the new plane when operations began again. Conceivably, he had made too few instrument approaches in the Electra to override habit patterns acquired during his thousands of hours in the slower-descending DC-7s. Fluet and Zamuda, like all experienced fliers, knew that a pilot who has dropped down to the four-hundred-foot legal minimum without breaking through a reported cloud ceiling is powerfully impelled to try going down fifty feet more to see if he isn't just about to pop out. If DeWitt had done that, he might have flown himself right into the water.

On Saturday, the fourth day after the accident, the police phoned Fluet in the afternoon to say that the diver had found the cockpit and that it would be raised late that night. Fluet immediately alerted all his group chairmen, and by 10 P.M. they were crowded onto the barge Constitution. At last, a little after midnight, the crane began to reel in its cables, and slowly the cockpit came to the surface, upside down, and was lifted out, with water cascading from it—a beautiful egglike shape, shorn horizontally across as if by some mighty scissors. With infinite caution, it was lowered to the deck of the barge. As it was settling on the deck, a barge hand played a flash-light inside. "He's in there!" he cried out. No one said a word.

The instant the cables had been cast off, Zamuda crawled under the cockpit in order to get a look at the instruments and controls before either handling or exposure to the air could change anything. He found himself in the grisly position of having to peer over the shoulder of Captain DeWitt, but he carried on, shouting out readings in the arcane jargon of his trade: "Captain's altimeter minus fifteen hundred feet. Setting twenty-nine point eighty-three. Radio compass heading two hundred and ten, slave indicator centered. Air-speed indicator showing twenty knots. Landing-gear handle in down position. Pitot heat switch on. Elevator trim minus nine degrees, nose up. Rudder trim minus one degree, nose right. Aileron trim zero." For five minutes, he went on calling off instrument and control positions. Then he relinquished his place to a C.A.B. electronics specialist named Rudolph Duncan, who read the roster all over again; Duncan was the chairman of the instruments group, and since the area of his investigation was so highly significant, it was important for a second complete set of readings to be on record. As Zamuda listened to Duncan's confirmation of his findings, he was painfully aware that the case was still proving an investigator's nightmare—devoid of clues, or even hints of trouble. All indications pointed only to a safe, uneventful landing. Both altimeters, to be sure, showed bizarre readings, but that was undoubtedly because of the water pressure they had been subjected to. The barometric settings on them, however, were still as Hlavacek and DeWitt had left them. Hlavacek's was almost exactly right, while DeWitt's was off a bit; still, his error would have amounted to only eighty feet, not five hundred. Once again the investigators had made progress only by reducing the zone of uncertainty a trifle more. At last, DeWitt's body was taken out and the instrument panel was detached from the cockpit. The body was sent to the New York Medical Examiner for autopsy, at Fluet's request, but the findings were negative; the possibility that DeWitt had become suddenly ill in the closing moments of the flight was ruled out. The instrument panel was carefully carried to American's flight-dispatch office, and there the instruments were removed from it and locked in a steel cabinet.

By the second week of the investigation, the various groups were pursuing their studies more or less independently, meeting only occasionally to compare progress. A C.A.B. aeronautical engineer named Bernard Doyle scrutinized every moment of the plane's recorded operational history (it had flown a little less than three hundred and two hours in all) and retrospectively stood by at every inspection and repair job it had ever undergone. There was nothing unusual to be found.

The structures group, charged with the examination of all the recovered material except the instruments, radio devices, and power plants, was going over every scrap of salvage for signs of failure or imperfection. Every trim lab, hydraulic piston, spar, and cable was examined clinically, but nothing incriminating turned up. In a vacant LaGuardia hangar, the group reconstructed, as best it could, some forty tons of wreckage—ranging from a forty-foot segment of fuselage to scraps of tubing no larger than a man's little finger—so as to see more clearly the precise pattern of impact and destruction. Bit by bit, over a three-week period, a master diagram was filled in, which showed beyond any doubt how the plane had hit the water—in a nearly level position, and travelling moderately fast. There was no longer any need to keep open the possibility of a sudden dive, spiral, or stall. DeWitt had flown the plane right into the river, and not even in the last terrible instant had he known the truth, for the underside of the tail showed no excessive destruction indicating that he had tried to pull up.

The work of the power-plant group was delayed for several weeks while Markelson tried to find the Electra's remaining two engines. The engineer's control panel had been examined piecemeal and the instrument readings had been found normal; perhaps the engines themselves would furnish a clue. When the other two engines were finally located and raised, all four were carefully crated and shipped off to the Allison plant in Indianapolis, followed by the C.A.B. power-plant chairman and his seven assistants—two men from Allison, two from Aeroproducts (the propeller manufacturer), one from

the airline, one from the F.A.A., and one from the engineer's union. In Indianapolis, the engines were hoisted up in slings, photographed for the record, and then disassembled. Everything was bent and corroded, but with much tapping and straining the Allison mechanics got nearly all of it to come apart, while the members of the power-plant group stood around like doctors watching an autopsy. After hours of study, the group concurred in a nineteen-page report crammed with figures, tables, and descriptions. Its net message could have been put in two words: Findings negative.

The only group that remained to be heard from was Rudolph Duncan's instruments group, and an added responsibility had been imposed upon them: A few days after the crash, General Elwood Quesada, Administrator of the F.A.A., had ordered all drum altimeters removed from commercial planes until further notice. He was merely being cautious, but to the public his order sounded rather like an indictment for murder. Duncan started work on the hypothesis that the altimeters had failed. "I began with the assumption that they suffered some mechanical defect of a sort that would mislead the crew by five hundred feet," he explained later. "But, you understand, I neither believed nor disbelieved this. I merely *assumed* it, in order to test the possibilities." All altimeters operate on the principle of an aneroid, or flexible sealed chamber containing air, which expands as it is carried to higher altitudes and in so doing turns a delicate watchlike series of gears that move a hand around the dial. In good condition and properly set for barometric pressure, the altimeter of a commercial transport plane flying at low altitudes and at landing-approach speeds is accurate to within fifty feet—this being the "static error" caused by the changing air flow around the inlet holes in the surface of the plane. All altimeters, of course, can be affected by dust, moisture, foreign particles, wax, or grease, any of which might cause them to jam completely or—what is worse—to stick temporarily at a crucial time. The old type seldom encountered such troubles, but Duncan thought that perhaps the new type, since they were more complicated and precise, might be more subject to sticking and jumping. While Duncan was waiting for the cockpit to be found, he had begun to search for reports of mechanical difficulties with drum altimeters. The instruments were made by the Kollsman Instrument Corporation, of Elmhurst, Long Island, which had spent years on their design and development and had only recently begun to sell them. Three or four hundred had been delivered to civilian customers, and about seven hundred to the military. At the Kollsman plant, Duncan and his group called on Walter Angst, the designer of the drum altimeter. Angst, a middle-aged Swiss-born engineer, was voluble about the merits of his altimeter. A search of the Kollsman records concerning drum altimeters that had been returned to the company for repair revealed nothing significant—a few complaints of an altimeter's jumping fifty or a hundred feet, but nothing like five hundred. The airlines using drum altimeters were asked to extract from their records all pilot complaints about them. Again, nothing of significance. If anything incriminating were to be found, it seemed, it would have to be in the cockpit.

On the Monday morning following the recovery of the cockpit, the entire instruments group, polite but guardedly mistrustful of one another, convened at Angst's workbench to watch him dissect Flight 320's controversial altimeters. Angst cautiously opened the cases and from each drained off nearly a tumblerful of liquid containing a cloudy white suspension, which proved, on subsequent analysis, to be sea water and the corrosion product of aluminum. But of wax (which might just conceivably have got in through the air inlet when the surface of the plane was being polished) there was no trace, nor of detergents (which might have got in when it was being washed). Angst then rinsed the mechanisms in distilled water, dried them in an oven, and started cautiously cleaning off the dried aluminum oxides with a tiny pointed wooden tool and a fine wire brush. Two hours later, when he had finished the first altimeter, he gently turned one of the wheels by hand, and the entire intimate little cluster of meshed gears moved lightly and silently, while the hand spun around the dial without hesitation. To the disappointment of some of the watchers, but the great relief of Angst, there was not the least flaw—certainly no indication

of faulty manufacture. The second altimeter gave a like result.

Meanwhile, the charges against the altimeters had been renewed, this time by the person from whom everyone had been waiting to hear. Frank Hlavacek, the co-pilot, was finally removed from the critical list and allowed by his doctors to talk—as best he could through a fractured jaw that had been wired together—to Zamuda's operations group on February 20th, seventeen days after the accident. Nine men, plus a doctor and Hlavacek's wife, crowded into his small hospital room that afternoon to hear his version of the crash. Everything Hlavacek told the group fitted in with the story told by Flight Engineer Cook. He confirmed the details of the speed and power used on the approach, the radio contacts, and DeWitt's use of the autopilot to control the plane. But his most interesting statements concerned the final part of the descent. Hlavacek said that he remembered reading exactly nine hundred feet on his altimeter as they passed over the marker of the range station on Clason Point and headed out across the East River. "As we went by the range, everything was normal," he said. "We were descending—the first part of the descent I recall being a little fast, but that was just for an instant. Al stopped it right there and put it back to a normal rate of descent for that approach."

"What rate is that?" prompted Zamuda.

"About two or three hundred feet a minute," Hlavacek said. "A slow—very slow—rate of descent." The plane had been in the clouds until the last second or so, he said, and he had not had the slightest suspicion that anything was wrong until they hit. Unlike Cook, Hlavacek got tangled in no contradictions or confusions concerning the last reading he had seen on the altimeter. The drum had shown between zero and one, and the hand had been on six, for a reading of six hundred; before the hand reached five hundred, he saw lights outside, and the plane hit.

Far from clarifying the case, Hlavacek's testimony threw the operations group into a new turmoil. The argument started as soon as the men left the hospital room, and it went on for hours. No man was better qualified than Hlavacek to report on the crucial readings over Clason Point and just before the crash; his recollections, furthermore, coincided with Cook's. But something was distressingly wrong all the same. If the altimeters had shown nine hundred feet at Clason Point, and the plane had descended at only two hundred or three hundred feet per minute from there on, it would never have got down to the runway in time but would have overshot it seriously. Either DeWitt had been guilty of flying much too high or Hlavacek's memory had played him false, possibly in his anxiety to exonerate DeWitt of any charge of flying too low.

Fluet had by now made much progress since his arrival at LaGuardia on the night of the disaster. Scores—perhaps hundreds—of possibilities had been slowly excluded as a good deal of valuable information was collected. Unfortunately, the information still left room for two different answers. A considerable amount of evidence tended to show that the plane had been flying too low from New Rochelle onward. If so, the altimeters must have read wrong—yet no precedent and no sufficient mechanical explanation for this had been found, nor was Hlavacek's testimony about the altimeter readings internally sound. On the other hand, there was a fair amount of evidence tending to show that DeWitt was new to the Electra and not very familiar (relatively speaking) with poor-weather I.L.S. approaches in the plane, and that the weather that evening had denied him the chance to recognize any errors he was making—yet for a man of his experience to have lost five hundred feet in any contemporary airliner without noticing it was almost unthinkable; moreover, no one in the plane had felt any stall or dive, and the structures group had proved that the plane had hit almost flat.

Fluet's major concern now was to exclude one of these two possibilities, if he could. Because he had no way of adding to his stock of information concerning the chance of pilot error, he figured he would start by trying to incriminate or exonerate the altimeters. Since nothing had yet been proved faulty in the design or assembly of the plane's drum altimeters, Fluet reflected, and since it was established that the two had read pretty nearly alike, perhaps the answer lay in some outside factor common to both—possibly in the static-air system, the independent tubes that lead from air-inlet holes to each altimeter.

Any icing, for instance, that might have affected one set of tubes could easily have affected the other.

Calling Jack Real, the chief flight-test engineer at Lockheed, in California, Fluet asked him to arrange tests and demonstrations of the static-air system under severe icing and sleet conditions. On March 9th, Zamuda and the operations group were all at the Lockheed test center, in Burbank. Real first delivered a lecture, illustrated with slides and films, to review for his select little audience the testing that had been done on the Electra static-air system before the plane was certified by the F.A.A. He showed them films of a refrigerated nose section with water being sprayed on it, and told how a prototype plane had for months chased freezing weather all over the Northwest and Alaska. But the designers had done their work well; nothing seemed to make the inlet ports or the tubing retain water or ice. Lockheed engineers, he said, had partly obstructed the inlets with metal plugs, tape, and various balsa-wood carvings simulating ice, and even then the greatest error they had been able to produce was around a hundred and fifty feet.

The following day, the committee went out to the Lockheed Air Terminal, where an Electra was waiting for them. A member of the ground crew squirted a powerful stream of water on an inlet port of the plane's static-air system, as though he were washing the plane carelessly, but all the water drained out quickly without getting near the altimeters. Next, he heaved buckets of frozen slush against the ports; the results were the same. Finally, the whole group climbed into the plane and took off for a rendezvous with a converted B-29 borrowed from the Air Force. At about fifteen thousand feet, the B-29, which carried a great water tank in its belly, put forth a spray of water that froze in the outside air; the Electra tagged along inside the stream of spray, sometimes flying close to the tanker and sometimes far behind it, in order to duplicate a wide range of natural icing conditions. For four hours the test continued, while ice built up on the exterior, now in the form of fine frost, now in the form of frighteningly heavy solid masses. But none of it caused the altimeters to vary from their proper readings. The group had come to another dead end. Still, if Fluet had not found what he was looking for, one of his alternative solutions to the accident had become a little less likely.

Whatever the tenor of Fluet's own thinking, he was only the chief investigator, not the judge and jury. In major accident cases, after the investigators have done most of their fact-gathering work, the C.A.B. holds a public hearing, at which the evidence is put on record, under oath, and the various interested parties have a chance to question witnesses and introduce new evidence. Afterward, analytical specialists at the Washington headquarters of the C.A.B. make a complete review of the evidence and prepare a written opinion, which is then subject to the critical revisions of as many as a score of other C.A.B. specialists. This labored-over analysis is finally presented to the five Presidentially appointed board members of the C.A.B., who, sitting as a tribunal, consider whether the evidence has been fairly dealt with by the investigators and review both the logic and the law of the written report. When they are satisfied with it, they sign it, and it becomes the C.A.B.'s official finding in the case.

At the end of February, most of Fluet's investigative groups had finished their studies and disbanded, and he and his several group chairmen busied themselves with the preparations for the hearing. All the reports, letters, maintenance records, maps, and witness statements they had collected were duplicated, collated, and made up into indigestible bundles, each half a foot thick and weighing several pounds. Each party to the case was given a bundle, so that each would know in advance of the hearing everything that would be put into evidence.

The public hearing on Flight 320 took place on Wednesday, March 18th, in the ballroom of the Governor Clinton Hotel, in New York. It lasted for six long, talk-filled days, sometimes intolerably dull, sometimes crackling with argument and punctuated by bangings of the C.A.B. Hearing Officer's gavel. Each of the group chairmen narrated his group's experiences on the case, and placed in evidence the documents he had gathered and the final report he had written. The F.A.A. traffic controllers, the Weather Bureau observers, the pilots of the DC-3, the F.A.A.

check pilot who had O.K.'d DeWitt's test on the Electra all told their stories again, under oath. So did everyone else who had had a part in the drama, either as a leading player or as an extra—Hlavacek, Captain Nickerson, Jack Real, and a score of others. Flight Engineer Cook, healthy once again, and no longer confused, testified that he now distinctly remembered seeing a reading of just over five hundred feet on DeWitt's altimeter the last time he glanced at it. His evidence was not taken at face value by everyone at the hearing, however; a representative of the Kollsman company read back what Cook had said from his hospital bed—"I saw Al's altimeter, and it was between zero and the hundred-foot mark on the drum . . . and I was just going to yell, and we hit"—and asked why Cook had been impelled to yell if he truly thought the plane had been at five hundred feet. "That was forty-eight hours after the accident," Cook said. "I was in shock and considerable pain." But an implication remained that Cook's last glimpse of De-Witt's altimeter—whatever its reading—had powerfully alarmed him.

One of the last witnesses to appear was one of the most important—Percy Tumber, the greenskeeper. A leathery, rawboned fellow dressed in sports clothes, he groped for words that would convey his impression of what he had heard and seen. "The noise was terrible," he said. "It was an eerie sound." When he looked up through the car's rear window, he said, he "saw this plane and it was terribly low and it looked eerie-like." Someone snickered, and Tumber bristled noticeably. Fluet asked him to describe the sound of the engines more fully. "It was like whistling in fir trees," he said. "It was like something you may hear in a ghost story." No one snickered.

On the afternoon of March 25th, the hearing was recessed and the accumulated heap of transcripts, reports, photographs, depositions, and charts was turned over to the C.A.B. analysts in Washington. The writing of an aircraft-accident report belongs to a species of literary art that is indigenous to our era. It involves the endless quibblings of multiple authorship, the calcification of style by official jargon, and the adulteration of clear thought by maddening digressions and qualifications. Yet, for all that, it represents a deliberate process jointly entered into by men with many special viewpoints, and is probably the most sensible way of handling such highly technical studies. The C.A.B. analysts, however, labor as they would behind their mountains of evidence, could get no closer to a clear-cut answer than Fluet had got before the hearing. Everyone was dissatisfied with the first draft of the report, and conferences and expert criticism did not help. "The whole thing would make such good sense and be so simple if it were only the altimeters," an instrument man said to Fluet at one point. Fluet sighed. "It certainly would," he replied, "but that isn't reason enough to say they were to blame. We just have to have more evidence, one way or the other."

So Kollsman's altimeters were put on the rack once again. A young C.A.B. instrument specialist named Thomas Collins was assigned to subject them to the most exhaustive tests his ingenuity could devise, and he went to work with a will. He spread mashed-up insects over the air inlets and measured the deviation from accuracy. He mounted altimeters in banks of ten and sent them through thousands upon thousands of simulated flights. He undertook immensely complicated studies of the effects of vibration. Week after week, he put altimeters by the score through every hoop he could conceive of.

Meanwhile, Cook's and Hlavacek's statements about the final moments of the flight were being separately rechecked. Fluet—who by late spring had been promoted to chief of the Operations Division of the C.A.B. but continued as chief investigator on the case—decided to fly out the conditions described by Hlavacek, rather than rely upon computations from them. In June, he and Zamuda took off in an Electra flown by an American Airlines pilot and made repeated approaches to Runway 22 under the conditions sworn to by Hlavacek and Cook. A movie camera in the plane and another in a police launch moored at the site of the crash recorded the flight path. In order to cross Clason Point at nine hundred feet and approach the point in the water where the launch waited, the plane had to be steeply dived—at a rate of two thousand to twenty-five hundred vertical feet per minute. The resulting angle of the plane and the rapid buildup of its speed—from a hundred and forty

knots to a hundred and ninety-five—could not have been missed by anyone but an absolute novice. On the other hand, at the slow rate of descent attested to by Hlavacek, the plane, in order to hit the water at the site of the crash, would have had to cross Clason Point at about five hundred feet. This disclosure advanced the reasoning one step further: If the plane *had* crossed Clason Point at about five hundred feet, then Hlavacek's statement that he had read nine hundred on the dial there became insupportable—always assuming that the altimeters were exonerated.

By autumn, Collins' tests were complete: The altimeters must be considered unequivocally exonerated. Not one altimeter had registered an error of five hundred feet at Flight 320's final altitudes—much less two altimeters at the same time. As these findings were summed up in the fifth, and final, draft of the C.A.B. report:

An identical and simultaneous malfunction . . . of the magnitude suggested by the crew testimony would involve such an extreme mathematical improbability that the Board is compelled to reject it. In rejecting the possibility of dual and simultaneous altimeter error, the Board must, as a consequence, reject portions of the testimony of one or both flight crew members.

Then, in mitigation of this harsh pronouncement, the report adds:

Considering that the flight crew members received physical injuries and that they were also under great emotional stress, such questioning of their testimony has a rational basis. Under such circumstances, the Board has frequently found that the recollection, particularly of events immediately preceding such an accident, is very difficult and often erroneous. Furthermore, we are mindful of the natural human tendency to assume conformance with standard operating procedures to fill in the voids or hazy areas of one's memory.

So all that was left was operational error. But explaining the accident in these terms might prove the hardest job of all. As Oscar Bakke, at that time director of the Bureau of Safety of the C.A.B., has said, "Where an investigation leans to operational error, there is almost never any physical evidence of what the pilot or co-pilot did, and we're practically limited to the use of deductive reasoning. And *that's* difficult work."

The investigators began with the now established altitude of five hundred feet over Clason Point, and deductively extended the flight profile in each direction. Evidently, the plane had dropped down too rapidly between New Rochelle and Clason Point; given this error, a routine descent from Clason Point on would produce a crash unless the pilot or co-pilot became aware of the situation. But there, of course, lay the real question: Why had neither one noticed it? Even at night and in foul weather, there are all sorts of safeguards and warnings at work. If a pilot fails to notice that his vertical-speed indicator, for instance, is showing too much of a dive, he can recognize the drop from his increasing forward speed, shown on the airspeed indicator, and his loss of altitude, shown on the altimeter, and similar cross-checks exist for the other major factors involved in flight. But once in a while, owing to an unfortunate combination of conditions, minor errors may go unnoticed and grow larger, or augment each other, until the situation is beyond the point of recovery. "In most cases of pilot error," Bakke has noted, "we've found that it has taken six, seven, or even more unfavorable circumstances, all working together, to cause the accident. If any single one of them had not been working against the pilot he would have recognized and corrected his situation in time—which, I suspect, is just what happens all the time in normal flights, and in our daily lives."

During the late fall, Fluet and half a dozen other investigators combed through the voluminous evidence from this point of view, trying to identify all the conditions that might have been unfavorable to both DeWitt and Hlavacek. From the papers dealing with DeWitt's training on the Electra, they culled the pertinent fact that although he had received five hours of ground practice in a Link trainer that incorporated the Electra's new autopilot system, he had not been exposed to the new drum altimeter; the trainer had been equipped with the old three-needle indicator. Moreover—and while this had not seemed serious until now, it was one more unfortunate circumstance—the vertical-speed indicator on the Link trainer was of a type widely used on planes slower than the Electra; for any given rate of climb or dive, the vertical-speed needle on the Electra moved less than half as far across the face of the dial. During an instrument approach, a pilot's eyes must flick incessantly across his instruments, and he tends to rely on needle angle rather than on a careful reading of numbers. DeWitt's ground training, therefore, had been of no help in preparing him for the two new instruments. And DeWitt's actual inflight experience with the Electra had been not only sparse but interrupted by flights in DC-6s, with the old-style instruments. In the stiff phrases of the final report:

> We regard it as significant that the ground trainer in which the captain received initial training . . . had installed the conventional vertical-speed indicator and not the instrument which was actually installed on the Electra. . . . The Board [also] finds it difficult to understand why American did not at least incorporate [the drum altimeter] in the Electra cockpit trainer used by the crews during their Electra training.

Thus there emerged the strong probability that DeWitt—with only forty-odd hours on the new instruments and more than twenty-eight thousand hours on the old ones—had dropped down too low between New Rochelle and Clason Point simply by misreading the vertical-speed indicator and passing over the evidence of the unfamiliar altimeter. (If so, it was deduced, his plane must have picked up a little extra forward speed—and a recomputation of the winds aloft that night, and the times at which Hlavacek called in both check points, verified this hypothesis.) Being preoccupied with the effort to head the plane down the back-course beam (he was off course at Clason Point), and using the autopilot to steer by, which put him in an awkward posture and gave him no "feel" of the plane, DeWitt was probably unaware of the excess loss of altitude. Hlavacek, meanwhile, was busy with navigational problems—making contact with Approach Control, returning his set for Local Control, and studying his navigation diagrams for local landing procedure.

The reasonable conclusion was that Flight 320 had flown over Clason Point in good order but at an altitude of some three hundred feet below the prescribed eight-hundred-foot minimum for that point. And here, again, two small but unfavorable conditions worked the wrong way for DeWitt. First, perhaps because of his preoccupation with making an instrument approach in a relatively unfamiliar plane, he had neglected to correct his altimeter to the latest barometric pressure, and it read eighty feet too high. Second, the "static error" inherent in every altimeter at this altitude and speed was in DeWitt's case an error in the wrong direction, amounting to perhaps forty-five feet. Over Clason Point, his altimeter therefore could well have read something like six hundred and twenty-five feet—a hundred and twenty-five feet too high. As soon as Flight 320 passed over the Clason Point marker, DeWitt started down, undoubtedly expecting at any moment to break out of the four-hundred-foot cloud ceiling over the East River and see the runway lying a mile ahead. But the unhappy fact, established by Captain Nickerson of the Teti, was that the ceiling over this section of the flight path was less than four hundred feet.

And now the minor disadvantages of the new cockpit environment, the dark night, and the poor weather, plus DeWitt's own small faults of judgment and practice, began to fuse into disaster. Probably because he again misread his vertical-speed indicator, DeWitt at first started down too rapidly (Hlavacek had himself testified to that). He was still having some difficulty staying on the back-course beam. Having been off to the left at Clason Point, he had swung a good bit too far to the right. (From the final report: "Since the captain was utilizing the autopilot, his corrections of altitude and direction were somewhat slower than would normally be expected in a manual approach.") Had he been under orders to go no lower than five hundred feet while still in cloud, he might have been a little less concerned about his back-course approach and a little more concerned about his altitude, but he had been granted a waiver from that extra margin of safety—and of inconvenience—by his own airline. (From the final report: "The Board questions the wisdom of the Company in exempting Captain DeWitt when he had but 12:32 hours of flying the Electra in scheduled operations.") The plane slid down to an altitude of about three hundred feet—more than four hundred on DeWitt's altimeter, if he was looking—within twenty seconds after passing the Clason Point marker. Now DeWitt had to correct that drift to the right, or the landing would be impossible; meanwhile, the plane continued down. Still intent upon the autopilot and the back-course needle, he may have been relying on Hlavacek to keep him informed of altitude. But Hlavacek called out no altitudes below six hundred feet. Although he testified that he had been monitoring the altimeter and air speed, the investigators now refused to accept this:

It is also not at all unlikely that the co-pilot was giving careful attention to the captain's efforts to maintain the localizer path, especially in view of the apparent difficulties being experienced. . . . Although preoccupation with this or any of the several elements of a new cockpit environment could reasonably explain the failure of Mr. Hlavacek to follow the procedure required in the Operations Manual with respect to monitoring and calling out altitude and air-speed below six hundred feet, the Board believes it more likely that he was anticipating breaking out beneath the overcast and, thereafter, having seen lights on the ground or water, was focussing particularly on visual identification of the airport and was no longer monitoring the flight instruments.

Even so, why did he not see the runway's threshold lights? One more unfortunate circumstance: A dike at the end of Runway 22, which keeps Flushing Bay from flooding it, cuts off the threshold lights below a certain point. DeWitt, by descending too low too soon, had made it impossible for Hlavacek to see them. And anything else that Hlavacek or Cook or DeWitt may have seen probably seemed reassuring because of a common sensory illusion; in the C.A.B.'s experience, flying over water in poor visibility often impairs pilots' sense of perspective. In any case, time passes quickly in such a situation, and there remained only a few seconds. Then, as the relentless logic of circumstance reached its conclusion, Flight 320 reached *its* conclusion, in the waters of the East River.

On January 6, 1960, more than eleven months after the accident, the final report was signed by the five board members of the C.A.B., and on Sunday, January 10th, it was given to the press for release. A number of people had strong reactions to it. Walter Angst was delighted with it. (Sweetening his weekend even more was the news that the F.A.A. had just rescinded its ban on the use of the drum altimeter in Electras.) American Airlines was glum but silent. The Air Line Pilots Association was less inhibited; the report, the Association president said, "maligned a dead pilot" and thus "conveniently wrote the accident off the books." As for Hlavacek, who received the gist of the report by telephone at his home the night before it appeared in the newspapers, he responded with a burst of temper; he was "furious," he said, and the C.A.B. was "trying to take the easy way out by blaming a dead pilot." Several days later, having read the report and found that he, too, was criticized, he described it to the press as "highly inaccurate and totally useless," adding, "This is one of the few bad accidents they've gotten a couple of crew members out of alive—and they simply disregard our testimony." A reporter asked what effect the report would have on him. "I don't expect it to have any," he said confidently. "In fact, I've just been O.K.'d by the F.A.A. as captain on DC-6s. That ought to prove something."

Fluet, for his part, experienced a sense of weary relief rather than one of triumph. "Well, it's done, but I don't exactly feel like cheering," he said. "It's a lot less agonizing for us when there's been, say, a fire, and we try to find out how it started, or an explosion, and we put the wreckage together to find out what caused it. There's always something more *satisfying* about a neat, simple conclusion like that, and generally we can work out a good quick fix to remedy the situation. The case of Flight 320 was something else. Within the first few days, I suspected it would narrow down to two major possibilities—instrument failure and operational error, both difficult to prove—and either way somebody had to be hurt. On the one hand, you had a poor, decent dead guy who couldn't defend his reputation, along with a lot of living pilots who would feel damaged by a finding of pilot error. On the other hand, you had a fine company—the Western world's leading maker of altimeters—with its good name and its latest and finest product at stake. It was a painful choice, and bound to result in a lot of bitterness either way. But every time I get discouraged, I try to remind myself of the statistics. Slowly but surely, it's getting safer and safer for the individual passenger to fly, and the C.A.B. can take some of the credit for that. No matter who criticizes our work, the statistics make it possible for us to be proud of what we're doing."

Chapter 16 Review Questions

1. How would you sum up the advice about ethical behavior in the public office suggested in Bailey's essay? How do his views on the subject differ from those of Paul Appleby, to whom Bailey refers in his essay? Whose approach to ethics in government—Appleby's or Bailey's—do you find the more persuasive? Explain your answer.

2. What factors influenced the behavior and decisions of Chief Investigator Joseph O. Fluet? Were his choices fundamentally moral and ethical?

3. Do you think Fluet's behavior in office met the ethical standards for public officials as outlined by Bailey's essay? On the basis of your reading of the case study, would you add any points to Bailey's essay regarding other criteria or standards for correct moral behavior by public officials?

4. Why do issues that arise in government always contain some degree of ethical or moral choice? In your opinion, are similar moral choices apparent in decision making in the private sector? Explain your answer.

5. Some observers argue that it is impossible to teach individuals who are preparing for public service careers to be moral and ethical—in other words, family background, religion, personal attitudes, and upbringing have more to do with a person's ethical orientation than does formal educational training. Do you agree? Or, are there ways formal education can inculcate ethical behavior in those persons who may someday fill government posts? If so, explain how.

6. Compare and contrast Case Study 1, "The Blast in Centralia No. 5," with Case Study 16 from the standpoint of their ethical lessons for public administrators. Can you extract from the cases a specific list of important lessons for practicing public administrators?

Key Terms

moral issues
ethical dilemmas
administrative responsibility
mental attitudes
public interest
moral sensitivity
contextual priorities
complexity of bigness

personal ethical codes versus
   organizational ethical codes
normative theory
higher law
predictable pathologies
moral virtue versus moral vice
paradoxes of procedures

Suggestions for Further Reading

Despite the enormous concern recently expressed about this topic, perhaps the most sensitive treatments remain those by earlier theorists: Chester Barnard, *The Functions of the Executive* (Cambridge, Mass.: Harvard University Press, 1938)—especially Chapter 17; Paul H. Appleby, *Morality and Administration in Democratic Government* (Baton Rouge, La.: University of Louisiana Press, 1952); and Frederick C. Mosher, *Democracy and the Public Service,* Second Edition (New York: Oxford University Press, 1982)—especially Chapter 8.

   The classic scholarly debate over this subject (though it is couched in terms of responsibility instead of ethics) is between Carl J. Friedrich, "Public Policy and the Nature of Administrative Responsibility," *Public Policy,* 1 (Cambridge, Mass.: Harvard University Press, 1940), pp. 3–24, and Herman Finer, "Administrative Responsibility in Democratic Government," *Public Administration Re-*

view, 1 (Summer 1941), pp. 335–350. Along with the Friedrich-Finer arguments, which remain highly germane even today, you should also read John M. Gaus, "The Responsibility of Public Administration," in Leonard D. White, *The Frontiers of Public Administration* (Chicago: University of Chicago Press, 1936), pp. 26–44, as well as Arthur A. Maass and Laurence I. Radway, "Gauging Administrative Responsibility," *Public Administration Review,* 9 (Summer 1949), pp. 182–192.

For more recent writings that have addressed this subject with varying degrees of success or failure, see Eugene P. Dvorin and Robert H. Simmons, *From Amoral to Humane Bureaucracy* (San Francisco: Canfield Press, 1972); Wayne Leys, *Ethics for Policy Decisions* (Westport, Conn.: Greenwood Press, 1968); John Rohr, *Ethics for Bureaucrats* (New York: Marcel Dekker, 1978); Edward Weisband and Thomas Frank, *Resignation in Protest* (New York: Grossman/Viking, 1975); Sissela E. Bok, *Lying* (New York: Random House, 1979), and *Secrets* (New York: Pantheon, 1983); Frederick C. Mosher, ed., *Watergate: Implications for Responsible Government* (New York: Basic Books, 1974); Herman Mertins, Jr., and Patrick Hennigan, *Applying Standards and Ethics in the 1980s* (Washington, D.C.: American Society for Public Administration, 1982); Ralph Nader, Peter J. Petkas, and Kate Blackwell, eds., *Whistle Blowing: The Report of the Conference on Professional Responsibility* (New York: Grossman/Viking, 1972); Victor Thompson, *Without Sympathy or Enthusiasm: The Problem of Administrative Compassion* (University, Ala.: University of Alabama Press, 1975); as well as such thought-provoking, sensitive essays as Dwight Waldo, "Reflections on Public Morality," *Administration and Society,* 6 (Nov. 1974), pp. 267–282; Marver Bernstein, "Ethics in Government: The Problems in Perspective," *National Civic Review,* 61 (July 1972), pp. 341–347; Mark T. Lilla, "Ethos, 'Ethics' and Public Service," *The Public Interest,* No. 63 (Spring 1981), pp. 3–17, or, in the same issue, Thomas C. Schelling, "Economic Reasoning and the Ethics of Policy," pp. 37–61. More recently, see York Wilbern, "Types and Levels of Public Morality" *Public Administration Review* 44 (March/April 1984), pp. 102–108; Barbara S. Romzek and Melvin J. Dubnik, "Accountability in the Public Sector: Lessons from the Challenger Tragedy," *Public Administration Review* 47 (May/June 1987), pp. 227–238; Terry L. Cooper, "Hierarchy, Virtue, and the Practice of Public Administration: A Perspective for Normative Ethics" *Public Administration Review* 47 (July/August, 1987), pp. 320–328; and Dennis F. Thompson, "The Possibility of Administrative Ethics," *Public Administration Review* 45 (September/October 1985) pp. 555–561. Perhaps the best recent summary of much of this literature is John P. Burke, *Bureaucratic Responsibility* (Baltimore: The Johns Hopkins Press, 1986).

Any in-depth review of this subject should include study of the Ethics in Government Act of 1978, as well as the enabling legislation and debates over such seminal oversight mechanisms as the War Powers Resolution of 1973, Freedom of Information Act 1967 (with 1974 amendments), Privacy Act (1974), the Inspector General's Office (1976), and the various ombudsman offices instituted within state and local governments. For many of these recent documents, see

Richard J. Stillman II, ed., *Basic Documents of American Public Administration Since 1950* (New York: Holmes and Meier, 1982).

Many novels focus on the role of ethics in public life. For an excellent discussion of how they contribute to our understanding of the subject, see Dwight Waldo, *The Novelist on Organization and Administration: An Inquiry into the Relationship Between Two Worlds* (Berkeley, Calif.: Institute of Governmental Studies, June 1968), or Marc Holzer, Kenneth Morris and William Ludwin *Literature in Bureaucracy* (Wayne, N.J.: Avery Publishing, 1979)

Topic Index

Budget and Finance

Bureaucracy

Citizens' Rights and Participation

Communications in Administration

Congress

Health and Human Services

Implementation

Intergovernmental Programs, Policies, and Problems

Intergovernmental Relations

National Defense and International Relations

Organizational Behavior

Organization and Management

Personnel and Civil Service

Planning and Policy Development

Power and Politics in Administration

Presidency

Regulation, Rule Enforcement, and Law in Administration

State and Local Government

The Study of Public Administration as a Discipline

Third-Party Government

Subject Index